CORPORATE BANKRUPTCY LAW IN CHINA

This fascinating study uses qualitative and quantitative data and insights from inter-views with judges, lawyers, government officials, entrepreneurs, bankers, consultants, and academics in China and abroad, to provide a new perspective on the problems that have hindered the implementation of the Enterprise Bankruptcy Law in China, and recent attempts at reform.

The analysis provides unique insights into China's business world and its interaction with the judicial and political system in China.

In addition, the book also provides important information about how the Enterprise Bankruptcy Law affects foreign companies, agencies and governments that are active in China. The author draws on empirical data, decided cases and her experience of how the law and surrounding practices deal with foreign stakeholders whose interests are affected by corporate bankruptcy in China.

The book will improve understanding of how China's corporate bankruptcy law has been used in practice, what has limited its practical effectiveness, whether it is desirable for the law to be used more readily in China, and the possible options for its reform.

T0395488

Corporate Bankruptcy Law in China

Principles, Limitations and Options for Reform

Natalie Mrockova

·HART·

OXFORD · LONDON · NEW YORK · NEW DELHI · SYDNEY

HART PUBLISHING

Bloomsbury Publishing Plc

Kemp House, Chawley Park, Cumnor Hill, Oxford, OX2 9PH, UK

1385 Broadway, New York, NY 10018, USA

29 Earlsfort Terrace, Dublin 2, Ireland

HART PUBLISHING, the Hart/Stag logo, BLOOMSBURY and the Diana logo are
trademarks of Bloomsbury Publishing Plc

First published in Great Britain 2021

First published in hardback, 2021
Paperback edition, 2022

A catalogue record for this book is available from the British Library.

Library of Congress Cataloging-in-Publication Data

Names: Mrockova, Natalie (Tereza Natalie), 1987- author.

Title: Corporate bankruptcy law in China : principles, limitations and options for reform / Natalie Mrockova.

Description: Gordonsville : Hart Publishing, an imprint of Bloomsbury Publishing, 2021. |
Includes bibliographical references and index.

Identifiers: LCCN 2020048391 (print) | LCCN 2020048392 (ebook) |
ISBN 9781509932443 (hardback) | ISBN 9781509945658 (paperback) |
ISBN 9781509932450 (pdf) | ISBN 9781509932467 (Epub)

Subjects: LCSH: Business failures—Law and legislation—China. | B ankruptcy—China. |
China. Qi ye po chan fa (2006) | Debtor and creditor—China. | Law reform—China. |
Corporate reorganizations—Law and legislation—China. | China—Politics and government.

Classification: LCC KNQ1942 .M76 2021 (print) | LCC KNQ1942 (ebook) | DDC 346.5107/8—dc23

LC record available at https://lccn.loc.gov/2020048391

LC ebook record available at https://lccn.loc.gov/2020048392

ISBN: HB: 978-1-50993-244-3
PB: 978-1-50994-565-8
ePDF: 978-1-50993-245-0
ePub: 978-1-50993-246-7

Typeset by Compuscript Ltd, Shannon

To find out more about our authors and books visit www.hartpublishing.co.uk. Here you will find
extracts, author information, details of forthcoming events and the option to sign up for our newsletters.

To Eric & Anička

PREFACE

China's corporate bankruptcy law is a fascinating topic. It lies at the intersection of law, politics, economics, finance, history, sociology and anthropology. Through the exploration of how the law is applied in practice, one gains an insight into how China operates more broadly. There are many conflicting goals and preferences: economic progress, international cooperation, attractive business environment, political control, prevention of unemployment, maintenance of social stability, local protectionism, and more.

In many ways, China's corporate bankruptcy law resembles bankruptcy laws in other countries. Indeed, China transplanted many concepts and provisions into its Enterprise Bankruptcy Law 2006 from foreign bankruptcy codes, most importantly from the US, Germany, Japan and England. However, the law has been implemented in a very particular way and in an environment that is underpinned by old Confucian values and guided by *the visible hand* of the Communist Party of China. This has led to biases and implementation that differs from how similar provisions are applied elsewhere. Exploration of how the Enterprise Bankruptcy Law 2006 works in China, what limits its practical use, and what are the possible improvements that could make the law a more efficient tool for enabling market exit and restructuring of distressed companies lies at the heart of this work.

This book is based on my doctoral thesis, which has been updated to cover subsequent turbulent years that have changed how corporate bankruptcy law is perceived and used in China. I am deeply indebted to many people who supported me throughout this process. I wish to thank two people in particular for their inspiration and support in my exploration of this area of law. I would like to thank Sandra Frisby, who introduced me to the wonderful world of bankruptcy law and supervised my undergraduate dissertation at the University of Nottingham. Her enthusiasm and energy are infectious. It was her support and encouragement that led me to pursue further study of corporate bankruptcy law. I also wish to express my deepest gratitude to John Armour, who supervised my doctoral thesis at the University of Oxford. He encouraged me to approach the subject from a completely new perspective, to use new analytical tools, to think deeply and creatively about the subject and to craft my arguments with precision. He helped me grow as an academic and as a writer, and I feel lucky to have had his support and advice over the years.

Many of the arguments in this book benefited from my attendance and participation at many academic and government-organised workshops and conferences. I wish to thank the participants and commentators for their invaluable feedback and suggestions. Many of the arguments and insights in this book are not described in the literature; instead, they were crafted with the help of my Chinese colleagues and interviewees who kindly shared their knowledge and gave their precious time to answer my questions and suggest additional arguments and new areas of research. In order to protect them and to allow them to speak freely, I anonymised all their contributions.[1] Nevertheless, I am incredibly grateful for all their help and I wish the acknowledge their contribution.

I am also deeply indebted to the examiners who read and commented on the thesis at various stages of the doctoral process at the University of Oxford. Louise Gullifer and Kristin van Zwieten – who examined the magisterial thesis – encouraged me to be bolder in my approach to the material and to go deeper in my analysis. Curtis Milhaupt and Horst Eidenmüller – who examined the doctoral thesis – provided valuable comments and suggestions that enriched this work and encouraged me to develop the thesis into this book. I wish to thank them all for giving up precious time to help me.

I have been very fortunate to have met many great people and colleagues – many of whom have become friends over the years – along the way. Although there are too many to name here, I wish to highlight a few for their time and care, and their inspiring questions and discussions which have helped shape my thinking and, ultimately, this book.

I wish to thank my colleagues at St John's College, Oxford – Simon Whittaker and Richard Ekins – for being so supportive and for having taught me so much. I also wish to thank my soon-to-be colleagues at Merton College, Oxford – Jennifer Payne and Mindy Chen-Wishart – with whom I have already shared so much. I look forward to our future cooperation. Of the many amazing people I have met in my academic life, I also want to thank Rebecca Williams for being the most wonderful and supportive mentor, who genuinely cared about me and my future and that of our students. I also want to thank Joshua Getzler for helping me view the problems and questions from unique and new perspectives and for the tremendous energy and enthusiasm that he seems to put into everything he does.

I also wish to thank Roberta Bassi, my wonderful and patient editor at Hart Publishing, for her support and understanding throughout this process. Her flexibility and positive attitude helped me in many dark moments. Similarly, I also want to thank Rosemarie Mearns and everyone at Hart Publishing for their work, professionalism and love which they put into all they do. I also thank the anonymous reviewers at Hart Publishing for their valuable, constructive and insightful comments and feedback.

Finally, I would like to thank my family, without whom none of this would be possible. My mother, brother and late father always believed in me and supported me in all my endeavours. I know how lucky I am to have you in my life. Most importantly, however, I want to thank my husband and daughter for their support, understanding and love. You remind me of all that is good in this life. This book is dedicated to you.

I hope that you enjoy the book that you now hold in your hands and find many useful and interesting insights that will help you understand China and its bankruptcy law at a more profound level. I really enjoyed writing it for you.

Natalie Mrockova
Oxford
15 July 2020

---

[1] I coded the identity of each interviewee so that the value of their insights can be more easily ascertained. See Section 1.3 for details.

CONTENTS

PART II
THE EBL AND ITS PRACTICAL LIMITATIONS

PART III
DESIRABILITY AND OPTIONS FOR REFORM

PART IV
FOREIGN STAKEHOLDERS AND THE EBL

LIST OF ABBREVIATIONS

ADR	Alternative dispute resolution
AMC	Asset management company
Big Four	Four biggest state-owned banks in China
CBIRC	China Banking and Insurance Regulatory Commission
CBRC	China Banking Regulatory Commission
Chapter 7	US Bankruptcy Code, Chapter 7 (Liquidation)
Chapter 11	US Bankruptcy Code, Chapter 11 (Reorganisation)
China	People's Republic of China
CIETAC	China International Economic and Trade Arbitration Commission
Constitution	Constitution of the People's Republic of China
CPPCC	Chinese People/'s Political Consultative Conferences
DDR	Diversified dispute resolution (a Chinese term for alternative dispute resolution)
EBL	Enterprise Bankruptcy Law
FDI	Foreign direct investment
FT	*Financial Times* (newspaper)
GDP	Gross domestic product
IMF	International Monetary Fund
JV	Joint venture
Med-Arb	A combination of mediation and arbitration, very popular in China
NBS	National Bureau of Statistics
NPC	National People's Congress
NPL	Non-performing loan
P2P	Peer-to-peer lending
Party, the	Communist Party of People's Republic of China
parties, the	Creditors and debtors eligible to use the EBL (see Section 4.3.2.2)

PBoC	People's Bank of China
RMB	Renminbi, official currency in China
SASAC	State-owned Assets Supervision and Administration Commission of the State Council
SCMP	*South China Morning Post* (newspaper)
SEZ	Special economic zone
SMEs	Small and medium enterprises
SOE	State-owned enterprise
SPC	Supreme People's Court
state company	A company that belongs to the state sector (see Section 2.5)
UNCITRAL	United Nations Commission on International Trade Law
WMP	Wealth management product(s)
WSJ	*Wall Street Journal* (newspaper)
WTO	World Trade Organisation

JUDICIAL AND POLITICAL
GUIDING DOCUMENTS

(ordered by date)

The Resolution of the Standing Committee of the National People's Congress concerning Improving Interpretation of the Law (10.6.1981)
全国人民代表大会常务委员会《关于加强法律解释工作》的决议

The Interim Order of the State Council concerning the Assignment and Transfer of Urban State-owned Land Use Rights in the People's Republic of China (19.5.1990)
中华人民共和国城镇国有土地使用权出让和转让暂行条例

The SPC Notice concerning Several Issues Concerning the Application of the Civil Procedure Law of the PRC (*Fafa* [1992] No 22)
最高人民法院印发《关于适用<中华人民共和国民事诉讼法>若干问题的意见》的通知

The Shenzhen Special Economic Zone Corporate Bankruptcy Regulations (18.12.1993)
《深圳经济特区企业破产条例》

The Chinese Communist Party's Regulation on Discipline Measures (18.2.2004)
《中国共产党纪律措施条例》

The SPC Provisions concerning the Appointment of Administrators (*Fashi* [2007] No 8)
最高人民法院《关于审理企业破产案件指定管理人》的规定

The SPC Provisions concerning the Remuneration for Administrators (*Fashi* [2007] No 9)
最高人民法院《关于审理企业破产案件确定管理人报酬》的规定

The SPC Notice concerning the Correct Hearing of EBL Cases and Judicial Guarantee to Maintain Orderly Market Economy (*Fafa* [2009] No 36)
最高人民法院《关于正确审理企业破产案件为维护市场经济秩序提供司法保障若干问题》的意见

The SPC Provisions concerning the Restriction on High Consumption and Related Expenses of Persons under Debt Enforcement Order (*Fashi* [2010] No 8)
最高人民法院《关于限制被执行人高消费》的若干规定

The SPC Provisions on Several Issues Concerning Implementation of Laws in Criminal Law Cases of Illegal Fundraising (*Fashi* [2010] No 18)
最高人民法院《关于审理非法集资刑事案件具体应用法律若干问题》的解释

The SPC Provisions (I) concerning the Application of the EBL (*Fashi* [2011] No 22)
最高人民法院《关于适用中华人民共和国企业破产法》若干问题的规定（一）

The SPC Memorandum concerning Handling of Listed Companies' Reorganisations and Liquidations (*Fa* [2012] No 261)
最高人民法院印发《关于审理上市公司破产重整案件工作座谈会纪要》的通知

The SPC Notice concerning Notice concerning Practising Justice for the People, Strengthening Fair Justice and Increasing Credibility of the Judiciary (*Fafa* [2013] No 9)
最高人民法院《关于切实践行司法为民大力加强公正司法不断提高司法公信力》的若干意见

The SPC Provisions (II) concerning the Application of the EBL (*Fashi* [2013] No 22)
最高人民法院关于适用《中华人民共和国企业破产法》若干问题的规定（二）

The Wenzhou Intermediate Court's Minutes on the Trial Implementation of Simplified Bankruptcy Case Procedures (27.3.2013)
温州市中级人民法院《关于试行简化破产案件审理程序》的会议纪要

The Zhejiang SPC Memorandum on Adjudicating Enterprise Bankruptcies in Simplified Procedures' (*Zhegaofa* [2013] No 153)
浙江省高级人民法院印发《关于企业破产案件简易审若干问题》的纪要

The Beijing Municipal SPC Notice concerning Procedural Rules of Enterprise Bankruptcy in Beijing Municipality (*Beijing Gaofafa* [2013] No 242) (Beijing, 22 July 2013)
《北京市高级人民法院企业破产案件审理规程》

The SPC Provisions concerning the Application of the Civil Procedure Law (*Fashi* [2015] No 5)
最高人民法院关于适用《中华人民共和国民事诉讼法》的解释

The SPC Notice concerning Providing Judicial Services and Safeguards to the Construction of the Belt and Road (*Fafa* [2015] No 9)
最高人民法院《关于人民法院为"一带一路"建设提供司法服务和保障》的若干意见

The SPC Provisions concerning Several Issues concerning the Application of Law in the Trial of Private Lending Cases (*Fashi* [2015] No 18)
最高人民法院《关于审理民间借贷案件适用法律若干问题》的规定

The SPC Notice concerning the People's Courts Further Deepening the Reform of the Diversified Dispute Resolution Mechanism (*Fafa* [2016] No 14)
最高人民法院《关于人民法院进一步深化多元化纠纷解决机制改革》的意见

The SPC Notice concerning Disclosure of Information on Enterprise Bankruptcy Cases (Trial) (*Fafa* [2016] No 19)
最高人民法院《关于企业破产案件信息公开》的规定（试行）

The Opinions of the Central Committee of the Communist Party of China and the State Council on Improving the Property Rights Protection System and Lawfully Protecting Property Rights (*Zhongfa* [2016] No 28)
中共中央、国务院《关于完善产权保护制度依法保护产权》的意见

The SPC Memorandum concerning Hearing Bankruptcy Cases in accordance with the Law and Actively and Steadily Promoting Rescue and Liquidation of Bankrupt Companies (*Fa* [2016] No 169)
最高人民法院《关于依法开展破产案件审理积极稳妥推进破产企业救治和清算工作》的通知

The SPC Memorandum concerning the Establishment of Liquidation and Bankruptcy Trial Divisions in Intermediate People's Courts (*Fa* [2016] No 209)
最高人民法院《关于在中级人民法院设立清算与破产审判庭》的工作方案

The SPC White Paper 'Outline of the Judicial Protection of Intellectual Property in China (2016–2020)'
中国知识产权司法保护纲要 (2016–2020)

The SPC Notice concerning Several Issues in the Transfer of Debt Enforcement Claims to Bankruptcy Case (*Fafa* [2017] No 2)
最高人民法院《关于执行案件移送破产审查若干问题的指导意见》

The Zhejiang Provincial Government's Several Opinions concerning the Acceleration of the Disposal of Zombie Companies (*Zhezheng Banfa* [2017] No 136)
《关于加快处置"僵尸企业"的若干意见》

The SPC Minutes of the National Bankruptcy Trial Work Conference (4.3.2018)
全国法院破产审判工作会议纪要

The SPC Memorandum concerning the Minutes of the National Work Conference on Bankruptcy Trials (*Fa* [2018] No 53)
最高人民法院关于印发 《全国法院破产审判工作会议纪要》的通知

The Shanghai Intermediate Court's Administrative Measures for Enterprise Bankruptcy Funds (Trial) (*Hugaofa* [2018] No 300)
企业破产工作经费管理办法（试行）

The Zhejiang Changxing Court's Corporate Bankruptcy Trial White Paper and Ten Typical Cases (2012–2018) (9.3.2019)
浙江长兴法院 ｜ 企业破产审判白皮书及十大典型案例（2012–2018）

The Shanghai Higher People's Court Guidelines on Simplifying Procedures and Accelerating the Advancement of Bankruptcy Cases 2019 (*Hugaofa* [2018] No 167)
上海市高级人民法院关于简化程序加快推进破产案件审理的办案指引

The SPC Provisions (III) concerning the Application of the EBL (*Fashi* [2019] No 3)
最高人民法院关于适用《中华人民共和国企业破产法》若干问题的规定（三）

The SPC Notice concerning the Provision of Judicial Services and Safeguards for the Construction of the 'Belt and Road' by Court (*Fafa* [2019] No 29)
最高人民法院《关于人民法院进一步为"一带一路"建设提供司法服务和保障》的意见

The SPC Notice concerning Compulsory Liquidation and Separate Performance Evaluation of Bankruptcy Cases (*Faban* [2019] No 49)
最高人民法院《关于强制清算与破产案件单独绩效考核》的通知

The SPC Memorandum concerning the Minutes of the National Civil and Commercial Trial Work Conference (*Fa* [2019] No 254)
最高人民法院. 关于印发《全国法院民商事审判工作会议纪要》的通知

The Notice of the National Development and Reform Commission and 13 other bodies concerning Reform Plan for Accelerating the Improvement of the Exit Regime for Market Entities (*Fagaicaijin* [2019] No 1104)
关于印发《加快完善市场主体退出制度. 改革方案》的通知

The Guidelines for People's Courts on Enforcement Work (2019–2023) (11.6.2019)
《人民法院执行工作纲要 (2019–2023)》

The Wenzhou Intermediate Court's Implementing Opinions on the Centralised Cleanup of Personal Debt (11.9.2019)
温州中院《关于个人债务集中清理实施意见》

The Dalian Municipal Intermediate Court's Guidelines on Simplifying Trial Procedures for Bankruptcy Cases in 2020
大连市中级人民法院发布《关于简化破产案件审理程序的工作指引》

The Jiangsu Bankruptcy Trial Work Report in 2019 (3.3.2020)
《2019年江苏法院破产审判工作情况通报》

The SPC Notice concerning the Promotion of Efficient Review of Bankruptcy Cases (*Fafa* [2020] No 14)
最高人民法院印发《关于推进破产 案件依法高效审理的意见》的通知

The Guangzhou Intermediate Court's Working Guidelines on Promoting Fast-track Bankruptcy Procedure (Trial) (*Sui zhongfa* [2020] No 30)
广州市中级人民法院关于推进破产案件快速审理的工作指引（试行）

The Opinions of the Central Committee of the Communist Party of China and the State Council on Accelerating the Improvement of the Socialist Market Economic System in the New Era (11.5.2020)
中共中央 国务院关于新时代加快完善社会主义市场经济体制的意见

TABLES AND FIGURES

1

Introduction

Following Deng Xiaoping's revolutionary economic reforms in the 1980s, China slowly transformed itself into a global economic power. Its GDP, standards of living, investment inflows and outflows, and other economic indicators multiplied over the last four decades. Nevertheless, many challenges also arose. One of them is the growing volume of debt – much of it non-performing – in China's banks and companies. In the past, corporate financial distress would be 'resolved' through bailouts or mergers. In a market economy, however, this is no longer possible. A mechanism was therefore needed to enable efficient market exit and, where appropriate, corporate restructuring. China's modern corporate bankruptcy[1] law – the Enterprise Bankruptcy Law 2006 (EBL) – sought to provide such a mechanism.

This book aims to answer four important questions. The first question focuses on how the EBL operates and why it is so rarely used in China. The second question considers whether it is desirable to use the EBL more. Concluding that it is, the third question explores China's reform options to ameliorate the identified shortcomings and improve the implementation of the EBL in practice. The fourth – and slightly separate – question then examines the role of foreign stakeholders in the making and implementation of the EBL.[2]

Important new insights are contained throughout the book which, unlike most other English-language books about China's corporate bankruptcy on the market,[3] includes extensive references to Chinese literature and is based on original empirical research. Chapter four discusses not only the black-letter EBL provisions but, importantly, also judicial guidance which influences how the provisions are applied in practice. Chapters five to nine provide functional insights into why the EBL is so rarely used. Chapter twelve presents an overview of recent local reforms that are largely ignored in English-language

---

[1] This book follows the Chinese tradition of using the term 'bankruptcy' to describe a legal process of resolving financial distress where a legal or natural person cannot repay their debts. The term 'bankruptcy' is used interchangeably with the term 'corporate bankruptcy', unless otherwise indicated in the text. The term 'insolvency' is used to describe a state of affairs where a legal or natural person is no longer able to pay their debts as they fall due or where their liabilities exceed their assets.

[2] For details, see Section 1.4 below, which explains the structure of this book.

[3] A few important exceptions exist, most notably an empirical study and excellent evaluation of corporate reorganisations between 2007 and 2015 in China in Z Zhang, *Corporate Reorganisations in China* (Cambridge University Press, 2018). See also H Zhao, *Government Intervention in the Reorganisation of Listed Companies in China* (Cambridge University Press, 2020).

literature. And Chapter thirteen provides details of cross-border bankruptcy issues and examines several foreign-related cases that have been decided in recent years.[4]

When reading this book, it is important to remember that China is a large and varied economy. Its 23 provinces, four municipalities, five autonomous regions and two Special Administrative Regions each have different GDP; different primary sources of income; different internal problems and pressure points; and different levels of ability and willingness to operate a market economy and let the forces of supply and demand determine prices, production decisions and corporate market exit for financially distressed companies. Shanghai, Shenzhen, Wenzhou, Guangzhou, Zhejiang, Jiangsu and other (mostly) coastal regions are at one end of the spectrum: they are modern market economies with advanced socio-legal infrastructure and many companies and professionals – judges, lawyers, accountants – who give advice and regulate activities within local markets. On the other hand, Gansu, Yunnan, Henan and other (mostly) inner regions have comparatively low GDP, high unemployment rates, low productivity, limited infrastructure and occasional challenges in the form of natural disasters. To illustrate the immense economic differences within China, one can compare the reported economic results: for example, in 2018, the GDP per capita was 140,211 RMB in Beijing but only 31,336 RMB in Gansu.[5]

As a result, any study that tries to provide a unified picture of China is bound to generalise and overlook local disparities in data and practices. This book has tried to strike a balance. The data and analysis are used to present a picture as close to reality as possible, but it is unable to show and explain every local discrepancy. Instead, it tries to present a picture that is true for most of China's market and, where relevant, point out important differences that may exist across provinces.

Moreover, the book presents data and functional insights from June 2007 to June 2020. Much has changed in those short 13 years, and much is likely to change in the future. This is particularly true of certain regions – such as Jiangsu and Zhejiang Provinces, which are at the forefront of the EBL reform – which further reinforces inter-provincial discrepancies.

The book deals with this problem in two ways. Firstly, it looks at the reasons why parties have been unable or unwilling to use the EBL more over the whole period. Some of the reasons were more pronounced initially, while others became more important later on. Secondly, it presents recent local reforms and initiatives in a separate chapter – Chapter twelve – in order to separate out the changes and improvements that are not yet fully reflected in the data and have not yet been able to influence EBL implementation and surrounding practices.

Finally, although some commentators try to explain Chinese data by saying that China is unique, this book tries to instead produce a more balanced, contextualised evaluation. It acknowledges, on the one hand, that there are some unique elements in China but, on the other hand, China is facing problems that are similar to those affecting other developing countries and other authoritarian regimes. What will work in China may be the same or similar to what works elsewhere, but at times it is important

---

[4] See Section 1.4 below for a complete overview of the structure of the book.
[5] Statista data.

to consider the 'Chinese characteristics' and adjust the rules and initiatives to fit into the local environment. This is the case in Chapter eleven, which discusses options for reform of the EBL – the proposals draw on experience and advice from other regions and countries but, ultimately, it acknowledges that the proposed reforms must be realistic and appropriate for China's political, legal, social and economic environment. International comparisons are included where appropriate, but it is not the aim of the book – nor could it be, given its scope – to provide an extensive comparison of China and other jurisdictions.

The remainder of this chapter provides some basic information about theoretical assumptions, methodology and structure of this book. Section 1.1 explains the theoretical framework of the book and the analytical tools that have been used to examine and evaluate China's corporate bankruptcy law. Section 1.2 then briefly summarises the findings of existing literature about the role and possible contribution of bankruptcy law to economic development. Section 1.3 describes the methodology that was used in collecting new qualitative data presented in this book. Finally, Section 1.4 explains the structure of the book.

1.1. Theoretical Framework: Economic Analysis of Law

When analysing parties' decision-making with regards to whether, when and how to use the EBL, this book relies on economic analysis of law – that is, the use of economic methodology to analyse and evaluate law.[6] Its aim is to understand parties' decision-making through studying their *incentives* created by the desirability of outcomes of different options that are open to them.[7] Following neo-institutional economics,[8] the analysis assumes that parties are influenced by and rely not only on written laws but on 'any form of constraint that human beings devise to shape human interaction'.[9] Thus, parties are influenced in their decision-making by *institutions*, that is all basic and stable mechanisms that govern players' incentives and coordinate activities in multilateral interactions. Informal social norms, therefore, coexist with laws and together create incentives that shape parties' choices, as is discussed in Section 2.3 and Chapter nine.

Traditionally, economic analysis of law relies on the assumption that all parties are *rational* – that is, that parties always make well-informed, prudent and logical decisions based on their analysis of the costs and benefits of each option that is open to them. Once they evaluate each option from this perspective – and so determine their predicted *payoffs* of each option – they choose the option that offers them the highest payoffs.[10] However, the book acknowledges that parties are not always rational in this way. They

---

[6] This approach dates back at least to the 1960s: *The Oxford Handbook of Law and Economics*, vol 1 (Oxford University Press, 2017) ch 1.

[7] On this view, law is treated as providing parties with price-like signals that guide them toward certain behaviour.

[8] See eg *The Oxford Handbook*, vol 1 (2017) ch 22.

[9] See D North, *Structure and Change in Economic History* (Norton, 1981) 4. See also C Xu, 'The Fundamental Institutions of China's Reforms and Development' (2011) *Journal of Economic Literature* 1076, 1078.

[10] See eg *The Oxford Handbook*, vol 1 (n 6) ch 2.

often rely on incomplete information, they may not know all their options, they may not know all the costs and benefits of each option, and they may not be able to evaluate what payoffs to expect in each option.[11] This is referred to as *bounded rationality*.[12] When examining parties' decision-making in this book – particularly in Chapters six to nine – it is assumed that parties rely on bounded rationality and the influence of a wide range of institutions is considered.

With assistance of economic analysis of law, as explained above, three key economic concepts are used throughout this book, namely incentives, payoffs, and efficiency. *Incentives* are concerned with motivating parties to act in a particular way. They can be remunerative (usually money-related); moral (eg guilt, admiration, social inclusion/exclusion); coercive (eg imprisonment, confiscation); and natural (eg fear, anger).[13] The basic incentive mechanism in economics is the price system. Economic analysis of law treats laws as conveying price-like signals; the new institutional economics extends this framework to other social institutions such as social norms. Laws and other rules are then seen as defining a preferred type of behaviour and deterring (ie increasing the cost of) all other. They can function as a carrot – carrying rewards for complying – or a stick – punishing non-compliance.[14] In the context of bankruptcy law, incentives encourage preferred modes of use of the law – to restructure or liquidate under court supervision – at a preferred point in time – once insolvent (in China) or before (other jurisdictions).[15] They order courts and administrators to carry out certain powers that can increase the pool of assets that are available for redistribution in bankruptcy.[16] They also encourage debtors to cooperate and accept a collective solution. Parties rarely act in isolation, and so their incentives – and interests – may clash with those around them. Similarly, parties may be incentivised to act in more than one way, which may lead them to consider particular trade-offs. These trade-offs may be inherent in the nature of the options, or they may be determined by the impact of expected choices of other parties.

Another important concept in economic analysis of law is the idea of parties' payoffs. A payoff is a value – monetary or otherwise – received as a result of a party's decision. However, because parties often consider the likely impact of their actions before making a decision (*ex ante*), this book mostly uses the concept of expected payoffs. This method uses backward induction to determine the likely outcomes and payoffs of parties' options. A party knows that they have several options for how they can act – for example, to repay a debt or not to repay. They then try to estimate what would be the outcome of these options – for example, imprisonment, a fine, other legal consequences, violence, threats, or nothing. Their payoffs are determined by the value of each action – for example, keeping all the money in case of non-repayment – in the light of the likelihood of each outcome.

---

[11] See H Simon, 'Rational decision-making in business organizations' (1979) *American Economic Review* 493, 502.

[12] Note that an additional field of study – behavioural economics – also questions the rationality of the decision-making process. One of the issues is that real-life parties are often influenced by their inner 'biases' – ie irrational personal fears and preferences, cultural preferences, etc: *The Oxford Handbook*, vol 1 (n 6) ch 4.

[13] See eg K Dalkir, *Knowledge Management in theory and practice* (Routledge, 2013).

[14] For more, see *The Oxford Handbook*, vol 1 (n 6) ch 21.

[15] See Sections 4.2.2, 6.3 and 11.1.4.1.

[16] See Sections 4.2.9, 4.2.13 and 8.2.

This payoff matrix takes into account unilateral decision-making. Often, however, parties make decisions in bilateral interactions where each party wants to maximise their own payoffs – monetary or otherwise[17] – while taking into account the likely decision or reaction of the other party.[18] This *strategic* interaction can be simulated, and outcomes predicted, using the game theory model.[19]

Finally, the quality of China's corporate bankruptcy law – on paper and in practice – is examined against the yardstick of *economic efficiency*. This involves a procedural assessment of whether resources are optimally allocated to carry out distributional goals of bankruptcy law with no or minimal waste. Bankruptcy law and practice can be said to be economically efficient where resources are allocated for the benefit of the whole and any one stakeholder's situation cannot be improved without making another stakeholder worse off.[20]

Economic analysis of law offers valuable insights into why parties decide to act in a particular way. In the context of this book, they help analyse why debtors and creditors in China often choose not to use the EBL. Although not perfect,[21] assuming (bounded) rationality delivers more tractable theoretical predictions than assuming irrationality. Moreover, economic tools offer a credible theory about why the EBL is so rarely used.[22] The theory is then supported by interviews with stakeholders and new data to provide more granularity and insight than prior data permits. Finally, the interview data – although not representative of *all* stakeholders in China – adds much-needed granularity to our understanding of how the EBL operates in practice and provides a platform for further study.

Finally, Chapter ten considers the desirability of further reform to the EBL in China. It reaches the conclusion that such reform is, indeed, desirable based on a functional approach to corporate bankruptcy law and its goals. Economists argue that it is not the role of bankruptcy law to *prevent* corporate risk or corporate failures.[23] Instead, key goals of bankruptcy law should include, firstly, the ability to differentiate between which companies should be reorganised and which should be liquidated; secondly, discouragement or prevention of abuse of bankruptcy law regime by debtors and creditors; thirdly, fair and value-maximising redistribution of assets; fourthly, the ability to maximise the pool of assets by reversing vulnerable transactions; and finally, the encouragement to use bankruptcy law in a timely manner in order to increase payoffs. The appropriate solution depends on why the company became financially distressed or insolvent in the first place. Collectively, these goals enhance corporate bankruptcy regime's efficiency

---

[17] Players' bounded rationality can influence this model and its inputs. See *The Oxford Handbook*, vol 1 (n 6) ch 19.

[18] The strategy that is best for both players when taking into account the other player's strategy, where neither player is better off by any other strategy – this is known as the Nash equilibrium.

[19] ibid.

[20] This is known as 'Pareto efficiency': see *The Oxford Handbook*, vol 1 (n 6) ch 2.3. See also R Posner, *Economic Analysis of Law* (Little, Brown, 1972).

[21] For an in-depth analysis and discussion, see *The Oxford Handbook*, vol 1 (n 6) ch 15.

[22] Nevertheless, it cannot identify which one of several causes is the primary one.

[23] Nevertheless, it can prevent companies from excessive over-indebtedness by imposing hard-budget constraints and reducing the moral hazard that arises from state bailouts and financial support. For more, see Section 10.1.

and justify the ex post redistribution of entitlements that arise from *ex ante* independently agreed contracts and relationships.[24]

1.2. Why Bankruptcy Law Matters

There are several studies about the role and impact of bankruptcy law and its reform on economic development. The studies suggest that improvements in bankruptcy law can have a positive impact on debtors and creditors, and that they contribute to economic development. Three such contributions – easier and cheaper corporate financing; more efficient allocation of resources; and more entrepreneurial activity – are considered below.

Firstly, the existing literature suggests that one of the major benefits of well-functioning bankruptcy law for the economy is the *increase in the availability and the decrease in the cost of credit*. In the absence of effective (legal) creditor protection, banks protect themselves against the risk of no or limited recovery by adjusting their lending practices by increasing interest rates, reducing loan amounts and shortening loan maturities.[25] Moreover, Comparatively higher creditors' recovery rates and lower duration of bankruptcy can lead to a significant reduction in the cost of debt and a big increase in the aggregate level of credit.[26] More timely repayments can also lead to cheaper credit.[27] Common to these improvements is an implied assurance that creditors will get back a larger part of the loan and these savings are passed on to the economy in the form of a greater amount of cheaper credit. Consequently, the protection of creditors' rights and the incentives at firm level often translate into an increase of private credit to GDP at macro level.

In addition, well-functioning bankruptcy law provides credible protection and repayment assurances to market participants (debtors, creditors, investors, shareholders), which enables strangers and one-time business partners to borrow at arm's length (without the need for personal trust or reputation).[28] As a result, better creditor

---

[24] Commentators do not agree on a closed list of goals of bankruptcy laws. For an overview, see J Armour, 'The Law and Economics of Corporate Insolvency: A Review' (2001) ESRC Centre for Business Research, University of Cambridge Working Paper 197/2001. For more, see eg T Jackson, *The Logic and Limits of Bankruptcy Law* (Beard Books, 1986) chs 2–3; A Casey, Bankruptcy's Endowment Effect (2016) *Emory Bankruptcy Developments Journal* 141.

[25] SA Davydenko and JR Franks, 'Do Bankruptcy Codes Matter? A Study of Defaults in France, Germany and the UK' (2008) *Journal of Finance* 565; K Bae and VK Goyal, 'Creditor Rights Enforcement and Bank Loans' (2009) *Journal of Finance* 823; S Visaria, 'Legal Reform and Loan Repayment' (2009) *American Economic Journal: Applied Economics* 59.

[26] G Rodano, N Serrano-Velarde and E Tarantino, 'The Causal Effect of Bankruptcy Law on the Cost of Finance' (2012) Oxford University Centre for Business Taxation Working Paper 12/18; B Funchal, 'The Effects of the 2005 Bankruptcy Reform in Brazil' (2008) *Economics Letters* No 101; X Giné and I Love, 'Do Reorganization Costs Matter for Efficiency? Evidence from a Bankruptcy Reform in Colombia' (July 2006) World Bank Policy Research Working Paper No 3970.

[27] L Klapper, 'Saving Viable Businesses' (2011) The World Bank, Viewpoint 328; S Djankov, O Hart, C McLiesh and A Shleifer, 'Debt Enforcement Around the World' (2008) *Journal of Political Economy* 1105.

[28] See Chapter 2.3.1 for further discussion.

protection leads to better-developed debt markets and more credit available for the private sector.

Secondly, well-functioning bankruptcy law can also help ensure *a more (economically) efficient allocation of resources*. One way it achieves this is through saving viable businesses and liquidating the rest.[29] This requires enabling the market forces to weed out unviable firms and release their assets to value-maximising new users. Studies suggest that lowering reorganisation costs can encourage a natural selection to occur where most weaker firms opt for liquidation while healthier firms choose to restructure.[30] Where a bankruptcy law allows such efficient selection, it has been shown to enable smooth and efficient resolution[31] and maintain an orderly and fair collective[32] distribution of the estate which put assets to the most (economically) efficient use[33] – all achieved for the benefit of creditors as a whole.

In addition, efficient allocation of resources is also promoted where bankruptcy law prevents or reverses preferential treatment of certain creditors and allows market forces to determine which enterprises should survive and which should fail.[34] The evidence suggests that allowing assets to go to the best user leads to improved efficiency of production[35] and lower transaction costs[36] – especially in more complex transactions (through property rights and enforceable contracts).[37] However, excessive cost of bankruptcy procedures may prevent efficient allocation of assets.[38] The problem is further exacerbated by indirect costs, which can grow uncontrollably if the bankruptcy proceedings are very long and supervision-heavy.[39]

---

[29] Giné and Love (n 26); Y Lim and C Hahn, 'Bankruptcy Policy Reform and Total Factor Productivity Dynamics in Korea: Evidence from Macro Data' (2003) NBER Working Paper 9810; JR Franks and G Loranth, 'A Study of Inefficient Going Concerns in Bankruptcy' (2004) CEPR Discussion Paper 5035.

[30] Giné and Love, 'Do Reorganization Costs Matter for Efficiency?' (2006).

[31] MJ White, 'Bankruptcy: Past Puzzles, Recent Reforms, and the Mortgage Crisis' (2009) *American Law and Economics Review* 1.

[32] Individual creditors have an incentive to grab and run rather than wait for an uncertain redistribution in a collective bankruptcy law procedure. Especially where the creditors are a numerous and heterogeneous group, their preferences are likely to vary, and voluntary agreement is highly unlikely, even though collective redistribution is most likely to preserve maximum value for the creditors as a whole: J Armour and D Cumming, 'Bankruptcy Law and Entrepreneurship' (2008) *American Law and Economics Review* 303; Klapper, 'Saving Viable Businesses' (2011).

[33] S Djankov, C McLiesh and A Schleifer, 'Private credit in 129 countries' (2007) *Journal of Financial Economics* 299; Lim and Hahn, 'Bankruptcy Policy Reform' (2003). This was achieved in Colombia through lowering bankruptcy costs: Giné and Love (n 26).

[34] In other words, bankruptcy law introduces a hard budget constraint which prevents the state from propping up inefficient enterprises. For an excellent example of the extreme losses to the economy in the form of non-performing loans and lost opportunities due to inefficient allocation of resources in China, see S Cho, 'Continuing Economic Reform in the People's Republic of China: Bankruptcy Legislation Leads the Way' (1996) *Hastings International and Company Law Review* 739.

[35] J Aron, 'Growth and institutions: A review of the evidence' (15/2000) *The World Bank Research Observer* 99.

[36] ibid: as compared with impossible or hard-to-do enforcement of deals between strangers based solely on relationships-based reputation and social norms.

[37] D North, 'Institutions' (1991) *Journal of Economic Perspectives* 97.

[38] JR Franks and O Sussman, 'Financial Distress and Bank Restructuring of Small to Medium Size UK Companies' (2005) *Review of Finance* 65; A Bris, I Welch and N Zhu, 'The Costs of Bankruptcy: Chapter 7 Liquidation vs. Chapter 11 Reorganization' (2005) *Journal of Finance* 1298.

[39] A Ogus, 'The Importance of Legal Infrastructure for Regulation (and Deregulation) in Developing Countries' (2003) CRC Annual Conference.

It is, therefore, important to ensure that only viable businesses are allowed to reorganise and that the costs of bankruptcy are not excessive. If assets are employed to highest valued use, unnecessary closure of good firms may be avoided and jobs could be saved.[40] Therefore, contrary to the oft-cited argument of protectionist regimes that bankruptcy law increases failure rates and so endangers employment and economy's performance, the reverse is true. Evidence clearly shows that improvements in bankruptcy law have the potential to lead to lowered failure rates[41] and increased recovery rates[42] in the long term.

Thirdly, the last major benefit of having a well-functioning bankruptcy law concerns the *increase in entrepreneurship*. Bankruptcy law deeply affects entrepreneurs who are subjected to external risks when starting and running their businesses. This applies to company owners as well as managers. It has been shown that forgiving personal bankruptcy laws can stimulate entry by 'latent' entrepreneurs who would otherwise be too risk-averse to start their own business.[43] By extension, a forgiving liability regime for managers in corporate bankruptcy laws is likely to have a similar effect of encouraging earlier resolution of financial distress and greater cooperation from the management in bankruptcy. At the same time, empirical studies further show that excessively strong protection of creditor rights can also be harmful to entrepreneurship because they discourage innovation[44] and entrepreneurship itself.[45]

Entrepreneurship can have a far-reaching impact on the whole economy since it improves the country's volume of economic activity which can introduce efficiency-inducing market competition, create value and boost the GDP. Greater entrepreneurial activity also creates new opportunities for investors, new jobs, tax revenue for the Government and increases the inflow of non-bank funds to entrepreneurs and their projects, which, in turn, supports innovation and creativity.[46]

China has not yet fully capitalised on these benefits. Although the law is written to be efficient, it is argued in Chapters ten and eleven that more needs to be done in order to make the EBL more efficient in practice.

---

[40] JB Berk, R Stanton and J Zechner, 'Human Capital, Bankruptcy, and Capital Structure' (2010) *Journal of Finance* 891.

[41] eg in Belgium the failure rate decreased by 8.4% as a result of the reform: N Dewaelheyns and C Van Hulle, 'Legal Reform and Aggregate Small and Micro Business Bankruptcy Rates: Evidence from the 1997 Belgian Bankruptcy Code' (May 2006) KU Leuven AFI Working Paper No 0607. In a Brazilian study, it was predicted that recovery rates will increase from 0.2% to 18.4% after reform: M Lu and Z Azar, 'Comparing the Old and New Brazilian Bankruptcy Law' (2005) Inter-American Trade Report (National Law Center for Inter-American Free Trade, Vol 12(3), March 2005).

[42] In India, timely repayments increased by 28% after the reform of debt enforcement mechanisms: Visaria, 'Legal Reform' (2009). In Thailand, there was a substantial decrease in the level of non-performing loans. However, recoveries were highest in countries with stronger overall creditor protection: Davydenko and Franks, 'Do Bankruptcy Codes Matter?' (2008); Funchal, '2005 Bankruptcy Reform' (2008).

[43] Armour and Cumming, 'Bankruptcy Law' (2008).

[44] V Acharya and K Subramanian, 'Bankruptcy Codes and Innovation' (2009) *Review of Financial Studies* 4949.

[45] Armour and Cumming (n 32).

[46] J Armour, 'Personal Insolvency and the Demand for Venture Capital' (2004) *European Business Organization Law Review* 87.

1.3. Methodology

Initially, very little was written about the EBL, and the empirical data was low in supply and of questionable quality. There were no reliable statistics and no publicly available details of EBL cases. The design of this research responded to these limitations by going directly to the source. I planned and conducted a series of interviews with those who are *authorised to invoke* the EBL – debtors and creditors – and those who *influence* whether and how the EBL is used in practice – most importantly judges, local government officials, practitioners, and other experts. The interviewees answered many of my questions and provided suggestions, information and hard-to-get documents which further informed the study.

In the end, I conducted 67 semi-structured interviews with practitioners, judges, entrepreneurs, policy-makers and experts in China and abroad. My approach to the selection of the interviewees was three-fold. Firstly, I relied on my existing contacts network consisting of my Chinese friends and colleagues from my undergraduate and postgraduate Law studies in the UK; experts I met during my academic stay in China, Australia and the US; and participants in China-related conferences and projects. Secondly, I relied on recommendations and referrals from my contacts and interviewees. And thirdly, I conducted a random search on the Internet, and in particular the Chambers and Partners database to identify top practitioners with relevant experience and insight. Interviewees were chosen according to their ability to provide insights about: (i) what mechanisms are used by creditors to enforce their debts and by debtors to resolve their insolvency/financial distress, and why; (ii) how courts view and use the EBL, and why; and (iii) what has shaped the particular rules and policies that determine how the EBL is implemented in practice.

In order to ensure confidentiality for my interviewees (for the purpose of enabling them to speak freely), however, identities of all interviewees are coded.[47]

I was also fortunate to be invited to take part in several high-level judicial and political projects in China and abroad, which opened my eyes to many practical difficulties that complicate the implementation of the EBL. I also hosted two Supreme People's Court judges at the University of Oxford for two months and benefited from many insightful conversations with them, for which I am very grateful. I have also presented parts of my research and taken part in many workshops, conferences, discussions, and arbitrations, which gave me further insights into how the EBL operates, why its efficient use is so important for China's economy and business environment, and what prevents more objective and efficient implementation of the law. Together, these insights further improved my understanding of the concerns of the primary decision-makers and

---

[47] Each interviewee is identified by an upper-case letter (which denotes their industry affiliation: Bank, Consultant, Entrepreneur, Informal Finance provider, Judge, Lawyer, Politician, Researcher) followed by a number (number within their category) and a lower-case letter (which denotes the method of selection: 'c' for connected through a conference, common project etc; 'r' for random, no connection; and 's' for snowball, by recommendation).

secondary influencers who, in the aggregate, determine whether and how the EBL gets used. These findings are discussed in Chapters six to nine.

Over time, more and more materials became available online, mostly in Chinese. Gaining access to the previously inaccessible primary and secondary sources helped to further support and refine many of my arguments and conclusions that are presented in this book. They also provided much-needed background and details that helped my understanding of the many issues raised in my interviews. Chapters four, six, eight, eleven and twelve, in particular, benefited from the increased availability of the primary materials.

Much of the data and information contained in this book comes from Chinese-language materials. I tried, wherever possible, to refer to English-language sources to enable the readers to dig deeper without the need to understand Chinese. For the Chinese speakers who wish to carry out further research, I tried to provide the names of key documents in Chinese. For that reason, I include a list of judicial and political guidance documents with their official Chinese name and identifier and with an English translation.[48] For some topics, most of the materials are only in Chinese. For example, the discussion of recent reform initiatives in Chapter twelve relies almost entirely on Chinese-language sources. In such cases, I tried to provide succinct summaries of the key issues and proposed rules so that non-Chinese speaking readers can also benefit and gain an insight into these materials.

Together, the newly collected qualitative and quantitative data and the primary and secondary materials offer valuable in-depth process insights to answer the four questions posed at the start of this chapter, namely the reasons for the limited use of the EBL, the desirability of greater and more efficient use of the EBL, the possible improvements, and the role of foreign stakeholders in the process.

1.4. Structure of the Book

This book contains 12 substantive chapters that are organised into four parts. Part I provides the basic background which makes this book and its arguments accessible to non-China experts and those with expertise in some but not all relevant areas. Chapter two explains the relevant developments in China's socio-economic environment, the structure of power, the role of laws, the role of courts and their relationship with the Party-state and corporate ownership. Chapter three focuses on debt finance, formal and informal debt enforcement, and challenges that prevent or limit debt enforcement in China.

Part II explores the Enterprise Bankruptcy Law 2006 (EBL) and its practical limitations. Chapter four describes the history and developments of bankruptcy law in China, the black-letter provisions of the EBL and the Supreme People's Court's guidance on how to apply these provisions. Chapter five examines the number of EBL cases and

---

[48] Note that these documents do not usually have an official English translation, and so they are identified under different names in different sources. That is why their Chinese identifier (eg *Fashi* [2007] No.8) is so important.

provides an overview of four interlinked constraints on the use of the EBL in practice. These constraints – informed by my interviews and new data from Chinese sources – are fully explored in Chapters six to nine. Chapter six focuses on the problems with the EBL as written, which reduce parties' payoffs (actual or perceived) under the EBL. Chapter seven discusses the problems in the surrounding rules and practices that are necessary for the EBL to function well in practice. The limitations of these rules also lead to reduced recoveries under the EBL. Chapter eight further proposes that the EBL enforcers – primarily judges and administrators, but also local governments in some cases – face internal and external limitations on their ability and willingness to enforce the law as written which results in biased implementation or refusal to accept EBL petitions altogether. And Chapter nine suggests that debtors and creditors perceive the EBL as offering them comparatively lower payoffs (versus extra-legal enforcement mechanisms) which is why they prefer not to use the EBL. Together, it is argued, these four sets of reasons have limited the effectiveness of the EBL in resolving corporate financial distress and, consequently, it has also reduced parties' willingness to use the EBL in practice.

Part III builds on the earlier discussion and considers whether it is desirable to ameliorate the practical implementation of the EBL in China and how it can be done. Chapter ten asks whether greater use of bankruptcy law is, in fact, desirable in China, and concluding that it is, it then provides a general discussion of the benefits that are likely to flow from such reform. It also outlines what would be the necessary focus of further reforms, what obstacles would likely hinder reform efforts, and which approach would likely work best in practice. Chapter eleven then proposes options for ameliorating the problems identified in Chapters six to eight. The reform proposals contained in this chapter were discussed and reviewed with many experts in China and abroad as part of a broader Chinese law reform project in which I have been actively involved. The proposals also provide new ideas and insights into what is needed but also what is feasible in today's China. Finally, Chapter twelve provides an overview of what has been happening since the Government identified bankruptcy law reform as one of its key political priorities in late 2015. It focuses on 10 major initiatives that have been trialled (mostly at a local level) between 2015 and 2020. It also considers the likely impact of these initiatives in the future.

Part IV, Chapter thirteen, completes the discussion by looking at how foreign bodies influenced the initial design and implementation of the EBL, considering the position of foreign creditors and debtors under the EBL rules and further guidance on cross-border bankruptcy cases, and examining several real-life cases in which foreign interests were affected.

This book aims to state the law as on 30 June 2020.

PART I

Background

Introducing and improving bankruptcy law has the potential to greatly improve China's business environment and further support the growth and development of its economy.[1] However, bankruptcy law operates within constraints of the environment in which it is implemented.[2] The next two chapters, therefore, outline EBL's institutional environment. Chapter two explores economic, social, political and legal developments that have prompted the need to introduce, and later to reform, bankruptcy law in China. The discussed developments have also shaped and continue to influence how bankruptcy law is used and perceived in China. Chapter three then examines the core element of bankruptcy law – debt and debt enforcement – and explains how they operate in China. The aim of Part I is to enable a deeper understanding and appreciation of the arguments about EBL's practical limitations in Part II and the discussion about the desirability and options of EBL reform in Part III.

[1] See Section 1.2.
[2] C Wihlborg, S Gangopadhyay and Q Hussain (2001) 'Infrastructure Requirements in the Area of Bankruptcy Law' (Wharton Financial Institutions Center Working Paper 01-09).

2

China's Socio-Economic, Political and Legal Environment

The People's Republic of China began its transition from central planning to a (socialist) market economy under Deng Xiaoping's leadership in 1978. Bankruptcy law was introduced as a part of these pro-market reforms in 1986, but almost as soon as it was brought in effect in 1988, the law was deemed insufficient. A search for a broader, more up-to-date law began almost immediately. The final product of the subsequent 12-year reform process, the Enterprise Bankruptcy Law 2006 (EBL), is the focus of this book. The motivation for introducing the law, its form, the implementation process, the behaviour of debtors and creditors who are entitled to use the law, the attitude of courts, the role of local governments and many other issues that shape whether and how the EBL gets used in practice, however, are heavily influenced by various socio-economic, political and legal issues in the surrounding environment.

This chapter provides a brief account of the institutional background in which the need for bankruptcy law arose and in which the law was passed, implemented and is being used. Section 2.1 of this chapter looks at economic and political changes over the past eight decades. The focus is on the period between 2007 to 2019 – same as the available data on the use of the EBL – but the discussion begins with the Mao era, which shaped later developments and still influences people's preferences and attitude to bankruptcy law today. Section 2.2 examines the role of the Chinese Communist Party and the Government, and looks at how they exercise power and make decisions. Section 2.3 discusses the role and interaction of rules and laws, the role of law, and the concept of the rule *of* (and *by*) law in China. Section 2.4 explores the relationship between courts and the Party-state and the resulting limitations of law enforcement. And Section 2.5 examines corporate ownership and control in China, and their impact on law enforcement.

2.1. Economic and Political Transformation of China

The People's Republic of China ('China') was established on 1 October 1949 following a victory of the Chinese Communist Party ('the Party').[3] Since then, China has been growing faster than any other country in history and developed from an economy based

---

[3] See eg M Meisner, *Mao's China and After: A History of the People's Republic*, 3rd edn (The Free Press, 1999).

on small-scale, localised trade and agriculture to one of the largest and most important economies of the early twenty-first century.[4] China's firms are among the largest
and most successful in the world, its GDP multiplies every few years, its FDI influences and shapes foreign economies, and its currency has become one of five Special
Drawing-Right currencies.[5] Bankruptcy law played its part in this transformation. Its
introduction was a natural response to an increasingly market-driven economy that
emerged following Deng Xiaoping's 1970s reforms,[6] and it also propelled China's growth
and development.[7]

The economy grew and matured steadily over the last eight decades, but the development was punctured by sharp drops and sudden increases that resulted from events that
continue to influence how China works and responds to economic shocks to this day.
As China opened up to foreign markets and influences post-1978, it became vulnerable to crises beyond its borders – most importantly the collapse of the Soviet Block
in 1989, the Asian financial crisis in 1997/98, the dot.com bubble burst in 2000/01,
and more recently the after-effect of the global financial crisis of 2009/10 and the
coronavirus pandemic in 2020. These domestic and international events influenced the
Government's willingness to introduce and reform bankruptcy law as well as people's
attitudes to doing business and dealing with crises – including corporate financial
distress. These key events and their continuing impact are briefly discussed below.

After the fall of the Qing Empire in 1911, China was engulfed in a 38-year civil
war which ended with the victory of the Party. Supported by the Party, Mao Zedong
declared the People's Republic of China on 1 October 1949, marking the beginning of a
new 'classless' era where the Party claimed absolute power in exchange for a promise to
deliver prosperity and progress to the people.[8] The Party banned private ownership and
all other capitalist concepts; all laws were abolished and replaced by high-level policies
that could be easily changed to serve the Party's needs; resources were diverted into the
nationalised heavy industry; farms were collectivised into communes; and from 1953
the economy operated under Five-Year Plans in a centralised Soviet-like command
economy.[9] In the mid-1950s, China moved away from Russian-style Marxist-Leninist
communism and towards Mao's new interpretation of communism (known as Maoism).
Its emphasis on 'strong Party' in the heart of China's future has survived until this day.[10]

---

[4] See eg L Brandt and TG Rawski, *China's Great Economic Transformation* (Cambridge University Press, 2008); B Naughton, *The Chinese Economy: Transitions and Growth* (MIT Press, 2007).

[5] ibid. For an account from the Chinese perspective see X Wu, *The Decade of Surge with Big Fishes and Flooding Water* (CITIC Press Corporation, 2017).

[6] B Gilley, 'Deng Xiaoping and His Successors' in WA Joseph (ed), *Politics in China*, 3rd edn (Oxford University Press, 2019).

[7] For a detailed discussion see N Mrockova, 'Does Law Matter for Economic Development: the Case of China' in L Scaffardi (ed), *The BRICS Group in the Spotlight: An Interdisciplinary Approach* (Edizioni Schientifiche Italiane, 2015). See also K Dam, *The Law-Growth Nexus: The Rule of Law and Economic Develop-ment* (Brookings Institution Press, 2006).

[8] See eg FC Teiwes, 'Mao Zedong in Power' in Joseph (ed), Politics in China (2019); Meisner, *Mao's China and After* (1999).

[9] The plans dictated when, what, and for how much SOEs produces their goods. The wages were deter-mined not by performance, but by reference to one's status (age, education, position, etc). The state owned, controlled and financed all projects, covering both losses and profits of its companies: see A Kipnis, L Tomba and J Unger (eds), *Contemporary Chinese Society and Politics* (Routledge, 2009).

[10] See eg WA Joseph, 'Ideology and China's Political Development' in Joseph (n 4).

With a vision to (re)build a 'great China', Mao initiated a set of far-reaching reforms in 1958–60. His Great Leap Forward was supposed to transform the country into an industrial and military superpower.[11] However, the reforms failed and instead led to the Great Famine that caused between 14 and 43 million excess deaths.[12] This historical experience has informed all post-Mao reforms and experiments in that all changes are first trialled locally. It has also influenced the initial testing and implementation of bankruptcy law.

To salvage the situation, the then-prime minister Zhou Enlai instituted several reforms which culminated in the 'Four Modernizations' programme (in agriculture, industry, science and technology, and defence) in 1964/65.[13] Their implementation was disrupted by the violent Cultural Revolution.[14] Between 1966 and 1976, Mao sought to ideologically 'purify' the Party – overthrowing his enemies and some ex-colleagues – and politically reinvigorate China's youth. Millions of people were killed, persecuted or publicly humiliated over their 'wrong' (ie non-communist or insufficiently zealous) political attitudes.[15] The ensuing chaos interrupted production and transportation of food, proper functioning of trade and exports, and normal life in the society, and caused another wave of famine.[16] Towards the end, Mao's deteriorating health and ultimate senility left China in the hands of his ambitious wife Jiang Qing and her Gang of Four.[17] When Mao died in 1976, China was impoverished and isolated. The Party had learned to be cautious and slow in making any far-reaching changes.

Zhou Enlai's reforms resurfaced after Mao's death, under the informal leadership of Deng Xiaoping, who took charge in 1978. Although never in a top political post, Deng became China's 'paramount leader' whose reforms transformed poverty-stricken China into an economic miracle between 1978 and his retirement in 1989.[18] Unlike Mao and his followers, Deng recognised the weaknesses of the planned economy and sought to learn from China's fast-developing market-oriented neighbours – Hong Kong, Taiwan, South Korea and Singapore – albeit adjusted to China's needs. The problems that China faced in the later 1970s were deep-rooted and ubiquitous: state-owned enterprises (SOEs) were inefficient, productivity was low, the financial sector was underdeveloped, and there was a lack of expertise and money due to China's isolation under Mao's reign. Deng gradually introduced select market tools that transformed China into a blend of socialism and capitalism but without sacrificing the central role of the Party-state.

---

[11] See eg Teiwes, 'Mao Zedong' (2019); R MacFarquhar, *The Origins of the Cultural Revolution 2: The Great Leap Forward, 1958–1960* (Columbia University Press, 1983).

[12] The estimates vary. See eg MacFarquhar, *Origins* (1983); T Bernstein, 'Stalinism, famine, and Chinese peasants Grain procurements during the Great Leap Forward' (1984) *Theory and Society* 339.

[13] See eg Gilley, 'Deng Xiaoping' (2019).

[14] See eg R MacFarquhar and M Schoenhals, *Mao's Last Revolution* (Harvard University Press, 2006); LT White, *Policies of Chaos: the organizational causes of violence in China's Cultural Revolution* (Princeton University Press, 1989).

[15] See eg J Andreas, 'Battling over political and cultural power during the Chinese Cultural Revolution' (2002) *Theory and Society* 463; FC Teiweis and W Sun, *The End of the Maoist Era: Chinese Politics During the Twilight of the Cultural Revolution, 1972–1976* (ME Sharpe, 2009); V Pollard, *State Capitalism, Contentious Politics and Large-Scale Social Change* (Koninklijke Brill, 2011).

[16] ibid.

[17] See eg Teiweis and Sun, *The End of the Maoist Era* (2009).

[18] See eg Gilley (n 4); E Vogel, *Deng Xiaoping and the Transformation of China* (Harvard University Press, 2011).

The resulting system is often referred to as 'socialist market economy'[19] with 'Chinese characteristics'.[20] Deng was a pragmatist who focused more on the effectiveness of his policies than ideology.[21] His reforms started opening the economy to foreign influence and expertise, international trade and cooperation, they led to more market-based production, and helped create a simple capital market.[22] The reforms focused on several key issues. Within China, Deng focused on reforming corporate ownership through reorganisation and privatisation of SOEs and communes, and expansion of private ownership.[23] These changes, however, disrupted the state's traditional role in social welfare provision – institutionalised through its policy of *iron rice bowl*, where everyone was employed and otherwise provided for from birth to death by the state through an SOE.[24]

Consequently, secondly, the reforms included reconceptualisation of employers' duties and depowering of state-controlled labour unions which previously regulated professional and social lives of their members.[25] As a result, people gained the freedom to move and live without the state's intervention, but they also lost the former certainty of a life-long social welfare provision.[26] Naturally, many people fear this growing insecurity, and so popular protests have been on the rise.[27] With an estimate of 200,000 public protests in 2010 alone,[28] local governments are careful to closely police and minimise disputes and controversies, which could give rise to mass uprisings.[29]

Many of Deng's reforms also sought to attract foreign investors, their know-how, skills and new products. First, four Special Economic Zones (SEZ) were opened in 1980 for that purpose – offering tax concessions and access to an untapped market in exchange for capital and technical knowledge[30] – and helped increase the contribution of foreign trade to China's GDP from 7 to 37 per cent between 1978

---

[19] See X Ding, 'The Socialist Market Economy: China and the World' (2009) 73 *Science & Society* 235.

[20] For discussion of ideological and economic transformation, see Brandt and Rawski, *China's Great Economic Transformation* (2008); Naughton, *The Chinese Economy* (2007). See also A Chan, R Madsen and J Unger, *Chen Village under Mao and Deng* (University of California Press, 1992) chs 11–12; M Meisner, *The Deng Xiaoping Era: An inquiry into the fate of Chinese socialism* (Hill and Wang, 1996).

[21] See R Baum, *Burying Mao: Chinese Politics in the Age of Deng Xiaoping* (Princeton University Press, 1996).

[22] Further see Pollard, *State Capitalism* (n 13) 157–58.

[23] See Section 2.5 below.

[24] Post-reform provision of healthcare outside the SOE structure has been difficult, especially in the countryside: G Chow, *Interpreting China's Economy* (World Scientific Publishing, 2010). See also JCB Leung, 'Dismantling the 'iron rice bowl': welfare reforms in the People's Republic of China' (1994) *Journal of Social Policy* 341; S Cook, 'After the Iron Rice Bowl: Extending the Safety Net in China' (2000) IDS Discussion Paper 377.

[25] Under the hukou户口 principle and the danwei 单位 principle. See eg M Gallagher, *Authoritarian Legality in China* (Cambridge University Press, 2017).

[26] China still does not have a functioning social welfare system: see Sections 7.2.1 and 11.2.1.

[27] For the numbers and examples of incidents see F Chen, 'Subsistence Crises, Managerial Corruption and Labour Protests in China' (July 2000) *The China Journal* 41; T Lum, 'Social Unrest in China' (2006) *Congressional Research Service* 19.

[28] C Goebel and LH Ong, 'Social Unrest in China' (2012) Long Briefing, Europe China Research and Academic Network.

[29] As a result, China's national budget for 'stability maintenance' (weihuwending 维护稳定, or weiwen维稳) is significant. In 2012 China spent 105 billion USD on defence, but 110 billion USD on stability maintenance: C Li, 'China's Communist Party-state: The Structure and Dynamics of Power' in Joseph (n 4).

[30] See eg J Chen, 'China: Constitutional Changes and Legal Development' in A Tay and A Leung (eds), *Greater China – Law, Society and Trade* (Law Book Company, 1995).

and 1998.[31] This also gave access to Chinese companies to foreign know-how and new export markets.

Deng adopted a dual-track approach to transition: a part of the economy (non-priority sectors like commodity production, light industry, services, etc) was liberalised and put under slowly-emerging market conditions, while the rest remained under state control (heavy manufacturing, energy, oil, etc).[32] His reforms were first tested in newly created SEZs before their nationwide implementation. A similar system remains in China to this day. Both the 1986 and the 2006 bankruptcy laws and the recent reforms discussed in Chapter twelve followed the same system.

Deng's reforms completely transformed China's economy and led to phenomenal economic growth. China's annual GDP (and GDP growth rates) increased steadily from just under RMB 68 billion in 1952 (when the records began) to RMB 368 billion in 1978 (when the reforms began). By the time of Deng's retirement in 1989, China's GDP stood at RMB 1.72 trillion – that is 465 per cent higher than when the reforms started in 1978 and 2529 per cent higher than in 1952.[33]

However, the massacre of the protesters at Tiananmen Square in Beijing in June 1989 and the crumbling of the Soviet Union in 1989 led to the reversal of many pro-market reforms.[34] The resulting economic stagnation was only reversed following Deng's famous Southern Tour (*nanxun* 南巡) in 1992[35] where he urged people to 'be a little bolder, go a little faster', which encouraged entrepreneurship and the resumption of pro-market reforms.[36] The 14th Party Congress in October 1992 – for the first time – formally endorsed Deng's idea of socialist market economy as its reform goal, and the results were impressive. The FDI increased, many new joint Sino-foreign companies were established, and several SOEs listed on overseas stock markets. Many poorly managed SOEs were restructured into corporations, internally reorganised, privatised, refinanced through FDI and many even made it to Fortune Global 500 list by 2009.[37] FDI also accelerated the development of China's non-state sector, which became the real engine of China's miraculous double-digit growth for several decades.[38]

The beginning of the twenty-first century marked China's formal entry into the global market, primarily through its accession to the World Trade Organization (WTO) in December 2001, after 15 years of negotiations. China agreed to introduce many substantial legal reforms to ensure China's smooth integration into the international trading system and to appease the existing WTO members and create market-style protections for foreign companies that operate in or with China. The Chinese Government agreed to make its legal system more transparent; to ensure uniform, impartial and reasonable

---

[31] G Chow, 'Economic Reform and Growth in China' (2004) *Annals of Economics and Finance* 127, 131.
[32] L Yueh, *Enterprising China* (Oxford University Press, 2009) 754; D Zweig, 'China's Political Economy' in Joseph (n 4).
[33] World Bank data.
[34] Z Yang, 'Legitimacy Crisis and Legitimation in China' (1996) *Journal of Contemporary Asia* 201, 217; S Breslin, 'Globalization, International Coalitions, and Domestic Reform' (2004) 36 *Critical Asian Studies* 657.
[35] Shortly after the final fall of the Soviet Union in late 1991.
[36] J Kynge, *China Shakes the World – The Rise of a Hungry Nation* (Weidenfeld & Nicolson, 2006) 25. See also n 16.
[37] See Section 5.1 below.
[38] See Section 2.5 below.

application of the law; to remove local protectionism, nepotism and red tape; and to provide for efficient judicial review.[39] An important law that needed to be made in order to deliver on these promises was an upgraded, market-driven bankruptcy law, which provided a further push for making a replacement of the 1986 law.[40]

Nevertheless, despite the promises to join the global market and follow its rules, the Chinese Government started slowing down the pro-market reforms in December 2006. It reinstated its control over the banks and revived some old-time protectionist measures in favour of the state sector.[41] The leadership's reluctance to follow the Western capitalist models was further deepened following the global financial crisis in 2008–2010.[42]

China's economy continues to benefit from the market reforms that were started by Deng in the late 1970s. China's GDP reached RMB 68.6 trillion in 2015 – a thousand times more than just six decades earlier.[43] GDP per capita also grew significantly – from RMB 385 in 1978 to RMB 49,992 in 2015.[44] Moreover, China's fast growth lifted over 70 million people out of poverty between 1981 and 2010.[45] Nevertheless, China has not become a full free-market capitalist economy where trade and industry would be controlled by private owners for profit. Instead, it is more accurately described as 'authoritarian capitalism' where the Party-state leaders allow the forces of supply and demand and private corporate ownership and management, but retain the ultimate control over economic actors and influence throughout the system.[46]

The success of China's economy since the late 1970s has been unprecedented. Nevertheless, China faces serious economic challenges.[47] Besides growing inequality and rapid urbanisation, the Chinese Government has had to adjust to the 'new normal' where GDP growth rates dropped from double-digits to about 6.5 per cent. In absolute terms, China's GDP remains significant and makes China one of the most productive countries in the world. Nevertheless, the economy needs to be restructured to resolve the enormous amount of debt[48] and to accommodate the changing socio-economic and political reality of the twenty-first century.[49]

The Party responded initially by changing its rhetoric from focusing on the speed of China's economic growth to ensuring economic stability and promoting innovation and quality of life.[50] This shift has also been reflected in the Party-state's refocusing on resolving some underlying economic issues, including excessive corporate debt and

---

[39] C Esplugues, 'China's Accession to WTO' (2009) *Chinese Business Law* 1.
[40] See Section 4.1.
[41] C Walter and F Howie, *Red Capitalism* (John Wiley & Sons, 2011) 4–5 and 20–22.
[42] Similarly, Western influence has also been rejected in judicial context: Section 2.4.1.
[43] World Bank data.
[44] ibid. The improvement stemmed from the combination of GDP growth and the positive economic impact of Deng's one-child policy (ie slower population growth and increasing living standards).
[45] In 1981, China had over 88% of its population living on less than 1.9 USD a day; by 2010, it was only 11.2% of the population: World Bank data.
[46] See RW Carney, *Authoritatrian Capitalism* (Cambridge University Press, 2018); MA Witt and G Redding, 'China: Authoritarian Capitalism' in MA Witt and G Redding, *Oxford Handbook of Asian Business Systems* (Oxford University Press, 2014).
[47] See Zweig, 'China's Political Economy' (n 30) 302–07.
[48] See Section 3.1.
[49] See Section 12.1.
[50] See Section 12.1 on how this shift influenced the Party-state's attitude to the EBL.

zombie companies (both of which require greater and more efficient use of bankruptcy law). As a result, the EBL has been in a spotlight and subject of many debates since late 2015.[51]

2.2. Power and the Party-State

The content, implementation and use of bankruptcy law in China have, to a large extent, been influenced by the pressure and preferences of the Party-state which holds power in China. Indeed, one of the major constraints on the use of the EBL is the reluctance of the Party-state to allow an independent implementation of the law.[52] The discussion below examines who holds the reins of power and how decisions are made in China. Section 2.2.1 briefly outlines the structures through which power is exercised. Sections 2.2.2 and 2.2.3 then look at the role of the Government and of the Party. And Section 2.2.4 concludes with a short analysis of the relationship between the two.

2.2.1. The Structure of Power in China

On paper, power in China is shared by six bodies: the Party holds political power (ie sets overarching policies); the People's Congresses and their committees hold legislative power (ie make laws); the State Council, its ministries and commissions hold executive power (ie make and carry out policies); the Supreme People's Court holds judicial power (ie adjudicates cases); the Supreme People's Procuratorate holds procuratorial power (ie investigates and prosecutes violations of the law); and the Central Military Commission holds military power (ie ensures internal and external security). Each has its role and responsibilities, but there is no clear separation of powers.[53] In practice, China is governed by so-called Four Big Organisations (*Sidabanzi*四大班子), namely the Party, the National People's Congress (NPC) and the State Council and the Chinese People's Political Consultative Conferences (CPPCC), which advises them all. In most cases, however, the Party oversees and controls the others, which makes it the real decision-maker and ruler of China.[54]

2.2.2. The Chinese Government and Legislature

China's Constitution states that the highest organ of state power is the NPC.[55] The NPC elects executive power-holders – the President (and Vice-President),[56] members of the

---

[51] See ch 12.
[52] See Section 8.3.
[53] See eg Li, 'China's Communist Party-state' (n 27).
[54] See Section 2.2.3–2.2.4.
[55] Art 2 of the Constitution of the PRC 1984, as amended 2004.
[56] Sometimes the word 'Chairman' is used instead. Both have the same Chinese translation *zhuxi* 主席. The Chinese word for a president, *zongtong*总统, is not used in China.

central Government called the State Council,[57] and the Government's chair called the Premier (and Vice-Premier). The NPC also chooses the Chief Justice of the Supreme People's Court. Delegates in the NPC are elected every five years and meet annually for about two weeks to discuss and vote on major political issues. When not in session, the NPC's power is exercised by its Standing Committee in their meetings (every two months).[58]

There are six levels of government: national (or central), provincial, municipal, county, township and village (or grassroots).[59] The central Government appoints and supervises governors in provinces and autonomous regions. Provincial leaders appoint and supervise municipal leaders, with higher-level bodies controlling those immediately below them.[60] Local governments are in charge of administration and management of social, political and economic affairs in their region – including dealing with unemployment and corporate financial affairs. Leading cadres at each level are subject to the cadre responsibility system (*ganbukaohezhidu*干部考核制度, or *gangweizerenzhi*岗位责任制)[61] and must sign political performance contracts with their immediate superior authorities.[62] These performance contracts always include a duty to promote local economic development, maintain economic and social stability, and collect state and local taxes, and all are measured against set targets.[63] The satisfaction of the targets is rewarded with better career opportunities and monetary rewards, while failing to fulfil one's targets leads to reprimands and loss of career progression opportunities,[64] and in some instances also a loss of the deposit paid when certain tasks are assigned.[65]

This multi-layered governance system enables easier control and accountability within the government hierarchy. At the same time, China's decentralised structure has enabled grassroots economic initiatives and innovative political solutions which were later successfully implemented nationwide[66] – for example, the first version of the

---

[57] ie the Premier, several Vice Premiers, several State Councillors, and 29 ministers and heads of State Council Commissions.

[58] See eg Li (n 27); JT Dreyer, *China's Political System: Modernization and Tradition* (Longman, 2010).

[59] Township and village level are sometimes put together as 'local' level. For an excellent, even if slightly out-of-date analysis see MS Tanner, *The Politics of Lawmaking in China* (Oxford University Press, 1999). For details of local-level governance, see M Xia, *The People's Congresses and Governance in China* (Routledge, 2008).

[60] The autonomous regions and the municipalities answer to the national level directly.

[61] See Z Wang, 'Seeking performance or control? Tethered party innovation in China's performance evaluation system' (2020) *Journal of Chinese Governance* 1; JP Burns and Z Zhiren, 'Performance management in the Government of the People's Republic of China' (2010) *OECD Journal on Budgeting* 1.

[62] See M Edin, *Market Forces and Communist Power* (Uppsala University Press, 2000); SH Whiting, *Power and Wealth in Rural China* (Cambridge University Press, 2006) 124.

[63] L Zhou, 'Governing China's Local Officials' (2007) *Economic Research Journal* 36; Y Jing, Y Cui and D Li, 'The Politics of Performance Measurement in China' (2015) *Policy and Society* 49.

[64] Also, it makes the leader more politically visible: ibid. Albeit, this is most pronounced at the provincial level, less so at lower levels of local Party-state: CE Nevitt, 'Private Business Associations in China: Evidence of Civil Society or Local State Power?' (1996) *The China Journal* 36, 39–40.

[65] See Edin, *Market Forces* (2000) 277.

[66] See eg Naughton (n 2); M Carney, D Shapiro and Y Tang, 'Business Group Performance in China: Ownership and Temporal Considerations' (2009) *Management and Organization Review* 167.

reformed bankruptcy law was tested in Shenzhen.[67] Some recent reforms of the EBL have also been inspired and carried out locally as grassroots initiatives.[68] Over time, local governments have become the new centres of power and influence, which, in the aggregate, have determined the growth of China's economy.

On the other hand, however, leaving so much discretion in the hands of local leaders has also led to harmful local protectionism, rent-seeking, and conflicting interests between the local and national levels of government.[69] As a result, although local officials are still appointed and dismissed by the central Government, the latter's ability to control and monitor local activities has been greatly diminished, while the local officials' position has been strengthened by their access to local information and resources.[70]

Under the leadership of President Xi Jinping, central Government reasserted its oversight over ministries and local governments and accumulated ultimate power over many political and fiscal issues[71] through a series of campaigns[72] and trials of high-ranking local officials.[73] Nevertheless, the relationship between central and local governments is not clearly hierarchical, and the central–local power divide continues to impact on the way laws are made and enforced in China.[74]

2.2.3. The Communist Party of China

The power-structure of the Party mirrors that of the Government (see Figure 2.1). The highest organ in the Party's organisational structure is the National Party Congress (in session once every five years) and its Central Committee. They elect the most powerful organs of the Party, namely the 25-man leadership group known as the Politburo, its seven-man Standing Committee, and the Party's leader, the General Secretary. In practice, however, the members of the outgoing Standing Committee of the Politburo influence the election choices to the highest positions in the Party.[75]

---

[67] See Section 4.1.

[68] See ch 12.

[69] See Section 2.4 below and Section 8.3. For further analysis, see Li (n 27).

[70] See G Montinola, Y Qian and B Weingast, 'Federalism Chinese Style' (1995) *World Politics* 50; H Cai and D Treisman, 'Did Government Decentralization Cause China's Economic Miracle?' (2006) *World Politics* 505.

[71] See eg B Naughton, 'Leadership Transition and the "Top Level Design" of Economic Reform' (30.4.2012) China Leadership Monitor No 37; Z Yang, 'Fragmented Authoritarianism' (2013) *China Journal of Social Work* 4.

[72] Including the powerful anti-corruption campaign: Gilley (n 4).

[73] eg the downfall of Bo Xilai, once a powerful Minister of Commerce (2007–12), a member of the Central Politburo (2007–12), a secretary of the Party's Chongqing branch (2007–12) and one of the most powerful men in China before his trial in 2013: K Zhai (22.8.2013, SCMP).

[74] Further discussed in Sections 2.4.2 and 8.3.2 in the context of bankruptcy law.

[75] For more see Li (n 27).

Figure 2.1 Comparison of the structure of the Party and the state

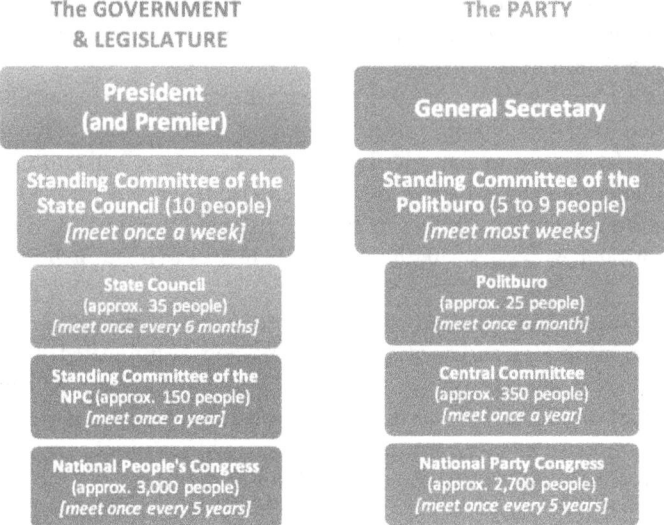

The Party exists at all levels of society in China. Its representatives – organised in so-called Party cells – operate at universities, in law firms, courts, companies (private and state-owned, Chinese and foreign), and even in non-profit and non-governmental organisations.[76] But the Party is not a representative institution: in 2013, there were 85 million members, which is only about six per cent of the total population.[77] The real power is concentrated in the hands of about 2,500 high-level cadres (*gaojiganbu* 高级干部),[78] and the most influential posts are held by the descendants of the old elite that led the Party in the 1920s.[79]

Party membership provides valuable networking opportunities for businesses and gives its members access to information and resources (most owners of private-sector enterprises are Party members). But membership also carries duties. Each new member must take an admission oath, promising:

> [T]o *uphold the Party's program*, observe the provisions of the Party constitution, fulfil a Party member's duties, *carry out the Party's decisions*, strictly observe Party discipline, guard Party secrets, *be loyal to the Party*, work hard, fight for communism throughout my life, *be ready at all times to sacrifice my all for the Party* and the people, and *never betray the Party*.[80]

[76] See LLP Gore, 'The Chinese Communist Party and China's Capitalist Revolution: The political impact of market' (Routledge, 2011) 35ff.

[77] D Roberts (12.6.2014, Bloomberg).

[78] K Brown, *The New Emperors: Power and the Princelings in China* (IB Tauris, 2014) 20.

[79] ibid 3–8.

[80] The Communist Party's admission oath (emphasis added).

Members must participate in regular indoctrination activities[81] and provide insider information through Party branches that exist in all businesses and law firms in China (often unknowingly to the owners).[82]

2.2.4. The Party-State

China has an authoritarian regime led by a strong decentralised government.[83] In practice, however, it is the Party that holds the ultimate control over central and local government institutions.[84] The complex overlay of the Party and state organs at national, provincial, municipal and county levels[85] result in a powerful Party-state hybrid which controls China's economy and society.

The Party exercises control over the Government in three important ways. Firstly, the members of the all-powerful Standing Committee of the Politburo (the Party) hold key roles within the country's governance structure.[86] Secondly, all voting delegates in the NPC are Party members who, therefore, took the oath of loyalty to the Party.[87] Moreover, the Party de facto appoints all members of the NPC Standing Committee and a member of the Politburo Standing Committee chairs the NPC Standing Committee meetings.[88] Thirdly, although the Party has no constitutional power to propose new laws, in practice, it has a significant influence both at the preparatory stage and during the consultations in the NPC Standing Committee and in the NPC itself.[89] The voting in the NPC by the delegates is then mostly a formality.

The form, substance, implementation and enforcement of laws and policies in China are, therefore, controlled by a Party-state hybrid.[90] The Party enforces its ideology[91] and goals[92] through its influence on various parts and levels of the government.

---

[81] There is a strong emphasis on this for high-level cadres: see F Pieke, *The Good Communist* (Cambridge University Press, 2015).

[82] The general manager usually acts as a secretary of the Party branch: R Callick, *The Party Forever* (Palgrave Macmillan, 2013) 16.

[83] Section 2.2.2.

[84] Section 2.2.3. PE Landry, *Decentralized Authoritarianism in China* (Cambridge University Press, 2008); R Gilson and C Milhaupt, 'Economically Benevolent Dictators: Lessons for Emerging Democracies' (2011) 59 *American Journal of Comparative Law* 227; S Heilmann (ed), *China's Political System* (Rowman & Littlefield, 2017) ch 2; Li (n 27).

[85] See Table 2.1.

[86] For example, in 2017 Xi Jinping was also the President of China and the Chairman of the Central Military Commission; Li Keqiang also chaired the State Council as the Premier; and Zhang Dejiang was also the Chairman of the NPC.

[87] See Section 2.2.3.

[88] See eg Li (n 27).

[89] Gore, 'The Chinese Communist Party' (2011) 26; Callick, *The Party Forever* (2013) 55.

[90] See eg D Lampton, *Following the Leader* (University of California Press, 2014).

[91] Broadly based on Marxism-Leninism, but significantly updated by the five generations of Chinese leaders: see Section 2.4.

[92] These are often intertwined with the goals of local governments. They are treated together in the remainder of this work.

At the same time, however, the Party itself is shaped and influenced by the government and various interest groups.[93]

2.3.   Laws and Rules in China

Bankruptcy law operates in a broader context of social norms, other laws and supplementary regulations that have evolved over time. Certain social norms have been instrumental in resolving debt-related disputes in the past and continue to influence bankruptcy law practice in China today. Similarly, surrounding laws and regulations significantly influence whether and how the EBL is used in practice.[94] Section 2.3.1 below, therefore, examines different types of social norms, laws and regulations, their interaction and inter-connectedness. Section 2.3.2 then focuses on the role of law and the rule *of* (and *by*) law in China.

2.3.1.   Rule-Layering in China: Social Norms, Laws and Regulations

Informal social norms are usually created over time in a given environment,[95] are based on social equilibria,[96] and are mostly unwritten but shared by a large part of society.[97] For centuries in China, social norms that codified acceptable behaviour and propriety (*li* 礼)[98] were more important than written law (*fa* 法).[99] Many of these social norms were reflected in Confucius's teachings,[100] in particular the focus on hierarchy and order in society, collective good (often over and above individual's needs), non-adversarial resolution of disputes through negotiations and mutual compromise,[101] and relational networks (*guanxi* 关系).[102] Confucianism remains influential in modern China, which

---

[93] My interviews and research support the work by Lampton, *Following the Leader* (2014) ch 3. But cf Tanner, *Politics of Lawmaking* (1999). For a more up-to-date discussion see Gore (n 74) 25.

[94] See Section 4.3 and ch 7.

[95] S Deakin, 'Legal Evolution: Integrating Economic and Systemic Approaches' (2011) Centre for Business Research, University of Cambridge Working Paper No 424.

[96] See A Greif, 'Reputation and Coalition in Medieval Trade' (1989) *Journal of Economic History* 857; L Bernstein, 'Opting out of the Leal System' (1992) *Journal of Legal Studies* 115.

[97] Some authors suggest that these underlying shared beliefs may not be derived from rational behaviour, but rather from 'culture', 'history' or 'precedent': H Gintis, *The Bounds of Reason* (Princeton University Press, 2009) 223; M Aoki, *Corporations in Evolving Diversity* (Oxford University Press, 2010) 131.

[98] J DeLisle, 'China's Legal System' in Joseph (n 4); Confucius, *Analects*, Book II, ch III.

[99] Because codified law was seen as being easily manipulated by the ruler to his benefit: W He, *In the Name of Justice: Striving for the Rule of Law in China* (Brookings Institution Press, 2012) 135–36.

[100] Confucius lived 551–479 BC. Confucianism was accepted as a state ideology during the Han dynasty (206 BC–221 AD) and still influences people's values in modern China: R Tomasic, P Little, A Francis, K Kamarul and K Wang, 'Insolvency Law Administration and Culture in Six Asian Legal Systems' (1996) *Australian Journal of Corporate Law* 248.

[101] See eg L Ladany, *Law and Legality in China* (University of Hawaii Press, 1992); KS Sim, *China in Transition*, vol 2 (Nova Science Publishers, 2003) 254. On the rule of law in China see R Peerenboom, *China's Long March Toward Rule of Law* (Cambridge University Press, 2002).

[102] K Fan, *Arbitration in China* (Hart, 2014) ch 8.II.

may explain why so many disputes are resolved in arbitration or mediation[103] rather than in an inherently adversarial court system.[104] In addition, a version of Confucianism is regularly invoked by Chinese leaders, albeit in a very selective manner – mostly focusing on pro-authoritarian statements that support the emperor, hierarchical order, collectivism and loyalty to the leader.

Social norms – as informal and simple constraints on people's behaviour – are effective in closely knit groups where the parties know each other, and in dealings that are straightforward, geographically close, short term and likely to be repeated. For example, when financing[105] a new project through relational lending (ie from family and friends), it is usually enough to rely on informal social norms since there is often no contract and no wish to involve any outsiders when enforcing debt repayment. Similarly, when a borrower considers whether or not to repay a loan from a *hui*, they need consider not only their legal position (ie their formal rights and obligations) but also the societal rules and consequences that would flow from failing to repay their neighbours (ie reputational loss, social exclusion).[106]

Formal law, on the other hand, is always written down and is mostly formulated and imposed from above (by a legislative body or a ruler). Unsurprisingly, many formal laws develop from stable, widely accepted social norms.[107] Although many interactions in China are still governed and resolved using non-legal principles and norms, laws are now more central to people's activities than before. In the context of corporate affairs and insolvency, laws come into play in agreements that are made at arm's length through commercial lending (ie debt finance from bank-like institutions, equity finance from the stock market) or other forms of public finance (ie finance with generalised, impersonal conditions known and accessible to a wide range of people). The parties are more likely to rely on formal law when enforcing repayment, especially where this is more efficient (ie faster, cheaper, more precise) than private ordering (eg private workout).

Social norms and laws create constraints that motivate people to behave in a certain way.[108] In some cases – often in a transition from planned to market economy – lenders and borrowers are not complete strangers, and the lending conditions tend to be more defined and explicit than in relational lending and more project-specific than in arm's-length lending.[109] Such hybridisation of the nature of transacting parties and their dealings can be observed in China since the reforms started in 1978. As trading partners become more heterogeneous and less well-known to each other, and as

---

[103] See eg Z Niu and G van Dijck, 'The Impact of Culture on Chinese Judges' Decision-Making in Contractual Damages Cases' (2017) *Asian Journal of Law and Society* 1; People's Court News (18.2.2009). See also Fan, *Arbitration* (2014) and Section 3.3.4.

[104] Derived from the Confucian ideal of harmony (*zhongyong*中庸): P Katz, *Divine Justice* (Routledge, 2008) 7–8; S Guo, *Chinese Politics and Government* (Routledge, 2013) 48.

[105] For types of debt financing in China, see Section 3.2.

[106] See Section 3.3.2.

[107] Deakin, 'Legal Evolution' (2011) 2; HP Glenn, *Legal Traditions of the World*, 3rd edn (Oxford University Press, 2007) 348–49. For further discussion of the evolution of social norms into formal law, see R Cooter, 'Law from Order' (1997) JMO Working Papers in Law, Economics, and Institutions.

[108] See eg R Posner, 'Social Norms and the Law' (1997) *American Economic Review* 365; R Ellickson, *Order Without Law* (Harvard University Press, 1991); Glenn, *Legal Traditions* (2007).

[109] For an interesting discussion of this categorisation, see R Cooter and H Shäfer, *Solomon's Knot* (Princeton University Press, 2011) 113–15.

the transactions become increasingly more complex, span longer periods of time, and become less frequent (or even not repeated),[110] the parties' needs change. Consequently, parties' preferred solutions often shift from pure reliance on social norms to a mixture of social norms and laws to enforce their agreements and secure their deals. This shift occurs because all dealings rely on individuals' ability to make credible commitments to one another *ex ante* with regards to their behaviour *ex post*. In simple relational dealings, parties can rely on trust and reputation because bad behaviour (ie non-payment) would be personally and professionally very costly.

In more complex arm's-length dealings, on the other hand, parties tend to use written contracts, fiduciary duties and other law-derived mechanisms because the existence of public ordering mechanism strengthens the credibility and reliability of private ordering.[111] During the transition, when formal law is still imperfect or outright non-existent, club enforcement mechanisms, private ordering tools, and state interference are often used to ensure enforceability of parties' promises (which, in turn, enables trade beyond one's immediate relational network).[112] As the nature of transacting changes, new, more formal rules are introduced, and they enrich – rather than replace – informal rules.[113] As a result, new layers of enforcement tools are added to suit the increasing complexity of parties' interaction, which in turn enables a greater amount of more diverse cooperation to take place because previously unenforceable promises can be comparatively efficiently enforced.[114] As is explored in Chapters three (in general) and nine (in the context of corporate bankruptcy), the whole spectrum of formal and informal rules plays an important role in debt enforcement in China.[115]

Laws, however, are often written with an insufficient level of detail, and so further guidance is needed to explain how the law should be applied and to fill the gaps.[116] The NPC has authorised the SPC to interpret the law with regards to a specific application of individual laws and decrees in court trials.[117] There are four types of normative judicial interpretations which bind lower courts (and are sometimes cited by them).

---

[110] For an excellent overview of legal anthropology, see Glenn (n 105) chs 1, 2 and 10.

[111] See A Morrison and AJ Wilhelm Jr, 'Trust, Reputation, and Law' (2015) *Journal of Legal Analysis* 363.

[112] See Cooter and Shäfer, *Solomon's Knot* (2011) 18: 'Under communism, state planning displaced markets, nationalised industries dwarfed private ownership, and public law crowded out private law. Even so, stable bureaucracies gave officials economic power somewhat like property rights, and political bargains created obligations resembling contracts.'

[113] Different rules coexist: R Cooter, 'Do Good Laws Make Good Citizens?' (2000) UC Berkeley Law & Economics Research Paper No 2000-8; Cooter and Shäfer (n 107) 35; C Milhaupt and K Pistor, *Law and Capitalism* (University of Chicago Press, 2008) 193. Moreover, formal rules often rely for their content and legitimacy on informal rules: D North, *Institutions, Institutional Change and Economic Performance* (Cambridge University Press, 1990); R Ellickson, 'Law and Economics Discovers Social Norms' (1998) *Journal of Legal Studies* 537; Posner (n 106); P Huang and H Wu, 'More Order without More Law' (1994) *Journal of Law, Economics, and Organization* 390.

[114] For a full discussion of the idea see eg K Thelen, *How Institutions Evolve* (Cambridge University Press, 2004); J van der Heijden, 'Institutional Layering: A Review of the Use of the Concept' (2011) 31 *Politics* 9.

[115] For a general discussion of the interaction between law and trust-based transacting, see D Chen, S Deakin, M Siems and B Wang, 'Law, Trust and Institutional Change in China: Evidence from Qualitative Fieldwork' (2017) *Journal of Corporate Law Studies* 1.

[116] See Section 4.1.

[117] The Resolution of the Standing Committee of the National People's Congress concerning Improving Interpretation of the Law (10.6.1981). This power was codified in Arts 45 and 104 of Legislation Law 2000, as amended in 2015.

They are Interpretations (*jieshi* 解释), Provisions (*guiding* 规定), Replies (*pifu* 批复) and Decisions (*jueding*决定).[118] The SPC also issues documents that must be complied with by lower courts but do not need to be cited by them. They include Opinions (*yijian*意见) and Conference summaries (*zuotanhuijiyao*座谈会纪要).[119] In addition, there are also regulatory judicial documents which include advisory guidance. These documents have an identifier *fafa* (法发).[120] Several such documents relating to the EBL are discussed later.[121]

The SPC has also been developing its own Chinese style case law (*anlizhidaozhidu*案例指导制度) in order to ensure uniform application of the law. Guiding cases (*zhidaoanli* 指导案例) are real-life cases that must be referred to by lower court judges in all similar cases – much like a precedent.[122] They are summarised by the SPC and include commentary about the key takeaways for lower courts. Typical cases (*dianxinganli* 典型案例) are also real-life cases that have been summarised and include commentary, but they can be released by the SPC or lower courts.[123] They are intended to illustrate how a particular problem can be addressed and how lower courts can apply the law.[124] The SPC has issued several such cases in relation to the EBL.[125]

2.3.2. The Role of Law and the Rule *of* (and *by*) Law in China

China had several legal codes before the fall of the empire in 1911,[126] but all laws were abolished and replaced by basic regulations in the aftermath of the 1949 Revolution. As a result, the Party enjoyed absolute power with no legal constraints on its exercise. The legal vacuum existed in China between 1949 and 1975 and was only disturbed by the Marriage Law and the 1954 Constitution.[127] The effect of the resulting legal uncertainty together with the Party's propaganda against the rule of law was that it became natural to distrust the law.[128]

China's current legal system dates back to the late 1970s. The NPC met after a decade of passivity (and civil war) in 1975. When Deng Xiaoping rose to power in 1976 and started his reforms in 1978,[129] laws were slowly reintroduced. Deng recognised that laws could be used to formalise and consolidate the achievements of economic reforms, to bring stability, and to enable future changes. The Ministry of Justice was re-established

---

[118] See SPC Monitor (10.7.2015).

[119] See SPC Monitor (28.8.2019).

[120] See SPC Monitor (19.5.2019).

[121] See Sections 4.3 and 12.1.

[122] See S Finder, 'China's Evolving Case Law System In Practice' (2017) *Tsinghua China Law Review* 245. But note that guiding cases are rarely referred to in practice: J Daum at China Law Translate (21.2.2017).

[123] For a hierarchy of cases see SPC Monitor (16.9.2016).

[124] Y Hu (29.1.2014, EPaper).

[125] See Section 4.3.

[126] Despite erroneous assumptions to the contrary in many Western texts. See eg DeLisle, 'China's Legal System' (n 96).

[127] The Party's position was that 'Laws are odious: they tie hands of the leaders': L Ladany, *The Communist Party of China and Marxism, 1921–85* (Hoover Institution Press, 1988) 55. See also Li (n 27).

[128] See eg Ladany, *Law and Legality* (1992) 69.

[129] See Section 2.1 above.

in 1979 (it had closed in 1959), and the 1980s saw a shift towards perceiving the legal system as a prerequisite for much-desired social and economic development.[130] The 1982 Constitution, although minimalistic, laid the foundations for a greater role of law in China. It was amended several times, inter alia in 1988 to legitimise the existence of the fast-developing private sector, in 1993 to formalise China's development into a 'socialist market economy', and in 2004 to recognise private ownership.[131]

As a result, much has changed since Mao's lawless era. Many new laws have been introduced and subsequently updated, and steps are being taken to ensure effective enforcement. Formal law has gained more weight in recent years – exemplified also in the 1999 addition of Article 5(1) to the Constitution which stipulates that the country is to be ruled 'in accordance with the law' and the emphasis on the rule *by* law since 2008.[132] Consequently, many of China's day-to-day activities are now governed by detailed laws and regulations. Moreover, certain elements of state power are restricted.[133] The Party-state's ideology has also changed significantly to provide for a greater role of law – including improvements in governance, new access to courts' decisions online,[134] creation of new procedures for communication of grievances and complaints, and more transparency and involvement of stakeholders in the law-making process.[135] Law now plays an important role in resolving (private sector) companies' arm's-length disputes. Similarly, more people are now turning to the law to resolve their disputes and seek redress for wrongdoing – even in purely personal disputes.[136]

Law, therefore, plays an increasingly important role in the running of China's internal and external affairs. Nevertheless – despite statements to the contrary by the Party-state[137] and some Chinese scholars[138] – China does not have a robust rule of law.[139] Laws are not adequately followed in China.[140] There is no separation of powers[141] as the law remains subject to the Party-state's will and influence both at the law-making level – through influencing the NPC's law-making activities – and at the law-enforcement level – through influencing legal professionals[142] and courts.[143] Moreover, there is no supremacy of law.[144] Instead, some say that Deng's reforms and subsequent laws simply

---

[130] See Y Zhang, 'On the Strengthening the Socialist Legal System' (1981) *Social Sciences in China* 1; Tay and Leung, *Greater China* (1995); Ladany (n 99).

[131] For commentary see S Chen (9.3.1994, Guangming Daily) 5; Legal Daily (2.1.1994).

[132] See K Blasek, *Rule of Law* (Springer, 2015) 43.

[133] For example, the revocation of land-usage rights: see sections 3.3.5 and 7.1.5.

[134] See wenshu.court.gov.cn.

[135] For an up-to-date overview of court-related developments, see court.gov.cn (or english.court.gov.cn in English).

[136] SZICA (18.2.2013).

[137] See Sections 10.2.7 and 12.1.

[138] See J Duan, 'Statement on the Rule of Law at the National and International Levels' (2008) *Chinese Journal of International Law* 509.

[139] Not even a thin version of it: for a discussion see Blasek, *Rule of Law* (2015) 10, 13–16. For a statement to this effect from the SPC see Section 2.4.3.

[140] China was ranked 72nd out of 102 surveyed countries in terms of their adherence to the rule of law: the World Justice Projects, Rule of Law Index 2015 (The World Justice Project, 2015) 6.

[141] Instead, China has a division of duties: Blasek (n 130) 19–32.

[142] See eg *The Economist* (15.6.2017).

[143] See Sections 2.4.2–2.4.3.

[144] Blasek (n 130) ch 4.2.

'replaced state-led growth with state-protected growth'.[145] Control is concentrated in the hands of the Party-state, without any meaningful checks and balances on its exercise.[146] The Party remains above the law,[147] it determines access to business opportunities and most bank-finance,[148] and protectionism is ubiquitous – especially at a local level – which often prevents fair and impartial enforcement of the law.[149]

It is, therefore, perhaps best not to think of China in terms of the rule *of* law – which many say is a Western concept and clashes with the idea of 'Chinese characteristics'[150] – but rather as a different legal tradition where the law is a tool used by the Government.[151] A more precise term to describe the role of law in China is perhaps the rule *by* law.[152] One of the consequences of such environment is that relational *guanxi* networks remain significant[153] – especially to private entrepreneurs who face severe credit constraints,[154] red tape, and are often unable to commence EBL proceedings at court.[155] The lack of the rule of law is illustrated by the de facto exclusion of state-protected debtor companies from the hard-budget constraints and consequences imposed under the EBL.[156]

2.4. Courts, the Party-State and Limited Law Enforcement in China

Many Chinese laws (including the EBL) are written at a 'high level' – ie without many details – and need proficient, effective and independent enforcers to apply them in practice.[157] However, courts in China are not independent[158] (Section 2.4.1 below)

---

[145] Cooter and Shäfer (n 107) 22.

[146] Blasek (n 130) ch 4.1.

[147] Chow, 'Economic Reform' (2004) 144.

[148] Loans are granted to companies based on their political connections rather than their profitability or promise: Y Zheng and Y Zhu, 'Bank lending incentives and firm investment decisions in China' (2013) *Journal of Multinational Financial Management* 146.

[149] For a discussion see Blasek (n 130) 10.

[150] I Castellucci, 'Rule of Law with Chinese Characteristics' (2007) *Annual Survey of International & Comparative Law* 35; B Sheehy, 'Fundamentally Conflicting Views of the Rule of Law in China and the West' (2005–6) *New Journal of International Law & Business* 225.

[151] See eg Peerenboom, *China's Long March* (2002). See also Section 2.3.1.

[152] In Chinese, the term *fazhi* 法治 can be translated as either a 'rule of law' or 'rule by law'. V Mair (20.10.2014, WSJ) explains the difference as follows: '"Rule of law" implies fairness and predictable application', he says. '"Rule by law" would include, for example, rule under Hitler's Nuremberg Laws (*Nürnberger Gesetze*), which were neither fair nor predictably applied'.

[153] As He, *In the Name of Justice* (2012, 73) has put it: 'Like most countries, China has a well-written constitution. China's constitution, however, does not tell how the state actually operates'. See also Tay and Leung (n 28) 1–10 and 182.

[154] Yueh, *Enterprising China* (n 30).

[155] J Kahn (28.12.2005, NY Times) reports that 'Courts legally must issue written rejection notices if they choose not to take the case. But to avoid appeals, court clerks often decline to take possession of legal papers. No rejection notice is needed if the case does not, in China's political-legal cosmos, formally exist'. See also Sections 8.3 and 9.2.

[156] See Sections 8.3 and 9.2.

[157] Dam, *Law-Growth Nexus* (2007) ch 5; LP Feld and S Voigt, 'Economic growth and judicial independence: cross-country evidence using a new set of indicators' (2003) *European Journal of Political Economy* 497.

[158] For a discussion about how this impacts their proficiency and effectiveness in the context of the EBL, see Section 8.1.1.

because their decision-making is subject to Party-state oversight and 'interference' (Section 2.4.2) which they allow and follow in practice (Section 2.4.3).[159]

China's court system has undergone many reforms since the late 1970s,[160] including several that concern the EBL directly.[161] Nevertheless, more needs to be done to improve judges' ability to deal with commercial cases[162] and to remove the Party-state's influence over how laws are applied and enforced in China.[163]

2.4.1. The Role of Courts and the Lack of Judicial Independence in China

Several studies suggest that strong independent judiciary is beneficial for economic development[164] and that the degree of judicial independence is correlated with economic growth.[165] Studies also find a correlation between having more independent and stronger judiciary and creating a better business environment and faster growth of companies.[166] Inter-regional studies in select countries further suggest that regions with stronger, more effective courts also enjoy comparatively better access to credit, more investment and greater corporate flexibility and willingness to switch to new (cheaper or better) suppliers because they can enforce their agreements and get remedies in court.[167]

Courts in China are not independent from the Party-state since judicial decision-making is influenced and limited by various forms of political actors.[168] Courts are treated as an administrative branch of the Party-state.[169] The Party-state's influence reaches all parts of the country's governance structure and various networks within society.[170] This state of affairs has been criticised by foreign commentators and some

---

[159] These issues are further explored in the context of the EBL in ch 8.

[160] See eg SB Lubman, *Bird in a Cage* (Stanford University Press, 2002); R Peerenboom (ed), *Judicial Independence in China* (Cambridge University Press, 2009).

[161] For more see ch 12.

[162] For a discussion in the context of the EBL, See Sections 8.1 (problems) and 11.3.1 (proposed reforms).

[163] ibid.

[164] Measured by eg length and cost of procedures, responsiveness to filed claims, ability and capability to cope with the caseload, etc: LJ Trebilcock and MM Prado, *What Makes Poor Countries Poor* (Edward Elgar Publishing, 2011) 114–15; K Dam, 'The Judiciary and Economic Development' (March 2006) University of Chicago John M Olin Law & Economics Working Paper No 287. But cf Gilson and Milhaupt, 'Economically Benevolent Dictators' (2011) who argue that there are other alternatives.

[165] Feld and Voigt, 'Economic growth and judicial independence' (2003); DM Klerman, 'Legal Infrastructure, Judicial Independence, and Economic Development' (2007) *Global Business & Development Law Journal* 427.

[166] R Islam, Institutional 'Reform and the Judiciary: Which Way Forward' (2003) World Bank Policy Research Working Paper 3134, 7–9.

[167] The same result was found in eg Argentina, Brazil, Mexico, Russia, Vietnam, etc: 'Doing Business in 2004: Understanding Regulation' (World Bank and Oxford University Press, 2004) 86.

[168] See R Peerenboom, 'Judicial Independence in China: Common Myths and Unfounded Assumptions' in Peerenboom, *Judicial Independence in China* (2009); DeLisle (n 96).

[169] D Clarke, 'Empirical Research in Chinese Law' in E Jensen and T Heller (eds), *Rule of Law: Legal and Judicial Reform in Developing and Transition Countries* (Stanford University Press, 2003); Peerenboom (nn 99 and 158).

[170] See Section 2.2.4.

Chinese scholars.[171] On the one hand, it is important to acknowledge that China's political system is different from Western liberal democracy[172] and that the SPC itself has repeatedly rejected what it described as 'erroneous influence from the West: "constitutional democracy", "separation of powers" and "independence of the judiciary"'.[173] On the other hand, however, an independent judiciary, the rule of law and a dominant party-state governance model can coexist.[174]

Moreover, China itself sends mixed signals about its legal and judicial system. Enhancing judicial independence was identified as one of the key reform goals at the end of 2015.[175] Many recent reforms have, in fact, increased judicial separation and independence from other branches of state governance.[176] In addition, written laws make Chinese judges fully independent final arbiters and balance-keepers who should ensure fair and impartial application of legal rules and principles.[177] In practice, however, the Party-state has made it clear that they may embrace enhanced courts' autonomy but are not willing to have a complete separation of power.[178] Instead, the Party-state retained its ability to interfere in complex and important cases.[179] At the same time, Chinese courts follow Party-state's guidance about which cases to hear and how[180] in order to protect Party-determined interests and goals.[181] This is problematic for bankruptcy law (and other corporate and market-facing laws) because, in order to deliver the benefits of greater use of bankruptcy law found in studies from around the world,[182] the law must be applied in an objective and predictable manner. Protectionism and other types of interference from outside distort parties' ability to arrange their affairs in a safe and predictable manner, which limits the expected benefits of bankruptcy law.[183]

2.4.2. Why does the Party-State Interfere?

The Party-state interferes in judicial decision-making for several reasons – albeit the exact motives depend on local needs.[184] There are four sets of reasons that incentivise

---

[171] KE Henderson, 'Halfway Home and a Long Way to Go' in Peerenboom (n 258); B Liebman, 'China's Courts: Restricted Reform' (2008) *Columbia Journal of Asian Law* 1; S Liu, 'Beyond Global Convergence: Conflicts of Legitimacy in a Chinese Lower Court' (2006) 31 *Law & Social Inquiry* 75.

[172] For an interesting discussion about the meaning and different forms of independence of courts in a party-state, see L Ang and J Wang, 'Judicial Independence in Dominant Party States: Singapore's Possibilities for China' (2019) *Asian Journal of Comparative Law* 337.

[173] Chief Justice Zhou Qiang's speech in 2017. See eg M Forsythe (18.1.2017, NY Times).

[174] See eg M Tushnet, 'Preserving Judicial Independence in Dominant Party States' (2015) *New York Law School Law Review* 107.

[175] See Section 12.1.

[176] See Ang and Wang, 'Judicial Independence in Dominant Party States' (2019).

[177] The EBL is no exception: Sections 4.2.9, 6.1 and 8.1.

[178] See discussion about the rule of law with Chinese characteristics in Section 2.3.2 above.

[179] See eg *People's Daily* (10.10.2015); Judicial Independence in the PRC (Congressional-Executive Commission on China).

[180] Interviews J1-c to J9-c, L2-s to L15-c, P1-r, P3-r, R6-c to R10-c, R14-s. See also Section 8.3, which discusses this issue in the context of the EBL.

[181] SPC Monitor (19.3.2017). See also Section 8.3.

[182] See Section 1.2.

[183] The question of judicial independence in the context of the EBL is further discussed in Section 8.3.

[184] All my interviewees stressed that the importance and impact of the discussed issues vary across provinces and regions in China and across national and local layers of the Party-state.

Party-state's interference – two at the institutional level and two at the personal level. These four incentives are discussed in detail below and, together, they shed light on why the Party-state interferes in judicial decision-making in China.[185]

2.4.2.1. *Different Roles and Focus of National and Local Governments*

At the institutional level, both national- and local-level government and the Party interfere with courts' decision-making in order to protect their interests and respond to their particular pressures. The difference in how and why they interfere stems from the natural divergence in the focus and interests of those who make the law (at the national level) and those who implement and enforce it (at the local level). The national Government is primarily concerned with the long-term interests of the country and the economy as a whole. As a result, national law reforms tend to focus on macroeconomic efficiency, on gaining access to the international market, and on ensuring continued growth of China's economy. On the other hand, local governments focus more on shorter-term[186] needs of their respective provinces because they are ultimately accountable for their performance in their region.[187] While the national Government faces pressure from the international community, local governments respond to the needs and pressure from individual (local) companies and particular problems which are often unique to their region.[188] Moreover, the national Government is concerned with overarching principles, ideology, the overall performance of the economy, overall levels of employment, and their appearance vis-à-vis the outside world (markets, investors, governments) and the Chinese people as a whole. In contrast, local governments are often concerned with local versions of such problems, they face the immediate effects of their policies and actions (such as labour strikes, lower taxes, lower FDI, etc), and so they have to be more pragmatic in their promises and approach to the rules created at the national level.[189] This divide was further reinforced by fiscal decentralisation,[190] which has given local governments greater powers with regards to the property and resources under their control – strengthening their incentives to maximise economic development and profits.[191] At the same time, however, local governments became responsible for raising most revenue for the local budget.[192] It has led to a boost in efforts to maximise the profitability of local enterprises, but the resulting financial pressure also led to the local preference for short-term revenue over potentially profitable but long-maturity projects.[193]

---

[185] The discussion is further developed in the context of the EBL in Section 8.3.2.

[186] Usually their term in office (five years).

[187] The accountability of local government translates into individual officials' duties and incentives, below.

[188] Interviews C1-c, C4-c, C5-r, C7-s, C11-c, J1-c, J4-c, J5-s, J8-c, J9-c, L2-s, L4-r to L6-s, P1-r, P3-r to P5-c, R1-r to R3-r, R6-c to R11-c, R21-c, R15-s.

[189] ibid.

[190] See C Xu, 'The Fundamental Institutions of China's Reforms and Development' (2011) *Journal of Economic Literature* 1076, 1084–87.

[191] JC Oi, 'Fiscal Reform and the Economic Foundations of Local State Corporatism in China' (1992) 45 *World Politics* 99–126, 100. See also Section 2.2.2.

[192] D Yang, *Remaking the Chinese Leviathan: Market Transition and the Politics of Governance in China* (Stanford University Press, 2004) 27.

[193] T Saich, 'The Blind Man and the Elephant: Analysing the Local State in China' in L Tomba (ed), *East Asian Capitalism: Conflicts and the Roots of Growth and Crisis* (Annali della Fondazione Giangiacomo Feltrinelli, 2002) 79.

Moreover, it also strengthened local governments' tendency to protect local companies regardless of their efficiency and competitiveness.[194]

2.4.2.2. Local Officials' Career Prospects

At the personal level, individual officials may trigger Party-state's interference in several circumstances, two of which are discussed below. The first type of personal-level incentives is tied to the career progression of local government officials. Each official's political career depends, to a large extent,[195] on their proven abilities to promote economic development and to maintain social and economic stability.[196] Individual officials who wish to advance their respective careers can demonstrate such abilities through a position in a local provincial government[197] – often in one of the more problematic or underperforming provinces.[198]

The satisfaction of this requirement is assessed primarily against easily measurable economic targets,[199] with the aim to incentivise the officials to maximise their region's economic development and economic output. However, such quantitative assessment is problematic. Most importantly, the targets are usually measured over one- or five-year period,[200] and so their use creates a bias towards short-termism. Moreover, research suggests that simple targets may not be able to incentivise sustained effort and performance.[201] As a result, officials' incentives are skewed towards protectionism and inefficiency.[202]

Similarly, officials have to show their ability to maintain social stability. This usually involves preventing or mediating large-scale disputes and disturbances, including labour unrest, which is now commonplace in China.[203] They are often triggered by calls

---

[194] Local governments' short-termism is further reinforced by the fact that top cadres in local governments usually only stay in power for five years and their performance is judged over one-year and the total five-year period.

[195] Persons' connections and ancestry are also important. Many of the most powerful posts are held by the princelings: K Brown, *The New Emperors* (2014).

[196] Interviews C5-r, C7-s, P1-r, P3-r to P5-c, R1-r, R3-r to R9-c, R12-c, R15-s. As we saw, this is formalised and further reinforced through the cadre responsibility system and political performance contracts: Section 2.2.2 above.

[197] ibid.

[198] ibid. A large majority of the past and current Chinese leaders made their way up through successful career in the provinces: Xu, 'Fundamental Institutions' (2011) 1098. See also Li (n 27).

[199] GDP, FDI, growth rates, import and export, trade volume, etc: Xu (n 188) 1098.

[200] ie a one-year period for the cadre performance system and a five-year period for local (provincial) governments' election period: 'People's Republic of China' in Concise Encyclopaedia of Democracy (Routledge, 2013) 94–98.

[201] GP Baker, MC Jensen and KJ Murphy, 'Compensation and Incentives: Practice vs. Theory' (1988) *Journal of Finance* 593; A Kohn, 'Why Incentive Plans Cannot Work' (Sept–Oct 1993) *Harvard Business Review* – confirmed in Interviews C5-r, C7-s, P1-r, P3-r to P5-c, R1-r, R3-r to R9-c, R12-c, R15-s.

[202] Local officials who fail to meet these targets do not get promoted and may face a fine or other punishment under the cadre responsibility system and the professional performance contract. As a result, data is sometimes falsified. My interviews (B1-c, B3-c, C1-c, C4-s to C7-s, C11-c, E1-c to E5-c, J1-c, J4-c to J9-c, L1-r to L17-c, P1-r, R2-r, R3-r, R6-c, R7-c, R9-c, R10-c) suggest that falsification of data is rampant and that, in their experience, it was very unlikely for the data to be checked in practice. See also Reuters (12.2.2014).

[203] There were about 2,770 large-scale labour strikes and protests in 2015: *China Labor Bulletin* (2016). For an in-depth discussion, see Gallagher, *Authoritarian Legality* (2017).

for higher wages, pay cuts, late or non-payment of wages, or factory closures (due to insolvency, reallocation, etc).[204] Local governments try to suppress them by declaring them illegal and threatening imprisonment and fines, often with the assistance of police who disperse the protesters.[205] However, all my interviewees suggested that local officials also try to exert influence over court cases that could lead to undesirable unrest. Since bankruptcy law can lead to large-scale unemployment and non-payment of debts, local governments are often – directly or behind the scenes – involved in bankruptcy law hearings.[206]

2.4.2.3. Pressure from Stakeholders on Local Officials

Another type of personal-level incentive that encourages local government officials to interfere in court decision-making is stakeholders' pressure. Although China is not a democracy, local governments do pay close attention to individuals' grievances, particularly where they could lead to disturbances of social stability.[207] This is due to the pressure from above and from below. From above, higher levels of government evaluate lower levels with regards to their ability to maintain a 'harmonious society' as a part of their career-progression evaluation process.[208] From below, stakeholders whose interests would be affected by objective law enforcement often exert pressure on local governments, and thereby indirectly on the courts. There are several methods that they use and four of them are discussed below, namely 'letters and visits', pressure through the media, protests, and exploitation of the interconnectedness of the Party-state and state sector companies.

Firstly, the practice known as 'letters and visits' (*xinfang* 信访) enables aggrieved individuals to lobby their local government through both written (letters) and personal (visits) pressure.[209] The tendency to avoid personal clashes and disagreements coupled with the fear of social unrest often encourage local governments to respond to such popular pressure and intervene.[210] Interestingly, the petitioning process handles significantly more cases per annum than courts.[211] However, responding to popular pressure may detract from objective delivery of justice, and so endangers the creation and

---

[204] J Hernandez (14.3.2016, *New York Times*).

[205] ibid.

[206] See Sections 4.3, 8.3, 9.2 and 12.12.

[207] Interviews C4-s, C5-r, C7-s, C11-c, J1-c, J4-c to J9-c, L2-s to L7-c, L9-c to L15-c, P1-r, P3-r, P5-c, R2-r, R3-r, R6-c, R7-c, R9-c, R10-c.

[208] See discussion above.

[209] Minzner argues that it enables citizens' political participation, and is a replacement for the inefficient judicial appeal process: CF Minzner, 'Xinfang: An Alternative to Formal Chinese Legal Institutions' (2006 103, 107 and 174–75. See also L Lin and J Yu, 'The Right of Letters and Visits & the System of Letters and Visits' (2008) 3 *Journal of Zhejiang University (Humanities and Social Sciences)* 1; I Thireau and L Hua, 'The Moral Universe of Aggrieved Chinese Workers' (2003) *The China Journal* 83.

[210] Interviews B3-c, C1-c, C4-c, C5-r, C7-s, C11-c, J1-c, J5-s, J7-c to J9-c, L2-s to L7-c, L9-s to L12-c, L15-c, P1-r to P5-c, R7-c to R10-c. See also Liebman, 'China's Courts' (2008) 22–25.

[211] eg in 2002, the national Xinfang bureau received 11.5 million cases, while courts handled 7.8 million cases (both numbers are from county level and higher): Interview with Zhou Zhanshun, Director of the State Bureau of Letters and Calls, Banyue Tan, 20.11.2003.

application of uniform rules,[212] which weakens the rule of law and empowers the rule of man instead.[213]

Media pressure is another method of influencing local governments and courts.[214] Existing research suggests that media can play an important role in exposing injustice and enforcing fairer judicial decisions.[215] Interviews with Chinese lawyers suggested that support from media is often 'the most important factor leading to a successful lawsuit'.[216] Media coverage of a particular story or case usually forces local Party-state to intervene and do what the pressure groups perceive as 'just'.[217]

A third way of putting pressure on local governments to intervene in one's favour is through threatening or actually staging a mass protest, which causes unwelcome publicity and draws attention to a local government's failure to fulfil one of their target duties – maintenance of social stability.[218] Officials' incentive to help aggrieved parties is further strengthened by the real possibility that the affected stakeholders' anger may turn into violence against local government officials.[219] Protesters sometimes forcibly enter government offices hoping to enforce officials' cooperation and protection because – the protesters believe – officials have the power and duty to help them.[220] To maximise their career prospects and safeguard their personal safety, local government officials often try to avoid controversial clashes and instead appease and prevent potential unrest.[221]

Finally, companies may also be able to exert influence over local governments where their management is interconnected with local Party-state institutions. My interviewees said that such connections could be established through close, long-term cooperation; part-ownership of a company by a local government; Party-state members serving in a company's management; or family ties between Party-state members and company owners.[222] The influence then goes both ways. On the one hand, the special relationship enables local Party-state to influence the company's actions – including its decision whether to invoke the law. But it also enables the company to lobby for special protection and help from the Party-state.[223]

As a result, local governments are incentivised – on an institutional level as well as individual officials' personal level – to influence whether and how laws are enforced, and often impose their preferred solution instead of letting courts apply the law objectively.

---

[212] Minzner, 'Xinfang' (2006) 103; Liebman (n 169).

[213] Minzner (n 207) 172.

[214] For an overview, see DeLisle (n 96).

[215] Liebman (n 169) 22.

[216] ibid. A similar sentiment expressed in my interviews (B3-c, C1-c, C4-c, C5-r, C7-s, C11-c, J1-c, L2-s to L7-c, L9-s to L12-c, L15-c, P1-r, R7-c to R10-c).

[217] ibid.

[218] The number of workers' strikes is significant and growing year-to-year. See eg *China Labour Bulletin* (7.1.2016); *China Labour Bulletin* (30.7.2019).

[219] Interviews B1-c, C1-c, C3-c to C5-r, C7-s, E1-c, E2-s, J1-c, J5-s to J9-c, L2-s, L4-r to L7-c, P1-r, P3-r to P5-c, R1-r, R3-r, R6-c to R10-c.

[220] ibid. Social unrest can have significant impact on the overall stability of the country, and so its prevention has been deemed the best safeguard for long-term development and success of China: Section 2.1 above.

[221] Y Cai, 'Local Governments and the Suppression of Popular Resistance in China' (2008) *China Quarterly* 24.

[222] And so they fall within the state sector: see Section 2.5 below.

[223] S Kennedy, *The Business of Lobbying in China* (Harvard University Press, 2005) 49.

2.4.3. Why do Courts Allow Party-State's Interference?

My interviewees identified three reasons why Chinese courts allow the Party-state to interfere in whether and how they apply the law. First, there are internal control mechanisms that ensure judges' cooperation with the Party-state. Second, some judges feel that they should not act without Party-state's blessing. And third, some judges feel that they cannot effectively act without Party-state's blessing and support.

Firstly, courts' cooperation with the Party-state is ensured through internal control mechanisms that align courts' interests with those of the Party-state. On the Party side, the mechanisms used include actual oversight of judicial decision-making through in-court Party branches[224] and the requirement that all judges must make an oath of loyalty to the Party where they promise 'to faithfully perform the sacred duties of a socialist-with-Chinese-characteristics legal worker; to be faithful to the motherland and the people; [and] to uphold the leadership of the Chinese Communist Party and the socialist system'.[225] In addition, local governments control judges' remuneration and career progression.[226] Furthermore, many senior judges at provincial courts are also members of the local Party leadership.[227] My interviewees suggested that judges are acutely aware of these restrictions and see them as a strong incentive to cooperate and follow Party-state's wishes.[228]

Secondly, my interviewees suggested that some judges feel that they should not independently accept and decide certain types of cases due to what they perceive as their 'proper role' as a judge in China.[229] As explained earlier, Chinese judiciary is not structurally independent from the Party-state, and Chinese courts are often perceived as an administrative extension of the Party-state whose instructions they follow.[230] Because the Party-state portrays itself as representing the people,[231] many judges do not see themselves as independent, objective arbiters – despite the laws being framed that way – but rather as state employees who should simply assist the Party-state in carrying out justice and ensuring order according to the Party-state's wishes, rather than the rule of law.[232] Some commentators suggest that such unquestioning obedience stems from an implied duty to take into account state-preferred socio-economic interests under the policy of 'participation in social management' (*canyuchenhuiguanli*参与社会管理),[233] which forces judges to look beyond particular facts of each case and consider a number of socio-economic issues[234] and the effect that their ruling could have on other

---

[224] See Section 2.2.3 above.

[225] *Legal Daily* (21.3.2012).

[226] ibid.

[227] For example, Xu Jianxin is the Vice-President of the Zhejiang Higher People's Court and also a member of the Zhejiang Party Leadership Group.

[228] Interviews C1-c, C5-r, C7-s, J1-c, J3-c to J9-c, R4-c, R6-c to R10-c.

[229] Interviews C7-s, J1-c, J3-c to J9-c, R9-c, R10-c. See also Section 2.4.1 above.

[230] See Section 2.2 above.

[231] See Sections 2.2 and 2.3.1 above.

[232] Interviews C7-s, J1-c to J9-c, L2-s, L4-r to L7-c, L10-s to L15-c, P1-r, P3-r, P5-c, R7-c to R10-c.

[233] See Y Qin, 'The Current Situations of Chinese Judges: Lost in a Cloud of Conflict and Confusion' (2011) *Zeitschrift fur Chinesisches Recht* 241, 241–42.

[234] In the context of the EBL, this is briefly discussed in Section 6.1: note that courts' pro-state, pro-employee biases go well beyond what the substantive EBL allows.

stakeholders. Judges are, therefore, expected to assist local governments in the organisation and management of the public by promoting 'harmonious society'[235] and social stability, helping safeguard the interests of the local and national economy, cooperating with the local government to ensure maximum employment and social welfare, encourage and assist in an informal resolution of disputes, etc.[236]

Judges' belief that they should not act independently of the Party-state is reinforced by China's central legal policy. A recent example that further emphasises courts' subordinated role within the broader state governance can be found in the speech by a senior member of the SPC Judicial Committee, Judge Liu Guixiang, which was delivered at the SPC Work Conference[237] in July 2019.[238] Judge Liu reminded the participants – mostly judges from lower courts – that 'the people's court is primarily a political organ. It must put political interests in the first place'. Courts must 'uphold the absolute leadership of the Party [which] is fundamental for socialism with Chinese characteristics'. He also reiterated that '"separation of powers" and "judicial independence" are erroneous Western ideas and must be decisively rejected and resisted'. Later, Judge Liu further reinforced the submission of law to the Party-state by stating that 'there is no rule of law that does not contain political positions or political views'. He then added that courts 'must integrate politics in civil and commercial trial work' and reminded courts that, when dealing with important and sensitive cases, courts must obey guidance from government agencies and organisation 'in order to understand the overall situation of social stability, social impact, and political impact'.

This restatement clearly shows that, although judges have an important role to play in private law cases, including EBL cases, they are instructed not to hear cases and make judgments without accepting the Party-state's guidance and influence. This has important implications for the whole legal system and the role of law in China.[239]

Finally, there is evidence to suggest that some judges also refuse to act independently because they believe that they cannot successfully resolve a large majority of cases in practice without Party-state's support.[240] Some believe that due to the complexity of many cases, a powerful mediator – the Party-state – is needed to persuade the parties to negotiate and cooperate in order to find a compromise. Similarly, some judges also fear that even if they did make an independent ruling, they would not be able to effectively enforce it without Party-state's assistance and support.[241] There is evidence that this issue is also affecting the implementation of the EBL.[242]

---

[235] See Section 2.3.1 above for a discussion of Confucianism and the law in China.

[236] S Wang (3.3.2011, *People's Court News*). For a detailed discussion see also H She (17.2.2014). Many of my interviewees – particularly from the more developed and pro-market regions – rejected such limitations on a judge's role: Interviews J3-c to J6-s, J8-c, J9-c, L2-s, L4-r to L7-c, L10-s to L15-c.

[237] The SPC Work Conference is a meeting of court representatives with the aim to unify central legal policy and court practices across China.

[238] See G Liu (3.7.2019, Weixin).

[239] See Section 2.3.2 above for a fuller discussion about the role of law and rule of law in China.

[240] Interviews J1-c, J6-s to J9-c, L4-r to L7-c.

[241] ibid.

[242] See Sections 8.3.3, 11.3.5 and 12.12.

2.5. Corporate Ownership and Control in China

Companies in China are an integral component of Party-state's governance structure. The Party-state acts as a regulator, but also a direct corporate participant and a decision-maker. Commonly, this is described as Chinese 'state capitalism',[243] which involves '(1) a comparatively high degree of direct state participation in the economy and (2) the use of capitalist forms of economic organisation – markets, corporations, and other investment vehicles – in combination with non-democratic forms of public governance'.[244] Research suggests that the way companies are owned and controlled in China codetermines whether and how their financial distress and insolvency are resolved. As a result, Section 2.5.1 below begins with a brief examination of how corporate ownership and control developed and how many companies there are in China today. Section 2.5.2 then explains the working definition of state and private sector of China's economy that is used throughout this book. Section 2.5.3 concludes by looking at the impact of corporate ownership and control on law enforcement in China.

2.5.1. Development of Corporate Ownership and Control in China

One of the primary building blocks of Chinese state capitalism are the SOEs – that is companies or corporations that are wholly or largely owned by a state department, organ or agency. When Deng Xiaoping started his reforms in 1978, China's economy was centrally planned, and people worked in state-owned companies and communes.[245] This created inefficient use of resources, overproduction of unwanted goods, and insufficient flexibility in responding to demand. To address these concerns, large communes were dismantled and replaced by a responsibility system in 1979 whereby each farm or farmer had to produce a certain amount of goods for the state and could keep or sell the rest. The process started illegally at first when several local political leaders – without approval from the central Government – allowed partial privatisation within their most poverty-stricken areas. The programme was so successful that communes were soon dismantled all over China,[246] and reforms were introduced to enable greater efficiency and responsiveness to consumers' needs within the state-owned economy.[247]

---

[243] Sometimes described as authoritarian capitalism or capitalism with Chinese characteristics: M Witt and G Redding, 'China: Authoritarian Capitalism' in Witt and Redding, *Oxford Handbook* (2014); J Hung and Y Chen (eds), *The State of China's State Capitalism* (Palgrave Macmillan, 2018); Y Huang, *Capitalism with Chinese characteristics: Entrepreneurship and the State* (Cambridge University Press, 2008).

[244] C Milhaupt and B Liebman (eds), *Regulating the Visible Hand?* (Oxford University Press, 2016) xiv. See also Section 2.2.4 above.

[245] R Hutcheon, 'Capitalist Bulls in the Socialist China Shop' in Tay and Leung (n 28) 40–47.

[246] For an excellent discussion of the grassroots initiatives see Xia, *The People's Congresses* (2008). As a result, grassroots initiatives have been supported ever since. Even the reformed EBL 2006 was partly based on Shenzhen local bankruptcy law – see Section 4.3.

[247] eg by allowing farmers to decide which crops to grow, to sell any surplus for profit, etc. Consequently, agricultural productivity grew by about 30% (from 305 million tonnes in 1978 to 407 million tonnes in 1984): Kynge, *China Shakes the World* (2006) 14.

Subsequently, most SOEs were sold off to gradually reduce the managerial burden on the state and to incentivise their greater efficiency and productivity.[248] The privatisation of SOEs helped dismantle rigid control and planning of the economy and lay the foundations for liberalisation of trade. Privatised SOEs attracted new investment and management. Some failed, others succeeded, but mostly they introduced a new stage of China's transition away from state-directed development to less predictable but potentially more rewarding market-based development.[249]

The state retained ownership and control of profitable SOEs in key industries (manufacturing, natural resources, infrastructure) but gave them partial autonomy in marketing, investment and production decisions in order to encourage greater productivity and efficiency.[250] In time, SOEs started operating under government's guidance rather than mandatory planning system, and from 1984 each SOE only had to give the government a fixed sum or goods and could keep or sell any surplus on an emerging internal market.[251] Several large SOEs were listed in the 1990s, albeit with the state usually keeping the majority stake in them. To monitor and supervise SOEs controlled by central or local government, the State Assets Supervision and Administration Commission (SASAC) was created in 2003.[252] Itself under direct state supervision, SASAC has been in charge of China's biggest SOEs – the national champions[253] – to supervise and ensure compliance with state guidance.[254] In recent years, the number of companies under SASAC's control fell from 189 to 97[255] – largely due to mergers which are hoped to increase the companies' competitiveness and global impact[256] – but SASAC's importance continues in ensuring political loyalty of China's national champions.[257] Additional indirect control mechanisms were also retained, such as the Party-appointed managers,[258] the Party cells operating within SOEs, and state-controlled access to bank finance.[259]

State ownership has its advantages – including easier provision of social welfare and implementation of state policies. Nevertheless, a growing body of literature identifies its disadvantages. Among other problems, SOEs' profits 'come from their monopolistic

---

[248] Privatisation was gradual in China, unlike the Soviet Union where it took only 500 days and led to dangerous instability and, unrest, and abuse by the insiders: see Chow (n 29).

[249] See Naughton (n 2).

[250] See Zweig (n 30).

[251] Pollard (n 13) ch 6; Sim, *China in Transition* (2003) 31–50; KX Zhou, *How the Farmers Changed China: Power of the people* (Westview, 1996); C Barbara-Francis, 'Quasi-Public, Quasi-Private Trends in Emerging Economies: The Case of China' (2001) *Comparative Politics* 276.

[252] There are also SOEs that are controlled by the Ministry of Finance.

[253] For an insightful analysis of their formation, interconnectedness and state influence, see L Lin and C Milhaupt, 'We are the (National) Champions: Understanding Mechanisms of State Capitalism in China' (2013) *Stanford Law Review* 697.

[254] See en.sasac.gov.cn. For an overview of the developments, see D Feng, 'Indigenous Evolution of SOE Regulation' in Milhaupt and Liebman, *Visible Hand?* (2016). See also S Tenev and C Zhang, *Corporate Governance and Enterprise Reform in China: Building the Institutions of Modern Markets* (World Bank & IFC, 2002) 20–28.

[255] See en.sasac.gov.cn.

[256] G Wildau (29.2.2016, FT); T Mitchell (31.12.2014, FT).

[257] W Wu (17.6.2017, SCMP).

[258] Tenev and Zhang, *Corporate Governance and Enterprise Reform in China* (2002) 20–28.

[259] Most bank loans go to provinces with heavy concentrations of SOEs: J Aziz and C Duenwald Growth-Financial Intermediation Nexus in China (2002) IMF Working Paper No 02/194.

positions, at the cost of private-sector business and their inefficient provision of public goods and services';[260] state-ownership can lead to inefficient allocation of resources and capital; it can also lead to conflicts of interests due to the state's role as both a shareholder and a regulator;[261] and, in China, it has also led to the creation of inefficient zombie companies.[262] Central and local governments have tried to deal with these problems but generally refuse to cede control over SOEs.[263]

SOEs remain important for China's economic development. By the end of 2018, only 1.8 per cent of all companies were SOEs, but they provided 15.7 per cent of all employment[264] and about 30 per cent of GDP.[265] Besides SOEs, however, much of China's growth in recent decades originated from private enterprises.[266] As mentioned earlier, privatisation started in the countryside as a response to the inefficiencies and inflexibility of the management of agricultural production. Besides privatisation of SOEs, local governments in Beijing and other large cities also allowed the creation of new private companies in the early 1980s when crowds of able, educated people flooded the cities – which had no jobs for them – after they were released from 're-education camps'.[267]

Allowing the migrants to start their own small businesses and provide for themselves proved to be an efficient solution. Private companies grew in number and importance. Their status was formally recognised in 1988 and fully legalised in 2004 when the Constitution was amended to confirm that private property[268] enjoys the same protection as state property (and private entrepreneurs have the same rights as SOEs). At first, the state retained at least partial ownership and control of new companies, but in time completely private and later also foreign enterprises were allowed to operate. In 1997, it was decided that the state would relinquish control of small and medium enterprises (SMEs) and their newly issued shares were offered to their managers and staff. The privatisation was substantial but relatively quiet, and state ownership fell by 40 per cent in the first five years alone.[269] Since then, the number of privately owned companies grew and soon overtook the total number of collectively owned and state-owned companies.

The expansion of the private sector heralded a new chapter in China's development.[270] By 2010, private enterprises provided more employment than SOEs,[271] produced twice as many exports than SOEs, introduced more technology and innovation, accounted for 80 per cent of all new urban jobs, re-employed 19 million workers laid off by SOEs,

---

[260] Milhaupt and Liebman (n 242) 4.

[261] M Pargendler, 'The Unintended Consequences of State Ownership: The Brazilian Experience' (2012) *Theoretical Inquiries in Law* 503.

[262] See Sections 9.2 and 10.1.2.

[263] Milhaupt and Liebman (n 242) 49, 133; G Wildau (14.9.2015, FT); L Hornby (14.7.2016, FT); G Wildau (9.1.2017, FT).

[264] NBS 2019.

[265] WIND data 2019.

[266] Both are important: AR Kroeber, *China's Economy* (2016, Oxford University Press) ch 5. See also Huang, *Capitalism with Chinese characteristics* (2008).

[267] Similar to Soviet gulags.

[268] Art 11 of China's Constitution.

[269] K Guo and Y Yao, 'Causes of privatization in China: Testing several hypotheses' (2005) *Economics of Transition* 211. See also B Naughton, *Growing out of the plan* (Cambridge University Press, 1996); Kynge (n 34).

[270] K Tsai, *Capitalism without Democracy: The private sector in Contemporary China* (Cornell, 2007).

[271] SOEs employed 60% of the working population in 1995, and only 30% in 2002: National Bureau of Economic Research.

and generated 800 billion RMB.[272] By 2015, private companies employed twice as many people as SOEs in urban areas.[273] There were about 10 times more private industrial enterprises by number,[274] but SOEs held almost twice as many assets by value[275] and each industrial SOE on average owned 13 times as many assets than each private industrial enterprise.[276]

The number of domestic[277] companies in China grew rapidly, from six million in 2006 to 17.8 million in 2017, ie a growth rate of about 10 per cent per year.[278] The fast growth was due to the increase in domestic and international economic activities but also Company Law amendments in 2013 that simplified company formation. However, data suggests that less than 70 per cent of companies remain active after five years, and less than 50 per cent survive the first nine years.[279] Some companies deregister, but many live on as zombie companies without liquidating or resolving their liabilities.[280] These companies should, ideally, be resolved using the EBL in order to protect release resources, protect relevant stakeholders and improve the business environment in China.[281]

2.5.2. Two Economic Sectors

Most literature divides China's economy purely according to ownership, ie into state-owned and privately owned sectors. This book uses a more nuanced classification which reflects not only ownership but also economic significance. The division is based on insights of all my interviewees who spoke of ownership as merely one of several factors that determine whether and how the Party-state exercises control over individual companies' decision-making, their access to finance and their access to courts. The division also builds on two recent projects. Firstly, in determining whether a particular company falls within a 'state sector' or 'private sector', it considers issues identified by Kennedy in the context of lobbying,[282] namely ownership, (absolute and relative) size, profitability, industry affiliation and location.[283] And secondly, the proposed division

---

[272] Li (n 27) estimates that the private sector contributes more than 60% of China's GDP. V Nee and S Opper, *Capitalism from Below: Markets and Institutional Change in China* (HUP, 2011) estimate it is 70% of China's GDP. See also: F Allen, J Qian and M Qian, 'Law, finance, and economic growth in China' (2005) *Journal of Financial Economics* 57; Huang, *Capitalism with Chinese characteristics* (2008).

[273] NBS 2016.

[274] 19,273 industrial SOEs v 216,506 private industrial enterprises: NBS 2016.

[275] Total assets amounted to 39.74 trillion RMB in industrial SOEs v 22.9 trillion RMB in private industrial enterprises: NBS 2016.

[276] Assets per enterprise: 2.02 billion RMB per each industrial SOE v 0.16 billion RMB per each private industrial enterprise: NBS 2016.

[277] ie not companies with foreign investment or funded from Hong Kong, Taiwan or Macau (they accounted for about 267 000 companies in 2017).

[278] NBS 2007–18.

[279] Judge Du Wanhua of the SPC, cited in C Zhang (3.5.2016, Weixin).

[280] ibid.

[281] See Sections 9.2.1, 10.1.2 and 12.7.

[282] The same issues were repeatedly mentioned in my interviews with stakeholders and practitioners.

[283] Kennedy, *Lobbying in China* (2005) argues that, contrary to the popular belief about doing business in China, companies' influence in the law-making process depends less on one's *guanxi* and more on

draws on a recent re-examination of the role of ownership by Milhaupt and Zheng in the context of corporate reforms in China.[284] The authors argue – and my interviewees agreed – that reforms of the state sector in China cannot focus purely on state-owned companies. Instead, they say, reforms need to focus on all companies that are under state control – including privately owned companies under state capture – in order to address the problems raised by state capitalism and make the corporate reform programme more effective.

The particular attributes of the state sector and the private sector are discussed below. The two sectors differ in many aspects, most importantly in terms of the presence/absence of both formal and informal state control and direction; the degree of protectionism and involvement from national and local governments in the resolution of their financial distress; debtors' and creditors' ability to file for a court-based bankruptcy procedure; courts' ability to accept such bankruptcy petition; and their individual economic significance. The resulting access to different sources of debt finance – from the state, shadow market or private sources[285] – is an additional factor which influences debtors' and creditors' choice of debt-resolution mechanism.[286]

2.5.2.1. State Sector

My interviewees suggested that there are two key characteristics which determine whether a given company falls within the *zhengfuying jingji* (政府营经济) – which means, literally, government-managed economy. The two characteristics are, namely, a company's state ownership, and, even more importantly, economic significance.

Much has been written about the protectionism of SOEs[287] in China to the point that it is often assumed only SOEs comprise the entirety of the state sector. However, that is not accurate. Firstly, state ownership is now more complex than it was in 1978. State ownership is no longer only direct but, increasingly, also indirect through SASAC and other vehicles and structures.[288] Furthermore, as the relative contribution of SOEs to local economies began to shrink[289] and several previously state-only sectors opened up to private competition, a number of private companies entered the market and some became important economic players in their own right. Local governments – incentivised by their new responsibility to raise funds for their respective local budgets[290] – responded to these developments by extending their (in)visible hand to economically

---

one's economic importance. His work also highlights that much of existing research overlooks important dimensions – such as size and industry affiliation – which seems to explain the divergence in one's access and influence far better than ownership or political connections alone.

[284] C Milhaupt and W Zheng, 'Reforming China's State-Owned Enterprises: Institutions, Not Ownership' in Milhaupt and Liebman (n 242).

[285] Section 3.2.

[286] Chapter 9 returns to this issue when discussing whether a company uses private or politically driven debt enforcement alternatives.

[287] See Sections 2.5.1 and 2.5.3. For the Party-state's reasons for interfering, see Section 2.4.2 (general) above and Section 8.3 (EBL-specific). For the ways of Party-state's interference, see Section 9.2 (debt enforcement).

[288] See Section 2.5.1. See also Milhaupt and Zheng (n 282).

[289] eg lower industrial output, profitability, employment, contribution to GDP and taxes: see Section 2.5.1.

[290] See Section 2.4.2.

significant privately owned companies.[291] As a result, a company's economic significance became more important for determining state control and protectionism than
mere state ownership.[292]

While there is no single commonly accepted definition, several characteristics
appear relevant to whether or not an enterprise is considered 'economically significant'. Economically significant companies tend to control a large number of assets,
have many employees,[293] or produce a large tax output and contributions to the local
or national GDP.[294] They are often important in terms of economic growth, innovation and research.[295] They are often connected with other important companies through
ownership, debt guarantees, trade agreements, etc.[296] In addition, they often also operate in key industries[297] and locations.[298] They are often listed on one of China's stock
exchanges, and possibly also abroad.[299] And they tend to have access to credit from
the state-owned banks. Most importantly, however, their collapse could have serious
consequences for the local economy and social stability in the region.[300] If a state-
sector company becomes financially distressed, the local government is usually heavily
involved.[301]

2.5.2.2. *Private Sector*

Private ownership was first permitted and grew as a response to SOEs' inefficiencies.[302]
There are now many important private companies whose operations and decisions are
significantly influenced by (local) governments and so, for the purpose of this book, fall
outside the scope of the private sector.[303] Nevertheless, *minying jingji* (民营经济which
means, literally, 'people-run economy') is crucial for China's economic development

---

[291] Milhaupt and Zheng (n 282) analyse this in terms of the mechanism use – namely state capture. The focus
here is on the reason for the state's control.

[292] Interviews B1-c to B3-c, C5-r, C7-s, E2-s, J1-s to J9-c, L2-s to L7-c, R10-c.

[293] See eg P Bharati, I Lee and A Chaudhury (eds), *Global Perspectives on Small and Medium Enterprises and
Strategic Information Systems: International Approaches* (Business Science Reference, 2010) 147.

[294] Local government officials' incentives are built so that they protect these companies: see Sections 2.4.2
and 8.3.1–8.3.2.

[295] Interviews B1-c to B3-c, C5-r, C7-s, E2-s, J1-s to J9-c, L2-s to L7-c, R10-c.

[296] Interviews C5-r, C7-s, J1-s to J9-c, L2-s to L7-c, L14-c, R2-r, R9-c, R10-c.

[297] Several industries are dominated by SOEs (eg the armaments, power generation and distribution, oil,
petrochemicals, telecommunications, coal, aviation and shipping industries: H Zhao (19.12.2006, *China
Daily*)). However, other significant industries (manufacturing, technology, IT, etc) are accessible to private
companies.

[298] Examples include SEZs, large cities, and areas designated for particular products (a remnant of planned
economy): ibid.

[299] Listing status is very hard to get in China. For this reason, listing carries with it a degree of protectionism
which is, in and of itself, a valuable asset. My interviewees suggested that this alone can be one of the reasons
why the courts are more willing to allow reorganisation petitions of listed companies: Interviews J1-c, J3-c to
J9-c, L2-s, L4-r to L7-c, P1-r, P3-r, R10-c.

[300] See eg Z Zhang, *Corporate Reorganisations in China* (Cambridge University Press, 2018) 85 (based on an
empirical study of reorganisations in 2007–15).

[301] See Sections 8.3, 9.2 and 11.3.4–11.3.5.

[302] See Sections 2.1 and 2.5.1.

[303] This does not mean that they are not privately owned. Instead, it is submitted that the nature of ownership
is secondary in determining whether the Party-state interferes in a resolution of the given company's financial
distress.

because it has been a breeding ground for many of China's subsequent economic success stories. Such private companies are usually comparatively small (compared to the state sector),[304] with fewer assets,[305] and with fewer employees. Consequently, they are of lesser importance for local taxes and GDP growth – and so the Party-state does not interfere in their day-to-day management or the resolution of their financial distress. One of the major hubs of the private sector is the city of Wenzhou, in Zhejiang Province, with approximately 400,000 companies[306] (many of which are SMEs) and deep-rooted acceptance and support for private entrepreneurs.[307]

2.5.3. Impact of Corporate Ownership and Control on Law Enforcement

Literature predicts that state ownership affects the implementation of laws.[308] State-owned companies are often protected from a strict application of the law and are instead protected by the state.[309] In the context of corporate bankruptcy, state-owned companies often do not have to face the consequences of their poor financial decisions when their budgetary constraints are breached.[310] Instead, the state influences whether and how creditors and courts enforce debt-related legal rights.

China-specific research confirms these claims.[311] There is evidence that privately owned companies without political connections – ie private-sector companies – cannot access bank finance and commercial opportunities (compared to SOEs), face heavy regulation, extra layers of bureaucracy ('red tape'), and local governments' rent-seeking.[312] Empirical studies also show that Chinese SOEs do not face hard-budget constraints and receive financial support from the Government.[313] Another study finds that SOEs' managers often make little effort, compared to their private-company counterparts, to ameliorate their company's financial distress because they expect the state to provide fresh finance or another solution.[314] My interviewees provide further support for these findings.[315]

---

[304] For our purposes, small private-sector companies are sole traders and family businesses. Medium private-sector companies are those who employ others outside the owner and their family and who are not so economically significant so as to fall within the state sector – and so under the state protection.

[305] Many smaller companies hire the machinery they need because they do not have the capital to buy their own.

[306] ie one company per 25 inhabitants.

[307] Interviews C1-c, C5-r, C7-s, C11-c, J1-c, J3-c to J9-c, L2-s to L15-c, P1-r, R2-r, R3-r, R6-c to R10-c.

[308] See eg A Shleifer, 'State versus Private Ownership' (1998) NBER Working Paper 6665; The World Bank, *Bureaucrats in Business* (Oxford University Press, 1995); K van Zwieten, 'Corporate Rescue in India: The Influence of the Courts' (2015) *Journal of Corporate Law Studies* 1.

[309] See eg A Szamosszegi and C Kyle, *An Analysis of State-Owned Enterprises and State Capitalism in China* (US-China Economic and Security Review Commission, 2011).

[310] ie they face soft-budget constraints: see eg J Kornai, 'Resource-constrained versus demand-constrained systems' (1979) *Econometrica* 801; J Kornai, *Economics of Shortage* (North-Holland, 1980).

[311] Szamosszegi and Kyle, *An Analysis* (2011).

[312] See J Du and S Girman, 'Red Capitalists: Political Connections and Firm Performance in China' (2010) *Kyklos* 530.

[313] See W Megginson, B Ullah and Z Wei, 'State ownership, soft-budget constraints, and cash holdings' (2014) *Journal of Banking and Finance* 276; R Cull and L Xu, 'Who gets credit?' (2003) *Journal of Development Economics* 533.

[314] See J Fan, J Huang and N Zhu, 'Institutions, ownership structures, and distress resolution in China' (2013) *Journal of Corporate Finance* 71.

[315] See Sections 6.1, 8.3 and 9.2.

3

Debt Finance and Enforcement in China

Bankruptcy law procedures in China – as is common in many other jurisdictions – are triggered when debts are not repaid as they fall due or when debts exceed assets.[1] This chapter, therefore, briefly explains how debt is acquired and debt repayment enforced in China. Section 3.1 of this chapter starts by examining the data on the volume of debt in China's economy. Section 3.2 then explores how companies acquire debt finance in China. It looks at various sources of formal and informal credit and discusses the particulars of China's shadow lending. Section 3.3 looks at informal, formal, individual and collective debt enforcement mechanisms other than bankruptcy law that are used by creditors to recover their money. And Section 3.4 briefly examines five general challenges that inhibit effective debt enforcement in China.

3.1. Debt Finance in China

China's economy has undergone a significant expansion and its total debt increased five-fold over just 10 years – from 36 trillion RMB in 2007 to 183 trillion RMB in 2016.[2] About two-thirds is corporate debt.[3] The growth of total debt is significant even when adjusted for China's spectacular GDP growth. China's debt-to-GDP ratio doubled between 2007 and 2016, from 146 per cent to 254 per cent of the GDP, and it exceeded 300 per cent by 2019.[4] Corporate-debt-to-GDP ratio grew at a similar pace, increasing from 99 per cent in 2007 to 166 per cent in 2016.[5]

Observers and Chinese regulators are worried about the speed and uncontrollability of debt expansion in China,[6] and warnings about the excessive indebtedness have been issued by many bodies including the Bank of International Settlement, Moody's and

---

[1] See Section 4.2.2.
[2] cf the IMF report suggests that China's debt is worth 225% of GDP: W Maliszewski, S Arslanalp, JC Caparusso, J Garrido, S Guo, JS Kang, WR Lam, D Law, W Liao, N Rendak, P Wingender, J Yu and L Zhang, 'Resolving China's Corporate Debt Problem' (October 2016) IMF Working Paper 16/203.
[3] Reuters (10.10.2016).
[4] Similar to the US and the Eurozone in 2017: Bank of International Settlement (BIS) and Institute of International Finance.
[5] ibid.
[6] For an excellent overview, see D McMahon, *China's Great Wall of Debt* (Little, Brown, 2018). See also Reuters (23.5.2017); G Wildau (12.10.2016, FT); F Tang (9.3.2017, SCMP).

Fitch Ratings. The credit-to-GDP gap[7] is an indicator that reflects the credit health of a country. Healthy economies maintain the credit-to-GDP gap between two and 10, but anything higher signals credit excess, with large gaps usually serving as early warning indicators of banking crises and systemic financial distress.[8] China's has been at the upper end and beyond the 10 mark since 2009, reaching almost 25 in 2015 and almost 27 in 2016.[9]

Many observers are also worry that the official data is incomplete – and that China's debt-related problems are much more severe. They point to four major gaps. Firstly, Chinese statistics are notoriously unreliable, and many commentators believe that official statistics underestimate the size of the problem.[10] Secondly, the dependence of some banks and non-bank financial institutions on wholesale borrowing may indicate that they are postponing debt-related problems.[11] Thirdly, the data does not reflect the debts that get repaid by the state – eg state bailouts and subsidies to financially distressed state-sector companies – and by state-owned banks – through forgiving debt, and guaranteeing and if necessary honouring SOEs' corporate bond repayments. This strategy has been severely criticised[12] because state-provided solutions often waste resources and only postpone financial distress without resolving the cause of the problem. Lastly, China's official figures fail to account for the enormous and largely unregulated shadow debt market which now drives China's private sector.[13] Although no official statistics exist, experts estimate that there is between five and 46 trillion RMB in shadow debt finance, depending on what is included.[14]

An additional problem that China faces are non-performing loans (NPLs). About five trillion RMB, or seven per cent of the GDP, is estimated to be bad debt.[15] Official statistics suggest that China's listed banks held 1.274 trillion RMB of NPLs in 2015.[16] However, most commentators agree that the real number is likely to be even higher as most bad debt in state-owned banks is concealed as bridging loans, reclassified as an investment, or resolved by turning debt into equity in the debtor company so as not to appear on the banks' books as non-performing assets.[17] There is also an unknown but significant amount of NPLs in the shadow debt market.

Finally, the total volume of corporate debt in China keeps rising, but companies' ability to service the debt remains problematic. Bloomberg estimated that in 2018, companies failed to repay corporate bonds worth 108.5 billion RMB.[18] The growing

---

[7] Defined by BIS as *the difference between the credit-to-GDP ratio (c_t/y_t) and its long-run trend* t_t: see www.bis.org/publ/qtrpdf/r_qt1609.pdf.

[8] M Drehmann and K Tsatsaronis, 'The credit-to-GDP gap and countercyclical capital buffers: questions and answers' (9.3.2014) BIS.

[9] 'BIS Quarterly Review March 2016', available at www.bis.org/publ/qtrpdf/r_qt1609.pdf.

[10] G Wildau (8.12.2016, FT).

[11] See eg I Kaminska (16.3.2017, FT).

[12] eg Dongbei Special Steel Group, which defaulted nine times in 2016.

[13] See Section 3.2.

[14] Wealth-management products and trust products are often not included.

[15] Maliszewski, Arslanalp, Caparusso, Garrido, Guo, Kang, Lam, Law, Liao, Rendak, Wingender, Yu and Zhang, 'Resolving China's Corporate Debt Problem' (2016).

[16] NBS 2016.

[17] G Wildau (30.10.2014, FT); C Balding (28.10.2015, FT). See also chs 3.III and 9.II.

[18] SputnikNews (20.12.2018).

number of missed bond payments – together with the increasing volume of corporate and government debt, the NPLs and the intense competition in the market – indicate that a functioning, efficient mechanism for liquidating and restructuring distressed companies is needed. Sections 5.1 and 10.1 build on the data above and argue that the number of EBL cases is far too low given the amount of bad debt in China's economy.

3.2. Companies' Access to Credit in China

Companies can fund their activities through internal or external finance (see Figure 3.1). The focus of this chapter is on external debt, which can be formal or informal.

Existing literature and many of my interviewees[19] suggested that access to formal bank finance depends on whether a borrower is sufficiently large and important.[20] In general, larger state-sector[21] companies have direct access to bank finance, while smaller private-sector companies tend to rely on private funding[22] and shadow lending.[23]

Figure 3.1 Overview of corporate debt finance in China

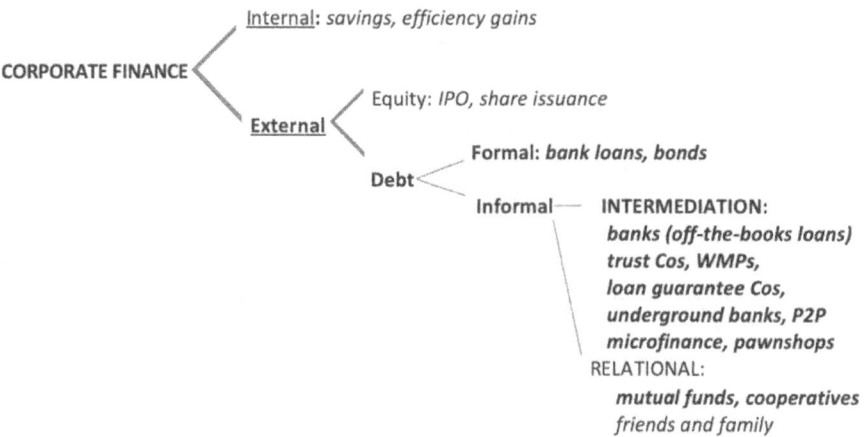

---

[19] Interviews B1-c to B3-c, C1-c to C5-r, E1-c to E5-c, IF1-s, IF2-c, L1-r to L7-c, L10-s to L14-c, R1-r to R3-r, R6-c, R7-c, R9-c, R10-c. A survey in 2000 suggested that lack of relationship with banks was a major constraint in accessing bank finance: N Gregory, S Tenev and DM Wagle, *China's Emerging Private Enterprises: Prospects for the New Century* (International Finance Corporation, 2000). Findings confirmed in G Hale and C Long, 'What are the Sources of Financing of the Chinese Firms?' (July 2010) Hong Kong Institute for Monetary Research Working Paper No 19/2010.

[20] See Section 2.5. Recently, there has been a push to provide bank loans to smaller companies who drive China's economic development: S Yu (30.12.2019, FT).

[21] See Section 2.5.2.

[22] Savings and money from friends and family are the main source of finance for start-ups in China: Gregory, Tenev and Wagle, *China's Emerging Private Enterprises* (2000).

[23] See discussion below. As previously discussed, a company affiliated with one sector can have activities or even whole departments affiliated with the other economic sector. The source of credit often determines the enforcement options and their payoffs in bankruptcy. See also Sections 3.3 and 7.3.

China's financial market is still dominated by large banks.[24] Bank loans are often secured over the company's assets. Common forms of security include a mortgage or a pledge, and they are granted over real estate (land, buildings, land use rights, fixtures), tangible property (machinery, raw materials, finished goods, etc), financial instruments (shares, negotiable instruments) or claims and receivables.[25] Security cannot be granted over future assets, certain public facilities, illegal constructions, and – in practice – security is not granted over fungible assets.[26] Bank finance in China is mostly controlled by the state. The 'Big Four' commercial banks are all owned and controlled by the central Government. There are also three policy banks through which the state finances its economic and trade development projects.[27] At the subnational level, there are 132 city commercial banks[28] which are owned or controlled by local governments and whose role is to provide credit to local companies and projects. Private banks entered the market in 2014,[29] but they have not been able to compete with the strong and established position of the Big Four state banks and the constraints imposed on the new entrants by the regulator.[30] Similarly, foreign banks have been allowed to operate in China for about a decade, but their operations are small – their total assets accounted for just 1.32 per cent of total banking assets at the end of 2017.[31]

Bank finance is heavily regulated by the People's Bank of China (PBoC) and the China Banking and Insurance Regulatory Commission (CBIRC).[32] Lending to certain types of companies – eg to real estate developers – has been restricted.[33] Similarly, the regulator prescribes maximum permissible proportion of non-performing loans (NPLs) on banks' balance sheets.[34] To comply with this limitation, many local banks have offered bridging loans and other masking mechanisms to replace NPLs; and bank credit officers have been made personally responsible for loans that turn sour, which has led to a degree of reluctance by banks to extend credit to borrowers who do not have state backing.[35] This has caused credit squeeze for private-sector borrowers.

China's corporate bond market provides an alternative source of external formal funding. Since January 2015, all corporates can issue corporate bonds; in practice, however, less than 30 per cent in number and 20 per cent in value of corporate bonds are

---

[24] A Schipke, M Rodlauer and L Zhang, *The Future of China's Bond Market* (IMF, March 2019) ch 1. In 2010, 82.9% of formal corporate funding was provided by banks: C Walter and F Howie, *Red Capitalism* (John Wiley & Sons, 2011) 15.

[25] X Zhang and M Liu, 'Lending and taking security in China: Overview' (1 July 2019) Practical Law Guide.

[26] This is because 'the relevant registration authority will require a clear description of the mortgaged or pledged property': ibid.

[27] This role was previously fulfilled by the Big Four banks.

[28] PR News (11.7.2016).

[29] R Morrow (6.6.2014, GlobalCapitalAsia); Xinhua (27.12.2016).

[30] G Wildau (12.12.2016, FT).

[31] P Danese (29.6.2019, EuroMoney).

[32] The China Banking Regulatory Commission (CBRC) was merged with the insurance regulator in 2018.

[33] Lending to real estate companies has been limited in order to manage the real estate bubble: Xinhua (6.12.2019); Caixin (11.9.2019); Reuters (9.8.2019).

[34] The CBRC was established in 2003 and one of its first tasks was to bring NPLs in the four big banks under control: RH Huang, 'Institutional Structure of Financial Regulation in China: Where Is It Now and Where Is It Heading?' in RH Huang and D Schoenmaker (eds) *Institutional Structure of Financial Regulation* (Routledge, 2014).

[35] R Smyth, OK Tam, M Warner and CJ Zhu (eds), *China's Business Reforms: Institutional Challenges in a Globalised Economy* (Routledge, 2015) 63.

issued by private companies.[36] Bond issuance helped raise between 0.5 and 2.8 trillion RMB per month in 2015/16.[37] By the end of 2018, China's corporate bond market grew to 19 trillion RMB.[38] However, the numbers are not entirely accurate because many corporate bonds are issued by local governments through special purpose vehicles (SPVs) in an attempt to circumvent their financing restrictions imposed by the national Government.[39] Moreover, there have been many cases of large-scale defaults in recent years[40] as local governments – themselves debt-laden – become less willing to step in to bail out local businesses, including politically well-connected businesses.[41]

Companies can also raise debt informally. China has an enormous 'shadow' finance market which consists of a number of financial intermediaries who provide credit to otherwise excluded borrowers.[42] Strong demand for shadow finances – from eg small private-sector companies and companies with cash-flow problems[43] – is reinforced by considerable supply from banks, (state) companies and general depositors with signifi-cant household savings[44] who look for profitable investment opportunities outside of (state) banks.[45] Moreover, there are very few onshore investment opportunities, and offshore investment is severely restricted,[46] and so those with extra cash look for profitable investment opportunities. It is, therefore, not surprising that China's infor-mal 'shadow' debt market is thriving despite the dangers associated with engaging in activities that are often risky and not entirely legal.[47]

Shadow lending encompasses an enormous range of activities. Some shadow finance is now fully legal and operating in full view – such as technology-supported P2P platforms[48] – while others form a part of China's unregulated and often semi-legal or outright illegal shadow lending.[49] An important source of shadow lending are official (state) banks that provide off-the-books loans and other financial products in order to increase profits and to counter their losses from state-directed lending and NPLs. They provide services such as letters of credit, loan commitments, wealth-management

---

[36] Data for 2014–18: FitchRatings, 'China Corporate Bond Market Blue Book' (2019).

[37] WIND Info.

[38] FitchRatings, 'Blue Book' (2019).

[39] See L Lin, 'Balancing Closure and Openness: The Challenge of Leadership Reform in China's State-Owned Enterprises' in C Milhaupt and B Liebman (eds), *Regulating the Visible Hand?* (Oxford University Press, 2016).

[40] Corporate bond default rate in 2018 climbed to 1.03% – or a total of 110.5 billion RMB: FitchRatings (n 38).

[41] See eg D Weinland (26.12.2019, FT).

[42] J Cai (6.1.2014, SCMP); K Tsai, *Back-Alley Banking: Private Entrepreneurs in China* (Cornell University Press, 2002).

[43] T Durden (10.12.2015, ZeroHedge).

[44] Household savings share of total savings in China was 71% in 1991 (R Cull and L Xu, 'Who gets credit?' (2003) *Journal of Development Economics* 533, 535) and about 60% throughout 2000–2003 (D Farrell, S Lund, J Rosenfeld, F Morin, N Gupta and E Greenberg, *Putting China's Capital to Work: The Value of Financial System Reform* (McKinsey Global Institute, 2006) 69).

[45] State banks often offer depositors interest rates that are lower than inflation rates. For example, PBoC's interest rates range from 0.3% for current accounts and 1.75% for a 12-month-term deposit, but inflation rates have been about 2% (5.45% in 2011): PBoC historic data. See also Reuters (29.9.2011).

[46] See eg L Wei (26.11.2016, WSJ).

[47] See Section 6.2.2.

[48] Note, however, that Chinese regulator has given all P2P platforms two years to become small loan-makers in November 2019 following a series of fraud scandals in the industry: Reuters (28.11.2019).

[49] For a detailed discussion see Tsai, *Back-Alley Banking* (2002).

products (WMPs) with risky underlying assets (often real estate), loan guarantees and entrusted loans. These are usually realised through trust companies and wealth-management vehicles to counter regulatory rules such as mandatory capital requirement and restrictions on lending to certain sectors (imposed by the CBIRC to reduce systemic risk). Trust companies take banks' illegal loans, repackage them as WMPs and sell them to investors (including banks) as bonds.[50] By 'selling off' these loans or classifying them as 'investment' WMPs, banks comply with the regulations without giving up profitable – albeit risky – shadow activities.[51] This is problematic because it exposes banks to unknown risks and most likely further worsens systemic risk by spreading the bad loans through WMPs.

Loan guarantees are provided by specialised companies or by enterprises with surplus capital (so-called 'red hats') which – in exchange for a percentage of the principal – guarantee loan repayment for others.[52] This service is particularly important for smaller borrowers who would otherwise not be able to access bank finance. The problem is four-fold. Firstly, it is often SOEs – who have access to credit from state-banks – who engage in this activity and so expose themselves to external risk. Secondly, loan guarantee companies have started lending directly. However, because they make no or limited background checks, their lending is more risky which, in turn, adversely affects their stability. Thirdly, loan guarantee companies take relatively risky positions without putting sufficient amount of capital aside in case they are called to repay the principal. And fourthly, loan guarantee companies are regulated at a local level, and so are more susceptible to political influence.[53]

Underground banks also provide shadow credit. They operate without a licence,[54] and so avoid CBIRC's regulation and oversight. They attract deposits by promising exceptionally high interest rates – usually about 20–30 per cent – and provide loans to private borrowers. As a result, they tend to operate in provinces with a strong private sector, such as Zhejiang. Their vulnerability stems from the lack of regulation and – as many believe – less sophisticated risk assessment.[55]

Another type of shadow lending is peer-to-peer (P2P) online lending. P2P plat-forms connect depositors and borrowers for a small commission. Interest rates are usually much higher than in bank loans, but credit is available to borrowers who do not ordinarily have access to bank finance. Lending platforms perform only limited risk assessment and make a recommendation to the lender who then decides whether to lend or not. P2P lending started in 2007 and, by the end of 2015, it was providing 982 billion RMB in loans.[56] However, following an increasing number of failures and fraud[57]

---

[50] This is illegal, but evidence shows that it is still happening. See eg G Wildau (23.11.2016, FT).

[51] See eg G Wildau (29.7.2016, FT).

[52] SOEs often guarantee loans for each other, and so create guarantee chains.

[53] N Borst, 'China Shadow Banking Primer' (1.11.2011, PIIE).

[54] Local officials tend to turn a blind eye because they provide finance to companies with no access to formal credit. Growth of these companies then enables regional development: ibid.

[55] See eg Wei (26.11.2016, WSJ); Tsai (n 42).

[56] Data from www.wangdaizhijia.com.

[57] eg the case of Ezubao where 900,000 depositors lost their money (approximately 7.6 billion USD) due to fraud in 2015: N Gough (1.2.2016, NY Times).

in the industry, it was decided at the end of 2019 that all existing P2P lenders would have to become small loan providers by the end of 2022.[58]

Smaller borrowers also rely on microfinance lenders and pawnshops. Microfinance lenders provide small unsecured loans at high interest rates and for additional fees.[59] Pawnshops provide short-term credit to small borrowers at very high interest rates – usually as temporary working capital or a bridge loan. The lending is less risky due to high collateral requirements.

Finally, some companies also rely on relational lending. Besides financing from family and friends, small companies can get small loans from local credit associations, local mutual assistance associations and assistance funds, local finance cooperatives, and other forms of profit-oriented community-based arrangements.[60] Because the members know each other, they can perform risk assessment, monitoring and enforcement without additional costs, and so defaults are practically unheard of.[61]

The main difficulty with shadow lending is that it increases systemic risk in China's economy.[62] This is mainly due to a lack of transparency; inherent difficulties in regulating, monitoring and managing the risks;[63] Ponzi scheme-like structures that promise unrealistic returns to depositors and investors;[64] and lending concentration, liquidity mismatches, and the resulting risk of liquidity shortages.[65] Many shadow lending activities are treated by national and local governments as semi-legal[66] or outright illegal.[67]

3.3. Debt Enforcement Mechanisms in China

Debt collection agencies were, for a long time, prohibited in China.[68] Instead, claimholders used to try to recover their debts by dealing directly with the debtor – in an 'informal' solution – or with the assistance of an authorised third-party decision-maker such as a court or an arbitrator – in a 'formal' solution. A claimholder can deal solely with their own claim – under an 'individual' approach – or join others – under a 'collective' approach. Claimholders have a range of formal and informal, individual and collective debt enforcement mechanisms, as summarised in Table 3.1.

---

[58] Reuters (28.11.2019).
[59] Borst, 'China Shadow Banking Primer' (2011).
[60] See eg Newsweek (17.11.2007).
[61] ibid.
[62] T Mitchell and G Wildau (6.5.2017, FT); G Wildau (4.12.2014, FT).
[63] As illustrated by a chain-failure of several underground banks in Wenzhou in 2011, the Ezubao ponzi scheme in 2015, the growing real estate bubble, and others.
[64] Tsai (n 42) 35–36.
[65] AC Herrero, S Schwartz, L Xia and G Xu, 'China's shadow bank lending: a threat to financial stability?' (BBVA, 2011).
[66] ie tolerated but not actually legal: Tsai (n 42) 35.
[67] Tsai (n 42) 35–36.
[68] Notice on Prohibition of Establishing Debt Collections Companies 1995; Notice on Revocation of Various Kinds of Debt Collection Companies and Attack on Illegal Debt Collections Activities 2000. cf individuals such as business consultants would sometimes assist others in collecting their debts for a fee: K Leggett (21.9.2000, WSJ).

Table 3.1 Overview of debt enforcement in China

	Individual	Collective
Informal	Contractual solutions	
	Threats / violence	Reputational mechanism
Formal	Payment order	EBL compromise
	Security enforcement	EBL reorganisation
		EBL liquidation
	Diversified dispute resolution	

The source of debt plays an important role when determining what enforcement mechanisms are available to unpaid creditors. This section deals with the options and rules for enforcing debt repayment outside of bankruptcy law. Further analysis and explanation of how these non-EBL alternatives affect the parties' perception of the EBL – and how they contribute to the low use of the EBL – are then found in Chapter nine.

3.3.1. Informal Individual Enforcement

In China, as elsewhere, unpaid lenders often first try to achieve repayment informally, by dealing directly with the borrower.[69] All of my interviewees agreed this commonly takes the form of an amicable private negotiation before turning to a more formal – and, therefore, also more costly – mechanisms.[70] This preference is reinforced by Chinese culture which has traditionally placed a particularly strong emphasis on informal, amicable conflict-resolution due to the underlying Confucian focus on harmony and maintenance of relationships.[71] This cultural preference still influences parties' negotiations in modern China.[72]

Private negotiations often result in a contractual deal that rewrites the original agreement. Such renegotiated deals are enforceable in law.[73] When a debtor company is still active and solvent, lenders try to agree on a repayment plan. Indeed, many corporate agreements include a provision that forces parties to negotiate before seeking third-party assistance in resolving their disputes.[74] This may involve part-forgiveness of the debt or substitution of other assets or services for some of the money due.[75] Alternatively,

---

[69] See eg O Shenkar and S Ronen, 'The Cultural Context of Negotiations' (1987) *The Journal of Applied Behavioural Science* 263.

[70] A recent survey of 3,900 private firms in China suggested that private companies are reluctant to use formal court enforcement and prefer using informal alternatives: YY Ang and N Jia, 'Perverse Complementarity: Political Connections and the Use of Courts among Private Firms in China' (2014) 76 *Journal of Politics* 318.

[71] See Section 2.3.1.

[72] Interviews C1-c, C4-c, C7-s, E1-c to E3-s, E5-c, L2-s, L4-r to L7-c, L9-s, L10-s, L12-c, L15-c to L17-cR3-r, R7-c, R9-c, R10-c.

[73] Arts 77 and 91(v) Contract Law 1999.

[74] Interviews C1-c to C5-r, L2-s to L6-s, R1-r to R3-r. See also M Moser (ed), *Managing Business Disputes in Today's China* (Kluwer Law, 2007) 8.

[75] Interviews B1-c, B2-c, C1-c, C4-c, C5-r, C7-s, E1-c to E5-c, IF1-s, L1-r to L13-c, R3-r, R9-c, R10-c.

lenders sometimes extend the maturity of the existing loan or offer a bridging loan with a longer maturity or lower interest rates.[76]

Debt-for-equity swaps have also been used in more sophisticated deals.[77] They enable further cooperation even where the debtor is cash-poor. Lenders often agree to it and hope that they would recoup some of the losses from the present dealings in the future.[78] Similarly, parties also sometimes agree on a merger or acquisition.[79]

Where negotiations fail, creditors sometimes use threats or violence to achieve repayment of their debt.[80] Creditors' threats come in many forms. My interviewees said that they include general threats to 'make life difficult',[81] but also more specific threats to use violence against debtor company's management or their families, or to damage debtor's and others' property.[82] Threats of – or actual – public shaming is another widely used method.[83] In some cases, creditors also threaten the debtor company with a feared tax or criminal investigation.[84]

The credibility of such threats is enhanced by numerous reported cases of kidnapping and detention of debtor companies' personnel and their family members in a hotel room until the debtor company repays.[85] Some interviewees also mentioned 'uninvited visits from the unpaid creditors and workers' who come as a group of five to 10 people and stay in debtor company's personnel's house to put pressure on them to repay.[86] Cases of actual violence against a person or property are rare, but some cases exist[87] despite the fact that violent collection of debts is illegal.[88]

3.3.2. Informal Collective Enforcement

It is sometimes possible to find a collective contractual solution between multiple stakeholders and the debtor. Involvement of more than two parties in contractual (re)negotiations has the benefit of finding a single solution to connected problems, but it also faces significant difficulties – primarily to do with coordination and conflicts of interests. Nevertheless, several interviewees suggested that multilateral negotiations are commonly used in two types of cases as an initial attempt to reach an agreement without court involvement.[89] The first type of cases is similar to the so-called

---

[76] ibid.

[77] Interviews B1-c, C1-c, C7-s, L2-s, L4-r, L6-s, R7-c, R9-c.

[78] Interviews B1-c, E1-c, C1-c, C7-s, E2-s, L2-s to L6-s, L9-s to L13-c, R7-c, R9-c, R10-c. See also Sections 8.3.5 and 9.2.3.

[79] Interviews C1-c, L2-s, L4-r to L6-s, R3-r, R9-c. See also Sections 8.3.5 and 9.2.3.

[80] This is not unique to China, and can be achieved directly or indirectly (by debt enforcers): C Fijnaut and L Paoli (eds), *Organised Crime in Europe* (Springer, 2004).

[81] Interviews L4-r, L6-s.

[82] Interviews C1-c, C4-c, L4-r, L6-s, L10-s, L11-c, L12-c, R9-c, R10-c.

[83] See eg Global Times (20.6.2016); Reuters (19.7.2016); K Elmer (4.5.2018, SCMP).

[84] ibid.

[85] Shanghai Scrap Blog (25.10.2008); D Harris (16.5.2016, ChinaLawBlog); J Kahn (1.11.2005, NY Times).

[86] Interviews C1-c, C4-c, C7-s, E2-s, E4-c, IF1-s, L2-s, L4-r, L6-s, L9-s, L11-c to L13-c, R7-c.

[87] See eg Want China Times (29.9.2011).

[88] ibid.

[89] Interviews B1-c to B3-c, C1-c, C4-c, L2-s, L4-r to L7-c, L9-s, L10-s, L12-c, R9-c.

London Approach:[90] the main lender presides over renegotiations with the debtor and its major claimholders – but without involving or informing smaller stakeholders whose claims continue to be honoured as if the debtor had no financial difficulties. The second type of cases involves large businesses which are interconnected by debt repayment guarantees or by triangular debt structures.[91] The negotiations take place behind closed doors, with no publicity, and very little is known about them.[92]

Alternatively, a creditor can rely on collective reputation mechanism to enforce debt repayment. Reputation mechanism involves no or limited direct contact between a debtor and its creditors. Instead, debt enforcement is ensured through the threat of the debtor company (or its personnel) losing its reputation, which would lead to its exclusion from future cooperation, and so also from future opportunities and profits. Reputation as an enforcement mechanism operates at a collective level because its efficiency relies on collective enforcement.

Game theory suggests that in a simple one-period exchange (one-off lending) with no enforcement, it is unlikely that a rational[93] lender would lend. Although the lender wishes to lend and be repaid with interest, the (rational) borrower ideally wishes to take the money and keep it together with any return made thereon.[94] Knowing this, a rational lender would not lend at all.[95]

Parties' incentives are altered with the introduction of a (potentially) multi-period interaction and the borrower's reputation. Firstly, the borrower's reputation provides the lender with information about the borrower's past ability and willingness to repay, which, in turn, can help ascertain the borrower's likely future behaviour. Secondly, the borrower can pledge his or her reputation as a costly *hostage* – which would be lost if they default – which enables him or her to credibly commit *ex ante* that they would repay *ex post*. Keeping or losing one's reputation in a multi-period interaction determines the borrower's future access to loans and often also their position in society, and so losing it is costly.[96]

For the reputation mechanism to work as described above, parties must interact repeatedly. It must also be clear to the parties what constitutes 'good' (repaying) and 'bad' (defaulting) behaviour and what are the consequences of cheating (losing future financial and social gains).[97] There also needs to be fast and effective detection of wrongdoing and information about borrowers' 'bad' behaviour must be communicated[98] quickly,

---

[90] J Armour and S Deakin, 'Norms in Private Insolvency: The "London Approach" to the Resolution of Financial Distress' (2001) *Journal of Corporate Law Studies* 21.

[91] ie non-mutual debts that create a chain of liabilities among these companies: Zhao and Qing (29.9.2011, Reuters).

[92] My interviewees heard of them, some hinted that they may have been involved in them, but they did not provide any details.

[93] See Section 1.1.

[94] ibid. (The model is based on the assumption that the players are self-interested.)

[95] In economic terms, 'not lend' is a strategy that is best for both players when taking into account the other player's strategy (the Nash equilibrium). cf OA Bedford and K Hwang, 'Guilt and Shame in Chinese Culture' (2003) *Journal for the Theory of Social Behaviour* 127: payoffs in rural societies may extend beyond purely financial interests.

[96] ibid.

[97] Desirable behaviour (in our context, repaying a loan) is often codified in social norms and laws.

[98] This is easiest in smaller, closely knit homogeneous groups with long-term relationships and repeated interactions: R Ellickson, *Order Without Law* (Harvard University Press, 1991); A Greif, 'Reputation and Coalition in Medieval Trade: Evidence on the Maghribi Traders' (1989) *Journal of Economic* History 857;

cheaply and in a credible manner to the other members. Moreover, it must be highly likely that default would be punished and cooperation rewarded by a sufficient number of other club members (other lenders) because, otherwise, the defaulting borrower could simply go to the non-enforcing parties and his wrongdoing would go unpunished. That would weaken the reputation mechanism and could lead to a collapse of the lending system due to the lack of effective enforcement.[99] Third-party enforcement may be personally costly for the third-party enforcers (other lenders),[100] and it carries no immediate reward. The resulting reluctance to punish a wrongdoer may be overcome with a rule that trading with a wrongdoer leads to exclusion from the club.[101] Moreover, members know that third-party enforcement benefits them in the long run because it minimises the incentive to defect and increases cooperation, which in turn enables each member to benefit from future trade gains and limited expenditure on individual monitoring. In addition, tolerating a member's default against a non-member harms the reputation of all members,[102] which incentivises intense internal monitoring and enforcement. Therefore, even self-interested members who suffered no harm punish defectors to discourage future bad behaviour in the group.[103]

Reputation mechanism may be extended beyond club members. Newcomers without established reputation may be prevented from cooperating with club members (the lending community) – due to their inability to signal their good behaviour – unless an existing member vouches for them (so-called reputation pooling).

In China, reputation-based debt enforcement is still relevant in relational lending from family, friends and neighbours and communal lending in less developed regions.[104]

3.3.3. Formal Individual Enforcement

Unpaid creditors can also rely on third-party assistance in debt enforcement. They can seek a payment order in a simplified pre-court procedure. Where the debt is undisputed, this is relatively straightforward. Once a court examines the validity of the claim, it issues an order against the debtor to repay which is enforceable 15 days after being delivered to the debtor.[105] A court can freeze debtors' assets or accounts to ensure enforceability of the award.[106] If a court refuses to enforce the debt, if the debtor disputes the debt, or if the debtor fails to repay its debt, the affected creditor can petition the court to start full civil litigation to determine the validity and enforceability of the claim.

J Landa, 'A theory of the ethnically homogeneous middleman group' (1981) *Journal of Legal Studies* 346. Monitoring and communicating in larger and more diversified groups (ethnically, culturally, geographically) is possible with assistance from modern technology: L Bernstein, 'Opting out of the Legal System: Extralegal Contractual Relations in the Diamond Industry' (1992) *Journal of Legal Studies* 115, 116.

[99] This relates to the idea of 'critical mass': T Shelling, *Micromotives and Macrobehaviour* (Norton & Co, 1978). Consequently, most membership groups have a rule that sanctions must be carried out by all members, and refusal to do so is punished: Greif, 'Reputation and Coalition in Medieval Trade' (1989); Bernstein, 'Opting out of the Legal System' (1992).

[100] The loss of trade opportunities and relationship network of the wrongdoer.

[101] So-called 'club mechanism': Bernstein (n 98).

[102] Due to an implied underwriting of each member's good behaviour: Greif (n 98).

[103] ibid.

[104] See Section 2.3.1.

[105] Art 189 Civil Procedure Law 1991.

[106] ibid.

Alternatively, a lender may have security for their debt – most commonly in the form of a mortgage or a pledge.[107] Security rights are usually enforced directly, but a secured lender can seek assistance from a court or an arbitral body where the provider of the security challenges its existence or scope. Mortgagor and mortgagee can agree on a sale or foreclosure of the mortgaged property without the court's assistance.[108] Failing that, a mortgagee can petition a court to sell or auction the mortgaged property. If the mortgage or the right to enforce mortgagee's security is challenged, the mortgagee must first obtain a judicial or arbitral award confirming their rights.[109] Similarly, enforcing a pledge is now significantly streamlined thanks to the Property Law 2007 and the PBoC's Credit Reference Centre's online registration system for pledges over receivables. A pledgee can unilaterally sell or auction the pledged property in case of non-payment. A court or arbitral body usually get involved where the pledge agreement is disputed, and where the pledgee seeks help in locating or recovering the pledged assets.

Where the debt and creditors' rights are undisputed, both payment order and enforcement of security rights are simple and quick. Otherwise, creditors may need to start a costly and time-consuming civil litigation. Irrespective of the above, additional enforcement assistance may be necessary to locate, appraise or freeze debtor's savings, income or assets, or to supervise the delivery of assets or documents by the debtor.[110]

3.3.4. Diversified Dispute Resolution

Diversified (elsewhere 'alternative') dispute resolution[111] (DDR) mechanisms offer less formal, more confidential options for resolving disputes and enforcing agreements. DDR is very popular in China[112] and has strong support from courts.[113] In many disputes, courts first insist that parties use DDR to find a solution before they can commence court-based litigation.[114] Three DDR mechanisms are outlined below, namely mediation, arbitration, and a combination of the two.

Mediation is an informal negotiation that is overseen by a professional mediator.[115] It may be triggered by an *ex ante* provision or an ex post agreement to mediate. There are four types of mediation:

- civil mediation run by People's Mediation Committees[116] in civil and economic disputes and minor criminal cases;

---

[107] See Section 3.2.

[108] Arts 196–197 Civil Procedure Law 1991.

[109] Property Law 2007.

[110] Wenfei Law (April 2014).

[111] *duoyuanhuajiufenjiejuejizhi*多元化纠纷解决机制.

[112] K Fan, *Arbitration in China* (Hart, 2014) 3 and section 1.3 and ch 8.

[113] In June 2016, the SPC issued a policy document to guide lower courts to use DDR more and in a more streamlined way: the SPC Notice concerning the People's Courts Further Deepening the Reform of the Diversified Dispute Resolution Mechanism (*Fafa* [2016] No 14).

[114] Interviews C1-c to C7-s, J1-c, J3-c toJ9-c, L1-r to L15-c, R1-r, to R4-c, R6-c, R7-c, R9-c, R10-c, R14-s.

[115] The role of the mediator depends on the particular circumstances, and can vary from a passive forum-provider to a proactive intermediary and negotiator: H Eidenmüller and D Griffiths, 'Mediation in Cross Border Insolvency Procedures' (2009).

[116] Art 111 of the Constitution.

- administrative mediation run by local governments or government departments in civil, economic or labour disputes;
- judicial mediation run by a court in civil disputes; and
- arbitration mediation (discussed below).[117]

There are very few rules relating to the procedures – mostly contained in the Civil Procedure Law 1991, the Constitution, and a set of SPC regulations.[118] A mediation agreement is only enforceable where all affected parties consent to it.[119] A written agreement resulting from mediation is legally binding and enforceable by the court.[120]

Arbitration is a structured formal dispute resolution mechanism that is run by a professional arbitrator. There are three types of arbitration: foreign arbitration; foreign-related arbitration; and domestic arbitration. Foreign arbitrators can only hear the first two. Chinese arbitrators only hear the last two. Foreign-related arbitration involve cases with a foreign element – for example, one of the parties is a foreign national or a company domiciled abroad; relevant legal facts took place outside China; or the subject matter of the dispute was situated outside China.[121] Since February 2015, the definition of 'foreign-related' has been expanded to situations where (i) the habitual residence of either or both contracting parties is located outside China, and (ii) there exist 'other circumstances' that can constitute a foreign-related element.[122] Foreign-related arbitrations are governed by the CIETAC Rules 2012 and enjoy more flexibility compared to domestic arbitration.[123]

This chapter focuses on domestic arbitration, which is governed by the Arbitration Law 1995. Domestic arbitration can be used instead of court-based litigation, but only if there is a valid arbitration agreement[124] – that is, an agreement showing a clear intention by each party[125] to resolve disputed matters through arbitration[126] at a designated arbitration institution.[127] A failure to designate an arbitration institution, or any uncertainty, invalidates the arbitration agreement.[128] Ad hoc arbitration is not possible.[129] Arbitrators are independent from administrative organs,[130] and the parties can choose their own arbitrators[131] in one of China's 200 arbitration institutions.[132]

---

[117] Arts 35 and 86–91 of the Civil Procedure Law 1991.

[118] The SPC Notice (*Fafa* [2016] No 14) (n 113).

[119] Art 88 of the Civil Procedure Law 1991.

[120] Art 51 of the Arbitration Law 1995.

[121] Art 304 of the SPC Notice concerning Several Issues Concerning the Application of the Civil Procedure Law of the PRC (*Fafa* [1992] No 22).

[122] Art 522 of the SPC Provisions concerning the Application of the Civil Procedure Law of the PRC (*Fashi* [2015] No 5).

[123] Fan, *Arbitration in China* (2014) sections 1.4.2–1.4.3.

[124] Art 5 Arbitration Law 1995.

[125] Unlike courts which derive their jurisdiction from statutory provisions or jurisdiction agreement, arbitral bodies derive their powers solely from a contractual agreement between the parties.

[126] Art 4 Arbitration Law 1995.

[127] Arts 6, 16 and 18 Arbitration Law 1995. Fan (n 112) 35.

[128] Art 18 Arbitration law 1995.

[129] Fan (n 112) 38–42.

[130] Art 14 Arbitration Law 1995.

[131] Art 31 Arbitration law 1995. Note that Art 13 of the Arbitration Law 1995 prescribes certain minimum requirements (quality and length of practical experience) with regard to professionals' eligibility to act as arbitrators.

[132] R Fung and S Wang, *Arbitration in China: A Practical Guide* (Sweet & Maxwell, 2003) 159.

Once made, the arbitral award is final and enforceable by courts.[133] Courts can review the arbitral award where there is strong evidence to suggest that there was insufficient evidence for the award; it was tainted by an error;[134] or that the law was wrongly applied.[135] My interviewees suggested that judicial review of arbitral awards is rare.[136]

Combining mediation and arbitration into a single procedure ('Med-Arb') is also very popular in China. Initially, a third-party professional acts as a passive mediator – giving the parties more freedom to agree. Where it becomes clear that the parties are unlikely to reach a solution, a mediator turns into an arbitrator who more forcefully navigates the parties towards a solution or, if that fails, imposes a solution on them.[137] To be able to use this mechanism, the parties must have a valid arbitration agreement. Enforcement of the final award follows the same rules as enforcement of an arbitral award.

3.4. General Challenges to Debt Enforcement in China

Debt enforcement in China faces numerous challenges which weaken the 'infrastructure for bankruptcy'[138] in which the EBL operates. This section examines five such challenges. Section 3.4.1 examines the insufficient amount of reliable financial information. Section 3.4.1 explores the difficulties in the verification of property rights. Section 3.4.3 considers problems arising from the limited protection of property rights. Section 3.4.4 looks at unpunished tunnelling, asset-stripping and the use of ghost companies. And Section 3.4.5 reviews the issues arising from the nature of land ownership and land usage rights. These challenges affect all types of debt enforcement. Their comparative effect on the EBL (versus non-EBL enforcement mechanisms) is discussed in detail in Section 7.1.

3.4.1. Insufficient Amount of Reliable Financial Information

The first general challenge to debt enforcement in China mentioned by all of my interviewees is the lack of reliable, publicly available financial information which, in their experience, hinders effective debt recovery in China because they are often unable to evaluate debtors' true financial situations, prove their full entitlements or enforce their rights. The lack of reliable financial information mostly stems from the use of forged and falsified documents, and problems with locating and identifying the real debtor. Despite many attempts to improve the situation,[139] much still remains to be done.

---

[133] Art 9 Arbitration Law 1995. See also Fan (n 112) ch 4.
[134] Art 63 Arbitration Law and Art 237(2) Civil Procedure Law 1991 (as amended in 2012).
[135] Fan (n 112) 87–88.
[136] Interviews L2-s to L17-c, R9-c.
[137] Arts 49–52 Arbitration Law 1995.
[138] C Wihlborg, S Gangopadhyay and Q Hussain, 'Infrastructure Requirements in the Area of Bankruptcy Law' (2001) Wharton Financial Institutions Center Working Paper 01-09.
[139] eg Property Law 2007 created institutional framework for acquiring, exercising and disposing of property rights. Similarly, Criminal Law 2015 makes it a crime to make or deal with forged documents.

Falsified information is used by some companies,[140] provincial governments[141] and the NBS.[142] Some companies use fake receipts, contracts and invoices, which distort the information about their financial health, assets and liabilities. The use of such documents is illegal in China,[143] but they remain widely available and easily accessible.[144] Moreover, determining asset ownership, allocation of responsibility for corporate (mis)management, and accurate risk assessment are further inhibited by so-called dual-accounting – a practice of having one 'official' set of accounts for outsiders and one true set of accounts for internal purposes[145] – which makes it difficult to identify asset owners, to allocate responsibility for corporate (mis)management, and to enable outside lenders to accurately assess lending risk.

Many of my interviewees suggested additional information-related problems arise in identifying and locating the real debtor. Ownership of assets and property interests apparently belonging to a debtor company is often unclear and can be manipulated to debtor's advantage as necessary – particularly in corporate groups which co-use land rights and assets without clearly defining each company's ownership rights.[146] In some SOEs, the confusion arises from the undefined division of rights between the state and the company.[147] This makes debt recovery particularly unpredictable and complicated.

3.4.2. Difficult Verification of Property Rights

The second general challenge to debt enforcement in China is that it is often difficult to verify ownership of property rights. Research suggests that economy flourishes where borrowers can use their assets as collateral – and so borrow against these assets – and lenders can perform risk assessment *ex ante* and have a greater chance of recovery ex post – and so are more willing to lend and do so with favourable conditions.[148] However, despite announcing and legislating for a national land registry in 2013/14,[149] releasing national guidelines on the protection of property rights in 2016,[150] and adopting the new Property Law in 2007, China still lacks a reliable and comprehensive national property registry.[151] As a result, verifying the ownership of assets remains difficult.

---

[140] T Durden (25.9.2014, ZeroHedge).

[141] T Hancock (18.1.2017, FT).

[142] G Wildau (8.12.2016, FT).

[143] See also Section 6.2.

[144] Forgeries are available from many sources: D Barboza (8.8.2013, NY Times).

[145] This is a well-known fact in China. Confirmed in Interviews B1-c to B3-c, C1-c to C5-r, E1-c to E5-c, J1-c, L2-r to L7-c, L10-s, L13-c, P3-r, R2-r, R9-c, R10-c. See also A Tang and A Ward, *The Changing Face of Chinese Management* (Routledge, 2003) 51–52.

[146] ibid.

[147] ibid. These are often explained as remnants of the planned economy where ownership, possession and use rights were owned by the state, and so there was no need to define anything.

[148] H de Soto, *The Mystery of Capital* (Basic Books, 2000); C Woodruff, 'Review of de Soto's Mystery of Capital' (2001) *Journal of Economic Literature* 1215. See also Section 1.1.

[149] In a report to the annual plenary session of the NPC in 2013, the then-Premier Wen Jiabao announced that the Government would release a statute on property registration by the end of June 2014.

[150] See eg Xinhua (27.11.2016).

[151] This is largely due to the resistance from local governments. See eg Reuters (10.1.2016).

This is problematic because companies often cannot use their property to assist with raising capital, which limits their ability to access safer and cheaper bank loans and often forces them to turn to riskier and more expensive shadow finance.[152]

3.4.3. Limited Protection of Property Rights

The third general challenge to debt enforcement in China is that protection of property rights which is crucial to ensuring maximum recovery and equal treatment of similar stakeholders is limited and inadequately enforced. All my interviewees suggested that land-related property rights[153] are sometimes disturbed by asset grabbing by claimholders who try to satisfy their claims independently, without debtors' or courts' authorisation, and without opposition from the police or punishment by courts.[154] This negatively affects *ex post* recoverability of debts which impacts borrowing ability *ex ante*.[155] Similarly, courts sometimes fail to protect intellectual property rights – as well as land rights – which negatively affects raising finance,[156] debt enforcement,[157] foreign direct investment,[158] and corporate spending on research and development.[159] The State Council and the Party released joint guidelines on protecting all property rights in November 2016,[160] but progress has been slow in practice.[161]

Furthermore, the actual protection of property rights in China often depends on the interests of the Party-state.[162] Many interviewees witnessed or heard of unjustified instances of violations of private property such as arbitrary sealing up, freezing and

---

[152] This is particularly problematic for private sector companies who cannot rely on state guarantee, and so are often excluded from formal finance: Interviews B1-c to B3-c, C1-c, C2-c, C4-c, C5-r, C7-s, E1-c to E5-c, IF1-s, IF2-c, J1-c, J5-s, L2-s to L7-c, R3-r, R2-r, R7-c, R9-c, R10-c. See also 5.2.1.2 for a discussion in the EBL context.

[153] Ownership and usage rights related to the company's land, as well as its moveable and immoveable assets.

[154] Interviews B1-c, B3-c, C1-c to C7-s, C9-c, C11-c, E1-c to E5-c, J3-c, L1-r, L2-s, L4-r to L7-c, L9-s to L14-c, R2-r, R3-r, R7-c, R9-c, R10-c. As a result, the use of land-related assets as collateral for formal finance is severely limited: C Bai, J Lu and Z Tao, 'Property rights protection and access to bank loans' (2006) *Economics of Transition* 611.

[155] See Section 1.2.

[156] Bai, Lu and Tao, 'Property rights protection' 2006); U Neelen, *Bankruptcy and Intellectual Property in the People's Republic of China* (Murdoch University, 2007); D Arner, C Booth, P Lejot and B Hsu, 'Property Rights, Collateral, Creditors Rights, and Insolvency in East Asia' (2007) *Texas International Law Journal* 515.

[157] ibid.

[158] TO Awokuse and H Yin, 'Intellectual property rights protection and the surge in FDI in China' (2010) *Journal of Comparative Economics* 217.

[159] C Lin, P Lin and F Song, 'Property rights protection and corporate R&D: Evidence from China' (2010) *Journal of Development Economics* 49.

[160] The Opinions of the Central Committee of the Communist Party of China and the State Council on Improving the Property Rights Protection System and Lawfully Protecting Property Rights (Zhongfa [2016] No 28).

[161] The SPC White Paper 'Outline of the Judicial Protection of Intellectual Property in China (2016–2020). Specialised IP tribunals launched in several cities in early 2017: Y Cao (30.8.2017, China Daily).

[162] This is not surprising given China's political structure: see Sections 2.4.2 and 8.3.1–2.

taking of private enterprises' assets.[163] Since local courts and police are controlled by the local Party-state, there is often no protection against such actions.[164]

3.4.4. Unpunished Tunnelling, Asset-stripping and the Use of Ghost Companies

The fourth general challenge to debt enforcement in China is that the rules that prevent asset-stripping are not properly enforced. Lack of effective enforcement of these rules makes companies in China vulnerable to asset depletion, which reduces the assets out of which debts could be repaid.[165] Directors and managers engage in activities such as tunnelling; asset-stripping; disadvantageous decapitalisation (eg increasing top management's wages); unsound investments motivated by corruption; and other examples of insider control abuse.[166] Thus depleted assets are then transferred to the insider or a connected party, or to a new company – leaving behind an empty shell called a 'ghost company' (*kongqiaogongsi* 空壳公司).[167] Criminal law includes provisions that are aimed at punishing – and preventing – such unauthorised asset-depletion by insiders.[168] Similarly, China's Company Law and Corporate Governance Code[169] also create incentives and punishment for self-dealing directors. However, many of my interviewees argued that these rules are commonly poorly enforced, and so asset depletion remains relatively common in China.[170]

Directors and managers may also strip the company's assets in order to avoid old liabilities. Company's valuable assets, its employees and selected contracts are transferred into a new company, leaving its liabilities[171] behind in the shell of what is now a ghost company.[172] Such practice is illegal, but the rules are not enforced.[173] As a result,

---

[163] Particularly in less developed regions: Interviews B3-c, C1-c, C2-c, C5-r, C7-s, E1-c to E3-s, L2-s to L6-s, L14-c, L15-c, R3-r, R9-c, R10-c. See also S Hsu (30.11.2016, Forbes).

[164] ibid.

[165] This is not unique to China. It stems from the agency conflicts which arise between companies' owners and management: J Armour, H Hansmann and R Kraakman, 'Agency Problems and Legal Strategies' in R Kraakman, J Armour, P Davies, L Enriques, H Hansmann, G Hertig, K Hopt, H Kanda and E Rock, *The Anatomy of Corporate Law: A Comparative and Functional Approach*, 3rd edn (Oxford University Press, 2017) ch 2.

[166] Y Cheung, L Jing, T Lu, PR Rau and A Stouraitis, 'Tunnelling and propping up' (2009) 17 *Pacific-Basin Finance Journal* 372. For a discussion of similar problems in Russia and elsewhere: A Kossov and D Lovyrev, *Related Party Transactions: International Experience and Russian Challenges* (OECD, 2014).

[167] Can be also translated as 'shell companies'.

[168] See Section 6.2. See also H Chen, *Financial Crime in China* (Palgrave Macmillan, 2016) 110.

[169] Poor corporate governance is believed to permit abuse of power and unreliable financial reporting: A Plazzi and W Torous, 'Does Corporate Governance Matter?' (2016) Swiss Finance Institute Research Paper No 16-54. Moreover, it is also believed to help reduce agency conflicts: A Dey, 'Corporate Governance and Agency Conflicts' (2008) *Journal of Accounting Research* 1143.

[170] Interviews C1-c, C5-r to C7-s, L1-r to L15-c, R2-r, R3-r, R6-c, R9-c, R10-c.

[171] These are the debts owed to the old creditors with whom the new company would not cooperate and statutory payments: Interviews C1-c, C4-c, C7-s, E2-s, L2-s to L7-c, L11-c to L14-c, R2-r, R10-c.

[172] Described in all my interviews. See e.g Law Time (17.2.2016); Sina (1.12.2015). This is different from UK-style phoenix companies where the old company is closed (and delisted) and a new company, with the same name, is established.

[173] Interviews B3-c, C1-c, C4-c, C5-c, C7-s, L1-r to L15-c, R2-r, R3-r, R6-c, R9-c, R10-c.

ghost companies are widely used – particularly in China's less-developed regions – as a debt-avoidance scheme.[174]

3.4.5. Issues Arising from the Nature of Land Ownership and Land Usage Rights

The fifth general challenge to debt enforcement in China arises from the nature of land ownership and land usage rights. Land in China is under state or collective ownership, and under the Party's control.[175] Only holders of so-called land usage rights can use and develop the land. Land usage rights last for 40 to 70 years – depending on the nature of the use[176] – and the state can claim the land after that period expires.[177] Renewal of the rights can be sought a year in advance, but the Government has complete discretion whether or not to grant it.[178]

Moreover, the Government can, in narrowly defined circumstances, cancel a land usage right, albeit it must provide adequate compensation.[179] My interviewees suggested that the state does sometimes revoke the rights in practice,[180] which impacts the value of these rights and any property on the land – making potentially valuable assets relatively valueless. This affects debt repayment because it reduces the overall value of companies' assets.

---

[174] ibid. Confirmed by an SPC judge: Y Cao (7.1.2016, China Daily).

[175] Land Administration Law 1986, last amended in 2019. Note that Art 70 Property Law 2007 permits private ownership of apartments.

[176] The Interim Order of the State Council concerning the Assignment and Transfer of Urban State-owned Land Use Rights in the People's Republic of China (19.5.1990). My interviewees (C1-c, C4-c, E2-s to E4-c, L4-r to L6-s, R2-r, R7-c, R9-c) suggested that private-sector companies must purchase land usage rights, but SOEs can get them for free. See China Briefing (19.2.2014).

[177] See eg Xinhua (4.11.2013).

[178] ibid – the regulations are decided locally, and so differ in form and substance. However, Art 22 of the Law on Urban Real Estate Administration 1994 (amended in 2007) states that the extension should be granted, unless the land is required for a public interest project (widely defined).

[179] Art 58 Land Administration Law 1986 (amended in 2004).

[180] Interviews B1-c, B3-c, C1-c, C4-c, C5-r, C7-s, E2-s, E3-s, IF1-s, IF2-c, J1-c, J6-s, L2-r to L7-c, L9-s to L14-c, P3-r, R2-r, R3-r, R7-c, R9-c, R10-c.

PART II

The EBL and its Practical Limitations

Many country-specific studies suggest that bankruptcy law can have a positive impact on economic development.[1] To reap the commonly observed benefits of having a well-functioning bankruptcy law, China introduced and later reformed corporate bankruptcy law in 1986 and 2006, respectively. The next six chapters look at the Enterprise Bankruptcy Law 2006 and its practical limitations. Chapter four provides a brief account of the development of corporate bankruptcy law in China, an overview of the Enterprise Bankruptcy Law 2006 on paper and additional guidance from the Supreme People's Court on how to use the law in practice. Chapter five examines the law's limited use in practice. Chapters six, seven, eight and nine present conclusions of the author's original empirical research. They each focus on one of four inter-connected constraints[2] on the use of the law that, the users suggest, reduce its uptake in practice.

[1] See Section 1.2.

[2] Halliday used the term 'implementation issues', but what the interviewees identified is broader than the issues dealt with therein. As a result, in this book, the term 'constraint' is used to describe practical obstacles that prevent or otherwise limit the use of the law.

4

Bankruptcy Law in China

The need to introduce a mechanism that would enable effective allocation of resources to the most efficient user and allow market exit or restructuring for financially distressed companies was recognised soon after Deng Xiaoping started his pro-market reforms in the late 1970s. Section 4.1 of this chapter, therefore, briefly examines the history of corporate bankruptcy law in China. The EBL was a product of a laborious reform process aimed at ameliorating its predecessor, the Enterprise Bankruptcy Law (Trial Implementation) 1986 ('the old law' or 'the 1986 law'). Although repealed, the 1986 law and practices still influence how the EBL operates. As a result, the discussion in this chapter explores the drafting and implementation of both the 1986 law and the EBL.

Section 4.2 then examines key features and provisions of the EBL. It is intended to provide an overview of the law and act as a reference section when considering arguments in later chapters. Section 4.3 looks at implementation guidance from the Supreme People's Court (SPC) that supplements the provisions of the EBL. They contain suggestions and well as mandatory instructions about various aspects of the EBL process. Finally, Section 4.4 briefly looks at personal bankruptcies in China.

4.1. History of Bankruptcy Law in China

China had no bankruptcy rules until the early twentieth century. Debt-related disputes were resolved informally, and debts were inherited following a Confucian convention that 'a son shall repay the debts of his father'.[1] In addition, trade was commonly conducted by family businesses through relational networks, and disputes were resolved using social norms and reputation as an enforcement mechanism.[2] China's first bankruptcy law was introduced in 1906, but it was repealed in 1908 by Emperor Guang Xu 'due to difficulties in implementation'.[3] During the period known as the Republic of China, between 1911 and 1949, two more bankruptcy laws were enacted: one in 1915 (locally, never implemented) and one in 1935 (implemented nationwide).[4] The latter

---

[1] S Li, 'Bankruptcy Law in China: Lessons of the Past Twelve Years' (2001) *Harvard Asia Quarterly* 1; P Little and R Tomasic, *Insolvency Law and Practice in Asia* (FT Law & Tax Asia Pacific, 1997) 51.

[2] See Section 2.3.1. See also R Parry, Y Xu and H Zhang (eds), *China's New Enterprise Bankruptcy Law: Context, Interpretation and Application* (Ashgate, 2010) 5.

[3] R Tomasic and M Wang, 'The Long March Towards China's New Bankruptcy Law' in R Tomasic (ed), *Insolvency Law in East Asia* (Aldershot, 2006); Li, 'Bankruptcy Law in China' (2001).

[4] ibid. Parry, Xu and Zhang, *China's New Enterprise Bankruptcy Law* (2010) 5–6.

was based on German and Japanese legal codes[5] and is still in force in Taiwan today. After 1949, all laws were abolished, and for 30 years there was no legal mechanism for dealing with corporate financial distress.[6] Instead, individuals continued using informal enforcement mechanisms, and the Government resolved corporate financial problems behind closed doors.[7]

Prior to the 1978 economic reforms, the absence of bankruptcy law was regarded as 'an attribute that made a socialist economy superior to its capitalist counterparts'[8] and so something to be proud of because there were no 'failures' in China. Nevertheless, in the 1980s – as the economy continued expanding and commercial dealings became increasingly complex – the desirability of bankruptcy law was slowly recognised[9] for its ability to liquidate (or sometimes restructure) failing companies, but also as a mechanism to incentivise companies to become more efficient and profitable.[10]

Naturally, there was strong opposition against such a capitalist concept, especially given that allowing struggling companies to fail could lead to large-scale unemployment which was undesirable in a communist state.[11] Similarly, market-promoting bankruptcy law was in sharp contrast with Soviet-style economic planning that China adopted after the 1949 revolution.[12] However, with financial and economic development came a greater awareness of the problems within the financial sector – in particular, the cost of continued inefficiency of the SOEs[13] and central planning – and increasing numbers supported the introduction of bankruptcy law.[14] Among them was Cao Siyuan, an economist and legal reformist who played an important role in the drafting process – first as a lobbyist and later as the head of the Bankruptcy Law Drafting team. Cao argued that it was necessary to introduce hard budget constraints into SOEs and to create a clear connection between effort and income to bolster productivity, encourage healthy competition, and so enable economic growth. Experiments in Wuhan, Shenyang and Chongqing suggested that bankruptcy law could promote efficiency to revive China's economy.[15] Eight SOEs in the test cities were given a warning about their state of finances and were told to restructure. Seven of them subsequently recovered.[16]

---

[5] U Neelen, *Bankruptcy and Intellectual Property in the People's Republic of China* (Murdoch University, 2007) 6.

[6] See Sections 3.1 and 3.3.

[7] Tomasic and Wang, 'The Long March' (2006) 94; Li, 'Bankruptcy Law in China' (2001).

[8] Tomasic and Wang (n 3) 94.

[9] S Cho, 'Continuing Economic Reform in the People's Republic of China: Bankruptcy Legislation Leads the Way' (1996) *Hastings International and Company Law Review* 739.

[10] S Cao, 'The Storm Over Bankruptcy' (1998) *Chinese Law and Government* 12.

[11] A Tang, *Insolvency in China and Hong Kong: A Practitioner's Perspective* (Sweet & Maxwell Asia, 2005) para 5.01.

[12] See eg L Brandt and TG Rawski, *China's Great Economic Transformation* (Cambridge University Press, 2008); B Naughton, *The Chinese Economy: Transitions and Growth* (MIT Press, 2007).

[13] The Legislative Work Committee recommended that 'it is most necessary to draw up an enterprise bankruptcy law since this would have a stimulating effect on state-owned enterprises that are poorly managed and whose economic returns are extremely poor': S Cao, 'Survey Report Concerning the Enterprise Bankruptcy Law' (May 1986) Appendix B.

[14] The first official call took place in 1984: see T Chang, 'The Making of the Chinese Bankruptcy Law: A Study In the Chinese Legislative Process' (1987) *Harvard International Law Journal* 333, 336.

[15] Cao's report (n 13, App A) to the Premier concluded that 'the enterprise bankruptcy law is both necessary and feasible and ... we should firmly and unswervingly bring it out as soon as possible'.

[16] H Zheng, Bankruptcy Law of the People's Republic of China: Principle, Procedure and Practice (1986) *Vanderbilt Journal of Transnational Law* 683, 688. See also Cao, 'The Storm' (1998) 33–37.

After two years of lobbying, testing and discussions, a draft bankruptcy law was taking shape. In the end, after what has been described as the 'most furious debate in Chinese legislative history',[17] China's first modern Corporate Bankruptcy Law was passed on 2 December 1986. It was implemented in November 1988 on a trial-only basis. The law was a compromise between the accepted need for bankruptcy law and the ideological opposition to the idea of corporate insolvency. It was limited in scope – it only applied to SOEs[18] – and the Government retained broad discretion in deciding whether an SOE could declare bankruptcy, who would be in charge and often also what should be the outcome. Creditors were largely marginalised in the process and were given a low priority in the distribution of debtors' property.

The 1986 law introduced many important concepts and mechanisms, but it was only rarely used. As Section 5.1 shows, there were only 98 cases in 1989, and the average number of cases in 1989–93 was 277. In 1994/95, the annual average rose to 2,000 cases each year and in 1996–99 to 5,500 cases each year.[19] The highest number of cases – 8,939 – was recorded in 2001.[20] Several thousand cases per year is not negligible. However, commentators in China and abroad agreed that it was still too low given the amount of non-performing corporate debt, SOEs' inefficiencies, and overall dysfunctionality of the Chinese economy.[21] Nevertheless, because SOEs still provided most urban employment and acted as central social welfare providers, local governments were under a lot of pressure to prevent corporate closures – which would naturally result from an objective implementation of the law – because they would lead to large-scale redundancies. Local governments responded by keeping the number of corporate bankruptcies artificially low and instead used bailouts, mergers and state-led negotiations to 'save' or at least cover up the underlying problems in financially distressed SOEs.[22]

As market reforms continued in China, it soon became clear that the 1986 law was inadequate and critical voices started calling for reform. There were multiple complaints levelled against the 1986 law.[23] First, to assist the implementation of the 1986 law, a myriad of other laws, regulations, SPC Opinions and policy documents were introduced.[24] Unfortunately, they created a mixture of frequently irreconcilable rules which were too complicated and difficult to follow.

The second complaint was that the law failed to address the complex economic reality of 1980s China. Professor Li Shuguang, one of the drafters, criticised the final version of the 1986 law for being vague and deficient in ignoring financial distress of

---

[17] W Wu, 'Commencement of Bankruptcy Proceedings in China' (2004) *Victoria University of Wellington Law Review* 239, 241.

[18] Corporate bankruptcies of non-SOEs were governed by Company Law 2005 (Chapter 8) and Civil Procedure Law 1991 (Chapter 19) and in some cases also local bankruptcy regulations: Tomasic and Wang (n 3).

[19] See also W Wang, 'Strengthening Judicial Expertise in Bankruptcy Proceedings in China' delivered at Forum for Asian Insolvency Reform in Indonesia on 7–8 February 2001.

[20] See Table 5.1 in ch 5.

[21] Li (n 1); Wu, 'Commencement of Bankruptcy Proceedings' (2004) 241; C Booth, 'The 2006 PRC Enterprise Bankruptcy Law: the wait is finally over' (2008) *Singapore Academic of Law Journal* 275, 279.

[22] Li (n 1) 3–5.

[23] For an excellent discussion of the problems with the 1986 law, see H Ren (21.4.2009, ChinaCourt.org).

[24] The corporate bankruptcy regime between 1986 and 2006 was governed by the 1986 law, Civil Procedure Law, Company Law, related judicial interpretations, policy decrees, administrative regulations, and local rules and regulations.

private enterprises, partnerships and natural persons. The private sector had grown in size and importance since its inception in the early 1980s, but the vast bulk of non-state companies existed and died in a legal void, which was inefficient and potentially value-destructive. Li also complained that the increasingly diversified creditors received insufficient protection, that there was no reorganisation procedure, and that there were serious inconsistencies between the 1986 law and existing government policies.[25] The problems further grew after China acceded to the WTO in 2001.

Third, the 1986 law was criticised that it simply codified state control over the fate of failing SOEs and failed to give courts enough real power to provide more efficient solutions. Some suggested that the Government wanted to use the law to warn SOEs that they *could* be closed due to bad performance (and so to put pressure on them) rather than intending actually to close them if necessary.[26] Government's involvement was described as short-sighted and harmfully inefficient (compared to developed market economies), and observers started calling for more transparency and independence.[27]

The final complaint was that, despite the early warnings from the pilot cities,[28] courts, lawyers, local governments and business community were uninformed and unprepared for the legal environment created by the 1986 law. The lack of understanding and legal training together with corruption and local governments' protectionism prevented any meaningful implementation of the 1986 law.

In 1993, the Government responded by setting up a reform committee that would look into the possibility of reforming the 1986 law. In March 1994, the NPC's Finance and Economy Committee was asked to draft a new law that would permit corporate rescue, prevent unnecessary unemployment, reduce direct state intervention, ameliorate the position and equal treatment of all creditors, comply with international standards, enable further economic development and attract FDI.[29] The process took 12 years due to numerous tensions and conflicts of interests. The drafting involved many Chinese and foreign experts, professionals, stakeholders, and even local governments. Many drafts were rejected after heated debates in the NPC and by various groups within the Party-state.[30] A four-year deadlock was only broken in 2000 to enable China's accession to the WTO. In the meantime, the economic importance of SOEs diminished, and further economic growth started relying on private companies and foreign trade.[31] The reform of the outdated 1986 law could no longer wait.

The drafting process was slowed down by several tensions between the interests of different stakeholders. Some of these tensions still affect whether and how the EBL

---

[25] ibid and L Qi, 'The Corporate Reorganization Regime under China's New Enterprise Bankruptcy Law' (2008) *International Insolvency Review* 13, 14.

[26] See eg C Booth and W Wang, 'Study on Alternative Approaches for Debt Restructuring of Enterprises in China' (World Bank Report for the State Economy and Trade Commission of China, 2002).

[27] See eg Qi, 'Corporate Reorganization Regime' (2008) 14.

[28] The experience and advice from Shenyang, Wuhan and Chongqing was submitted to the Premier and the National Congress in May 1986 (Cao (n 13) fns 524–25).

[29] See R Tomasic and M Wang, 'Reforming China's Corporate Bankruptcy Laws' (2005) 18 *Australian Journal of Corporate Law* 220.

[30] See eg J Shi, 'Bankruptcy Law Reform in China' (The Second Forum for Asian Insolvency Reform, Bangkok Thailand 16–17 December 2006); T Halliday, 'The Making of China's Corporate Bankruptcy Law' (2007) The Foundation for Law, Justice and Society, University of Oxford; Wu (n 17).

[31] See Section 2.5.3.

is applied today. One of the key conundrums in China's socialist system – and the reason why the reform process took so long – was the question whether to prioritise claims from 'the people' – ie debtors' employees – or the money-providers – ie debtors' (secured) creditors.[32] On the one hand, protecting employees is crucial given that China still lacks a fully functioning social welfare system[33] which means that the employees who are dismissed following corporate restructuring or liquidation face a loss of livelihood and existential uncertainty. As a result, there is a real danger of social instability.[34] This is particularly problematic in large-scale corporate bankruptcies where fast re-employment is particularly difficult.[35]

On the other hand, giving priority to secured creditors in bankruptcy may benefit the whole economy. Lenders' expected *ex post* recovery in bankruptcy plays an important part in their *ex ante* risk-assessment,[36] which in turn informs their decision whether to lend and with what conditions (term, costs). Without credit and stability, companies would suffer, which would – in the long run – affect employment. Moreover, unlike creditors, employees can be given protection through other means.[37] As a result, the tension was resolved by affording secured creditors priority over employees' interests.[38]

Equally difficult was the question of what role the Party-state should have in bankruptcy law. The new law had to balance, on the one hand, bankruptcy law's need for objective and independent enforcement, and, on the other hand, the ideological setting where the Party-state – as a representative of the people – needs to have a say in the process to protect its financial and non-financial interests.[39] In the end, the central Government took the view that, in the long term, not allowing inefficient companies to reorganise or liquidate may lead to serious economic problems which would undermine its image as a strong, capable leader. Consequently, the EBL as written puts courts in charge of EBL procedures and removes the Party-state's influence.[40]

Finally, China was under a lot of pressure to comply with international demands.[41] In exchange for its ability to access international markets[42] and to attract FDI, China agreed to update its laws – including bankruptcy law – to comply with international standards. To support China's effort, foreign governments and international bodies offered expertise and funding but also sought to ensure that the new regime would provide equal playing field, prevent local protectionism, protect efficiency-driven competition, and ensure more transparency and objectivity in law enforcement.[43]

---

[32] See eg B Carruthers and T Halliday, 'Negotiating Globalization: Global Scripts and Intermediation in the Construction of Asian Insolvency Regimes' (2006) *Law & Social Inquiry* 521.

[33] See Section 7.2.1.

[34] See Sections 2.4.2 and 8.3.1–8.3.3.

[35] Cao (n 13) point 3.

[36] See Section 1.2.

[37] See Sections 6.1 and 11.1.2.

[38] See Section 4.2.11.

[39] At the time, many SOEs would have to be liquidated if the insolvency law test was applied to them. This would cause large-scale unemployment and disruption in supply of social welfare. Neither was desirable: Shi, 'Bankruptcy Law Reform' (2006).

[40] See Sections 4.2.4–4.2.6 and 4.2.9. But cf Sections 2.4 and 8.3. See also Section 12.12 about future proposals.

[41] See Section 13.1.

[42] Most importantly since its accession to the WTO in 2001.

[43] For more about foreign influence in the EBL, see ch 13.

As a result, the EBL applies to all companies – Chinese or foreign – and it contains rules on cross-border bankruptcies.[44] In addition, numerous foreign concepts – such as moratorium, cramdown, *pari passu* and post-petition financing – have been included in the final draft of the EBL.

In the end, after many local experiments,[45] the EBL was finally enacted on 27 August 2006 and it came into effect on 1 June 2007. It received praise for its progressive drafting,[46] but also criticism for the remaining difficulties and warnings about the amount of work that still remained.[47]

4.2. Black-letter Overview of the Enterprise Bankruptcy Law 2006

The EBL 2006 represents an amalgamation of, on the one hand, China's non-economic interests – most importantly the desire to maintain legitimacy and social stability, and to retain control over state assets – and, on the other hand, the international best practice derived from American, English, French and German bankruptcy laws[48] and recommendations of the WTO, the IMF and the UNCITRAL Legislative Guide on Insolvency Law 2005 ('UNCITRAL Guide').[49] With 136 Articles in 12 chapters (compared to 43 Articles in six chapters in the 1986 law), the EBL as written *significantly contributes to the creation of a robust framework for a modern market economy*. The law broadens the scope of bankruptcy application to cover all legal persons and financial institutions; establishes an administrator system; introduces strict time limits for bankruptcy proceedings; provides better creditor protection; makes creditors active players in bankruptcy procedures; punishes fraud and wrongdoing; enables court-driven restructuring; enhances courts' role; diminishes government's influence; and recognises cross-border bankruptcies. The remainder of this section examines key functions and tools[50] that the EBL introduced. Later chapters build on and refer to the discussion below in order to explain how the written provisions have been applied in practice (Chapters five to eight) and how the law as written and as applied needs to change in order to ensure a more effective resolution of corporate bankruptcies in China (Chapters ten to twelve).

---

[44] For more, see Sections 13.3.2–13.3.3.

[45] Especially the successful local bankruptcy regulation from Shenzhen (implemented locally in November 1993): C Booth and X Zhang, 'Chinese Bankruptcy Law in an Emerging Market Economy: The Shenzhen Experience' (2001) *Columbia Journal of Asian Law* 1. See also Section 12.8.

[46] See eg Tomasic and Wang (n 3).

[47] Neelen, *Bankruptcy and Intellectual Property* (2007) 2; Halliday, 'China's Corporate Bankruptcy Law' (2007). See also chs 11 and 12.

[48] See eg M Falke, 'China's New Law on Enterprise Bankruptcy: A Story with a Happy End?' (2007) *International Insolvency Review* 63.

[49] See R Tomasic, 'The Conceptual Structure of China's New Corporate Bankruptcy Law' in Parry, Xu and Zhang (n 2).

[50] The primary purpose of this book is to present empirical findings of how the EBL 2006 is used in practice and how it should be reformed. For an in-depth black-letter analysis of the EBL 2006, see Parry, Xu and Zhang (n 2).

4.2.1. Scope, Principles and Objectives of the Enterprise Bankruptcy Law 2006

Unlike the old law that only applied to SOEs,[51] the EBL applies to all legal persons.[52] Given the fast expansion of the private sector,[53] extending bankruptcy law to all companies regardless of their ownership status was seen as crucial and, as a result, did not face too much opposition. There was some debate about whether SOE bankruptcies should have a special regime.[54] The 1995 draft included a special government-driven procedure for resolving SOEs' financial distress which provided additional consideration for employees and state-owned banks which are usually the main creditor.[55] No such provision was included in the 2000 draft or the final version of the EBL which treats all companies equally. Nevertheless, state's interference was explicitly permitted on a temporary basis in resolving 2,116 hand-picked SOEs[56] – which were particularly vulnerable or operated in a sensitive industry (eg military and mining) – but only until the end of 2008 when the special status expired.[57]

The EBL also applies to bankruptcies of financial institutions, such as commercial banks, securities companies and insurance companies.[58]

The EBL includes several important guiding principles and objectives that provide a framework for its application in practice.[59] Article 1 of the EBL provides four general principles that are further expanded in later provisions.[60] Firstly, corporate bankruptcies should be administered according to legal rules – the EBL and other laws – rather than through politicised administrative mechanisms as was the case under the 1986 law. This is further reinforced in Article 3 of the EBL, which gives complete control and oversight of the process to courts (and administrators[61]) rather than state bodies (compared to the 1986 law). The EBL as written, therefore, clearly aims to adhere to the rule of law.[62]

---

[51] Previously, there were separate bankruptcy proceedings for different types of corporate entities: Bankruptcy Law 1986, Civil Procedure Law 1991, and local laws and regulations.

[52] Art 2 EBL, in line with the UNCITRAL Guide paras 8–10. Note that this means that some commercial parties are excluded – eg partners in partnerships, sole traders, etc: see Sections 11.1.6 and 12.9.

[53] See Section 2.5.

[54] This is not unique to China. Similar issues arose in Russia, Eastern Europe, South America, and others.

[55] W Wang, 'The Order of Payment of Workers' Claims and Securities Interests under China's New Bankruptcy Law' (2006) presented at Fifth Forum for Asian Insolvency Reform (FAIR) on 27–28 April 2006 in Beijing, China, 16–17.

[56] Out of about 100,000 SOEs: J Li (22.6.2004, China Daily).

[57] Art 133 EBL.

[58] Art 134 EBL. For a detailed discussion, see Y Xu and W Zheng, 'Bankruptcies of Financial Institutions' in Parry, Xu and Zhang (n 2).

[59] These objectives and principles need to be understood in the context of the EBL's legislative history and the environment in which they are implemented. The former was discussed earlier in Section 4.1, the latter is discussed in chs 5–9.

[60] For an in-depth discussion and its context, see Tomasic (n 48).

[61] See Section 4.2.9.

[62] Although the rule of law is an important feature for many foreign investors, and so it matters to China whether it appears to respect it, the concept is still underdeveloped in China. For further discussion, see Section 2.3.2.

Secondly, the EBL should be applied so as to ensure a fair settlement of all claims and debts. This broad principle is reinforced in later provisions which impose strict time limits on making decisions,[63] demand timely assumption of duties by an administrator,[64] and give decision-making power to expert administrators and judges.[65] There are also detailed provisions about the filing of claims[66] and a clear definition of what is included in the bankrupt's estate[67] – including set-off rights[68] and rules about avoidable transactions.[69] In addition, there are also detailed provisions on the priority of distribution of assets that the law deems fair.[70] Together, these rules aim to define stakeholders' entitlements and create a mechanism for getting it in a timely and transparent manner.

Thirdly, the EBL aims to protect the lawful interests of creditors and debtors. This is ensured through a clear definition of which claims can be filed and how;[71] direct creditor and debtor participation;[72] rules about the priority of distribution;[73] and importantly also avoidance of certain pre-petition transactions.[74]

Finally, although the EBL borrows extensively from other jurisdictions, it inserts 'Chinese characteristics'[75] into the process in order to protect its existing socio-political environment. The fourth principle in Article 1, therefore, states that the law should be applied with a view to maintain orderly socialist market economy,[76] which has been interpreted as allowing courts to take into account other-than-purely-financial considerations when hearing corporate bankruptcy cases.[77] Subsequent SPC guidance reiterates this principle and orders courts to protect socialist market order and to keep in mind the 'social responsibility *inherent* in the EBL cases'.[78] An important implication of this principle is the protection of employees in all bankruptcy cases. Article 6 reinforces this when saying that courts shall safeguard the legitimate rights and interests of the employees of the debtor company, often ahead of other (unsecured) creditors.[79] Article 8 further states that debtor's EBL petition must include a resettlement plan for its employees in order to be accepted. This degree of employee protection is uncommon in market economies, but the problems with Chinese social welfare provision make it necessary.[80]

---

[63] Arts 10–14, 69 and 111 EBL.

[64] Arts 20–21 EBL.

[65] Arts 13 and 24 EBL.

[66] For details see B Ye, 'Filing of Claims' in Parry, Xu and Zhang (n 2).

[67] Arts 30–40 EBL. For details see J Xiao, 'Bankruptcy Estate' in Parry, Xu and Zhang (n 2). See also Arts 1–5 of the SPC Provisions (II) concerning the Application of the EBL (*Fashi* [2013] No 22) – hereafter the 'Judicial Interpretation No 2'.

[68] Art 40 EBL. See also Arts 41–46 Judicial Interpretation No 2.

[69] See Section 4.2.13.

[70] See Section 4.2.11.

[71] Arts 44–58 EBL. For details see Ye, 'Filing of Claims' (n 65).

[72] See Sections 4.2.8 and 4.2.7, respectively.

[73] See Section 4.2.11.

[74] See Section 4.2.13.

[75] This is used to describe deviance from commonly understood concepts as adapted to Chinese circumstances and socio-political needs: eg capitalism with Chinese characteristics.

[76] See Section 2.1.

[77] For how this has been used in practice, see Sections 6.1 and 11.1.1.

[78] Preamble to the 2018 typical cases, first point – see Section 4.3.

[79] See Section 4.2.11, 6.1.2–6.1.3 and 11.1.2.

[80] See Sections 4.2.10, 6.1 and 11.1.2.

Besides the four principles in Article 1, the EBL also introduces a comprehensive corporate rescue regime.[81] In doing so, it follows other modern bankruptcy laws in encouraging efficient rehabilitation and reorganisation of viable companies (or core business) rather than their liquidation.[82] Two separate restructuring procedures were introduced – reorganisation[83] and composition[84] – to support this aim, and courts are encouraged to allow corporate restructuring, where possible. However, unlike the US Bankruptcy Reform Act 1978 and the UK Insolvency Act 1986 (especially since the introduction of the UK Enterprise Act 2002), which place predominant focus on saving ailing companies and providing 'breathing space' under the protection of the law, the EBL appears to be closer to the German insolvency law which is more concerned with a fair (re)distribution of assets and rights.[85] The wording of Article 2 of the EBL speaks of liquidation as the primary procedure and only mentions reorganisation as an alternative in the second sentence. Nevertheless, the inclusion of the reorganisation procedure in the law is a significant step forward which has been celebrated in China and abroad.[86]

4.2.2. Entry Requirements

Under the 1986 law, (local) government's permission was needed to declare bankruptcy.[87] This was logical at the time when all companies were owned and controlled by the state. The requirement was removed in the EBL. Similarly, the EBL empowered debtors and creditors to file a bankruptcy petition[88] (creditors only under the 1986 law) provided the debtor satisfies the insolvency test.[89]

The EBL replaced the broader entry requirements of 'serious losses' which 'result from … poor operations and management' because such test was deemed vulnerable to subjective, politically susceptible interpretation.[90] Instead, the EBL introduced an objective insolvency test.[91] A *creditor*[92] who files an EBL petition must satisfy a one-limb cash-flow test by showing that the debtor is unable to pay off debts as they fall due.[93]

---

[81] The 1986 law also provided for reorganisation of SOEs (Arts 18–20 EBL 1986), however, the procedures were cumbersome and largely state-driven. They were, therefore, never successfully used. For details, see H Zhang 'Corporate Rescue' in Parry, Xu and Zhang (n 2) 208.

[82] Li (n 1). See also Section 1.1.

[83] See Section 4.2.4.

[84] See Section 4.2.5.

[85] s 1 German Insolvency Law 1994.

[86] See eg an excellent empirical study by Z Zhang, *Corporate Reorganisations in China* (Cambridge University Press, 2018).

[87] Art 8 EBL 1986.

[88] Art 8 EBL 2006 stipulates that the petition must contain, inter alia, a contingency plan for employees' resettlement, and payment of employees' wages and social insurance premium.

[89] Art 7(1) EBL.

[90] Tomasic and Wang (n 3) 9.

[91] The simplification (see the UNCITRAL Guide para 21) was introduced in the 1995 draft despite calls to retain the requirement for 'serious losses': W Wang, 'Institutional Reasoning in Drafting New Bankruptcy Law of China' (2000) Chinese Insolvency Law Symposium.

[92] Or investors holding more than 10% of the debtor's registered capital: Art 70 EBL.

[93] Art 7(2) EBL. Arguably, it would be unreasonable to ask the petitioning creditor to prove balance-sheet insolvency since creditors do not usually have access to debtor's accounts.

The EBL does not specify any qualifying minimum amount or length of time for which the debt is due.[94]

A petitioning *debtor*, on the other hand, must satisfy a two-limb test, namely the cash-flow test (as for creditors) and a balance-sheet test where he must show that the debtor company's liabilities exceed its assets.[95] Moreover, Article 8 of the EBL further stipulates that the debtor must also include a proposed employee resettlement plan[96] and an up-to-date summary concerning the payment of employees' wages and social insurance premium. This is a stringent requirement, especially when interpreted as a precondition for accepting EBL applications. Usually, resettlement of employees is a matter for the Government, but the EBL pushes this responsibility onto the debtor company.[97]

The EBL allows pre-insolvency use of reorganisation (but not liquidation or composition). Article 2(2) of the EBL states that a debtor can apply for reorganisation where it is 'obviously likely to become insolvent' – a requirement that closely reflects the German requirement of imminent illiquidity.[98] The drafters followed the broad guidance in the UNCITRAL Guide[99] but did not go as far as the US Chapter 11 which allows restructuring in a wide set of circumstances, regardless of debtor's ability to pay its debts. For a comparison, see Table 4.1.

Once filed, the petition is considered by a court.[100] Under the 1986 law, courts had no procedural requirements or time limit for responding to the application. In contrast, the EBL imposes strict time limits. Where the petition is filed by a debtor, the court must decide whether to accept or reject the application within 15 days.[101] Where the petition is filed by a creditor, the court has five days to notify the debtor. The debtor can then object within seven days. The court must decide whether to accept or reject the application within 10 days after the seven days expire. Their ruling must then be communicated to the petitioning creditor within five days after the ruling was made. That is a total of 27 days.[102] If the petition is rejected, the petitioning creditor can appeal to a higher court within 10 days to have the decision affirmed or reversed within further 15 days.[103] The court can in 'special circumstances' extend the hearing by 15 days.[104] If the petition

---

[94] cf s 123 of the UK Insolvency Act 1986, which states that the debt must exceed £750. See eg S Wang and W Chen, 'Empowering Creditors in Filing for Bankruptcy: Lessons from the UK' (2014) *Hebei Law Science* 45; X Wang, 'Case Registration and Bankruptcy Filings' (2015) *Journal of Law Application* 36.

[95] ibid. The Standing Committee insisted on the two-limb test for voluntary petitions to prevent much-feared floodgates and debt-avoidance by the debtors. It broadly complies with the UNCITRAL Guide para 21. cf the UK and Germany where debtor only needs to satisfy one of the two tests.

[96] Note that in reorganisations involving listed companies, it must be a 'practical and feasible employee resettlement plan': Art 3 of the SPC Memorandum on Handing of Listed Companies' Reorganisations and Liquidations (*Fa* [2012] No 261) – hereafter 'Listed Companies Memorandum'.

[97] See also Sections 6.1 and 12.12.

[98] s 18 German Insolvency Law 1994 states that debtor can use insolvency procedures if it is highly probable that at some date in the future it will be unable to pay its debts as they fall due.

[99] The UNCITRAL Guide paras 48–49.

[100] Note that reorganisation and liquidation petitions of listed companies must have an advance permission from the SPC: Art 4 of the SPC Listed Companies Memorandum.

[101] Art 10(2) EBL.

[102] Arts 10(1) and 11 EBL.

[103] Arts 12(1) and 10(2) EBL.

[104] Art 10(3) EBL.

is accepted, the court must notify all known creditors within 15 days and make a public announcement of the ruling.[105] The bankruptcy process then formally begins. If the petition is rejected, the court must provide its reasons within five days after making the ruling[106] and the petitioner can appeal to a higher court within 10 days.[107]

Table 4.1 Entry requirements into bankruptcy procedures in China, England, the US and Germany

	CHINA (post-2007)	UK	US	GERMANY
Who can apply?	Debtor Creditors Some investors*	Debtor Creditors Company directors	Debtor** Some creditors***	Debtor Creditors Company directors, officers
Insolvency test(s)	**Debtor:** Cash-flow test *and* Balance-sheet test **Creditor:** Cash-flow test	Cash-flow test *or* Balance-sheet test	No requirement of insolvency (Good faith, with intention to restructure *or* to sell the company)	Cash-flow test *or* Balance-sheet test
Pre-insolvency entry?	YES, but only debtor's reorganisation application: an obvious possibility that it will lose the capability to repay its debts	YES (likely to become unable to pay its debts as they fall due)	YES (same as above)	YES, but only debtor's application: highly probable that at some date in the future it will be unable to pay its debts as they fall due

* *Those holding more than 10 per cent of the debtor's registered capital: Art 70 EBL.*
** *Creditor can submit counter-petition to have the Chapter 11 proceedings closed down.*
*** *Creditors holding unsecured non-contingent undisputed claims that amount to more than $12,300 (in large company), or where the debtor company is 'generally not paying debts as such debts become due'.*

4.2.3. Moratorium

The EBL introduced the concept of a moratorium.[108] There are two types of moratoria: a main moratorium and an interim moratorium.[109] A main moratorium is imposed as soon as the court accepts the bankruptcy petition and stays all judicial measures

---

[105] Art 14 EBL.
[106] Art 12(1) EBL.
[107] Art 12(2) EBL.
[108] In compliance with the UNCITRAL Guide recommendations 39, 45–47, and 49–51.
[109] Arts 19–20 EBL.

against debtor's property and all security enforcement by secured creditors (unless a court decides otherwise).[110] An interim moratorium is also imposed from when the court accepts the bankruptcy petition, but it only lasts until the administrator's appointment with an effect of temporarily staying pending civil and arbitral cases that involve the debtor.[111] This two-stage moratorium conception is another transplant from the German Insolvency Law,[112] but the fully automatic nature of the moratorium is closer to the US and UK regimes.[113]

4.2.4. Reorganisation

Under the 1986 law, restructuring was theoretically possible, but the process was limited in scope,[114] cumbersome,[115] politically determined[116] and rarely used.[117] The EBL established a widely accessible, court-supervised and time-limited reorganisation procedure[118] which follows international best practice.[119] The EBL drafters put a lot of emphasis on this procedure because it was seen as a tool that could 'rescue enterprises in difficulties while fairly clearing their debts'.[120] Following the increased interest in the EBL in China since late 2015, courts have been encouraged to use restructuring (or a merger) rather than liquidation wherever possible,[121] and this policy was further highlighted in SPC's typical cases released in 2018 and 2020.[122]

To commence the reorganisation procedure in China, a debtor or creditor files a general EBL petition[123] but specifies a preference for reorganisation.[124] It is then at the

---

[110] Arts 19 and 75 EBL. Secured creditor can be permitted by court to enforce their security rights where the secured asset is at the risk of being destroyed or its value is at the risk of being reduced dramatically to the extent of impairing the rights of secured creditors.

[111] Art 20 EBL.

[112] Under German *Insolvenzordnung*, an interim moratorium is discretionary, and a main moratorium is automatic. Where secured creditors wish to enforce security rights over moveable assets, the administrator has the right to sell and distribute proceeds to secured creditor: see eg A Remmert, *Introduction to German Insolvency Law* (Justiz, 2007).

[113] The US and the UK only have one moratorium that starts at acceptance (UK) or filing (US) of the petition and lasts until the end of the administration (UK) or reorganisation (US).

[114] Only creditors could petition: Art 3 EBL 1986.

[115] The petitioning creditor had to prove not only that their debt was due, but also that the corporate failure was a result of debtor's management's incompetence, irrationality or poor decision-making.

[116] For an excellent discussion, see H Zhang, 'Corporate Rescue' in Parry, Xu and Zhang (n 2).

[117] See eg W Wang, 'Adopting Corporate Rescue Regimes in China: A Comparative Survey' (1998) *Australian Journal of Corporate Law* 234. See also empirical research in Zhang, *Corporate Reorganisations* (2018).

[118] Arts 70–94 EBL.

[119] C Han, 'The Legislative Evolvement of the Bankruptcy Enterprise Law in China and Its Lessons' (2009) *Citizenship and Law* 2.

[120] See Wang, 'Institutional Reasoning' (2000) 9–10, which discussed a report about the 1995 draft of the EBL.

[121] See Section 12.6.

[122] See Sections 4.3–4.4.

[123] See general entry requirements (Section 4.2.2). The 1995 draft also required that the debtor could show that rehabilitation was possible: Wang (n 90) 10. Note that in EBL cases involving listed companies, the petitioning debtor must also submit a report on the feasibility of restructuring and the relevant provincial government must submit a stability maintenance plan and other information regarding the listed company: Art 3 of the SPC Listed Companies Memorandum.

[124] Art 70(1) EBL.

court's discretion whether it considers the case to be appropriate for restructuring.[125] Alternatively, a debtor or a capital contributor holding more than 10 per cent of debtor's registered capital[126] may request that a creditor's petition for liquidation be reclassified as reorganisation once the general bankruptcy petition is accepted by a court.[127] As was highlighted in Section 2.2 above, Article 2 of the EBL allows pre-insolvency use of reorganisation where the debtor company is 'obviously likely to become insolvent'.[128] Unfortunately, pre-insolvency reorganisation cases are rare in practice.[129]

Once reorganisation petition is accepted by a court, a main moratorium and an interim moratorium are automatically triggered.[130] At the same time, the court appoints an administrator to manage the business.[131] Alternatively, the debtor can apply to the court to remain in control of its business,[132] albeit under the administrator's supervision.[133] As such, the Chinese regime is closest to the German Insolvency Law, which gives courts a discretionary power to allow debtors to stay in possession. Chinese reorganisation procedure is, therefore, quite different from the US Chapter 11, where the debtor remains in control during the proceedings and is only replaced if the management is deemed to be incompetent.[134] It is also different from the UK administration where the debtor is automatically replaced by an administrator.[135]

The debtor or administrator in charge has six months to propose a reorganisation plan.[136] A three-month extension can be given by a court.[137] If a plan is not submitted within the time period, the court can terminate the proceedings, and the debtor is automatically put into liquidation.[138] The plan must cover, inter alia, an operational and business strategy; classes of creditors; adjustment of claims; repayment scheme of claims; proposed implementation time period; a supervisory period for implementing the plan; and other arrangements that are relevant.[139]

---

[125] Listed companies need advance permission from the SPC: see Section 4.2.2. Moreover, some provincial and local courts also require advance permission from the relevant intermediate court before and EBL reorganisation petition can be accepted: Zhang (n 85) 18.

[126] This is imported from Japan and Taiwan, where shareholders can file for reorganisation: X Wang and Y Xu, 'Several Issues of Making the Enterprise Bankruptcy Law' (2007) *Politics and Law* 89, 90.

[127] Art 70(2) EBL. For a discussion of several cases where this was allowed, see Zhang (n 85) 50–51.

[128] See Section 4.2.2 for details. See also ss 16 and 17–19 of German Insolvency Law 1994.

[129] See Sections 6.3 and 11.1.4.1.

[130] See Section 4.2.3.

[131] See Section 4.2.9.

[132] Arts 13, 73–74 and 89 EBL. Note, however, that the Chinese debtor-in-possession model is different from elsewhere as many major tasks are still carried out by the administrator: Zhang (n 85). See also Section 3.3.2.

[133] The power-sharing, details of the debtor-in-possession (DIP) regime, and administrator supervision are unclear. An empirical study of all reorganisations in China between 2007 and 2015 suggests that every third reorganisation was managed by the debtor and in many cases the supervision was quite extensive: Zhang (n 85) 89 and 101–05.

[134] RI Patel, 'A Practical Evaluation of the PRC's 2007 Enterprise Bankruptcy Law' (2009) *UC Davis Business Law Journal* 109. But some believe that debtor-in-possession regime should be the starting point, same as in the US: H Zou, 'China's Corporate Rehabilitation System – Theories and Practice' (2007) *Journal of China University of Political Science and Law* 48.

[135] Insolvency Act 1986, Sch B1, para 67.

[136] Arts 79(1) and 80 EBL.

[137] Art 79(2) EBL.

[138] Art 79(30 EBL.

[139] Art 81 EBL.

The supervising court then convenes a creditors' meeting[140] where creditors vote on the plan in four predefined groups (secured creditors; employees; tax claimants; and other general claimants).[141] The court can sanction the creation of further groups within any of the existing general groups.[142] The plan is deemed adopted if in each group creditors representing more than a half in number and two-thirds in value accept the draft plan.[143] The reorganisation plan must then also be approved by the court.[144] Importantly, the court can reject the plan even if the stakeholders voted in its favour.[145]

The EBL empowers a debtor or an administrator-in-charge to negotiate with the group that failed to approve the plan.[146] If the dissenting group refuses to vote again or rejects the plan one more time, the debtor or administrator can petition the court to cram down the dissenting class – that is, a court can de facto force the dissenting class to agree.[147] Article 87(2) of the EBL 2006 specifies that cramdown is only possible if:

(i)   secured creditors' rights are not infringed;
(ii) labour and tax creditors voted for the reorganisation plan or are fully paid;
(iii) general creditors are not worse off than they would be in liquidation;
(iv) corporate investors voted for the reorganisation plan, or the reorganisation plan is fair and impartial;
(v)   the reorganisation plan treats creditors within the same class fairly and in accordance with the priority of repayment order in Art 113 EBL; and
(vi) debtor's proposed plan is feasible.[148]

It appears that the court can cram down dissenting stakeholders and approve the reorganisation plan even if no other class voted in its favour.[149]

Once the plan is approved, reorganisation is terminated, and the plan becomes binding.[150] The reorganisation plan is then implemented by the debtor under the administrator's supervision.[151] The administrator submits a supervision report to the court at the end of the supervision period.[152] The administrator must apply to the court for termination of reorganisation if the business and financial situation of the debtor worsens making corporate rescue unlikely; if the debtor acted fraudulently or in an

---

[140] Art 84 EBL.

[141] Art 82 EBL. Moreover, Art 85 EBL allows shareholders to vote if the plan adjusts or cancels their equity stake.

[142] Art 82(2) EBL.

[143] Arts 84 and 86 EBL. This is identical with the US Chapter 11.

[144] Art 86 EBL. This is the same as in Germany. There is no such requirement in the UK or the US. The need for such approval has been questioned as it adds another layer of bureaucracy and, arguably, does not add to the regime's efficacy: Zhang (n 85) 173–74.

[145] Art 88 EBL. There is no further guidance as to why or when a court may use this power.

[146] This is very similar to German law.

[147] Some scholars worry that this power may be abused in China. See also Section 6.1.4.

[148] The US Chapter 11 also empowers courts to cram down a dissenting class(es), but the scope is broader.

[149] W Wang, 'The New Enterprise Bankruptcy Law: a Contemporary and Advanced Legislation' (2006) *The People's Congress of China* 17.

[150] Arts 86(2) and 92(1) EBL.

[151] Arts 89–90 EBL.

[152] Art 91 EBL. Chinese system here lies half-way between the German regime where the debtor is in charge with optional administrator's supervision and the English regime where the administrator is fully in charge. It is furthest away from the US where the plan is implemented by the debtor alone.

otherwise wrongful manner; or where debtor's acts make it impossible for the administrator to perform their duties.[153]

Notably, the EBL introduced several options for post-petition financing.[154] A debtor can use any unencumbered assets as security for a new loan.[155] In practice, this is unlikely to be useful as financially distressed or insolvent companies tend not to have such assets.[156] Nevertheless, it may also be possible to grant a second charge over one asset to the extent that the first secured creditor is over-secured.[157] Alternatively, an administrator (or a debtor if in control of reorganisation) is allowed to take out an unsecured loan.[158] In general, an unsecured loan would not be helpful either as there is unlikely to be enough assets to satisfy the new unsecured creditor in case the reorganisation failed.[159] Any lender who provides money on this basis is running the risk of not getting their money back. Finally, the only real option for post-petition financing relies on a narrow exception that allows grant of super-priority to unsecured loans for the specific purpose of payment of wages and social security insurance. Under Articles 42(4) and 43 of the EBL, such debt ranks ahead of other unsecured claims.[160] Given the difficulties in obtaining post-petition finance, it is hardly surprising that most reorganisations do not rely on loans but rather on partial business or company sale where the new buyer injects money into the reorganised company.[161]

4.2.5. Composition

A simpler, quicker and comparatively cheaper alternative to reorganisation is the composition procedure.[162] A debtor (but not its creditors)[163] can apply for composition directly, or it can ask a court to reclassify a pending liquidation application as composition.[164] Together with the application, the debtor must also submit a draft composition agreement.[165] Once the court is satisfied that the debtor is insolvent, it opens the proceedings, makes a public announcement thereof, and convenes a creditors'

---

[153] Art 78 EBL.

[154] See also the SPC Provisions (III) concerning the Application of the EBL (*Fashi* [2019] No 3) – hereafter the 'Judicial Interpretation No 3'.

[155] Art 75 EBL.

[156] Albeit there have been a few cases where such assets did exist and security was granted: see Zhang (n 85) 110.

[157] Art 35 Guarantee Law 1995. But it may be difficult in practice: X Ying, 'Risks of New Financing in Listed Company Reorganisations' (2012) *Chinese Lawyer* 46.

[158] Art 69 EBL (or Art 73 EBL).

[159] Zhang argues that it should be possible to classify post-petition unsecured loan as a common-interest debt which is to be repaid ahead of other unsecured creditors. This argument relies on a broad reading of Arts 42 and 43 EBL which is problematic: Zhang (n 85) 109.

[160] See Section 4.2.11.

[161] See empirical data in Zhang (n 85) 113–14.

[162] Arts 95–106 EBL. Sometimes translated as conciliation, reconciliation or compromise.

[163] Interestingly, in the old law and the early drafts of the EBL, the Government was put in charge of the process. See eg Wang (n 90) 7.

[164] Art 95 EBL.

[165] ibid.

meeting to discuss the draft composition plan.[166] The procedure is overseen by an administrator and a court, albeit in a much more limited manner than in reorganisation.

Unlike reorganisation, composition usually involves only some of the debtor's creditors.[167] In this sense, it is very similar to the English Schemes of Arrangement,[168] which is also commonly used to agree with some but not all creditors. Unlike in reorganisation, secured creditors in composition can realise their collateral freely with the court's permission.[169] There are no voting classes, and the debtor has only one chance to persuade the creditors to accept its composition plan. The plan is deemed adopted if approved by a majority in number and two-thirds in value of the creditors present and entitled to vote, and if sanctioned by the court.[170] Otherwise, the procedure is terminated, and the debtor is declared bankrupt.[171]

Composition is not commonly used in China.[172] An interview with a leading member of the EBL drafting team suggests that the procedure was always intended as an option for 'small companies and simple cases', and it was assumed that it would be rarely used.[173] The EBL drafting team discussed the possibility of not including composition in the EBL – following France and Germany – but it was concluded that it was better to 'cultivate a small garden with a hoe rather than a tractor'.[174] As a result, inspired by the multi-procedure regime in the UK, composition remained as an alternative to the other two (comparatively costly and complex) mechanisms.

4.2.6. Liquidation

Liquidation[175] is a widely used fall-back option in the EBL which is intended for unviable companies that 'have lost operating value'.[176] A petition for liquidation can be submitted by a debtor or its creditors so long as the relevant entry test in Article 2 of the EBL is satisfied.[177] When a court declares the debtor bankrupt, it must make a public announcement to that effect and notify the administrator and the creditors within five and 10 days, respectively.[178] Secured creditors can then enforce their claims over specific assets, and the remainder of the debtors' assets becomes known as general assets.[179]

---

[166] Art 96(1) EBL.

[167] Art 100 EBL.

[168] cf J Payne, *Schemes of Arrangement: Theory, Structure and Operation* (Cambridge University Press, 2014).

[169] Art 100 EBL.

[170] Arts 97–98 EBL.

[171] Art 99 EBL.

[172] For a discussion of one example of its use, see X Ge, 'Composition in Parry' in Xu and Zhang (n 2). But note that in 2018, courts in Jiangsu Province concluded 123 composition cases: Jiangsu Higher People's Court's Report on the Commercial Trial Work of Provincial Courts (28.5.2019). See also the first typical cases (2020) in Section 4.3.4.

[173] See Li (n 1); interview with Professor Li in Legal Daily (12.2.2007).

[174] Wang (n 90) 8.

[175] Also translated as winding up. See Arts 107–24 EBL.

[176] Preamble to the 2018 typical cases, first point: see Section 4.3. See also Section 1.1.

[177] See Section 4.2.2.

[178] Art 107 EBL. Liquidation can be reversed if all due debts are paid off, or where a third party provides good security for the outstanding debts: Art 108 EBL.

[179] Arts 109–10 EBL.

An administrator then 'promptly' formulates a disposition plan – which must comply with the statutory priority of distribution[180] – and submits it to the creditors' meeting and the court for approval.[181] Debtor's remaining assets are then usually sold in an auction and are distributed[182] in accordance with the statutory priority rules. The distribution plan is implemented by the administrator.[183]

If a debtor has no available property to distribute,[184] an administrator must ask a court to terminate the procedure. Otherwise, liquidation is terminated by a court upon receipt of the administrator's distribution report.[185]

4.2.7. Debtors

There are three types of parties empowered by the EBL to get involved in EBL procedures: debtors, creditors and courts (assisted by administrators). Debtors can propose composition, both debtors[186] and creditors can initiate insolvent liquidation and reorganisation, while courts – usually assisted by an administrator – manage and oversee all three procedures and have the final word in cases of dispute. This section looks at the powers and duties of debtors. Section 4.2.8 below explores the position of creditors and Section 4.2.9 looks at courts and administrators.

Where a debtor fulfils the EBL insolvency test,[187] the law states that it may choose to file a petition to apply for reorganisation, liquidation or composition. The law does not, however, impose a legal duty on the debtor to monitor its financial health and liquidate or restructure where it becomes insolvent. Nor does it – unlike the earlier EBL drafts – impose personal or criminal liability on the management of the debtor company where they 'were or should have been aware of the company's inability to pay off debts as they fall due, but still unreasonably spend money and property or squander the property'.[188] In that sense, the law is similar to the US Bankruptcy Code, which does not impose any duty related to insolvent trading. In contrast, both the UK and German systems do require the debtor to monitor its financial health and to submit to bankruptcy law if insolvent.

Debtors can object to creditors' EBL petition.[189] However, once the court accepts the EBL petition, the debtor personnel become subject to a number of duties. They must submit to the court all details of debtor's property, debts and claims, financial and accounting reports, and information about employee's wages and social insurance premium.[190] Debtors' senior personnel must cooperate with the court and administrator,

---

[180] See Section 4.2.11.
[181] Arts 111 and 115 EBL. A court has the final say (Art 65 EBL), but its decision can be appealed (Art 66 EBL).
[182] Arts 112 and 114 EBL.
[183] Art 116 EBL.
[184] Note that some local courts have tested the use of a bankruptcy assistance fund: see Section 12.10.
[185] Art 120(1)–(2) EBL.
[186] And certain capital contributors: Art 70 EBL 2006.
[187] See Section 4.2.2.
[188] This was included in the 1995 EBL Draft and worked well in the test cities: Booth and Zhang, 'Chinese Bankruptcy Law' (2001). See Section 11.1.5.1.
[189] Within five days: Art 10(1) EBL.
[190] Art 11 EBL.

they must attend creditors' meetings as non-voting delegates,[191] and they cannot act as senior officers in another company or leave their place of domicile without the court's permission.[192] These rules are in compliance with the UNCITRAL Guide.[193]

The debtor may remain in control in reorganisation, but only with the court's or administrator's permission and under the administrator's supervision.[194] Where left in charge, the debtor is responsible for formulating and submitting a reorganisation plan, explaining it to and negotiating with creditors, and implementing it if accepted.[195] If the debtor refuses to cooperate or to implement the plan, the court can punish the responsible personnel[196] and declare the debtor bankrupt.[197]

The debtor has no rights or powers in liquidation, but – similar to the UK and Germany – may be subject to legal liabilities for their pre-EBL activities.[198]

4.2.8. Creditors

As mentioned in Section 4.2.1 above, the second and third of the overarching principles in Article 1 of the EBL – ie fair settlement of claims and debts and protection of creditors' lawful interests – aim to ensure that creditors' rights are resolved in an objective, predictable and transparent manner. To this end, the EBL has greatly enhanced creditors' position and powers (compared to the 1986 law).[199] Creditors can petition a court to reorganise or liquidate a debtor who is unable to pay off their debts as they fall due.[200] If the petition is accepted, the court decides a timeframe for filing claims.[201] Immature claims,[202] conditional claims, claims with a time limit and pending claims under litigation or arbitration can be declared[203] to the appointed administrator.[204] The administrator verifies the claims and makes a list which is submitted to the first creditors' meeting for verification.[205] If the debtor and creditors agree on the list, the court confirms the list.[206]

Creditors' meetings have a central role in the EBL.[207] They address conflicts of interest and effective coordination of claims. Moreover, they also provide a forum where creditors vote on liquidation, composition and reorganisation plans; the management and

---

[191] Arts 15(1)–(3) and 68 EBL.
[192] Art 15(4)–(5) EBL.
[193] In particular Recommendations 108–16.
[194] See Section 4.2.4.
[195] ibid.
[196] Arts 125–29 and 131 EBL.
[197] Art 93 EBL.
[198] See Section 6.2.
[199] See eg X Ge, 'Creditors' Meeting and Creditors' Committee' in Parry, Xu and Zhang (n 2).
[200] See Section 4.2.2.
[201] Usually between 30 days and three months: Art 45 EBL. Late claims may be filed but any distribution made prior to such filing will not be affected: Art 56 EBL.
[202] Art 46 EBL.
[203] Art 47 EBL.
[204] Art 48 EBL.
[205] Arts 57 and 58 EBL.
[206] Art 58(2) EBL.
[207] So much so that an entire chapter of the EBL – Chapter VII – is devoted to it. This is a major upgrade from the 1986 law which only contained four simple provisions. Moreover, the Judicial Interpretation No 3 adds further details about how to challenge the validity of creditors' meeting resolutions and the role of creditors' committee.

distribution decisions relating to the debtor's property; and the remuneration and replacement of an administrator.[208]

All creditors who successfully submitted their claim (and whose claim were confirmed by the court) can attend and vote.[209] Note, however, that secured creditors who have not waived their security rights cannot vote on a composition or liquidation plan.[210] It is unclear whether employee representatives, who can attend creditors' meetings, can also vote, but on a literal reading of the law, it is unlikely.[211] The first creditors' meeting must be convened within 15 days after the deadline for filing claims.[212] Its main purpose is to examine and confirm the list of claims. Later creditors' meetings may be called by the court, an administrator, or creditors' committee of any creditor(s) representing at least one quarter of creditors' rights.[213] A resolution is passed if approved by a simple majority of creditors present at the meeting, provided that they represent more than a half of the creditors with voting rights and that their claims amount to more than a half of all unsecured creditors' claims.[214] Creditors can also establish a creditors' committee (subject to a court's approval) of up to nine members who have additional powers and represent the creditors as a whole.[215]

Creditors' role and powers are particularly pronounced in reorganisation because the moratorium prevents enforcement of their claims,[216] and the drafters believed – in line with the international practice and recommendations – that creditors are entitled to have a degree of control over the process.[217] Once the administrator (or the debtor-in-possession) makes a reorganisation plan, secured and unsecured creditors vote on the plan as two of several classes.[218] The plan is adopted if accepted by voting members who amount to more than a half in number and two-thirds in value in each group.[219] If creditors reject the plan, the administrator or debtor may negotiate with them, or can ask a court to cram down the dissenting group.[220] A court retains the final power of oversight.[221]

Creditors in liquidation also discuss and vote on the administrator's distribution plan.[222]

---

[208] Arts 59(1) and 61 EBL.

[209] Art 59 EBL.

[210] Arts 59(3), 61(7) and 61(1) EBL.

[211] Art 59(5) EBL states that employee representatives can attend creditors' meetings and voice their opinions, but it does not mention voting. In addition, employees' claims are not 'confirmed' in the usual way (Art 48 EBL) which means that they do not satisfy the requirements in Art 59(1) EBL. For further discussion see Ge, 'Creditors' Meeting' (n 197) 190–92.

[212] Art 62 EBL.

[213] Art 62(2) EBL.

[214] Art 64(1) EBL.

[215] Art 68 EBL.

[216] Arts 19–20 (unsecured creditors) and 75 (secured creditors) EBL.

[217] This is similar to the UK and Germany and complies with the UNCITRAL Guide recommendations 126–134. It is more extensive than in the US Chapter 11 where their rights are said to be protected by an administrator.

[218] See Section 4.2.4.

[219] ibid.

[220] ibid.

[221] See Section 4.2.9.

[222] See Section 4.2.6.

4.2.9. Courts and Administrators

Courts have extensive powers under the EBL.[223] They have the final say in deciding, inter alia, whether to accept bankruptcy petitions,[224] whether a creditor's claim is recognised and coverable under the chosen EBL procedure,[225] whether to permit the use of reorganisation instead of liquidation,[226] and whether to enforce a reorganisation plan despite its rejection by a class of creditors ('cramdown').[227] They also decide whether to terminate reorganisation and composition.[228] Courts' role is particularly pronounced in reorganisation where all key decisions by the administrator and creditors' committee – including the reorganisation plan, the cramdown of dissenting voting classes, and administrators' appointment and remuneration – have to be ratified by the court.[229]

In addition, courts are also charged with preventing and punishing malpractice, fraud and incompetence.[230] To this end, courts must always investigate whether debtor's managers acted in breach of their legal duties.[231] If they did – for example by submitting no or false statements, or by fabricating or destroying evidence[232] – the court can impose a fine. In addition, courts can also fine administrators who fail to perform their duties loyally and diligently.[233] Finally, courts can also detain managers to prevent their escape[234] and fine them if they leave without prior consent[235] in order to enable proper investigation

Such prominent role of courts sets the Chinese system apart from the UK, Germany and the US – where courts primarily only rule on the validity of a bankruptcy petition and, in varying degrees, act as final arbiters and high-level supervisors. Instead, the role of Chinese judges brings the EBL closer to the French system, where courts have a more proactive role.[236] The extent of courts' involvement in bankruptcy cases is a matter of national preference. Where the bankruptcy administrators are seen as insufficiently experienced or professional, for example, court involvement is particularly useful. However, it may be that once the administrators became better trained and gain more experience, it may be preferable to transfer more managerial powers to them. At the same time, given the Party-state's interference in courts' law enforcement – both generally[237] and in the context of the EBL[238] – it may be better to reduce the court involvement in EBL cases to permit more objective and independent bankruptcy hearings.

---

[223] Unlike under the 1986, which put the Government in charge. See Section 8.3.1.
[224] Art 10 EBL.
[225] See Section 4.2.8.
[226] Art 72 EBL.
[227] Arts 86–87 EBL.
[228] Arts 78–79, 96 and 98 EBL.
[229] See Section 4.2.4. See also Zhang, *Corporate Reorganisations* (2018) 224–26.
[230] See Section 4.2.12.
[231] Art 6 EBL. Breaching the fiduciary duty results in a three-year ban to manage any enterprise: Art 125(2) EBL.
[232] Art 127 EBL.
[233] Serious violations may give rise to criminal liability: Arts 130–31 EBL.
[234] All my interviews with lawyers and entrepreneurs confirmed that this happens in China. See also Sections 6.2 and 10.2.2.
[235] Art 129 EBL.
[236] French Insolvency Code 1985 and 2005 (*Redressement judiciaire*). See also recent *L'ordonnance pour des procédures préventives plus faciles* (12.3.2014), which encourages collaboration and informal reorganisation.
[237] See Section 2.4.
[238] See Section 8.3.

Courts' work is supported by administrators whom they appoint from a local register of administrators[239] as soon as an EBL petition is accepted.[240] Courts also supervise administrators.[241] Administrators are professional, impartial managers[242] who largely replaced politically controlled liquidation committees which operated under the 1986 law. A liquidation committee can, in practice, still be appointed to manage a bankruptcy procedure under the EBL. Their role was retained at the request of China National State-Asset Management Commission in order to allow their use in resolving policy bankruptcies of exempted SOEs. Nevertheless, the wording of Article 24 of the EBL allows liquidation committees to act as administrators regardless of the type of whether the bankrupt is an SOE or a private company.[243] Subsequent guidance from the SPC specifies that liquidation committees should be appointed in four circumstances: in bankruptcies of financial companies (eg banks or securities companies); SOEs whose resolution is included in the national bankruptcy plan; where the use of a liquidation committee is required by another statute; and where the court considers the use of a liquidation committee to be appropriate – such as in cases of significant public importance.[244]

Administrators supervise EBL procedures, recommend whether to close or sell or otherwise reorganise the debtor company before the first creditors' meeting; manage the debtor company, its property and information; investigate and sometimes formulate reorganisation and liquidation plans; make interim decisions (often subject to a court approval); assist creditors; and in general act as intermediaries between the parties.[245] They are subject to duties of due diligence and loyalty to the creditors and to the company as a whole,[246] and once appointed, they are not allowed to resign without justifications that would be accepted by the supervising court.[247]

Administrators report to the court[248] and, to a lesser extent, creditors' committee.[249] They must investigate and apply to the court to reverse certain transactions that put creditors at a disadvantage.[250] They also have to police and report cases of malpractice, fraud and incompetence from debtors' personnel[251] so long as they took place within a

---

[239] Art 15 of the SPC Provisions concerning the Appointment of Administrators (*Fashi* [2007] No 8) – hereafter the 'Appointment Provisions.' See also Section 4.3.

[240] Art 13 EBL.

[241] Arts 22–23 EBL. Administrators are chosen at random from administrators' register, which is managed by local courts: Art 20 of the Appointment Provisions.

[242] They can be individuals or organisations such as specialist liquidation firms, law firms, accountancy firms etc: Art 24 EBL. Preference is normally given to organisations: Art 16 of the Appointment Provisions. Individuals should only be appointed in simple cases: Art 17 of the Appointment Provisions. This is similar to the US where organisations can also act as administrators: US Bankruptcy Code Title 11 para 321.

[243] X Wang, 'Government-Organized Liquidation Committees in Corporate Bankruptcies' (The China National Bankruptcy Annual Conference, Beijing China, 2.5.2017).

[244] Art 18 of the Appointment Provisions. See also SPC's ninth typical case (2018) in Sections 4.3 and 8.3.5.

[245] Chapter III, Arts 23 and 25 EBL. For a detailed discussion see J Xiao, 'Bankruptcy Administrator: Status, Powers and Duties' in Parry, Xu and Zhang (n 2).

[246] Art 27 EBL.

[247] Art 29 EBL and Art 35 of the Appointment Provisions.

[248] Art 23 EBL.

[249] The administrator must attend creditors' meetings and answer any questions that they may have: Art 23(2) EBL. The administrator must also report to creditors' committee upon occurrence of certain events such a transfer of ownership, transfer of property rights, or granting a loan or collateral over debtor's property: Art 69 EBL.

[250] See Section 4.2.13.

[251] See Section 4.2.12.

certain period prior to the acceptance of the EBL application. In addition, administrators must also collect unpaid capital contributions from shareholders.[252]

Administrators also have a broad range of powers. An administrator can affirm or terminate a contract entered into before the EBL application.[253] This power is much more extensive than that of administrators in the US and UK. In Germany, an insolvency administrator may choose to affirm or terminate some types of contract. The broad-ranging powers given to EBL administrators far exceed those found in many other jurisdictions, but they are still firmly within the recommended guidelines in the UNCITRAL Guide.[254]

Administrators' remuneration is determined by a court[255] following SPC's seven-grade system (Table 4.2) according to the total value of debtor's liquidated assets and the administrator's likely workload.[256] Nevertheless, local courts can adjust the remuneration to reflect local circumstances and the actual performance by the administrator so long as they make the new guidelines known through a well-known media and report the same to the SPC.[257] Administrators' remuneration is paid in priority as a bankruptcy expense.[258]

Table 4.2 Guidelines for determining administrators' remuneration

	Total value of liquidated assets	Maximum compensation
Grade 1	Up to RMB 1 million	12% or less
Grade 2	More than RMB 1 million but less than RMB 5 million	Not more than 10%
Grade 3	More than RMB 5 million but less than RMB 10 million	Not more than 8%
Grade 4	More than RMB 10 million but less than RMB 50 million	Not more than 6%
Grade 5	More than RMB 50 million but less than RMB 100 million	Not more than 3%
Grade 6	More than RMB 100 million but less than RMB 500 million	Not more than 1%
Grade 7	More than RMB 500 million	Not more than 0.5%

The court can replace the administrator in some circumstances,[259] acting of its own volition or following a written request from the creditors' committee.[260] Finally, the

---

[252] Art 35 EBL.

[253] Similarly, a contract is automatically terminated if administrator fails to respond within one month to a formal notice served by the other contracting party: Art 18 EBL.

[254] In particular, the UNCITRAL Guide recommendations 87–92.

[255] Art 28 EBL. For a detailed discussion see R Parry, 'Administrator: Appointment and Remuneration' in Parry, Xu and Zhang (n 2).

[256] Arts 2 and 4 of the SPC Provisions concerning the Remuneration for Administrators (*Fashi* [2007] No 9) – hereafter the 'Remuneration Provisions.' See also Section 4.3.

[257] ibid. Also Arts 8–9 of the Remuneration Provisions.

[258] Art 12 of the Remuneration Provisions. See also Section 4.2.11.

[259] For example, where the administrator disappears (or is dissolved or bankrupt in case of organisations acting as administrators), where the administrator made deliberate or gross errors which damages creditors' interests, or where the administrator is being investigated for alleged violation of the law: Arts 33–4 of the Appointment Provisions.

[260] If the administrator cannot perform their function in an impartial way or where they are not able to perform their duties or functions: Art 31 of the Appointment Provisions. See also Art 22 EBL.

administrator can resign from office if they have 'legitimate reason' for doing so.[261] If the court does not allow the administrator to resign, but the administrator insists on resigning, they may be fined by the court.[262]

4.2.10. Employees

The EBL gives special protection to employees.[263] It stems from the flaws in China's social welfare provision[264] and its socio-political environment.[265] Courts are ordered to protect 'legitimate rights and interests of employees of the insolvent company'.[266] A debtor must submit an employee resettlement plan and an explanation of how employee wages and social insurance have been paid.[267] In reorganisation, employees are represented at creditors' meetings[268] (and creditors' committee if there is one[269]), and they can vote on the reorganisation plan.[270] Moreover, the restructuring debtor must notify the labour union or provide an explanation to all its employees 30 days in advance if it plans to dismiss more than 20 employees (or at least 10 per cent of the total number of employees).[271] Finally, employees' claims rank ahead of secured creditors if they were incurred prior to 1 June 2007 (when the EBL came into effect), otherwise, they rank ahead of other preferential claims (tax, social insurance claims) and unsecured claims.[272] These measures seek to ensure social stability and are reinforced through the duty on courts to maintain orderly socialist market economy in Article 1 of the EBL.[273]

4.2.11. Priority of Distribution

Outside bankruptcy law, creditors get their money back on a first-come-first-served basis. Such an approach is inefficient and results in destruction of value and unequal

---

[261] However, the Court will only accept the resignation if one of the above-mentioned reasons is present: Art 35 of the Appointment Provisions.

[262] Art 130 EBL and Art 39 of the Appointment Provisions.

[263] This is reiterated in many internal documents, including the SPC Notice concerning the Correct Hearing of EBL Cases and Judicial Guarantee to Maintain Orderly Market Economy (*Fafa* [2009] No 36): see section 4.3.

[264] See Sections 4.1 and 7.2.1.

[265] See Section 2.1.

[266] Art 6 EBL.

[267] Both required in debtor's petition, the latter in creditor's petition: Arts 8 and 11 EBL.

[268] Art 59 EBL. Note that where there are 25 or more employees, they must be allowed to form a labour union: Art 10 Labour Union Law 2009.

[269] Art 67 EBL.

[270] Art 82(2) EBL.

[271] Art 41 Employment Contract Law 2007.

[272] Arts 113 and 132 EBL. See also Section 4.2.11.

[273] See Section 4.2.1.

or unfair distribution of debtors' assets.[274] Bankruptcy law offers a collective recovery mechanism that regulates the priority of distribution of debtors' assets.

The issue of priority was one of the reasons why the reform took 12 years.[275] When the EBL was finally enacted in 2006, it contained an uneasy compromise in order to accommodate China's transition from a centrally planned socialist (pro-employee) regime to market (pro-creditor) system. To allow the Chinese Government time to expand its social welfare provision for the unemployed and to appease the powerful Labour Unions,[276] Article 113 of the EBL states that, after expenses, employees rank ahead of all other claims. However, Article 132 of the EBL qualifies this by saying that this preferential treatment only extends to employee claims that were incurred before the new law came into effect, ie before 1 June 2007. As a result, employee claims now rank behind those of secured creditors, similar to bankruptcy laws elsewhere.[277] Nevertheless, employee claims remain recoverable ahead of other unsecured creditors and even tax and social insurance (Table 4.3).

Table 4.3 Priority of distribution in China, England, the US and Germany

	CHINA (post-2007)	UK	US	GERMANY
1st	Secured creditors	Secured creditors (fixed charges)	Secured creditors	Secured creditors *
2nd	Bankruptcy expenses and Debts of common interest	Bankruptcy expenses	Bankruptcy expenses	Bankruptcy expenses
3rd	Preferential creditors FIRST: Employees' claims SECOND: Social insurance contributions, taxes	Preferential unsecured creditors (wages, pension contributions)	Preferential unsecured creditors (wages, pension contributions, taxes)	Unsecured creditors
4th	General unsecured creditors	Secured creditors (floating charge)	General unsecured creditors	Subordinated claims (shareholder loans)
5th		General unsecured creditors (including taxes, shareholder loans)	Subordinated claims (discretionary)	

* In Germany, an administrator can take their fee from the proceeds of sale of movable secured assets before paying the secured creditor

---

[274] R Goode, *Principles of Corporate Insolvency Law*, 4th edn (Sweet & Maxwell, 2011) paras 2-04 and 2-05; J Armour, G Hertig and H Kanda, Transactions with Creditors in R Kraakman, J Armour, P Davies, L Enriques, H Hansmann, G Hertig, K Hopt, H Kanda and E Rock, *The Anatomy of Corporate Law: A Comparative and Functional Approach*, 3rd edn (Oxford University Press, 2017).
[275] See Section 4.1. Note that this dilemma is not unique to China: see eg H Eidenmüller, 'Comparative Corporate Insolvency Law' ECGI Law Working Paper 319/2016, 7–12.
[276] ibid.
[277] See also the UNCITRAL Guide paras 62–75 and recommendations 185–93.

Claims incurred after 1 June 2007 are, therefore, paid out in the following order:[278]

(i)   outstanding secured creditors' claims;[279]
(ii) bankruptcy expenses[280] and debts of common interest;[281]
(iii) employees' claims;[282]
(iv) other social insurance premiums and taxes; and
(v)   (declared) general unsecured debts.

The EBL does not expressly mandate the use of *pari passu* principle, but in practice, unsecured debts are treated equally.[283]

4.2.12. Misconduct, Fraud and Liability

Signalling it is serious about preventing and punishing malpractice, fraud and incompetence, the EBL introduces strict provisions on civil[284] and criminal[285] liability for defined wrongdoings by debtors' management and administrators.[286] The court must always investigate whether the company directors, supervisors or senior managers acted in breach of their legal duties of honesty and diligence,[287] which led to the financial distress of the debtor company.[288] Breaching the fiduciary duty results in a three-year ban to manage any enterprise;[289] civil liability for the loss caused;[290] and criminal liability in cases of misappropriation or bribery.[291]

Once an EBL procedure begins, any staff member of the debtor can be admonished or detained and fined if they leave their place of domicile without the court's prior consent.[292] The debtor and its representatives may be fined if they fail to attend creditors' meeting without a justifiable reason, if they refuse to answer, or if they lie.[293]

---

[278] Arts 43, 113 and 132 EBL.
[279] Secured creditors are not stayed from enforcing their security in liquidation (unlike in reorganisation: Art 75 EBL), but if they fail to enforce their security, then their claims are satisfied first: Art 109 EBL.
[280] ie litigation costs; cost of administration, appraisal and distribution of debtor's property; and administrator's remuneration: Art 41 EBL and Art 12 of the Remuneration Provisions. See also the Judicial Interpretation No 3.
[281] ie debts incurred by enforcing performance of unfinished contracts; debts incurred from voluntary service to the debtor's property by a third party; and the wages and social insurance premiums for continued operations: Art 42 EBL.
[282] ie medical/disability fees and compensations, and support payments owed to employees and their families; employees' basic pension and medical insurance premiums; and any other compensations payable to the employees: Art 113(1) EBL.
[283] All my interviews. See also Zhang (n 85) 147–56 who notes that *pari passu* is mostly applied but, in some situations, it is relaxed in favour of smaller unsecured creditors.
[284] Art 125 EBL. Moreover, Art 148 of the Company Law creates the management's general duty of loyalty and care to their company.
[285] The Criminal Law 1997 was amended in 2011.
[286] For a detailed discussion of what this involves in practice, see Section 6.2. See also B Wang, 'Improper Trading in bankruptcy and Director Liabilities' in Parry, Xu and Zhang (n 2).
[287] Imposed, generally, in Arts 21, 149, 150, 152 and 153 Company Law.
[288] Arts 6 and 125 EBL.
[289] Art 125(2) EBL (and Art 147 Company Law).
[290] Art 150 Company Law 2018.
[291] In some very limited cases. See Section 6.2.
[292] Arts 15(4) and 129 EBL.
[293] Arts 15(3) and 126(1) EBL.

Similarly, the debtor and its representatives may be fined if they fail to submit or submit false documents and if they fabricate or destroy evidence.[294] The debtor or its representatives may also be criminally liable if they falsely file for bankruptcy in order to defraud the creditors.[295]

Administrators can also be liable if they fail to perform their duties with loyalty and diligence.[296]

4.2.13. Avoidable Transactions

The EBL contains several provisions that prevent pre-bankruptcy asset dissipation and deprivation and put an administrator in charge of their enforcement. The provisions seek to maximise the total value of the bankrupt's estate that is available for distribution to the debtor's creditors and to disincentivise asset dissipation and fraudulent or self-serving behaviour by insiders. Under the EBL, an administrator must investigate and apply to the court to reverse certain activities that affected debtor's property[297] within one year before the acceptance of the EBL application.[298] They include transactions at an undervalue;[299] security given for past value;[300] payments of undue debts;[301] and waivers of claims or other transactions by the debtor company that defrauded creditors.[302] An administrator must also claw back preferential payments made within six months before the EBL procedure commenced.[303] Moreover, irrespective of when they happened, an administrator must seek and claim back property hidden or transferred to evade debts;[304] and uncover and claw back money and property paid over in satisfaction of fabricated debts.[305] The EBL also makes void any payment from the debtor to a creditor that was made following the acceptance of an EBL petition.[306] In addition to transactions vis-à-vis outsiders, an administrator must also investigate and recover any inappropriate income acquired and property misappropriated by any director, supervisor and other managerial officers of the debtor who took advantages of their position.[307] These are powerful and important provisions which have the potential to enlarge the amount of assets that are available to creditors.[308]

---

[294] Arts 8(2) and 127 EBL. See also Art 6 of the SPC Provisions (I) concerning the Application of the EBL (*Fashi* [2011] No 22) – hereafter the 'Judicial Interpretation No 1'.

[295] Art 131 EBL and Art 162(2) Criminal Law.

[296] Art 27 EBL gives rise to this duty. Serious violations may give rise to criminal liability: Arts 130–31 EBL.

[297] Art 34 EBL.

[298] If he does not, he can be personally liable to compensate the estate for any resulting loss: Art 10 Judicial Interpretation No 2.

[299] ie free of charge, at an unreasonably low price: Art 31(1)–(2) EBL.

[300] ie for an unsecured debt: Art 31(3) EBL.

[301] This gives an unfair preference to one creditor over the others: Art 31(4) EBL. See also Art 32 EBL.

[302] Art 31(5) EBL.

[303] Art 32 EBL. Not if the payment took place longer than six months before the bankruptcy: Art 12 Judicial Interpretation No 2.

[304] Art 33(1) EBL.

[305] Art 33(2) EBL.

[306] Art 16 EBL.

[307] Art 36 EBL.

[308] See also Section 4.3.1 for further guidance.

4.3. Supreme People's Court's Interpretations and Judicial Cases

The EBL provides a legal framework for resolving corporate bankruptcies in China. The Supreme People's Court (SPC) has issued several documents to provide non-binding guidance[309] to instruct lower courts on how to apply the law.[310] The guidance is very important for ensuring consistency in judicial decision-making as well as transparency and predictability of the law in China as a whole.

This chapter considers several SPC documents that contain important EBL-related guidance to lower courts. Section 4.3.1 below briefly examines seven SPC guiding documents that focus on the EBL directly.[311] Section 4.3.2 considers SPC guidance on how to transfer individual debt enforcement hearings and orders to an EBL hearing. Finally, Sections 4.3.3 and 4.3.4 give a brief overview of the SPC 'typical cases' – 10 in 2018 and eight in 2020. Together, these documents expand and explain how to apply the EBL in practice.[312] Where relevant, the substantive rules discussed below have also been included or referenced throughout the summaries in Section 4.2 above. The SPC and lower local courts have also recently issued several policy documents which have not yet influenced the practice, and so are discussed in chapter twelve together with other recent reforms.

4.3.1. SPC Judicial Interpretations of the EBL

The SPC released five important normative judicial interpretative provisions (*guiding* 规定) concerning the EBL directly. The SPC Provisions concerning the Appointment of Administrators (*Fashi* [2007] No 8) was adopted on 4 April 2007 and came into effect together with the EBL on 1 June 2007. It sets out rules about preparing a register of eligible administrators (both individuals and organisations) and reviewing the membership of the register; it says that an administrator for a particular case must be appointed from the register; and it provides guidance about when to appoint an organisation, an individual or a liquidation committee as an administrator. It explains how administrators and courts should deal with conflicts of interests. And it provides several guidelines about when and how administrators should be replaced.

The SPC Provisions concerning the Remuneration for Administrators (*Fashi* [2007] No 9) was also adopted on 4 April 2007 and promulgated together with the EBL. It establishes the right for administrators to receive remuneration for their services. Importantly, it provides guidance about the usual limits of such remuneration, but it also empowers the court to adjust the remuneration if certain circumstances arise. It also clarifies that the administrator's remuneration is paid in priority as a bankruptcy expense.[313]

---

[309] See Section 2.3.1.

[310] For an excellent discussion, see SPC Monitor (19.5.2019).

[311] This is not an exhaustive list. Other documents exist, some of which are incorporated into the discussion in Section 4.2 and ch 12.

[312] For a discussion of the role of these rules, see Section 2.3.1.

[313] See Section 4.2.11.

The SPC Provisions (I) concerning the Application of the EBL (*Fashi* [2011] No 22) became effective on 26 September 2011. It provides further guidance about how to apply the insolvency test, what evidence a debtor may be required to submit, and how to confirm and deal with EBL petitions vis-à-vis applicants (including additional time limits). It also states that, where a court fails to accept the EBL petition within the time limit, the applicant may file the petition with a court at a higher level which may order the lower court to review it.

The SPC Provisions (II) concerning the Application of the EBL (*Fashi* [2013] No 22) came into effect on 16 September 2013. It further specifies what is and what is not included in a debtor's estate.[314] It also provides further details concerning the administrator's duty to rescind certain transactions under Articles 31–33 of the EBL, and it establishes the administrator's liability for failing to exercise their powers under Articles 31 and 32 of the EBL to rescind certain transactions.[315] The administrator must also collect unpaid capital from shareholders and seek repayment of the debts owed to the debtor. The document also clarifies that the EBL is a collective procedure and so individual arrangements cannot be accepted by the court unless they involve payment of wages or otherwise benefit the debtor's property.[316] The guidance also contains rules on how to deal with the passing of title in transfers to third parties and how to set off claims in accordance with Article 40 of the EBL.

Finally, the SPC Provisions (III) concerning the Application of the EBL (*Fashi* [2019] No 3) came into effect on 28 March 2019. It provides further explanation about what can be claimed as bankruptcy expenses. It also clarifies rules about the availability and priority of post-petition lending. It deals with the issues arising from insolvency of a debtor's guarantor, creditors' rights confirmed before the EBL petition was accepted, disagreements about the nature or extent of creditor's right(s), the possibility to challenge the validity of the creditors' meeting resolution, and the role and powers of the creditors' committee.

In addition, there are also two important regulatory judicial guidance documents (*Fafa* 法发). The SPC Notice concerning the Correct Hearing of EBL Cases and Judicial Guarantee to Maintain Orderly Socialist Market Economy (*Fafa* [2009] No 36) highlights the importance of the EBL in managing the global economic crisis in 2009. It reiterates the importance of working closely with local governments and Party representatives in order to maintain social stability and coordinate the interests of various stakeholders. The document urges courts to use reorganisation and composition rather than liquidation. At the same time, however, it acknowledges that some companies should be liquidated and it calls for a full consideration of employees' as well as creditors', debtors' and other stakeholders' interests.

The SPC Notice concerning the Promotion of Efficient Review of Bankruptcy Cases (*Fafa* [2020] No 14) provides further guidance on how to improve the efficiency of the EBL. It focuses on five broad areas, namely improving the process of case announcement and acceptance; improving how bankruptcy assets are investigated and taken over; improving the convening of and voting at creditors' meetings; exploring a simplified EBL procedure;[317] and strengthening the prevention and punishment of debt evasion. The SPC

---

[314] See Section 4.2.1.
[315] See Section 4.2.13.
[316] Arts 15–16 Judicial Interpretation No 2.
[317] See Section 12.8.

hopes that resolving these issues will help make EBL hearings more efficient and reduce the cost involved in the resolution of corporate financial distress in China.

4.3.2. SPC Guidance about Transfer of Debt Enforcement Cases to EBL Cases

In many cases, creditors – in China and elsewhere – first try to recover their debts using individual enforcement mechanisms.[318] However, once the debtor becomes insolvent, these individual enforcement hearings and orders (from a court or an arbitral body) need to be brought into a single collective EBL proceeding. Indeed, one of the greatest advantages of using corporate bankruptcy law is that it allows for a collective solution which, in the aggregate, ensures greater recovery for the creditors as a whole. It is, therefore, important to resolve the technical issues surrounding the transfer of individual debt enforcement cases to a collective EBL case. The EBL itself is silent on the matter, but subsequent SPC guidance has been released. This has taken two forms: normative guidance in SPC rules; and soft guidance in guiding and typical cases.

The SPC Notice concerning Several Issues in the Transfer of Debt Enforcement Claims to Bankruptcy Case (*Fafa* [2017] No 2) was released to provide much-needed guidance for lower courts, which felt unable to deal the increasing volume of EBL cases that involved individual debt enforcement cases and claims. The Notice created procedural rules that helped standardise and promote such transfers, which is necessary for effective implementation of the EBL. In order to satisfy the entry requirements of the EBL itself,[319] the transfer is only possible if the debtor is a legal person; and if the debtor satisfies the EBL insolvency test (unable to pay off debts as they fall due and assets exceed liabilities or obviously lack solvency).[320] At the same time, however, the debtor or the creditor who applied for the enforcement order must agree in writing with the transfer into an EBL case.[321] The Notice also provides detailed rules on jurisdiction, deadlines, the court's role in the transfer, duty to notify, guidelines for dealing with perishable and other goods, fees, and consequences of acceptance or rejection by the receiving court.[322] Once the transfer is confirmed, all seizure or freeze orders remain in place until an EBL case is commenced and an EBL moratorium is imposed.[323] This is very important for the continuity of legal enforcement and protection of the creditors as a whole. The SPC Notice also provides a list of materials that should be transferred to the EBL court[324] and imposes a deadline of 30 days after receiving the transfer documents in which the receiving court must decide whether they accept the case.[325]

The SPC provided further guidance in its guiding and typical cases in 2016, 2018 and 2020. The SPC Guiding Case No 73 concerns a case where two parties reached a settlement of debt agreement in an arbitration which gave the claimant creditor priority

---

[318] See Section 3.3.3.
[319] See Sections 4.2.1–4.2.2.
[320] Arts 2(1) and (3) of the SPC Notice.
[321] Art 2(2) of the SPC Notice.
[322] Arts 3–8 and 15–19 of the SPC Notice.
[323] Art 9 of the SPC Notice.
[324] Art 10 of the SPC Notice.
[325] Art 13 of the SPC Notice.

in repayment. Later on, the debtor entered EBL proceedings in the Anhui Provincial High Court,[326] and one of the issues was whether the pre-existing arbitral settlement was valid under the EBL. The court confirmed the validity and priority of the right to be compensated in construction project price in accordance with the general spirit and the rule in Art 18 of the EBL.[327]

Similarly, the second typical case (2018)[328] provides further guidance on how to deal with a transfer of individual debt enforcement hearings and orders into an EBL hearing. In that case, 1,384 debt enforcement judgments had to be transferred into an EBL liquidation. The SPC commentary highlighted that the case illustrates that transfer of debt enforcement orders to an EBL procedure not only ensures fair protection of the legitimate interests of the stakeholders, but it also deals with and clears from courts' books debt enforcement cases which were impossible to execute and ended up congesting the courts. Speed and protection of employees were seen as particularly important for ensuring a successful conclusion of such cases.[329] The SPC released another typical case in 2020, which illustrated these issues in the context of reorganisation.[330]

Further guidance has been provided at local level. For example, Zhejiang Higher Court released a report containing general guidance and 10 typical cases in April 2018.[331] The report noted that there were 1,640 transfer-to-bankruptcy cases in 2017. It also highlighted the importance of

> promoting the link between debt enforcement and bankruptcy procedures. The enforcement procedure focuses on the realization of individual creditors' claims, and the bankruptcy procedure focuses on the fair and orderly settlement of all creditors. An important reason for 'difficult enforcement' is that some individual enforcement cases are not simply 'difficult' but rather 'impossible to execute', that is, some companies have become severely insolvent following an individual debt enforcement, and so they should have entered bankruptcy. A bankruptcy procedure pays off all creditors in a fair and orderly manner, and finally withdraws the debtor from the market. Bankruptcy procedures are not only a standardized exit channel in the market, but also an important way to resolve the 'difficult implementation' problem.[332]

This commentary highlights the practical problems facing individual debt enforcement and, more importantly, the importance of enabling smooth transfer from individual enforcement hearings into an EBL case.

---

[326] (2014) Wanmin Yizhongzi No 00054.

[327] This Article gives an administrator a right to cancel contracts that the debtor entered prior to the acceptance of the EBL case. For more see eg cgc.law.stanford.edu/guiding-cases/guiding-case-73 (in English); m.zichanjie.com/article/139884.html (in Chinese).

[328] See Section 4.3.3.

[329] The case can be found, in full, at www.chinacourt.org/article/detail/2018/03/id/3219365.shtml (in Chinese).

[330] See also the seventh typical case (2020) in Section 3.4.4.

[331] See the press release by Xu Jianxin, a member of the Party Leadership Group and Vice President of the Zhejiang Higher People's Court, on 16.4.2018: 'Zhejiang Court Advances the Structural Reform of the Bankruptcy Trial Service Supply Side and Economic Transformation and Upgrade'.

[332] ibid.

4.3.3. SPC Typical Cases (2018)

The SPC also released 10 typical EBL cases (*dianxinganli* 典型案例)[333] on 6 March 2018 following the annual plenary sessions of the National People's Congress (legislative power) and the Chinese People's Political Consultative Conference (the Party).[334] These hand-picked real-life cases with SPC's commentary are not binding (compared to common law precedents), but they guide and educate judges in lower courts about how to deal with typical problems that arise in corporate bankruptcy cases in practice. Eight cases are reorganisations; two are liquidations. Half concern SOEs and half concern private companies. All the companies involved are large.

The first case (2018) – *Bankruptcy Liquidation of Zhejiang Nanfang Petrochemical Industry Ltd et al* – concerns three interconnected private companies whose assets were liquidated within 54 days and distribution was completed within 10.5 months. The case shows how the Court can help a company in liquidation protect business continuation, save jobs and ensure fast and flexible liquidation and distribution of assets of related companies through joint-administrator and joint creditors' meetings (albeit separate voting for each company).

The second case (2018) – *Transfer of Enforcement Hearings in Songhui Industry (Shenzhen) Ltd into Bankruptcy* – concerns a private company which faced 1,384 debt enforcement judgments. Its assets were auctioned off, but the money raised barely covered employees' claims. The case was transferred into insolvent liquidation. The SPC uses this case to illustrate how to handle, firstly, transfer of debt enforcement claims into an EBL liquidation case;[335] and, secondly, how to balance competing claims from unpaid employees and creditors (the EBL's priority of distribution rules were used to resolve the conflict of interests). The commentary also highlights the importance of a speedy resolution and efficiency in 'putting idle assets back into use'.

The third case (2018) – *Insolvent Reorganisation of Chongqing Iron & Steel Ltd* – concerns a large listed SOE, the first of its kind to go through EBL restructuring. The SPC uses it to illustrate how the Court can guide an administrator to achieve successful restructuring in a transparent, market-driven way through identifying the cause of the financial distress and finding solutions such as a sale of inefficient and ineffective assets, management replacement, change of production and asset structure, and the use of industrial structure adjustment fund and capital markets.

The fourth case (2018) – *Insolvent Reorganisation of Jiangsu Textile Industry (Group) Import & Export Ltd and its subsidiaries* – concerns a group of six SOEs. The SPC comments that the case shows the advantage of using a joint administrator and a merger of the affected debtor companies (especially if their assets and governance structures are intertwined) in order to achieve a recovery of the whole group. The SPC also highlights the benefits of using a settlement that involves providing cash as well as debt-for-equity swaps.

---

[333] These are not part of the SPC guiding cases – see Section 2.3.1.
[334] The cases were released alongside the SPC Notice concerning the Minutes of the National Work Conference on Bankruptcy Trials (*Fa* [2018] No 53): see www.sohu.com/a/225145138_481798.
[335] See Section 4.3.2.

The fifth case (2018) – *Insolvent Reorganisation of Yunnan Coal Chemical Industry Group Ltd et al* – concerns a provincial-level group of SOEs in the coal industry. The SPC uses it to show how EBL reorganisation can be used to cut excessive industrial capacity (a reform objective since 2015[336]) through structural adjustments – in this case by closing 18 unprofitable coal mines, reducing unwanted coal capacity and settling claims from 14,552 laid-off employees. The case involved a series of mini-reorganisations in order to detangle a complex web of internal and external debt structures.

The sixth case (2018) – *Insolvent Reorganisation of Beijing Institute of Technology ZTE Corp* – involves a pre-packaged use of the EBL reorganisation in a large SOE. It was the first reorganisation case filed by a non-listed public company on the Securities Trading Automated Quotations System (STAQ) and the NET System. The SPC praised the local court for using a pre-pack: the Court, assisted by an administrator, ran initial negotiations and consultations which resulted in a business plan and a restructuring plan being fully agreed by the key parties even before the EBL reorganisation officially began. The Court and local Government also played a key role in securing an outside investor and financing.

The seventh case (2018) – *Insolvent Reorganisation of Zhuangji Group Ltd et al* – concerns a reorganisation of four private companies that over-expanded prior to an economic downturn and got into financial difficulties. Because of the interconnected nature of the four companies, the Court approved a merger of their assets and liabilities and appointed a joint administrator. The SPC uses the case to illustrate when and how the cramdown powers can and should be used (here, the dissent did not concern the reorganisation plan per se). Moreover, the case also illustrates that the Court's assistance may be needed even after the proceedings end – eg to help with further financing or tax benefits.

The eighth case (2018) – *Insolvent Reorganisation of Fujian Anxi Tieguanyin Group Ltd. and affiliated companies* – concerns one of three oldest state-owned tea factories in China. The SPC uses the case to illustrate how the Court can help upgrade and transform a traditional agricultural company through the use of reorganisation (new processes, marketing, research and products were introduced). There was no need for a merger because the assets, transactions and account books of the involved companies were largely separate. Nevertheless, a joint administrator managed both reorganisations, and one key investor was brought in to invest in both companies.

The ninth case (2018) – *Insolvent Reorganisation of Zhongshun Automobile Holdings Ltd* – concerns a private carmaker. As the company had been closed for a long time and there were fears about its impact on social stability, a liquidation committee was established to manage the process. The situation was complex, and the Court had to balance a fair settlement of creditors' rights against the debtor company's interests and future profitability. The Court was guided and supported by the local government in bringing in new investors and refocusing the company's production to renewable energy vehicles. The local Government also helped coordinate the work of various departments and overcome red-tape and delays which would otherwise prevent effective restructuring. Moreover, the SPC highlighted that the Court assisted the local Government in achieving the (national) goal of revitalising an old industrial base of northeast China – in line with the national policy supporting technological innovation.

---

[336] See Section 12.1.

Finally, the tenth case (2018) – *Insolvent Reorganisation of Guilin Guangwei Wenhua Tourism Culture Industry Ltd* – concerns a private company and was the first EBL case in China to be accepted directly by a High Court. The SPC agreed with and praised the Court's decision to allow the debtor to remain in possession (given the particular circumstances) and to run the asset without the Court's interference. The Court played a purely supporting role and assisted the debtor in resolving its debts and promoting local economic development.

All 10 cases stress the importance of maintaining social harmony and stability and, where possible, achieving a win–win outcome. They also illustrate the key role that the SPC perceives local governments playing in corporate bankruptcy cases – usually to resettle employees, bring in new funding, find a buyer, help coordinate rescue efforts, or more broadly maintain social stability of the affected region.

4.3.4. SPC Typical Cases (2020)

On 31 March 2020 the SPC also released eight typical EBL cases[337] which focus on reorganisation and composition. They were released in response to the coronavirus pandemic and subsequent economic slowdown in order to showcase how the EBL restructuring tools can 'promote the resumption of work and production'.[338] The SPC highlighted the key functional values of the EBL restructuring regime, namely

(i) the company's ability to continue operations during the procedure and achieve an efficient allocation of market resources;
(ii) the protective and restructuring functions of the EBL regime combined with a focus on resolving creditors' rights and claims and promoting regeneration of companies; and
(iii) the judicial guarantee system which can help companies overcome difficulties and continue producing essential goods.

The first case (2020) – *Composition of Guangdong Xingangxing Concrete Ltd* – concerns a company with long-term cash-flow problems. It was transferred from liquidation into composition, and a draft composition plan was made. Its implementation was disrupted by the coronavirus epidemic, and the Court stepped in and renegotiated a new timetable for repayment of debts. The SPC praised the Court's proactive and inventive approach. It also highlighted the importance of seeing composition as a complex 'package' regime rather than merely repayment of creditors' claims.

The second case (2020) – *Reorganisation of Jiangsu Panyu Technology Ltd* – concerns a medical device manufacturing company which suffered a liquidity crisis due to poor management. It was transferred from liquidation into reorganisation because the Court felt that its market access and unique resources could not be sufficiently protected in liquidation. The reorganisation plan was severely affected by the coronavirus epidemic, but the crisis also created new opportunities as the company was able to produce medical masks which were, globally, in short supply. The SPC used this case to show that a reorganisation plan needs to be changed where there is a national policy adjustment,

---

[337] See pccz.court.gov.cn/pcajxxw/pcdxal/dxalxq?id=29B484A2B4A754E9DD67165D4285144B.
[338] ibid.

legal change, or other objective reasons. The SPC also highlighted the crucial role of the local government in coordinating the process and streamlining new opportunities for the business.

The third case (2020) – *Reorganisation of Zhejiang Yuansheng Pharmaceutical Chain Ltd* – concerns a pharmaceutical company that was no longer able to operate and was winding down with many stores closing or closed. To respond to the increased demand in the pandemic, the court transferred the business and all the employees to a new company under the administrator's supervision. The SPC praises the smooth operation of the administrator regime and the maintenance of the business operation. It also highlights the role that the Court played in securing a new investor.

The fourth case (2020) – *Reorganisation of Anshun City Shuzheng Market Development Ltd* – concerns a company that runs a major fruit and vegetable wholesale market, but which became heavily indebted and was mismanaged. The debtor was allowed to remain in possession and continue to operate its business under the supervision of the administrator and the Court. The SPC highlights the role of EBL reorganisation in internal corporate restructuring and safeguarding creditors' rights and trust. It also emphasises the necessity of ensuring the involvement and cooperation of a local government and local chamber of commerce.

The fifth case (2020) – *Reorganisation of Shandong Wanxin Tire Ltd* – concerns a company that was unable to pay its own significant debts or debts that it guaranteed. The reorganisation plan was interrupted by the coronavirus epidemic. The SPC notes that this case shows how courts (and administrators) can actively support and guide a distressed company to resume production and implement its restructuring plan during an epidemic crisis.

The sixth case (2020) – *Merger and Reorganisation of Jiangsu Soul Wine Ltd and affiliated companies* – was a joint-stock company producing alcoholic beverages and disinfectant alcohol. A merger and reorganisation were agreed, but the coronavirus epidemic disrupted the subsequent two-month supervision period by the Court. The SPC praises the Court's proactive approach, which involved regular visits to the company, communication with the management and employees, and advice about other issues.

The seventh case (2020) – *Transfer of enforcement hearings to Reorganisation of Sichuan Southwest Medical Equipment Ltd* – concerns a company with large debts and significant debt guarantees. The debtor applied to the Court to transfer debt enforcement orders into reorganisation. The Court considered the necessity and feasibility of bringing all the claims under the EBL reorganisation umbrella, the desirability of allowing the protection of moratorium (an automatic consequence of allowing reorganisation) and the likely positive impact of the resumption of production. The SPC presents the case as an illustration of how the transfer of enforcement hearings into an EBL procedure can help a company recover and restart production (rather than simply liquidate to repay its debts).

The eighth case (2020) – *Liquidation of Yinjing Medical Technology (Shanghai) Ltd* – concerns a company that was mismanaged and overindebted. The Court accepted the liquidation petition, but when the coronavirus epidemic struck, and medical equipment was suddenly in short supply, the Court guided the administrator to negotiate with creditors and arrange for the company's supply of masks to be sold and for the company to resume production. The SPC praises the agility of the court and the administrator, but also highlights the important role that the Government played in ensuring timely changes and reopening of production lines in the company.

All eight cases stress the importance of flexibility and judicial support in cases where an unexpected event (an epidemic outbreak in this case) prevents full implementation of previously approved restructuring or liquidation plan. The SPC commentary again highlights that it perceives local governments as key coordinators and helpers, particularly in complex cases.

4.4. Personal Bankruptcy Law

The EBL modernised and unified the rules for dealing with corporate bankruptcies. However, bankruptcies of natural persons – including partners in partnerships, sole traders, some guarantors of insolvent enterprises, consumers and other individual debtors – are excluded. The 1935 bankruptcy law provided for personal bankruptcies,[339] but the statute was repealed following the Communist revolution in 1949.[340] Since then, many have called for the introduction of personal bankruptcy rules[341] – or at least some form of a resolution of insolvent partners and sole traders[342] – but without success.[343] Section 11.1.6 explores the arguments in favour of having a national personal bankruptcy law and suggests that such law should be introduced in China.

The significant exclusion in the scope of the EBL sets it apart from other jurisdictions, including the UK, US and Germany, where natural persons can go bankrupt. In some countries, corporate and personal bankruptcies are dealt with under a single regime (Germany and the US: chapters seven and eleven). Other countries have a parallel regime specifically designed for natural persons (the UK and US: chapter thirteen).

Although the EBL itself does not deal with personal bankruptcies, there have been some recent developments in this context. In 2018, the President of the SPC called for the introduction of a personal bankruptcy system. Subsequently, the SPC launched a pilot programme in select regions where courts hear personal bankruptcy cases and collect data about the process and its challenges. The pilot programme is to run from 2019 to 2023. Section 12.9 provides more details about this initiative.

---

[339] Arts 2–3 of the 1935 bankruptcy law: Section 4.1.

[340] See Section 2.1.

[341] See Sections 11.1.6 and 12.9.

[342] In order to, inter alia, bring the law in compliance with the UNCITRAL Guide para 1.

[343] Limiting the scope of the law to legal persons was strongly favoured since the 1995 draft, and was maintained in the final version of the EBL: Wang (n 90) for a discussion of the drafters' reasons.

5

Limited Use of the Enterprise Bankruptcy Law 2006 and its Causes

The passage of the EBL received much attention and praise from abroad, being called 'a landmark in the legislative history of China'[1] and 'a watershed moment for Chinese capital markets'.[2] The new law addressed many problems of the 1986 law and caught up with China's economic reality.[3] Significant improvements in resolution of corporate financial distress have been achieved – especially with regards to enabling all forms of companies to access formal resolution of insolvency and introducing a workable formal restructuring that has been successfully used in an increasing number of cases.[4] Nevertheless, several problems still need to be resolved[5] because they reduce the law's efficiency and practical utility.

Since the EBL came into effect on 1 June 2007, it has been only comparatively rarely used. Section 5.1 of this chapter discusses the annual number of EBL cases between 2007 and 2018.[6] As was discussed in Chapter one, one of the main purposes of this book is to explain the reasons for the EBL's limited use in practice. New data and existing literature suggest that there are four groups of reasons, four 'constraints' on the use of the EBL. They are summarised in Section 5.2 and discussed in full in Chapters six, seven, eight and nine.

5.1. Limited Use of the Enterprise Bankruptcy Law 2006

The EBL's predecessor, the 1986 law, was initially used in several hundred, and later several thousand, cases per year – which was criticised for not being enough.[7] However, despite the expectation that the new, improved law would be used more often to resolve corporate bankruptcies,[8] the problem of low use affected the EBL as well. The need for greater use of the EBL stemmed from the fact that the number of insolvent companies

---

[1] R Tomasic, The Conceptual Structure of China's New Corporate Bankruptcy Law in R Parry, Y Xu and H Zhang (eds), *China's New Enterprise Bankruptcy Law: Context, Interpretation and Application* (Ashgate, 2010).

[2] DL Eaton, LE Norley, H Huang and KM Asimacopoulos, 'China's New Enterprise Bankruptcy Law' Kirkland & Ellis LLP (October 2006).

[3] See Section 4.1.

[4] See Z Zhang, *Corporate Reorganisations in China* (Cambridge University Press, 2018).

[5] See ch 12 for a discussion of recent local reforms.

[6] See Section 10.1 for a further analysis.

[7] S Li, 'Bankruptcy Law in China: Lessons of the Past Twelve Years' (2001) *Harvard Asia Quarterly* 1; SJ Arsenault, 'The Westernization of Chinese Bankruptcy: An Examination of China's New Corporate Bankruptcy Law through the Lens of the UNCITRAL Legislative Guide to Insolvency Law' (2008–09) *Penn State International Law Review* 45.

[8] See eg C Han (31.5.2007, People's Court News) 5.

was clearly much greater than the number of EBL cases. Moreover, the economy was expanding fast and, simultaneously, there was also a steep increase in the total number of companies – including failed start-ups and redundant older companies. Nevertheless, as Figure 5.1 shows, the number of cases actually *fell* after the EBL came into force in 2007[9] and remained low for a decade.

Figure 5.1 Concluded corporate bankruptcy cases in China (1989–2018)

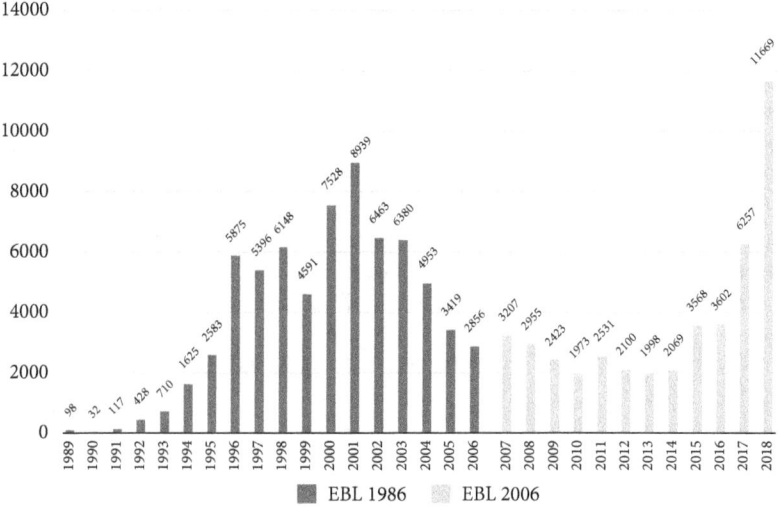

Source: SPC, NBS.

Admittedly, several thousand cases per annum is not negligible. However, as is discussed in Section 10.1, it is unlikely to represent the real need and demand for bankruptcy law in China.[10] This view is shared by some Chinese commentators, who also see the number as too low.[11]

There were, on average, between 2,000 and 3,000 EBL cases each year from 2007 until 2015. Since then, the numbers have been growing: in 2016, Chinese courts closed 5,665 EBL cases, in 2017 they closed 6,257 EBL cases, and in 2018 they closed 11,669 EBL cases.[12] This increase is to be celebrated. Nevertheless, it is still limited – both in absolute and in relative terms[13] – because the real need for the use of the EBL in China is much higher.[14] Moreover, the recent increase coincides with the Government's recent efforts to remove zombie companies from the market.[15] As such, it appears to

---

[9] See eg K Watson (30.9.2008, SCMP).

[10] In terms of ratio of bankruptcies to the number of firms, the US has the ratio of 3.65 and the UK ratio of 1.85. There is insufficient data to calculate such ratio for China (but it is likely to be very low, probably similar to the ratio of 0.22 in Russia): S Claessens and L Klapper, *Bankruptcy Around the World: Explanation of its Relative Use* (World Bank, 2002) Table 1.

[11] See eg Y Li (12.6.2017, Weixin). The SPC itself acknowledges that the EBL case number is low – see Section 12.1.

[12] SPC data.

[13] See Section 10.1.3.

[14] See Section 10.1.2.

[15] See Sections 10.1.2, 10.3, 12.1 and 12.3. These are companies that are technically insolvent and are surviving only with regular state financial injections. As such, they are an enormous drain on China's state finances. See eg G Wildau (23.6.2016, FT). See also Sections 9.4.2 and 10.1.

be (largely) politically driven use similar to that in 2001 – which recorded the highest number of cases decided under the 1986 law – when the old law was used to cleanse the system as a part of China's accession to the WTO.[16]

Following the nationwide lockdown in China in response to the coronavirus pandemic in early 2020, it is reported that some 247,000 companies have become insolvent.[17] This is likely to keep the courts busy for some time. Consequently, it is expected that the number of EBL cases will continue to grow. Nevertheless, in order to resolve all corporate bankruptcies efficiently and fairly, several issues and obstacles – as described below – must be resolved and ameliorated first. Only then will the EBL be able to ensure efficient resolution of corporate bankruptcies in all regions of China.

Moreover, although the legislators intended that the EBL should be used as a restructuring tool in the first instance[18] – a policy that has been reiterated by the SPC in subsequent years[19] – the number of reorganisation cases has been comparatively very low.[20] There were only 19 reorganisation cases in 2007, albeit the volume rose steadily to 353 cases in 2015 and 1,163 cases in 2017.[21] In percentage terms, reorganisation cases accounted for less than two per cent of the total number of cases in the first few years, going up to about 18 per cent of all EBL cases in 2016 and 2017.[22] The data is summarised in Figure 5.2.

Figure 5.2 Concluded corporate reorganisation cases in China (2007–2017)

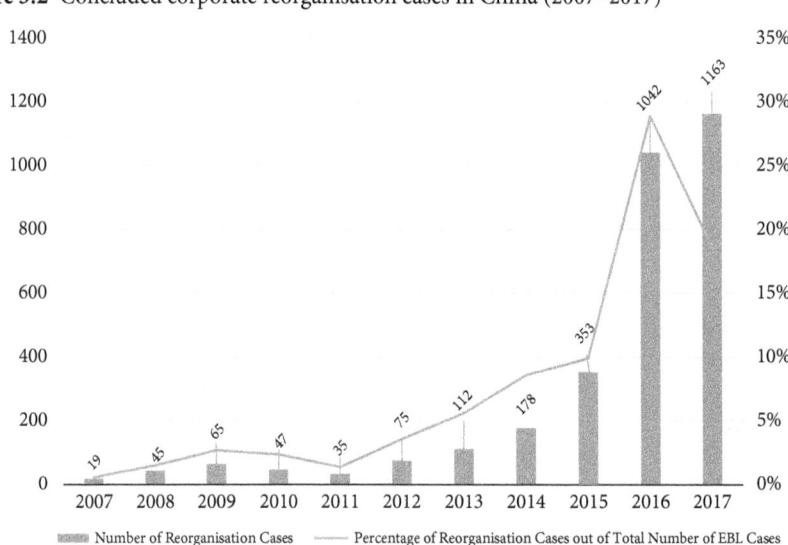

Number of Reorganisation Cases —— Percentage of Reorganisation Cases out of Total Number of EBL Cases

Source: SPC, NBS.

[16] See Sections 8.3, 9.2.3, 10.3.3, 11.3.5 and 12.12.

[17] J Feng (9.4.2020, SupChina).

[18] See Section 4.2.4. See also H Zhang, 'Corporate Rescue' in Parry, Xu and Zhang, *China's New Enterprise Bankruptcy Law* (2010).

[19] The SPC National Bankruptcy Trial Work Conference in Shenzhen in 2018: see Section 12.1.

[20] Zhang argues that this has always been the expectation of higher courts: Zhang (n 4) 17. However, compare this view with official SPC guidance to lower courts – see Chapter 12.1.

[21] Data for 2007–15 are provided in Zhang, *Corporate Reorganisations* (2018) 30; data for 2016/17 provided in the SPC Memorandum concerning the Minutes of the National Work Conference on Bankruptcy Trials (*Fa* [2018] No 53).

[22] For a discussion of the political pressure to reorganise (and to save jobs) rather than liquidate regardless of the underlying economic reality, see Section 12.6.

5.2. Reasons for the Limited Use
of the EBL – The Four 'Constraints'

China has undergone large-scale economic changes[23] which have facilitated a rapid increase in the number of companies, the level of corporate indebtedness, and increasing complexity in commercial dealings – which should, one might expect, lead to a greater number of instances of corporate bankruptcies. As Section 4.1 explained, reformed corporate bankruptcy law was introduced in 2006 to keep up with these changes. Nevertheless, the data presented in the previous section show that the number of court-run bankruptcy cases did, in fact, *decrease* after the EBL was introduced. Moreover, despite the recent increase in the number, the use of the EBL remains limited. Despite this, there is surprisingly little in-depth research into why the law has been so rarely used. This book seeks to fill this gap. The next four chapters present insights from the author's interviews and new research that may explain why eligible debtors and creditors (hereafter 'the parties') may be unwilling or unable to use the EBL.

The identified issues have been grouped into four broad categories of constraints on more effective and efficient operation of the EBL. It is proposed in this book that these four constraints help explain why the law has not been used more.[24] The first constraint focuses on the EBL as written and the parties' perception that the law insufficiently protects their interests. The second constraint concerns the surrounding rules and practices – flaws in debt enforcement and problems relating to certain types of lending – that reduce or prevent recoveries under the EBL. The third constraint arises from the limitations and biases of EBL enforcers – lawyers, administrators, courts and local governments – which prevent effective operation of the EBL, and so further reduce recoveries under the law. The fourth and final constraint on the use of the EBL which reinforces debtors' and creditors' unwillingness to use the EBL is that the parties (often inaccurately) perceive non-EBL debt enforcement alternatives as comparatively more effective or attractive than the EBL, and so use them instead. The four constraints are discussed in detail in Chapters six to nine. The reform options proposed in Part III – especially Chapters eleven and twelve – then build on these constraints and the issues they uncover.

Before delving into the discussion, two caveats should be noted. First, China is a large country with uneven levels of development and many social, political, economic and cultural differences across provinces and between the north and the south, coastal and inner regions, cities and the countryside. Much effort and resources have gone into minimising these differences and trying to improve the bankruptcy system and business environment more generally, especially since early 2016.[25] Nevertheless, the application, understanding and willingness to use the EBL continue to vary across different regions and groups. As a result, it is extremely difficult to capture every little variation and divergence in this book. Every effort has been made to avoid over-generalisations and to

[23] See Section 2.1.
[24] This book uses economic analysis of law to understand creditors' and debtors' incentives regarding the use of the EBL: see Section 1.1.
[25] See ch 12.

discuss important differences. The book also tries to draw on a variety of sources in order to reflect the variations in the real-life application of the EBL in China. However, the book does not aim to provide an encyclopaedic account of every detail of the EBL practice. Instead, the next four chapters offer an account of the practical difficulties and challenges that have been encountered by debtors, creditors, their advisors, courts, administrators and local governments when dealing with corporate bankruptcies in practice.

Second, the data collected and presented in the following chapters span over a decade of EBL practice. Some issues have been ameliorated over time, others remain unchanged or have deteriorated. Some are more acute in certain provinces, others ebb and flow depending on the current socio-economic and political climate. Together they represent a broad range of issues that have prevented the users of the law – ie debtors and creditors – from choosing to use the EBL. Nevertheless, anyone studying or applying the law needs to be aware that these issues have prevented efficient implementation of the EBL.

6

The First Constraint – Creditors and Debtors Feel Insufficiently Protected under the EBL

The EBL as written and applied in practice contains several provisions which may discourage creditors and debtors from using the law to resolve their financial distress and recover their debts. The interviewed experts highlighted three of them as particularly important. Section 6.1 below examines the argument that the courts' EBL-derived duties to protect employees affect creditors' willingness to use the EBL. Section 6.2 discusses the argument that several EBL provisions increase the likelihood of scrutiny and imposition of liability on a debtor and its management upon initiation of an EBL procedure[1] and so discourage debtor companies from filing to use the EBL in the first place. Finally, Section 6.3 considers the argument that the unclear drafting of the entry requirements and consequent de facto requirement of insolvency as a precondition to using the EBL disincentivises the parties from using reorganisation. Table 6.1 summarises the impact of each of these issues on the relevant stakeholders.

Table 6.1 Overview of the impact of the problematic EBL provisions

	Secured creditors	Unsecured creditors	Debtors	Employees
Courts' duties to protect employees (Section 6.1)	–	–	–	+
Heightened threat of scrutiny and liability (Section 6.2)			–	
Insolvency as de facto entry requirement in reorganisation (Section 6.3)	–	–	–	–

– denotes harmful effect, + denotes beneficial effect

---

[1] Or once the news of their financial distress becomes publicly known through their initiation of a bankruptcy procedure.

6.1. Implications of Courts' Duties to Protect Employees

The question of how to deal with employees in corporate bankruptcies had caused a lot of difficulties and disagreements when the EBL was being drafted.[2] When the policy ensuring absolute protection of SOEs was formally removed in 2000, there was a protracted discussion whether employees should be afforded any special protections under the EBL, and what should be the status of their claims vis-à-vis other stakeholders. In the end, the EBL was enacted with several provisions that aim to protect debtor's employees. Four such provisions are discussed here. Section 6.1.1 below examines the requirement that debtors' EBL applications must contain a plan for employee resettlement which likely disincentivises debtors from using the law. Section 6.1.2 considers the conflicting guidelines in the EBL as to whether courts should prioritise secured creditors' or employees' interests and the clear preference for the latter in practice which disincentivises secured creditors from using the EBL to seek recovery of their money. Section 6.1.3 discusses the position of unsecured creditors and their near certainty of limited or no recovery pursuant to EBL rules, which also reduces the parties' incentive to use the EBL. Finally, Section 6.1.4 explores courts' power and practice of cramming down dissenting voting classes in reorganisation to protect employees' interests.

6.1.1. Plan for Employee Resettlement

According to Article 8 of the EBL, debtor's EBL petition – whether for liquidation or reorganisation – must contain an employee resettlement plan. The EBL provides no further details, and the SPC guidance only adds that, when reorganising listed companies, the resettlement plan must be 'practical and feasible'.[3] The interviewed Chinese judges and practitioners suggested that, in practice, courts tend to interpret the requirement strictly, as a pre-condition to hearing EBL cases. They all agreed that it was a burdensome requirement, and several of the lawyers said that they knew of insolvent companies which could not produce such a plan and so were not able to use the EBL.[4] Half of the interviewed judges and several consultants suggested that requiring the resettlement plan hinders the use of the EBL.[5]

The reasons for such strict interpretation are unclear. Nevertheless, requiring that a debtor submits a plan for employee resettlement in order to gain access to the EBL procedures shows how highly politicised the EBL is.[6] Some interviewees saw the requirement as a necessary 'balancing tool' to ensure that corporate bankruptcies have minimal impact on employees' social welfare.[7] The underlying problem is that China still does

---

[2] See Section 4.2.10.

[3] Art 3 of the SPC Memorandum on Handing of Listed Companies' Reorganisations and Liquidations (*Fa* [2012] No 261).

[4] Interviews L1-r, L2-s, L7-c, L8-c, L10-s, L11-c, L14-c, L15-c.

[5] Interviews J1-c, J2-c, J8-c, J9-c, C5-r, C6-c, C7-s.

[6] For more on this point, see Sections 8.3, 9.2 and 11.1.4.1.

[7] Interviews J3-c, J9-c, L14-c.

not have a functioning social security system, and the EBL is used to fill this gap.[8] In doing so, courts not only adjudicate the case in front of them but also implement wider socio-economic policies of their immediate superior – local governments[9] – who are particularly concerned about maintaining social stability. Since large-scale redundancies have, in the past, caused significant social upheaval, the EBL is used in such a way which would minimise social unrest.[10] Unsurprisingly, therefore, local government influence was identified in all my interviews as an important reason for the strict interpretation of the requirement to submit an employee resettlement plan.

Regardless of the reasons why the courts impose this strict requirement, all the interviewed enterprise representatives, consultants and lawyers agreed that financially distressed debtor companies are likely to be disincentivised by this requirement because its fulfilment costs them resources and slows them down at the time when 'time is of essence if we want to restructure or effectively liquidate a struggling business'.[11] At the same time, it also strengthens the argument that a successful application of the EBL requires the support of local governments who can help a debtor fulfil this requirement by coordinating with other companies in their region and extracting concessions and resettlement agreements which would be inaccessible to the debtor alone.[12]

6.1.2. Courts' Conflicting Duties: Secured Creditors and Public Policy

Secured creditors have two main options for recovering their debts – individual security enforcement[13] and collective debt enforcement under the EBL. They usually prefer using individual, small-scale security enforcement pursuant to which they can recover their money directly and relatively cheaply and quickly.[14] However, where they fail to complete the enforcement of their security before an EBL petition is accepted by a court, their enforcement is stayed under an interim moratorium until the court appoints an administrator.[15] In reorganisation, secured creditors are then further stayed from freely realising their claims under a main moratorium.[16] The EBL states that in liquidation, the moratorium should be lifted and secured creditors should be allowed to enforce their claim. However, my interviewees suggest that secured creditors are often prevented from enforcing their claims freely in liquidation.[17] The discussion below examines

---

[8] Interviews C2-c, C3-c, C5-r, C7-s, C8-s, J1-c, J3-c, J5-s, J6-s, J8-c, L1-r, L3-r, L4-r, L7-c, L9-s, L11-c, L13-c, L14-c, L15-c, P1-r, P3-r, R1-r, R3-r, R4-c, R10-c.

[9] See Sections 2.4 and 8.3 for details about this relationship.

[10] ibid.

[11] L6-s. The sentiment was echoed in most interviews.

[12] This argument was made by a number of judges and advisors in support of courts' following local government guidance: see Section 8.3.3. It is, however, problematic: see Sections 11.3.4–11.3.5 and 12.12.

[13] See Section 3.3.3.

[14] cf delays and costs of EBL cases: Section 8.1.2.

[15] See Section 4.2.3.

[16] See Section 4.2.4. A court may grant a special exemption in limited circumstances: Art 75 EBL.

[17] Interviews B1-c, B2-c, B3-c, C2-c, C5-r, C7-s, E1-c, E5-s, J1-c, J5-s, L1-r, L2-s, L5-c, L13-c, R2-r, R3-r, R9-c.

general provisions and reorganisation-specific provisions that guide courts' dealings with secured creditors. Together, these rules give rise to uncertainty, delays and decrease the likelihood of recovery, and so contribute to secured creditors' preference for avoiding the EBL. Given the difficulties in recovering their loans, lenders in China are often reluctant to lend – or lend with higher interest rates, if possible.[18]

My interviewees who had dealt with secured debt in bankruptcy suggested that where secured creditors are forced to recover their debts under a collective EBL procedure, their rights were more often than not compromised in favour of employees' claims.[19] The capture of the judiciary by the Party-state's political interests plays a role,[20] but some courts are also influenced by the conflicting guidance in the EBL which enables courts to read in and prioritise employees' interests – despite the EBL also affording priority to secured creditors. On the face of it, the EBL protects and gives priority to secured creditors.[21] Article 109 of the EBL states that 'secured creditors are entitled to obtain payment in priority over debtor's specific asset', that is regardless and ahead of claims from any other party. However, the reality is sometimes different. Ancillary provisions which enable consideration of other non-market interests are scattered throughout the EBL. These provisions – discussed below – do not explicitly direct courts to prefer socio-economic interests, but they have, nevertheless, given the courts a scope to circumvent otherwise clear priority of secured creditors.[22] The reasons *why* the courts exploit these conflicts in the EBL provisions to the advantage of employees and socio-economic interests are explored later.[23] First, however, it is important to look at the provisions themselves.

Article 1 of the EBL states that, besides protecting 'the legitimate rights and interests of creditors and debtors', the law is intended to 'maintain the order of the socialist market economy'.[24] Article 6 of the EBL then orders courts to 'safeguard the legitimate rights and interests of the employees of the insolvent enterprise'.[25] Note that these general provisions expressly enable only protection, not a prioritisation of the socialist market and the employees. Nevertheless, many of my interviewees suggested that they have been interpreted as enabling the courts to provide preferential treatment to employees in all EBL procedures.[26]

These protections are further reinforced by additional powers given to employees in the EBL. One example is a debtor's duty to submit an employee resettlement plan, discussed above. Another example is the supervisory power given to employee and labour union representative(s) who can attend creditors' meetings and voice any concerns with a proposed liquidation or reorganisation plan.[27] If a creditors' committee is

---

[18] See Sections 1.2 and 10.2.4.

[19] Interviews B1-c, B2-c, B3-c,C4-c, C5-r, C6-c, IF1-c, IF2-c, J1-c, J3-c, J5-s, J6-s, J8-c, L1-r, L2-s, L4-r, L6-s, L7-c, L9-c, L10-s, L11-c, L14-c, L15-c, P1-r.

[20] Discussed in Sections 2.4 and 8.3.

[21] See Section 4.2.11.

[22] Interviews B1-c to B3-c, C7-s, IF1-c, IF2-c, J1-c, J3-c to J6-s, J8-c, L1-r, L2-s, L4-r, L6-s, L7-c, L9-c, L10-s, L11-c, L14-c, L15-c, P1-r.

[23] See Section 8.3.1.

[24] See Section 4.2.1.

[25] Note that Art 6 EBL does not impose an equivalent direct duty to consider creditors' rights.

[26] Interviews C2-c, C5-r, C7-s, C9-c, J1-c, J3-c, J7-c, J8-c, J9-c, L1-r, L2-s, L4-r, L5-c, L8-c, L9-c, L12-c, L13-c.

[27] Art 59 EBL.

established, the representative must be one of its nine constituent members.[28] Moreover, the court can cram down dissenting voting classes (eg secured creditors) for any reason – which, in practice, can include protection of employee interests.[29]

The practical application of these EBL provisions resembles the approach taken under the 1986 law. On paper, secured creditors were to enjoy absolute priority,[30] but in practice, these were overridden by policy decrees which prioritised employees' interests and resettlement protection.[31] This was seen as problematic, and the reform committee empathically stressed in many drafts and reports that reliable protection of secured creditors' rights is a crucial element of modern bankruptcy law.[32] Nevertheless, my research suggests that, in some cases, courts have continued to treat secured creditors according to political interests rather than the clearly set-out priority in the EBL.

Probably most controversial, however, are the provisions regulating EBL reorganisation. As discussed earlier, secured creditors cannot enforce their claims under a separate enforcement procedure once a court accepts the reorganisation petition, and a main moratorium is automatically triggered which stays individual debt enforcement.[33] Secured creditors and employees[34] each form one of several classes for the purpose of voting on a reorganisation plan.[35] If a voting class fails to approve the plan, it can be crammed down by the court.[36] Article 87(1) of the EBL provides that secured creditors' rejection is fatal to the plan, as secured claims must be repaid in full. Nevertheless, some of my interviewees suggested that this is not always respected[37] and data shows that secured creditors were crammed down in about 10 per cent of all reorganisations between 2007 and 2015.[38] As a result, despite the absolute priority of secured creditors in Article 109 of the EBL, secured claims are often subordinated to employees' claims based on EBL's broad ancillary provisions.

The result of interpreting the conflicting duties in the EBL in favour of employees and against secured creditors is that the latter often lose the very priority which customarily defines their position and are instead treated as de facto unsecured creditors. For example, a paper published by the Maoming Intermediate People's Court examined 61 liquidations carried out under the 1986 law and the EBL between 2000 and 2008. It found that employees' claims were paid out first and generally in full.[39] The question of priority is particularly important for institutional finance providers – banks – who then refuse to lend without additional guarantees, and often end up lending only to state-sector companies which receive an implied guarantee from the state.

---

[28] Art 67 EBL.
[29] See Section 6.1.4.
[30] Arts 32 and 37 of the 1986 law.
[31] C Booth, 'The 2006 PRC Enterprise Bankruptcy Law: the wait is finally over' (2008) *Singapore Academic of Law Journal* 275, 307–08.
[32] ibid. See also Section 4.1.
[33] See Sections 4.2.3–4.2.4.
[34] This is defined broadly – see Section 4.2.11.
[35] ibid.
[36] See Sections 4.2.4 and 6.1.4.
[37] Interviews B1-c, B2-c, C1-c, C4-c, C6-c, IF1-s, IF2-c, J1-c, J6-s, L2-s, L6-s, L14-c, L15-c.
[38] See Section 6.1.4.
[39] 'A Study on Corporate Liquidations in Maoming Court' in X Wang and Z Yi (eds), *The Chinese Bankruptcy Summit* (Law Press, 2010) 527.

6.1.3. Priority of Repayment: Unsecured Creditors versus Employees

Ostensibly, the pool of assets for satisfying unsecured creditors' claims appears to be relatively larger in China than elsewhere due to the aforementioned general tendency to ignore security rights[40] and because many (private) companies rely largely or exclusively on unsecured credit.[41] However, the finance providers and consultants that I interviewed suggested that unsecured creditors commonly recover very little or nothing at all under the EBL.[42] This conclusion is supported by several local court reports. Shandong Provincial Supreme People's Court published a study of 1,899 EBL cases from 2007 to 2015 and concluded that, on average, unsecured creditors recover virtually no money.[43] Similarly, the Zaozhuang Xuechen County People's Court studied 102 corporate liquidations between 1995 and 2016 – ie under both the 1986 law and the EBL – and concluded that average recovery by unsecured creditors was 1.03 per cent (and zero per cent in 93 of the 102 studied cases).[44]

In contrast, some studies suggest that unsecured creditors do recover a sizeable part of their debt under the EBL. A study of 99 EBL cases by the Xuecheng Court in Shandong Province found that, on average, unsecured creditors recovered 14.01 per cent in liquidations, 30.02 per cent in reorganisations and 24.25 per cent in compositions.[45] However, 44 of the studied cases were listed companies, which makes the data unrepresentative since listed companies – large and important – receive a lot of additional support and attention under the EBL.[46] In a recent study, Zhang analysed data of a quarter of all reorganisations in China between 2007 and 2015 and found that unsecured creditors, on average, recovered 28.74 per cent of their claims (and 100 per cent in 12 cases).[47] Unfortunately, the three-quarters of reorganisation cases where data was not available would likely decrease the average recovery rates, and so Zhang's findings have to be treated with caution as well. Similarly, the recovery rates in reorganisation cases include debt-for-equity swaps and other techniques, which are often heavily opposed by unsecured creditors, but which are, nevertheless, enforced and count as 'full recovery'.[48]

The EBL puts unsecured creditors' claims at the bottom of the repayment order, similar to the position in many other jurisdictions.[49] However, what is different compared to other jurisdictions is that, firstly, employees are entitled to recover all their claims first,[50]

---

[40] See Section 6.1.2.

[41] Access to secured (mostly state-bank) credit is often limited to SOEs and few economically important private companies: see Sections 3.1–3.2.

[42] Interviews B1-c to B3-c, C1-c to C11-c, IF1-s and IF2-c.

[43] Shandong Provincial People's Court, 'A Study Dealing with Zombie Companies in Shandong' (2016) *People's Judicature* 10.

[44] Zaozhuang Xuecheng Court, Unsecured Creditor Protection in Corporate Liquidations (30.11.2016).

[45] China Bond Rating Co Ltd and Y Hum (9.4.2014, Finance.ce.cn).

[46] See eg ch 4.2.4; H Zhao, *Government Intervention in the Reorganisation of Listed Companies in China* (Cambridge University Press, 2020).

[47] Z Zhang, *Corporate Reorganisations in China* (Cambridge University Press, 2018) 144–45.

[48] See Section 6.1.4.

[49] See Section 4.2.11.

[50] This is similar to the French system.

and secondly, employees' claims are particularly large and with no cap on how much they can recover.

Employees' claims under the EBL include past and a portion of future wages. Dismissed employees are entitled to severance pay in the form of a month's wage for each year worked for the employer.[51] Moreover, employees' claims are defined broadly. Apart from employees' wages they also include, importantly, basic pension entitlements and medical insurance premium defaulted by the debtor, and other compensations payable by the debtor to the employees in accordance with other applicable laws and rules.[52] Social insurance payments are also included and recoverable ahead of unsecured debts.[53] As a result, unsecured creditors in most cases face no or only limited recovery.[54]

Such generous pro-employee policy operates as a substitute for China's incomplete social security system. It also assists local governments in keeping employees content in order to maintain public order.[55] Nevertheless, many of my interviewees expressed a view that, in the long term, unlimited employee protectionism is very harmful to the economy as creditors are unlikely to use the EBL in a timely manner – which may lead to inefficient resolution and value-destruction.[56] Moreover, unsecured creditors are incentivised not to submit to a collective debt recovery under the EBL and instead try to recover their money through private enforcement alternatives,[57] which they perceive as offering a greater chance of at least part-satisfaction of their debt and, therefore, better payoffs than the EBL.[58]

6.1.4. Political Use of Cramdown Powers in Reorganisation to Protect Employee Interests

Chinese courts have a power to cram down dissenting voting classes in reorganisation.[59] This is not unique to China and, in fact, its introduction was inspired by the US Chapter 11. However, the proper scope and use of such power are not well defined. Article 87 of the EBL says that where a reorganisation plan fails to be adopted by any voting class, the debtor or administrator can renegotiate and the dissenting class can

---

[51] Labour Contract Law 2008. In SOEs, where many people work most of their lives, the sum of such compensation packages can be significant.

[52] 'Other compensations' include employer's compulsory contributions to the insurance, to a pension fund and to a housing fund – up to 50% of each employee's salary (with some regional variations): Art 1-56 of the Social Insurance Law 2011. See also A Livermore (21.2.2012, China Briefing).

[53] See Section 4.2.11.

[54] Interview IF1-s. Especially if the reorganisation is run without local government support: interviews B1-c, C2-c, C3-c, C5-r, E3-s, IF1-s, IF2-c, L2-s, L7-c, L11-c, L17-c, R9-c. For data, see Zhang, *Corporate Reorganisations* (2018) 144–45 and local court studies cited earlier.

[55] See Sections 2.4 and 8.3.

[56] Interviews E1-c to E5-c, IF1-s, IF2-c, C2-c, C4-c, C7-s, L2-s, L4-r, L5-c, L6-s, L11-c, L15-c For the importance of timely resolution, see Section 11.1.4.1.

[57] Discussed in Section 9.1.

[58] Interviews B1-c, B2-c, C1-c, C3-c, C5-r, C7-s, E2-s, E3-s, IF1-s, IF2-c, L2-s, L9-s, R9-c, R10-c. See Section 10.2.1 on why this is limiting and inefficient.

[59] See Section 4.2.4.

vote again. If the dissenting class refuses to vote or again rejects the draft reorganisation plan, the debtor or the administrator can ask the court to cram down the dissenting class(es) and forcibly approve the plan.

The use of cramdown is a controversial topic in China. Scholars, practitioners and the media worry about the courts abusing this extensive power, which has been invoked in 25.68 per cent of reorganisation cases between 2007 and 2015.[60] In response, the SPC has urged lower courts to only use the cramdown powers with caution and only in exceptional circumstances.[61]

A particularly problematic issue that has arisen in practice is whether a court can cram down *all* voting classes, in other words, whether a court can forcibly approve a reorganisation plan under Article 87 of the EBL where that plan has been rejected by all voting classes.[62] There is strong support for a literal reading of the cramdown provision among Chinese scholars[63] and practitioners,[64] who say that the answer must be in the negative.[65]

Nevertheless, the issue was discussed, and a requirement that at least one voting class should support a reorganisation plan was dropped by the NPC when the EBL was being drafted.[66] Furthermore, several senior Chinese scholars suggest that a court is justified in forcibly approving a reorganisation plan that has been rejected by all voting classes because the purpose of reorganisation is the protection of public good, most importantly ensuring social stability, protecting employment and saving businesses.[67] Some also argue that, in a socialist market economy, any conflict between a (private) creditor's interest and public interests should be resolved in favour of the public.[68] Admittedly, cramdown of all voting classes is rare.[69] Nevertheless, its existence and support suggest that many view the EBL – and particularly the reorganisation procedure – as a political tool for supporting China's socialist market economy[70] and its aims – including the

---

[60] Zhang (n 47) 200–20.

[61] Art 7 of the SPC Notice concerning the Correct Hearing of EBL Cases and Judicial Guarantee to Maintain Orderly Socialist Market Economy (*Fafa* [2009] No 36). See also Art 18 of the SPC Notice concerning the Minutes of the National Court Work Conference on Bankruptcy Trials (*Fa* [2018] No 53).

[62] This would be the case where the court – or someone who controls the court – makes a restructuring plan with an aim that does not directly and personally benefit any one of the classes. For example, a plan that prioritises employees at the expense of all other voting groups.

[63] See eg D Yan, 'Government Intervention in China's Listed Company Reorganisations' (2016) *Legal Forum* 122; X Wang, 'Theories and Practice of the Corporate Reorganisation Regime' (2012) *Journal of Law Application* 10; X Xin, 'Cramdown Approvals in China's Corporate Reorganisation Law' (2011) *Journal of Law Application* 57.

[64] See C Yu, 'Protecting Bank Creditors in Corporate Reorganisation Cramdown Approvals' (2017) *China Urban Finance* 52; C Mai (10.10.2016, China Stock Times).

[65] This was recently endorsed by the SPC in Art 18 of the SPC Memorandum concerning the Minutes of the National Work Conference on Bankruptcy Trials (*Fa* [2018] No 53).

[66] W Tang, 'Several Problems of the Proposed Bill of Enterprise Bankruptcy Law on Reorganisation' (2005) 2 *Jurists* 33.

[67] W Wang, 'The New Enterprise Bankruptcy Law: a Contemporary and Advanced Legislation' (2006) *The People's Congress of China* 17.

[68] H Zou, 'An Analysis of China's Corporate Rehabilitation Regimes' (2007) *Journal of China University of Political Science and Law* 48.

[69] There have been at least two reorganisation cases in China where the court crammed down all the voting classes and forcibly approved the rejected reorganisation plan, in Guangxia Limited in 2011 and Qufu Jinghuang Piston Limited in 2015: Zhang (n 47) 202.

[70] See Section 2.1.

protection of employment – rather than as a market tool that maintains efficiency and order in the market.[71] Sophisticated creditors complain about this as it weakens their ability to make *ex ante* decisions about their *ex post* risks and so are unable to price finance accurately.

Less objectionable but still problematic are cases where at least one voting class approves the reorganisation plan, but the others are crammed down. In general, the real winner of cramdowns tends to be the employees of the debtor company (and, after them, the tax creditors) who get paid in full – often at the expense of creditors who are forced to take less in full satisfaction of their debt.[72]

Data shows that, between 2007 and 2015, secured creditors were crammed down in 40.82 per cent of cases that involved a cramdown.[73] That is despite the fact that Article 87(2)(1) of the EBL expressly states that the cramdown power can only be used if secured creditors' rights are not infringed. A closer inspection of reorganisation cases reveals that secured creditors usually reject reorganisation plans because they worry about delays, being underpaid or being forced to accept worthless debt-for-equity swaps.[74]

In the same period, unsecured creditors were crammed down in 44.90 per cent of the cramdown cases. They were primarily concerned about low recovery rates under the proposed reorganisation plans, and so they used their power to vote as a tool in negotiations.[75]

Many of my interviewees suggested that both secured and unsecured creditors are aware of the courts' power to cram them down – especially where this would ensure the protection of employees' claims – and fear that their rights could be unilaterally altered or outright suppressed in an EBL reorganisation.[76] This makes them perceive EBL reorganisation as insufficiently protecting their interests and look for other options to recover their debts.[77]

6.2. Heightened Threat of Scrutiny and Liability under the EBL

A second major objection to the EBL raised by the interviewees is that debtor companies' personnel[78] often feel that using the EBL increases the likelihood of being investigated and facing liability arising from the company's bankruptcy. Such liability arises directly from the EBL provisions, explored in Section 6.2.1 below, and indirectly from non-bankruptcy laws and practices, which are triggered, inter alia, when a company uses the

---

[71] See eg R Goode, *Principles of Corporate Insolvency Law*, 4th edn (Sweet & Maxwell, 2011).
[72] This protection is anchored in Art 87(2) which states that the cramdown power can only be used where the employee and tax creditors voted in favour of the plan or are fully paid under the plan.
[73] The rest involved mostly shareholders: Zhang (n 47) 203–06.
[74] ibid.
[75] ibid. 207–08.
[76] Interviews B1-c to B3-c, C3-c to C5-r, C7-s, C10-s, E1-c to E5-c, L1-r to L17-c, R2-r, R3-r, R6-c, R7-c.
[77] Contrary to Art 1 EBL. cf ch 4.2.1.
[78] ie directors and supervisors, but 'relevant personnel' is defined broadly in Art 15(6) EBL as including – if a court so decides – 'financial and accounting personnel as well as other managerial personnel'.

EBL, discussed in Section 6.2.2. Due to the scarcity of literature that deals with liability under both the EBL and such other laws, on paper as well as in practice, this section first provides a short description of the rules governing each type of liability before delving into the discussion of how they affect a debtor's decision (not) to use the EBL.

Many liability provisions in China are vaguely defined, which – as many of my interviewees highlighted – creates much *ex ante* uncertainty in practice.[79] This is further exacerbated by the way that they are applied in practice. The interviewed practitioners argued that the vague EBL provisions are often interpreted by courts and governmental bodies in a manner which imposes liability regardless of any actual wrongdoing or proven fault[80] of those being punished.[81] It is hardly surprising that debtor companies' personnel are reluctant to use the EBL given that such extensive and, in many ways, unpredictable liability is triggered by the debtor company's EBL petition – particularly where, without such trigger, the provisions would probably never be invoked even where the company or its personnel were, in fact, guilty of wrongdoing.[82]

6.2.1. Liability Arising Directly from the EBL

One of the novel elements in the EBL is that Article 6(2) creates a general duty for courts to investigate the bankrupt company's personnel for their 'legal liabilities'. Articles 125 to 131 of the EBL then explain the circumstances under which courts can impose criminal, personal or professional liability, and when they can impose career-affecting sanctions. Several examples are discussed below.[83]

6.2.1.1. Criminal Liability

Firstly, Article 131 of the EBL states that where a violation of any provision contained in the EBL constitutes a criminal offence, courts must investigate potential criminal liability of the debtor company's personnel.[84] Detailed provisions are found in the criminal law.[85] Many of the relevant provisions can be invoked outside the EBL. However, all my interviewees agreed that, in practice, the likelihood of criminal investigation is significantly increased if a company uses the EBL.

---

[79] Interviews with all consultants (C1-c to C10-s), all entrepreneurs (E1-c to E5-c), IF1-s, IF2-c, L1-r, L2-s, L5-c, L6-s, R3-r, R6-c, R7-c, R9-c.

[80] As is widely accepted, financial distress may result from bad management, but also changes in trends and consumer demand, new technology, etc: R Cooter and H Shäfer, *Solomon's Knot* (Princeton University Press, 2011) ch 10.

[81] Interviews C1-c, C2-c, C5-r, C7-s, C10-s, all lawyers, R1-r, R2-r, R3-r, R9-c.

[82] ibid.

[83] Two interviewees (L4-r, L6-s) argued that courts in different provinces and regions impose the sanctions with varying degrees of severity.

[84] There are slight variations, but this most often includes directors, supervisors and managers.

[85] China's Criminal Law was introduced in 1979 and has been amended nine times. The key changes took place in 2010 (limitations on the use of the death penalty, stricter rules on imprisonment, criminalisation of refusal to pay employee remuneration), in 2009 (tax-related crimes added, Ponzi schemes and some shadow lending market activities criminalised), and in 2006 (provision of false information criminalised, concealment of property and fabrication of debts to avoid having to repay criminalised, detailed account of directors' duties and criminalisation of their breach, deception in obtaining loans criminalised).

There is a wide range of circumstances where courts impose criminal liability – mostly leading to fines and imprisonment.[86] This section explores three examples, which my interviewees identified as particularly significant. Firstly, personnel of bankrupt companies can be liable for white-collar crimes, which range from interference with company accounts[87] to 'seriously injuring' the company's creditors and stakeholders.[88] 'Injury' is then defined as including taking the property of 'comparatively large value' which properly belongs to the company, and keeping it for one's benefit.[89] However, there is no definition of what 'serious' injury means, which affords broad discretion to courts.[90] If the property thus taken is 'public property', and is taken by a state official or a person authorised by state organs or SOEs, the maximum punishment is a death sentence and confiscation of the wrongdoer's property.[91]

Secondly, endangering collection of taxes is also considered a crime in China.[92] Several interviewees suggested that this is particularly relevant in the EBL context where debtors and outside providers are often guilty of common business practice of making[93] or forging and selling[94] invoices with the purpose of gaining a tax advantage.[95] If these invoices cause 'seriously heavy losses to the state interests', the guilty parties face life imprisonment or a death penalty and confiscation of property.[96] My interviewees all agreed that, regardless of whether tax evasion is an express aim or an unintended consequence, opening company's books to an outsider (courts, administrators, creditors) by filing an EBL petition exposes the company to a much greater likelihood of liability.[97] It is, therefore, contrary to the interests of debtor companies' personnel to voluntarily use the EBL since it may expose existing, but previously undiscovered criminal transgressions and expose them to potentially significant liability.

Finally, SOEs' personnel may also face criminal liability for 'causing [an SOE's] insolvency or serious financial distress'[98] and for 'causing great financial loss to [an SOE]'.[99] The provided illustrative list of relevant examples contains several situations that give

---

[86] These are discretionary, and go up to 10 years in prison and 500,000 RMB. The sanctions occasionally exceed this level – see particular examples below.

[87] The common business practice of dual-accounting and a provision of false, adjusted accounts to a court under the EBL may also lead to liability for 'obstruction of justice' – in particular under Arts 305 and 306 of the Criminal Law, which deal with destroying or fabricating evidence and making false statements under oath. See also Sections 3.4.1 and 7.1.1.

[88] Art 162 EBL.

[89] Art 271 Criminal Law 2015.

[90] Falsely declaring bankruptcy to avoid having to repay one's debts where the company has enough assets to do so also counts as 'serious' injury: Art 162(2) EBL. Several interviewees (J1-c to J9-c, L2-s, L4-r, L6-s, L14-c, L16-c) suggested that courts are particularly proactive in protecting employees' interests and only step in to protect creditors' rights in extreme cases.

[91] The particulars depend on the value of the misappropriated assets: Art 383(1)–(4) Criminal Law 2015.

[92] Failing to repay or underpaying and hiding property to avoid paying taxes: Arts 201 and 203 Criminal Law 2015.

[93] Art 205 Criminal Law 2015.

[94] Art 206 Criminal Law 2015.

[95] Interviews L1-r, L2-s, L4-r, L6-s, L9-s, L10-s, L11-c, L12-c, L160c, J6-s, C2-c, C5-r.

[96] Art 205(2) Criminal Law 2015.

[97] Interviews E1-c to E5-c, C1-c, C2-c, C5-r, C7-s.

[98] Art 168 Criminal Law.

[99] Art 169 Criminal Law.

courts further discretion and create uncertainty.[100] For example, imposing criminal sanctions where the SOE's personnel loan their company's assets to persons or companies who are 'clearly unable to repay'[101] is problematic due to the state of company accounts in China and the low quality and amount of information about companies.[102] Similarly, providing a repayment guarantee for a person or a company where SOE's personnel have 'no reasonable grounds for giving the guarantee' is also a crime.[103] However, many interviewees stressed that providing repayment guarantees for other SOEs or connected private companies is fairly common in China, and it often takes place at the request of a local government.[104] The lack of a definition and guidance about the meaning of 'reasonable grounds' for giving a guarantee creates further uncertainty and gives courts scope to punish those SOEs whose personnel acted without local government support since governmental approval seems to be regarded as fulfilling the reasonableness requirement.[105] As a result, debtor SOEs are unlikely to use the EBL procedures unless they receive express permission from a local government because they fear that 'the web of rules and liabilities which would trip them up if [the SOE personnel] act independently'.[106]

Such vague language enables courts to impose criminal liability even for activities that are commonplace and relatively unobjectionable[107] so long as they coincide with a company's financial distress. Courts do not always require strict causation.[108] Instead, several interviewees proposed that courts often presume director and supervisor guilt[109] because – unlike in the West – directors in China are actively involved in their company's daily activities and so are deemed to have participated or at least supervised (and so explicitly or implicitly sanctioned) their company's criminal activities.[110] The resulting threat of multifaceted, unpredictable criminal liability is, therefore, sufficiently serious that – even if a financially distressed company could be saved under EBL reorganisation – many debtors in China find the prospect of using the EBL highly undesirable.[111]

---

[100] Interviews C5-r, C7-s, L1-r, L2-s, L4-r, L5-c, L6-s, L9-s, L11-c, L13-c, L14-c.

[101] Art 169(3) Criminal Law 2015.

[102] See Sections 3.4.1 and 7.1.1.

[103] Art 169(4) Criminal Law 2015.

[104] Interviews E1-c to E5-c, L1-c to L6-s, L12-c, L14-c, P1-r, R1-r, R3-r, R6-c.

[105] ibid.

[106] Interview L4-r, similar views in C2-c, C3-c, C7-s, E2-s, J1-c, J5-s, J9-c, L1-r, L2-s, L4-r, L5-c, L6-s, L8-c, L12-c.

[107] eg providing guarantees, inter-company loans, etc: Interviews C2-c, C5-r, C8-s, L1-r, L2-s, L4-r, L6-s, L8-c, L9-s, L14-c, L15-c, R1-r, R4-c, R6-c, R9-c.

[108] Interviews J1-c, J4-c, L2-s, L4-r, L6-s, L7-c, L8-c, L14-c, L15-c, R1-r, R4-c, R6-c, R9-c. For details see Section 7.3.

[109] Interviews C2-c, C5-r, C10-s, E2-s, E3-s, J1-c, J4-c, L2-s, L4-r, L6-s, L7-c, L8-c, L14-c, L15-c, R1-r to R4-c, R6-c, R7-c, R9-c. This is particularly pronounced in less commercially active provinces where the stigma of bankruptcy continues.

[110] ibid. This view is particularly pronounced in less developed regions.

[111] This provides some support to White's proposal that the *ex ante* costs of ex post manager/director liability are potentially the most significant of all: MJ White, 'The Cost of Corporate Bankruptcy' in JS Bhandari and LA Weiss, *Corporate Bankruptcy: Economic and Legal Perspectives* (Cambridge University Press, 1996) ch 30.

6.2.1.2. *Personal or Civil Liability*

Besides criminal liability, directors of bankrupt companies can also face personal or civil liability under the EBL. Under Article 125(1) of the EBL, debtor company directors[112] can be found personally liable if their breach of fiduciary duties of loyalty and diligence results in their company's bankruptcy. A breach of these duties gives rise to a fine and a duty to compensate affected stakeholders.[113] Further details are provided in the Company Law,[114] but the duty of loyalty is only broadly defined,[115] and the duty of diligence is not defined at all. Instead, the law offers an illustrative list of activities which would breach directors' duties.[116] Importantly, punishable activities include illegally (ie shadow-market) lending their company's funds and accepting as their own the commissions of a transaction between another person and the company – both of which are fairly common.[117]

The list also includes a catch-all category of 'other acts' that violate directors' fiduciary obligation to the company.[118] Several interviewees suggested that the open-endedness of the list makes debtor companies' directors particularly worried due to courts' manifested readiness to punish activities which are generally accepted by the business community, but which contravene informal state policies and so are seen by courts as giving rise to liability under the last catch-all category – often at the request of local officials.[119]

Although the EBL expressly states that liability only arises where the breach of the above causes the company's bankruptcy, some of my interviewees argued that, in practice, courts often do not require proof of causality and impose liability where a breach and company's bankruptcy simply exist at the same time.[120] Courts, therefore, have very wide and far-reaching discretion and the resulting increase in the threat of civil liability acts as an additional reason for avoiding the EBL when dealing with one's financial distress.

6.2.1.3. *Career-related Consequences*

Finally, debtor company's personnel also fear career-related consequences of using the EBL, such as losing their respective jobs – a natural consequence of corporate bankruptcy – and facing an automatic three-year disqualification from acting as directors,

---

[112] And under Art 147(1) Company Law also company supervisors and senior officials.

[113] Art 149 Company Law. The 2013 amendment to the Company Law added new guidelines on compensation.

[114] First introduced in 2005, amended in 2013 and 2018.

[115] As 'a ban on taking advantage of one's position and powers in the company to collect or accept bribes or other illegal income and to encroach upon the company's property': Art 147(2) Company Law.

[116] Art 148 Company Law.

[117] ibid.

[118] ibid.

[119] Interviews C2-c, C5-r, E1-c to E5-c, L1-r to L6-s, L11-c, L15-c, L9-c.

[120] Interviews C2-c, C5-r, C10-s, E2-s, E3-s, J1-c, J4-c, L2-s, L4-r, L6-s, L7-c, L8-c, R1-r to R4-c, R6-c, R7-c, R9-c.

supervisors and senior managers in any company in China.[121] The disqualification is imposed regardless of whether the person actually caused the bankruptcy. Moreover, unlike the other employees whose interests are vigorously protected by courts and local governments, senior managers and directors are not treated as employees in bankruptcy. Their unpaid wages are generally not recoverable.[122] In addition, courts and administrators can adjust managements' contractual provisions regarding their compensation for termination of employment if they deem it appropriate.[123] These EBL-specific consequences, therefore, further discourage debtors' senior personnel from using the EBL and instead encourage the use of alternative enforcement mechanisms.[124]

6.2.2. Increased Scrutiny and Liability under Non-bankruptcy Laws and Practices that are Triggered by the Use of the EBL

The previous section detailed liabilities that arise directly from the EBL where a company is insolvent.[125] This section, on the other hand, discusses the liabilities that arise regardless of a company's financial health, where the EBL merely acts as a trigger or a catalyst for scrutiny, but where the EBL itself does not directly give rise to the liability. The discussion considers criminal liability arising due to one's involvement in shadow lending activities; personal liability to repay company's debts where repayment guarantee was provided; career- and remuneration-related consequences for SOEs' management under regulations and Party rules; and detention and other consequences facing debtor company's representatives in cases of non-payment.

6.2.2.1. *Criminal Liability for Involvement in Shadow Market Activities*

Firstly, debtor companies' representatives can face imprisonment and large fines for their involvement in shadow lending activities. Many of my interviewees spoke of managers' liability if they borrowed from 'too many people'.[126] Article 176 of the Criminal Law defines the crime as 'illegally taking deposits from the general public or through an equivalent activity whereby disrupting the financial order'. Borrowing even small sums from many individuals – other than one's family and friends – and from lenders who found out about the opportunity through social channels (eg social media, promotion meetings, leaflets, wide-range advertising, etc) falls within this definition.[127] Many – particularly private – companies are financed in this way because they do not have

---

[121] Art 125(2) EBL. They are also under a duty not to take up or hold any other managerial post in another company: Art 15(5) EBL.

[122] Interviews C2-c to C8-s, E1-s, E3-s, E4-c, L2-s to L8-c. See also Legal Advice 110 (24.9.2013).

[123] ibid. See also Legal Advice 110 (15.11.2012).

[124] Discussed in ch 9.

[125] Or financially distressed, which is sufficient for using EBL Reorganisation: Section 4.2.2.

[126] Interviews E1-c to E5-c, C2-c to c7-s, C10-s, L6-s to L10-s, R2-r, R3-r, R9-c, R10-c.

[127] Clarified in the SPC Provisions on Several Issues Concerning Implementation of Laws in Criminal Law Cases of Illegal Fundraising (*Fashi* [2010] No 18). Interviewees L2-s, L4-r said that this is usually 'more than 200 people', but neither could point to a particular provision which defines a precise number. Rather, they suggested, the law sets the standard broadly, and courts tend to determine what 'many people' means.

access to bank finance, and their entry into an EBL procedure significantly increases the likelihood that their 'illegal' borrowing activities may be discovered and punished.[128]

Similarly, several interviewed practitioners reported that their clients (debtors and creditors) often do not want to use the EBL because they have taken out bank loans and reinvested the money in the shadow market.[129] Legally speaking, it is a crime for a company to obtain a bank loan in order to relend the money at high interest rates.[130] My interviewees suggested that this is particularly problematic for state-sector companies,[131] which are often coerced by the (local) government to carry out money-losing projects but are – at the same time – made responsible for the overall financial health of the company.[132] Therefore, they often try to make additional gains by 'gambling in the shadow market' using bank finance which is available to them, because shadow market is perceived by many as an opportunity to 'make [them] rich, quickly'.[133] Using the EBL triggers scrutiny and where it becomes apparent that these activities gave rise to 'relatively large' illegal gains, then those responsible face imprisonment and a discretionary fine.[134] As a result, those in charge of state-sector companies are further incentivised to avoid the EBL.

Moreover, both private- and state-sector companies are further incentivised not to use the EBL if they are involved in the shadow market in any other way because courts[135] have an additional power to criminalise any other activities they deem to be a 'disruption of the market order'.[136] Many interviewees felt that this is an extreme and rarely used measure, but it is nevertheless considered a threat, particularly by large players in the market who are often heavily involved in shadow market activities as lenders, borrowers and intermediaries.[137]

6.2.2.2. *Personal Liability under a Personal Guarantee*

Secondly, directors can also find themselves liable to repay their company's debts where they provided a personal guarantee that the company would repay and it does not. Such guarantees are particularly common in smaller and less well-connected companies which would otherwise not be able to access arm's-length finance.[138] Several interviewees argued that while an ordinary Chinese creditor may try to renegotiate the repayment conditions or find another solution,[139] creditors with a personal

---

[128] Interviews C2-c to C7-s, C10-s, C11-c, IF1-s, IF2-c, J6-s, L1-r to L6-s, L8-c to L17-c, R1-r to R3-r, R6-c, R9-c, R10-c.

[129] Interviews L1-r to L6-s, L9-s, L11-c to L15-c, C5-r.

[130] Art 175 Criminal Law. For further discussion, see Section 7.3.

[131] See Section 2.5 for the definition.

[132] Interviews C2-c, C5-r, C7-s, L2-s, L4-r, L6-s, P1-r to P3-r.

[133] ibid, a quote from interview L2-s.

[134] Art 175 Criminal Law 2015.

[135] Or, in practice, the local government: see Section 2.4.

[136] Art 225(3) Criminal Law.

[137] Interviews L1-r to L9-s, L11-c to L15-c, C1-c, C5-r.

[138] ibid.

[139] All my interviews agreed that in China the first step is always to try to renegotiate the loan before enforcing them – see Section 9.1.

guarantee can go beyond debtor company's assets and into its directors' personal funds and property.[140] This raises further difficulties, not only because it incentivises directors who provided personal guarantees to avoid entering the EBL even where a formal restructuring or liquidation would be beneficial to the company and its stakeholders, but also because China does not have personal bankruptcy rules.[141] As a result – some interviewees proposed – there are stories of run-away directors, particularly in regions with a strong private sector and an economy reliant on smaller businesses whose financing comes from non-banks and is often secured by personal guarantees from the directors.[142]

6.2.2.3. Career- and Remuneration-Related Consequences under Other Regulations and Rules

Thirdly, managers of SOEs are sometimes discouraged from using the EBL because of the threat of career- and remuneration-related consequences of SOEs' bad financial performance that are enforced under Party disciplinary regulations. Article 122 of the Regulation on Disciplinary Measures of the Chinese Communist Party 2003 states that if a director or any other person in an SOE violates regulations of state-owned assets management and in doing so causes financial loss, they face investigation by the Central Commission on Disciplinary Inspection, which can result in a warning, a severe warning, removal from the post and personal inspection, and in serious cases an outright dismissal.[143]

In addition, the management in companies under SASAC supervision also faces potential consequences for bad financial performance under SASAC-specific regulations. Article 32 of the Measures for Implementing the Investigation of Responsibility for Investment of Central Enterprises in Violation of Regulations (Trial) 2018 states that, depending on whether the losses are normal, large or significant, those responsible may be publicly criticised, admonished, suspended or removed from office. Those in positions of responsibility may be demoted, ordered to resign or removed from office and restricted in further activities. In addition, the performance part of the salary and any additional incentives of those responsible (directly, in a supervisory capacity or as a leader of the group) can be withdrawn by up to 100 per cent, and personal liability for the losses may be imposed.

These are severe consequences, especially when combined with those that are imposed directly under the EBL.[144] As a result, SOEs and central companies under SASAC supervision are often discouraged from using the EBL to resolve their financial distress as the key personnel may fear personal consequences for the companies' bad financial results.

---

[140] Interviews B1-c to B3-c, C2-c to C7-s, E2-s, E3-s, IF1-s, IF2-c, L2-s, L10-s to L16c, R9-c.

[141] Interviews C1-c, C5-r, J1-c, J6-s, L4-r to L8-c, L14-c to L16-c. See also Sections 11.1.6. and 12.9 for proposed and recent developments in this regard.

[142] ibid. See also Section 10.2.2.

[143] The Chinese Communist Party's Regulation on Discipline Measures (18.2.2004).

[144] See Section 6.2.1.3 above.

6.2.2.4. Detention

Finally, if the fact of bankruptcy becomes publicly known,[145] debtor company's representatives can also find themselves forcibly detained to ensure repayment of debts. This is an extreme measure that is not often used, but many of my interviewees confirmed that they know of cases where this happened. As was discussed earlier, the EBL orders debtor company personnel not to leave their place of domicile without court approval,[146] and if they try to leave, a court can issue a warrant to detain them.[147] However, several interviewees suggested that courts often act too slowly[148] and so – to prevent debtor's representatives from fleeing (and so enable subsequent court enforcement) – creditors sometimes (illegally) detain debtor's representatives without court's assistance.[149]

The combination of personal and professional liability that arises directly from the EBL and indirectly from non-bankruptcy laws, but which is triggered when the EBL is used, therefore, incentivises debtor company representatives not to use the EBL and, where possible, cover up their financial distress or at least resolve their problems through alternative mechanisms.[150] As such, it is another plausible explanation for the limited use of the EBL.

6.3. Insolvency as De Facto Entry Requirement for Reorganisation

A third and final major constraint on the use of the EBL that arises from the wording of the law itself is the de facto requirement of insolvency as a pre-condition to using EBL reorganisation.[151] The entry requirements, discussed in Section 4.2.2, state that insolvency is needed in most cases, but that a debtor can apply for reorganisation where it is 'obviously likely to become insolvent'. On the face of it, the EBL, therefore, allows and encourages[152] pre-insolvency use of reorganisation. Unfortunately, there is no guidance in the EBL or elsewhere that explains how and who can determine whether a company is 'obviously likely' to become insolvent. The term can be defined broadly or narrowly. If defined too broadly, it may allow debtor companies to enter the protection of a moratorium too early and gain unfair and unjustified protection from its creditors. If, on the other hand, it is defined too narrowly, pre-insolvency use of reorganisation is barred and

---

[145] In the Lipu County, in Guilin, there were no EBL cases because, reportedly, people would do 'anything to avoid the public large-scale monster process': People's Daily (10.10.2015).

[146] Art 15(4) EBL.

[147] Confirmed in all my interviews.

[148] As was the case in Zhejiang in 2011 where more than 200 business owners went into hiding to avoid repayment of debts. See eg SCMP (12.10.2011).

[149] Interviews L1-r to L7-c, L11-c to L15-c, C2-c to C5-r, C7-s, E2-s, R2-r to R4-c, R7-c, R9-c to R11-c. Unpaid creditors sometimes resort to extreme methods so as to enforce repayment of their money, such as a case of a Guangdong businessman who was put in a cage for three months for defaulting on a loan of 1 million RMB owed to the local government: SCMP (4.12.1999). See also D Harris (11.1.2016, Forbes).

[150] See Sections 9.1 and 10.2.2.

[151] For details, see Section 4.2.2.

[152] L Wang, 'Problems of Amending the Bankruptcy Law' (2005) *Legal Science* 3, 11.

efficient, timely restructuring may be impossible. In practice, courts in China tend to come closer to the latter extreme, reading the test 'likely to become insolvent' narrowly and so, de facto, not allowing pre-insolvency petitions in order to avoid abuse[153] and possibly also due to the lack of courts' experience and expertise that would enable them to understand and apply the test within the spirit of the EBL.[154]

Such restrictive reading of the entry test is problematic because the parties perceive insolvent restructuring as less able to save the company, a part of the business, or even to offer the parties comparatively higher payoffs than those that they would receive outside the EBL regime because the restructuring takes place too late.[155] If reorganisation commences late, it is more difficult to find an investor, to undo bad operational decisions, to change structural and marketing issues and to save the company or at least its business. In such cases, the company may become unable to restructure without the help of a local government – which is why successful insolvent reorganisation cases are usually driven by a local government and a liquidation committee.[156]

That is undesirable, however, because local governments generally only interfere in state-sector companies – large, economically significant players in local economies – and smaller companies are left out. The consequences are felt by creditors who are less likely to recover their claims, by debtors who lose a chance to restructure, by employees who lose their jobs, and by society at large due to, inter alia, the resulting fall in tax income, provision of fewer goods or services, and – depending on the circumstances – possible industry- or economy-wide impact.[157]

---

[153] Y Jiang, 'The Curious Case of Inactive Bankruptcy Practice in China: A Comparative Study of US and Chinese Bankruptcy Law' (2014) *Northwestern Journal of International Law & Business* 560.

[154] See Section 8.1.1.

[155] All interviewees expressed their misgivings about this test. Some were particularly sceptical, stating that successful restructuring was very difficult to achieve in practice: interviews C3-c, C5-r, E2-s, E4-c, L2-s, L4-r, L6-s, P1-r, R10-c. Nevertheless, see an excellent empirical analysis of EBL Reorganisation cases in China in Zhang (n 47).

[156] See Zhang (n 47).

[157] For a comparative discussion and a discussion of why pre-insolvency use of reorganisation is important, see Section 11.1.4.1.

7

The Second Constraint – Reduced Recoveries under the EBL

The first constraint on the use of the EBL was concerned with certain flaws in the EBL which reduce expected payoffs of the parties and so discourage them from using the EBL in the first place. This second, complementary, constraint is concerned with how the parties' expected payoffs and ability to use the EBL are affected by the shortcomings in the institutional environment in which the EBL is enforced. Based on my interviewees' experience and insights, this chapter proposes that the flaws in surrounding rules and practices reduce or outright prevent recoveries under the EBL, and so disincentivise creditors from using the law.[1]

The discussion focuses on three broad issues. Creditors' expected payoffs under the EBL are reduced due to missing or incomplete supporting mechanisms and rules. This includes, firstly, general flaws in debt enforcement that affect EBL recoveries (Section 7.1) and, secondly, shortcomings in surrounding rules and practices that specifically affect EBL enforcement and which affect creditors' decision whether to use the EBL (Section 7.2). Finally, recoveries under the EBL are further limited due to existing rules that regulate lending and other debt-related activities, which also disincentivise or outright bar certain creditors from recovering under the EBL (Section 7.3). In the aggregate, these surrounding rules and practices reduce creditors' expected and actual recoveries, and so – my interviewees suggested – contribute to the low use of the EBL.

Table 7.1 Overview of the impact of the problematic surrounding rules and practices

	Cause of reduced recoveries	Scope of impact – type of enforcement
General flaws (Section 7.1)	Incomplete or missing rules	All debt enforcement
EBL-specific flaws (Section 7.2)	Incomplete or missing rules	EBL only
Restrictions on lending (Section 7.3)	Rules restricting lending activities	Certain credit contracts
		All debt formal enforcement

---

[1] It also provides further weight to claims that bankruptcy law cannot function well unless surrounded by effective institutions and norms that help define, support and enforce it: C Wihlborg, S Gangopadhyay and Q Hussain, 'Infrastructure Requirements in the Area of Bankruptcy Law' (2001) Wharton Financial Institutions Center Working Paper 01-09.

7.1. General Flaws in Debt Enforcement that Negatively Affect Recoveries under the EBL

Section 3.4 outlined five general problems that weaken the 'infrastructure for bankruptcy'[2] in which the EBL operates. These problems are further explored here, in the context of EBL enforcement. Section 7.1.1 below examines the problems arising from unreliable financial information. Section 7.1.2 explores the difficulties with the verification of property rights. Section 7.1.3 considers the problems arising from the limited protection of property rights. Section 7.1.4 looks at tunnelling, asset-stripping practices and the use of ghost companies. And Section 7.1.5 examines the issues that arise from the revocability of land usage rights. Many interviewees argued that, in the aggregate, these flaws further disincentivise creditors from using the EBL because they make the recovery of their financial claims *ex ante* uncertain and *ex post* limited or non-existent.[3] Possible improvements are discussed in Section 11.2.1.

7.1.1. Recoveries under the EBL are Affected by Lack of Reliable Financial Information

Section 3.4.1 suggested that the lack of reliable and publicly available information – due to the use of forged and falsified documents and dual accounting – hinders debt enforcement in China by complicating the verification of creditors' claims and determination of asset ownership. Several interviewees argued that, in EBL enforcement, the information-related issues also complicate or outright prevent an accurate assessment of debtor company's financial health. As a result, it is often very difficult to determine whether a debtor satisfies the EBL insolvency test – a precondition to using the law.[4] For example, where debtors use forged invoices, their assets – which would otherwise be available to creditors – are artificially reduced or augmented. Similarly, the use of dual accounting hinders any meaningful determination of debtor's financial health.[5]

The lack of reliable financial information may also prevent creditors from filing reorganisation petitions of listed companies because the SPC guidance requires that creditors' reorganisation petition concerning listed companies must be accompanied by a reorganisation plan.[6] In some regions, courts require that creditors' reorganisation petitions for any type of company must also satisfy this requirement.[7] However, it is very

---

[2] Wihlborg, Gangopadhyay and Hussain, Infrastructure Requirements (2001).

[3] Interviews B1-c, B2-c, C2-c, C3-c, C5-r, C7-s, J1-c to J9-c, L1-r to L15c, P1-r, R1-r to R4-c, R9-c, R10-c.

[4] Interviews B1-c to B3-c, C2-c, C3-c, C5-r, C10-s, J1-c, J3-c, J5-s, L2-s to L6-s, R1-r to R3-r, R9-c, R10-c. See also RI Patel, 'A Practical Evaluation of the People's Republic of China's 2007 Enterprise Bankruptcy Law' (2009–10) *UC Davis Business Law Journal* 109.

[5] Interviews B1-c to B3-c, C2-c, C3-c, C5-r, C10-s, J1-c, J3-c, J5-s, L2-s to L6-s, R1-r to R3-r, R9-c, R10-c.

[6] Art 3 of the SPC Memorandum on Handing of Listed Companies' Reorganisations and Liquidations (*Fa* [2012] No 261).

[7] See eg Art 15 of the Beijing Municipal SPC Notice concerning Procedural Rules of Enterprise Bankruptcy in Beijing Municipality (*Beijing Gaofafa* [2013] No 242).

difficult for creditors to produce such a plan in practice because they lack the necessary financial information.

Furthermore, some interviewees expressed concerns that the lack of reliable financial information makes it very difficult for courts and administrators to carry out their respective duties under the EBL.[8] These include duties to claw back wrongly transferred assets, to cancel vulnerable pre-EBL transactions,[9] and to fulfil their general duty under Article 1 of the EBL to 'fairly liquidate debts [and] to protect legitimate rights and interests of creditors and debtors'. The interviewees doubted whether 'fair' allocation and protection of parties' interests are possible under the EBL in its current institutional environment where the size of the pool of assets and the identity of all stakeholders are difficult to ascertain.[10] Consequently, the lack of accurate and available financial information leads to imperfect enforcement, great uncertainty and lower payoffs to creditors.

An additional problem – albeit not unique to China – is that the inherent information asymmetry between the insiders (asset owners) and outsiders (potential buyers) makes it difficult to liquidate debtor's assets effectively.[11] Information asymmetry exists in all markets, but the situation in China is worsened by the lack of reliable, commonly available financial information. Without reliable information about the quality and actual value of the assets, there are only two types of willing buyers of the distressed assets: insiders who know the real value of the assets, or opportunistic speculators. Both know that bankruptcy sends a negative signal about the assets' quality and that, due to the information asymmetry, very few people are willing to buy, and so they can successfully offer very low prices for distressed assets. This further reduces the recovery rates under the EBL and disincentivises creditors from resolving their claims under the EBL. This adverse selection problem is – several interviewees suggested – more pronounced in less-developed regions of China where the stigma of failure makes people particularly suspicious of anything and anyone connected with bankruptcy.[12]

Although private enforcement mechanisms[13] should, in principle, face similar information issues, several interviewees suggested that, in practice, it is often comparatively easier to recover debts using alternative enforcement mechanisms.[14] They argued that, firstly, imperfect financial information is less of a problem in informal enforcement since a creditor usually does not have to prove their claim to any third party. Instead, they observe and enforce their claim directly, without assistance from any third party.[15] Secondly, creditors using informal enforcement often do not respect the legal limitation

---

[8] Interviews B1-c to B3-c, C2-c to C5-r, C10-s, J1-c, J5-s, L2-s to L7-c, R1-r, R9-c, R10-c.

[9] For details see Section 4.2.9.

[10] Interviews B1-c to B3-c, C2-c to C5-r, C10-s, J1-c, J5-s, L2-s to L7-c, R1-r, R9-c, R10-c.

[11] See eg M Nishihara and T Shibata, 'Dynamic bankruptcy procedure with asymmetric information between insiders and outsiders' (2018) *Journal of Economic Dynamics and Control* 118.

[12] The stigma issue has been largely overcome in large, developed cities and market zones, but remains problematic in interior and northern provinces: Interviews C1-c, C2-c, C5-r, C10-s, E1-c to E4-c, L1-c to L6-s, L9s, L10s, L13-c, R1-r, R10-c.

[13] See Section 9.1.

[14] Interviews C2-c to C5-r, C7-s, E2-s, IF1-s, IF2-c, L1-c, L2-s, L4-r to L6-s, L9s, L10s, L13-c, R1-r, R10-c.

[15] cf the idea of 'incomplete contracting', which is motivated by a concern that verification to a third party is often more costly than observation by a contracting party: see eg O Hart and J Moore, 'Incomplete Contracts and Renegotiation' (1988) *Econometrica* 755.

of only recovering from company-owned assets, and they are willing to threaten debtors' representatives or even their next-of-kin with violence and use other means to enforce repayment.[16] And thirdly, creditors using non-EBL mechanisms do not need to prove that the debtor company satisfies the EBL insolvency test. It is, therefore, not surprising that many creditors perceive non-EBL debt enforcement alternatives as more efficient, and so better than the EBL.

7.1.2. Recoveries under the EBL are Affected by Difficult Verification of Property Rights

Further two challenges to debt enforcement in China relate to property rights, namely parties' limited ability to prove entitlements and interests in property (discussed here); and insufficient protection of property rights (discussed in Section 7.1.3 below).[17] Although significant steps have been taken to finalise and bring up to date China's property registry[18] – and so to ameliorate the first challenge – its limitations during the first decade of EBL implementation have had an impact described below.

One of the crucial roles that the EBL performs is the collection and subsequent redistribution of debtor's assets according to a predetermined order. However, this function has been severely impaired due to the parties' inability to check and prove ownership of property and property-related interests and rights due to the lack of a fully functioning property rights registration system. Several interviewees suggested that this has had a significant impact on the size of the pool of assets due to administrators' inability to collect all relevant assets. As a result, creditors' expected payoffs in the EBL have been reduced because they have had to share a smaller amount of assets which, in turn, has made them less willing to use the law to recover their debts from insolvent debtors.[19] This has been particularly problematic in the EBL – as a collective mechanism – because most other enforcement mechanisms involve individual enforcement and so do not necessarily rely on the aggregation of debtor's assets prior to debt enforcement.

Moreover, several interviewees also pointed out that the difficulties in the verification of creditors' property rights in debtor's assets have hindered creditors' ability to prove their claims – as required under Article 49 of the EBL – and so have made it difficult for them to recover, pro rata, for the entirety of their claim.[20] On the other hand, unlike the EBL, creditors using informal enforcement have not had to prove their claim to any third party – and so could function without a property rights register – as they enforce directly against the debtor.[21]

---

[16] See Section 9.1.
[17] See Sections 3.4.2–3.4.3.
[18] See Section 11.2.1.2.
[19] Interviews C2-c to C5-r, C7-s, E2-s, IF1-s, IF2-c, L1-c, L2-s, L4-r to L6-s, L9s, L10s, L13-c, R1-r, R10-c.
[20] ibid. This is particularly difficult for secured creditors.
[21] ibid. Note that without a registration system – even if such enforcement usurps another's right – there is no way of proving that the informal enforcement was unfair: Interviews C5-r, L2-s, L6-s, R1-r, R10-c.

7.1.3. Recoveries under the EBL are Affected by Limited Protection of Property Rights

In addition to the problems with verification of financial information and property ownership, debt enforcement in China is also affected by severe limitations in the protection of property rights. As was discussed in section 3.4.3, the disregard for and failure to protect property rights is not unique to China, nor does it only affect enforcement under the EBL. However, my interviewees suggested that protection-related issues are particularly severe under EBL enforcement.

One example of this issue has already been discussed in the context of subordinating secured creditors' rights.[22] Another example is the asset-grabbing and looting of the debtor's property by claimholders – employees and creditors – who react to the news of the debtor's petitioning to use an EBL procedure by racing to recover their claim instead of waiting for an uncertain recovery in the future.[23]

Arguably the best protection of debtor's property rights would involve *ex-ante* prevention of asset-grabbing and looting by affected claimholders. Unfortunately, many of my interviewees agreed that, in practice, local governments and police are often unable or unwilling to step in to prevent debtors' angry employees and creditors from satisfying their claims informally and directly, without going to court or waiting for a collective resolution under the EBL.[24] A second-best solution would be *ex-post* protection through, for example, clawing back and recovering debtor's misappropriated assets. Asset-grabbing is reversible under the EBL: once located, the stolen objects can be returned to the debtor company.[25] However, several interviewees said that, in practice, this is often not done due to the perceived costs and practical and evidential difficulties.[26]

Moreover, the damage caused by looting is, in many ways, irreversible. Although illegal and punishable by a prison sentence under the Criminal Law,[27] looting of a debtor company and accompanying public disorder almost invariably destroy or devalue the debtor's property. This, in turn, reduces the amount and value of the debtor's assets and so diminishes creditors' payoffs in the aggregate. Some value may be recovered by imposing fines on the looters,[28] but the interviewees suggested that courts tend not to

---

[22] Section 6.1.2 showed that security rights are often subordinated to employees' claims by courts. As a result – several interviewees concluded – any meaningful pre-lending analysis and costing of the provided credit become meaningless, and so disincentivise creditors from using the EBL in the first place: Interviews B1-c to B3-c, C2-c, C5-r, L2-s, R3-r, R9-c.

[23] For a general discussion of race to collect see eg J Armour, 'The Rise of the 'Pre-Pack': Corporate Restructuring in the UK and Proposals for Reform in RP Austin and Fady JG Aoun' (eds), *Restructuring Companies in Troubled Times: Director and Creditor Perspectives* (Ross Parsons Centre of Commercial, Corporate and Taxation Law, 2012).

[24] Interviews B1-c to B3-c, C2-c to C5-r, C7-s, E2-s, IF1-s, L2-s to L7-c, L10-c, L14-c to L16-c, R1-r to R4-c, R8-s to R10-c.

[25] See Section 4.2.13.

[26] Interviews B1-c to B3-c, C2-c to C5-r, C7-s, E2-s, IF1-s, L2-s to L7-c, L10-c, L14-c to L16-c, R1-r to R4-c, R8-s to R10-c.

[27] Arts 268 and 270 (gathering with the aim to seize and seizure of another's property), and 275 (looting, intentional damage to another's property) of Criminal Law 2015.

[28] Or clawing back the stolen assets, where possible: ibid.

impose criminal sanctions for such behaviour in practice, which means that no money is recovered and looting is not sufficiently deterred.[29]

Many of my interviewees[30] and numerous news stories[31] suggest that asset-grabbing and looting are often triggered by the news of a debtor's financial problems, which is often brought about by the company petitioning for or entering into an EBL procedure. It is, therefore, often not in the creditors' best interests to commence EBL procedures either because they prefer to enforce directly, or because they may fear that petitioning to use the EBL may trigger a race to collect and looting, which may, in turn, lead to value destruction and so limit their recovery under the EBL.

7.1.4. Recoveries under the EBL are Affected by Unpunished Tunnelling, Asset-stripping and Creation of Ghost Companies

Besides asset-grabbing by claimholders, debtor companies are also vulnerable to tunnelling and asset stripping by directors and managers. In addition, directors sometimes also transfer valuable assets into a new company, and leave the liabilities and valueless assets behind in a shell known as a ghost company. Section 3.4.4 suggested that these practices affect all types of debt enforcement by reducing the volume of assets available for repayment of the debts. Nevertheless, several of my interviewees – who had first-hand experience with these practices – suggested that, although asset-stripping and the use of ghost companies can and do happen in a normal course of business, their use is particularly pronounced at a brink of insolvency.[32] They argued that, often, once it becomes clear that the debtor company would not recover – and especially where a creditor petitions or threatens to petition a court to start an EBL procedure – directors and managers take their company's assets and run away[33] or transfer valuable assets to a new company in a way that makes them hard to trace or claw back.[34] Then they start afresh with the stolen assets in a new company – leaving behind the shell of a ghost company.

The creation of ghost companies and asset-stripping practices are reversible by courts and administrators under the Company Law and the EBL.[35] Nevertheless,

---

[29] See n 15. Some limited exceptions do exist. Nevertheless, the restoration of social order is usually the primary concern of the relevant local government and its enforcement agents: see Section 2.4.2.

[30] ibid. This is not very different from the pre-EBL era when, as one banker put it, one could only recover one's unsecured loan if they 'react immediately to early distress signals and obtain immediate payment or additional collateral by using all kinds of threats against the firm and its managers and owners as long as they are legal.': S Tenev and C Zhang, *Corporate Governance and Enterprise Reform in China: Building the Institutions of Modern Markets* (World Bank & IFC, 2002).

[31] See eg T Durden (10.12.2015, ZeroHedge); J Kaiman (9.1.2016, Los Angeles Times).

[32] Interviews C2-c, C3-c, C5-r, E2-s, L2-s, L4-r, L6-s, R3-r, R10-c. See also Y Zheng, Y Lu and LT White (eds) *Politics of Modern China* (2010, Routledge) 315–42.

[33] The problem of run-away bosses is discussed in Sections 6.2.2 and 10.2.2.

[34] Eg through a seemingly *bona fide* third party purchaser so that the law would not allow these to be clawed back.

[35] For the details of the administrators' duties and its enforcement in practice see Sections 4.2.9 and 8.2, respectively.

several interviewees argued that these reversal mechanisms are only rarely used in practice – especially in corporate bankruptcy cases, which are seen by many judges as 'already difficult enough without the added difficulty of reversing hard-to-trace transfers'.[36] As a result, my interviewees argued, creditors sometimes fear that their payoffs under the EBL would be severely diminished compared to their expected recovery in informal enforcement mechanisms, and so creditors are disincentivised from using the law.[37]

7.1.5. Recoveries under the EBL are Affected by Revocability of Land Usage Rights

Finally, an additional but independent issue which further diminishes expected and actual payoffs to creditors under the EBL stems from the nature of land ownership in China. As was discussed in Section 3.4.5, land in China is under state or collective ownership. Therefore, most companies can only acquire land usage rights from the state (or a state-controlled collective) and only for a fixed period of time. However, in contrast with the general protections of these rights when the right-holder is solvent, land usage rights that are held by an insolvent company[38] can be cancelled immediately and without compensation.[39]

Many of my interviewees reported that the state does, in fact, use this power in practice, and thereby makes it practically impossible to sell the land usage right or the buildings and other immovable property on such land once the holding company becomes insolvent.[40] This significantly reduces the assets out of which creditors and other stakeholders can be repaid.[41] And so, unsurprisingly, my interviewees argued that debtors who use state-owned land and their creditors often avoid using the EBL. This is mainly because they believe that by avoiding a formal declaration of bankruptcy under the EBL, they ensure that the Government does not revoke debtor's land usage rights, or that if it is revoked under one of the predefined circumstances,[42] the debtor would be compensated according to the law.[43] Consequently, creditors' payoffs under the EBL are lower than under other debt enforcement mechanisms, which disincentivises creditors from using the EBL in the first place.

---

[36] Interview J1-c. Similar views that courts are often unwilling to engage in a search for misappropriated assets were expressed by several other judges (J4-c, J7-c), lawyers (L2-s to L4-r, L6-s, L11-c to L13-c) and consultants (C2-c to C5-r, C8-s, C9-c).

[37] Interviews C2-c to C5-r, C8-s, C9-c, L2-s, L4-r, L6-s, L9-s to L13-c, R3-r, R10-c.

[38] Insolvency is not defined, but my interviewees suggested that acceptance of EBL petition is needed in practice: Interviews C2-c, C5-r, C7-s, E1-c, E2-s, J1-c, J3-c to J9-c, L2-s to L9-s, R1-c to R3-r, R9-c, R10-c.

[39] This is confirmed in Art 38 EBL.

[40] Or, in practice, once it becomes official that the company is insolvent because the court accepted their EBL petition: Interviews C2-c, C5-r, C7-s, E1-c, E2-s, J1-c, J3-c to J9-c, L2-s to L9-s, R1-c to R3-r, R9-c, R10-c.

[41] ibid.

[42] See Section 3.4.5 for details.

[43] Interviews C2-c, C5-r, C7-s, E1-c, E2-s, J1-c, J3-c to J9-c, L2-s to L9-s, R1-c to R3-r, R9-c, R10-c.

7.2. Shortcomings that Specifically Affect EBL Enforcement

In addition to the general shortcomings that affect all debt enforcement, my interviewees also identified two further problems in surrounding rules and practices that specifically affect debt enforcement under the EBL. The first shortcoming concerns China's incomplete social security system and is discussed in Section 7.2.1 below. The second shortcoming arises out of the interconnectedness of large companies in China, and is discussed in Section 7.2.2. Unlike the general flaws discussed in Section 7.1 above that operate at creditor and debtor level by affecting their willingness to use the EBL, the issues discussed below affect the willingness of courts and local governments to allow the parties to use the EBL. Consequently, these shortcomings further explain why local governments influence courts – as discussed in Sections 2.4 (general) and 8.3 (EBL-specific) – and forbid certain corporate bankruptcies to be resolved under the EBL. The threat of such interference disincentivises some creditors and debtors from wanting to use the EBL in the first place. Alternative mechanisms are then used instead of the EBL.[44] Possible improvements to the two shortcomings are proposed in Section 11.2.2.

7.2.1. Incomplete Social Security System

Economic reforms and the legalisation of private companies eventually led to the dissolution of the 'iron rice bowl' regime under which SOEs provided employment and social security for every Chinese citizen from birth to death.[45] The introduction of the 1986 law (and its reform in 2006) then enabled and regulated corporate closures and large-scale redundancies which, in the aggregate, contributed to the increasing uncertainty for people who were used to life-long social provision from the state. Although the Government introduced a new set of rules for social security provision which, it was hoped, would remove this uncertainty, the system was simplistic, incoherent and fragmented.[46] A new, unified regime was then introduced and codified in Social Insurance Law in 2011. For the first time, it created a comprehensive social security system that clearly explained employees', employers' and government's responsibilities. Nevertheless, problems remain.

The 2011 law introduced comprehensive coverage, procedural rules and clear entitlements to workers, retired persons and the unemployed.[47] However, most interviewees argued that, in practice, its implementation has been problematic.[48] The new Chinese regime for unemployment benefits relies on both employees' and employers'

---

[44] See Sections 9.1 (private alternatives) and 9.2 (state-driven alternatives).

[45] See Section 2.1.

[46] The rules were scattered across many laws and regulations, including Labour Law 1994, the State Council's Regulations on Unemployment Insurance 1999, and Labour Contract Law.

[47] For an excellent overview, see China Labour Bulletin (29.6.2016).

[48] Interviews C1-c, C4-c, C5-r, C7-s to C11-c, J1-c, J4-c to J9-c, L2-s, L4-r to L6-s, L14-c to L16-c, P1-r, R1-r to R4-c, R6-c to R10-c.

contributions to an unemployment insurance fund. However, by the end of 2015, only 22.3 per cent of all workers – about 173 million out of 775 million workers[49] – were participating. Moreover, the law states that unemployment benefits must be lower than local minimum wage – which is generally very low and considered to be less than a living wage[50] – and are determined by the length of employment[51] and the contributions to the unemployment fund, with a maximum of 24 months of payments. In addition, my interviewees also suggested that, in many places where the unemployment insurance contributions have been collected, the system, nevertheless, failed due to the lack of an effective mechanism for distribution of unemployment benefits to their rightful recipients.[52]

All my interviewees suggested that the failure to implement an effective and holistic social security system has had a significant impact on the use of the EBL. Until 2011, there was no system in place. As a result, local governments had been actively avoiding and preventing the use of the EBL in order to respond to significant popular pressure to deal with large-scale redundancies,[53] to appease the unemployed[54] and to fulfil their duty to ensure social stability in their region by preventing further protests.[55] Although the new system has the potential to improve the situation, it appears to have failed to ameliorate the situation in any meaningful way in practice.

The lack of a functioning social security system appears to be one of the motivating factors why local governments force courts to ignore EBL petitions – particularly from companies with a significant number of employees.[56] My interviewees suggested that this may also help explain the courts' insistence on having an employee resettlement plan before authorising reorganisation[57] and their tendency to interpret conflicting guidelines in the EBL as affording priority to employees over secured creditors.[58]

Moreover, this shortcoming in the institutional environment in which the EBL is enforced also diminishes expected (and often also actual) recoveries by creditors under the EBL. The issue also affects debtors who, even if they wish to, cannot use the EBL to reorganise their company and start afresh where local governments and courts do not let them. As a result, the lack of unemployment safety net is a further reason for the limited use of the EBL.

---

[49] Statistical Bulletin of Human Resources and Social Security Development in 2015 (30.5.2016, Ministry of Human Resources and Social Security).

[50] In 2016, the minimum wage in small cities was about 1,000 RMB (149 USD) and in most major cities around 1,600 RMB (239 USD) per month. The national average income was about 3,300 RMB (492 USD) per month, and in most major cities around 4,000 RMB (597 USD): NBS and Statista.

[51] Full benefits are only available after 10 years of previous employment – ibid.

[52] Interviews C1-c, C4-c, C5-r, J1-c, J4-c to J8-c, L2-s, L4-r to L6-s, P1-r, R1-r to R4-c, R6-c to R10-c.

[53] ibid.

[54] Local governments fear that large-scale use of EBL liquidation (some suggested that even if they allowed reorganisation under the EBL, as the signalling effect of entering the EBL would suffice) may trigger strikes by the affected employees: Interviews C5-r, E3-s, J1-c, L4-r, L6-s, R1-r, R7-c, R10-c.

[55] Local governments fear that using the EBL would cause social unrest, 'publicise the local government's failure to deal with the situation', and otherwise 'cause trouble': Interviews C2-c to C5-r, C7-s, C10-s, E2-s, E3-s, J1-c, J6-s to J9-c, L2-s to L6-s, P1-r, P3-r to P5-c, R1-r to R3-r, R7-c to R10-c. See also section 2.4.2.

[56] ibid.

[57] See Section 6.1.1.

[58] See Section 6.1.2.

7.2.2. Interconnectedness of (Large) Companies

Many of my interviewees also suggested that local governments are reluctant to permit the use of the EBL where there is a danger that bankruptcy of one company may lead to other bankruptcies or have a significant adverse effect on the financial health of other companies, a particular industry or the economy in general.[59] The interviewees identified two main sources of this dangerous interconnectedness, namely mutual debt guarantee chains[60] and triangular debts.[61] The problem seems to be particularly pronounced in state-sector companies in traditional, protected industries (eg manufacturing, mining) where these mechanisms are commonly used.[62] As a result, my interviewees argued, many (usually large) companies are not allowed to use the EBL – either at all or independently without state assistance.[63]

Firstly, many SOEs provide debt repayment guarantees for other SOEs who, in turn, provide debt repayment guarantees for them. As a result, these companies are interlocked in a web of mutual obligations to pay to third-party lenders in case of the other's inability to do so (including its insolvency). Many of my interviewees suggested that large companies in China are often involved in entire chains of such guarantees, and for significant sums.[64] This makes them vulnerable, because one corporate bankruptcy may trigger a chain of other bankruptcies where the other companies guaranteed the debt but are unable to service it and so are pushed into bankruptcy themselves.[65] In an extreme case, this may have a serious, destabilising effect on the local economy as a whole.[66]

In addition, large companies are also often involved in significant non-mutual debts among themselves – often referred to as 'triangular SOEs debt structures' – which have a similar effect to debt guarantees. If one of the lending companies in this structure declares bankruptcy under the EBL, its debts are repayable immediately,[67] which may trigger bankruptcy in other companies in the debt structure. Alternatively, if one of the borrowing companies in this structure declares bankruptcy under the EBL, its debts may not be repaid in full – regardless of whether the lender is secured or not[68] – which may also trigger a chain of financial distress or bankruptcies in other companies in the debt structure. As a result, my interviewees suggested that local governments often prefer individual, politically driven alternatives to the publicity and limitations of the safeguards in the EBL procedures, focusing in particular on the need to manage the

---

[59] Interviews B1-c, B3-c, C1-c, C4-c, C5-r, C7-s, E5-c, all judges (J1-c to J9-c), L4-r to L7-r, L10-s to L12-c, L16-c, P1-r, P3-r, R1-r to R4-c, R10-c, R13-c.

[60] These guarantee chains survive EBL procedures: Art 124 EBL. See eg D McMahon (23.11.2014, WSJ); G Wildau (28.4.2014, FT).

[61] See Section 3.3.2 for a non-EBL solution.

[62] See n 60.

[63] ibid.

[64] Interviews B1-c to B3-c, C1-c to C7-s, C10-s, C11-c, E1-c to E3-s, IF1-s, J1-c, L2-s to L6-s, L8-c, L11-c to L15-c, P1-r, P4-c, P5-c, R1-r to R3-r, R6-c, R9-c, R10-c.

[65] ibid.

[66] ibid. Note that, in 2015, a member of the special Committee for Bankruptcy and Reorganisation within Chinese Lawyers' Association warned of the systemic risk that this may pose: Judicial Independence in the PRC (Congressional-Executive Commission on China).

[67] Art 46 EBL states that all immature claims at the time of the case being accepted become mature.

[68] See Section 6.1.

systemic risk that the interconnectedness of the companies poses.[69] As above, this then reduces the value of creditors' expected recoveries under the EBL and prevents debtors from using the EBL as they wish. This limits the EBL's utility, and so may partly explain the low use of the law in practice.

7.3. The EBL not Viable for Certain Types of Debt Contracts

Finally, it appears that the EBL is not available to creditors in certain types of debt contracts[70] due to the circumstances in which the loans were made. This section considers three such cases. It first examines how the use of the EBL is prevented if the loans originated in China's shadow market.[71] Section 7.3.1 below examines a situation where loans may not be recoverable under the EBL because they were not made by state-authorised lenders and, as a result, are not enforceable in court. Section 7.3.2 considers a situation where the lenders charge interest that is higher than the permitted maximum, and so any excess is not recoverable. Using the EBL in either case would also draw undesirable attention to such lenders' activities, which may be an additional reason why shadow lenders in either case prefer to avoid using the EBL. Section 7.3.3 then looks at a situation where creditors – often state-related – are technically allowed to use the EBL but tend not to do so because doing so may expose their lending activities which contravened policy restrictions on lending into certain sectors. The consequences of being discovered range from the Party-state's displeasure and disciplinary measures to criminal and other sanctions.

7.3.1. The Origin of Debt Finance

As was discussed in Section 3.1, China's shadow finance market is vast and increasingly important for the economy. Until recently, its unauthorised private lending activities would not be recognised by courts, and many types of shadow activities have been forbidden by the state. And although in recent years shadow lenders in a few provinces have been able to enforce their credit contracts in court,[72] many of my interviewees suggested that – even in those provinces – shadow lenders remain unable or at least reluctant to use the EBL.[73] My interviewees pointed to two main reasons. First, shadow lenders' activities are often illegal, and so there is a risk that their claims would not be recognised.[74]

---

[69] See n 66.

[70] This section focuses on the position and incentives of creditors. The corresponding impact on debtors is triggered under the EBL investigation provisions, and are discussed in Section 6.2.

[71] For details on sources of corporate funding, see Section 3.1.

[72] Available data show that shadow lenders are slowly getting comfortable using formal individual debt enforcement mechanisms in select provinces such as Zhejiang. For an excellent summary, see S Finder (26.3.2015, The Diplomat).

[73] Interviews C2-c to C7-s, IF1-s, IF2-c, J1-c, J4-c, J7-c, J8-c, L1-c to L17-c, R1-r to R3-r, R6-c, R10-c.

[74] ibid.

Second, shadow lenders moreover face a particularly high risk of scrutiny and significant criminal liability pursuant to an EBL case, which – the interviewees suggested – shadow lenders believe can be avoided if they use non-EBL enforcement mechanisms.[75] This belief draws support from the fact that EBL procedures typically affect many stakeholders, and so attract unwanted attention.[76] To avoid it, shadow lenders prefer to use non-EBL enforcement mechanisms instead.[77]

My interviewees pointed to the fact that the fear of increased scrutiny of shadow lenders' activities under the EBL is particularly pronounced among creditors in regions with a small private sector[78] and little support for pro-market measures.[79] Until recently, shadow lenders could be sentenced to death for their illegal activities.[80] And even though this is no longer the case, creditors[81] involved in unauthorised borrowing from the general public, relending bank loans in the shadow market, carrying out any other 'unauthorised activities' which 'disrupt' the market, or collecting deposits and setting up financial institutions without regulator's permission[82] nevertheless face severe fines and long-term imprisonment. As a result – many interviewees claimed – shadow creditors are disinclined to use the EBL procedures.[83]

7.3.2. Usury Laws

Besides the difficulties that shadow lenders face in general, the lenders who charge 'high' or 'usurious' interest rates also face an increased probability that courts would not protect their claims even in provinces where shadow lenders enjoy some judicial recognition and that their activities – once exposed – may lead to the imposition of criminal liability. The discussion in Section 6.2 showed that private lending with high interest

---

[75] ibid. For an overview of criminal provisions concerning shadow lending, see Section 6.2.2. For a discussion of non-EBL alternatives, see Section 3.2 and ch 9.

[76] ibid – Interviewees L2-s, L4-r and L6-s spoke of several examples where their clients were subjected to such unwanted attention and compared it to other, similar cases where private enforcement through negotiations or bilateral arbitration led to 'more desirable, less heated, and more efficient results' (Interview L4-r).

[77] ibid.

[78] For a definition see Section 2.4.2.

[79] Interviews C2-c to C7-s, IF1-s, IF2-c, J1-c, J4-c, J7-c, J8-c, L1-c to L17-c, R1-r to R3-r, R6-c, R10-c. However, two of my interviews (L4-r and L6-s) argued in the regions with a particularly strong private sector and pro-market courts – most importantly Zhejiang Province and Wenzhou City – the shadow lenders are treated like normal lenders, and their claims are often satisfied even under the EBL because the local government and the courts fear that ruling any other way would cause serious social unrest, which they wish to avoid. Moreover, R10-c also suggested that – according to their extensive research in China – courts may in some cases be so worried about violent enforcement against private persons by shark lenders that they give them full protection and priority to their claims, including full interest rate repayment.

[80] eg the notorious case of Wu Ying, a 31-year-old tycoon who raised and lent about USD 122 million through the private capital market, who was given a death sentence for fraud (reduced to life imprisonment after public protests): J Li, N He and J Xu (14.2.2014, China Daily). The death penalty in this context has now been abolished (through state policy, not in Criminal Law): Y Cao (26.11.2014, China Daily).

[81] And debtors: Section 6.2.

[82] Arts 176, 175, 225(3) and 174 Criminal Law (amended 2015), respectively. For full details see Section 6.2.

[83] Interviews C2-c to C7-s, IF1-s, IF2-c, J1-c, J4-c, J7-c, J8-c, L1-c to L17-c, R1-r to R3-r, R6-c, R10-c.

rates is a criminal offence punishable by imprisonment and fines,[84] and until 2014 – in particularly serious cases – by life imprisonment or even a death penalty.[85]

Although there is no definition of 'high interest rate,' many of my interviewees suggested that, until recently, it was a flexible concept allowing for a degree of judicial (and political) discretion, but usually meaning more than the official lending rates.[86] The SPC has now confirmed that it means more than 24 or 36 per cent.[87] However, this guidance is only relevant for cases from late 2015 onwards – and has, therefore, very little explanatory power for earlier cases. The threat of severe punishment for the vaguely defined crime of lending with high interest rates was, therefore, present in creditors' minds and influenced their decision whether to use the EBL between 2007 and 2015.[88] Moreover, even post-2015, it is proposed that the restriction of permissible level of interest rates is likely to affect the preferences of many shadow lenders – who often charge very high annual interest rates and are often able to recover them using non-EBL enforcement alternatives.[89]

Besides the issue of recoverability, many interviewees also suggested that shadow creditors fear that using the EBL would increase the likelihood that their activities would be scrutinised under Criminal Law provisions.[90] If so, they could face criminal liability for their unauthorised lending activities[91] as well as fines and imprisonment for their usurious lending practices.[92] Several interviewees suggested that courts are 'ready and willing to punish shark lenders', particularly given the

> keen attention that the Party and the government pay to resolve the problems associated with shadow banking, and in particular with exorbitant interest rates, which can weaken the financial health of otherwise strong companies and can affect the macroeconomic stability of the whole country.[93]

As a result, shadow market creditors who charge high interest rates – however determined – have a strong incentive not to use the EBL, especially where they have alternative means for enforcing their claim.[94]

---

[84] See Section 6.2.

[85] See n 80.

[86] Interview C1-c to C7-s, C10-s, E1-c to E3-s, IF1-s, IF2-c, J5-s, J6-s, J8-c, L2-s to L6-s, L12-c, L13-c, L16-c, R1-r to R3-r, R6-c, R9-c, R10-c. See also X Zhang and M Liu, 'Lending and taking security in China: Overview' (1.7.2019) Practical Law Guide.

[87] The SPC suggested that courts would not enforce any claim for the interest repayments exceeding 24% (and in some cases 36%): the SPC Provisions concerning Several Issues concerning the Application of Law in the Trial of Private Lending Cases (*Fashi* [2015] No 18). For an overview see SA Li (3.11.2015, CrowdFundInsider).

[88] Interviews C2-c to C5-r, C11-c, IF1-s, IF2-c, J1-c, J6-s, L1-r to L6-s, L8-c to L11-c, L14-c to L17-c, R1-r to R3-r, R6-c, R7-c, R9-c, R10-c.

[89] See Section 3.1 and ch 9. See also Reuters (29.9.2011).

[90] Interviews C2-c to C7-s, C10-s, C11-c, IF1-s, IF2-c, J6-s, L1-r to L6-s, L8-c to L17-c, R1-r to R3-r, R6-c, R9-c, R10-c.

[91] See Sections 3.2–3.3 and 7.3. See also Section 11.2.3.

[92] See n 87. They propose that the regulator has a good reason to prevent such high-interest-rate lending. The problem is not only its immorality but also the fact that it pushes objectively healthy companies into factual insolvency, leading to the destruction of companies and jobs and to very few people getting rich from it.

[93] Interview R10-c, similar views were also expressed in Interviews C2-c to C5-r, C11-c, IF1-s, IF2-c, J1-c, J6-s, L1-r to L6-s, L8-c to L11-c, L14-c to L17-c, R1-r to R3-r, R6-c, R7-c, R9-c.

[94] These alternatives are explored in Section 9.1.

7.3.3. Policy Restrictions on Lending

While the main reasons for avoiding the EBL in the previous two sections were attributable to the affiliation of the creditor, in this section, it is the affiliation of the debtor that diminishes creditors' ability to recover. My interviewees used the example of lending to real estate companies, but suggested that this issue concerns any sector that is affected by policy restrictions on lending.[95] Although Chinese real estate projects once enjoyed an almost unlimited supply of bank finance – being perceived as low-risk, certain growth – the market regulator started imposing restrictions on the supply of finance in 2001 to cool growth of the property market and manage what was feared to be a growing property bubble.[96] Instead of slowing down, however, property developers turned to shadow lenders who readily extended large loans to them. A Credit Suisse study estimated that at one point, about 60 per cent of all shadow lending went into the real estate sector.[97] As a result, there is an increasing number of empty houses and so-called ghost towns where new blocks of flats fail to attract purchasers and occupants.[98] Nevertheless, real estate companies keep building, and property prices continue climbing. This trend further fuels the property bubble and could be extremely dangerous for China's fragile economy, and so it needs to be managed by the regulator.[99]

Many interviewees argued – and numerous newspaper stories support – that many real estate companies have been financially distressed and even insolvent.[100] Recent large-scale defaults or near-defaults included 10 billion RMB in debt by Tianyu Construction company in 2012 and 3.5 billion RMB in debt by Zhejiang Xingrun Real Estate in April 2014.[101] However, to date, many real estate companies avoid using the EBL to resolve their financial problems.[102] My interviewees suggested that one of the reasons is that creditors – and in particular state-related creditors – with claims against real estate companies prefer to recover their claims informally, where possible, because they wish to avoid drawing too much attention to their activities which contravene express policy restrictions on lending.[103] Alternatively, the interviewees suggested, if a

---

[95] Interviews B1-c, C1-c to C7-s, E3-s, IF1-s, IF2-c, L1-r to L6-s, L9-s to L15-c, R1-r to R3-r, R6-c, R7-c, R9-c, R10-c.

[96] See eg B Powell (22.3.2010, The Times); AsiaNews (28.11.2011); Y Yang (19.12.2016, FT); S Rabinovitch (2.12.2012, FT).

[97] A large proportion of the 2008/09 financial stimulus from the state – aimed at counteracting the effects of the global financial crisis – ended up in the real estate sector. This took place directly as new loans and indirectly as bridge loans to repay the outstanding bank loans: Credit Suisse, Case Studies on the Monitoring of Informal Credit Markets (Credit Suisse Economics Research, 28.9.2011) 1 and 3.

[98] BBVA, 'China's shadow bank lending: a threat to financial stability?' (23.11.2011) China Banking Watch, BBVA Research, 1 and 7.

[99] See n 96.

[100] Interviews B1-c, B2-c, C2-c to C5-r, C7-s, IF1-s, IF2-c, L2-s to L6-s, L9-s to L17-c, P1-r, R1-r to R3-r, R6-c, R7-c, R9-c, R10-c, R13-c.

[101] Reuters (3.4.2014). The problems – and corresponding restrictions – are likely to continue: S Hsu (16.1.2015, The Diplomat).

[102] But note that real estate companies do occasionally use the EBL – especially if they are particularly large or listed: see Z Zhang, *Corporate Reorganisations in China* (Cambridge University Press, 2018) 43 and 105.

[103] Interviews B1-c, B2-c, C2-c to C5-r, C7-s, IF1-s, IF2-c, L2-s to L6-s, L17-c, R1-r to R3-r, R7-c, R9-c, R10-c.

failure of a large, economically significant real estate company would lead to significant redundancies or a region-wide social and economic disturbance, the affected creditors can often rely on politically driven alternatives[104] which can give them superior payoffs to what they could recover under the EBL.[105] Therefore, most creditors lending to real estate borrowers affected by policy restrictions on lending – and, indeed, debtors thus affected – either do not want to or do not need to use the EBL.

---

[104] Or increasingly also an EBL procedure with heavy influence from local government: see the reorganisation of a real estate developer Ganzhou Yingxin Developer Ltd in Zhang, *Corporate Reorganisations* (2018) 105.

[105] ibid. See also Section 9.2.

8

The Third Constraint – Limitations and Biases of EBL Enforcers

My interviewees suggested that the problems surrounding the quality of enforcement – and of EBL's direct[1] and indirect[2] enforcers – also contribute to the limited use of the EBL. Section 8.1 of this chapter looks at courts' and lawyers' internal limitations that affect their perceived ability to deal with bankruptcy cases in an effective, fair, objective and predictable manner. Section 8.2 examines the passivity of some administrators when carrying out EBL pro-creditor duties and powers, and discusses how it reduces the parties' potential payoffs. Section 8.3 concludes by looking at when and how the Party-state interferes with courts' enforcement of the EBL, and how that adversely affects the parties' incentives and ability to use the EBL. The causes of enforcers' limitations and biases and their impact on debtors' and creditors' expectations are summarised in Table 8.1.

Table 8.1 Overview of EBL enforcers' limitations and biases

	Cause of enforcers' limitations and biases	Impact on debtors' and creditors' expectations
Courts' & lawyers' limitations (section I)	(i) lack of expertise and experience (ii) delays, length and cost (iii) courts' internal quotas (iv) judicial corruption	(i) Limits debtors' and creditors' trust that enforcement of the EBL is effective, fair and objective (ii) Reduces creditors' expected payoffs (iii) Possible inability to use the EBL
Administrators' passivity (section II)	(i) general enforcement issues (ii) courts do not force administrators to use their powers (iii) pressure from the Party-state not to act	(i) Loss of a major advantage of using the EBL

(continued)

---

[1] ie judges, lawyers and administrators.
[2] ie local governments and local Party representatives.

Table 8.1 *(Continued)*

	Cause of enforcers' limitations and biases	Impact on debtors' and creditors' expectations
Party-state's influence over courts (section II)	(i) lack of judicial independence due to interference from local Party-state in EBL cases	(i) Limits debtors' and creditors' trust that enforcement of the EBL is effective, fair and objective (ii) Reduces creditors' expected payoffs (iii) Possible inability to use the EBL

8.1. Courts' and Lawyers' Internal Limitations

As was discussed earlier, courts have a central role in EBL procedures and, as such, are empowered to ensure that the parties carry out their respective duties and powers according to the EBL.[3] Courts have the final say in cases of conflict, they can sanction or prevent agreements from going ahead, and they can impose their own 'best solution' on the parties.[4] Many of my interviewees expressed sincere appreciation for the work of Chinese courts and judges who, as one interviewee put it, 'do their best given the circumstances'.[5] However, they also suggested that, in many cases, there are serious limitations regarding courts' abilities, capacity and power to deal with EBL cases effectively.[6] Some of these internal limitations disincentivise creditors and debtors from using court-driven EBL procedures and make them use alternative enforcement mechanisms[7] which they perceive as relatively cheaper, quicker, easier and more accessible.[8] My interviewees suggested that there are three key groups of limitations. Section 8.1.1 below examines the lack of courts' and lawyers' commercial and bankruptcy-related expertise and experience. Section 8.1.2 considers the relative length and cost of the EBL process, and Section 8.1.3 looks at courts' internal quota system. Finally, Section 8.1.4 considers the potential role and impact of judicial corruption on EBL cases.[9]

Although most of the issues below relate to judges, some of my interviewees highlighted that the limitations and biases of lawyers – as corporate advisors and problem-solvers – also influence whether and how the EBL is used.[10] Lawyers' roles and limitations are mostly ignored in prior literature, but their ability to understand, offer

---

[3] See Sections 4.2.9 and 6.1.

[4] ibid.

[5] Interview L6-s. Similar views were also expressed in Interviews C2-c, C5-r, C7-s, L1-r to L5-c, R1-r, R3-r, R10-c.

[6] Much effort and resources have gone into improving the judicial expertise in recent years. See also Sections 12.3, 12.4 and 12.6.

[7] See Section 9.1.

[8] See ch 9. For a discussion why this may be problematic, see Sections 10.1 and 11.3.4–11.3.5.

[9] Further limitations on the courts' power and ability to act stem from biases arising from the Party-state's interference, which are explored in Section 8.3.

[10] Interviews C2-c, C7-s, J7-c, J8-c, L4-r to L6-s.

and explain EBL procedures to financially distressed companies and unpaid creditors was repeatedly highlighted during my participation in workshops and legal training programmes in China. The relevant insights are, therefore, included in the discussion below.

8.1.1. Expertise, Experience and Consistency when Applying the EBL

Most Chinese judges are not well versed in corporate bankruptcy matters. There had been calls for developing greater judicial expertise in commercial and bankruptcy matters under the 1986 law,[11] which have been reiterated repeatedly in recent years in the context of the EBL.[12] China started experimenting with specialised bankruptcy courts (and specialised sections within general courts) in several regions[13] in 2016 and their progress – along with debtors' and creditors' experience with specialised courts – is discussed in Section 12.4.

This section, on the other hand, focuses on debtors' and creditors' experience with general courts as the majority of EBL petitions are still heard by generalist judges. My interviewees suggested that many debtors and creditors perceive Chinese judges as lacking sufficient understanding of commercial and technical matters, which disincentivises them from using the EBL.[14] This is particularly pronounced in lower courts and in less developed and less commercially active regions.[15] A number of my interviewees – mostly themselves potential creditors or advisors to creditors and debtors – said that companies are often reluctant to give up control over their claims to a generalist judge who has 'limited appreciation of the particular practices and norms of their trade',[16] and so is more likely to 'ignore [their] interests and protect the state and employees instead'.[17]

The lack of judges' expertise and experience in EBL-related matters is particularly problematic in reorganisation cases. Two issues arise in this context. Firstly, judges are often unable or unwilling to allow pre-insolvency entry of debtors into the reorganisation procedure despite it being expressly allowed in Article 2(2) of the EBL.[18] The key

---

[11] Critique of the 1986 bankruptcy law: W Wang, 'Strengthening Judicial Expertise in Bankruptcy Proceedings in China' (2001) presented at the Forum for Asian Insolvency Reform (FAIR), Bali, 7–8 February 2001.

[12] See eg interview with Professor Li: Legal Daily (12.2.2007).

[13] Local testing of new laws and measures is common in China – see eg recent reforms in ch 12.

[14] Interviews B1-c, C1-c to C5-r, C7-s, C10-s, all entrepreneurs (E1-c to E5-c), IF1-s, IF2-c, L2-s to L6-s, L9-s to L15-c, R1-r to R3-r, R6-c, R7-c, R9-c, R10-c.

[15] ibid.

[16] Interview E4-c, similar views expressed in Interviews C1-c, C4-c, C5-r, C7-s, E2-s to E5-c, IF1-s, IF2-c, L1-s to L6-s, L10-s.

[17] Interview L4-r, similar views expressed in Interviews C1-c, C4-c to C7-s, E2-s to E4-c, IF1-s, IF2-c, L1-r to L6-s, L9-s, L10-s. In this regard, their arguments are similar to the reason why the diamond traders elected to contractually opt out of the legal system and instead operate under their own rules and judges: L Bernstein, 'Opting out of the Legal System: Extralegal Contractual Relations in the Diamond Industry' (1992) *Journal of Legal Studies* 115. See also Section 2.3.1.

[18] For details, see Sections 4.2.2, 4.2.4 and 6.3. For reform proposals, see Section 11.1.4.1. See also Z Zhang, *Corporate Reorganisations in China* (CUP, 2018) 19 and 38–39.

issue appears to be the lack of guidance with regards to what constitutes a company being 'likely to become insolvent'.[19] In general, judges are not willing to determine how close to insolvency a company has to be in order to satisfy this test, and so demand that the company be insolvent before it can use the EBL reorganisation procedure. Some judges lack the experience required to confidently determine whether the entry test has been satisfied, while others fear that the EBL moratorium – which is triggered automatically upon acceptance of the petition[20] – may be abused, and so they usually refuse to allow pre-insolvency use of reorganisation.[21] That is problematic because international experience suggests that timely – usually pre-insolvency – start of reorganisation is one of the most important determinants for its success.[22]

Secondly, judges' varying levels of experience and expertise mean that their approach to EBL petitions and the criteria that they apply when considering EBL reorganisation petitions vary greatly. Empirical research suggests that courts only accept EBL reorganisation petitions from large companies.[23] Such size-related requirement is not found in the EBL, and so it is not clear what determines whether a company is 'large' for this purpose. In practice, it appears that it is broadly equivalent to 'state sector' companies[24] – ie economically significant (large by local standards, many assets, sometimes listed) and usually with many employees.[25] Reserving EBL reorganisations to large companies has been unofficially endorsed since the later drafts of the EBL,[26] and it was identified as the correct approach in the SPC guidance in 2009[27] and in some provinces through local-level guidance.[28] This is problematic as the EBL itself does not exclude smaller companies from applying. Nevertheless, in practice, smaller companies are often discouraged from even considering the EBL reorganisation as an option and are instead directed by the SPC to use composition or liquidation instead.[29]

Similarly, courts have been instructed by the SPC[30] to pay particular attention to companies that fall within a broad list of national strategic industries identified by the State Council and the National Development and Reform Commission.[31] However, being in an industry that appears on the list does not automatically ensure that a court will accept the reorganisation petition[32] – it merely makes it more likely that a court

---

[19] See Section 11.1.4.

[20] See Section 4.2.3.

[21] See Zhang, *Corporate Reorganisations* (2018) 19.

[22] See eg T Jackson, *The Logic and Limits of Bankruptcy* Law (Beard Books, 1986) ch 8.

[23] See Zhang (n 18) 20–22.

[24] See Section 2.5.2.

[25] See Zhang (n 18) 40–22.

[26] Z Jia, 'Explanation on the Draft Law of the People's Republic of China on Enterprise Bankruptcy' (2006) *Journal of the China People's Congress* 575.

[27] Art 6 of the SPC Notice concerning the Correct Hearing of EBL Cases and Judicial Guarantee to Maintain Orderly Market Economy (*Fafa* [2009] No 36).

[28] eg in Zhejiang Province: Art 12 of the Zhejiang SPC Memorandum on Adjudicating Enterprise Bankruptcies in Simplified Procedures' (*Zhegaofa* [2013] No 153).

[29] Art 6 of the SPC Notice concerning the Correct Hearing of EBL Cases and Judicial Guarantee to Maintain Orderly Market Economy (*Fafa* [2009] No 36). Note that simplified EBL procedures are being developed for smaller companies: see Section 12.8.

[30] The SPC Notice concerning the Correct Hearing of EBL Cases and Judicial Guarantee to Maintain Orderly Market Economy (*Fafa* [2009] No 36).

[31] The latest list was issued in 2017. See www.sdpc.gov.cn/gzdt/201702/W020170204632980447904.pdf.

[32] See Zhang (n 18) 22–23 and 43.

will pay close attention to the application.[33] This further reduces the predictability and transparency of the process, and so discourages some creditors and debtors from considering EBL reorganisation as a viable option.

In addition, some courts also appear to be applying what could be described as a feasibility or survivability test. This requirement does not appear in the EBL either,[34] but some argue that it naturally follows from the spirit of the EBL provisions.[35] This test has been endorsed by the SPC in the 2018 and 2020 typical cases.[36] The feasibility test is also applied in cases involving listed companies.[37] It has also been recognised in some provinces where the petitioning debtor or creditor must explain whether and how the company can successfully complete the reorganisation procedure.[38] Naturally, successful completion can take many different forms – from survival to full return to the pre-insolvency level of performance (or better) – and can be measured in different ways, which has led to the test being applied very differently across China.[39] This is problematic for potential petitioners because proving feasibility may be difficult or outright impossible,[40] and it is likely to delay the potential entry into restructuring which is very time-sensitive.[41] Moreover, the application of these tests has not been consistent or predictable. The variable levels of scrutiny by courts and vastly different levels of courts' enthusiasm, experience and expertise in the relevant fields make creditors and debtors reluctant to use the EBL.

Unfortunately, except for a few EBL-active provinces, judges in general are unlikely to learn more about finance, commerce and effective corporate restructuring and liquidation in the natural course of their job because they do not hear enough EBL cases.[42] Generalist judges, therefore, remain mostly ill-prepared to deal with the increasing demand for[43] and complexity of EBL hearings[44] which result from China's gradual transition to a more market-driven economy.[45]

Notably, many corporate lawyers in China are also affected by the lack of an in-depth understanding and experience with the EBL. However, unlike courts which only get involved after the parties decide to use the EBL, lawyers play a role even before a

---

[33] Such companies are economically significant, and so fall into the state sector: see Section 2.5.

[34] See eg G Pen and T Zhang, 'Entry of Corporate Reorganisation Procedures' (2012) *Academic Forum* 72.

[35] See eg L Wang, 'Problems of Amending the Bankruptcy Law' (2005) *Legal Science* 3; H Tang and Y Shi, 'Judicial Experiment of Hearing Corporate Reorganisation of Private Companies' (2011) *Legal Research* 102.

[36] See the preambles to both batches of typical cases and seventh typical case (2020) – see sections 4.3–4.4.

[37] Art 3 of the SPC Memorandum concerning Handling of Listed Companies' Reorganisations and Liquidations (*Fa* [2012] No 261).

[38] eg Art 11 of the Zhejiang Memorandum (n 28); Arts 14–15 of the Beijing Municipal SPC Notice concerning Procedural Rules of Enterprise Bankruptcy in Beijing Municipality (*Beijing Gaofafa* [2013] No 242).

[39] For a discussion and examples from practice see Zhang (n 18) 45–46.

[40] Due to problems with the quality of publicly available information and property rights: Sections 7.1.1–7.1.2.

[41] See Section 8.1.2.

[42] Interviews C1-c, C4-c to C7-s, E2-s, E4-c, IF1-s, IF2-c, L1-r to L6-s, L10-s, P1-r, R1-r to R3-r, R6-c, R7-c, R10-c.

[43] See Section 10.1.

[44] As the Chinese economy started slowing down, the courts have allowed more cases in 2015. The Government also ordered the courts to liquidate so-called zombie companies in 2016, which is likely to lead to a further increase: see Section 12.3.

[45] See the analysis of policy-making in this regard in RL Kuhn, *How China's Leaders Think* (Wiley & Sons, 2011) ch 21.

debtor becomes insolvent and long before the parties decide to go to court. It is, therefore, crucial that lawyers understand how the EBL operates, what it offers to debtors and creditors, and what are its major advantages and disadvantages. Unfortunately, my interviewees suggested that comparatively few lawyers have such understanding, and most of them work in select few regions of China.[46] It is, therefore, likely that some creditors and debtors that would otherwise consider using the EBL are simply not aware of the option,[47] or do not perceive it as a sufficiently viable option due to the incomplete understanding of what the law offers.[48] Moreover, until recently, lawyers had no definitive source of this information.[49] Traditionally, there have been very few local bankruptcy practitioners' associations,[50] and the practice varies significantly across provinces depending on the preferences of local governments and the guidance and abilities of local courts.[51]

Consequently, an increasing number of voices have been calling for widely available specialised bankruptcy courts and bankruptcy training for judges and practitioners[52] in the hope that courts' newly acquired skills and knowledge and the competency improvements could eventually lead to a quicker and cheaper resolution of financial distress,[53] which may then increase the parties' willingness to resolve their case in a court-driven EBL procedure.[54]

8.1.2. Delays, Length and Cost of the EBL Process

My interviewees all agreed that, in their experience, the relative length and cost of EBL procedures (compared to alternative mechanisms) are also directly relevant to whether creditors and debtors choose to use them.[55] This section, therefore, looks at the length and cost of using the EBL and considers their impact on the parties' willingness to use the law.

The EBL and subsequent SPC guidelines introduced tight deadlines for all stages of the EBL process.[56] However, my interviewees suggested that the law on paper is not

---

[46] Mostly in large cities and coastal regions: interviews C5-r, C7-s, J4-c, J8-c, L2-s, L4-r to L7-c, P1-r, R3-r, R10-c.

[47] Interviews L6-s, R3-r, R10-c.

[48] Interviews C5-r, J8-c, L4-r, L6-s, R10-c.

[49] See Section 12.5.

[50] However, note that there has been an increase in recent years: see Section 12.4.

[51] Interviews C5-r, C7-s, J4-c, J8-c, L2-s to L7-c, P1-r, R1-r, R3-r, R9-c, R10-c. The degree of interference from local governments also varies: see sections 2.4, 8.3 and 11.3.5.

[52] See Sections 11.3.2 and 12.4.

[53] cf a study of bankruptcy law reform in Brazil: A Araujo, R Reffeira and B Funchal, 'The Brazilian bankruptcy law experience' (2012) *Journal of Corporate Finance* 994. There are some promising early results from those provinces in China that introduced specialised courts: see Section 12.4.

[54] Based on informal discussion with a number of corporate and bankruptcy lawyers who participated in my practitioners' workshop about the EBL in China in 2016.

[55] This is not unique to China. Most commercial parties in China and abroad consider the costs and benefits of their options and decide accordingly what is the best strategy. However, due to the weak enforcement of the EBL and non-existent monitoring thereof, the parties in China are, in practice, often able to avoid using the law altogether and choose to resolve debtors' financial distress informally.

[56] See Sections 4.2.4–4.2.6. The time limits have recently been reiterated in the SPC 2018 typical cases: see Section 4.3.

reflected in reality. Many petitioners never hear back about whether their petition was accepted,[57] and even if they do, it rarely happens within the authorised 37 days.[58] The interviewed practitioners felt unable to provide a representative estimate of the average length of an EBL procedure. They said that the main reasons are that each case and each province is very different and that the court and Party-state's response usually depends on several issues. These include the debtor's size, relative economic importance, affiliation with the private or state sector, interconnectedness in the economy and with other large companies, interests of the local government, the number of employees, the difficulty with finding alternative employment for the redundant workers,[59] courts' and administrators' experience and willingness to hear EBL cases, the complexity of the given case, whether the debtor's assets are located in one or several provinces, whether there are foreign elements present, and whether the case is likely to receive attention from the international observers and media.[60] Moreover, given the low number of cases in many courts, they felt it was not possible to provide a representative estimate of an average length 'because the [EBL] cases are so widely different'.[61]

There is limited data on the duration and delays within the EBL process. The SPC does not release statistics about the length of EBL cases. A recent empirical study surveyed the duration of 885 cases between 2005 and 2016 and found that an EBL case in their sample took, on average, over 520 days from when the petition was accepted to when the case was closed.[62] That is broadly consistent with an analysis from the end of 2015 that estimates that the average length of EBL procedures is two to four years.[63] Similarly, the SPC typical cases released in 2018 provide further insights, albeit the data should be treated with caution because these cases were handpicked by the SPC to showcase the EBL in its full force rather than to be a representative sample of the EBL practice.[64] Of the 10 typical cases in 2018, the liquidation cases took eight to 10.5 months to complete, while the reorganisation cases took between six and 22 months to complete. In some cases, EBL hearing is shortened through so-called pre-packs.[65]

Steps are being taken to speed up the process.[66] But until the reforms become effective across China, EBL procedures are likely to take much longer than is prescribed by the EBL. All my interviewees agreed that, for now, EBL procedures are perceived as being long in their own right and comparatively much longer than many non-EBL

---

[57] The SPC acknowledged this as a problem (eg Liu Guixiang's speech introducing the 2018 typical cases – see Section 4.3) and the SPC Provisions (I) concerning the Application of the EBL (*Fashi* [2011] No 22) makes it possible for such a petitioner to turn to a higher court.

[58] Interviews C5-r, C7-s, L2-s, L4-r to L7-c, L9-s to L15-c, R3-r, R10-c.

[59] This was identified as the single most important cause of delay in EBL procedures since courts often refuse (following local government's guidance) to close an EBL case without sufficient number of the redundant employees being reemployed: Interviews C2-c, C5-r, C7-s, J1-c, J6-s, L1-r to L6-s, L9-s, L11-c, L13-c, P1-r, P3-r, R1-r, R3-r, R10-c.

[60] Interviews C2-c to C5-r, C7-s, J1-c, J6-s to J8-c, L1-r to L7-c, L9-s, L11-c, L13-c, L14-c, P1-r, P3-r, R1-r, R3-r, R4-c, R10-c.

[61] Interview L2-s – this view was shared by all the Chinese lawyers that I interviewed (L1-r to L15-c).

[62] B Li and J Ponticelly, 'Going Bankrupt in China', available at ssrn.com/abstract=3251570.

[63] Euler Hermes, 'Collection Profile: China' (December 2015).

[64] See Section 4.3.

[65] See Sections 8.3.5 and 9.2.3. See also the sixth typical case (2018) in Section 4.3.

[66] See ch 12 for details.

alternatives, which disincentivises creditors from using the EBL.[67] The reason for such perception, they suggested, was that in many cases there is a significant delay, firstly, between the time when a petition is submitted and when it is actually accepted, and secondly, between the commencement and the resolution of an EBL case.[68] Such delays enable grabbing and stripping of debtor's assets, and it also provides an opportunity for debtor's representatives to run away.[69] Both problems were highlighted as important obstacles to the functioning of the EBL in a recent in-depth report by Ma Jian, who examined data and law users' experiences in EBL cases between 2003 and 2012.[70]

The issue of relative cost also appears to be an important consideration when deciding whether to use the EBL (compared to alternative mechanisms). Many of my interviewees argued that EBL procedures are too expensive for smaller companies.[71] This is one of the reasons why the SPC suggests that reorganisation should only be used by large companies[72] and why several local courts started exploring the option of simplified EBL hearing.[73] Nevertheless, even larger players – whose financial distress is often more complex and who may, therefore, conceivably benefit from external coordination under the EBL – often perceive the cost as too high due to the problems (both general and particular to the EBL) with enforcing the EBL in practice.[74]

The cost of liquidation can be high,[75] but it is usually particularly high in reorganisation. This is because EBL enforcement includes not only (often significant) fees paid to the practitioners and courts – some of which may also be charged in alternative debt enforcement mechanisms – but also the indirect cost of the relocation of laid-off workers,[76] the costs imposed on crammed-down creditors in politically driven EBL cases,[77] the macro-economic costs imposed through implied state guarantees to repay state companies' debts,[78] and the costs and debt write-offs imposed by the state on creditors in many state-sector corporate bankruptcies.[79] As a result, despite the advantages of collective procedures,[80] the EBL can become much more expensive than alternative mechanisms.[81]

---

[67] All my interviews agreed with this statement, and those with international experience (Interviews C1-c to C3-c, C7-s, L2-s, L4-c to L6-s) also added that particularly the overall length (when taking into account the pre-EBL negotiations as well as the court time under the EBL) is relatively greater than elsewhere.

[68] Interviews B1-c, C2-c, C5-r, C7-s, E3-s, E4-c, L10r to L6-s, L8-c to L13-c, R10-c.

[69] See Sections 3.3.1 and 7.1.3–7.1.4.

[70] J Ma, 'Analysis of 10 years of People's Courts hearing bankruptcy cases' (China INSOL, 27.6.2014).

[71] Interviews C4-c to C7-s, E1-c, E2-s, IF2-c, J1-c, J6-s to J9-c, L2-sto L6-s, R10-c. NB: this is not unique to China.

[72] For a discussion, see Section 8.1.1.

[73] See Section 12.8.

[74] Interviews P1-r, R3-r, R6-c, R7-c. See also Section 8.1.1.

[75] See eg Section 4.3, the second typical case (2018) concerning the Liquidation of Songhui Industry, where bankruptcy expenses accounted for 6.85 million RMB and the remaining 9.38 million RMB covered most of the employees' claims. No other claims were satisfied.

[76] See Sections 6.1 and 8.1.1.

[77] See Sections 8.3.4 and 9.2.

[78] ibid.

[79] ibid.

[80] Such as preservation of asset value, higher sale price in liquidation, higher chance of saving the business or the whole company in reorganisation – see Sections 1.1 and 10.1 for discussion.

[81] See eg an interview with Professor Li (n 12). The same view was expressed in Interviews C4-c to C7-s, E1-c, E2-s, IF2-c, J1-c, J6-s to J9-c, L2-sto L6-s, P1-r, R10-c.

When combined with the fact that, historically, many EBL reorganisations have failed to save the company or its business[82] and that EBL liquidation cases evidence a preference for repayment of state-preferred stakeholders,[83] the EBL as currently implemented often not only fails to create value due to the inefficiencies in the way it is implemented,[84] but it also destroys value through the attendant direct and indirect costs. It is, therefore, hardly surprising that creditors and debtors are reluctant to use the EBL regime.[85]

8.1.3. Courts' Informal Quota System

Besides creditors' and debtors' reluctance to entrust their case to courts whom they perceive as lacking in expertise, experience and ability to deal with their case comparatively quickly and cheaply, judges themselves are often reluctant to allow technically insolvent companies to invoke the EBL. Several of my interviewees suggested that one of the reasons for this reluctance is that courts face internal quotas of how many cases they should hear and resolve in any given period to 'satisfy the internal performance requirements [and] look good to [their] boss – the local government'.[86] This attitude is clearly widely shared, as confirmed in several reports and articles. In a recent newspaper interview, one judge said that 'Some courts' assessment systems are based on quantitative heroes. It may take several years to process a bankruptcy case, which affects the enthusiasm of the judge to deal with corporate bankruptcy cases'.[87] Another commentator said: 'The court's handling of bankruptcy cases is time-consuming and unsatisfactory, which affects the closing rate, so there is no enthusiasm'.[88]

The problem is that many EBL cases, and particularly large-scale reorganisations, are often complex and, therefore, take a long time to resolve.[89] As a result, generalist[90] courts do 'not want to clog [their] books with cases which either take too long or may be too expensive and too difficult to resolve'.[91] This adds to courts' tendency to prioritise the use of their limited resources to deal with 'more urgent issues'[92] rather than difficult, lengthy and controversial EBL cases. As a result, the interviewees suggested, courts sometimes ignore EBL petitions.[93]

---

[82] These conclusions are drawn from a summary of the EBL cases in Wenzhou from the period of 2012–15 (privately acquired dataset with the author).

[83] See Sections 6.1, 7.2 and 8.3.

[84] As discussed in ch 6 and Section 7.1.

[85] See Sections 11.3.1 and 11.3.3 for proposed improvements.

[86] Interview R10-c – similar views were also expressed in Interviews C2-c, C5-r, C7-s, C9-c, J1-c, J6-s to J8-c, P1-r, R1-r, R4-c, R7-c. See also interview with Professor Li (n 12).

[87] Sina (28.3.2016).

[88] ibid.

[89] ibid. See also People's Daily (10.10.2015) and Section 12.8.

[90] cf specialised courts. See Sections 11.3.2 and 12.4.

[91] Interview J1-c. Similar views expressed in Interviews C2-c, C5-r, C7-s, C9-c, J7-c to J9-c, P1-r, R1-r, R4-c, R7-c, R10-c.

[92] Interview J1-c, same views also expressed in Interviews C5-r, C7-s, J3-c, J5-s to J9-c, L4-r to L6-s, P1-r, R1-r, R3-r, R10-c.

[93] ibid. Several of them (C7-s, J10-c, J9-c, L4-r, L6-s, P1-r, R1-r, R10-c) suggested that the Government does not wish to look bad when compared with other countries, and so there is a lot of pressure to be seen as resolving cases quickly and effectively. The quota system is one of the incentives that they use to achieve a quicker turnover of cases.

This attitude is completely natural but problematic for China's market and the economy. The EBL is crucial for ensuing efficient resolution of corporate financial distress, better allocation of resources through the introduction of hard-budget constraints, and greater willingness of banks to provide cheap credit through easier and more certain debt recoveries.[94] For a discussion of reform options and recent reform initiatives, see Sections 11.3.3.3 and 12.11, respectively.

8.1.4. Judicial Corruption

Several academics and observers further blame courts' unwillingness to hear certain cases on systemic judicial corruption in China.[95] It is true that judicial corruption has been a real problem in China, and there had been several high-profile cases – including one involving SPC's Vice-President – where judges were stripped of rank and sentenced for corruption.[96] However, it is unclear whether judicial corruption also affects EBL cases. My interviewees neither confirmed nor rejected this as a potential issue for the enforcement of the EBL[97] and there is no evidence to suggest that judicial corruption is any more or less relevant in EBL cases than in other court-based enforcement mechanisms. It was, therefore, not possible to confirm or disprove the role of judicial corruption in the parties' willingness to use the EBL.

8.2. Administrators' Passivity

Administrators are specialists – usually lawyers, but also accountants or other experts – who assist courts in overseeing and managing debtors' day-to-day activities under the EBL.[98] They have several pro-creditor duties that are aimed at reversing certain vulnerable transactions and clawing back wrongfully transferred assets.[99] These duties and corresponding powers could – in theory – be one of the greatest advantages and a potential selling point of EBL procedures to creditors since they could help increase the value and amount of the debtor's assets available for distribution[100] and lead to greater, less risky recoveries than the use of imperfect and often illegal private enforcement. However, many of my interviewees reported that, despite the importance and

---

[94] See Sections 10.1 and 10.2.

[95] See eg Reuters (12.7.2015); L Li, 'The "Production" of Corruption in China's Courts: Judicial Politics and Decision making in a One-Party State' (2012) *Law & Social Inquiry* 848.

[96] SPCM (10.7.2016). Generally see also L Li, 'Corruption in China's Courts' in R Peerenboom (ed), *Judicial Independence in China* (Cambridge University Press, 2010).

[97] Some interviewees stated that creditors and debtors do not wish to use the EBL because the court decision-making process is perceived as 'biased' (Interviews C1-c, C5-r, C7-s, E1-c, L1-r to L7-c, L14-c, L16-c, R10-c). However, this has been most strongly linked to the Government's influence rather than judicial corruption per se.

[98] See Section 4.2.9.

[99] Including eg preferential payments, hidden or transferred property, payments of fabricated debts, and with court's approval also transactions at an undervalue, etc. See Section 4.2.13.

[100] Including *ex ante* disincentive and ex post reversal of asset stripping and looting, which we discussed in Sections 7.1.3–7.1.4.

in some cases the imperative mode of the provisions,[101] administrators are often unable or unwilling to exercise such powers and duties fully.[102] This, in turn, further disincentivises creditors from using the EBL.[103]

My interviewees thought that there were three main reasons for the administrators' passivity. Firstly, administrators face the general enforcement obstacles explored earlier, such as a lack of reliable information, resources and time.[104] Secondly, although courts can supervise and force administrators to perform their duties with loyalty and due diligence, my interviewees argued that administrators are only rarely held liable for their breaches.[105] Finally, administrators often face pressure from the local Party-state *not* to act, or at least not to act in line with their duties under the EBL, in circumstances where it would go against the state's wishes.[106] The role of state interference in EBL cases and its influence on courts' and administrators' passivity are further explored in Section 8.3 below.

Regardless of the reasons, effective enforcement of the EBL relies on administrators to carry out their duties proactively, objectively and without outside interference. Otherwise, as is the case in China, potential payoffs are reduced, which makes creditors less inclined to use the EBL.

8.3. The Party-state's Influence over Court Enforcement of the EBL

The previous two sections were concerned with the issues in EBL enforcement that reduce the parties' relative payoffs and so discourage them from using the EBL. This section, on the other hand, looks at the reasons and circumstances in which the Party-state influences when and how EBL enforcers deal with EBL cases or outright prevent the parties from using the law even if they wish to do so.

The discussion below builds on the earlier general examination of the interaction of courts and the Party-state in China. Section 2.4 looked at the Party-state's influence over Chinese courts; the reasons why the Party-state interferes in courts' decision-making; and the reasons why courts accept Party-state's guidance. The discussion below follows the same structure in the context of the EBL. Section 8.3.1 below examines data about the Party-state's interference in EBL cases. Section 8.3.2 considers the reasons why the Party-state interferes in EBL cases. Section 8.3.3 explores courts' reasons for allowing such interference in the context of the EBL. The discussion then shifts to two important issues which are not discussed in prior literature. Section 8.3.4 summarises new

---

[101] Note the use of 'have to' in Arts 32–33 EBL.

[102] Interviews B1-c, B3-c, C2-c, C4-c to C7-s, C9-c, L1-r to L15-c, P1-r, R1-r, R3-r, R4-c, R6-c, R7-c, R9-c, R10-c. However, two of the interviewees (L4-r, L6-s) – both practising in regions with strong markets – suggested that, in their regions, administrators carried out their duties diligently. All the other interviewees, however, mentioned inactive administrators who often fail to carry out some of their pro-creditor duties.

[103] ibid.

[104] See Sections 2.4, 3.4, 7.1 and 8.1.

[105] The reasons are explored in Sections 2.4 and 8.3.

[106] Interviews B1-c, B3-c, C1-c, C2-c, C5-r to C7-s, J1-c, J3-c, J6-s to J9-c, L1-r to L6-s, L10-c to L15-c. The reasons for state interference are explored in Section 2.4.2.

insights into the types of situations when the Party-state intervenes in EBL enforcement. And Section 8.3.5 looks at the methods that the Party-state uses to achieve its goals in the context of corporate bankruptcies.

8.3.1. The Party-state Interferes in Court Enforcement of the EBL

As was discussed earlier, China is not governed by the rule of law, and written laws are enforced in a way that supports the Party-state's policies and interests.[107] Similarly, Chinese courts are not independent from the Party-state.[108] This influences how the laws are implemented and limits the predictability of judicial decision-making. In the context of the EBL, the supremacy and interference of the Party-state lead to the biased implementation of the law in favour of employees and politically protected interests rather than objective enforcement of the law as written.[109] All my interviewees expressed concern about not knowing what rights they may have under the EBL and cited it as a consideration when deciding whether to use the law (or whether to advise their clients to use the law). The interviewed judges acknowledged that the resulting uncertainty likely reduces the perceived advantages of using the EBL.[110] The problems are often comparatively more severe (compared to other laws) given the political sensitivity surrounding corporate bankruptcies – most importantly, the risk of a rise in unemployment and reputational and economic damage caused by corporate failures.

Local governments used to play a central role under 1986 law.[111] This was criticised and was removed during the 12-year-long reform process which led to the passing of the EBL in 2006. On paper, this recalibration of power was successful and local governments and the Party-state in general were removed from the process of resolving corporate bankruptcies. However, my interviewees and other empirical studies suggest that, in practice, the removal was only partly successful and that local governments in particular continue to interfere in some types of cases.[112]

Local governments used to have a say in whether or not a company could use the old law and how its liquidation or restructuring would be done. Local governments' interference has become more difficult under the EBL, and local governments or the Party do not, in fact, have any formal role in the corporate bankruptcy process according to the EBL as written.[113] Nevertheless, all my interviewees and several observers clearly indicate that local governments' influence remains significant behind the scenes even under the EBL regime.[114] In an interview in 2013, Ren Yimin, the head of the Bankruptcy

---

[107] See Section 2.3.2.
[108] See Section 2.4.1.
[109] See Section 6.1.
[110] See suggestions in Section 11.1 and recent local reforms in Section 12.6.
[111] See Sections 4.1 and 4.2.2.
[112] See Section 8.3.4.
[113] Note, however, that it is still possible in some circumstances to appoint a liquidation committee: see Sections 4.2.9 and 8.3.5.
[114] See discussion in Zhang (n 18) 71; Sina (28.3.2016).

and Restructuring department of the Zhejiang Lawyers Association, admitted that it is still the case that 'bankruptcy and restructuring of a large enterprise cannot occur without certain support from government'.[115] Indeed, the involvement of local governments is supported and encouraged in the typical cases that were recently published by the SPC to guide lower courts in how to use the EBL in practice.[116] In a recent empirical study, it was found that over 90 per cent of reorganisation cases in 2010 were controlled by local governments.[117] My interviewees confirmed this trend, especially in certain types of cases,[118] and there is no sign that such interference is going to be removed any time soon.[119]

Although direct political interference in judicial decision-making is uncommon in the US, the UK or Germany – ie countries whose bankruptcy codes were influential when the EBL was drafted – China's courts are not alone in facing political pressure when dealing with corporate bankruptcies. Existing literature suggests that courts in developing countries are often influenced by those in power and that state ownership creates biases in whether and how bankruptcy law is used.[120] Nevertheless, studies also found that where such biases and external influences were removed, it led to better outcomes for the economy as it helped to initially differentiate between viable companies which could be restructured and the rest which must exit the market, and eventually it also forced the companies that were capable of restructuring to remove unprofitable production lines, reform their production processes, change financing structures, and take other steps in order to survive and thrive in the long term.[121]

8.3.2. Why does the Party-state Interfere in EBL Cases?

Section 2.4.2 examined some of the reasons why the Party-state interferes in judicial decision-making in China. The reasons included local officials' career prospects being affected by judicial decisions and local governments being under pressure from local stakeholders to intervene in their favour. These reasons are equally relevant in the context of the EBL and do not need to be discussed further. However, the third reason that was discussed earlier – different roles and focus of national and local governments and the resulting divide between the goals and incentives at national and local levels – requires a closer inspection here in the context of the EBL.

The Party-state's institutional-level interests are not uniform at national and local levels. An important consequence of such divergence is that the focus and priorities differ in the EBL as written (by the national-level Party-state) and as implemented (by the local-level Party-state). The EBL was written by the national Government with

---

[115] L Hook and P Davies (21.3.2013, FT).
[116] See Sections 4.3–4.4.
[117] Zhang (n 18) 85. See also Section 8.3.5.
[118] See Section 8.3.4 for details.
[119] See Section 12.12. cf the discussion in Section 11.3.5.
[120] See Section 2.5.
[121] For a fuller discussion, see Section 1.2. For a discussion of reform options, see ch 11.

a long-term focus on macroeconomic benefits that bankruptcy laws can create.[122] However, the law has been implemented at a local level with a short-term focus on immediate needs of the provinces and the need to protect its primary contributors to the local budget – large and economically significant state-sector[123] companies – following the fiscal decentralisation.[124] The EBL was written by the national government as a part of a package of reforms with the intention to attract international trade and FDI. As a result, the EBL, as written, creates a pro-creditor environment and puts emphasis on objective, independent and professionally driven enforcement. However, in practice, the EBL is strongly pro-employee in focus, and it is only rarely enforced objectively, without local government's interference.[125] Similarly, professionals (courts and administrators) are often guided by the local Party-state.[126]

Many of my interviewees suggested that the national Government has been pushing for greater and more efficient use of the EBL in practice.[127] It has also instructed the SPC to provide further guidance to encourage and educate lower courts about the EBL.[128] The necessary changes and improved guidance have been slow in coming. Some have been tested locally in recent years[129] while others are yet to be considered or implemented.[130] However, in most cases, these attempts have only had limited success so far. There has been an increase in the number of cases in the last few years, but many problems still remain. The lack of independence, predictability and objectivity in the law's application as well as the limited expertise and experience of EBL enforcers remain significant and complicate efficient use of the EBL.[131]

My interviewees argued that, in many cases, local governments do not share the national Government's enthusiasm for greater use of the EBL, and instead prefer to use non-EBL alternatives which give them more scope to protect local interests.[132] Alternatively, they allow the use of the EBL but interfere in the work of the court and administrator, or sometimes outright take over the process.[133] Given that local governments oversee the day-to-day decision-making of Chinese courts,[134] their reserved attitude to the EBL appears to contribute significantly to the law's limited use in practice.

In addition, enforcing the EBL as written would mean closing down many local companies, which may trigger temporary decreases in local economic activity and cause social unrest. Following on from the earlier discussion of personal-level incentives of

---

[122] The national Government was heavily influenced by pro-market experts, in China and abroad: see Sections 4.1 and 13.1.

[123] See Section 2.5.2.

[124] See Section 2.4.

[125] See Section 8.3.1.

[126] See Sections 8.3.3 and 8.3.5.

[127] Interviews C1-c to C5-r, C7-s, C9-c, C11-c, J1-c to J9-c, L2-s to L17-c, P1-r to P5-c, R2-r, R3-r, R6-c, R7-c, R9-c, R10-c.

[128] See Sections 4.3, 12.1 and 12.6.

[129] For a discussion, see Section 12.6.

[130] See Section 11.1, 11.2.3 and 11.3.1.

[131] See Sections 10.1 and 10.3.

[132] Interviews C1-c to C5-r, C7-s, C9-c, C11-c, J1-c to J9-c, L2-s to L17-c, P1-r to P5-c, R2-r, R3-r, R6-c, R7-c, R9-c, R10-c.

[133] See Section 8.3.5.

[134] See Section 7.3.

local Party-state representatives, this would negatively affect Party-state officials' career prospects.[135] Although greater use of the EBL would most likely lead to healthier local economies in the medium-to-long term, officials' performance is assessed by reference to annual quantitative targets that need to be satisfied over their five-year term.[136] This form of assessment may have incentivised the production of false information which is then relied on at higher levels of government.[137] It also incentivises local governments to cover up or bail out large-scale bankruptcies in order to avoid drawing their superiors' attention and triggering an investigation into the veracity of the economic data.[138] These incentives are further reinforced by popular pressure and protests calling to keep troubled companies open, and by individual pressure from stakeholders through the media and visits in local government offices.[139] Consequently, instead of allowing or even encouraging the (efficient) use of the EBL, local governments often prefer non-EBL alternatives[140] and engage in local protectionism – both of which are likely to damage the economy and compromise economic development.

8.3.3. Why do Courts Allow and Accept the Party-state's Interference in EBL Cases?

Section 2.4.3 examined three broad reasons why Chinese courts follow the Party-state's guidance. The first reason – the internal control mechanisms that align court interests with those of the Party-state and so ensure the courts' cooperation and compliance with the Party-state's guidance – is relevant but does not need to be discussed further as its application is not altered in the EBL context. The second and third reasons, however, are affected by the EBL context and so are discussed below.

The second reason why courts follow Party-state's guidance is that many judges feel that they *should not* act without Party-state's blessing. Judges' internalised moral obligation to follow Party-state's instructions in EBL cases is illustrated in a recent article in which Judge Ren (district-level court) argued that:[141]

> [C]orporate bankruptcy cases involve vital interests of many people and directly affect social harmony and stability. Thus, it is the social dimension of bankruptcy that determines that courts cannot act alone in bankruptcy cases. Some local governments do not want companies to go bankrupt for statistical, performance, maintenance of stability and other considerations.

Although such an attitude may be foreign to a non-Chinese audience, many of my interviewees stressed that Judge Ren's views are widespread in China.[142] Several interviewees also added that the courts accept Party-state's guidance because they believe that the

---

[135] See Section 2.4.2.
[136] ibid. Officials then usually move to another province.
[137] ibid.
[138] Interviews C1-c to C5-r, C7-s, J1-c, J4-c to J9-c, L2-s to L7-c, L9-s, L10-c, L14-c, L15-c, P1-r to P5-c, R2-r, R3-r, R6-c, R7-c, R9-c, R10-c.
[139] For details see Section 2.4.2.
[140] See ch 9.
[141] P Ren (19.1.2016, Weixin).
[142] Interviews C1-c, C3-c, C7-s, J1-c, J3-c to J9-c, L6-s, P1-r, R7-c, R9-c, R10-c.

Party-state is best positioned to decide what is best for the people and the economy.[143] Therefore, the view that following Party-state's guidance is 'the right thing to do' needs to be duly considered when trying to understand courts' reluctance to accept EBL petitions and hear EBL cases independently.

This attitude is further supported by the SPC in its regulatory judicial guidance and recently released typical EBL cases. The SPC Notice concerning the Correct Hearing of EBL Cases and Judicial Guarantee to Maintain Orderly Market Economy[144] directs lower courts to follow Party-state guidance and reminds them that the courts are merely a branch of the Party-state. Moreover, a senior SPC judge in charge of promoting the EBL, Du Wanhua, called for greater cooperation of courts and administrators with local governments in his speech at the Shenzhen National Bankruptcy Trial Work Conference in December 2017.[145] The message has been recently repeated in the introductory note to the 2018 typical EBL cases and in the commentary to some of the typical cases.[146] The top-down guidance further reinforces judges' feeling that they should not accept and decide EBL cases without the Party-state's support and guidance as their proper role is merely to support the Party-state rather than independently adjudicate and apply the law.

Finally, the third reason why courts allow and accept Party-state's interference in EBL cases stems from judges' belief that they *cannot* effectively act without Party-state's blessing and support. The 1986 law gave local governments control over which companies can declare bankruptcy and how the court could hear and resolve the case.[147] Indeed, courts using the 1986 law did not accept bankruptcy petitions without the Government's agreement, and they played 'an assisting role in the shadow of strong government intervention'[148] when the case was heard.

The EBL removed local governments' involvement in corporate bankruptcies. Nevertheless, courts often remain reluctant to hear EBL cases independently. Speaking about his local-level experience with hearing EBL cases, Judge Ren said:

> Courts should actively seek support of the local government where the debtor is located in order to ensure reallocation of workers of the bankrupt company, payment of wages, and disposal of the bankrupt company's factory or other fixed assets. By communicating with relevant departments, judges can ensure political support to help pay taxes, apply for transfer [of property], coordinate the interests of creditors, debtors, investors, employees and other stakeholders.[149]

This view is further supported by the SPC. In its 2018 typical cases, the SPC highlighted the importance of courts accepting and making most of local government support when hearing EBL cases.[150] The 10 cases illustrate that local governments can help the court protect employees by ensuring that their wages are repaid and that they are resettled to

---

[143] Interviews C7-s, J1-c, J3-c to J9-c, R9-c, R10-c.
[144] *Fafa* [2009] No 36.
[145] See also Section 12.1.
[146] See Section 4.3. The message of courts' subordination to the Party-state in general has been recently repeated: see Liu Guixiang's speech at the SPC Work Conference in July 2019: G Liu (3.7.2019, Weixin) and Section 2.4.3.
[147] See Sections 4.2.2 and 4.2.8.
[148] See Zhang (n 18) 17.
[149] Ren (n 141).
[150] See Section 4.3.

other jobs following a debtor company's closure or restructuring. Local governments can also safeguard the interests of creditors by ensuring that new finance is available (particularly in reorganisation cases), and help struggling but valuable companies access new finance and ensure the cooperation of their lenders in the restructuring process by, inter alia, providing guarantees and putting pressure on the affected lenders.[151]

Local governments can also force the affected stakeholders, who would normally refuse to negotiate and instead insist on being repaid in full, to sit down with the debtor and find a solution. As my interviewees said, no court has the power to do that just as effectively. In addition, local governments can provide the support that makes recovery of reorganised companies more likely – for example, by promising tax breaks or by providing guarantees with regards to the protection and continuity of the distressed company. Local governments are often regarded as crucial in complex reorganisation cases which require high-level coordination and effective cooperation of various departments.[152] These steps may make the difference between the restructuring being successful or not, and so may influence whether creditors, trading partners and customers support the restructured company during the process and in the future.

There is now an increasing body of evidence that shows the importance of local government assistance in resolving EBL reorganisations.[153] This was confirmed more broadly by many of my interviewees, who said that local governments play an important role in EBL cases and that courts cannot resolve many of the EBL cases without such support.[154] They said that courts often do not feel able to act independently because EBL cases tend to be complex, involve coordination of many parties and require the ability to enforce whatever arrangement is agreed in the end. As one interviewee put it: '[EBL procedures], and in particular reorganisation, cannot succeed without local government's help, and so it is preferable for the local government to take charge of the process and only use courts when necessary'.[155] It is undeniable that the Party-state has played an important role in enabling courts to hear and effectively resolve complex corporate bankruptcies. However, it is equally important to ask whether such interference leads to efficient and fair results. That is a separate matter which is dealt with in Section 11.3.

Together, the three reasons ensure courts' cooperation and willingness to follow Party-state guidance in EBL cases. The belief that the proper and only possible role of the court is to support the Party-state and its wishes – rather than act as an independent adjudicator, as written in the EBL[156] – contributes to the limited use of the EBL in practice.

8.3.4. In what Situations does the Party-state Interfere in EBL Cases?

The previous section explored why courts allow, and at times even welcome, Party-state guidance and interference in EBL enforcement. However, the extent of that interference

---

[151] For details of how the Party-state assists in corporate bankruptcies, see Section 9.2.
[152] See the ninth typical case (2018) in Section 4.3.
[153] See in particular Zhang (n 18).
[154] Interviews C7-s, J1-c, J3-c to J9-c, R9-c, R10-c.
[155] Interview J1-c.
[156] See Section 4.2.1.

is not uniform across different types of companies and cases. This section identifies four types of situations where the Party-state – especially local governments – is most like to interfere. The discussion builds on the findings of prior literature – that state ownership affects the implementation of corporate bankruptcy law – and my research – that the Party-state's interference largely depends on the insolvent company's economic significance rather than its ownership.[157]

Firstly, the Party-state prevents enforcement of the EBL against a group of SOEs called 'special treatment companies', which were exempted from falling under the EBL by the law itself.[158] Although these cases of corporate financial distress were supposed to be resolved once the EBL came into force in June 2007, several of my interviewees suggested that certain (mostly publicly listed) SOEs still receive special protections and privileges well beyond those otherwise generally available to state-sector companies.[159]

Secondly, the Party-state – in particular local governments and local political-legal committees of the Party – is also heavily involved in 'cases of significance'.[160] My interviewees suggested that significance is usually measured in terms of the financial and socio-economic impact of the given bankruptcy on the local economy. As a result, the key issue is not ownership, but rather the affected company's affiliation with the state sector.[161] Financial problems in particularly large or otherwise important companies, therefore, attract a great deal of attention and command significant resources from local governments.[162] Traditionally, such cases would not be resolved using the EBL because local governments saw it as incapable of affording sufficient protection to employees and other state-preferred interests.[163] More recently, however, EBL procedures have been used to resolve some cases of significance, but Party-state representatives tend to play an important role in the process,[164] or the EBL is merely used to formally legitimise previously agreed politically acceptable solutions.[165]

Examples include the recent Bohai Steel reorganisation, the largest corporate restructuring in China's history. Owned by the Tianjin local Government, the former Fortune Global 500 company collapsed in 2016 under more than 200 billion RMB of unpaid debt. The local Government oversaw much of the restructuring process and put a lot of pressure on the final implementation of the reorganisation plan which involved a partial repayment from the proceeds of sale of the steel-making part of the business

---

[157] As was explained in Section 2.5.

[158] Art 133 EBL. See Section 4.2.1.

[159] Interviews B1-c, B2-c, C1-c, C2-c, C5-r, C7-s, C11-c, J1-c, J6-s, J8-c, J9-c, L1-r to L6-s, L9-s to L13-s, P1-r, P3-r, R1-r, R3-r, R10-c. See also Legal Daily (1.3.2016).

[160] Interview with the emigrated lawyer Chen in R Callick, *The Party Forever: Inside China's Modern Communist Elite* (Palgrave Macmillan, 2013) 63. Also Interviews B1-c to B3-c, C1-c, C2-c, C5-r, C7-s, C10-s, C11-c, J1-c, J6-s, J9-c, L1-r to L7-c, L9-s to L15-c, P1-r, P3-r, R1-r, R3-r, R9-c, R10-c.

[161] ibid. This is contrary to what most authors assume when writing about Chinese commerce: see Section 2.5.

[162] Interviews B1-c to B3-c, C1-c, C2-c, C5-r, C7-s, C10-s, C11-c, J1-c, J6-s, J9-c, L1-r to L7-c, L9-s to L15-c, P1-r, P3-r, R1-r, R3-r, R9-c, R10-c.

[163] ibid. For discussion of these interests see Section 2.4.2.

[164] See Sections 8.3.5 and 9.2. For a real-life example, see eg Y Mao (18.6.2020, Yunqingsuan).

[165] In other words, the solution is pre-packaged, and so the Party-state avoids having to deal with the interests that would have to be considered and protected under the EBL, most importantly creditors' interests: ibid. See also Section 9.2.3.

and partial satisfaction of the debts through forced debt-for-equity swaps.[166] The typical cases that were issued by the SPC in 2018 and 2020[167] are also cases of significance where the EBL was used with heavy involvement of local governments.

Thirdly, (local) Party-state representatives are also heavily involved in cases which are particularly politically or publicly sensitive, such as scandals and high-profile cases. Past examples include the Sanlu Group's milk scandal and bankruptcy. Formerly one of China's largest agricultural companies, Sanlu collapsed after it transpired that they were adding a harmful chemical into baby milk powder to make it appear more nutritious. At least six babies died and about 300,000 fell ill following its consumption.[168] Similarly, the Government took charge of the high-profile bankruptcy of EastStar Airlines, a Hubei-based, privately owned company which owed 752 million RMB in unpaid debt. The company was liquidated in 2009 after the court rejected its 'unfeasible' reorganisation plan.[169] It was the first Chinese airline to collapse. One thousand employees lost their jobs as a result.[170]

Finally, listed companies also usually receive special attention. Although some have been allowed to use EBL reorganisation, a significant number of my interviewees suggested that for many years this was used as a backdoor way of selling its key asset – its listed status – which is very hard to acquire in China and so is very valuable.[171] Such EBL reorganisation is, therefore, not a typical restructuring process which aims to save the viable part of a business or the company as a going concern, but it is rather a way of gaining listed status by acquiring the listed shell. Although it does often raise more money than if the company was liquidated and so more stakeholders are repaid, many of my interviewees saw it as controversial use of corporate bankruptcy law.[172]

More recently, listed companies have been using the EBL more readily, albeit with extensive interference and guidance from the Party-state[173] and with additional requirements imposed by the SPC.[174] The SPC guidance was produced in conjunction with the China Securities Regulatory Commission in order to 'refine relevant procedures and regulations, […] optimise the allocation of social resources, and promote healthy development of the capital market'.[175] To that end, the guidance directs courts to cooperate with local governments in order to better coordinate rescue process, achieve better cooperation of various departments, and to get access to financial guarantees for the distressed company.[176] It also states that local government and local securities regulator need to be involved in the EBL process.[177]

---

[166] Reuters (21.8.2019).

[167] See Section 4.3 for details.

[168] See eg T Branigan (2.12.2008, The Guardian); K Cai (13.2.2009, China Daily).

[169] Xinhua (27.8.2009); Reuters (27.8.2009).

[170] 600 of the laid-off employees were resettled in the state-owned Air China: 'East Star Airline goes bankrupt with huge debts' (28.8.2009, China.org).

[171] Interviews C2-c, C5-r, C7-s, J1-c, J5-s to J9-c, L1-r to L15-c, P1-r, R3-r, R10-c.

[172] Interviews C2-c, C5-r, C7-s, J6-s, J8-c, J9-c, L2-s to L6-s, L13-c to L15-c, P1-r, R3-r, R10-c.

[173] For a recent empirical study of this issue see H Zhao, *Government Intervention in the Reorganisation of Listed Companies in China* (Cambridge University Press, 2020).

[174] The SPC Memorandum on Handing of Listed Companies' Reorganisations and Liquidations (*Fa* [2012] No 261).

[175] ibid, Preamble.

[176] ibid, Art 1(3).

[177] ibid, Art 4.

Many of my interviewees suggested that if a distressed company does not fall into any of the above-mentioned categories – which is the case for many smaller private-sector companies – it falls outside the Party-state's scope of interest and so does not receive the Party-state's express blessing to use the EBL[178] nor does it receive direct or indirect political support in resolving its financial distress.[179] Without the Party-state's permission to use the EBL, my interviewees argued, a petitioning debtor or creditor may find it difficult to persuade a local court to accept their EBL petition[180] and may instead be limited to private non-EBL debt enforcement alternatives.[181] The situation was particularly difficult in the first few years after the EBL was brought into force. The courts' willingness to accept EBL cases on their merits has been slowly improving as judges gain more experience and expertise in EBL-related matters.[182] Nevertheless, courts' reluctance to accept EBL petitions remains an obstacle to the effective resolution of corporate bankruptcies in less developed regions.[183]

8.3.5. How does the Party-state Interfere in EBL Cases?

My interviewees reported that representatives of the Party-state, usually local government officials,[184] tend to interfere in EBL enforcement in three important ways. Firstly, they can prevent the parties from filing EBL petitions. Secondly, they can force the court to reject EBL petitions. And thirdly, they can allow EBL petitions to be filed and accepted, but local governments can interfere or take over the EBL process. This section examines each type of interference in turn.[185]

Firstly, local governments can effectively prevent directors and managers of creditor and debtor companies from filing an EBL petition.[186] Several interviewees reported that such interference is mostly seen in bankruptcies of state-sector companies.[187] In the case of state-owned parties – such as SOEs and state banks – a local or national government can, as the main shareholder, refuse to give the company the necessary permissions to

---

[178] Interviews B1-c to B3-c, C1-c, C2-c, C5-r, C7-s to C11-c, J1-c, J3-c, J5-s to J9-c, L1-r to L15-c, R1-r, R3-r, R9-c, R10-c.

[179] See Section 9.2.

[180] ibid. See also S Li, 'Bankruptcy Law in China: Lessons of the Past Twelve Years' (2001) *Harvard Asia Quarterly* 1; Legal Daily (12.2.2007). A rare exception to this rule has been the situation in Wenzhou province, where small private debtors and creditors have been able to use the EBL without the local Government's support. This is because the private sector is particularly strong and important there (see section 2.5) and the courts are used to acting with less guidance from the local government than is customary in other parts of China: Interviews C1-c, C5-r, E3-s, J4-c to J8-c, R1-r, R10-c.

[181] See Section 9.1.

[182] See Sections 5.1, 12.1, and 12.3.

[183] The situation is slowly improving in some regions: see Chapter 12.

[184] My interviewees observed that the interaction of courts and the Party-state is particularly pronounced at the local level where local governments often put direct pressure on courts. At the same time, there are Party cells in each court which enforces the Party discipline: See Sections 2.2 and 2.4.

[185] This section focuses on the enforcement of the EBL and the Party-state's interference in the process. A related question of what alternative mechanisms the Party-state employs instead of the EBL is discussed in Section 9.2.3.

[186] Interviews C2-c, C5-r to C7-s, J1-c, J6-s, J8-c, L2-s to L7-c, L13-c to L15-c, R1-r, R9-c, R10-c. See also Li Shuguang, 'Six Problems of Enforcing the Corporate Bankruptcy Law' cited in Zhang (n 18); Sina (28.3.2016).

[187] For a definition, see Section 2.5.2. Interviews C2-c, C5-r, C7-s, L2-s to L7-c, L13-c to L15-c, R1-r, R10-c.

declare bankruptcy and use the EBL.[188] My interviewees argued that local governments sometimes also put pressure on non-state-owned creditors and debtors that fall within the state sector for the reasons explained in Section 8.3.2 above – most importantly to limit the negative impact on the local economy, social stability and employment.[189]

A notable example of such limitations is the position of state-owned banks, which are mostly prevented from exercising their creditor rights.[190] This is so even though they are now supposedly independent bodies which are fully responsible for their financial decisions and affairs.[191] The bank responsibility system has, on the one hand, incentivised banks to avoid the accumulation of more bad debt by putting their debtors into reorganisation or liquidation or enforcing their security.[192] However, in practice, banks are often dissuaded from petitioning to use EBL procedures against state-sector debtors without express permission from the local Government. Instead, they follow the instructions of their (direct or indirect) majority stakeholder, the Government, and wait or lend more money to the distressed SOE instead of being able to use the EBL when financial problems arise.[193]

Secondly, apart from influencing creditors and debtors, local governments also sometimes discourage courts from accepting any EBL petitions that are not expressly sanctioned by them.[194] As was discussed earlier, courts allow and accept the Party-state's interference in EBL cases because many judges feel unable or unwilling to proceed without its support.[195] As one judge put it, the 'ties between judges and Party officials are often close ... It's very difficult for judges to be impartial'.[196] External and internal pressure to cooperate with the Party-state is overwhelming and courts typically yield to it, some willingly and others by coercion.[197]

At times, courts do accept EBL petitions without the Party-state's permission. But if their decision conflicts with local government's preferences or interests (eg a desire to keep the local debtor companies alive and so its workers employed at any cost), the

---

[188] A Tang and A Ward, *The Changing Face of Chinese Management* (Routledge, 2003) 50-51. A company must seek permission to exit the market from its majority shareholder. For SOEs, this is the national or local government: Interviews C2-c, C5-r, C7-s, J1-c, J5-s to J9-c, L2-s to L7-c, L13-c to L15-c, R1-r, R10-c.

[189] ibid.

[190] Interviews B1-c to B3-c, C5-r, P1-c, R10-c. See also Reuters (21.5.2012).

[191] The bank responsibility system has been established through a series of central government's policies: Interviews C1-c, C5-r, C7-s, L4-c to L6-s, R3-r, R9-c, R10-c. For details, see R Smyth, OK Tam, M Warner and C Zhu (eds), *China's Business Reforms: Institutional Challenges in a Globalised Economy* (Routledge, 2015).

[192] Interviews B1-c to B3-c, C1-c, C5-r, C7-s, L2-s, L4-r, L6-s, L10-s to L13-c, R2-r, R3-r, R6-c, R9-c, R10-c.

[193] Interviews B1-c to B3-c, C1-c, C2-c, C5-r, L4-c to L6-s, R10-c. See also J Anderlini (15.5.2015, FT); J Qian and P Strahan, 'How law and institutions shape financial contracts: The case of bank loans' (2007) *Journal of Finance* 2803. The banks might also be unable or unwilling to recognise their poor lending decisions by declaring the debtor bankrupt and instead lend again to roll the debt over. This is called zombie loans: see A Ahearne and N Shinada, 'Zombie firms and economic stagnation in Japan' (2005) *International Economics and Economic Policy* 363; R Caballero, T Hoshi and A Kashyap, 'Zombie Lending and Depressed Restructuring in Japan' (2008) *American Economic Review* 1943.

[194] Interviews C2-c, C5-r, C7-s, J1-c, J3-c to J9-c, L4-r, L6-s, P1-r, P3-r, R1-r, R6-c to R10-c. See also The Economist (9.10.2008). See also Li Shuguang, 'Six Problems of Enforcing the Corporate Bankruptcy Law' cited in Zhang (n 18); Sina (28 March 2016).

[195] See Sections 2.4.3 and 8.3.1.

[196] Callick, *The Party Forever* (2013) 71.

[197] Interviews C2-c, C5-r, C7-s, J1-c, J3-c to J8-c, L2-s, L4-r to L7-c, P1-r, R2-r, R7-c, R9-c, R10-c.

judicial decision may be ineffective and the EBL protections in favour of the creditors and other stakeholders may become practically worthless.[198] Several of my interviewees said that they had seen a few cases where courts disregarded the wishes of a local government and accepted an EBL petition. In such cases, the EBL hearing was interrupted by a technicality or by the local Government calling a police-led criminal investigation of the debtor company and its directors, which takes precedence over civil proceedings, including the EBL.[199] The debtor's financial distress was then resolved in line with the state-orchestrated solution,[200] or the company was allowed to fail, and the management was made to face full liability in order to make an example of them to deter others from rebelling against the Party-state.[201] Several interviewees suggested that judges are aware that in certain types of cases local governments want to have a say, and so it is rare for courts go against the local government's instructions.[202]

Finally, there has been an increasing number of cases where corporate distress is resolved using the EBL.[203] However, in many of these cases, the EBL process is driven by the Party-state rather than a court. As was discussed earlier, local governments are particularly concerned about protecting employees and maintaining social stability in their region.[204] This is achieved in practice in five different ways.

In some cases – commonly very complex cases or where multiple companies are involved – the local government takes full control of the EBL process, and the court merely assists with administrative tasks and rubber-stamps the final solution.[205]

Similar in substance, but different in form, is the use of a pre-negotiated deal which is legitimised under the EBL, commonly known as 'pre-packs'.[206] Pre-packs are used in other jurisdictions, but usually without the involvement of the Government.[207] The local Government negotiates with key stakeholders behind closed doors, without involving smaller stakeholders or the public. A compromise is agreed and all key terms are decided prior to the debtor company entering the EBL.[208] The local Government usually plays a key role in the negotiations and in rushing the final agreement through the courts under the auspices of the EBL.

A third way in which local governments interfere in the EBL process is by assembling 'liquidation committees' akin to those which existed under the old law to resolve SOEs' financial distress.[209] Although there was an intention to limit the scope of such

---

[198] My interviews (B1-c, C2-c, C5-r, J1-c, J4-c, J6-s to J8-c, L4-r to L6-s, R10-c) confirm these propositions in R Tomasic and Z Zhang, 'From Global Convergence in China's Enterprises Bankruptcy Law 2006 to Divergent Implementation' (2012) *Journal of Corporate Law Studies* 295, 322.

[199] Interview C1-c, J1-c, L4-r, L6-s, R10-c. This happened in Hubei EastStar Airline where a criminal investigation into the CEO's activities was launched because the company and the creditors refused to 'cooperate with the government organs', ie refused to accept the local Government's solution: Sina (16.3.2009).

[200] See Section 9.2.

[201] Interviewees C1-c, C5-r, L4-r, L6-s, L14-c, and L15-c spoke of personal experiences when this happened.

[202] Interviews C2-c, C5-r, C7-s, J1-c, J3-c to J9-c, L2-s, L4-r to L7-c, P1-r, R3-r, R7-c, R9-c, R10-c.

[203] For the number of EBL cases see Sections 5.1, 10.1.1 and 12.3.

[204] See Section 8.3.2.

[205] See Section 9.2.3.

[206] ibid.

[207] ibid.

[208] A report released by the Hangzhou Intermediate People's Court in 2015 suggests that the local Government was heavily involved prior to the EBL application in most reorganisation cases it handled: 'A Report of handling Corporate Bankruptcies' cited in Zhang (n 18) 85.

[209] See Sections 4.2.9 and 11.3.5.

committees to the resolution of SOEs and some special types of cases,[210] courts were given the discretion to appoint a liquidation committee as an administrator under the EBL. As a result, they are still widely used.[211] A study of cases between 2007 and 2015 found that a liquidation committee was appointed as an administrator in 30.63 per cent of reorganisations.[212] That is surprisingly high. Although the SPC guidance suggests that liquidation committees should be used primarily when resolving SOEs and financial companies, the data suggests that this is not the case in practice. Liquidation committees were used in private companies as well as foreign-invested companies.[213] The extensive use of liquidation committees has been criticised by some scholars and practitioners as contravening the spirit of the EBL and the underlying intention to establish a professional and independent regime for resolving corporate bankruptcies.[214] The criticism also highlights the fact that liquidation committees consist of politicians rather than lawyers[215] – meaning that they lack legal knowledge and expertise in dealing with corporate bankruptcies – and that it is difficult to hold them accountable as they are often powerful government officials.

On the other hand, some scholars and judges welcome the extensive use of liquidation committees because many bankruptcy practitioners are not yet sufficiently experienced, able to coordinate various departments and deploy government resources as effectively as government officials, and able to protect broader socio-economic stability which may be affected by corporate bankruptcies.[216] Nevertheless, even the supporters recognise that, eventually, liquidation committees should be phased out.[217]

A fourth way in which local governments influence EBL cases is where they exert significant influence over the appointed administrator, acting as a 'shadow' administrator. About 54 per cent of the reorganisation cases in 2010 had a bankruptcy practitioner firm appointed as an administrator. However, in at least 45 per cent of these cases, the EBL process was controlled by government officials.[218] They were in charge of negotiating key terms with stakeholders and choosing the buyer of the debtor's business.[219] The Government stepped in as a shadow administrator to help resolve state-sector companies – all the cases in 2010 involved SOEs and economically significant private companies – in order to ensure the continued existence, tax revenue and employment provided by these big companies, and to protect socio-economic stability in the region.[220]

---

[210] See Section 4.2.9, which explains the scope of Art 24 EBL.

[211] Interviews C2-c, C5-r, C7-s, J1-c, J3-c to J9-c, L1-r to L7-c, P1-r, R2-r, R7-c, R9-c, R10-c. See also section 4.2.9.

[212] Zhang (n 18) 68.

[213] For a discussion of examples, see Zhang (n 18) 69–70.

[214] Legal Daily (9.6.2008); X Lu, 'The Balance between Court Control and Autonomy of Affected Parties in Corporate bankruptcy Administrator Appointments' (2015) *People's Judicature* 75.

[215] However, note that liquidation committees increasingly do include lawyers and bankruptcy practitioners as a part of the broader team: Zhang (n 18) 72.

[216] B You, 'Risk Management for China's Insolvency Practitioners' (2009) *People's Judicature* 33; X Jiang, 'The Roles of Insolvency Practitioners in Corporate Reorganisation' (2009) *Journal of Law Application* 77; Z Ke, 'Commencement of Listed Company Reorganisations in China' (2009) *People's Judicature* 38.

[217] For an alternative, less objectionable involvement of the government, see Section 11.3.5.

[218] See Zhang (n 18) 80–81.

[219] ibid.

[220] See Section 2.5.2 and Zhang (n 18) 80–85.

Finally, courts and lawyers are also subject to indirect influence from local government and Party interests. My interviewees pointed to several mechanisms through which the Party-state ensures that courts and lawyers closely cooperate and support their preferred outcomes.[221] As was discussed earlier, judges are monitored by a political-legal committee of the local Party branch and have to promise in an oath loyalty to the Party and its ideology.[222] Similar mechanisms are used to ensure lawyers' cooperation. All lawyers now have to take the same oath of loyalty to the Party in order to 'firmly establish … faith in socialism with Chinese characteristics … and effectively improve the quality of lawyers' political ideology'.[223] In addition, Party cells have been created in most law firms to monitor their activities.[224] This is a stark reminder of the status that courts and lawyers have in China in general, and under the EBL in particular.

As a result of the internal (Sections 8.1 and 8.2) and external (Section 8.3) limitations discussed in this chapter, enforcement of the EBL is ridden with protectionism and fails to maximise creditors' recoveries. When combined with the parties' perception that the EBL does not sufficiently protect their interests (discussed in Chapter six) and that the problems in the surrounding rules further reduce recoveries under the EBL (discussed in Chapter seven), it is hardly surprising that creditors are often unwilling to use the EBL – and that debtors do not trust courts to help them resolve their financial distress effectively. My interviewees, however, identified one final element that motivates the parties not to use the EBL: the existence of alternative debt enforcement mechanisms which the parties perceive as offering them relatively higher payoffs than they would receive under the EBL. This is the focus of the next chapter.

---

[221] Interviews C2-c, C5-r, J1-c, J3-c to J8-c, L2-s to L6-s, L9-s, L13-c to L15-c, R10-c.
[222] See Section 2.4.3.
[223] China's Ministry of Justice, 'New lawyers must make an oath of loyalty' (21.3.2012), available at www.moj.gov.cn/index/content/2012-03/21/content_3445267.htm?node=7318.
[224] ibid.

9

The Fourth Constraint – Non-EBL Debt Enforcement Mechanisms

The final constraint that limits the use of the EBL in China, as identified by my interviewees, concerns the parties' perception that non-EBL alternatives offer comparatively greater payoffs than the EBL. Many of the non-EBL alternatives have been used since long before the 1986 bankruptcy law was introduced.[1] Most of them developed incrementally, building on users' experiences and expectations over a long period of time. The resulting familiarity and simplicity of many of the alternative mechanisms together with stakeholders' ability to remain in control both in private and in the politically driven alternative mechanisms appear to make them a much more attractive option[2] than the complex EBL which relies on incomplete supporting institutions, inefficient courts and administrators, and often unwelcome intrusions by the courts or the local Party-state.[3] In other words, the perceived payoffs under the EBL are not sufficient to persuade the parties to use it instead of these familiar, immediately available alternatives.

Parties' tendency to rely on less formal, more familiar debt enforcement mechanisms in the first instance is not unique to China[4] and is consistent with people's tendency to combine social norms and formal laws to resolve their disagreements.[5] Where lenders and borrowers know each other, or where the case involves only a handful of parties or small amounts of debt, it is possible and often quicker and cheaper to enforce debt repayment informally, without involving paid third parties. Private negotiations, pressure and enforcement through reputation mechanisms tend to be preferred initially by all creditors to enforce, individually, repayment of their debt. When the simpler methods fail, parties move to stronger or more sophisticated mechanisms which involve third-party adjudicators and enforcers.

My interviewees suggested that, besides the complexity and seriousness of the financial distress, the preferred method of enforcement may also depend on whether

---

[1] See Section 3.3.

[2] Interviews B1-c to B3-c, C2-c to C7-s, C9-c, C11-c, E1-c to E5-c, IF1-s, IF2-c, J7-c, L2-s to L15-c, P1-r, P3-r, R1-r to R4-c, R6-c, R7-c, R9-c, R10-c, R12-c.

[3] ibid. Some of my interviews (C5-r, C9-c, J7-c, L11-c, R1-r) and some existing research speak of 'cultural preference for the non-legal dispute resolution'. However, the use of extralegal alternatives may be readily explicable as creditors' and debtors' preference for using the more effective, accessible and understood tools.

[4] Indeed, extralegal alternatives and simplified legal debt enforcement are commonly used around the world. Similarly, there has been a global shift towards informal restructuring and the use of pre-packs.

[5] For a detailed discussion see Section 2.3.1.

debtors' activities fall within the state sector or the private sector.[6] Parties operating in the private sector are often limited to informal private alternatives or the EBL. State-sector companies, on the other hand, are often forced to rely on politically driven alternatives or politically driven use of the EBL[7] in order to ensure that the socio-economic interests are protected.

This chapter presents an overview of parties' non-EBL debt enforcement alternatives.[8] Section 9.1 examines private alternatives where parties resolve their debt-related disputes individually or with limited help of a third party. Section 9.2 focuses on politically driven alternatives where the Party-state controls and decides the outcome of the case.

The alternatives are summarised in Table 9.1.

Table 9.1 Overview of non-EBL alternative debt enforcement mechanisms

	Private alternatives (Section 9.1)	**Politically driven alternatives** (Section 9.2)
Informal (only affected parties)	(i) Private negotiations (ii) Violence, threats (iii) Reputation mechanism	(i) Politically driven negotiations → State-enforced compromise → State-led mergers and acquisitions → State-led financial assistance → State-led private restructuring
Formal (third party involved)	(i) Enforcement of contract (ii) Enforcement of security (iii) Diversified dispute resolution (mediation, arbitration)	(i) State-led use of the EBL

9.1. Private Alternatives and their Perceived Advantages

Private alternatives are commonly used by private-sector companies. State-sector players sometimes use them before the Party-state gets involved to try to find a solution without its knowledge and interference. Section 9.1.1 below looks at why the parties use these alternatives. Section 9.1.2 examines when and why the parties prefer private informal alternatives – most importantly private negotiations, violence, threats, and reputation mechanism – rather than the EBL. Section 9.1.3 concludes by considering when and why the parties use private formal mechanisms – most importantly court-based enforcement of contracts, court-based enforcement of security rights, and diversified dispute resolution mechanisms – rather than the EBL.

---

[6] As was discussed in Section 2.5, the determinants of state influence include not only ownership but also an array of other issues such as industry, relative economic importance, employment considerations, etc.

[7] See discussion in Section 8.3.

[8] See Section 3.3 for a general overview.

9.1.1. Why the Parties Use Private Alternatives

Section 3.3 provided an overview of the most common debt enforcement options without the use of the EBL or the Party-state's help.[9] This chapter builds on that discussion, but the focus shifts to consider the reasons why stakeholders prefer to use these alternatives rather than the EBL. Besides the comparatively higher expected payoffs under the non-EBL alternatives,[10] my interviewees identified three further reasons why the parties often prefer to using non-EBL debt enforcement alternatives.

Firstly, as was mentioned earlier, private alternatives are familiar to all stakeholders, and they have been used for a long time. The EBL, on the other hand, is a relatively new and little-understood mechanism.[11] Consequently, the parties perceive the alternative mechanisms as a trusted fall-back option for dealing with corporate financial distress on an individual as well as collective level.

Secondly, the parties often perceive non-EBL alternatives as comparatively cheaper and quicker than the EBL. Small private companies[12] usually prefer non-EBL alternatives because their financial distress tends to be less complicated, more localised, their assets and net worth are generally smaller, and so the impact of their potential failure is also less significant for the economy and social stability.[13] As a result, the EBL would probably be disproportionately expensive and unnecessarily lengthy.[14] Medium-sized private companies[15] often face greater complexity and their size might justify the cost of an EBL procedure, but because they are not sufficiently economically significant (so as to warrant Party-state protection[16]) their EBL petitions are often ignored by the courts,[17] and so they, too, have to rely on private alternatives.

Thirdly, the parties often prefer the privacy and informality of non-EBL alternatives. This is most pronounced in cases where creditors or debtors engaged in shadow market or lent to politically prohibited industries,[18] and so they either cannot rely on the Party-state's assistance, or they prefer not to draw attention to themselves and instead choose to resolve their disputes without its help.[19]

9.1.2. Private Informal Mechanisms

Sections 3.3.1 and 3.3.2 discussed several informal mechanisms which the parties use to enforce debt repayment without having to resort to laws and court enforcement. The parties know how these mechanisms operate, they are relatively low-cost, and

---

[9] See Sections 3.3.1–3.3.2.
[10] See chs 6–8.
[11] See Sections 8.1.1 and 11.3.1. See also recent improvements in Sections 12.4–12.7.
[12] See Section 2.5.
[13] Note, also, that small companies are directed by the SPC not to use EBL Reorganisation: Section 8.1.1.
[14] See Sections 7.2.1, 8.1.2 and 12.8.
[15] See Section 2.5.
[16] See Section 8.3.
[17] See Sections 7.2, 7.3 and 8.3.
[18] See Sections 7.3.1 and 7.3.3.
[19] See Sections 7.3 and 8.3.

they enable them to enforce repayment directly, which creates a perception that the alternative mechanisms are better than the EBL.

9.1.2.1. Private Negotiations

Probably the most prevalent – and used initially by most parties – is private negotiations.[20] Cheap and often effective, negotiations between a debtor and its creditor(s) is a universally preferred method which often achieves repayment, or at least a renegotiation of terms followed by a repayment.[21] Theoretical literature suggests that the parties could use the threat of invoking the EBL as a way of motivating the debtor to negotiate in good faith so as to avoid losing control of their company.[22] However, there is no evidence in empirical literature or from my interviewees that the threat of invoking an EBL procedure would be used as a bargaining tool.[23] If anything, two of my interviewees expressed their doubt whether the threat of using the EBL would be credible due to the known complexity and difficulty of using the law in China.[24] Moreover, in some cases, debtors and creditors need to avoid formal enforcement under the EBL because of their involvement in the shadow market or otherwise prohibited lending activities.[25]

9.1.2.2. Threats and Violence

If a creditor is not willing to give their debtor another chance to repay, or if the initial negotiations fail, creditors in China use threats and, in some cases, violence.[26] Although the use of violence to enforce payment is illegal and punishable by fines and imprisonment, several interviewees suggested that it is often successfully used because it makes debtor's default position – non-payment – as inconvenient and 'miserable' as possible.[27] In other words, knowing that court enforcement is slow and expensive (or unavailable), creditors try to credibly decrease debtor's payoffs for non-payment through harassment and credible threats of further trouble.[28] This makes non-payment more difficult, costly and unpleasant than payment.[29]

---

[20] See Sections 3.3.1–3.3.2.

[21] This is not unique to China. But my interviewees (J1-c to J9-c, L2-s toL15-c, P1-r, R1-r to R10-c, R12-c) suggested that the courts in China do not accept a case without evidence that the parties tried to settle their dispute informally first.

[22] See eg J Armour, A Hsu and A Walters, 'Corporate Insolvency in the United Kingdom: The Impact of the Enterprise Act 2002' (2008) *European Company and Financial Law Review* 1613.

[23] Two interviewees (L4-r, L6-s) who operate in a developed city expressed some faith in legal enforcement. But even they did not report that the parties would be bargaining in the shadow of the EBL.

[24] Interviewee L6-s said: 'Few companies are concerned about the threats of civil litigation. Based on my experience and that of my colleagues, this is rational and perfectly reasonable given the local conditions'. Similar vie was expressed by Interviewees L2-s, L4-r, L5-c and L10-s.

[25] See Section 7.3.

[26] See Section 3.3.1.

[27] Interview C1-c, C4-c, E2-s, E4-c, IF1-s, L2-s to L7-c, L9-s to L13-c, R7-c, R9-c.

[28] Interviewee L2-s said: 'In my experience, people in China and elsewhere do what they think they need to do – and no more – and obey rules which they think will be enforced'; this was also stressed in Interviews L4-r to L7-c, L10-s to L14-c.

[29] ibid.

In addition, creditors who choose to enforce repayment of their debts using threats or violence often operate in the shadow market. As a result, the debtor is incentivised to cooperate because they do not want their involvement in the shadow lending to become public, because – as was explored in Sections 6.2 and 7.3.1 – borrowing from shadow lenders is itself a criminal offence.[30]

9.1.2.3. Reputation Mechanism

In situations where the debtor and creditors are a part of a club – including shadow lenders and small-scale lenders – they can also rely on the reputation mechanism to enforce debt repayment by a financially distressed debtor.[31] Looking at the situation from a creditor's perspective, the reputation mechanism provides them with a valuable hostage against a debtor and those associated with it, which can help ensure recovery of the loan. In small companies that rely on relational finance,[32] the hostage is their personal relationship with the lender and their standing in society. In larger companies or in arm's-length lending, the hostage is the company's relationship with various stakeholders and the benefits arising from it, the potential liability of the company's directors and managers, and the career prospects of local government officials. Using the reputation mechanism – where it is available – instead of the EBL is considerably more efficient.[33]

From a debtor's perspective, the news of its financial distress and its failure to honour its obligation to repay a debt adversely affect its reputation in two ways. Firstly, it impacts upon the company itself and harms its relationships with other companies, potential investors and shareholders,[34] and possibly also its ability to attract good employees in the future.[35] Moreover, where a debtor gained access to the lending market with the assistance of a reputation intermediary – such as local government or Party officials, or an established company willing to act as an informal guarantor or agent – such an intermediary risks losing their own reputation, and so puts extra pressure on the debtor to repay.[36]

---

[30] Although, arguably, the creditor is just as liable to be punished, some of my interviewees (C2-c, C4-c, C5-r, C7-c, E1-c, E3-s, IF1-s, IF2-c, L2-s, L4-r, L6-s, P1-r, R3-r, R9-c, R10-c) suggested that they are more accustomed to the risks associated with shadow lending and so are more willing to use criminal methods to enforce repayment.

[31] For an overview, see Section 3.3.2.

[32] See Section 3.1.

[33] It is costless and almost immediate. Some experts and stakeholders speak about the influence of the threat of reputational loss on their conduct in business: R Tomasic, P Little, A Francis, K Kamarul, and K Wang, 'Insolvency Law Administration and Culture in Six Asian Legal Systems' (1996) *Australian Journal of Corporate Law* 248. Another study also shows that reputation loss is far more important a concern resulting from firm failure than economic loss or legal/safety consequences: F Allen, J Qian, and M Qian, 'Law, finance, and economic growth in China' (2005) *Journal of Financial Economics* 57, 94.

[34] This is either because they guaranteed repayment and so have to repay borrower's debt, or because they start perceiving the borrower as an unreliable counterparty: Interviews B1-c, C1-c, C4-c, C7-s, E1-c to E5-c, IF1-s, IF2-c, L1-r to L6-s, L11-c, L14-c, R3-r, R6-c, R7-c, R9-c, R10-c.

[35] See also Sina (28.9.2015).

[36] See Section 2.3.1.

Secondly, the news of debtors' financial distress also affects the individuals associated with the company – most importantly, its directors and managers,[37] and in some cases also local government officials – because their career prospects and personal social standing may be affected by their company's failure.[38] Several of my interviewees commented that debtor companies and their representatives, therefore, often do their best to repay their debts and avoid using the EBL because, for many Chinese, bankruptcy still means 'utter and complete failure [which] carries the stigma of not just economic failure, but a lifetime non-reversible declaration and admission of guilt and defeat in the person of the debtor'.[39] Many practitioners stressed the importance of reputation for their corporate clients in China, and the fear they have of losing it.[40] The implications of reputational loss then incentivise debtors to repay.[41]

9.1.3. Private Formal Mechanism

Sections 3.2.3 and 3.2.4 showed that unpaid creditors could also seek (limited) third-party assistance to enforce their debts. These include court-based contract and security enforcement and diversified dispute resolution mechanisms. My interviewees all argued that, to an average creditor, these mechanisms have the advantage of formal enforcement – similar to the EBL – but are less complex, cheaper and quicker than the EBL. However, what creditors often fail to fully acknowledge – the interviewees argued – is that these alternatives suffer from similar enforcer-related problems as the EBL[42] and may be ill-suited for resolving more complex cases of financial distress with multiple (types of) claimholders and conflicting interests.[43] Nevertheless, the parties often try to enforce repayment through one of the following alternatives.

9.1.3.1. Court-based Enforcement of Contract

A lender can seek recovery of their contractual debt in court.[44] However, similar to the reputation mechanism, for the threat of enforcement to be credible, it is important that it can be carried out where necessary. All my interviewees suggested that courts

---

[37] This is further reinforced by the fact that managers and directors can be held personally liable if the borrower company fails to pay its debts (Interviews C1-c to C4-c, C7-s, C9-c to C11-c, E1-c, E3-s, J1-c, L2-s to L7-c, L11-c). If the situation further worsens, they can also be liable under the EBL and can be banned from managerial activities for three years: see Section 6.2.

[38] This is further reinforced by the low mobility of personnel between provinces in China.

[39] A Tang, *Insolvency in China and Hong Kong: A Practitioner's Perspective* (Sweet & Maxwell Asia, 2005) 8. Also Interviews C1-c to C4-c, C7-s, C9-c to C11-c, E1-c, E3-s, J1-c, L2-s to L7-c, L11-c. See eg an interesting interview in K Leggett (21.9.2000, WSJ) with a debt collector who claims that 'The Chinese don't like to lose face. But if they don't pay their bills, that's exactly what I do to them'.

[40] Interviews C1-c to C4-c, C7-s, C9-c to C11-c, J1-c, L2-s to L11-c.

[41] ibid. Debtors' fear of losing their reputation as a capable, healthy company may, however, make debtors avoid using court-driven EBL – in particular reorganisation – since they fear that even if it succeeded in saving the business, the company would be finished because of the loss of reputation.

[42] See chs 7 and 8.

[43] See Section 10.2.1.

[44] See Section 3.3.3.

enforce bilateral lending contracts with significantly lower costs and fewer delays than when they deal with EBL claims. A court can issue a payment order – giving the debtor 15 days to repay.[45] So long as a debtor does not dispute any of the claimed debts and so long as there is enough money to repay all the claimants, this alternative provides a far more efficient method of recovery – even where there are multiple claiming creditors – and should be used instead of the EBL.

However, if a debtor makes a defence or brings a counterclaim, the case must be dealt with in a full-court hearing, which can slow things down.[46] Similarly, this method is inappropriate where the debtor cannot satisfy all its debts in full – ie is insolvent – and where enforcement of individual contracts would necessarily unfairly prejudice the other creditors.[47] Once this happens, enforcement of individual debt contracts and issuing payment orders becomes unavailable and will likely be transferred into a full EBL procedure.[48] Nevertheless, my interviewees suggested, individual creditors do not want to – and due to courts' passivity often do not need to – consider other claimants' position other than so far as it concerns their ability to recover.[49] As a result, creditors do seek – and often get – payment orders from courts due to the information asymmetry (and courts' ignorance that they should be using the EBL) and courts' reluctance to allow EBL petitions.[50]

9.1.3.2. Out-of-court and Court-based Security Enforcement

Similarly, secured creditors also prefer to use non-EBL alternatives. In China, as elsewhere, secured creditors' claims can be – and commonly are – enforced outside of bankruptcy law proceedings because security rights attach to a particular asset which can be sold and the proceeds used to repay the secured debt. As was discussed in Section 3.3.3, security enforcement usually takes place out of court or through a simple court procedure whereby the secured asset is identified sold, and the proceeds are used to repay the secured creditor. Where done successfully, the procedure is quicker and cheaper than recovery under the EBL – and without the risk to secured creditors that courts may postpone or cram down their rights to protect public policy interests instead.[51] This process, however, faces similar difficulties as the EBL, namely information asymmetry, misleading accounting, and limited willingness of courts to go beyond the assets known to and identified by the petitioning creditor as belonging to the debtor.[52]

To deal with the difficulties associated with contract and security enforcement, lenders sometimes use contractual guarantees and pawnshop-style lending to increase their ability to recover their money. A contractual guarantee makes repayment more likely

---

[45] ibid.
[46] Interviews C1-c, C4-c, C5-r, C7-s, J1-c, J4-c, J6-s to J9-c, L2-s to L7-c, L9-s to L15-c – most claims are disputed.
[47] eg whose claims are not yet mature, or who have not yet realised that the debtor is in financial trouble.
[48] See Sections 4.2.13 and 4.3.2.
[49] Interviews C1-c, C4-c, C5-r, C7-s, E1-c, E2-s, J1-c, J4-c, J6-s to J9-c, L2-s to L7-c, L9-s to L15-c, P1-r, R1-r, R3-r, R6-c, R7-c, R9-c, R10-c.
[50] ibid. See also Sections 7.1.1 and 8.3.3.
[51] See Sections 4.2.4 and 6.1.2.
[52] See Sections 3.4 and 7.1.

because it nominates a third-party (guarantor) who would pay if the debtor becomes unable or unwilling to repay. My interviewees suggested that, so long as the requisite formalities are satisfied, courts only have to confirm the guarantor's duty to repay.[53] So long as the guarantor is able to make the payment, the lender can recover their money.

Pawnshop-style lending in another mechanism used to increase the likelihood of debt recovery. It circumnavigates the problems associated with court enforcement altogether because the lender becomes a full legal owner of the liquid asset(s) which the borrower provides as a quasi-security.[54] If he fails to repay, the pawnshop owner can sell the asset and keep the money in satisfaction of the borrower's debt.

9.1.3.3. *Diversified Dispute Resolution (DDR)*

Finally, as Section 3.3.4 suggested, parties often resolve with the help of a mediator, an arbitration panel, or a combination of the two. DDR is more formal than self-help debt enforcement mechanisms but less public than court-assisted contract and security enforcement or the EBL. As a result, it is very popular with private companies in China, particularly if informal attempts to resolve the dispute failed or the issue is too complex for the simpler mechanisms.

My interviewees suggested several reasons why parties tend to use mediation instead of the EBL. Mediation is often preferred where the parties hope to maintain a cooperative relationship but are themselves unable to reach an acceptable compromise.[55] It is also used where the parties wish to safeguard their reputation, which – they fear – could be tarnished by a public court hearing, but where they cannot rely on the reputation mechanism.[56] The perception of mediation's relatively higher speed and efficiency and comparatively lower cost were also highlighted in some of my interviewees.[57] Mediation is also encouraged by the state, which seeks to maintain public order and harmony, and by over-burdened courts.[58] Once made, a final mediation settlement is enforceable in court.[59]

If the parties are unlikely to reach an amicable compromise but do not want to hand their case to a court, they can use arbitration – but only where they agreed and incorporated a valid arbitration clause into the relevant contract *ex ante*, or if they make an arbitration agreement ex post.[60] Where allowed, arbitration cases are heard in one

---

[53] Unless instructed not to do so by the Party-state: see Section 8.3. Interviews C1-c, C4-c, C5-r, C7-s, E1-c, E2-s, J1-c, J4-c, J6-s, L2-s to L7-c, L9-s to L14-c, R1-r, R3-r, R6-c, R7-c, R9-c, R10-c.

[54] ibid.

[55] Interviews B2-c, C1-c to C5-r, C7-s, C8-s. C10-s, E1-c to E5-c, J1-c, L2-s to L7-c, L9-s to L12-c, L14-c, L16-c, P1-r, R3-r, R9-c, R10-c.

[56] eg where the parties do not have a functioning club enforcement mechanism: see Section 2.3.1. Interviews C5-r, E1-c, E4-c, E5-c, L2-s to L7-c, L9-s to L12-c, L14-c, L16-c, R3-r, R6-c, R7-c, R9-c, R10-c.

[57] Interviews C1-c, C5-r, C7-s, E1-c to E5-c, L2-s to L7-c, L9-s to L12-c, L14-c, L16-c, P1-r, R3-r, R9-c, R10-c.

[58] Arbitration and mediation institutions are not in competition with courts in China; instead, they coexist and support one another. As we saw in Section 3.3.4, many DDR cases are managed by judges or are heard in centres which are associated with local courts. See eg SPC Monitor (5.7.2016), which summarises the progress in preparing the SPC guidelines and further reform of DDR in China, suggesting that courts are encouraged to offer a 'one-stop shopping' for dispute resolution.

[59] Art 51 Arbitration Law 1995.

[60] See Section 3.3.4.

of the numerous authorised domestic and international arbitration centres in China.[61] Several interviewees proposed that the main advantages of arbitration over litigation include the speed,[62] secrecy[63] and independence[64] of the process, and the adjudicators' expertise.[65] Moreover, an arbitral award is final[66] and internationally enforceable.[67]

China also makes use of Med-Arb, a combination of mediation and arbitration.[68] Arbitrators – who initially act as mediators – can have private hearings with the parties to establish their respective bottom lines and assess whether their expectations and demands are likely to result in a mutually acceptable compromise. Some of my interviewees suggested that this is one of the key advantages of MedArb because adjudicators are able to determine early on whether there is a realistic chance of a voluntary settlement, or whether a more adversarial, centrally managed procedure is necessary to impose a top-down solution.[69] Another big advantage is that, without wasting the time necessary to start a new procedure and allow adjudicators to familiarise themselves with the case, arbitrators can start off as quasi-mediators and immediately switch into arbitration when necessary.[70] Moreover, regardless of the stage at which the award is made – in the early mediation or later arbitration stage – it is fully enforceable. Several of my interviewees suggested that this makes MedArb more like litigation, but with the advantages of speed and privacy.[71]

Although mediation, arbitration and MedArb have many advantages, my interviewees doubted that, in their present form, they are optimal for all types of cases. Firstly, several interviewees highlighted that it might be problematic that arbitrators and mediators focus solely on the parties' financial interests instead of emulating courts' holistic approach of taking into account socio-economic needs and political preferences – especially in cases that involve state-sector companies.[72] However, the

---

[61] There were 176 domestic arbitration centres in 2006: J Zheng, 'Competition Between Arbitral Institutions in China – Fighting for a Better System?' (Kluwer Arbitration Blog, 16.10.2015).

[62] The parties do not face excessive delays leading up to a hearing, and the arbitration hearing can only last for six months. Interviews C1-c, C5-r, C7-s, E1-c to E5-c, L2-s to L7-c, L9-s to L14-c, L16-c, P1-r, R3-r, R9-c, R10-c.

[63] Interviews C1-c, C5-r, C7-s, E1-c to E5-c, IF1-s, IF2-c, L2-s to L7-c, L9-s to L12-c, L14-c, L16-c, P1-r, R3-r, R9-c, R10-c and Art 40 Arbitration Law 1995.

[64] Local governments are expressly excluded from the arbitration regime, and my interviews suggest that they play no significant role in practice: Interviews C1-c, C5-r, C7-s, E1-c to E5-c, IF1-s, IF2-c, L2-s to L7-c, L9-s to L12-c, L14-c, L16-c, P1-r, R3-r, R9-c, R10-c.

[65] Art 13 of Arbitration Law 1995 states that members of the arbitration commission must have at least eight years of work experience in arbitration or in law or in the judiciary or in research and teaching at a senior level.

[66] Art 9 Arbitration Law 1995. A report suggests that, although in theory possible, courts do not often overturn arbitral awards in practice: S Wang and M McKee, 'Litigation and arbitration in China: Which is better?' (2015) Lehman Law briefing paper.

[67] Because China is a signatory of the New York Convention. Judicial decisions, on the other hand, are problematic: Interviews C1-c to C7-s, C9-c, J5-s to J8-c, L2-s, L4-r, L6-s, R3-r, R10-c. cf cross-border bankruptcy decisions: ch 13.

[68] See Section 3.3.4.

[69] Interviews C1-c, C4-c, C5-r, L2-s to L7-c, L9-s to L12-c, L14-c, L16-c, R3-r, R6-c, R7-c, R9-c, R10-c.

[70] As we saw, the shift can be initiated by the arbitrators or the dispute parties: K Fan and G Kaufmann-Kohler, 'Integrating Mediation into Arbitration: Why It Works in China' (2008) *Journal of International Arbitration* 479.

[71] Interviews C1-c, C5-r, C7-s, E1-c to E5-c, IF1-s, IF2-c, L2-s to L7-c, L9-s to L12-c, L14-c, L16-c, P1-r, R3-r, R9-c, R10-c.

[72] Interviews C5-r, C10-s, J1-c, J7-c, J9-c, L1-r, L14-c, L15-c, P2-s, R10-c. One of the interviewees suggested that the arbitrators 'cannot be trusted [because] they are not loyal to the nation'.

problem with this criticism is that courts are slow and often distrusted partly because of such a holistic approach. This may also be why China's arbitration decisions are often regarded with greater respect than court decisions and enjoy greater enforceability internationally.[73]

Secondly, some of my interviewees doubted the abilities of arbitrators in smaller cities and less developed regions.[74] However, although the overall level of experience and expertise may be lower than in booming commercial centres, many of my interviewees thought that the knowledge and understanding of local arbitrators tend to be comparatively much better than that of local judges.[75]

Thirdly, some of my interviewees also complained that mediators and arbitrators do not have sufficient power to make their decision-making meaningful.[76] For example, they cannot order interim measures such as asset freezing, and instead have to rely on a relevant court to safeguard goods and evidence.[77] Nevertheless, mediators and arbitrators can take steps to strengthen their power – eg by seeking a court order for interim measures. Similarly, at times, enforcing arbitral awards can be slow. However, the problems in enforcement are less frequent and less severe than those facing the enforcement of court decisions.[78]

On balance, therefore, many parties consider the DDR mechanisms to be a good alternative for resolving corporate financial distress in China.

9.2. Politically Driven Alternatives and their Perceived Advantages

To complement the discussion of private alternatives in the previous section, this section examines politically driven non-EBL mechanisms that have been used to resolve financial distress of certain types of companies. Section 8.3.4 summarised four broad types of cases where the Party-state is most likely to interfere: 'special treatment' SOEs that were listed before the law came into force by the State Council under Article 133 of the EBL[79] as falling outside the normal EBL rules; 'cases of significance' whose distress would have wide-ranging financial and socio-economic impact; politically sensitive cases such as high-profile cases and scandals; and listed companies.[80] These companies are referred to as 'politicised debtors' for the purposes of the discussion in this chapter.

My interviewees argued that 'special treatment' SOEs and state companies are usually not free to resolve their financial distress as they wish. Instead, they are a part of

---

[73] Interviews C4-c, L2-s, L4-r, L6-s, L7-c, P1-r, R3-r, R9-c, R10-c.
[74] Interviews C1-c, C4-c, L4-r, L6-s.
[75] Interviews C1-c, C4-c, C5-r, C7-s, E1-c, L2-s, L4-r to L6-s, R10-c.
[76] Interviews C1-c, C5-r, C7-s, E2-s, L4-r, L7-c, L10-s, L16-c, R10-c.
[77] ibid. See also Wang and McKee, 'Litigation and arbitration in China' (2015).
[78] ibid.
[79] Art 133 EBL states: 'The bankruptcy of the state-owned enterprises within the time limit and to the extent stipulated in regulations issued by the State Council before this law goes into effect shall be dealt with in accordance with the relevant regulations made by the State Council'. See also Sections 4.2.1 and 8.3.4.
[80] See Section 8.3.4.

the state-run economy, and so the resolution of their financial distress must accommodate Party-state's financial and non-financial interests, in particular, ensure maximum employment, social stability and (particularly short-term) economic prosperity.[81] Instead of letting money-losing state companies fail,[82] the Party-state often uses a variety of mechanisms to resolve their financial distress.[83] The mechanisms that they use include many of those used by private companies discussed above – albeit driven by both financial and political interests rather than solely financial interests – and many other top-down restructuring tools and solutions which are described in this section.

High-profile cases and listed companies are often resolved behind closed doors or under the EBL driven by a local government rather than a court. For both types of cases – my interviewees stressed – it is important to send 'the right signal to the Chinese people and to the market that the Party and the government are in charge and keeping the economy stable and safe'.[84] The ability to steer the process and influence or determine the outcome of corporate bankruptcy in these important cases helps the Party-state maintain the appearance of power and stability which, in turn, strengthens its credibility as a good leader.[85]

The discussion below is divided into three parts. Section 9.2.1 brings together several discussions from earlier chapters to highlight why the affected parties accept the Party-state's interference and preferred solutions. Section 9.2.2 then looks at when and why the Party-state prefers to use politically driven informal mechanisms rather than the EBL. And Section 9.2.3 concludes by examining the circumstances and reasons why the Party-state allows the use of the EBL and how it interferes in EBL procedures to protect its interests. Together, the findings provide important insights into how the Party-state resolves corporate financial distress of certain companies which, in turn, helps explain the limited use of the EBL in practice.

9.2.1. Why do the Parties Accept the Party-state's Solutions?

As was discussed earlier, the Party-state representatives have many personal and institutional reasons which make them interfere in judicial decision-making in general,[86] and in debt resolution and bankruptcies of state companies in particular.[87] At the same time, courts have several reasons why they accept and follow the Party-state wishes[88] and why,

---

[81] See Section 8.3.1.

[82] We saw earlier that where a state sector company becomes financially distressed, the Party-state – most importantly the local governments – often order the court not to accept the EBL petition or they control the way the EBL procedures are run through their own committees: See Section 8.3 for details.

[83] See eg T Halliday, 'The Making of China's Corporate Bankruptcy Law' (2007) The Foundation for Law, Justice and Society, University of Oxford 5. See also R Pedone and H Liu, 'The Evolution of Chinese Bankruptcy Law: Challenges of a Growing Practice Area' (2009) available at www.nixonpeabody.com/-/media/Files/Alerts/China_Bankruptcy_Law_Pedone.ashx.

[84] Quote from Interview P4-c. Similar views were also expressed in Interviews B2-c, C1-c to C4-c, C9-c to C11-c, E1-c, E3-s, J1-c, J3-c to J9-c, L4-r, L5-c, L7-c, L9-s to L12-c, L15-c, P1-r to P3-r, R4-c, R6-c, R9-c, R13-c, R14-s.

[85] See Section 2.2.

[86] See Section 2.4.2.

[87] See Section 8.3.2.

[88] See Sections 2.4.3 (in general) and 8.3.3 (in the context of the EBL).

in cases of financial distress involving state-sector companies, they often welcome and feel that they need to rely on the Party-state's help.[89] This section builds on these discussions in order to determine why the affected parties – state-company debtors and their creditors – allow such interference from the Party-state, and why – in many cases – they welcome and even prefer such state-provided solutions to objectively applied EBL.

Politicised debtors[90] and their claimholders also tend to accept – and in many cases welcome – Party-state's interference.[91] For the debtors, this usually means that their company will be saved instead of them having to face hard budget constraints and market-driven resolution of their distress. Party-state's interference also often gives them comparatively higher payoffs (compared to the EBL) because where a debtor is bailed out or where new finance-provider is found, claimholders are often repaid in full or at least receive more than they would under objectively enforced EBL. In addition, there are minimal or no redundancies. On the other hand, however, Party-state's interference may not always be welcome. Where a politicised debtor and its claimholders do not agree with Party-state's guidance or its preferred solutions, they have little say and no choice but to accept Party-state's guidance. My interviewees suggested that many stakeholders are unhappy with Party-state's interference because their interests are subordinated contrary to the wording of the law (eg secured creditors' claims, banks that are forced to accept debt-for-equity swaps, etc[92]). Although the Party-state may listen to their preferences and demands, my interviewees suggested that the Party-state makes its final decision largely according to its own interests and preferences.[93]

9.2.2. Informal State-led Mechanisms

There are many mechanisms which the Party-state uses to resolve financial distress in politicised debtor[94] companies instead of independently run EBL procedures. Companies can be quietly suspended or written off. The problem arises where there are unresolved claims and clashing interests that need to be addressed before a company can be closed effectively. EBL liquidation and reorganisation offer a regime for dealing with such issues. The Party-state, however, often refuses to allow market-driven EBL to be used and instead imposes its preferred solutions.

The discussion below examines four informal techniques that the Party-state employs to resolve politicised debtors' financial distress. Firstly, the Party-state uses its vast influence to force creditors not to insist on being repaid as originally agreed and to grant loan extensions or forgive some or all of the debt instead. Secondly, ailing companies can be 'resolved' by the Party-state forcing a merger with another, healthy state company in the hope of creating a stronger whole. Thirdly, the Party-state may provide

---

[89] See Section 8.3.3 for further details.

[90] As defined at the start of Section 9.2.

[91] Interviews B1-c, C4-c, C5-r, C7-s, J1-c, P1-r, L7-c, L14-c, L15-c, R10-c. See also Section 8.3.5.

[92] See Section 6.1.

[93] Interviews C1-c, C5-r, C-s, L2-s to L6-s, L10-s to L15-c, R9-c, R10-c. See also C Milhaupt and B Liebman (eds), *Regulating the Visible Hand?* (Oxford University Press, 2016); and Section 8.3.2. For evaluation, see Sections 10.1 and 11.3.4–11.3.5.

[94] As defined at the start of Section 9.2.

financial assistance to struggling companies, usually in the form of financial guarantees, bailouts, bad debt buyouts, or regular injections of money that lead to the creation of zombie companies. And finally, in some cases, Party-state representatives take charge and devise a restructuring plan behind closed doors with the key players. Each mechanism is discussed in turn below.

9.2.2.1. Creditors to Politicised Debtor Companies Forced to Compromise

If a debtor knows that they may not be able to repay all debts in accordance with the original agreement(s), they often try to renegotiate the terms or reach a deal that would be satisfactory to both parties.[95] However, many of my interviewees suggested that where such private negotiations with a politicised debtor fail, the Party-state representatives often 'forcefully encourage'[96] the creditors to reach a compromise.[97] This usually takes one of three forms: loan term adjustments, debt-for-equity swaps or debt forgiveness.

Firstly, the Party-state – usually a local government – can order a bank[98] to extend the maturity of a company's loan, or to provide a bridging loan.[99] Where a debtor company is in temporary financial distress, creditors often willingly agree.[100] However, my interviewees suggested that banks in China are increasingly reluctant to offer extra time or new loans to severely financially distressed SOEs and other politicised debtor companies due to the responsibility system which makes bank representatives responsible for unpaid loans.[101] At the same time, however, local banks are acutely aware that they need to cooperate closely with local governments for three main reasons. Firstly, many local banks are branches of large state-owned banks, and so are under direct or indirect state influence.[102] Secondly, local governments are often important customers of the bank and so, in order to survive commercially, banks work closely with local governments and follow their instructions.[103] Finally, alienating the local Government may lead to significant operational difficulties for the bank as the Government may impose restrictions and excessive bureaucratic burdens known as 'red tape'. As one interviewee put it, 'local banks and local branches of national banks rely on the goodwill of the local governments to gain access to the local market',[104] and so a good working relationship

---

[95] As discussed in Section 9.1.2.

[96] Interviews B1-c to B3-c, C1-c to C5-r, C7-s, J1-c, J8-c, J9-c, L2-s to L7-c, L10-s to L15-c, P1-r, P3-r to P5-c, R1-r, R2-r, R9-c, R10-c.

[97] See discussion in Section 8.3.5.

[98] State sector companies have access to state-controlled bank finance, as discussed in Section 4.1.

[99] Also called 'shifting loans' or 'zombie loans' where the debtor borrows money to repay old loans: Interviews B1-c to B3-c, C1-c, L2-s, L4-c, L6-s. See also A Ahearne and N Shinada, 'Zombie firms and economic stagnation in Japan' (2005) *International Economics and Economic Policy* 363; R Caballero, T Hoshi and A Kashyap, 'Zombie Lending and Depressed Restructuring in Japan' (2008) *American Economic Review* 1943.

[100] See Section 9.1.2.

[101] See Section 2.5.1 for the details of the responsibility system. Interviews B1-c to B3-c.

[102] See eg W Liu, Base III and Bank Regulation in China (2014) *Journal of Legal Technology Risk Management* 1.

[103] For a discussion of actual examples, see Z Zhang, *Corporate Reorganisations in China* (Cambridge University Press, 2018) 117–18.

[104] Interview B1-c. Similar sentiment was shared in interviews B2-c, B3-c, C1-c, C5-r, C8-s, L2-s, L4-c, L6-s, L9-s, L10-s, L13-c, P1-r, P3-r, R9-c, R10-c.

with local officials is necessary for business. Banks, therefore, regularly extend the terms of bad loans and provide bridging loans if ordered to do so.[105]

Secondly, Party-state officials can force banks and individual creditors of politicised debtors to forgive a part or all of the debt owed to them.[106] This also includes agreeing to unwanted debt-for-equity swaps which may be less valuable than the debt owed. Similarly, state banks and state companies are often prevented from exercising their creditor rights, including security enforcement and debt recovery.[107] Several interviewees suggested that creditors' main reason for agreeing and cooperating is their need to maintain productive relationships with local officials who can ensure that business and scarce resources are channelled to them in the future.[108]

9.2.2.2. State-led Mergers

State-led mergers – where the Party-state orders a merger of the ailing company with a healthy one – have been used on several occasions in the last few decades. The first time that the Party-state experimented with the use of mandated mergers as a substitute for formal bankruptcy proceedings was in the 1990s in response to the fears of the impact of large losses arising from the Asian economic crisis in 1997[109] and the considerable unemployment problem.[110] The policy was initially tested in 18 cities in 1994 and later expanded to 111 cities in 1997. As a result, the number of bankruptcy cases dropped dramatically in those years.[111] Ultimately, however, it was recognised that, instead of resolving underlying issues, such mergers simply shifted them onto another enterprise. Also, the merged entity often failed to ameliorate the pre-existing issues of its distressed part and in some instances caused financial distress of the newly merged company. In time, it became apparent that this policy could, in the long term, reduce the number of profitable companies and even lead to a total collapse of the state economy. What's more, after several unsuccessful mergers, there was a growing opposition from healthy SOEs against the merger policy,[112] and so politically driven mergers were officially abandoned in 2000 when the Government started promoting the use of bankruptcy law again.

Regardless of the utter failure of the merger policy under the old 1986 bankruptcy law, my interviewees suggested that mergers have been used again in more recent times

---

[105] ibid.

[106] My interviews (B1-c to B3-c, R10-c) suggest that this is mostly the case in SOEs.

[107] See Sections 6.1 and 8.3.5.

[108] Interviews B1-c to B3-c, C3-c, C7-s, E1-c, L2-s to L10-s, L14-c, L15-c, P1-r, R3-r, R7-c, R9-c, R10-c. See also Z Zhou, J Chen, W Zhu and L Yang, 'Firm capability and performance in China' (2014) *Journal of Business Research* 77; M Peng and Y Luo, 'Managerial Ties and Firm Performance in a Transition Economy' (2000) *Academy of Management Journal* 486.

[109] In 1996, banks were owed RMB 26.1 billion, but they only managed to recover RMB 11.4 billion due to bankruptcies – see S Li, 'Bankruptcy Law in China: Lessons of the Past Twelve Years' (2006) *Harvard Asia Quarterly* 1.

[110] According to the official statistics, China had 5.76 million (ie 3.1%) unemployed people in urban areas in 1997. Additional at least 10 million people must be added to account for so-called *xiagang* (下岗) who were laid off but paid a nominal wage by their previous working unit. It was feared that allowing more bankruptcies would exacerbate this problem and could lead to much-feared social unrest: Li, 'Bankruptcy Law in China' (2006).

[111] See ch 4.

[112] See eg the case of Shanxi Textile Dyeing Plant case in Li (n 109) 2.

under the EBL, to deal with important, large-scale bankruptcies.[113] Some of my interviewees proposed that one of the key reasons why local governments opt for a merger is because they believe that it is the only viable alternative to liquidation – an option which they see as politically unacceptable.[114] Others suggested that mergers are sometimes driven by a desire to create national champions – big brand names with national and international significance – for the sake of local and national economic development or as vanity projects (*mianzigongcheng*面子工程).[115]

The use of mergers in lieu of resolving the financial distress under the EBL has been encouraged by the Party-state, the SPC and local courts in the most recent wave of EBL-related reform. Section 12.1 provides further details and discussion.[116]

9.2.2.3. *Financial Assistance from the State*

Forced loan extensions and debt forgiveness are, of course, problematic, because the Party-state effectively rescues its preferred company, but the cost of such rescue is borne by the creditors. Similarly, forced mergers compel a healthy company to absorb debts and inefficiencies of an ailing one, but often without being permitted to then make its ailing part more efficient by – most importantly – laying off superfluous staff. Given that many of the creditors who are forced to accept less than was originally agreed, and all the companies involved in the mergers, are wholly or partly state-owned (and all are controlled by the state), the above can be viewed as examples of the Party-state providing indirect financial assistance to ailing state debtors at the expense of state and other (usually minority) creditors. In some cases, however, the state also provides direct financial assistance, which – at least in the short term – benefits debtors, their creditors, employees and other stakeholders. Four mechanisms are considered below, namely state-provided unsecured loans, one-off financial assistance (bailouts), bad debt buyouts, and continuous financial support to 'zombie' companies.

In some cases, local governments provide unsecured direct loan (or an indirect one through one of its companies).[117] These loans are commonly provided to make sure that employees' wages are repaid[118] which, in turn, helps avoid widespread protests and so ensure social stability. Given the purpose of these loans and the influence that the Party-state has over the courts, it is hardly surprising that the SPC issued judicial guidance that such loans should be treated as employee claims.[119] As such, these local government unsecured loans are repaid ahead of regular unsecured claims and so gain de facto priority over other claims.[120]

---

[113] Interviews C1-c, C4-v, C5-r, C7-s, C9-c, J1-c, L2-s, L4-r to L7-c, L9-s to L12-c, L14-c, L15-c, P1-r, P3-r to P5-c, R3-r, R6-c, R9-c, R10-c.

[114] Interviews C4-v, C5-r, C7-s, C9-c, J1-c, L4-r to L7-c, L10-s to L12-c, L14-c, L15-c, P1-r, P3-r to P5-c, R3-r, R6-c, R9-c, R10-c.

[115] Interviews C1-c, C5-r, C7-s, L2-s, L4-r to L6-s, L9-s to L10-s, L14-c, L15-c, P1-r, P5-c, R3-r, R6-c, R9-c, R10-c.

[116] See Sections 4.3.3, 4.3.4 and 12.6.

[117] See a discussion of actual examples in Zhang, *Corporate Reorganisations* (2018) 118–19.

[118] See Zhang (n 103) 119–20.

[119] Art 5 of the SPC Notice concerning the Correct Hearing of EBL Cases and Judicial Guarantee to Maintain Orderly Market Economy (*Fafa* [2009] No 36).

[120] See Section 4.2.11.

My interviewees also mentioned one-off financial injections (bailouts) which the Party-state provides to overcome financial distress and return a state company to financial health – or at least delay the problem until the politician in charge moves on to another job in another province.[121] Bailouts were regularly used under the 1986 law and they continue to be used as a quick-fix solution under the EBL.[122] Several interviewees suggested that the decision to bail out a state company is often motivated by government officials' personal incentives – most importantly the desire to have good economic results, save jobs and ensure social stability[123] rather than by any genuine financial analysis realistically showing that the distress is, indeed, temporary, or that the one-off assistance can return the company back to health in the long term.[124] Financial injections usually succeed in pulling the company out of financial distress, and – in the short term – the EBL is not needed.

Similar to a bailout, albeit less obvious and often less costly, is a bad debt buyout. The most significant – and most controversial – buyout took place in the early 2000s. NPLs started accumulating in China's financial system because of directed lending based on administrative orders rather than commercial principles.[125] When banking regulations later limited the permissible amount of bad debt that banks can hold, banks immediately replaced all NPLs with new loans and introduced the responsibility system.[126] To prevent the resulting credit squeeze, looming defaults and asset depreciation, it was decided to move SOEs' bad debt from the books of China's Big Four banks to four newly created state-owned asset management companies (AMCs). Formed and financed by the Government with the aim to assume and liquidate the banks' NPLs, the AMCs were wholly state-owned, non-bank financial institutions with registered (state-provided) capital of 10 billion RMB each. The AMCs bought the NPLs at face value, ie without reference to the (much lower) market valuation, which was entirely unrealistic and caused large losses to the Government, but it helped prevent the indebted SOEs being officially insolvent.[127] At first, the AMCs seemed to be making good progress in disposing of the NPLs through collecting and restructuring the debts, and selling and leasing associated real property. Much of the NPLs were repackaged and sold as securities with state-provided guarantees, which greatly enhanced its marketability. Some securities were bought by foreign investors, some by ordinary people through government-organised online auctions, and some by domestic companies and investors.[128] Unlike banks, the AMCs could sell the NPLs at a discount to face value which enabled them to renegotiate and recover at least some of the debts.[129] Often, the discounted debt was collateralised with hard assets like buildings, machinery and land rights, which made

---

[121] Which happens every five years: see Section 8.3.2. Interviews C1-c, C5-r, C7-s, L2-s, L4-r to L6-s, L9-s to L10-s, L14-c, L15-c, P1-r, P5-c, R3-r, R6-c, R9-c, R10-c.

[122] ibid. See also Reuters (21.5.2012).

[123] As discussed in Sections 2.4.2 and 8.3.1–8.3.2.

[124] ibid. See also T Durden (11.7.2016, ZeroHedge).

[125] See Section 3.1.

[126] ibid.

[127] D Pierce and L Yee, 'China's Bank Asset Management Companies: Gold in Them Thar Hills?' O'Melveny & Myers LLP (July 2001) *Topics in Chinese Law* 2–5.

[128] J Sternberg (28.10.2011, WSJ).

[129] Interviews B3-c, C1-c, C5-r, C7-s, L2-s, L4-r to L7-c, L10-s, L14-c, L15-c, P1-r, P2-s, P5-c, R3-r, R6-c, R7-c, R9-c, R10-c. See also L Gesteland (22.4.2002, ChinaOnline).

it easier to sell.[130] Individual reported recovery rates ranged from eight to 60 per cent, the median being about 25 per cent (although some argue that it was as low as five per cent).[131] Certain assets were disposed of quickly while others had to be written off. However, although all the losses were ultimately absorbed – directly and indirectly – by the Government, the AMCs have been perceived for the past 15 years as a successful alternative to the slow and uncertain bankruptcy law procedures in China. Additional 53 city- and provincial-level AMCs were established between 2015 and 2017, and another national-level AMC was created in March 2020.[132]

Bad debt buyouts have been encouraged by the state and, in many cases, the state provides guarantees which made it easier for creditors to sell to interested investors and recover at least some of their money. Securitisation of banks' NPLs has been perceived as a simple and effective mechanism for dealing with bad debt.[133] The securitised distressed debt market functioned in China until 2009 and was reopened again in May 2016 to enable the banks to deal with the mounting NPL problem.[134] China's distressed debt market opened to specialist foreign investors at the start of 2020.[135]

Finally, some companies have become reliant on regular financial injections from the state. Such companies are known as 'zombie' companies (*jiangshiqiye* 僵尸企业). Many interviewees suggested that they are a significant drain on state's resources, but instead of letting them fail, local governments prop them up with regular financial injections, claiming that these companies are too big to be effectively restructured, and that the impact of their failure on the local economy, employment and social stability would be devastating.[136] Nevertheless, zombie companies present a real challenge to the short-term and long-term prosperity and stability of their home provinces, but they are also a direct result of local governments refusing to deal with their financial distress early on, which allows them to grow without taking any measures to ameliorate their situation. Although resolving zombie companies under the EBL would be painful, it is the only efficient long-term solution. This was recognised by the national Government in 2015 when formal resolution of zombie companies and their exit from the market became an official economic target for 2016 and subsequent years, as is discussed in Section 12.3. The top-down push to use the EBL led to a significant increase in the number of EBL cases in the last few years.[137]

9.2.2.4. *State-driven Private Restructuring*

State-sector companies often benefit from short-term direct and indirect financial support from the state, with little or no role played by the EBL. However, in some cases,

---

[130] See Asiaweek (30.11.2001). Interviews C1-c, C4-c, C5-r, C7-s, C11-c, L2-s, L4-r to L15-c, R3-r, R6-c, R7-c, R9-c, R10-c. The ability to use land rights, unlike the position under the EBL (Section 7.1.3), greatly enhances this alternative.

[131] Enterprises' auction data in Allen, Qian and Qian, 'Law, finance, and economic growth' (2005) 77.

[132] K Yeung (30.3.2020, SCMP).

[133] Interviews C1-c, C5-r, C7-s, C9-c, L2-s, L4-r to L7-c, L10-s to L14-c, P1-r, R1-r, R0-c, R10-c.

[134] See eg D Weinland (20.5.2016, FT).

[135] Yeung (n 131).

[136] Interviews C1-c, C5-r, C7-s, L2-s, J1-c, J4-c to J7-c, L4-r to L6-s, L9-s to L10-s, L14-c, L15-c, P1-r, P5-c, R3-r, R6-c, R9-c, R10-c.

[137] See Sections 5.1 and 10.1.1.

more is needed and the state has to get involved over an extended period of time. In such cases – several interviewees suggested – the state runs corporate restructuring by arranging new management, choosing new business partners, providing money and guarantees, negotiating or enforcing compromises in existing contracts, and forcing parties to cooperate.[138] One such method has been developed to respond to the variations in companies' ownership structure and sources of credit and has been used repeatedly in the past instead of the EBL. Locally it became known as 'purchase-sale restructuring', and nationwide as 'Changchun-style restructuring'.[139]

In essence, the Government takes debtor's liquid profitable assets and leases land to a new company (NewCo) which then becomes a multi-shareholder entity.[140] The NewCo, the distressed company and the primary creditors (the bank which originally extended credit to the distressed company usually becomes the principal lender) enter into a common agreement. The bank lends an amount of money close to the valuation of the profitable assets to the NewCo which then acquires the said profitable assets from the debtor company. The process is similar to EBL reorganisation, with the exception that most employees are transferred to the NewCo, and the Government plays a major role both in the negotiations and in the disposition of the assets to protect the employees.[141] The bank ends up with security over NewCo's assets, and debtor company's creditors get paid from the consideration received from the NewCo. The difficult part here is differentiating between profitable and non-profitable assets. Also, since the valuation is performed by state-authorised specialists and sanctioned by the SASAC and the primary creditor (usually a state-owned bank), there is real danger that a pro-state (ie low) valuation will be favoured and that non-state creditors will be effectively abandoned with recourse only to the now-empty debtor company with no profitable assets from which to repay its debts.[142] In some cases, non-state creditors can also receive equity in the NewCo which may remedy any bias in valuation and reimburse some of their claims, but several interviewees suggested that this rarely takes place where the creditors are not affiliated with the state sector.[143] Unsold (ie unprofitable) assets in the distressed company are then usually resolved through Company Law liquidation or a quick EBL liquidation, and the debtor company is officially dissolved.[144]

Together, the four mechanisms described above enable the (local) Party-state to resolve financial distress of some debtor companies without the use of the EBL. Many

---

[138] Interviews B1-c to B3-c, C1-c to C5-r, C7-s, C10-s, L2-s to L6-s, L9-s to L15-c, P1-r, P3-r to P5-c, R3-r, R6-c, R9-c, R10-c.

[139] It was named after an old industrial city in north-east China with many SOEs dragged down by two decades of heavy debt, redundant workers, low-quality assets, inefficient management, and old technology and equipment. It is similar to the UK pre-packs and the 19th-century US equity receivership. See also H Zhang 'Corporate Rescue' in R Parry, *China's New Enterprise Bankruptcy Law* (Routledge, 2010).

[140] Many companies are now partly owned by private shareholders, while the controlling stake remains with the government. See eg A Szamosszegi and C Kyle, *An Analysis of State-Owned Enterprises and State Capitalism in China* (US-China Economic and Security Review Commission, 2011).

[141] W Wang, 'Changchun Approach: A New Scheme for Debt Restructuring in China' (2002) presented at The Second Forum for Asian Insolvency Reform, Bangkok, Thailand, 16–17 December 2002.

[142] Similar to a ghost company: see Sections 4.1.3.4 and 5.2.1.4.

[143] Interviews C3-c, to C5-r, E1-c to E5-c, L2-s, L4-r to L7-c, L11-c, L14-c, L15-c, P1-r, P4-c, P5-c, R2-r, R7-c, R9-c, R10-c.

[144] Where this happens, the cases show up in bankruptcy statistics, which makes the real number of bankruptcies even lower than thought.

of the solutions are inefficient and costly in the long term. Nevertheless, their existence and use help partly explain the limited use of the EBL in practice.

9.2.3. Politically Driven Formal Mechanisms: State-led Use of the EBL

In some instances, the EBL is formally used to resolve financial distress of state companies, but the EBL process is shaped and controlled by the Party-state.[145] Such cases are reflected in the total volume of EBL cases, which is misleading because they are not EBL cases in the normal sense. The process is not controlled by an independent judge, but rather by a representative or a liquidation committee staffed and run by the local Government.[146] Similarly, the normal EBL safeguards and rules on priority are not fully observed. The politically driven use of the EBL takes on several forms.

9.2.3.1. State Takes Over the EBL Process

The most direct way of influencing the outcome of an EBL case is where a local government steps in and runs the whole process – either directly or through a liquidation committee.[147] The role of the court is reduced to mere rubber-stamping of the final plan. In particularly sensitive or complex cases, the local Government may decide that it is best to coordinate various stakeholders, governmental departments and regulatory bodies in order to achieve timely resolution while also protecting social stability and minimise the negative impact on the local economy. The local Government usually uses informal mechanisms that were discussed in Section 9.2.2 but under the umbrella of the EBL. This often involves the Government forcing a creditor bank to lend more money or finding a new finance provider to inject new funds for further functioning of the firm.[148] In other cases, it may involve arranging for a healthy company to buy a part of the business or merge with the struggling debtor company.[149] Direct financial assistance from the state is not that common, but indirect financial support in the form of an unsecured loan is quite popular, especially in reorganisation.[150] Similarly, bailouts are not that common in state-run EBL cases, but buying bad debts from, particularly, SOEs or providing state guarantees for distressed companies' securities happens quite often.

---

[145] For a general discussion of how the Party-state interferes in EBL cases – by preventing creditors and debtors from petitioning, forcing courts to reject such petitions, or interfering with how the case is run – see Section 8.3.5. See also a recent empirical study of the Party-state interference in reorganisations of listed companies in China: H Zhao, *Government Intervention in the Reorganisation of Listed Companies in China* (Cambridge University Press, 2020).

[146] See Sections 4.2.9 and 8.3.5.

[147] ibid.

[148] In some cases, banks provide bank loans indirectly (as lending to insolvent companies is often forbidden by internal regulations) through a third-party vehicle which then relays the money to the company in reorganisation. See Zhang (n 103) 117–20. See also Sections 8.3.3 and 9.2.1.

[149] See Section 9.2.2.

[150] There are several real-life examples in Zhang (n 103) 118–19.

9.2.3.2. *State Using Pre-packs*

At times, the Party-state may decide to devise a restructuring plan with the assistance of key stakeholders – such as the main creditor(s) and employee representatives – behind closed doors, with only the parties present knowing about the debtor's financial distress.[151] Once a plan is approved, the state allows the debtor company (or the principal creditor) to officially petition for EBL reorganisation[152] in order to legitimise the pre-agreed deal under the EBL. The process is similar to the UK pre-packaged administration[153] in which a sale is negotiated, due diligence completed, price is agreed, and all transaction documents prepared and held in an escrow before an administrator is formally appointed.[154] The data from China suggest that something similar is taking place there,[155] albeit the time period between the petition and ultimate sale or rescue plan implementation is slightly longer. In addition, in Chinese pre-packs, the state is heavily involved through a liquidation committee which de facto replaces the administrator and the court.[156] The problem with this approach is that the process is carried out without the safeguards and due processes set out in the EBL. Nevertheless, the SPC has recently endorsed the use of state-devised pre-packs and other out-of-court restructuring in the introduction to the 2018 typical cases.[157]

9.2.3.3. *EBL Used as a Deterrent or a Punishment*

Alternatively – my interviewees suggested – the EBL is sometimes used as an ex ante deterrent or an ex post public punishment. State companies usually enjoy an informal state guarantee that if they get into difficulties, they will be rescued.[158] This is dangerous because it creates a potent moral hazard problem. Such state companies are likely to take more risks than they would otherwise because they will enjoy the upside (ie they will be rewarded for the success of the business), but they will not share in the downside (ie the losses are absorbed by the state). The state is aware of this and uses two tools to control it.[159] Firstly, there is a real threat that criminal and personal liability may be

---

[151] Interviews B1-c to B3-c, C5-r, C7-s, L2-s, L4-r to L14-c, P1-r, P4-c, P5-c, R2-r, R7-c, R9-c, R10-c.

[152] Liquidation is sometimes used in this scheme, but only rarely: ibid.

[153] See eg S Frisby, 'A preliminary analysis of pre-packaged administrations' (August 2007) Report to The Association of Business Recovery Professionals; J Armour, 'The Rise of the "Pre-Pack": Corporate Restructuring in the UK and Proposals for Reform' in RP Austin and Fady JG Aoun (eds), *Restructuring Companies in Troubled Times: Director and Creditor Perspectives* (Ross Parsons Centre of Commercial, Corporate and Taxation Law, 2012).

[154] Generally, see also B Xie, *Comparative Insolvency Law: The Pre-pack Approach in Corporate Rescue* (Elgar Publishing, 2016).

[155] Tang, *Insolvency in China and Hong Kong* (2005) 1–3: Art 79 EBL gives the parties six to nine months to negotiate the terms of reorganisation proposal. Most companies in this empirical study needed less than 100 days, in five cases less than two months, and in one case, it took only 33 days to finish the procedure. Such speed is inconsistent with my interviewees' experience and may be readily explained by pre-EBL negotiations taking place. See also Sections 8.3.4–8.3.5.

[156] See Sections 4.1 and 4.2.9 and 8.3.5.

[157] See in particular Art 22: Section 4.3 and Sohu (8.3.2018).

[158] Interviews B1-c to B3-c, C1-c to C7-s, C11-c, E4-c, J1-c, L2-s to L15-c, P1-r, P3-r to P5-c, R1-r to R3-r, R6-c, R9-c, R10-c, R13-c.

[159] ibid. See also Li (n 109); Legal Daily (12.2.2007).

imposed against those in charge of an insolvent company.[160] And secondly, the state tries not to rescue each and every state company which needs its help. In some cases, the state steps in and forces the state company to reorganise or liquidate publicly under the EBL to warn and deter the others. A recent example is the forced liquidations of several heavy-industry companies to deal with their overcapacity and over-indebtedness.[161] Similarly, as is discussed in chapter twelve, the central Party-state ordered local governments in 2015 to deal with – ie restructure or liquidate – zombie companies in their region using the EBL and other rule-of-law mechanisms.[162] A senior SPC Judge, Du Wanhua, instructed lower courts to assist local governments and to 'become hospitals for sick companies'.[163]

Besides managing moral hazard, the state occasionally forces a state company to use the EBL to signal the state's determination to prevent certain types of activities. This was the case in the Sanlu Milk scandal, where the company knowingly sold contaminated powdered milk, which led to the death of several babies and made further 300,000 babies sick.[164] The case raised serious questions about food safety and political corruption, and so directly endangered social stability and the interests of many powerful figures.[165] Those involved in the scandal were criminally prosecuted, two were executed, one received a suspended death penalty, and three were imprisoned for life.[166] The company itself did not fare much better. The brand was tarnished, and so the company was broken up, and parts of the business were sold in EBL liquidation. Several interviewees suggested that there was a lot of political pressure to use the EBL to show to the people that the issue had been dealt with, to signal to the market that such transgressions will not be tolerated, and to avoid any further allegations of corruption and cover-ups.[167] Some further believe that the EBL was used to publicly shame the company and those involved in the scandal, and to show that the acquirers of the assets should not be tainted by the scandal, as they are 'a new and different body from the disgraced Sanlu'.[168]

Although politically driven EBL cases are reflected in the EBL statistics, it is submitted that they are not genuine EBL procedures since stakeholders' interests are not sufficiently protected and balanced according to EBL provisions. Moreover, in state-driven EBL cases, independent administrators are only rarely appointed, and courts often play no or minimal role – usually mere rubber-stamping and oversight over the implementation of the pre-negotiated deal as approved by the local government.[169] Therefore, the number of genuine EBL cases is likely to be even lower than the statistics show.[170]

---

[160] See Section 6.2.

[161] G Wildau (29.2.2016, FT).

[162] As explained in the introduction to Section 9.2.2, zombie companies are state companies that rely on state bailouts for survival.

[163] Quoted in the SPC Monitor (3.3.2016).

[164] For details, see Section 8.3.4.

[165] Interviews C1-c, C5-r, C7-s, J1-c, J4-s to J7-c, L2-s, L6-s, P1-r, R10-c.

[166] Z Zhu (23.1.2009, China Daily).

[167] Interviews C1-c, C5-r, C7-s, C8-s, C11-c, J1-c, J4-s to J9-c, L2-s, L4-r to L6-s, P1-r, P3-r to P5-c, R2-r, R6-c, R9-c, R10-c.

[168] Interview P3-r.

[169] See Section 2.4.

[170] For a further discussion, see Sections 5.1 and 10.1.

PART III

Desirability and Options for Reform

The four constraints that are discussed in Part II of this book have contributed to the limited use of the EBL in practice. The next three chapters consider whether the Government should be trying to remove the issues that reduce the overall utility of the EBL and ameliorate the implementation of the EBL in practice. Chapter ten considers whether greater use of bankruptcy law is, in fact, desirable in China. Concluding that it is, it provides a general discussion of the benefits that are likely to flow from greater use of the (reformed) EBL. It also outlines what would be the necessary focus of further reforms, what obstacles would likely hinder the reform efforts, and which approach would likely work best in practice. Chapter eleven returns to the issues identified as the four constraints in Part II and examines what steps need to be taken in order to ameliorate these issues and so enable more efficient use of the EBL. Chapter twelve then provides an overview of recent reform initiatives that have taken place in China between 2015 and 2020 – mostly at a local level – and it considers their likely development and impact in the future.

10

Desirability of Reforming
Bankruptcy Law in China

Before discussing what needs to be changed in order to achieve greater, more efficient use of the (reformed[1]) EBL in China, it is first important to consider whether reforming China's corporate bankruptcy law is even desirable. Section 10.1 of this chapter puts forward a number of reasons why bankruptcy law matters in China and why it should be used more. Section 10.2 then examines the potential benefits of greater and more efficient use of the (reformed) EBL in practice. Building on this debate, Section 10.3 considers what is the best way to carry out the necessary reforms. It examines three key issues that are likely to arise in the process – the proper focus of such reforms; likely obstacles to the reforms; and best format for carrying out the proposed reforms. The discussion connects, on the one hand, the positive analysis of the constraints on the use of the EBL in Chapters six to nine and, on the other hand, the substantive reform proposals (which encapsulate the key elements of the 'reformed' EBL mentioned throughout this chapter) in Chapter eleven.

10.1. Is a Greater Use of Bankruptcy Law in China Desirable?

Bankruptcy law is an important tool that support the proper functioning of a market economy. Ever since China started its transformation into a 'socialist' market economy in the late 1970s,[2] corporate financial distress and bankruptcies became a part of everyday reality in China and a mechanism to deal with them had to be introduced. The 1986 law was the first attempt to create a functioning mechanism for resolving insolvent companies. It gave extensive powers of interference to the state, partly because the key beneficiary of that law's procedures were the SOEs. Nevertheless, within a few years of its implementation, the 1986 law was deemed insufficient to deal with the changing needs to corporate bankruptcies in China.[3] The EBL was introduced

---

[1] For detailed suggestions, see ch 11.
[2] ie a market economy combined with socialist elements under the auspices of 'Chinese characteristics': see Section 2.1.
[3] See Section 4.1.

in 2006 in response to these shortcomings. Unfortunately, the law's implementation has been limited by a number of issues[4] which have prevented its efficient use in practice. Nevertheless, it is argued below that greater, more efficient use of the EBL in practice is crucial for distressed companies, their lenders and the economy at large, and so it is, indeed, desirable that the law should be reformed and the identified issues ameliorated.

There are three arguments that support the need for greater use of bankruptcy law in China. Section 10.1.1 below looks at the number of EBL cases per year and compares it with historical and international use of corporate bankruptcy law. It concludes that, by this metric, the EBL is not used enough. Section 10.1.2 proposes that there is an economic need to improve the functioning of the EBL. It points to a large number of insolvent or nearly insolvent companies whose financial distress is either ignored or is dealt with using comparatively less efficient methods (compared to insolvency law). Finally, Section 10.1.3 examines the calls for reform from the Chinese Government. Together, it is proposed, these are strong arguments to support the call for greater and more efficient use of bankruptcy law in China.[5]

10.1.1. Limited Use of Bankruptcy Law in China

The number of bankruptcy law cases in China has been low, even when taking into account the recent increase in the total volume of cases. This holds true both in terms of the total number of bankruptcy law cases and in terms of the ratio of bankruptcy law cases to the total number of companies in China (compared to several other jurisdictions).

In terms of the total number of bankruptcy law cases, the data presented in Chapter five showed that China had, on average, about 2,000 EBL cases per year from when the EBL was implemented in 2007 to the end of 2015.[6] Importantly, that was significantly lower than the volume of cases heard under the 1986 law which was criticised for being very narrow in scope (it only covered SOEs' bankruptcies) and for being only rarely used.[7] Following the Government's call for cleaning up heavily indebted zombie companies in December 2015, the number of cases started increasing. Courts concluded 5,665 EBL cases in 2016 and 6,257 EBL cases in 2017. Nevertheless, it wasn't until 2018 when courts concluded 11,669 EBL cases and so finally exceeded the annual number of cases that had been heard under the 'underutilised' 1986 law.[8] This recent increase in the total number of EBL cases is encouraging. However, it only gives rise to limited optimism. The increase has clearly coincided with the political push to clear out zombie companies under the EBL.[9] It remains to be seen whether the upward trend

---

[4] See chs 6 to 9.
[5] Indeed, some of the reasons explored below have been used to call for a new wave of reforms since late 2015, as explored in Sections 12.1 and 12.3.
[6] See Section 5.1.
[7] See Section 4.1.
[8] The courts accepted, on average, about 6,000 cases annually in 1996–2003, and almost 9,000 cases in 2001 when China acceded to the WTO: see Sections 5.1 and 12.3.
[9] See Section 12.3.

continues in the future.[10] This is particularly important given that there has been a jurisdiction-wide spike in the total number of cases in 2018.[11]

Moreover, the reported number of EBL cases is inaccurate. As Section 9.2 explained, many EBL cases are, in fact, politically driven and fail to apply the safeguards and rules of the law. The real number of independently run, objectively enforced EBL cases is, therefore, even lower than the statistics suggest.[12]

As a result, even when considering the recent increase in the total number of EBL cases, the EBL has so far failed to fulfil the high hopes of its drafters that it would be used to resolve all cases of corporate financial distress that cannot be effectively resolved under any of the alternatives.[13]

The total number of EBL cases in China is low by international standards, too. As Figure 10.1 illustrates, the number of bankruptcy law cases in China is significantly lower than the numbers in other jurisdictions. For example, in 2015–16 (ie after the end of the global financial crisis) there were, on average, 15,500 cases in England, 26,000 cases in the US, and 14,500 cases in Russia – but there were, on average, only 4,500 cases in China.

Figure 10.1 Total number of corporate bankruptcies in China, Russia, England and the US in 2010–18

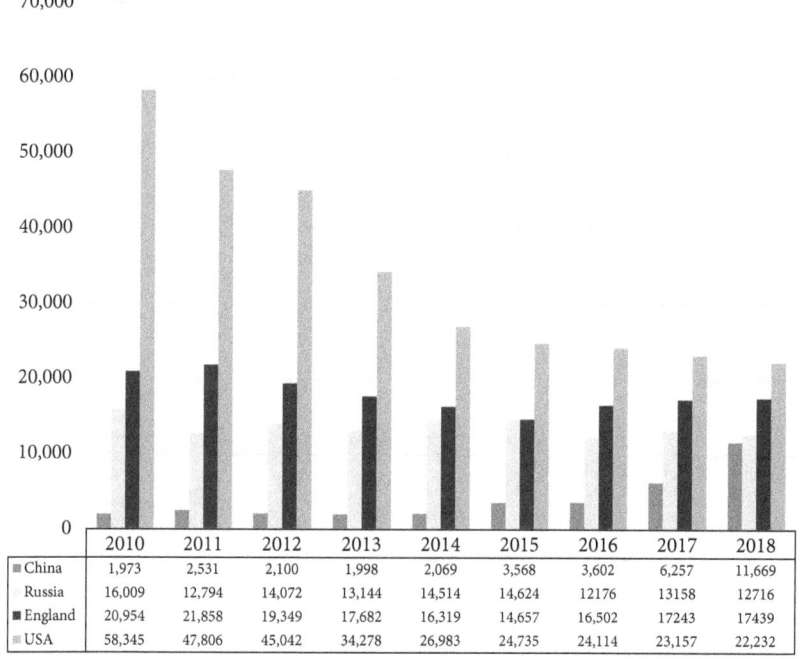

	2010	2011	2012	2013	2014	2015	2016	2017	2018
China	1,973	2,531	2,100	1,998	2,069	3,568	3,602	6,257	11,669
Russia	16,009	12,794	14,072	13,144	14,514	14,624	12176	13158	12716
England	20,954	21,858	19,349	17,682	16,319	14,657	16,502	17243	17439
USA	58,345	47,806	45,042	34,278	26,983	24,735	24,114	23,157	22,232

Sources: NBS, SPC, gks.ru, Company register UK, The Insolvency Service, census.gov, abi.org.

[10] Note that in the aftermath of the coronavirus pandemic in early 2020, 247,000 companies declared bankruptcy: see Section 5.1. These cases should be resolved by the courts using the EBL in the next few years.

[11] The annual SPC Report, delivered at the meeting of the 13th National People's Congress on 9.3.2018, showed a 55.6% increase in the total volume of closed cases heard at local courts nationwide compared with previous five years.

[12] See Section 9.2.

[13] See the excerpts from Wang Liming's 2004 speech to the NPC in section 10.1.3. See also Section 4.1.

Admittedly, comparing the total numbers of cases is a crude metric.[14] Each of these economies is different, and although the size of China's economy is similar to that of the US, China is still a developing country with many notable differences. Nevertheless, the comparison of this kind can be a useful indicator of the general trend in the given country if considered in a broader context and alongside other indicators.

The international comparison can become more precise, and therefore more useful, if the numbers are contextualised. Figure 10.2, therefore, shows each country's ratio of the number of bankruptcy law cases to the total number of registered companies. Interestingly, the numbers tell a similar story. In 2015/16[15] – despite being one of China's highest levels of use since the EBL was implemented – only about 0.03 per cent of companies used bankruptcy law in China, while it was 0.29 per cent in Russia (approximately 10 times more than in China), about 0.45 per cent in the US and England (approximately 15 times more than in China), and about 0.66 per cent in Germany (approximately 30 times more than in China in 2015, and 20 times more than in China in 2016).[16]

Figure 10.2 Ratio of corporate bankruptcies to total number of companies in China, Russia, England and the US (2010–16)

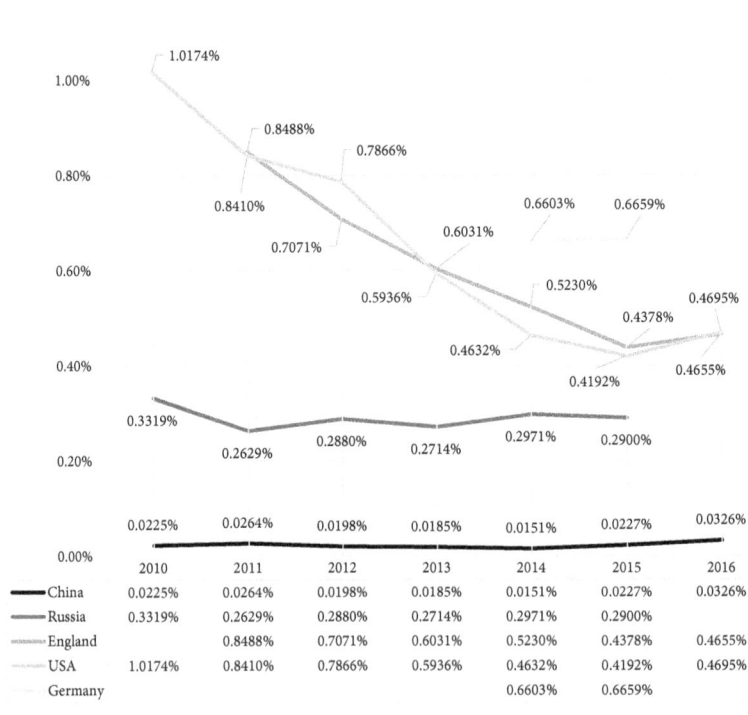

Sources: NBS, gks.ru, Company register UK, census.gov, abi.org; author's calculations.

---

[14] For a discussion of the problems in comparing numbers of cases across different jurisdictions see eg Z Zhang, *Corporate Reorganisations in China* (Cambridge University Press, 2018) 34–38.

[15] This period was chosen in order to minimise the impact of the global financial crisis 2007–10.

[16] Note that this table only provides data until 2016 because of gaps in the available statistics since then.

Although one must be careful with relying on comparisons with other jurisdictions and another era, the data above suggests that the real volume of insolvent companies in China is likely to be much higher than the existing number of EBL cases. The strength of this claim is further bolstered by the economic data, discussed next, and by the Government's own admission that China's economy would benefit from greater use of the EBL, discussed last.

10.1.2. Economic Need for a More Efficient Resolution of Corporate Bankruptcies in China

Another argument in favour of greater and more efficient use of the (reformed) EBL rests on the fact that China is harbouring a potentially large number of companies in financial distress, at the brink of insolvency or actually insolvent. The examination of China's economic data shows that the economy has been slowing down, the profitability of companies has been decreasing, and companies' indebtedness and banks' non-performing loans have multiplied over a short period of time. Together, these indicators suggest that there may be a large number of insolvent (or seriously struggling) companies whose financial distress has not been resolved under the EBL (given how few EBL cases there are each year). In fact, we know that some large-scale defaults and insolvencies of high-profile companies have not been resolved under the EBL. Similarly, there are certain types of debtors and creditors who cannot use the EBL. These cases have been resolved outside the court system – often using comparatively less efficient non-EBL alternatives (compared to bankruptcy law). The aim of EBL's drafters was to introduce discipline and fiscal responsibility into the state sector and to empower the private sector to use courts' assistance to deal with their financial distress.[17] The data, newspaper stories, decided cases and my interviewees suggest that this aim has not been fulfilled yet. Nevertheless, the five problems discussed below illustrate why China's economy would benefit from greater and more efficient use of the EBL.

10.1.2.1. Problem 1: Economic Slow-down

China's stellar growth was long unaffected by the global slow-down. Nevertheless, in 2011 China's annual GDP growth rate began falling[18] and reduced to around 6.5 per cent in recent years.[19] This means that China is growing more slowly, despite the rapidly increasing number of registered companies – as illustrated by the columns in Figure 10.3.

[17] See Section 4.1. See also Wang Liming's overview of the potential benefits of the EBL in Section 10.1.3.
[18] See Section 2.1.
[19] NBS 2008–19. Note that China's economy contracted by 6.8% following the nationwide lockdown during the coronavirus pandemic in the first quarter of 2020. This will have further consequences for the economy.

Figure 10.3 China's contextualised GDP growth rate (2007–18)

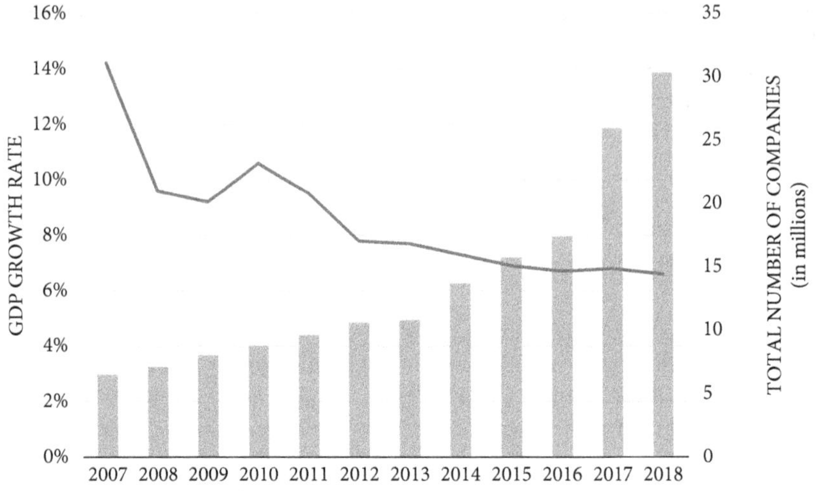

Source: World Bank, NBS, statista.com.

On its own, a slower rate of growth is not necessarily problematic. Indeed, slower economic growth can signal greater maturity of the economy[20] and can lead to greater economic stability in the longer term. However, it also leads to a slower increase in living standards, fewer new jobs, less public spending, and lesser ability of the state to manipulate its currency and inflation (deflation) rates. At the same time, slower economic growth is often correlated with lower consumer demand, lesser appetite for (corporate) risk-taking or expansion, slower investment, and more restrictive lending policies – all of which have an adverse effect on trade and so may cause financial difficulties for some companies.

The economic slow-down in recent years in China has been further exacerbated by decreasing profitability and increasing levels of (bad) debt – discussed below – which make China's economy unstable. Together, it is, therefore, reasonable to expect an increase in the number of financially distressed companies.

10.1.2.2. Problem 2: Falling Profitability and Returns on Assets

Another economic problem that is likely to result in companies encountering financial problems is the decreasing profitability of many companies in China. The profitability of Chinese SOEs is comparatively low (compared to private companies). Between 2000 and 2014, the percentage of loss-making SOEs was approximately twice as high as the percentage of loss-making private companies, despite the state's financial and other support to the former.[21]

---

[20] See eg D Vollrath, *Fully Grown: Why a Stagnant Economy Is a Sign of Success* (University of Chicago Press, 2020) – but note that his argument is based on economic slowdown in rich nations.
[21] In 2000, about 17% of all private companies and 35% of all SOEs were loss-making: SASAC, NBS, Credit Suisse.

Moreover, the profitability of SOEs between 2007 and 2015 was falling despite a high level of state investment and consistently increasing amount (and value) of assets that they held.[22] By mid-2018, SOEs accounted for 28 per cent of China's industrial assets but only contributed 18 per cent of the total profits.[23] The falling profitability was partly caused by the increased costs[24] (most importantly the cost of labour,[25] taxes, and materials) and partly by local governments' interventions which have prevented restructuring efforts that would reduce SOEs' overcapacity (due to the fear of unrest resulting from large-scale redundancies[26]).

However, SOEs have been showing much lower returns on assets than private companies, despite the fact that they received most (cheap) bank finance and a lot of state support. Before 2007, the rates of return on assets in private- and state-owned companies were nearly the same. But the Government's periodic stimulus efforts in the mid-2000s eventually led to excessive growth in production capacity and, without improved productivity, a significant decrease in SOEs' profitability. By mid-2018, the rates of return on assets in private companies were 9.9 per cent but only 3.9 per cent in SOEs.[27]

In the most extreme cases, these policies enabled the creation of zombie companies which rely on continuous state support to survive, and so are a drain on public finances.[28] Because these zombie companies have been concentrated in regions with significant economic problems – often due to their over-reliance on traditional industries such as coal mining and manufacturing – they could destabilise local economies. They have, therefore, attracted significant political attention and protectionism. As a result, for many years, the cause of their financial difficulties has been ignored, and the distress has been patched up using short-term bailouts and measures that only postponed the core problem.[29]

Zombie companies were finally recognised as a significant macro-economic problem at the end of 2015, and they have been liquidated en masse using the EBL.[30]

Nevertheless, zombie companies contributed to the economic problems in China until recently, and so they remain relevant. Moreover, they also highlight a deeper problem, namely that the local governments are generally unwilling to let unviable, unprofitable companies face hard budget constraints which would be imposed by objectively enforced bankruptcy law, and instead keep many of them alive.

10.1.2.3. *Problem 3: Growing Volume of Corporate Debt and NPLs*

In addition, the increasing volume of debt – and in particular non-performing corporate debt – also suggests that China's economy is harbouring many failed and financially

---

[22] ibid.

[23] The Rhodium Group research, cited at ZY Zhang (29.5.2019, China Briefing).

[24] But those affect private companies in the same way.

[25] An annual average wage more than tripled in a decade, from 21,000 RMB in 2006 to 68,000 RMB in 2016. Similarly, minimum annual wage grew from 8,280 RMB in 2006 to 27,600 RMB in 2016: data from www.tradingeconomics.com.

[26] See Section 8.3 for further details and discussion.

[27] The Rhodium Group research, cited in Zhang (n 23).

[28] See Section 9.2.2.

[29] ibid. For a discussion of local governments' short-termist incentives, see Section 2.4.2.

[30] See Section 12.3. See also G Wildau (23.6.2016, FT).

distressed companies. As was shown in Section 2.1, the amount of total debt in China doubled between 2012 and 2016, and the debt-to-GDP rate grew by 30 per cent in the same period.[31] The amount of bad debt in China's largest banks almost quadrupled between 2010 and 2015, reaching 1.27 trillion RMB in 2015.[32] Similarly, the credit-to-GDP gap – which indicates credit health of a country – is three times higher than is deemed safe, which may signify systemic financial distress.[33] Cleaning these up is estimated to have already cost the Government over USD 900 million (about 6.3 billion RMB).[34] Moreover, many problems are concealed by rolled-over loans which the banks use to cover up the real extent of the problem.

The amount of bad debt in China's economy is further increased due to the volume of NPLs in the shadow finance market.[35] However, unlike in bank lending, there is no official data about the size of shadow lending, there is no effective regulation of its activities, and there are many who fear that the size and riskiness of China's shadow credit market is a ticking bomb waiting to set off systemic financial distress which may destabilise the entire Chinese economy.[36]

The extent of financial distress in Chinese companies can be further illustrated in the increased demand for short-term loans to finance operational costs such as bills and wages.[37] Companies' inability to pay debts as they fall due is one of two insolvency tests in the EBL which allow a company to petition a court to use bankruptcy law to restructure or liquidate its business. However, the increase in demand for such short-term loans is not matched by a similar increase in the limited number of EBL cases in Chinese courts.

10.1.2.4. *Problem 4: There are Insolvent Companies that are not being Resolved Using the EBL*

Furthermore, the need for greater use of bankruptcy law in China is also apparent from the number of recent high-profile cases of corporate distress and corporate failures which were not resolved through the EBL (or where Party-state's heavy interference prevented courts from implementing the EBL objectively). These include high-value bond defaults – 29 in 2016 alone – including nine defaults by partly-state-owned Dongbei Special Steel Group worth 5.8 billion RMB and four defaults by Dalian Machine Tool Group worth 2.9 billion RMB;[38] failures of many real estate companies in recent years;[39] failures of 800 online P2P online lending platforms in 2015;[40] and numerous zombie companies which are factually insolvent but are still supported by the (local) Party-state.[41]

---

[31] See Section 3.1.
[32] ibid.
[33] ibid.
[34] See Section 9.2.2.
[35] See Section 3.1.
[36] Y Huang (6.12.2016, FT); J La Roche (10.2.2016, Business Insider).
[37] T Durden (10.12.2015, ZeroHedge). See also Section 3.2.
[38] Bloomberg (2.4.2017).
[39] See eg W Lin, J Wang and Y Guo (19.12.2019, Caixin); P Liu (26.7.2019, SCMP); S Yan (19.3.2014, CNN).
[40] Including Ezubao where 900,000 investors lost 50 billion RMB.
[41] Many zombie companies have been liquidated under the EBL in recent years (Section 12.3), but in many cases the EBL was not applied objectively.

Concurrently, there are many so-called ghost companies[42] – corporate corpses with unresolved liabilities, whose valuable assets were stripped and transferred to another company. In these cases, the use of bankruptcy law would empower an administrator to cancel the transfers, claw back the transferred assets, and distribute these assets to all entitled claimholders. Instead, the EBL is not used in China, the wrongdoers can keep the spoils, the wrongdoing is not disincentivised, systemic uncertainty continues, and claimholders are left unsatisfied. This is inefficient and undesirable, especially given that the EBL could deal with this problem and improve the situation.

In addition, all my interviewees agreed that, in their experience, most demand for the EBL comes from creditors – which is similar to what happens in the UK, US, Russia and elsewhere. Nevertheless, a recent statistical analysis by Ma Jian for INSOL China[43] reveals that almost 70 per cent of the *accepted* EBL petitions[44] are filed by the debtor. There are several possible explanations. Mr Ma suggests that creditors do not trigger the EBL because they do not know the true state of the financial health of its debtor; or they know but hope that the debtor recovers. Although these may be true in some cases, my research points to other explanations. My interviewees suggested that some market creditors submit their EBL petition but never hear back – either because their claim is not recognised by courts (eg shadow market participants),[45] or because the Party-state does not authorise the petition.[46] Alternatively, some creditors wish to use bankruptcy law but are not willing to initiate an EBL procedure because of the low expected payoffs.[47] Regardless of the reason, the high proportion of debtor-initiated EBL cases does not appear to be consistent with creditors' high demand for EBL procedures. This apparent lack of creditor-initiated EBL cases may be further evidence that there is a greater demand and need for EBL cases than is currently represented in the volume of use of the EBL in China.

A similar discrepancy in the data concerns the geographical distribution of EBL cases which does not correspond with the distribution of corporate distress across provinces. For example, in 2015, the courts in Zhejiang Province heard 638 EBL cases (or 18 per cent of the total number). Although Zhejiang has a very active corporate market, Zhejiang's companies accounted for a much smaller proportion of total corporate losses in loss-making enterprises than other provinces in China – mainly in northern and central China – where the EBL was hardly used.[48]

10.1.2.5. Problem 5: There are Insolvent Companies that are not able to Use the EBL

Finally, many of my interviewees argued that there are debtors and creditors who wish to use the EBL, but are not allowed to do so by courts and Party-state representatives.

---

[42] See Section 3.4.4.
[43] SPC Monitor (14.11.2015).
[44] This is not the same as *filed* petitions. See also Sections 6.1 and 8.3.5.
[45] See Section 7.3.
[46] See below.
[47] Instead, they use non-EBL alternative mechanisms which they perceive as giving them higher payoffs: see ch 9.
[48] See the data and maps showing total losses in loss-making industrial enterprises in 2015: NBS.

Courts sometimes ignore EBL petitions from the parties who do not have the Party-state's express approval.[49] Furthermore, as was discussed in Section 7.3, debt contracts concluded by shadow lenders and borrowers are not able to use the EBL because their debt contracts are often not recognised by courts.[50] Moreover, by coming forward, they may face liability for being involved with the shadow market or for lending into restricted sectors. Finally, several interviewees also suggested that the parties are also sometimes pressurised into not using the EBL by an interested Party-state body.[51]

Together, these problems highlight the fact that the real market-driven demand for the use of the EBL is likely significantly higher than the existing number of EBL cases. As is discussed later, the recent increase is likely a consequence of political pressure on courts to resolve zombie companies, and in the next few years, it may also be pushed up by the number of bankruptcies that have resulted from the coronavirus pandemic lockdown in early 2020.[52] Nevertheless, as was argued earlier, the EBL needs to be allowed and encouraged to be used more often but, importantly, to be used in an objective, efficient manner in order to help all companies that need to use one of its mechanisms and to fully maximise the potential benefits that greater use of the EBL may bring.[53]

10.1.3. Government's Calls for Reform and Greater Use of the EBL

Finally, the Chinese Government has repeatedly acknowledged the need to use the EBL more to help resolve corporate under-productivity, over-capacity, inefficiency and bad debt. The need to introduce corporate bankruptcy law was recognised early on in Deng's economic reforms which led to the introduction of China's first bankruptcy law in 1986.[54] That law was soon deemed insufficient and was replaced with the EBL in 2006.[55] In the final push to get the EBL passed, Wang Liming, a member of the Law Committee of the NPC and a vice-dean of the Renmin University Law Faculty urged the NPC in 2004 to pass the modern, market-driven EBL.[56] He set out five reasons why China needs a market-driven corporate bankruptcy law. These reasons remain valid and relevant to this day.

Firstly, Wang believed the EBL could 'improve China's market economy [because] companies must follow the rules of survival of the fittest in fierce competition'.[57] He highlighted the need to maintain a fair market competition order and to allow effective exit for bankrupt companies. Secondly, he believed that the EBL could help

---

[49] See Sections 6.1 and 8.3.

[50] See also FW Engdahl, 'The Role of Debt and China's Shadow Banking System: Is Baoshang Bank China's Lehman Brothers?' (8.7.2019) Global Research.

[51] See Sections 8.3 and 9.2.

[52] See eg S Leng (6.4.2020, SCMP); J Feng (9.4.2020, SupChina).

[53] See Section 10.2.

[54] See Section 4.1.

[55] ibid.

[56] L Wang, 'Corporate Bankruptcy Legal System' (6.4.2004) lecture to the NPC.

[57] ibid.

'maintain the normal order of the market economy and reduce financial risks'.[58] He warned that inefficient bankruptcy law enables over-indebted companies to continue operating without others realising it. This may lead to excessive borrowing and non-payment, which increases banks' non-performing debt. Effective bankruptcy law, he said, would allow much-needed timely liquidation or reorganisation of indebted companies. It would also allow early detection of financial distress and so help prevent unnecessary financial risks. Thirdly, Wang believed that the EBL could assist with regulating and ameliorating SOEs, given that much had already been achieved under the (imperfect) 1986 law.[59] The EBL promised to introduce further market discipline and hard-budget constraints. Fourthly, Wang believed that the EBL could help 'strengthen the protection of creditors and curb debt evasion'.[60] He warned that the market economy was based on the availability of credit and that non-repayment of debts leads to reduced or no availability of credit. As a result, he said,

> it is necessary to strengthen the protection of creditors by establishing and perfecting the bankruptcy liability system and the disciplinary mechanism for fraudulent and false use of bankruptcy mechanism so as to curb the occurrence of various debt evasion and establish and maintain good social credit.[61]

Finally, Wang also highlighted the importance of bankruptcy law for 'improving the efficiency of asset utilisation and realising the optimal allocation of resources'.[62] He warned that bankrupt companies that continue borrowing money wasted resources, which should be prevented. Moreover, he said, the EBL would provide a mechanism that could save resources and prevent wasteful liquidations if struggling companies were able to restructure and benefit from a temporary breathing space (moratorium).

The EBL was then passed in 2006 and implemented in June 2007. Wang's high hopes were, however, only partly fulfilled – primarily due to internal and external issues that accompanied its implementation in practice, which were discussed in Chapters six to nine.

In 2015, the Chinese Government acknowledged that the EBL was not working well – it was not used enough, and its use was riddled with a series of problems – and put it on the reform agenda. Such call for reform and greater emphasis on using the EBL better have been repeated several times since then.[63] The Government recognised that the law should be used more often and in a more efficient manner in order to deal with the general problem of growing levels of non-performing corporate debt in China and with SOEs' overcapacity and inefficiency.[64] Finding a solution to these problems is particularly pressing in the current climate as China's economy keeps slowing, and SOEs' overcapacity and inefficiency are being openly discussed and criticised as excessively

---

[58] ibid.
[59] ibid.
[60] ibid.
[61] ibid.
[62] ibid.
[63] See Section 12.1 for details.
[64] All these problems were discussed at length at the Economic Work Conference in December 2015 and again in the regional and national government meetings at the annual sessions of the NPC and Chinese People's Political Consultative Conference in Beijing in March 2016. See Section 12.1.

costly and problematic[65] in China and abroad.[66] As a result, national and local governments, courts, experts and academics have started discussing possible improvements to the EBL. Beijing, Chongqing, Shanghai, Tianjin and several provincial capitals have been designated pilot regions to trial new approaches[67] that are aimed at improving the EBL. Their work and recent reforms are discussed in detail in Chapter twelve.

10.2. Benefits of Greater Use of (Reformed) EBL

Greater use of the (reformed) EBL has the potential to deliver several economic benefits. First, Section 10.2.1 below suggests that the (reformed) EBL may deliver comparatively more efficient solutions to financial distress than the non-EBL alternatives currently used, particularly in more complex cases.[68] Second, Section 10.2.2 argues that the (reformed) EBL may offer a better solution to creditors and other claimholders than the currently used avoidance mechanisms which lead to non-payment. Third, Section 10.2.3 explains that earlier interventions under the (reformed) EBL are likely to enable better control of bad debt. Fourth, Section 10.2.4 discusses the likely improvements to the cost and amount of credit in China[69] pursuant to improvements in the EBL. Fifth, Section 10.2.5 considers the improvements in the allocation of resources[70] that China would experience once the EBL and its surrounding rules and practices are improved. Sixth, Section 10.2.6 looks at the possible improvements to China's business environment, including more investment and entrepreneurship,[71] which could result from the (reformed) EBL regime. And seventh, Section 10.2.7 focuses on the possible improvements to the rule of law in China. Many of these proposed benefits have been observed elsewhere,[72] and many were highlighted by the proponents of the EBL when the law was being drafted and enacted.[73]

10.2.1. Limitations of Alternative Debt Enforcement Mechanisms in Post-2007 China

Non-EBL alternatives – discussed in Chapter nine – are often used instead of the EBL because the parties believe that they would produce higher payoffs or because the

---

[65] See eg G Wildau (22.9.2015, FT).

[66] The economic problems include stock market crash in early 2016 and the general macroeconomic slowing resulting in, inter alia, lower GDP growth rate, lower imports and exports, stacking non-performing loans (which cost the government some USD 900 million to clean up) and zombie loans (ie rolled over without hope of repayment or given through state direction as a de facto periodic bailout), etc. All these problems were discussed at length in the regional and national government meetings at the annual sessions of the NPC and Chinese People's Political Consultative Conference in Beijing in March 2016.

[67] SPC Monitor (30.6.2016).

[68] Some forms of sophisticated private workouts and state-led use of the EBL may, in some cases, also achieve this: see ch 9. However, the former may be hard to enforce, and the latter are often politically driven and protectionist.

[69] Similar to the predictions in empirical literature: Section 1.2.

[70] ibid.

[71] ibid.

[72] ibid.

[73] See Sections 4.1 and 10.1.3.

parties are prevented from using the EBL.[74] Allen, Qian and Qian argue that informal mechanisms always dominate any formal mechanisms.[75] However, although it may be true that – particularly in the earlier stages of development – informal mechanisms such as reputation mechanism, bailouts and private workouts play an important role,[76] it is not accurate at this stage of China's economic development to suggest that informal mechanisms are superior or are alone sufficient to deal with financial distress.[77] This is mainly because, as transactions grow increasingly complex, finding a resolution for the aggrieved parties becomes more difficult or outright impossible without an outside adjudicator.[78]

Moreover, the increase in complexity is often accompanied by an increase in the number of stakeholders involved – and so a much higher chance of encountering coordination problems and conflicts of interests. In addition, many transactions now take place at arm's length, and so the parties often do not have sufficiently developed relationships to rely on informal relational solutions.[79] Although there is no doubt that most parties first try to resolve their disagreements and force repayment informally, my interviewees agreed that this is often unsuccessful and so the parties have to rely on more formal enforcement – either through DDR or in courts. As a result, formal mechanisms become crucial for resolving more complex transactions where the parties cooperate at arm's length. Therefore, as Thalen and others argue, at a certain stage, informal and formal mechanisms start coexisting and create a menu of solutions[80] to suit parties' individual needs and limitations. Arguably, China is at that stage.

What's more, some informal debt enforcement mechanisms in China involve criminal or otherwise undesirable behaviour, which should be disincentivised. For example, threats against debtors' personnel and their families often lead to violence and occasionally even death.[81] Similarly, the use of violence and looting against a debtor company[82] often lead to personal and property damage, which should be avoided. In the same way, the (legal) mechanism of detaining debtor's personnel to achieve repayment[83] is unsafe, it limits personal freedom, and damages China's image as a good investment destination. Moreover, Party-state-led non-EBL mechanisms[84] are often costly (eg bailouts), inefficient as they only protect certain parties and their interests (eg employees) at the expense of other worthy claimants (eg secured creditors), and they are limited as they

---

[74] See chs 6 and 7 and Section 7.3, respectively.

[75] F Allen, J Qian, and M Qian, 'Law, finance, and economic growth in China' (2005) *Journal of Financial Economics* 57.

[76] ibid. See also CF Minzner, Xinfang: 'An Alternative to Formal Chinese Legal Institutions' (2006) *Stanford Journal of International Law* 103.

[77] For a general discussion of the limitations of the informal system see L Yueh, *China's Growth* (Oxford University Press, 2013) ch 2.

[78] ibid. For a longer discussion of this issue see N Mrockova, 'Does Law Matter for Economic Development: the Case of China' in L Scaffardi (ed), *The BRICS Group in the Spotlight: An Interdisciplinary Approach* (Edizioni Schientifiche Italiane, 2015).

[79] In particular, the most informal mechanisms such as reputation mechanism, personal pressure, etc.

[80] See also Section 2.3.1.

[81] L Hornby and A Zhang (30.3.2017, FT): the debtor's mother was attacked and sexually assaulted in front of the debtor who then killed one of the attackers.

[82] See Sections 3.3.1 and 9.1.2.

[83] ibid.

[84] See Sections 9.2.2 and 9.2.3.

may temporarily fix a particular problem, but they often fail to address the root of the problem (eg mergers of healthy and distressed SOEs, or financial support of zombie companies).[85] Local governments' solutions may also be short-termist[86] and inefficient (eg shielding SOEs from competition from a more efficient private sector, or forcing banks to provide bridge loans to zombie companies).

Consequently, formal mechanisms may, in certain situations and for certain types of claimants, offer a comparatively more efficient solution and disincentivise undesirable behaviour better than informal mechanisms.

10.2.2. Non-payment Pursuant to Avoidance Mechanisms in China Limited under the EBL

The low use of the EBL is also problematic for the economy as the parties sometimes avoid repaying their debts altogether by using avoidance mechanisms. This section examines three types of avoidance mechanisms that result in non-payment. Firstly, it looks at how debtors try to avoid having to repay. Secondly, it examines how state banks choose to forego debt enforcement, where this would reflect poorly on their financial performance. And finally, it looks at how local governments prevent (timely or full) debt enforcement in order to make SOEs and state banks under their control look healthier[87] – and so improve the perception of their leadership qualities and fulfilment of the career-progression criteria. These avoidance mechanisms are summarised in Table 10.1.

Table 10.1 Avoidance mechanisms that result in non-payment of debt in China

	Aim	Mechanisms used
Debtor mechanisms	To avoid having to repay	(i) bosses run away (ii) ghost companies
Bank mechanisms	To not enforce payment	(i) extend/roll over existing loan (ii) new (bridge) loans (iii) IPO (iv) debt-for-equity swap agreements*
Local government mechanisms	To find and enforce a preferred solution	(i) provide state guarantees (ii) force state banks to write off bad debt (iii) force state banks to swap debt for equity* (iv) transfer bad debt from state banks to asset-management companies*

* Denotes that some payment may be received; nevertheless, the mechanism is not more efficient than the (reformed) EBL.

---

[85] See Sections 11.3.4–11.3.5.

[86] See Sections 2.4.2 and 8.3.2.

[87] It not unusual that banks make soft loans and that state steps in to help state-owned companies resolve their financial distress: J Fan, J Huang and N Zhu, 'Institutions, ownership structures, and distress resolution in China' (2013) *Journal of Corporate Finance* 73–74.

10.2.2.1. *Debtors' Avoidance Mechanisms*

Informal and shadow lending agreements are often initially enforced through threats or actual violence. Debtors' common response to such threats is paying up – even if they have to borrow from their family and friends or the shadow market to do so.[88] However, several of my interviewees suggested that – where debtors do not have the money to repay or where avoidance is less costly than repayment,[89] and if they think that they can act quickly enough – debtors may go into hiding or run away to another province or abroad to avoid having to repay their debts.[90] This is often the case where the debts are very large,[91] or where debtors may face serious criminal liability for their involvement in the shadow lending market.[92] Probably the most famous case of 'the run-away bosses' took place in Wenzhou in 2011 where several bosses of both large and small private companies ran away to avoid the consequences of what one observer described as 'reputation and violence [replacing] laws and courts'.[93] Although only a few entrepreneurs can afford to and dare to disappear like this,[94] several interviewees suggested that if the EBL worked better, debtors would be incentivised to stay and resolve their debts,[95] which would be more efficient and more desirable for creditors and debtors alike.

Besides running away, debtor company's management also sometimes transfer all valuable assets out of the ailing company and into a new company. What is left behind is known as a 'ghost company'. Such transfers are often left unreversed and unpunished.[96] If the EBL was used to resolve such cases, the administrator would be able to reverse such transfers and claw back the assets for the benefit of debtor's claimholders.[97] As such, avoiding debt repayment would become much more difficult.

10.2.2.2. *State Banks' Avoidance Mechanisms*

Interestingly, creditors also sometimes choose not to enforce repayment of their debts. Although bank officials are now personally liable for failed loans,[98] even more important is the overall image and financial performance of the bank as a whole. This is because, firstly, banks are now subject to macro-prudential regulation which defines the maximum permissible level of bad assets,[99] and secondly, because bank managers' career progression into other managerial positions within the state-owned sector or bank regulator depends on their performance.[100] As a result,

---

[88] Interviews C1-c to C5-r, C7-s, C11-c, E1-c to E3-s, IF1-s, IF2-c, L1-r to L6-s, L9-s to L14-c, L16-c, R2-r, R3-r, R6-c, R7-c, R9-c, R10-c.
[89] In terms of a cost–benefit analysis.
[90] See Section 6.2.2 and Reuters (29.9.2011).
[91] ibid.
[92] For details see Sections 6.2 and 7.3.
[93] EEO (8.10.2011); C Yap and T Orlik (15.2.2012, WSJ).
[94] Consequently, creditors' threats remain, in general, a powerful debt enforcement tool.
[95] Interviews C5-r, C7-s, E1-c to E3-s, IF1-s, L2-s, L4-r, L6-s, L10-s, L14-c, R3-r, R6-c, R9-c, R10-c.
[96] See Section 3.4.4.
[97] See Sections 4.2.9 and 4.2.13.
[98] See Section 3.1.
[99] ibid.
[100] Interviews B1-c to B3-c, C1-c, C4-c, C5-r, E1-c, E3-s, J1-c, J3-c, J4-c, J6-s to J8-c, L4-r to L8-c, L10-s, L14-c, L16-c, R2-r, R4-c, R7-c, R10-c.

non-performing debt is often restructured so as to be reclassified from a bad asset to a good asset (or as an investment). This can be done by providing bridging loans – ie repaying an old loan with a new one or by changing the terms of existing loans – eg by extending the maturity, or by agreeing to accept non-monetary or non-cash assets in satisfaction of the debt.[101] In some cases, banks also use trust mechanism or WMPs to securitise and sell off bad loans.[102] The EBL would not necessarily stop these practices, but it would offer an efficient alternative option for resolution of bad debts which would make these practices unnecessary.

10.2.2.3. *Local Governments' Avoidance Mechanisms*

The Party-state influences political, social and economic activities and decisions in China. As was discussed in Section 2.4.2, Party-state officials in local governments who wish to progress their careers have to meet certain socio-economic targets. At the same time, they control local SOEs and local branches of banks which rely on their protection for access and ease of doing business.[103] As a result, the officials make and enforce the rules against their own companies, which creates a significant conflict of interests.

The national-level Party-state tried to resolve this conflict by liberalising management and decision-making of both SOEs and state banks to make them more independent from the state – and so able to make efficient market-driven decisions. However, in reality, state-sector companies[104] and banks are still perceived by many local governments as administrative extensions of the Party-state which, consequently, have to comply with the (local) Party-state's ideology and directions. Several interviewees suggested that, as a result, state-sector debtors and creditors are often prevented from using the EBL at a local level.[105] Instead, state-controlled creditors are forced to write off their debts, or they have to accept (possibly worthless) debt-for-equity swaps in ailing companies in full satisfaction of their debts.[106] These mechanisms often lead to unsatisfactory outcomes – either non-payment or an unwanted form of part-repayment – which is inefficient for the economy and undesirable for individual creditors. If the EBL was enforced objectively, without Party-state's interference, it could ensure that creditors are treated fairly, according to the principles as stated in the law which would enable them to arrange their affairs in a predictable manner. It would also enable the credit market to determine the risk and likelihood of repayment in individual cases.[107]

Local governments also try to prevent corporate failures by providing state guarantees – and paying up when the debtor company fails to repay – and by creating asset-management companies that buy bad debt off banks and SOEs at full price and

---

[101] See Section 9.2.2; D McMahon (22.12.2014, WSJ).

[102] See Section 3.1.

[103] See also Sections 2.3 and 3.1.

[104] See Section 2.5.

[105] Interviews C1-c to C5-r, C7-s, C11-c, IF1-s, L1-r to L6-s, L9-s to L14-c, L16-c, R2-r, R3-r, R6-c, R7-c, R9-c, R10-c.

[106] ibid. See also Sections 9.2.1 and 12.6. eg in the reorganisation of Dongbei Special Steel Group, large unsecured institutional investors had to choose between a 22.1% repayment in cash or a 100% debt-for-equity swap. See also Ren S (10.3.2016, Barrons); Reuters (3.4.2014).

[107] See Section 10.2.4.

dispose of the bad debt through the collection, collateralisation and securitisation.[108] Although these mechanisms, prima facie, result in the full repayment of creditors' claims, the solution is sometimes inefficient where bad debt is simply buried and paid off using public money which could and should be better spent elsewhere. If the EBL was allowed to be enforced objectively, it would introduce hard-budget constraints and market discipline into the state sector. That would, in turn, enable the EBL to differenti-ate between the viable companies that should be reorganised and the rest which should be liquidated,[109] and it could limit excessive borrowing by risky borrowers.[110]

10.2.3. Control of Bad Debt under the (Reformed) EBL

The size of corporate and state debt is enormous and growing in China – as was discussed in Section 3.1 – and much of it is non-performing. The (reformed) EBL could help. Timely use of liquidation – where a debtor company cannot be efficiently saved – and reorganisation – where a part or whole business can be restructured and saved – could help manage the existing bad debt and prevent further piling up of bad debt in already distressed debtors. It could also provide comparatively high return to creditors because timely closure and sale of assets would most likely attract a better sale price. For this to work – and to disincentivise and prevent healthy companies from taking on exces-sive amounts of risky debt – the EBL would have to be allowed to impose hard-budget constraints on all companies. It would also be helpful if the EBL imposed a duty[111] to reorganise or liquidate financially distressed companies. This would introduce more market discipline, and companies would only be able to borrow a limited amount of money – which would constrain the maximum amount of bad debt that they can accu-mulate if (or by the time) they fail.

In addition, greater use of the (reformed) EBL may also prevent deepening of finan-cial distress of companies that are run in an inefficient manner by closing them down or reorganising them. The EBL could then redistribute (sell) their assets to more efficient users or enable restructuring to remove the impediment(s) that was responsible for the initial inefficiency. For this to work, however, it is necessary to change state-controlled parties' incentives. At the moment, state creditors (mostly banks) and state debtors (mostly SOEs) expect to be bailed out or otherwise assisted in case of financial distress. This creates moral hazard where state-controlled debtors have no incentive to try to improve their indebtedness[112] because of their belief that they would be assisted by the state, and they also take great risks because they would benefit from the upside and would be bailed out if the risk materialises and they become financially distressed.[113] Several interviewees explained this phenomenon by pointing to local governments'

---

[108] See Section 9.2.
[109] See Section 1.1.
[110] See Sections 10.2.3 and 10.2.5.
[111] Such duty existed in the original Shenzhen Bankruptcy Regulations 1993 – see Sections 4.1 and 11.1.4.1.
[112] See Section 9.2.3.
[113] See eg J Tirole, *The Theory of Corporate Finance* (Princeton University Press, 2006) ch 1; MV Pauly, 'The Economics of Moral Hazard' (1968) *American Economic Review* 531, 535.

short-term incentives to maintain socio-economic stability – and so save failing companies – and their reliance on the maintenance of employment and tax revenue.[114] This is particularly pronounced in cases of large, important companies which are interconnected with other important players in the economy, and which are, as a result, not usually allowed to fail because of the rippling effect that would have on the local economy.[115] Instead, they are resolved behind closed doors with heavy involvement of local Party-state representatives.[116]

These consequences of the non-use of the EBL create serious problems for the economy because soft-budget constraints and near-certainty of state solution incentivise healthy state companies to take on too much risk. Changing these incentives, and not allowing distressed companies to continue without changing their financial strategy or direction would also help reduce governments' debt and the waste of public resources in rescuing over-indebted enterprises. That could be achieved by allowing objective enforcement of the (reformed) EBL. It is likely that, in the long term, this is the only way how China can manage its growing bad debt burden.

10.2.4. Improved Availability and Lower Cost of Credit Pursuant to Objective Enforcement of the (Reformed) EBL

Another potential improvement resulting from better enforcement of the (reformed) EBL relates to the availability and cost of credit. Empirical studies suggest that the high cost and the low amount of credit is a fairly common problem in emerging markets because creditors respond to the difficulties that they face when seizing assets and liquidating distressed companies to recover their debts.[117] Traditionally, debt provision in China suffered from the same shortcomings.[118] Many policies have been released to ameliorate the situation. However, much still remains to be done as many private-sector companies still struggle to access enough cheap credit to grow and expand.

As was discussed in Section 1.2, one of the elements that may contribute to increased availability and lower cost of credit is an efficient bankruptcy law regime. The reformed EBL would likely enable such provision of credit. Even if state banks only continue lending to the state-sector companies, there is an increasing number of other sources of credit.[119] However, reasonably priced[120] arm's-length lending is provided only where it is possible to predict that a lender would be able to recover their debt and under what conditions. In China, such risk-analysis has been difficult, which makes arm's-length finance scarce and expensive.[121]

---

[114] Interviews C1-c to C5-r, C7-s, C11-c, IF1-s, L1-r to L6-s, L9-s to L14-c, L16-c, R2-r, R3-r, R6-c, R7-c, R9-c, R10-c. For details see Section 2.4.2.

[115] Note the similarity with the too-big-to-fail phenomenon. See eg AR Sorkin, *Too Big to Fail* (Penguin Books, 2010).

[116] Note that, more recently, several local governments refused to bail out or otherwise assist large debtors in order to reduce the moral hazard: see Sections 5.1 and 12.3.

[117] See eg Fan, Huang and Zhu, 'Institutions' (2013). See also Section 1.2.

[118] See Sections 2.5 and 3.1.

[119] See Sections 3.1 and 3.2.

[120] Excessively expensive shadow lending is available, but is very prohibitively costly and risky: see Section 3.1.

[121] ibid.

Building on the predictions and observations in prior literature,[122] the access to and the cost of arm's-length finance is likely to improve if debt enforcement becomes more predictable, if arm's-length finance providers receive objective and equal treatment, and if state protectionism is limited or (ideally) removed – all of which may be achieved under the (reformed) EBL.[123] Similarly, arm's-length lending would likely become much easier and cheaper if courts respected the priority of security rights[124] – which can also be achieved under the (reformed) EBL. Given China's stage of development – where further growth and economic opportunities arise largely from arm's-length, cross-provincial and cross-border relationships – a functioning bankruptcy law is crucial. Most of the expansion of China's economy in recent years relied on the private sector which, in turn, was often forced to rely on expensive and highly volatile shadow finance where credit contracts are often hard to enforce or are enforced using undesirable methods.[125] However, going forward, greater and more objective enforcement of the (reformed) EBL will likely be necessary to enable further expansion of the private sector without the risk and instability that have been associated with its growth so far.

10.2.5. More Efficient Allocation of Resources and Fewer Value-destroying Activities under the (Reformed) EBL

Greater use of the (reformed) EBL is also likely to lead to a more efficient allocation of resources – as predicted in empirical literature[126] – and fewer value-destroying activities by financially distressed companies. Resources – labour, credit, input materials – are scarce, and so they need to be allocated to the most efficient user[127] to ensure maximum returns. Similarly, the limited supply of credit and raw materials also needs to be allocated based on efficiency – measured by return on assets, productivity and profitability – rather than political connections and protectionism. Unlike the initial period of growth when China could rely on a seemingly unlimited supply of cheap labour, China has now reached a stage where further growth is driven by improvements in efficiency and profitability.[128]

When exposed to an objective market-based application of the (reformed) EBL, financially distressed companies would either retain their resources but put them to a better use following restructuring,[129] or liquidate and so free up their resources for more efficient use elsewhere. This would ensure, firstly, credit being allocated to efficient, profitable companies – many of which have no access to legal credit at the moment – rather than to prop up distressed SOEs; and secondly, materials and workforce from closed inefficient companies (SOEs and private) being re-employed in more profitable and productive projects. The ability of bankruptcy law to do these things – and the

---

[122] See Section 1.2.
[123] See Chapters 11 and 12.
[124] See Sections 4.2.11, 11.1.2.2 and 11.1.4.3.
[125] See Sections 3.2 and 10.2.1.
[126] See Section 1.2.
[127] Or at least relatively more efficient than the previous user.
[128] Yueh, *China's Growth* (2013).
[129] Where informal attempts failed.

importance of these functions for a market economy – was recognised when the EBL was being drafted[130] and again recently in the context of resolving overcapacity and inefficiency of SOEs – and in particular zombie companies – since December 2015.[131]

Moreover, timely use of EBL reorganisation and liquidation may also prevent further destruction of value. It is generally accepted that if reorganisation is used too late, it may not be possible to save the company or its business which could have been done earlier in the process by, for example, changing production methods, refocusing on different regions, upgrading technology, changing company policies, replacing management, or making other necessary changes. Similarly, if liquidation is used too late, it is likely that more resources had been wasted in an attempt to save the company; the need for a fast sale of assets is likely to push the sale prices even lower; the situation may worsen and become more complex in the meantime which may, in turn, make the process longer and more costly; and, in China, there is also the danger of looting by angry employees when the firm is closed.[132] A timely, more predictable use of bankruptcy law has the potential to minimise a lot of these negative effects present in China at the moment, and so minimise destruction of value.

10.2.6. Better Business Environment, more Investment and more Entrepreneurship Pursuant to Objective Enforcement of the (Reformed) EBL

More objective enforcement of the (reformed) EBL may also have a positive impact on the business environment in China. It is likely that resolving SOEs' financial distress using objectively enforced bankruptcy law could lead to a short-term reduction in exports and sales of domestic products in certain industries. However, in the long term, greater use of the (reformed) EBL is likely to lead to higher profitability;[133] greater recoverability of debts;[134] lower levels of bad debt;[135] reduced or no need to provide wasteful subsidies to inefficient SOEs;[136] greater amount of cheaper credit that would be allocated using market mechanisms rather than protectionism and connections;[137] better use of resources;[138] the stronger rule of law, more transparency and predictability;[139] and more opportunities for private companies to grow and become national champions – as many have already done.[140] Together, these improvements would also lead to a dramatic improvement in the business environment which – all my

---

[130] See Sections 4.1 and 10.1.3.
[131] See Sections 12.1 and 12.3.
[132] See Section 7.1.3.
[133] See Sections 10.1.3 and 10.2.5.
[134] See Section 10.2.2.
[135] See Section 10.2.3.
[136] See Sections 10.2.3 and 10.2.5.
[137] See Sections 10.2.4 and 10.2.5.
[138] See Section 10.2.5.
[139] See Section 10.2.7.
[140] See Section 2.5.

interviewees agreed – would encourage more domestic, intra-provincial and international investment and more entrepreneurial activity.[141]

In terms of increased investment and new trade cooperation, many of my interviewees suggested that domestic and international investors are worried about the slow-down and problems in China's economy.[142] Although not yet reflected in the data, my interviewees revealed some of their clients are considering alternatives and exit strategies if Chinese economic indicators continue to decline and if the local business environment does not improve further.[143] Restoring investors' trust is crucial for receiving further investment from within China and from abroad. For investors and lenders that already operate in China, enhanced enforcement of bankruptcy law would lead to greater predictability of business outcomes as well as greater procedural and legal transparency, which would lower the risk of doing business in China. Similarly, the increased certainty that security rights will be protected that would result from more efficient implementation of the EBL could also enable these companies to invest more time and money in potentially profitable ventures and engage in more complex transactions than is possible at the moment. For new market entrants who are considering potential cooperation with China, but have so far deemed it too risky or too unpredictable, greater and fairer enforcement of bankruptcy law would help alleviate their fear and encourage them to expand their operations and cooperation with Chinese counterparts which, if planned well, could benefit both sides.

In addition, improved enforcement of the (reformed) EBL may also encourage more entrepreneurship – both in terms of greater creativity and (healthy) risk-taking by existing entrepreneurs, and entry of new entrepreneurs onto the Chinese market. More entrepreneurial activity leads to a healthier private sector and a stronger economy. As was discussed in Chapter 2.5, China's private companies are crucial for its economy – they now provide most new jobs, they export more goods than SOEs, generate a large amount of tax, and significantly contribute to China's GDP growth. However, a precondition for entrepreneurial activity is that those with good ideas have access to sufficient funding and resources. Since both are scarce, it is important to ensure that it is possible to close down unsuccessful ventures and recycle the resources from failures to successes quickly and efficiently to feed further economic growth.[144] Bankruptcy law provides a collective mechanism through which such liquidations and recycling can be done.

Similarly, (potential) entrepreneurs also care about the existence of clear, fairly enforced rules that govern the consequences of potential failure, enable fresh start, and so also encourage creativity and enable risk-taking. Personal bankruptcy law[145] and corporate bankruptcy law can ensure that entrepreneurs are only punished for actual

---

[141] Commercial parties are increasingly enraged and discouraged by the Party-state's interference because 'it is impossible to do business in an environment like this.' (Interview E2-s). See also G Wildau (27.7.2016, FT).

[142] Interviews B1-c to B3-c, C1-c to C7-s, C9-c, C11-c, E1-c, E2-s, E5-c, J6-s to J9-c, L2-s, L4-r to L7-c, L9-s to L17-c, P1-r, P2-s, P4-c, P5-c, R1-r to R4-c, R6-c, R7-c, R9-c, R10-c, R12-c, R13-c.

[143] Interviews B1-c to B3-c, C1-c to C7-s, C9-c, C11-c, E1-c, E2-s, E5-c, J6-s to J9-c, L2-s, L4-r to L7-c, L9-s to L17-c, P1-r, P2-s, P4-c, P5-c, R1-r to R4-c, R6-c, R7-c, R9-c, R10-c.

[144] R Cooter and H Shäfer, *Solomon's Knot* (Princeton University Press, 2011) 157; K Dam, *Law-Growth Nexus: The Rule of Law and Economic Development* (Brookings Institution Press, 2006) 195.

[145] See Sections 4.4 and 12.9.

wrongdoing, and that, instead of fearing failure or punishment, they are incentivised to be creative. Failure and new beginning are vital elements of a well-functioning market economy. Where the rules are enforced predictably and fairly, private entrepreneurs are more likely to start new ventures and, in many cases, succeed thanks to the lessons learnt from their previous failure(s).[146]

10.2.7. Improved Rule of Law in China Pursuant to Objective Enforcement of the (Reformed) EBL

Finally, improved enforcement of the (reformed) EBL could also strengthen the rule of law[147] in China. The importance of the rule of law for China was discussed at length at the Fourth Plenary Session of the 18th Congress of the Communist Party in October 2014. The Party leadership concluded that China's stability and further economic development need to be underpinned by clear, accessible legal norms that apply equally to all, without unnecessary use of discretion or special treatment.[148] Nevertheless, in most cases of corporate bankruptcy, courts either ignore the parties' EBL petitions or cede control of the case to the local Government, which then determines the outcome without reference to stakeholders' rights and duties as defined in the EBL and in pursuance of its own interests and preferences.[149] The officials in charge usually protect important local companies (state-sector companies) through subsidies, forced debt forgiveness, and other unfair commercial techniques rather than allowing bankruptcy law to determine which companies are fit to survive and which should be liquidated.[150] This puts private and foreign companies at a disadvantage and unfairly affects their profitability and ability to survive. Objectively enforced EBL would put an end to most or all such interventions, and so create a level playing field for all domestic and foreign companies. In the long term, this could benefit everyone as all companies would be incentivised to focus on efficiency rather than special status or relationship with those in power.

The rule of law relies on transparency, predictability, and non-discrimination. Without these qualities, my interviewees suggested, the Chinese market remains unattractive to many investors and companies that are mindful about the level of risk that they are willing and able to undertake. Improved enforcement of bankruptcy law would enhance the rule of law in China, create a level playing field, and – as a result – it would also encourage more risk averse companies and investors to come to China, and to enable (foreign) companies already in China to start new projects (eg long-term cooperation, high-volume projects, intellectual property-related projects, etc) without unacceptable risks.

---

[146] See Section 1.2.

[147] See Section 2.3.2.

[148] This definition is closer to the rule by law since it does not elevate law above politics. See eg N Malcolm (ed), *Thomas Hobbes: Leviathan (1647)* (Oxford University Press, 2012); B Tamanaha, *On the Rule of Law: History, Politics, Theory* (Cambridge University Press, 2004) 3.

[149] See Section 8.3.

[150] See Sections 2.4.2 and 8.3.2.

10.3. Nature of Further Reform

With China's economy slowing down, particularly since late 2012, and with the dramatic increase in the amount of state and corporate bad debt,[151] the Chinese Government and courts have slowly come to acknowledge that the current regime for resolving financial distress – which often entails avoiding the use of the EBL and employing various private and state-led alternative enforcement mechanisms[152] – is insufficient.[153] As a result, some limited steps have been taken to permit a more market-driven debt resolution, to enable more predictable enforcement of creditors' rights, and to allow inherently inefficient, insolvent companies to liquidate in order to recycle their resources and restart the economy. It was also acknowledged that, in the long term, it would be necessary to enhance the rule of law and provide more predictable and transparent protection to credit-providers who may then, as empirical studies suggest, release a greater amount of cheaper credit into the economy.[154]

The reform proposals that are contained in the remainder of this chapter and in Chapters eleven (proposed reforms) and twelve (recent local reforms) are set against this background. However, unlike previous attempts to reform bankruptcy law in China – which focused solely or largely on the written law – the recommendations that follow take a broader view and focus also on improving how the law is implemented and enforced in practice. Section 10.3.1 below discusses the over-arching aims on which further reforms need to focus. Section 10.3.2 then looks at the likely obstacles to the process. Section 10.3.3 concludes by providing a high-level outline of the reforms that are proposed in Chapter eleven.

10.3.1. Necessary Focus of Further Reforms

The Chinese Government and its various agencies have made many attempts to improve the functioning of the EBL through SPC interpretations,[155] local experimentation, and recently also top-down political pressure on local governments to use the EBL to deal with local zombie companies.[156] Their aim has been to enable further, sustainable economic growth by removing systematic inefficiencies that have led to a credit squeeze, misallocation of resources and scarcity of entrepreneurial activity.[157]

However, the primary focus of most of the reforms so far has been the law itself or only a very limited number of issues that prevent EBL's enforcement[158] rather than the environment in which it is enforced and the general ability and willingness of the authorised enforcers to implement the law as written. Unfortunately, without a more

---

[151] See Sections 2.1 and 3.1.
[152] See ch 9.
[153] See Section 12.1.
[154] See Sections 1.2 and 10.2.
[155] See Section 4.3.
[156] See Section 12.3. See also Section 12.6.
[157] Interviews P1-r, R5-r, R10-c. For a discussion, see Section 1.2.
[158] eg the SPC guidelines and limited judicial reforms.

holistic approach, it is unlikely that any reform will achieve more efficient use of the EBL and deliver economic benefits that were discussed in the previous section.

10.3.1.1. Key Issues to be Addressed

There are several over-arching issues which need to be addressed by the reform. They are summarised in Table 10.2.

Table 10.2 Key issues and necessary focus of further EBL reforms

Key issues	Necessary focus of reform
Improve payoffs	Payoffs under the EBL are comparatively lower
	Perception that payoffs are comparatively lower
Clarification	Clarify aim(s) and goals of the EBL (efficiency)
	Clarify preferred interests and priorities
	Clarify how to apply the surrounding rules under the EBL
Enable use	Enable all parties to use the EBL
	Enable timely use
Knowledge	Insufficient understanding of the EBL by the parties
	Insufficient understanding of the EBL by enforcers
Willingness	Local governments to allow use of the EBL
	Courts to accept EBL petitions
Objectivity	Ensure objective enforcement of the EBL

Firstly, the reforms must focus on parties' payoffs – both actual and as perceived. The new rules must create a regime which is capable of giving the parties comparatively greater payoffs than they would receive under non-EBL alternatives.[159] It was proposed in Section 10.2.1 that, in many cases, the reformed EBL would likely provide a comparatively more efficient mechanism for dealing with debtor's financial distress than non-EBL alternatives. This can be achieved through a combination of changes to the EBL and the surrounding rules and practices, and by addressing the shortcomings and biases of the enforcers. Moreover, the data presented and analysed in Chapter nine suggests that the parties often perceive non-EBL alternatives as giving them better payoffs than the EBL (regardless of whether this perception is accurate or not). The reforms, therefore, also need to alter the parties' perceptions of the expected payoffs under the EBL once the functioning of the EBL is improved so that the parties know that the EBL can offer them a better solution than the familiar non-EBL mechanisms that they used in the past.

Reformers' efforts to increase the parties' payoffs under the EBL are more likely to succeed if they also focus on five additional issues, namely further clarification of the rules; the ability of all parties to use the EBL; a better understanding of the EBL by the

---

[159] See ch 9.

parties and enforcers; a greater willingness of local governments and courts to allow the use of the EBL; and objective enforcement of the law. These five issues are outlined below.

Firstly, further clarification of the EBL[160] and the surrounding rules and practices[161] are necessary to enable – ex post – smoother application and a better understanding of the EBL in bankruptcy cases and – ex ante – to enable lenders and other parties to carry out a risk assessment of doing business in China. There are several areas where such clarification is needed. For example, the EBL needs to provide a fuller statement of EBL's aims and goals. Similarly, it is necessary to remove the contradictions in courts' duties under the EBL and clarify which interests take priority in order to enable a smoother and more predictable resolution of conflicts of interests. Moreover, further clarification is needed in the context of how the surrounding rules – most importantly those that impose criminal liability – should apply under the EBL.

Secondly, dealing with the parties' ability to invoke the EBL where needed and desired must also be addressed by the reforms. This is particularly important for certain debt contracts – eg those originating in the shadow market and those involving activities that contravene policy restrictions[162] – and for private-sector debtors whose EBL petitions are sometimes ignored by courts.[163] Similarly, it involves enabling the parties to use the EBL in a timely manner – in particular where it is possible to save the debtor under EBL reorganisation.[164]

Thirdly, improving the parties' and enforcers' knowledge of what the EBL can do, and deepening the understanding of how the EBL can assist financially distressed companies are also important issues that should be addressed in further reforms.[165] The parties – and their legal advisors – need to know that the EBL provides a menu of options that can help them deal with their or their debtor's financial distress. Parties' ability to decide whether to use a less formal method or the EBL depends, inter alia, on the level of their understanding of how the EBL operates and how it is different from the alternatives. At the same time, the authorised enforcers – courts and lawyers-administrators – also need to be aware of what the EBL does, how to use it, when to use it, and why it matters.

Fourthly, local governments' and courts' willingness to permit the use of the EBL is also important. The Party-state plays an important role in law enforcement in China, and so local governments have to understand the role and functioning of the EBL. But understanding may not be enough. As was discussed in Sections 2.4 and 8.3, the Party-state interferes with EBL enforcement – it is, therefore, important to incentivise Party-state officials to allow the EBL to be used. The increased willingness of local governments to allow the use of the EBL together with several other changes would then also incentivise courts to accept all EBL petitions that comply with the entry requirements.[166]

---

[160] See Section 11.1.
[161] See Section 11.2.
[162] See Section 7.3.
[163] See Section 11.2.3.
[164] See Sections 11.1.4–11.1.5.
[165] See Sections 11.3.1–11.3.2.
[166] For details see Sections 4.2.2 and 11.3.3–11.3.4.

And finally, the reforms need to enable (more) objective enforcement of the EBL. In other words, it is necessary to prevent Party-state's intervention in the enforcement of the EBL to ensure that the law is enforced in an objective and transparent manner.[167]

10.3.1.2. Gradual Reform

The necessary changes should be delivered in stages, similar to the reforms in Deng's era.[168] A variety of tools should be used. The key provisions should be anchored in national law. The changes which require local adaptations can be made through local laws and regulations. In addition, some changes can be implemented through SPC's guidance, conferences with local courts, and cross-postings of EBL experts in less developed regions. At the Party-state level, changes can be introduced through officials' training, conferences, intra-provincial and national meetings, top-down agenda setting, and bottom-up initiatives with corresponding rewards from the superior level of the Party-state.[169]

As is usual in China,[170] the changes should be first tested in selected regions – which should include a combination of rich and poor, coastal and interior, industrial and agricultural regions – in order to learn about different types of obstacles and allowing for regional variations.[171] With the benefit of this understanding, the reformed EBL should then be implemented nationally. Where regional variations lead to significantly different results in terms of a boost in efficiency to the resolution of corporate financial distress, cost and availability of credit, allocation of resources, and entrepreneurial activity,[172] it may be more appropriate to make some of the changes through local rules[173] and SPC guidance in order to give the struggling regions more time to implement the changes. Nevertheless, extra time and flexibility should only be given subject to clearly defined responsibilities and timetables for local governments and courts regarding when and how the EBL should be fully implemented in their province in order to achieve full national harmonisation. Moreover, the fulfilment of these aims should be included in local government officials' career-progression targets to ensure their full cooperation.[174]

---

[167] See Section 11.3.5.

[168] See Section 2.1. For a discussion of benefits of gradual changes with local adaptations of the rules (also known as the Beijing Consensus) over a shock approach where new rules are introduced everywhere at once, without preparatory stages (known as the Washington Consensus), see M Myant and J Drahokoupil, *Transition Economies: Political Economy in Russia, Eastern Europe, and Central Asia* (Wiley, 2011). In comparison, Lin and Milhaupt argue that the implementation of some changes may be easier in authoritarian regimes. However, the problem in China is that a significant amount of decision-making power has been devolved to local levels of government, which means that China's central Government is not able to unilaterally implement the changes that it wants without having to deal with local government opposition: L Lin and C Milhaupt, 'We are the (National) Champions: Understanding Mechanisms of State Capitalism in China' (2013) *Stanford Law Review* 697. See also Section 10.3.2.

[169] For the structure, see Section 2.2.

[170] For details, see Sections 2.3 and 4.1.

[171] This has been done in the recent initiatives: see ch 12.

[172] All of these are the predicted benefits of reforming bankruptcy law – see Section 1.2.

[173] For example, Wenzhou has introduced additional local regulations which enable its court to function better in EBL cases, making the process quicker and cheaper. However, people in Wenzhou are more entrepreneurial and pro-market than most provinces, and so its additional regulations may not be well-suited for other regions: Interviews C5-r, C7-s, J4-c to J9-c, L4-r, L6-s, P1-r, R6-c, R7-c, R9-c, R10-c.

[174] See Sections 2.4.2 and 8.3.2.

10.3.2. Likely Obstacles to Further Reform

My interviewees suggested that there is strong support for further reform of the EBL as written and enforced.[175] However, they also highlighted that some of the changes are likely to face opposition and obstacles. These insights are discussed below.

10.3.2.1. Supporters of Further Reform

All my interviewees suggested that there is strong support for further reform from law-makers, law-users, and law-commentators. The central Government (including the Legislative Affairs Committee of the NPC Standing Committee and the Ministry of Finance) and the SPC are already supporting improvements to bankruptcy law in China.[176] They are likely to further support these efforts both in terms of monetary and other backing. Their support will also be crucial in incentivising local governments to cooperate and in finding, financing and enforcing practical ways of improving the expertise, abilities and willingness of courts and local governments to implement the reformed EBL.

Moreover, some local governments – most importantly those in Zhejiang (including Shenzhen and Wenzhou), Jiangsu, Guangdong and Shanghai – have already started implementing centrally suggested as well as locally devised improvements to bankruptcy law.[177] Other local governments – mainly from interior regions such as Yunnan, Inner Mongolia, and Guilin – have been more passive. Nevertheless, several interviewees argued that there are some officials and judges even in these regions who understand the importance of bankruptcy law and would likely support its reform.[178] However, they need support from the outside with enhancing the understanding and appreciation of the potential benefits of bankruptcy law. Central government agencies, bankruptcy law centres, and enthusiastic experts will be crucial to changing the environment in which the EBL is enforced and in delivering information and training to potential users and enforcers of the EBL. Overall, my interviewees suggested that there is now a sufficient level of interest and a growing momentum across China, and so it is very likely that a change of attitude – which is crucial for better implementation and enforcement of bankruptcy law in China – is possible.[179]

Furthermore, many potential law-users – businesses and business chambers in China and abroad – as well as expert consultants have been very supportive of greater use of bankruptcy law because it helps create a safer and more stable business environment, and so enables greater business cooperation and economic growth.[180] Similarly, many banks and finance providers in China also support further reforms to bankruptcy law – primarily to gain the ability to assess the riskiness of individual loans and to recover more regardless of whether the borrower is a state company or not.[181] However,

---

[175] See Chapter 12, especially Section 12.1.
[176] See eg SPC Monitor (5.7.2016). See also Chapter 12.
[177] See Chapter 12.
[178] Interviews C5-r to C9-c, J3-c to J9-c, P1-r, P3-r to P5-c, R7-c, R10-c, R13-c.
[179] ibid.
[180] Interviews C1-c to C11-c, E1-c to E5-c, L2-s to L15-c, R10-c. See also Section 6.1.2.6.
[181] Interviews B1-c to C3-c, C1-c, C4-c, C5-r, IF1-s, IF2-c, L2-s, L4-r, L6-s, R9-c, R10-c.

several interviewees also warned that state-controlled banks in China would not be able to go against the wishes of the same-level Party-state, and so winning the support of – in particular – local governments first will be crucial.[182]

Academics and other expert observers have also been calling for better implementation and enforcement of bankruptcy law for several years now. Key voices include Li Shuguang, Shi Jingxia, Ren Yongqing, Wang Liming, Wang Xinxin, Wang Weiguo and, more broadly, also the Beijing-based Research Centre for Bankruptcy Law at Renmin University to name just a few.

10.3.2.2. Obstacles to Further Reform

However, not everyone supports the reforms – even within the generally supportive groups discussed above. Key obstacles to further reforms are likely to include, firstly, the opposition from those who fear that more efficient use of the EBL would negatively affect their interests, and secondly, the slow pace at which these changes are likely to proceed.

Many reform initiatives in China are stalled due to the opposition from local governments. In the context of the EBL, *some local governments* fear that more EBL cases would necessarily involve large-scale unemployment, social instability and weaker economic performance. Their opposition is translated into courts' reluctance to hear EBL cases.[183] Although the short-term drawbacks may be surpassed by the long-term economic benefits, in the current environment – with short-term incentives and limited accountability[184] – it is rational for local governments to oppose further reforms of the EBL and its greater use.

The EBL reform is also opposed by the *entrenched parties* – most importantly employees and SOEs – who benefit from the current regime. Under local governments' alternative solutions,[185] employees only face a limited chance of company closures and subsequent redundancies. Moreover, employees know from experience that local governments are likely to intervene in their employer's financial distress if enough of them put pressure on the Government.[186] If the EBL was used to resolve all insolvent companies, the likelihood of corporate closures, redundancies, and increased pressure to work harder to keep a job would ensue. In the short term, employees are, therefore, incentivised to oppose reforms that would result in more efficient use of the EBL.

Similarly, the *SOEs* also benefit from the national and local governments' support in the form of easy access to bank finance – without having to face hard budget constraints or competition from the private sector for credit – as well as limited competition from non-state companies due to local governments' protectionist policies, and direct and indirect financial support from the Government.[187] Reforms and more efficient use of the EBL would most likely result in banks extending finance to more private companies

---

[182] Interviews B1-c to C3-c, C5-r, L2-s, L4-r, L6-s, R9-c, R10-c.
[183] As explained in Section 8.3.3.
[184] ibid.
[185] See Section 9.2.
[186] See Sections 2.4.2 and 8.3.1.
[187] See Sections 8.3.5 and 9.2.2.

which would increase competition for credit and market competition for the SOEs. It could also impose hard budget constraints and would force many SOEs to either restructure or liquidate due to their current low profitability and financial problems.[188]

Finally, many of the proposed changes in Chapter eleven will require time. In a way, changing the written law – although requiring some time to research, rewrite and pass through the NPC – may be the fast part of the reform. On the other hand, issues that are likely to take more time include changing people's attitudes towards the concept of bankruptcy and debt forgiveness (for companies and individuals); disseminating information about the EBL, its procedures, and its benefits; training lawyers and judges; retuning local Party-state officials' incentives to enable greater use of the EBL; persuading local governments that they stand to benefit from allowing objective enforcement of the EBL; and many other issues that will only become known as the process unfolds. In addition, the reforms will have to adapt to local differences – including different stages of economic development, different social norms and business environments, and different levels of experience, ability and willingness of local courts and governments to enforce the EBL. As was suggested in the previous section, these differences can be managed through a combination of hard national and local rules and soft guidance from the Party-state and courts. In the end, a coordinated effort and a lot of work will be needed to reform the EBL successfully.

10.3.3. What is Likely to Work in Practice?

Having concluded that China's economy stands to benefit from greater and more efficient use of the (reformed) EBL – but also bearing in mind the nature of likely opposition to the changes – this section argues, as an introduction to chapter eleven, that it is best to adopt a gradual approach to the reform.[189] The reform proposals are structure in the same way as the discussion of the constraints on the use of the EBL in China in Chapters six to eight.[190]

Firstly, changes are proposed to the wording of the EBL. The proposals build on and add to the issues identified in Chapter six and are set out in Section 11.1. Secondly, changes are proposed to the rules and practices that form the environment in which the EBL is enforced. The proposals address the shortcomings identified in Chapter seven and are contained in Section 11.2. Thirdly, there are also several reforms aimed at improving the quality and capacity to enforce the EBL in China. The proposed reforms tackle the issues identified in Chapter eight and are contained in Section 11.3. Together, the changes proposed in Chapter eleven also address the fourth constraint identified in Chapter nine – the factual and perceived superiority of payoffs of non-EBL alternative mechanisms – by, firstly, improving the payoffs under the EBL, and secondly, by informing the (potential) parties of what the EBL has to offer.

---

[188] See Sections 2.5, 3.1 and 10.1.3.

[189] This is similar to the way all successful reforms since Deng's era have been carried out. During the 1980s reform, the intention was to maintain the planned economy while expanding the private sector, and gradually grow out of the plan: see Section 2.1.

[190] Ch 9 examines non-EBL alternatives, and so is not discussed in this context.

11

Options for Reform

Previous chapters discussed the EBL and other debt-enforcement mechanisms,[1] the environment in which they operate,[2] the low use of the EBL,[3] the constraints that appear to contribute to such limited use,[4] and the desirability of EBL's greater use.[5] This chapter turns to the proposed reforms which aim to alleviate the identified issues and thereby enable and incentivise greater and more efficient use of the EBL. This process requires very careful balancing and sensitivity to the existing socio-economic environment in which the law operates.[6] In particular, the reform has to take into account the particular sensitivities such as the employee protection and the political interests of the ruling Party-state.[7] Much has changed and improved since the first bankruptcy law was introduced in China in 1986. National and local governments have been trying hard to improve the business environment in order to protect and support further economic development. Bankruptcy law is an important part of the infrastructure that supports a functioning market economy,[8] but its potential is yet to be reached. This chapter offers a few thoughts and proposals about how this can be changed.

This chapter builds on the earlier discussion of the nature of further reform.[9] The structure of the proposals closely follows the structure of Chapters six, seven and eight, which identified and explored the key constraints to the operation of the EBL in China. Section 11.1 below explains the first set of proposals which focus on direct, substantive improvements to the EBL as written. Section 11.2 presents the second set of proposals which look at the possible improvements to the surrounding rules and practices that are necessary for the implementation of the EBL. And Section 11.3 explores the third set of proposals which suggest possible improvements to the quality and objectivity of EBL enforcers. Each section explains the proposals in detail and assesses the likelihood of the given reform proposal being implemented in the current socio-political environment in China.

---

[1] See chs 3–4.
[2] See ch 2.
[3] See Section 5.1.
[4] See chs 6–9.
[5] See ch 10.
[6] For the discussion on the importance of the socio-economic context, see N Mrockova, 'What can the West learn from China's failed bankruptcy law reform' in R Parry (ed), *Designing Insolvency Systems* (INSOL Europe, 2016). See also Section 10.3.
[7] See Sections 2.4 and 8.3.
[8] See Section 1.2, 2.1 and 4.1.
[9] See Section 10.3.

The implementation of these three sets of reforms could, in the aggregate, help ameliorate the key issues that must be addressed in order to improve the functioning of the EBL in practice. Section 10.3.1 identified six such issues, namely the need to increase the parties' payoffs under the EBL; clarify the law and its most misapplied rules; enable greater and more timely use of the EBL; improve the parties' and enforcers' knowledge and understanding of the law; improve the willingness of local governments to permit the use of the EBL; make courts more willing and able to deal with EBL cases; and ensure more objective implementation of the EBL.[10]

Importantly, some of the reform proposals discussed below have now been picked up and tested in various regions in China. However, all the recent reforms have been limited in scope, and none of the proposals has been fully implemented. As a result, this chapter focuses on all proposed reforms, and Chapter twelve examines the main reform initiatives that have recently been implemented in China. Where relevant, reform proposals and recent reform initiatives are cross-referenced in the main text or the footnotes.

11.1. Reforms Aimed at Improving EBL Provisions

Most reform attempts so far have focused on improving the black-letter law. Overall, however, the EBL is written well. The EBL was introduced as a response to the complaints levelled against the old 1986 law. As a result, the EBL covers private and foreign stakeholders, it has a comprehensive rescue mechanism, it enables imposition of a moratorium, it introduces hard-budget constraints, it provides detailed rules on the priority of repayment, and it also removes government involvement in bankruptcy procedures by putting an independent bankruptcy practitioner in charge.[11]

Nevertheless, Chapter six identified several outstanding issues in the written provisions of the EBL. Six changes are proposed in response, as summarised in Table 11.1. The first five are based on existing provisions; the last one proposes to introduce two new provisions to enhance the existing rules. Section 11.1.1 calls for clarification of EBL's aims and goals. Section 11.1.2 highlights the need to explain the courts' role in employee protection in EBL procedures. Section 11.1.3 suggests that there need to be more guidelines about when and how to impose criminal liability in EBL cases. Section 11.1.4 examines possible improvements to EBL reorganisation such as reformulation of the entry requirements to enable its timely use and more guidance about how and when to use the cramdown power. Section 11.1.5 argues that two further provisions should be inserted into the EBL, namely directors' duty to monitor their company's health and a fast-track EBL hearing for small companies. Next, Section 11.1.6 argues in favour of introducing a personal bankruptcy law.

---

[10] The proposals in this chapter have been discussed with many China experts with experience in practice and academia, in China and abroad, when I was writing a report for the UK and Chinese Governments about the possible reform projects that would help improve the enforcement of the EBL in China. I am grateful for all comments and insights of those who contributed their time and knowledge to this project. All mistakes are my own.

[11] See Section 4.2.

Section 11.1.7 concludes by drawing the proposals together to consider their likely cumulative impact in practice.

Table 11.1 Proposed reforms of the EBL as written

	Content of reform	**Timing of reform**
Clarify existing rules	Clarify aims and goals of the EBL (Section 11.1.1)	Any time
	Clarify courts' role in employee protection in EBL procedures (Section 11.1.2)	Implement after social security system becomes operational (Section 11.2.2)
	More guidelines about imposition of criminal liability in EBL procedures (Section 11.1.3)	Any time, but best together with judges' training (Section 11.3.1)
Change existing rules	Improvements to EBL reorganisation (Section 11.1.4)	Implement together with reforms aimed at enforcers (Section 11.3)
Introduce new rules	Introduce additional provisions (Section 11.1.5)	Any time, but effective only after reforms aimed at enforcers (Section 11.3)
	Introduce personal bankruptcy law (Section 11.1.6)	

11.1.1. Clarify Aims and Goals of the EBL

The EBL provides only limited insight into law-makers' intended aims and goals of the EBL. Article 1 states that the EBL's aim is 'to fairly liquidate claims and debts, to protect the legitimate rights and interests of creditors and debtors, and to maintain the order of the socialist market economy'. Article 6 then adds that courts, when applying the EBL, 'shall safeguard the legitimate rights and interests of the employees of the insolvent enterprise and hold officers of the insolvent enterprise accountable for their liabilities in accordance with the law'.[12] However, neither the EBL nor later regulations or public policy documents explain what are the parties' 'legitimate rights and interests', or how to balance the conflicts between its aims of 'fairly' liquidating claims on the one hand and the protectionist measures that the Party-state often deems necessary to 'maintain … socialist market economy'.[13]

A clearer statement – in the EBL or otherwise – is, therefore, needed to ensure greater predictability of outcome for the parties, and to achieve greater harmonisation of the way how the rules are applied across China. In Germany, traditionally, the predominant aim of bankruptcy law has been to ensure effective allocation of the remaining resources,[14] and requiring insolvency does not per se hinder that aim. On the other hand, the language used by Chinese officials and SPC judges when describing

---

[12] See Section 4.2.1.

[13] See Section 6.1.

[14] For an overview, see A Remmert, *Introduction to German Insolvency Law* (Justiz, 2007). But note that the German regime has been refocusing on the need to enable restructuring in recent years: Clifford Chance (January 2012).

EBL's objectives brings it closer to the US and UK bankruptcy laws[15] in that its primary aim is to enable value-creating or at least value-preserving restructuring of financially distressed debtor companies.[16]

If the aim of the EBL reform is to support further economic development,[17] the law should facilitate ex ante lower cost and greater availability of credit by increasing the predictability and likelihood of greater recovery of debts ex post.[18] Furthermore, bankruptcy law should enable efficient allocation of resources – away from inefficient projects and companies and to the most efficient users – by imposing hard budget constraints, reorganising distressed debtors who can be made more efficient and liquidating all others.[19] Similarly, bankruptcy law should aim to encourage more entrepreneurial activity by providing clear rules about the consequences of corporate failure – and so enable more risk-averse parties to engage in potentially value-creating projects.[20] In addition, timely use of the correct procedure – reorganisation or liquidation, depending on which is most efficient in the circumstances – should also be encouraged.[21]

All these goals can be encapsulated – and should be reflected in EBL's framing provisions – as an aim to enhance the economic efficiency of resolution of corporate financial distress. It could then be explained and illustrated by the SPC in a guidance document.[22] By moving to the yardstick of economic efficiency,[23] the law could be applied in a more predictable and comparable fashion across provinces regardless of their social and economic differences. This change can be made at any time.

11.1.2. Clarify Courts' Role in Employee Protection in EBL Procedures

Linked to the question of EBL's aims and goals is the issue of courts' role in employee protection. Section 6.1 pointed to several EBL provisions which have been interpreted as protecting employees at the expense of other stakeholders. This section argues that two elements of this regime need to be changed, which would put employees on par with other regular stakeholders. Section 11.1.2.1 below suggests removal of the requirement for employee resettlement plan as a pre-condition to filing an EBL petition. Section 11.1.2.2 suggests additional guidelines on how to resolve courts' conflicting duties.

The timing will be critical. Making these changes immediately would most likely face (potentially insurmountable) opposition from local governments. Therefore, the changes should be carried out after fully implementing the social security system,[24] which would reduce the pressure from employees on local governments.[25]

---

[15] And the latest changes in Germany: ibid.
[16] Interviews P1-r, R5-r, R10-c. See also Section 12.1.
[17] See Sections 1.3 and 10.3.1.
[18] See Section 1.2. See also Sections 10.1.3 and 10.2.4, and ch 12.
[19] See Section 1.2.
[20] ibid.
[21] cf the discussion in Section 10.2.
[22] See Sections 2.3.1 and 4.3.
[23] As defined and discussed in Sections 1.1.
[24] See Sections 7.2.1 and 11.2.2.1
[25] At the moment, dismissed employees face existential difficulties unless they have their own savings or support from their next of kin when they are between jobs: ibid.

11.1.2.1. Limit Employee Protectionism

The first change that is necessary in order to ensure more efficient – and fairer – treatment of all stakeholders is the removal of the requirement to provide a resettlement plan for debtor company's employees *as a pre-condition* to filing an EBL petition.[26] This duty is only imposed in debtors' EBL petitions (although my research suggests that some courts require it in creditors' EBL petitions, too).[27] Although this provision conveniently shifts the responsibility for dismissed employees from local governments to a debtor, it is submitted that it provides wrong incentives for financially distressed debtor companies. Firstly, a financially distressed debtor is usually in no position to be able to reshuffle its employees to new jobs. This requirement may have made sense at the time when all companies were owned by the state because employees would be, de facto, moved from one branch of the state economy to another. However, it makes no sense in the current environment where most companies operate as independent entities. In addition, a financially distressed debtor should focus on finding a solution to its distress rather than having to redirect some of its efforts and concern itself with finding replacement jobs for its employees. Such requirement can, at best, slow down the finding of a solution because managers' attention is divided, and, at worst, it can jeopardise the resolution efforts by diverting too much attention away from the crucial – ie saving the company, or liquidating it to maximise value – to the less important – ie resettling employees if the company fails.

Moreover, if a debtor fails to provide an employee resettlement plan, it cannot use EBL reorganisation. This, in turn, bars them from using a mechanism which may be the only way of preventing its corporate failure in the first place. At the same time, it also ignores the fact that a plan for employee resettlement may only be successfully put together in the course of EBL reorganisation, but not at the time of filing to use it.

This requirement leads to four undesirable outcomes. Firstly, most users of the EBL are politically connected players where local governments provide an implicit guarantee of employee resettlement. Secondly, some parties may instead use pre-packaged reorganisation where they reach an agreement before filing an EBL petition.[28] Such use of the EBL negates one of the reasons for wishing to use the law in the first place, namely the desire to use a collective, structured mechanism where all stakeholders have pre-defined rights and duties. Thirdly, EBL petitions are sometimes accepted even without a clear employee resettlement plan, but this is only possible in market-driven regions – such as Wenzhou – where the provision is not applied literally and a resettlement plan can be supplied later, or only in vague terms.[29] And finally, although the desire to protect employees is understandable, in the long run, it leads not to the protection of employment and employees, but to the continued operation of inefficient companies – which is costly due to direct and indirect financial support that they need[30] – and it traps limited resources in inefficient use instead of allowing them to be reallocated to the most efficient user with the help of bankruptcy law, thereby further harming the economy.

---

[26] See Sections 4.2.2 and 6.1.1.
[27] ibid.
[28] See Section 9.2.3.
[29] Interviews J1-c, J4-c to J9-c.
[30] See Section 10.1.

Efficient use of liquidation and reorganisation relies on speed, which is compromised where debtors have to make a resettlement plan for its employees. It is, therefore, suggested that this requirement should be removed. Bankruptcy law cannot work efficiently if it has to act as a quasi-social security system.[31]

11.1.2.2. Provide Clearer Guidelines on How to Resolve Courts' Conflicting Duties

Section 6.1 argued that courts face conflicting duties with regards to their treatment of various stakeholders' rights. This is ultimately a political question. The EBL embodies a classical tension between the desire to protect lenders' interests – to incentivise greater and cheaper lending[32] – and the importance of keeping struggling companies alive in order to protect employment and to avoid potential social instability and political crisis.[33] The EBL does not clearly prefer one or the other. This creates harmful unpredictability and divergence in the way the law is enforced across China.

To ameliorate the situation, additional, clearer guidance should be provided about how to resolve the conflicts between employees' and (secured) creditors' interests. This guidance should clearly state that secured creditors' interests must be protected even where this would reduce employees' recovery.[34] More broadly, the EBL needs to provide more details about creditors' participation in important decisions such as an appointment of an administrator,[35] voting and cramdown,[36] and major property disposals.[37] As argued above, bankruptcy law cannot and should not be used to replace a social security system.

11.1.3. Provide More Guidelines about Imposition of Criminal Liability in EBL Procedures

Section 6.2 suggested that debtors face heightened risk of scrutiny and liability under the EBL because courts are under a general duty to investigate the personnel of insolvent companies for their 'legal liabilities' and to examine whether a violation of any provision contained in the EBL constitutes a criminal offence. But while scrutiny and liability are not per se bad, more guidance is needed in order to ensure that managers and directors are only punished for their specific wrongdoing. What is particularly problematic

---

[31] See also Section 11.2.2.1.

[32] See Section 1.2.

[33] See Sections 2.2, 2.3, 3.1 and 8.3.2.

[34] For example, a quasi-insurance fund could be established by each local government that would serve as short-term support for dismissed employees following corporate bankruptcies. Note that other types of social insurance (medical and pension insurance) are being supplemented by local governments, unemployment social insurance is not: China Labour Bulletin (29.6.2016).

[35] This was also proposed by Professor Li Shuguang at the Seminar on the 10th Anniversary of the Implementation of the Corporate Bankruptcy Law in B Lu (12.9.2017, People's Court News).

[36] ibid. See also Section 6.1.4.

[37] This was recently proposed by Judge Yang Linping, a deputy to the NPC and President of the Chongqing Higher People's Court, at the NPC meeting: People's Court News (24.5.2020).

is that, often, courts do not sufficiently investigate whether debtors' personnel caused the financial collapse. Instead – several interviewees suggested – being in power at the time of insolvency (ie correlation) is often taken to satisfy the causation element.[38] This can lead to an excessive imposition of liability and deters debtors' personnel from using the EBL.

A way to deal with this problem is to provide more guidance to courts – ideally from the SPC – to explain that causation, and not merely correlation, is needed to establish criminal liability under the EBL. Such guidance should also give an illustrative list of what evidence is permissible and clarify that there is no presumption of guilt.[39] If the EBL is excessively and unfairly punitive, it disincentivises the parties who are least affected by the information asymmetry – managers and directors of distressed companies – from using the EBL in a timely manner. This is particularly problematic for reorganisation, where timely use matters the most.

Moreover, to encourage greater use of debtor-invoked EBL reorganisation courts should be encouraged to impose lesser punishment and reward timely use in cases of genuine financial distress.[40] This could be included in the guidance to courts, and it should be accompanied by a training session or a conference where judges can meet and discuss their views and experiences.[41]

11.1.4. Improvements to EBL Reorganisation

Section 4.2.4 highlighted the special role of reorganisation within the EBL and its promise to restructure (and, where possible, save) rather than close distressed companies.[42] Nevertheless, my interviews and existing data suggest that reorganisation is still comparatively rarely used. This criticism stands even in light of the recent increase from 178 reorganisation cases in 2014 to 1,163 reorganisation cases in 2017.[43] Moreover, some commentators suggest that, in practice, courts are often unwilling to permit the use of reorganisation in other types of companies than those that are large listed companies[44] – to buy the valuable listed status[45] – and in politically driven restructuring to legitimise a pre-agreed deal.[46] As courts gain experience and learn more about the EBL process, they become more willing to permit reorganisation cases. Nevertheless, although the number of reorganisation cases has been increasing, the

---

[38] Interviews C2-c, C3-c, C7-s, E2-s, J1-c, J5-s, J9-c, L1-r, L2-s, L4-r, L5-c, L6-s, L8-c, L12-c.

[39] Several interviewees (C5-r, C7-s, J1-c, J2-c, J8-c, J9-c, E3-s t E5-c, L2-s to L7-c, L13-c to L15-c, P1-r, R6-c, R7-c, R9-c, R10-c) suggested that some judges view managers who cannot prevent their company's distress as inherently guilty.

[40] Naturally, it is equally important to prevent fraudulent use of the EBL.

[41] More about this in Section 11.3.

[42] See also Section 12.6.

[43] See Section 5.1.

[44] See H Bi, 'The Role of Court in Corporate Reorganization' (2009) *Shandong Judicial Review* 68. See also Sections 8.1.1, 8.3.4 and 9.2.

[45] Interviews J1-c, L2-s, L4-r, L6-s. See also J Kynge, *China Shakes the World – The Rise of a Hungry Nation* (Weinfeld & Nicolson, 2006) 176; A Szamosszegi and C Kyle, *An Analysis of State-Owned Enterprises and State Capitalism in China* (US-China Economic and Security Review Commission: Washington, 2011).

[46] See Section 9.2.3.

total use is still very limited.[47] EBL reorganisation should be used in all cases where there is a financially distressed company that is struggling, but either the whole company or its business are viable and the use of reorganisation would be more efficient than liquidation or the non-EBL alternatives.

In terms of how the reorganisation procedure is set up on paper, there are three important changes that should be implemented in order to enable its greater use. Section 11.1.4.1 below considers the importance of allowing the use of reorganisation before the company becomes insolvent. Section 11.1.4.2 looks at the need to provide explicit guidance about who are the intended users of reorganisation. Section 11.1.4.3 examines why courts need more guidance about voting and cramdown of dissenting stakeholders in reorganisation.

11.1.4.1. Expressly Allow Pre-insolvency Use of Reorganisation

The entry requirements in China's EBL were inspired by the German Insolvency Law in that they both require some form of (actual or threatened) insolvency as a pre-condition to using the law's restructuring mechanism.[48] However, as Section 6.3 discussed, in practice, Chinese courts often interpret the entry requirements narrowly so as to only allow actually insolvent companies to use EBL reorganisation. This needs to be addressed in order to enable earlier restructuring and so more efficient use of the range of tools in the EBL.

As a general rule, the choice of entry requirement is linked to the core justification for allowing alteration of the parties' initial (substantive and procedural) entitlements. Insolvency is often seen as the only legitimate justification for such ex post interference in private actors' dealings. In Germany, the primary aim of bankruptcy law is to ensure effective allocation of the remaining resources, and requiring insolvency does not per se hinder that aim.[49] On the other hand, EBL's primary aim – similar to bankruptcy laws in the US and the UK – is to enable efficient restructuring of financially distressed debtor companies.[50] In order to achieve that, however, it may be necessary also to follow the American and English entry requirements for a reorganisation procedure where debtor's actual or threatened insolvency is not required.

Allowing the use of reorganisation without relying on actual or narrowly defined threatened insolvency has several benefits. Many interviewees pointed out that, in practice, creditors often petition a court to use the EBL after – and not as soon as – the debtor becomes technically insolvent (by either test) because – due to the information problems – they may not know when the debtor became insolvent.[51] Similarly, debtors may not petition to use reorganisation as soon as they become insolvent because they try to find an internal solution and return the company back to health without

---

[47] See Section 5.1 and generally Z Zhang, *Corporate Reorganisations in China* (Cambridge University Press, 2018).
[48] See Sections 4.2.2 and 4.2.4.
[49] Section 11.1.1.
[50] ibid. Interview P1-r, R10-c.
[51] See Section 11.2.1.1.

any third parties.[52] However, more often than not, financial problems continue and often also get worse over time, and so by the time the debtor company petitions to use reorganisation, there is nothing to save in the company, and so the court automatically pushes the debtor into liquidation.[53] The fire sale of assets further depresses the value of the debtor company, and any delays in negotiating with the creditors lead to further loss of value.[54]

If, on the other hand, companies are allowed and encouraged to enter into reorganisation before they become insolvent (or obviously likely to become insolvent[55]) – some of my interviewees argued – two major positive outcomes may occur. Firstly, distressed companies would have more time to benefit from the expertise of outside specialists and so save a part of the business or at least provide better-than-liquidation outcome for the parties.[56] And secondly, because entering into reorganisation would no longer signal one's insolvency, it may encourage more voluntary debtor petitions without risking reputational damage.[57] Although – strictly speaking – such procedure would no longer be 'insolvency' procedure, it would play a crucial role in the prevention of corporate bankruptcies, and so should be considered in this context.

Moreover, the international trend is increasingly to focus on the importance of timely intervention, including pre-insolvency collective restructuring.[58] The UNCITRAL Guide encourages early intervention in financial distress, but also warns against abusive use of bankruptcy law.[59] If China wanted to prevent abuse, it could introduce provisions to punish strategic use of the EBL where fraud or misuse can be proven by creditors. Alternatively, courts could be given discretion in precisely explained circumstances – details of which would be collated from experience from the trial implementation of this provision in several regions – to deny petitions for the reason of abuse and to order the debtor to pay associated costs. This would comply with the UNCITRAL suggestion that 'it may be desirable that the bankruptcy law focuses upon discouraging improper use rather than making commencement more difficult to the potential detriment of all eligible applicants'.[60]

Potential benefits of earlier use of reorganisation were also highlighted in a report that accompanied the 1995 draft of the EBL and in many discussions since. The report suggested that financially distressed companies should be allowed and encouraged

> to explore the possibility for rehabilitation by applying [in a timely manner] for Reorganisation or Composition … in the new law. Even in case that an enterprise is not recoverable,

---

[52] Interviews C1-c to C7-s, C9-c, E1-c to E3-s, J1-c, J5-s to J9-c, L1-r to L6-s, L9-s to L13-c, R1-r to R4-c, R6-c to R11-c.

[53] ibid – in line with Arts 43, 78, 79, 88 EBL.

[54] This is further aggravated by the slow and unresponsive courts both when deciding whether to accept the petition and when making subsequent decisions in the course of reorganisation: Interviews C3-c, C5-r, L1-r to L9-s, L15-c, P1-r, R9-c, R10-c.

[55] See Section 4.2.2.

[56] Interviews B1-c, B2-c, C2-c to C7-s, E1-c to E4-c, J3-c to J9-c, L1-r to L6-s, L8-c to L15-c, P3-r, R1-r, R3-r, R9-c, R10-c.

[57] ibid.

[58] See eg the European Commission's proposal for the Directive on preventive restructuring frameworks, second chance and measures to increase the efficiency of restructuring, bankruptcy and discharge procedures – COM (2016) 723.

[59] Para 46 UNCITRAL Guide.

[60] Para 47 UNCITRAL Guide.

earlier commencement of bankruptcy liquidation is more beneficial to both creditors and the society in the sense of saving assets and reducing losses as far as possible.[61]

Unfortunately, the final version of the EBL retained the requirement of actual or imminent insolvency. Nevertheless, several politically connected interviewees suggested that the Chinese Government and the SPC are slowly realising how important it is to allow companies to restructure in a timely manner, and are slowly recognising that pre-insolvency entry into reorganisation may be needed.[62]

It is, therefore, proposed that earlier entry into reorganisation procedure should be enabled by removing the insolvency requirement and replacing it with courts' discretion to reject those petitions where the court has grounds to believe – and the petitioner fails to disprove – that allowing the petition would enable abuse of the EBL regime.[63]

11.1.4.2. More Explicit Guidance about who are the Intended Users of EBL Reorganisation

Section 8.1.1 argued that judges' varying levels of experience, and the lack of further guidance, lead to courts being unsure about the intended users of reorganisation, which has led individual courts and judges to impose additional limitations on who can use the EBL. They include accepting only petitions from large companies and requiring a feasibility or survivability test before a company is allowed to use reorganisation.[64] In addition, the SPC has also encouraged courts to prefer applications from national strategic industries. The justification for imposing these further limitations on the use of reorganisation is unclear. Moreover, these additional restrictions are applied in an unpredictable and ad hoc manner, which makes the application of the EBL incoherent and non-transparent.

Some commentators suggest that the reason for adopting such a selective approach is based on the international experience – most importantly the US Chapter 11 – which suggests that corporate restructuring is expensive and so it is felt that most small companies do not have the necessary resources to pay for such process.[65] However, this argument is flawed because, in fact, most Chapter 11 reorganisations concern small companies.[66]

Moreover, some point to the fact that the formal corporate reorganisation laws in Taiwan and Japan – which were also influential when drafting the EBL – only allow restructuring of (large) public companies and that this approach has also influenced the restrictive approach to the scope of permitted users of EBL reorganisation.[67]

---

[61] W Wang. 'Institutional Reasoning in Drafting New Bankruptcy Law of China' (2000) at the Chinese Insolvency Law Symposium.

[62] Interviews C2-c, C5-r, C7-s, J6-s, L14-c, L15-c, P1-r, P3-r to P5-c, R10-c. See also Section 11.1.1.

[63] This is similar to the argument that courts should approve reorganisation plans under the current regime unless they have 'justifiable reasons' for rejecting them (albeit, naturally, it is important to define what such justifiable reasons would be): L Wang, 'Several Issues of Amending China's Bankruptcy Law' (2002) *China Legal Science* 78.

[64] See Section 6.3.

[65] See Zhang, *Corporate Reorganisations* (2018) 20–21.

[66] See E Warren and JL Westbrook, 'The Success of Chapter 11: A Challenge to the Critics' (2009) *Michigan Law Review* 603.

[67] See eg Wang, 'Amending China's Bankruptcy Law' (2002).

However, this argument is also flawed because Japan and Taiwan have a separate restructuring regime for SMEs.[68]

There is pressure in China to allow a broader range of companies to use EBL's reorganisation. Some suggest this should be possible under a single regime,[69] while others call for a special SME-specific regime with simplified and so cheaper and quicker procedures aimed at the special needs of the SMEs.[70] Either way, greater use and more coherent and predictable application of EBL reorganisation can only be achieved if the additional requirements at a local level are banned or if they are properly justified, explained and incorporated into the national rules as the new entry requirement test in Article 2 of the EBL.[71]

11.1.4.3. More Guidance about Voting and Courts' Power to Cram Down Dissenting Stakeholders in EBL Reorganisation

The EBL contains several detailed provisions about creditors' voting and gives courts the power to cram down dissenting creditors. Both the voting and the use of cramdown are problematic. More guidance is, therefore, needed.

Firstly, courts often fail to provide sufficient protection to small unsecured claims. Article 82 of the EBL states that, if necessary (ie where the claims are different in nature), courts may create an additional voting group within reorganisation to provide sufficient protection to these claims. However, empirical research shows that courts generally ignore this provision and make small unsecured creditors vote within a single group with large unsecured creditors. This means that, given the voting rules,[72] the interests of small creditors are often ignored in practice.[73] An additional problem arises where local banks hold large amounts of unsecured debt and vote (often under pressure) in favour of a reorganisation plan preferred by local government at the expense of small trade creditors.[74] The wording of Article 82 of the EBL should, therefore, be changed and courts should be under a duty to create a special voting class for small unsecured claims.

Moreover, several interviewees also argued that reorganisation is often hindered by courts' inability to apply the cramdown powers effectively.[75] Similar to the US Chapter 11, China's EBL enables courts to prevent individual creditors from hijacking the process by refusing to cooperate or to make any compromises.[76] Without a cramdown power,

---

[68] See eg S Bufford and K Yanagida, 'Japan's Revised Laws on Business Reorganization: An Analysis' (2006) *Cornell International Law Journal* 1; J Kaufman Winn, 'Creditors' Rights in Taiwan' (1998) *North Carolina Journal of International Law and Commercial Regulation* 409.

[69] D Fan (24.1.2014, The Nanfang Weekend); Y Mao, 'Informal Reorganisation of SMEs' (2012) *China Entrepreneur* 112.

[70] See Sections 11.1.5.2 and 12.8.

[71] See also Zhang (n 47) 38–46.

[72] See Section 4.2.4: a group is deemed to approve the plan if more than a half in number and two-thirds in value vote in its favour.

[73] See Zhang (n 47) 194–95.

[74] ibid 195–96.

[75] Interviews C5-r, C7-s, J2-c, J6-s to J9-c, L2-s, L4-r, L6-s, L13-c to L15-c, R3-r, R6-c, R7-c, R10-c.

[76] See Section 4.2.4.

reorganisation would lack the ability to bind dissenting stakeholders, which is one of the important advantages that differentiate it from out-of-court restructuring.

Empirical evidence shows that courts in China do use cramdown to bind dissenting stakeholders.[77] However, the rules are not clear, which causes confusion and, in the most extreme application, unfair results in practice.[78]

It is, therefore, proposed that courts should be given more guidance about when, how and why they can use the cramdown power. This guidance can initially come from the top down, as a document from the SPC or additional details that would be added into Article 87 of the EBL itself. Ideally, the additional guidance should be explained with reference to the key principles that underpin the functioning of the EBL,[79] and it should be informed by real-life experience and insights of individual judges. Local courts should also share their experience through an online platform or in conferences.[80]

11.1.5. Introduce Additional Provisions

Besides changes to the existing provisions, two new provisions should also be introduced that could improve the functioning of the EBL. Section 11.1.5.1 below argues that the directors' duty to monitor their company's health should be (re)introduced to ensure more timely and efficient use of the EBL. Section 11.1.5.2 further proposes that a simplified, fast-track EBL procedure should be created to enable smaller-scale bankruptcies to be resolved more quickly, cheaply and efficiently under the EBL. Both of these provisions have been successfully trialled in several pro-market regions in China,[81] but have not yet been implemented nationwide.

11.1.5.1. (Re)Introduce Duty to Monitor Company Health

The EBL should include a provision that the company's directors must monitor the company's health and submit to one of the EBL procedures once they are insolvent or once insolvency becomes imminent. When a company is still solvent, owners of the business – whose interests are represented by the directors – are the main financial stakeholders. But as soon as the company becomes insolvent, it is the creditors who bear the losses suffered if the debtor continues to trade, which makes them the new main financial stakeholders.[82] Many other regimes – including in Germany and the UK – try to regulate the resulting moral hazard and, even more importantly, the information

---

[77] See Zhang (n 47) 200–18.
[78] ibid. See also Sections 4.2.4 and 6.1.4.
[79] See Section 10.3.1.
[80] See also Section 11.3.1.
[81] Interviews J3-c to J9-c, R10-c. See also ch 12.
[82] R Kraakman, J Armour, P Davies, L Enriques, H Hansmann, G Hertig, K Hopt, H Kanda and E Rock, *The Anatomy of Corporate Law: A Comparative and Functional Approach*, 3rd edn (Oxford University Press, 2017) ch 5.4.

asymmetry between the debtor and its creditors[83] by shifting the duty of monitoring and disclosure onto the debtor as the party with the lowest cost and the best access to the necessary information. Thus, insolvent debtors in Germany have a duty to file for bankruptcy within three weeks after they become insolvent, failing which they face criminal liability. Similarly, in the UK, debtors' directors[84] can be criminally liable where they continue to trade when they 'knew, or ought to have concluded that there was no reasonable prospect of avoiding insolvent liquidation' and they did not take 'every step with a view to minimising the potential loss to the company's creditors'.[85]

On the other hand, some commentators argue that it is not economically efficient to push the duty to monitor onto directors because welfare gains by creditors are minimal due to the increased costs associated with directors demanding higher pay for a riskier job.[86] Instead, they propose, creditors can ascertain and protect themselves contractually because pushing the entire responsibility onto directors over-compensates the lender and does not allow directors to use their judgment and commercial common sense freely.[87] The US bankruptcy law follows this rationale and it, therefore, has no insolvent trading provisions. If a creditor wants wrongful-trading-style protection, they have to insert a special term into their contract,[88] or they have to rely on tortious remedies.

Given that the substantive provisions of China's corporate legal regime are closer to the UK and Germany, it is proposed that China should introduce a new provision into the EBL to impose a duty on company directors to monitor the organisation's financial health and to apply to use the EBL once it becomes (or is likely to become) insolvent. Such duty was included in an early draft of the EBL that was successfully trialled in Shenzhen.[89] The wording can focus on factual insolvency, as was the case in Shenzhen. Alternatively, the duty could be phrased in terms of actual or constructive knowledge, as in the UK. Regardless of the precise wording, imposing a duty to monitor and submit to the EBL on the company's directors is desirable in China.

The reason why it is proposed that China should follow the UK/German model rather than the US is that, in China, the sophistication and ability of many players to protect themselves contractually are limited, and enforcement thereof slow. Moreover, courts' ability and willingness to investigate directors' activities are also limited.[90] The proposed duty to self-monitor would make it the directors' duty to prove that they petitioned to use the EBL as soon as it was reasonable for them to know that the company became (or was about to become) insolvent.

---

[83] Where directors and owners have better access to information about the debtor company's financial affairs.

[84] This can include shadow and de facto directors.

[85] Known as wrongful trading: Insolvency Act 1986, s 214.

[86] See the review of the literature and a rejection of this argument in MJ Whincop, 'The Economic and strategic structure of insolvent trading' in IM Ramsay (ed), *Company Directors' Liability for Insolvent Trading* (University of Melbourne, 2000) 44–45 and 54–60.

[87] ibid.

[88] See DA Oesterle, 'Corporate directors' personal liability for "insolvent trading" in Australia, "reckless trading" in New Zealand and "wrongful trading" in England: a recipe for timid directors, hamstrung controlling shareholders and skittish lenders' in Ramsay, *Company Directors' Liability* (2000) 22.

[89] C Booth and X Zhang, 'Chinese Bankruptcy Law in an Emerging Market Economy: The Shenzhen Experience' (2001) *Columbia Journal of Asian Law* 1.

[90] Therefore, following the US model would most likely not work.

11.1.5.2. Introduce Simplified, Expedited Use of the EBL for Small Companies

The EBL should also offer a simplified, expedited mechanism that would be available to smaller companies[91] in order to enable a quicker, more cost-effective solution for companies that are usually excluded from the EBL restructuring.[92] Small companies are special because their distress is usually simpler, involves fewer stakeholders and concerns fewer assets. Moreover, China's economy contains a large number of smaller private companies which makes it important that their distress is resolved efficiently.

The need for an expedited mechanism is particularly acute in the context of corporate restructuring. Reorganisation is currently limited in scope in practice so that it excludes most SMEs from its scope.[93] This is problematic because there are many smaller companies that are not politically connected – and so cannot usually use reorganisation in practice – but which would greatly benefit from getting access to a formal collective restructuring mechanism.[94]

The proposed expedited mechanism could improve small companies' access to cheaper credit, and it could also enable quicker recycling of resources back into the economy to enable the development of other projects. The desirability of SME-specific tools has already been recognised in China[95] and has been trialled in several Chinese regions.[96]

11.1.6. Introduce Personal Bankruptcy Law

The EBL was enacted to provide a collective mechanism for reaching a binding, expert-driven resolution of corporate financial distress in state and private companies. It is much wider in scope than its predecessor, the 1986 law, but it does not extend to non-corporate bankruptcies. This is problematic for two reasons: allowing discharge of personal debts using personal bankruptcy law is good for the economy; and it is the right thing to do.

Firstly, introducing personal bankruptcy law would be good for the economy. The EBL only covers legal persons[97] which means that some commercial parties – eg partners in partnerships or sole traders – are excluded from the scope of the law. Resolving the debts of individuals who are involved in commercial activities is crucial for economic stability and for establishing a strong and efficient business environment. Personal bankruptcy law would provide a collective framework which would deal with

---

[91] A definition of a small company could be left to local laws, as it will depend on the commercial reality and context in each province.

[92] See Section 8.1.1.

[93] See Sections 8.1.1 and 11.1.4.

[94] Note that in China SMEs include companies with several hundred employees (the exact number depends on the industry).

[95] Weihai Intermediate People's Court, 'Enhancing the Reorganisation of Limited Liability Companies in China' (2013) *Shandong Justice* 32.

[96] See Section 12.8.

[97] See Sections 4.2.1 and 4.4.

all claims simultaneously, under clear and predictable rules, with the aim to maximise the value of debtor's assets and redistribute it fairly to creditors.[98]

Similarly, in many corporate bankruptcies, natural persons provide guarantees for the company's debts. It is quite common for owners of a small private company to provide such guarantee when obtaining external finance, or for shareholders to provide guarantees for debts of their company. Indeed, the lack of personal bankruptcy rules was one of the reasons why the bosses ran away in several corporate bankruptcies where they provided personal guarantees for their company's debts.[99] However, in the absence of personal bankruptcy law, where the company is unable to pay a debt or where it goes bankrupt and the individual guarantor does not have enough assets to repay the company's debts, it may become impossible for courts to enforce debt repayment according to the law. Zhou Qiang, the President of the SPC, reported to the Standing Committee of the NPC in 2018 that about 18 per cent of civil and commercial cases were 'unable to execute' cases (due to the problems with personal guarantees), which blocks the judicial system, damages courts' reputation,[100] and harms economic stability and social order.

Moreover, in recent years, a large number of bosses of P2P and private equity institutions ran away because of the lack of personal bankruptcy resolution mechanism, which further reflects the urgency of the construction of a personal bankruptcy regime. Due to the increasing complexity of corporate debt and associated personal debts, it is difficult to effectively solve all debt-related issues by relying on the current debt enforcement system and credit reporting system.[101] China's economy relies on entrepreneurs, but entrepreneurship involves innovation and risk-taking, which in turn involves a high probability of failure. Personal bankruptcy law would provide a mechanism for dealing with excessive indebtedness, it would ensure part-repayment of debts, and it would then allow the debtor to have a fresh start.[102]

Secondly, introducing personal bankruptcy law is the right thing to do given China's stage of social and economic development. The ratio of household debt to GDP increased from 11 per cent in 2006 to 55 per cent in 2019.[103] Moreover, consumer spending increased from 25 per cent of China's GDP in 2011 to 54 per cent in 2017.[104] With the reorienting from production to consumption, it is only natural that an increasing number of individuals face excessive indebtedness and personal insolvency. A law that would ensure effective and fair treatment of creditors while at the same time allowing the debtor's eventual return to normal life is highly desirable. Moreover, China's recently introduced social credit system[105] means that, in early 2019, there were almost

---

[98] See eg MJ White, 'Economics of Bankruptcy' in F Parisi (ed), *The Oxford Handbook of Law and Economics*, vol 2 (Oxford University Press, 2017).

[99] See Sections 6.2.2 and 10.2.2. See also Sections 4.3.1 and 12.9.

[100] Yunqingsuan (27.8.2019).

[101] ibid.

[102] Empirical studies suggest that personal bankruptcy law would also likely encourage more entrepreneurship and healthy risk-taking which is necessary for growth and innovation: see Section 1.2.

[103] BIS data.

[104] NBS data.

[105] See eg F Liang, V Das, N Kostyuk and M Hussain, 'Constructing a Data-Driven Society: China's Social Credit System as a State Surveillance Infrastructure' (2018) *Policy & Internet* 415.

14 million people with a bad social credit rating in China who could face being banned from travelling, being publicly shamed, being restricted from which jobs they could apply to, etc. It is clear that being stuck on a bad rating due to one's inability to repay their debts is problematic and a better solution – personal bankruptcy law – needs to be found.[106] This is especially true in cases of honest but unfortunate debtors who became unable to repay their debts due to ill health or ill fortune.[107]

For these and other reasons, many commentators have called for an introduction of personal bankruptcy law in China in recent years. Among the most vocal is Professor Li Shuguang.[108] When asked to provide specific proposals for reform at a forum celebrating the EBL's first decade, Professor Li said that the EBL

> must really enter the Chinese economic life, enter the market to determine the allocation of resources, and play an important role. In the absence of personal bankruptcy provisions, the EBL can only be counted as half of a bankruptcy law. Only when the content of personal bankruptcy is incorporated into the EBL, the law has more institutional value and significance.[109]

The Government has finally accepted that there are important reasons for introducing personal bankruptcy law and ordered local experiments in several regions of China. The local reform initiatives are discussed in Section 12.9.

11.1.7. Practical Impact and Conclusion

Reforming EBL provisions alone is unlikely to result in a greater or more efficient use of the law. This is because flaws in the written EBL are only one of many constraints on its use.[110] Nevertheless, the written EBL can and should be improved so that the rules are the best that they can be for when the shortcomings in enforcement – arguably the major constraint – improve over time.[111] The effectiveness of the proposed reforms of the EBL provisions would be significantly improved by the introduction of the proposed reforms of EBL enforcement practices and surrounding rules, which are discussed next.

11.2. Reforms Aimed at Improving EBL Enforcement Practices and Surrounding Rules

In order to improve the functioning of the EBL as a whole, it is necessary to improve EBL's supporting infrastructure – surrounding rules and practices – which lower parties' payoffs under the EBL or outright prevent the EBL from being used. The proposed

---

[106] Q Wang (20.7.2019, CGTN).

[107] ibid.

[108] See eg S Li, 'Some Problems of Drafting the Chine New Bankruptcy Law' (2002) *China Legal Science* 78, 79.

[109] See the Seminar on the 10th Anniversary of the Implementation of the Corporate Bankruptcy Law in B Lu (12.9.2017, People's Court News).

[110] See chs 7 to 9.

[111] Following the reform proposals in Sections 11.2 and 11.3.

reforms – summarised in Table 11.2 – focus on three sets of issues that were identified in chapter seven. Section 11.2.1 below proposes several reforms which aim to ameliorate general flaws in debt enforcement that also negatively affect recoveries under the EBL. Section 11.2.2 describes several changes which aim to ameliorate the rules and practices that specifically affect recoveries under the EBL. And Section 11.2.3 recommends to clarify and harmonise the treatment of the parties engaged in shadow market activities in China. The proposals are then drawn together to consider their likely cumulative impact in practice in Section 11.2.4.

Table 11.2 Proposed reforms of surrounding rules and practices

	Content of reform	**Timing of reform**
Ameliorate general flaws in debt enforcement (Section 11.2.1) to increase payoffs under the EBL	Strategies for reducing information asymmetries (Section 11.2.1.1)	Any time, but effective only after reforms aimed at enforcers (Section 11.3)
	Introduction of national property rights register (Section 11.2.1.2)	Any time, but more likely to be effective only after reforms aimed at local governments (Section 11.3.3)
	Better protection of property rights (Section 11.2.1.3)	Any time, but effective only after reforms aimed at enforcers (Section 11.3)
	Better enforcement of directors' duties and reversal of transfers to new companies (Section 11.2.1.4)	Any time, but best together with judges' training (Section 11.3.1)
Ameliorate rules and practices that specifically affect the EBL (Section 11.2.2) to remove opposition for local governments	Full implementation of social security system (Section 11.2.2.1)	Any time, but effective only after reforms aimed at local governments (Section 11.3.4)
	Reduce state companies' interconnectedness, triangular debts, and guarantee chains (Section 11.2.2.2)	Any time, but effective only after reforms aimed at local governments (Section 11.3.4)
Clarify and harmonise treatment of the parties engaged in shadow lending (Section 11.2.3)	Clarify and harmonise political and legal approach to shadow market activities (Section 11.2.3)	Any time, but effective only after reforms aimed at local governments (Section 11.3.4)

11.2.1. Ameliorate General Flaws in Debt Enforcement

As was discussed earlier, there are several issues that affect recoveries under both the EBL and general debt enforcement mechanisms.[112] The improvements proposed in this section aim to increase payoffs which the parties can expect to receive under the (reformed) EBL.

---

[112] See Sections 3.4 and 7.1.

Section 11.2.1.1 below examines possible strategies for reducing information asymmetries. Section 11.2.1.2 then discusses the need for a fully functional national property rights register. Section 11.2.1.3 considers how better protection of property rights may improve the functioning of the EBL. Section 11.2.1.4 concludes by looking at possible improvements to the Company Law. In the aggregate, these proposed reforms are likely to increase actual recoveries under the EBL, and so encourage greater and more efficient use of the EBL.

11.2.1.1. *Strategies for Reducing Information Asymmetries*

The Chinese business environment is negatively affected by the scarcity of reliable, publicly available information.[113] In the context of bankruptcy law, this causes several problems which make the EBL process comparatively slow and expensive. The information asymmetry complicates the determination of whether a company is, in fact, insolvent. It hinders proving debtors' assets and liabilities. It also impedes a proper implementation of the safeguards and procedures contained in the EBL.[114]

Improvements in this area are likely to be gradual because an effective reform requires multiple changes in China's business environment and the parties' attitude. The strategies can be divided into two groups. Internal changes come from parties' increased understanding that a greater amount of reliable information is efficient for the economy at large and so, in time, also for themselves. However, such understanding alone is unlikely to result in any measurable improvements. Therefore, parties must also be incentivised – with encouragement and a threat of punishment – to publish truthful information in sufficient quantity and which is freely and easily accessible. This may be achieved through the creation of online platforms where company information could be accessed freely and easily; random checks of the submitted information and severe punishment for submitting (knowingly or carelessly) untrue information; a requirement that the information must be submitted in a unified form (to allow easier comparison); better enforcement of China's Company Law and Corporate Governance Code; and liability for accounting firms which recklessly or fraudulently cover up or allow a cover-up of false information. Effective enforcement of these strategies will be crucial to their success.[115]

11.2.1.2. *Introduction of National Property Rights Register*

Although the Property Register was formally introduced in 2013/14, its implementation in practice remains incomplete.[116] As a result, it is often unclear who owns particular property and property rights. It is also difficult to protect security rights effectively. This makes the verification of claims and collection of assets in bankruptcy difficult and enables fraudulent asset stripping at the expense of creditors.

---

[113] See Section 3.4.1.
[114] See Section 7.1.1.
[115] Note that there have been recent reforms in this area. For a discussion see Sections 12.4–12.6.
[116] See Sections 3.4.2 and 7.1.2.

It is, therefore, proposed that national and local governments should prioritise the completion of the Property Register in China. Technically, they should face no significant obstacles. Once implemented, the register would enable quicker, cheaper and more reliable verification of parties' rights and claims, it would help determine their priority and enforceability, and it would increase transparency and ease of doing business in China – all of which are likely to have a positive impact on investment and access to credit. Although independent from other reforms, the implementation is likely to be quicker and more effective after reforms aimed at improving local government understanding of the role and importance of bankruptcy law in China's economic development.[117]

11.2.1.3. *Better Protection of Property Rights*

The lack of effective protection of property rights – which, inter alia, enables asset-grabbing and unpunished looting – hinders business activities.[118] Under the EBL, it negatively affects the value and amount of assets that are available for satisfying stakeholders' claims.

Asset-grabbing can be prevented by the police and, under the EBL, by administrators.[119] Similarly, looting of debtor companies can also be prevented by the police. Nevertheless, as was discussed in Section 7.1.3, the police often fail to intervene to protect debtors' assets from damage or misappropriation. Regardless of whether such failure to act is due to their unwillingness or inability, the police play a crucial role in property protection. It is, therefore, suggested that the Government – both at national and local levels – must allow and order it to act. The ability to protect property may be added to local government performance targets to incentivise their proactivity in this matter.[120]

Similarly, courts must also be willing to step in and protect property rights. The impact of this issue goes far beyond individual cases and claimholders. In a system where owners of assets cannot rely on the absolute nature of their right – and its protection where needed – their ability to borrow is reduced, which limits their ability to compete and engage in new projects. In the aggregate, the resulting incomplete protection of property rights has a negative impact on economic development.

11.2.1.4. *Better Enforcement of Directors' Duties and Reversal of Transfers to New Companies*

Similar to the previous issue, there are rules and mechanisms which can prevent unauthorised transfers of assets that aim to defraud claimholders – most notably through tunnelling, asset-stripping and creation of ghost companies. Besides provisions in the EBL,[121] the Company Law also empowers courts to reverse asset stripping by companies' insiders. Furthermore, it imposes duties of diligence and loyalty on company

---

[117] See Section 11.3.3.
[118] See Sections 3.4.3 and 7.1.3.
[119] More about administrators' role in Section 11.3.3.1.
[120] See also Section 11.3.4.2.
[121] ibid.

directors. However, my research suggests that these rules are not strictly enforced, and asset transfers are de facto permitted due to courts' passivity.[122]

It is therefore proposed that courts should be directed to pay more attention to these issues and more strictly enforce these provisions in practice. This includes EBL hearings. The change will be slow and difficult. China, like many developing countries, is facing difficulties that arise from imperfect law enforcement.[123] However, there is no practical replacement for courts in this context. The success of this particular reform will, therefore, depend on the outcome of the proposed court-related reforms.[124]

11.2.2. Ameliorate Rules and Practices that Specifically Affect the EBL

In order to reduce local government opposition to EBL enforcement, it is also important to address two further issues.[125] Section 11.2.2.1 below discusses the need to implement China's national social security system in full. Section 11.2.2.2 then examines the need to incentivise (or order) local governments to reduce state companies' interconnectedness, triangular debts and guarantee chains.

11.2.2.1. Full Implementation of Social Security System

It was argued in Section 7.2.1 that local governments fear that letting (large) local companies fail may lead to a significant number of redundancies, which often leads to social unrest. One of the main reasons why the newly unemployed take to the streets is because – without a functioning social welfare system – losing a job means losing their livelihood. As a result, local governments often interfere or prevent bankruptcy cases from being tried independently and in accordance with the EBL rules because they want to prevent company closures.[126]

In the early stages of China's economic development, when all companies were owned by the state, social welfare was provided through the tradition of iron rice bowl whereby SOEs would provide lifelong employment and take care of people's material needs from birth to death. This system was abolished during the 1970s economic reforms.[127] For this reason, the concept of a social security fund was introduced in the 1990s, with further changes in 2011. However, by 2015, only about a quarter of all companies were contributing to the fund.[128] Moreover, there is still no mechanism for paying out unemployment benefits from this fund once a person becomes unemployed. As a result, the Government continues to protect the employees. To highlight the seriousness of this problem, Premier Li Keqiang said at the end of the annual NPC

---

[122] See Sections 3.4.4 and 7.1.4.
[123] See Section 2.3.
[124] See Sections 11.3.1–11.3.3.
[125] See Section 7.2.
[126] See Section 8.3.5. Alternatively, local governments sometimes force the debtor to resettle all the laid-off employees before using the EBL to restructure or liquidate: see Section 6.1.1.
[127] See Section 2.1.
[128] For details, see Section 7.2.1.

meeting in 2016: 'We must proceed with reducing industrial capacity, but the great numbers of employees cannot lose their rice bowls, and we must strive to find them new rice bowls'.[129] Although the old iron rice bowl regime was abandoned following Deng's reforms,[130] it is clear that the state continues to look after employees' interests – even at the expense of creditors[131] – in order to safeguard social stability.

However, it is proposed that efficiency cannot be introduced – and further economic growth facilitated – without liquidating and restructuring at least some (and ideally all) of the distressed companies in China. It is true that corporate closures and restructurings necessarily involve redundancies, but the recycled resources and resulting efficiency also provide further opportunities to grow existing projects and to create new ones. When this happens, new jobs are created, the unemployed are re-employed in more efficient projects, and the economy develops and grows. Nevertheless, there is usually a time gap between an employee's dismissal from a distressed company and re-employment in a new company. For this period, there needs to be some support mechanism which provides for the unemployed persons' basic material needs – a temporary rice bowl. One such mechanism is unemployment benefits paid out of a social security fund.

It is, therefore, proposed that national and local governments must prioritise the completion of social security system in each region and nationwide. All companies must be forced to contribute to the fund, and each local government must create a mechanism and a publicly accessible set of rules that regulate[132] and explain the provision of unemployment benefits in their region. Such full implementation of the social security system would remove one of the main reasons for local government opposition to bankruptcy law.

This proposal is crucial to change the attitude of local governments. However, realistically, the change is unlikely to happen until local government officials understand the importance of this project and the EBL for their economy.[133] Employment and tax law experts should be consulted, and support from the national Government, the Party, and their local agencies will be needed for this project to succeed. To speed up the process, the successful establishment of a social security system could become one of the measures in local leaders' career progression assessment. Once local governments understand and their incentives are changed, they will be more likely to allow courts to apply EBL provisions more objectively, without employee protectionism which now hinders the enforcement of the EBL.[134]

11.2.2.2. Reduce State Company Interconnectedness, Triangular Debts, and Guarantee Chains

Section 7.2.2 argued that another reason why local governments do not allow parties to use the EBL concerns their fear of systemic risk that arises from the interconnectedness

---

[129] C Buckley and J Hernandez (16.3.2016, New York Times).
[130] See Section 2.1.
[131] cf Section 4.2.11. But see also Section 6.1.
[132] The system would ideally be linked to the *hukou* 户口 registration system.
[133] See Section 11.3.4.
[134] See Sections 6.1 (employee protectionism by courts), 6.2.1 (incomplete social security system), 8.3.1 (why the Party-state interferes) and 9.2 (politically driven alternatives).

of state-sector companies. This interconnectedness stems from the unique ownership structure of the SOEs,[135] but also the use of mutual guarantee chains and triangular debts among large companies.[136] Together, these mechanisms increase the risk of economy-wide distress because they increase the likelihood of a domino effect of insolvencies.

In the short-term, local governments may see it as a good idea[137] to rescue individual companies in distress where their insolvency would cause financial distress in other companies in their region that are connected to it through debts and mutual guarantees. However, it is proposed that, in the long term, shielding companies from hard-budget constraints in this way leads to moral hazard because state-sector companies know that they will be rescued and so make limited or no effort to manage their risk. Moreover, this attitude leads to wasteful bailouts and other forms of financial support,[138] which should be discouraged.[139]

It is, therefore, proposed that local governments should be forced to reduce corporate interconnectedness in the state sector. They should not allow companies under their control to become too big and too interconnected so as to avoid the too-big-to-fail dilemma.[140] This would also reduce the risk of systemic distress and enable healthy competition in the economy. Similarly, triangular debts and mutual guarantees and guarantee chains should be banned, and this ban should be monitored and strictly enforced. Consequently, the bankruptcy of one company would be (comparatively) less likely to affect the financial health of the others. These changes are likely to be implemented once local government incentives are amended from a short- to a long-term focus.[141]

11.2.3. Clarify and Harmonise the Treatment of the Parties Engaged in Shadow Lending

One of the most fundamental changes, which is likely to ensure that the EBL becomes used by all eligible companies whose financial distress would be most efficiently resolved under the EBL, is the inclusion of shadow lenders and borrowers.[142] For this to occur, the Government needs to change its attitude towards shadow credit, and it needs to clarify and harmonise the rules on how to treat the activities of the shadow market participants – both in and out of insolvency.

There are two major reasons why these changes are necessary. The first reason is connected with the wide use of undesirable enforcement techniques by shadow lenders which is partly caused by the lack of recognition of their claims in Chinese courts.[143]

---

[135] See Section 2.5.
[136] For details see Sections 3.2.2 and 7.2.2.
[137] See Section 8.3.1.
[138] See Section 9.2.
[139] See Sections 10.2 and 12.3.
[140] AR Sorkin, *Too Big to Fail* (Penguin Books, 2010).
[141] See Section 11.3.4.2.
[142] They are mostly excluded under the current system: Section 7.3.
[143] For examples, see Section 10.2.1.

Moreover, shadow credit is crucial for China's fast-growing private sector,[144] but a party's involvement in the shadow market – whether as a lender or a borrower – can give rise to criminal liability, with the maximum penalty (until recently) being capital punishment.[145] As a result, creditors and debtors usually do not wish to use the EBL and instead opt for private enforcement mechanisms[146] and avoidance of repayment techniques,[147] respectively. This is problematic because shadow creditors often use violent and otherwise undesirable methods to enforce debt repayment which – many of my interviewees argued – could be significantly reduced if shadow lending contracts were recognised in and enforced by courts.[148] Similarly, allowing shadow borrowers to use the EBL would be beneficial because there would be a mechanism for debtors to restructure or otherwise resolve their liabilities and have a chance for a fresh start instead of having to fear violence or face exile in order to avoid it.

The second reason why shadow lending and borrowing need to be legalised is that, otherwise, they pose a large threat to the stability of China's financial system. This threat arises from the riskiness and vastness of the shadow lending activities, and the fact that shadow finance is still largely unregulated. Shadow lending is risky because lenders usually do minimal or no background checks and so they lend to sub-prime borrowers – which ex ante increases the likelihood of a default. In addition, they charge high interest rates to compensate for the increased risk of default. However, it is often the high interest rates that cause or significantly contribute to borrowers' financial distress.[149]

Moreover, shadow lending permeates China's entire economy. Private as well as state-controlled parties are involved. As was discussed in Sections 3.1 and 7.3, shadow lending includes any arm's-length provision of credit that comes from an unauthorised (usually private) entity – eg underground banks – or that involves unauthorised activities by an authorised body – eg WMPs and unauthorised lending into real estate sector by state banks. Borrowers are usually private sector companies and struggling SOEs which try to conceal their distress from the Party-state.

Furthermore, shadow lending is still largely unregulated. This often leads to unstable lending models and fraud – leading to collapses of underground banks and lending platforms, causing losses to depositors, and sending shock waves through the entire economy because so many players are involved. The Government has been trying to contain the risk for years,[150] but with limited success. Shadow lending is growing and is riddled with fraud, collapses and quickly concealed local crises that threaten the stability of China's economy.[151]

Shadow lending is unlikely to disappear so long as there is demand – from credit-starved private companies – and supply – from depositors seeking returns at rates

---

[144] See Section 3.1.

[145] See Section 6.2.

[146] See Section 9.1.

[147] See Section 10.2.2.

[148] Interviews C4-c, C5-r, C7-s, C11-c, E1-c, E2-s, IF1-s, IF2-c, J4-c to J9-c, L2-s, L4-r to L15-c, P1-r, P5-c, R3-r, R7-c, R9-c, R10-c.

[149] Interviews C1-c, C4-c, C5-r, C7-s, C11-c, E1-c to E4-c, IF1-s, J3-c to J6-s, J8-c, J9-c, L1-r to L15-c, R2-r, R3-r, R6-c, R7-c, R9-c, C10-c, R13-c.

[150] See eg D Choyleva (21.6.2017, FT).

[151] See eg A Collier (26.6.2017, FT).

higher than those of the banks and companies seeking extra profits from their idle funds. Demand will remain so long as banks remain controlled by the state. And supply will remain so long as there is money to be made – mostly through high interest rates.

It is, therefore, proposed that there need to be clearer national guidelines about the treatment of each type of shadow lending activity.[152] This is likely to be a staged process. First steps must be taken by the Chinese Government through a public statement and subsequent specialised legislation that would deal with the permitted and forbidden lending activities, and their consequences. Courts should also receive detailed guidelines on how to deal with non-bank lending activities and shadow debt contracts in general and under the EBL. The drafting of both is likely to take time and should not be rushed. Experience from local courts and governments should be shared in intra-provincial sessions.[153]

11.2.4. Practical Impact and Conclusion

Improving EBL's enforcement environment is as important as improving the EBL itself. The changes proposed in Section 11.2.1 are needed for enabling the EBL to offer higher payoffs, and so incentivise the parties to use the law more. On the other hand, the changes in Section 11.2.2 are likely to reduce the opposition from EBL's enforcers, and so enable the law's greater use. Finally, the changes in Section 11.2.3 affect both the parties' expected payoffs under the EBL and the enforcers' ability and willingness to deal with a particular type of claimants in financial distress. In the short term, the reform efforts should focus on the first two sets of changes – in particular improvement to the quality and quantity of available information in Section 11.2.1.1 above, completion of the national property rights register in Section 11.2.1.2 above, and full implementation of social security system in Section 11.2.2.1 – without which the EBL is unlikely to function effectively. In the medium-to-long term, however, the third set of reforms – aimed at shadow lenders and borrowers – will also have to be implemented to enable a fuller application of the EBL to all eligible cases.

11.3. Reforms Aimed at EBL Enforcers

The findings in Chapter eight suggest that reforms aimed at improving the efficiency of the EBL in practice also need to focus on improving enforcers' understanding, appreciation and willingness to allow greater and more efficient use of the EBL. There are five proposals which address the key issues identified in Chapter eight. First three sets of reforms focus on improving the problems associated with EBL's direct enforcers – judges, lawyers and administrators. Section 11.3.1 below looks at ways how to improve courts' and lawyers' expertise and experience. Section 11.3.2 considers the desirability

---

[152] Many types of shadow lending activities are treated differently in different provinces: see Section 4.1.
[153] See Section 11.3.1.

of introducing specialised bankruptcy courts. And Section 11.3.3 explores the options for ensuring more accurate and objective enforcement of the EBL by the courts. The final two sets of reforms focus on indirect enforcers who influence the procedures from behind the scenes, without EBL-derived power – most importantly local governments.[154] Section 11.3.4 examines how and why to change local government incentives to ensure that they understand and are willing to support the more efficient use of the EBL by the parties. Finally, Section 11.3.5 considers how to ensure greater judicial independence while retaining the possibility of efficient and appropriately limited support from the state. Section 11.3.6 then summarises the proposals and considers their likely cumulative impact in practice.

The reform proposals and their timing are summarised in Table 11.3.

Table 11.3 Proposed reforms aimed at EBL enforcers

	Content of reform	Timing of reform
Changes that affect courts and lawyers (Section 11.3.1–3)	Improve expertise and experience of judges and lawyers (Section 11.3.1)	Any time (staged)
	Introduce specialised bankruptcy courts (Section 11.3.2)	Any time, but best together with judges' training (Section 11.3.1)
	Ensure that administrators carry out their duties (Section 11.3.3.1)	Any time, but best together with judges' training (Section 11.3.1)
	Ensure that priority of repayment is respected (Section 11.3.3.2)	Any time, but best together with judges' training (Section 11.3.1) and local government training (Section 11.3.4)
	Remove judges' internal quotas (Section 11.3.3.3)	Any time, but best with local government training (Section 11.3.4)
Changes that affect local governments (Section 11.3.4)	Enhance local government understanding of the need for the EBL (Section 11.3.4.1)	Any time
	Change structure and substance of local government officials' incentives (Section 11.3.4.2)	Any time
Changes that affect both courts and local governments (Section 11.3.5)	Enable and safeguard judicial independence (Section 11.3.5)	Implement after reforms aimed at local governments (Section 11.3.4)
	Optional appropriately limited state assistance (Section 11.3.5)	

The reforms proposed in this section are particularly sensitive in terms of timing. Their ultimate aim is to enable courts to apply the EBL with skill and independence. Skills and experience are built over time through actual decision-making and training, but independence requires that local governments permit judges to hear cases without

[154] See ch 8.

political interventions.[155] To that end, local governments must first be persuaded – through changed incentives, greater understanding, and top-down orders – that the EBL matters and that it has much to offer to their local economy if applied independently.

11.3.1. Improve Expertise and Experience of Judges and Lawyers

Improving judges' and lawyers' knowledge and skills that are necessary for dealing with EBL cases is crucial because judges and lawyers play a crucial role in EBL enforcement.[156] The reforms that are proposed below are aimed at helping them appreciate the importance of bankruptcy law for China, to know what the EBL says, and to understand how to use the law in practice. If implemented successfully, the reforms should help ameliorate one of the key limitations that my interviewees identified in Section 8.1, namely judges' and lawyers' lack of expertise and experience in applying the EBL in practice.[157] This section, therefore, first looks at the challenges that face judges and those that face lawyers. It then examines possible ways of ameliorating them and considers likely difficulties with implementing the proposed changes.

Much criticism has been levelled against Chinese courts.[158] However, my interviewees insisted that many judges – particularly in higher courts – are very competent and exceptionally hard-working.[159] Nevertheless, judges' work is affected by internal and external limitations which make them reluctant or unable to deal with EBL cases more effectively.[160] Several interviewees also stressed that some judges are unaware of the purpose and procedures in the EBL, which is why they do not use it.[161] Nevertheless, given their central position in EBL enforcement, they must know and understand the law to be able to apply it effectively. In time, as courts' expertise and experience grow, creditors and debtors will become more likely to entrust their case to a judge.[162] An increase in courts' expertise and experience is also expected to lead to a decrease in the length and cost of bankruptcy proceedings.[163]

Improving lawyers' EBL-related expertise and experience is equally important. Lawyers' role in resolving corporate financial distress starts even before debtors submit an EBL petition because companies in distress often rely on advice and knowledge of their legal advisors when deciding whether and how to deal with their financial problems. Moreover, some lawyers also act as administrators who are central to the day-to-day administration of EBL cases. It is, therefore, crucial that they understand their role in the process and their many duties.[164]

---

[155] For details, see Sections 2.4 and 8.3.
[156] See Sections 4.2.9 and 8.1.
[157] See People's Daily (10.10.2015).
[158] See Section 2.4.
[159] In particular interviews C2-c, C5-r, C7-s, J2-c, L1-r to L7-c, L9-s to L14-c, L16-c, P1-r, R3-r, R6-c to R10-c, R15-s.
[160] ibid. For details see ch 8.
[161] Interviews C4-c, C5-r, C7-s, J1-c, J2-c, J4-c to J8-c, L2-s, L4-r to L7-c, L14-c, L15-c, P1-r, R2-r, R8-s to R10-c.
[162] See Section 8.1.1.
[163] Interviews B1-c, C3-c to C5-r, C7-s, C8-s, C10-s, E1-c to E5-c, IF1-s, IF2-c, L2-s to L6-s, L9-s to L15-c, R1-r, R3-r, R6-c, R7-c, R9-c, R10-c. See also Section 8.1.2.
[164] See Section 4.2.9.

Five ways to ameliorate the situation are proposed.[165] Firstly, all regions in China should introduce specialised bankruptcy courts, or specialised branches within existing general courts which would enable judges with relevant education and background (eg finance, business, accounting, restructuring) to become experts in dealing with bankruptcy cases. This is discussed in detail in Section 11.3.2 below.

Secondly, the Government could also call on selected regions – with various degrees of economic development, in different geographical regions, with a different number of EBL cases – to become pilots for further reform. Local governments in the selected regions would be encouraged – through incentives and rewards (if successful) – to experiment with ways how to enable and encourage more efficient use of the EBL. This would be similar to the 1970s and 1980s approach to reform where local governments were successfully encouraged to achieve large-scale improvements through local experiments.[166]

Thirdly, the SPC should provide additional detailed guidance on the procedural elements of the EBL – such as criminal liability of managers of insolvent companies, a priority of repayment, acceptance or rejection of EBL petitions – to inform judges at lower courts about the likely challenges in the process and SPC's preferred solutions. The SPC could also provide guiding cases – akin to precedents[167] – showing how liquidation and reorganisation should be used in different circumstances depending on size, industry, region and ownership type. Some limited guidance has been produced in recent years and is discussed in Section 12.4.

Fourthly, many interviewees suggested that their preferred way of learning about the EBL and its application would be through conferences and practical training sessions.[168] They suggested that the conferences should be led by Chinese and foreign experts, and the content should be practical. Expert-led training sessions should then share the guidelines and advice in a workshop-style environment where judges and lawyers could learn from practical examples and problems. Several local courts have already held several sessions and produced reports for local governments and local Party committees about the EBL process.[169] Others have been holding training sessions, either in courts or together with local governments.[170] Many more of these initiatives are needed across China.

And finally, practical insights and guidelines for hearing EBL cases could also be shared through online platforms, which would maximise their practical impact and geographical reach. Several courts have already released guidance on hearing EBL cases.[171] Guidelines have also been released for dealing with specific types of cases.[172]

Some changes have been made and implemented with a degree of success in recent years. Nevertheless, the recent increase in the number of EBL cases is likely to

---

[165] Some local examples of the below already exist and are discussed in ch 12.

[166] See Sections 2.1 and 4.1.

[167] See Section 2.4.2.

[168] Interviews C1-c, C3-c to C5-r, C7-s, C9-c to C11-c, J1-c to J9-c, L2-s to L15-c, P1-r, P3-r to P5-c, R2-r to R4-c, R6-c to R10-c, R13-c.

[169] See Section 12.6.

[170] ibid.

[171] See Section 12.5.

[172] ibid.

be temporary[173] unless more in-depth changes are carried out. After all, the number of cases that were heard under the much-criticised old law temporarily reached to almost 9,000 cases in 2001 when the Government put pressure on the courts to use the law just before its accession to the WTO.[174] Similarly, despite the push to create specialised bankruptcy branches in all Chinese courts, most courts still do not have one.[175]

There appears to be an increase in appetite and willingness to learn about these issues, which should make the delivery of the proposed interventions in this section relatively straightforward. Nevertheless, when implementing the proposed changes, it is important to bear in mind that most court-related changes rely heavily on a change in local government attitudes. Training the lawyers, on the other hand, is likely to prove less problematic.

11.3.2. Introduce Specialised Bankruptcy Courts

It is desirable that China introduces specialised bankruptcy courts in all regions. Thanks to the concentration of EBL cases in the hands of relatively few judges, specialisation and experience would grow over a relatively short period of time even with a small number of EBL cases. The calls for specialised judges first appeared when the old law came into force in 1988[176] and have been reiterated in recent years. Professor Li Shuguang has been a prominent proponent of specialised EBL courts, but he stresses that – in order to achieve more efficient implementation of the EBL – they must be not only physically removed from normal courts but also 'professional, independent, authoritative and impartial in the process of bankruptcy proceedings. This requires special status and legal support to achieve'.[177] Specialised bankruptcy courts have been introduced in some Chinese regions in the last few years. Their progress is discussed in Section 12.4 below.

11.3.3. Ensure More Accurate and Objective Enforcement of EBL Rules

Besides improving courts' and lawyers' expertise, it is also important to ensure that the powers and duties in the EBL are actually carried out. Although it is generally accepted that the EBL is well written, many of its provisions which have the potential to make it a particularly useful debt-resolving mechanism are not enforced in practice.[178] To address this, three improvements are proposed. Section 11.3.3.1 below argues that administrators' duties must be properly enforced. Section 11.3.3.2 further proposes that the EBL

---

[173] See Section 10.1.
[174] See Sections 5.1 and 10.1.
[175] For details, see Sections 11.3.2 and 12.4.
[176] For details see Section 8.1.1.
[177] See the Seminar on the 10th Anniversary of the Implementation of the Corporate Bankruptcy Law in B Lu (12.9.2017, People's Court News).
[178] See Sections 6.1 and 8.2.

rules on the priority of distribution must be respected and enforced as written. Finally, Section 11.3.3.3 suggests that judges should not be subject to simplistic quotas that discourage them from accepting EBL petitions. The success of the second and third interventions is conditional on a change in local governments' attitude – discussed in Section 11.3.4 – and on proactive cooperation from judges and lawyers, and so should be included in the training sessions mentioned in Section 11.3.1 above.

11.3.3.1. *Better Enforcement of Administrators' Duties*

Section 4.2.9 pointed out that, besides being in charge of day-to-day management in reorganisation, administrators must also identify and claw back certain preferential payments, hidden or transferred property, fraudulent payments, and they must ask a court to revoke transactions at an undervalue and other transactions the seek to defraud creditors. My interviewees argued[179] that these extensive duties and corresponding powers could be one of the greatest advantages of the EBL to creditors because they could help increase the total amount of assets available for distribution and lead to greater, less risky recoveries (compared to illegal or costly private enforcement). However, despite the importance and in some cases the imperative mode of the provisions,[180] many of my interviewees suggested that administrators are often unable or unwilling to exercise such powers and duties fully which negatively affects the likelihood of meaningful recovery by creditors.[181]

It is therefore proposed that this issue should be addressed as a part of judges' and lawyers' training and that the SPC should direct lower courts to police and enforce administrators' duties more closely. The key obstacles are likely to be administrators' ignorance of the relevant provisions, and lawyers' and judges' fear of being overburdened.

At the same time, there is evidence to suggest that local governments sometimes control administrators' work or that local governments actually carry out the duties of administrators in reorganisation as liquidation committees.[182] Where this is the reason for administrators' passivity, it would first be necessary to address the local governments' insistence on interfering in EBL procedures and persuading them to let courts and administrators work independently, without local government interference[183] – unless assistance is called for by a court.[184] In any case, it is very important that administrators' passivity is reversed in order to make EBL procedures truly collective and efficient.

11.3.3.2. *Priority of Repayment under the EBL*

In addition, it is also important that judges respect and apply the law as written because the parties arrange their affairs and make decisions ex ante based on what the law suggests they can expect to happen ex post. If the law cannot be trusted, lenders are likely

---

[179] See Section 8.2.
[180] Note the use of 'have to' in Arts 32–33 EBL.
[181] Interviews B1-c to B3-c, C1-c, C3-c to C5-r, C7-s, C9-c, E2-s, J12-c, J4-c to J9-c, L2-s, L4-r to L7-c, L10-s to L15-c, P1-r, R1-r to R3-r, R9-c, R10-c, R13-c.
[182] See Section 8.3.5. See also Zhang (n 47) 80–85.
[183] See Section 11.3.4.
[184] See Section 11.3.5.

to consider lending risky and, consequently, not lend or make credit more expensive.[185] The EBL stipulates that 'secured creditors are entitled to obtain payment in priority over debtor's specific asset'[186] – regardless and ahead of all other claims. However, as was argued in Section 6.1, courts have afforded preferential repayment to employees' claims by interpreting ancillary EBL provisions as enabling *prioritisation* of socio-economic interests.[187] This failure to respect the written provision of the EBL is problematic and should be rectified.

As above, it is proposed that the rules about the priority of distribution and their practical importance should be discussed in judges' training sessions. A shift in court practice is only likely to occur after a shift in local government understanding and attitude to the issue.[188] Full implementation of the social security system[189] will also likely play an important role in encouraging local governments to stop interfering in EBL cases to protect employees. The SPC and central Party-state should also support this initiative with further guidelines and orders to lower courts and local governments.

11.3.3.3. Remove Judges' Internal Quotas

It was also proposed earlier that judges' reluctance to accept EBL petitions has been partly caused by an internal quota system which obliges each judge to hear a certain number of cases per month.[190] This crude metric ignores the fact that certain cases – such as bankruptcy cases – need significantly more time (and resources) to be resolved. As a result, judges often refuse to accept EBL cases which they see as preventing the fulfilment of the quotas (and, consequently, negatively affecting their career).

There are three possible ways to deal with judges' quotas. Firstly, the quota system can be removed completely. This is the simplest solution, but it is unlikely to happen in the short term. Secondly, the quota system can be adjusted to reflect that certain cases are more complex and take longer to resolve than others. One possible way is to assign credits to each case whereby resolving a simple case would earn the judge one point, while resolving a complex case – like many EBL cases – would earn them five points. The advantage of this system is that it considers the complexity of some EBL cases and rewards judges for resolving them. The downside, however, is that it is complicated and prone to subjective interpretation. A third option is to de-emphasise the role of case quotas and incorporate them as one of many metrics of judges' performance. As above, adjusting the quota system is subject to approval from the national and local government, and possibly also the SPC. Without their cooperation – and understanding – the change is unlikely to take place due to the political control of the judiciary.[191]

---

[185] See discussion in Section 3.2.2.

[186] Under Art 113 employees' claims enjoyed absolute priority, but this only applies to those claims which occurred prior to the promulgation of the EBL (Art 132), and so is by now ineffective.

[187] See Sections 4.2.11, 6.1.2–6.1.3 and 10.2.4–10.2.6.

[188] See Section 11.3.4.

[189] See Section 11.2.2.1.

[190] See Section 8.1.3.

[191] See Section 2.4.1.

The SPC recognised this problem and issued guidance in 2019, ordering a change in judges' performance evaluation in the context of the EBL. This initiative is examined in Section 12.11.

11.3.4. Change Incentives of Local Governments

Once practitioners and judges know how to use the EBL, the last major obstacle to the independent enforcement of the EBL are the protectionism and interference from local governments.[192] Two sets of reforms are proposed so as to encourage local governments to allow greater and more independent use of the EBL. Section 11.3.4.1 below examines various ways which can help the local governments appreciate that bankruptcy law holds immense potential for the economic development of their regions.[193] Section 11.3.4.2 suggests that the structure and substance of local government incentives must be changed in order to help encourage local government support for greater use of the EBL.

The interventions proposed in this section must be carried out with utmost respect and sensitivity to the political economy of China and the individual needs of each province.[194] The Chinese (as well as international) understanding and expertise in bankruptcy law, the insights offered by the economic theory and the practical implications of development will be useful as guides when finalising the details of the reform.

11.3.4.1. *Enhance Local Government Understanding of the Need for the EBL*

Sections 8.3 and 9.2 suggested that local governments prevent courts from accepting EBL petitions and that, even where EBL cases are allowed, local governments often interfere in the process. Some of the reasons why local governments interfere were addressed elsewhere – most importantly those relating to China's social security system (in Section 11.2.2.1 above) and systemic interconnectedness of state companies (in Section 11.2.2.2 above). This section focuses on local government attitudes towards bankruptcy law in general, and proposes that greater willingness to allow local courts to hear EBL cases can be achieved through improving local government officials' understanding of the benefits of using the EBL.

One way to achieve this is to organise a series of local and intra-provincial conferences and sessions led by bankruptcy law experts with the aim to explain and persuade local governments to allow greater use of the EBL. Close cooperation should be established with the Party School as well as the SASAC, SAIC and representatives of local

---

[192] Such interference appears to be fairly frequent: Section 8.3.

[193] The local governments in some provinces already understand this. For example, the local governments and courts in Zhejiang Province and Jiangsu Province have been very active and have proposed and have been testing many of the recent reform initiatives discussed in ch 12.

[194] My interviewees (C1-c, C3-c, C5-r to C7-s, C11-c, J1-c to J9-c, L2-s to L6-s, L10-s to L15-c, P1-r, C3-r, R10-c) suggested that the political pressure and protectionism are more pronounced in less developed, inland provinces.

governments in regions where the EBL is widely used in order to gather their views and experience, and take note of their fears and needs.

The next step would be to deliver a series of training sessions where an expert would outline why China (or a particular region) needs to use the EBL more and what are the benefits of faster-paced, more objective judicial involvement (this can focus on private, smaller companies in the first instance, but the rationale is similar to SOEs, too). It is also important that, in each province, the sessions address the particular reasons for local government opposition to the EBL. The key focus is on showing local governments that aside from short-term costs, using the EBL produces many medium- and long-term benefits in terms of economic development, increased FDI flows, increased business activity and greater availability of cheaper credit. It is essential to illustrate all claims with case studies from China as well as other (similar) countries.

The sessions should also explain why the (reformed) EBL may be more efficient than alternative solutions to corporate distress such as bailouts and other financial support to ailing companies (as is the case with many SOEs and zombie companies); why debt-for-equity swaps (currently preferred in zombie companies) may be problematic; how to deal with employees (drawing on the issue of implementation of social security system in China and elsewhere); the benefit of better information sharing by companies and what local governments can do about it (drawing on the issue of information sharing and property register in China and elsewhere); the distortions caused by the exclusion of shadow finance creditors from bankruptcy law regime; and the benefit of allowing and encouraging courts to hear more EBL cases – even those concerning non-protected, non-state-controlled companies. My interviewees further suggested that the sessions' impact can be maximised by being as practical as possible. This could involve examples of well-executed liquidation and reorganisation cases in other provinces and abroad.[195]

A similar session could also be arranged as a roundtable or a workshop that would bring together representatives such as practitioners and judges, companies, state and non-state lenders, and possibly also academics and consultants to talk with local government representatives about the EBL (its challenges and opportunities) from their perspective.

11.3.4.2. *Change Structure and Substance of Local Government Officials' Incentives*

Besides persuasion, local governments are also likely to respond to additional pro-EBL incentives. Sections 2.4.2 and 8.3.2 discussed how local government officials have to fulfil simple targets that measure economic development and maintenance of social stability in order to progress their career. However, the way that these targets are set up means that officials tend to focus on delivering local, short-term benefits through protectionism, cover-ups of corporate financial distress, and inefficient allocation of

---

[195] A different format of this has already been implemented when the SPC released the typical cases in 2018 and 2020: see Sections 4.3–4.4 and 12.6–12.7.

funds and other resources – at the expense of longer-term, sustainable economic growth and slower, efficiency-enhancing projects. In light of China's economic slowdown, such short-termist behaviour cannot be allowed to continue.

To deal with this issue, the simple targets should be de-emphasised and changed to include other elements that will be rewarded. These should include, inter alia, rewarding innovation and competition-enhancing, long-termist policies. Rewarding innovation would encourage local experimentation and localised risk-taking, including allowing EBL cases to be heard by courts where this would be likely to lead to economic development. Similarly, rewarding local governments for encouraging long-term efficiency and for policing healthy competition among local companies would also most likely encourage greater and more efficient use of the EBL because local governments would be rewarded for permitting hard budget constraints and survival of the fittest – rather than being punished for temporary drops in productivity and economic growth which are natural consequences of using bankruptcy law.

Such positive encouragements should also be backed up by a credible threat of punishment for certain (clearly defined) types of wrongdoing. This should include, in particular, severe punishments for falsifying data and for cover-ups as well as increased likelihood of discovery through, eg, more checks in order to change the payoffs of officials' options when reporting economic data to their superiors.[196]

11.3.5. Judicial Independence and the Possibility of Limited Assistance from the Party-state

The initiatives proposed earlier in this chapter would ameliorate courts' and lawyers' limitations and improve their understanding and willingness to use the EBL as written. They would also help local governments understand why they should limit or altogether avoid intervening in EBL cases. Together, the proposed reforms would serve as a foundation that would enable (greater) judicial independence in hearing EBL cases.

At the moment, Chinese judges are not independent[197] and, realistically, any intervention aimed at full judicial independence in China in the short term is unlikely to succeed. Nevertheless, this section explores three reasons why it is crucial for greater and more efficient use of the EBL to enable and strengthen judicial independence in the medium-to-long-term. The discussion concludes by acknowledging that Party-state's assistance can be helpful in more complex cases, but that such assistance must not – and does not need to – be in conflict with judicial independence. Instead, it should only ever come at the court's request and must be limited in scope.

There are three reasons why it is important to enable and protect judicial independence in China. Firstly, judicial independence ensures objective enforcement of the law. It was argued in Section 10.2 that objectively enforced EBL could lead to improved control of bad debt, a greater amount of cheaper credit, more efficient allocation of resources, a

---

[196] ie make it more costly to lie. See Section 2.4.2.
[197] See Sections 2.4 and 8.3.

better business environment which encourages more investment and entrepreneurship, and the improved rule of law. Unfortunately, at present, courts often cannot enforce the EBL without Party-state's interference. Similarly, creditors and debtors are also influenced by representatives of their local government when deciding whether and how to resolve their or their debtor's financial distress.[198]

Objective enforcement of the EBL would have its costs, but they would be far outweighed by the likely benefits. On the one hand, state-sector companies benefit from state protectionism, support and subsidies – which would be (largely) lost if the law was objectively enforced. However, on the other hand, the cost of such protectionism is that they also have to follow state orders and preferences. State interference may lead to localised short-term gains – such as more employment and social stability – but local protectionism and biased law enforcement is also very costly and potentially damaging to the economic efficiency and market development in the long term.[199] Moreover, state interference in corporate financial distress makes doing business more unpredictable and risky.[200] Similarly, state protectionism creates moral hazard whereby, if the Government always steps in to rescue state-sector businesses, these businesses do not need to be careful in their decision-making and their investments.[201] Such protectionism also distorts market competition. All my interviewees suggested that a withdrawal of local government interference would allow companies and banks to decide whether to use the EBL depending on economic rather than political reasons. Moreover, they also agreed that it would enable judges to accept and decide EBL cases on their own merit rather than based on local governments' preferred interests. Such development is highly desirable.

Secondly, courts, debtors and creditors obey the Party-state's orders, but many fundamentally disagree with such political interference. Several of my interviewees suggested that many state-sector companies and banks do not like state interference in law enforcement and the resolution of their financial affairs, but that they feel unable to do anything about it.[202] Similarly, in another study, many state-sector companies complained that despite recent financial reforms there are 'few fathers-in-law, but still too many mothers-in-law'[203] – meaning that there is less protectionism from national ministries and bureaus than before the marketisation of China's economy commenced, but there are still too many intervening local government agencies, regulators and other local bodies which, like proverbial Chinese mothers-in-law, chase SOEs – their daughters-in-law – and make them do their bidding.[204] State interventions are also

---

[198] For details, see Sections 2.4, 8.3, 9.2 and 10.2.3.

[199] See Section 2.4 and discussion below. See also eg S Heilmann (ed), *China's Political System* (Rowman & Littlefield, 2017) ch 4; M Pei, *China's Trapped Transition* (Harvard University Press, 2006) 126–27; CC Coughlin, KA Chrystal and GE Wood, 'Protectionist Trade Policies: A Survey of Theory, Evidence and Rationale' (January/February 1988, Federal Reserve Bank of St Louis).

[200] ibid.

[201] See Section 10.2.4.

[202] Interviews B1-c to B3-c, C1-c, C4-c, C5-r, C7-s, E5-c, J1-c, J3-c to J9-c, L1-r to L15-c, P1-r, R2-r, R3-r, R6-c, R7-c, R9-c, R10-c, R13-c.

[203] gonggong shaole, popo hai henduo (公公少了，婆婆还很多): A Tang and A Ward, *The Changing Face of Chinese Management* (Routledge, 2003) 49.

[204] This is confirmed in Interviews B1-c to B3-c, C1-c, C4-c, C5-r, C7-s, E5-c, J1-c, J3-c to J9-c, L1-r to L15-c, P1-r, R2-r, R3-r, R6-c, R7-c, R9-c, R10-c, R13-c.

increasingly resented among the judiciary.[205] A recent SPC study stated that over 68 per cent of interviewed judges thought that local protectionism was one of the main reasons for unfairness in judicial decisions.[206] An empirical study of reorganisations of listed companies in China also heavily criticised local government interference for being justified, inefficient and harmful to the economy.[207]

Finally, without an independent judiciary, many parties are forced to use non-EBL alternatives to resolve their financial distress which is problematic and often also inefficient. State-sector companies often have little or no say in how their distress is resolved – and are often forced to use politically driven alternatives.[208] Similarly, many private-sector companies are left without a formal mechanism for resolving their financial distress because courts in many provinces are reluctant to accept EBL petition without an express blessing from the Party-state.[209] However, available data and my interviewees suggest that debt enforcement through non-EBL alternatives[210] is often problematic because private alternatives may involve undesirable behaviour (eg violence) and state-led alternatives can be inefficient compared to the reformed EBL.[211] Therefore, it is undesirable for the Party-state to continue using these alternatives in most cases.[212] Instead, courts should be allowed to apply the EBL objectively, and the parties should be encouraged to arrange their affairs in accordance with the law as written.

There are many examples of state interference in EBL cases.[213] Indeed, the typical EBL cases that were released by the SPC in 2018 and 2020 highlighted local government assistance and praised its importance for resolving EBL cases.[214] However, the unlimited ability of local governments to step in and interfere with the EBL's implementation is harmful – as explained above – and undesirable. Excessive state powers in the bankruptcy process were identified as problematic under the 1986 law and were removed in the final version of the EBL.[215] Even before the EBL was finalised, during a discussion of one of its later drafts in 2004, Wang Liming delivered a powerful speech in the NPC[216] where he called for the removal of state interference and its replacement by market-driven application of China's bankruptcy law in order to introduce healthy market competition, ensure the survival of the fittest (and exit of inefficient companies),

---

[205] As one judge (J8-c) put it: 'Many judges would be perfectly capable of making independent decisions and help companies devise good solutions, only if they had the freedom to do so'. Interviews C5-r, C7-s, L2-s to L7-c, L10-s to L17-c also expressly shared this view.

[206] Congressional-Executive Commission on China, 'Judicial Independence in the PRC', available at www.cecc.gov/judicial-independence-in-the-prc.

[207] H Zhao, *Government Intervention in the Reorganisation of Listed Companies in China* (Cambridge University Press, 2020) chs 3 and 5.

[208] See Section 9.2.

[209] See Section 8.3.

[210] See ch 9.

[211] See Section 10.2.1.

[212] Arguably, there are limited circumstances in which state intervention is desirable – such as to prevent financial crisis or failure of a core element in financial infrastructure (eg a bank). However, such interventions should be exceptional, not regular.

[213] See Sections 8.3 and 9.2.

[214] See Section 4.3.

[215] See Section 4.1.

[216] See Section 10.1.3.

prevent avoidable financial risk and excessive lending to over-indebted companies (which leads to the creation of more NPLs, which burden the economy), and improve the business environment for current and future market participants.

Independent application of the EBL is very important. However, that does not mean that the Party-state's support in EBL cases is undesirable or unhelpful. On the contrary, the Party-state can provide invaluable assistance and support to the courts. Such assistance is especially important in more complex cases that require coordination and support from various departments in order to reach a solution in a timely and efficient manner.[217] The Party-state can help by arranging new funding, making introductions, finding partners for future cooperation, resettling employees, encouraging state agencies to speed up administrative processes and remove red tape.[218] Unfortunately, to date, the Party-state has not only helped resolve EBL cases, but it has done so while protecting state-preferred interests. That is unacceptable and harmful to the economy.

However, it may be possible to have the best of both regimes: to allow and encourage the Party-state to continue in helping the courts resolve EBL, but limit such assistance to acts and support that do not in any way restrict judicial independence in hearing and deciding the EBL cases. For such court–government cooperation to work, it is crucial that the EBL cases are primarily driven by the courts and that any state assistance (note, not intervention, which would denote a change in the power structure in this context) is provided at the court's request and only to the extent necessary to force the relevant departments to cooperate and encourage the parties to talk. Therefore, the assistance should be limited to the formal enabling of a smooth process rather than substantive influencing of the outcomes. This would ensure that procedural delays and conflicts among various state branches that are involved in listed companies and large interconnected companies would be removed or at least minimised.[219] At the same time, the law would be applied objectively and independently. This would improve parties' ability to foresee the likely outcome of their actions and enable them to plan ex ante their behaviour according to the law, which would, in turn, enhance proper functioning of the market.

Section 12.12 discusses some recent development in the relationship between courts and the Government. This discussion is important, but it is crucial that judicial independence is maintained and that state support is only permitted within the limits of judicial independence. There is no substitute for judicial independence in this context. That is the only way how the rule of law can be reinstated in this area, how the resolution of financial distress can lead to more predictability and efficiency in the market, and how excessive overindebtedness and further creation of zombie companies and similar problems can be avoided. So long as local governments are allowed to protect their own interests in the context of corporate distress – whether under the EBL or through the use of non-EBL alternatives – the EBL will not be able to maintain market order and the benefits of bankruptcy law seen elsewhere (greater availability

---

[217] The importance of state support in coordinating EBL case has been highlighted by Professor Li Shuguang at the Seminar on the 10th Anniversary of the Implementation of the Corporate Bankruptcy Law in B Lu (12.9.2017, People's Court News). See also section 8.3.3.

[218] See section 8.3.5.

[219] See section 12.12.

of cheaper credit, more efficient allocation of resources, entrepreneurship)[220] will not materialise in China.

11.3.6. Practical Impact and Conclusion

The proposals contained in this final subset of reforms are likely to pose many challenges to the reformers, but their implementation is crucial for achieving efficient use of the EBL in the long term. The key challenge – in particular with regards to judicial independence, discussed in Section 11.3.5 above – arises from the fact that change cannot be effectuated simply by writing more laws or changing existing rules. Instead, change needs to come from an adjustment of enforcers' attitude and understanding – both of which are likely to face opposition and take time.

Some of the proposals in this chapter – especially in Sections 11.3.1–11.34 above – concern areas with recent reform initiatives. Chinese courts have undergone several major reforms[221] – some local, others national – and as a result their level of professionalism, knowledge and skills have been increasing steadily over the last few years.[222] With the economy slowing down – particularly since late 2014 – and with the increase in the amount of NPLs, financially distressed companies, and changes in demand patterns (domestically and internationally), China's courts and Government have slowly come to admit that the current regime for resolving financial distress is insufficient and that more needs to be done.[223] Several reform initiatives have been tested locally in recent years, and their progress is discussed in Chapter twelve.

The EBL has returned to the Government's and courts' agendas, and steps have been taken to improve the system for dealing with corporate financial distress. If this trend continues and as a result courts' and lawyers' understanding is improved, court enforcement of the EBL as written is strengthened, and local government understanding and incentives are ameliorated to allow greater use of the EBL, then independent judicial enforcement may – one day – become a reality. If that happens – that is, if the courts become able to decide each case on its merits, and not based on the Party-state's wishes – it would most likely result in a number of benefits, most importantly greater efficiency of EBL procedures in practice which would, in turn, help deliver the predicted benefits – ie greater availability of cheaper credit, better allocation of resources and better business environment.[224] Until then, reform efforts should continue to focus on proposals in Sections 11.1, 11.2 and 11.3.1–11.3.4.

---

[220] See Section 1.2.

[221] For a critique of the limitations of the reform see B Liebman, China's Courts: Restricted Reform (2008) *Columbia Journal of Asian Law* 1.

[222] The reforms have been on the agenda since China's entry into the international market in 2001, but they have become particularly pronounced since the SPC released its Notice concerning Practising Justice for the People, 'Strengthening Fair Justice and Increasing Credibility of the Judiciary' (*Fafa* [2013] No 9). See eg S Finder (26.3.2015, The Diplomat); R Peerenboom, 'A Tale of Two Judiciaries: Judicial Enforcement of Economic and Social Rights in China and India' (2013), available at ssrn.com/abstract=2211911.

[223] For government reactions see eg L Lopez (21.12.2015, Business Insider).

[224] See Section 1.2.

12

Recent Reform Initiatives 2015–20

This chapter seeks to complete the discussion of China's EBL, its limitations and the options for reform, with a summary of important developments and reform initiatives that took place between October 2015 (when the Party-state identified improving the EBL as one of its priorities) and June 2020 (where this book ends). Section 12.1 below considers the key steps that led to the refocusing on the EBL as a political priority and it summarises what has happened so far. Section 12.2 then provides a summary of key local initiatives and locally tested national initiatives. The discussion refers back to the reform proposals in chapter eleven and evaluates the scope of the initiatives and the obstacles that they have faced in practice. Sections 12.3 to 12.12 then contain detailed discussions of the reform initiatives. Where possible, real-life cases and detailed rules have been provided to allow the reader to dig deeper if they wish. Finally, Section 12.13 considers the likely impact of these initiatives on the EBL and China's economy in general.

12.1. What Set Off Recent Bankruptcy Law Reform?

The EBL moved into the spotlight from late 2015 to late 2017, but it has remained an important supporting mechanism for other reforms since then. With the economy slowing down – particularly since late 2014 – and with the increase in the volume of NPLs and financially distressed companies, and the changes in demand patterns (domestically and internationally), China's courts and the Party-state have slowly come to admit that the current regime for resolving corporate financial distress is insufficient and that more needs to be done.[1] This set the wheels in motion. In October 2015, the 5th Plenary Session of the 18th Central Committee of the Party announced that it is necessary to allow market mechanisms and the rule of law to resolve corporate over-capacity and improve market exit of insolvent companies. In December 2015, China's Central Economic Work Conference – an important annual meeting where China's President and Premier present the economic achievements of the previous year and set the economic agenda for the following year – announced that tackling underproductivity was one of the five big national goals for 2016, which led to a renewed interest in bankruptcy law and the question of its greater use.[2] Their concluding report emphasised

---

[1] For government reactions see eg L Lopez (21.12.2015, Business Insider).
[2] For a summary see Xinhua (24.11.2015).

that market forces would play a bigger role in the allocation of resources, and those struggling to keep up with the forces of demand and supply and those who are unable to manage their finances would be pushed to 'exit the market'.[3] The EBL was identified as the key rule-of-law solution which could resolve inefficient overcapacity, optimise the allocation of resources, and improve the quality of the business environment and the efficiency of companies in China.[4]

Improving the implementation of the EBL also became a central part of China's 13th Five-year Plan (2016–20).[5] In order to help deal with structural overcapacity, the EBL were to be allowed to be applied as written; the process was to become more market-driven; the trials were to become quicker and more efficient; disposal of the NPLs and re-employment of laid-off workers was to be of primary interest; and courts were told to 'merge and reorganise' rather than liquidate the struggling companies.[6]

Commenting on the 2015 report of the Central Economic Work Conference, Wang Xinxin highlighted the report's emphasis on market-driven implementation of the EBL. He said:

> The implementation of bankruptcy laws in different regions in China, especially the imple-
> mentation driven by market forces and hard budget constraints, is uneven. [...] In some
> places where there are few bankruptcy cases, the acceptance of bankruptcy cases must be
> resolved first, and then the marketization problem can be gradually solved. [...] There are
> many deficiencies and defects. However, only by actively and steadily accepting bankruptcy
> cases can we achieve market-driven implementation of the EBL. [...] The task of 'creating
> conditions to improve bankruptcy procedures' is not to push the government back to the
> old policy-based bankruptcy path of non-market and illegal governance of administrative
> intervention. The market-oriented implementation of the bankruptcy law is a profound social
> revolution, everyone still needs to work hard![7]

His comments clearly show the importance of removing the Party-state' interference in EBL cases, similar to what was argued in Sections 11.3.4 and 11.3.5. Many small steps have been taken in the interim. Nevertheless, so far, his call has not been answered.

The changes initially focused on resolving zombie companies – ie heavily indebted SOEs which cannot survive without state financial support.[8] One of the first official meetings where the new strategy was discussed was the SPC's 8th National Conference for Civil and Commercial Judges in late December 2015, where senior judges from across China convened to discuss trends and developments over the past year and in the near future. It was at this conference where Judge Yang Linping of the No 2 Civil Division of the SPC provided some guidance on how the courts should deal with EBL cases.[9] Judge Yang said that the judges should make it easier for zombie companies to petition for and go through EBL procedures. Judges must distinguish between real and fraudulent bankruptcies in order to prevent malicious avoidance of debt repayment,

---

[3] Xinhua (21.12.2015).
[4] ibid. See also the Preamble to the SPC Provisions (III) concerning the Application of the EBL (*Fashi* [2019] No.3).
[5] Xinhua (12.12.2019).
[6] ibid.
[7] X Wang (6.12.2016, People's Court News).
[8] See Sections 9.2.2, 10.1.2, 10.2.1 and 10.3.
[9] For an overview in English, see SPC Monitor (16.1.2016).

and they must always ask whether the financial distress was caused by the criminal conduct of those in charge, and if so, punish it. She also said that judges should monitor administrators to make sure that they are recovering assets,[10] and higher courts should monitor lower courts to ensure correct handling of EBL cases. In addition, EBL reorganisation should be used, particularly for large companies with a valuable business worth saving. Other-than-zombie companies were, however, not discussed at this stage.

Further guidance was provided in February 2016, when the SPC held a conference in Zhejiang to discuss how to deal with zombie companies. Judge Du Wanhua, a senior SPC judge in charge of national EBL reform efforts, presided over the proceedings. He echoed Judge Yang in supporting more reorganisation and composition cases. He also said that modern technology should be used to inform the people of the possibility of using the EBL, in particular the reorganisation mechanism, so as to enable maximum recoveries. Local courts should also establish bankruptcy divisions and judges receive expert training to enable them to hear EBL cases. Procedures for hearing an EBL case should be consolidated across courts, and administrators should be given more guidelines and better status. He also added, however, that courts must protect interests of the state, then those of employees, then creditors, and finally investors.[11] Courts were instructed to devote more resources to the resolution of zombie companies which 'occupy valuable credit, land resources and market space. Therefore, it is important to either restructure or liquidate such companies under the bankruptcy law'.[12] Following the official guidance, many zombie companies were closed down since 2016. The SPC as well as the Ministry of Finance and governmental agencies were heavily involved in the process.[13]

The importance of resolving zombie companies was reiterated by the Central Economic Work Conference in December 2016 and removing zombie companies from the market was set as a target for 2017.[14] In addition, it was also agreed that corporate debts need to be properly resolved rather than ignored or temporarily replaced by bridging loans. To this end, the experts agreed that 'It is necessary to support the market-oriented and rule-of-law debt-to-equity swaps of enterprises, increase equity financing, strengthen the debt constraints of enterprises' own debts, and reduce the leverage ratio of enterprises'.[15] Excess capacity in traditional industries was to be reduced in 2017. The experts also agreed that the Government and courts should focus on strengthening the protection of property rights and reduce funding into real estate development in order to deflate the real estate bubble.[16]

In June 2017, China celebrated 10 years since the implementation of the EBL. A seminar was held to discuss the law and its achievements. The experts celebrated the many successes,[17] but they also mourned the fact that the EBL is rarely used in practice

---

[10] As discussed above in Section 8.2.
[11] cf Section 4.2.11 (priority of distribution under the EBL).
[12] Sina (28.1.2016).
[13] For a summary, see SPC Monitor (26.2.2017).
[14] People's Daily (17.12.2016).
[15] ibid.
[16] Following a motto: 'houses are for living, not for speculation' (ibid).
[17] See Section 4.1.

and that the law represents an 'unfinished reform'.[18] They called for further reform, more clarity of certain EBL provisions, more speedy use of the law, and generally more efficient exit for insolvent companies.

Even more important EBL-focused conference was the SPC Shenzhen National Bankruptcy Trial Work Conference in December 2017.[19] It brought together many senior judges and Party-state leaders to summarise what has been achieved and make a plan for further improvements to the EBL. Importantly, it built on the work and decisions of the 19th National Congress of the Communist Party in October 2017 which highlighted the importance of the EBL for the economy and resolution of problems in the corporate sector in the following few years.[20] The summary of the conference highlighted important EBL-related policies and contained many proposals and calls for further reform.[21] The President of the SPC, Judge Zhou Qiang, reiterated the preference for merging and reorganising over liquidating distressed companies. He also called for an establishment of specialised bankruptcy courts in intermediate courts in larger cities and economically developed areas.[22] In addition, he also suggested that the courts should explore the use of a simplified EBL procedure and a pre-reorganisation system (akin to the English pre-packs).[23] More broadly, he also reminded the courts that they must follow the Party's leadership and policies.

Judge Du Wanhua, who was in charge of the EBL reform until his retirement in 2017, called on lower courts to improve the professionalism of courts; improve and upgrade the bankruptcy administrator system (including the establishment of an expenses fund to make sure that bankruptcy expenses are covered even where debtor's property is insufficient); speed up the resolution of EBL cases; maximise the use of market-driven reorganisation; beware of excessive use of cramdown powers in reorganisation; introduce a streamlined EBL mechanism for simpler cases; establish a government-courts coordinated system;[24] be careful when dealing with cases that involve guarantees and cases involving corporate affiliates; encourage debt-for-equity swaps and other pro-survival mechanisms; and improve cross-border bankruptcy. Professor Li Shuguang also delivered a speech in which he identified several challenges facing courts when hearing EBL cases. He said that the relationship between the state and courts in EBL cases is often unclear;[25] many courts refuse to accept EBL petitions and some established additional (unreasonable) barriers to filing EBL petitions; the rules about selection, oversight and day-to-day operation of administrators need to be more detailed; rights of creditors and debtors must be protected according to the EBL rather than to please the local governments; and the need to expand on the rules about liquidation. He also

---

[18] See the Seminar on the 10th Anniversary of the Implementation of the Corporate Bankruptcy Law in B Lu (12.9.2017, People's Court News).

[19] For an overview and commentary, see SPC Monitor (31.12.2017).

[20] See eg Xi Jinping's report delivered at the NPC on 18.10.2017, available at www.xinhuanet.com/english/download/Xi_Jinping's_report_at_19th_CPC_National_Congress.pdf.

[21] The SPC Minutes of the National Bankruptcy Trial Work Conference (issued on 3.4.2018).

[22] See Section 12.3.

[23] See Section 12.8. Note that pre-packs are already being used in China: see Sections 8.3.4–8.3.5, 9.2.3 and 11.1.2.1.

[24] See Section 11.3.5.

[25] This concerns eg political interventions in court hearings and the legal status of any pre-EBL deals made with the assistance of a local government.

echoed Judge Du with regards to cases involving corporate affiliates and the importance of clarifying the rules about cross-border bankruptcies.[26] Overall, said Professor Li, the EBL in its current form is inadequate and the SPC alone cannot fill the many gaps to make the law work.

At the next Central Economic Work Conference in December 2017, it was decided that further EBL-driven resolution of zombie companies should be encouraged in order to support the shift in the focus of China's economy from traditional manufacturing to modern innovation, and from speed to quality. It followed the 19th National Congress of the Communist Party in October 2017 which made a top-down decision to move China 'toward the mid-to-high end of the global value chain and cultivate world-class advanced manufacturing clusters'.[27] The EBL was seen as an important tool also in its aim to improve property rights protection, ensure market-based allocation of resources, and speed up reform and opening up.

The EBL continued to play a supporting role for the goals identified at the Central Economic Work Conference in December 2018 as well.[28] The economic goals for 2019 focused on reducing local government debt and improving the business environment. The latter goal was supported by several proposals. Firstly, the aim was 'to steadily promote the survival of the fittest, accelerate the disposal of zombie enterprises, formulate implementation measures for [market] withdrawal'.[29] The language and focus on removal of zombie companies echo the earlier policies. And secondly, the Government was to 'adhere to the principles of separation of government and enterprise, separation of government and capital'.[30] In short, it was acknowledged that government intervention in corporate affairs could be harmful and lead to short-term, inefficient outcomes. It was, therefore, decided that it was 'necessary to effectively change the government's functions, significantly reduce the government's direct allocation of resources [...]. Whenever the market can adjust itself, let the market adjust, and if the company can, let the enterprise do it'.[31] The importance of limiting local government intervention was highlighted in Sections 11.3.4–11.3.5, but there has been no significant shift in this regard in the context of EBL hearings in practice.

The SPC has also been contributing to further clarification of the EBL rules. In March 2018, the SPC released 10 typical EBL cases to educate lower courts about their role in EBL procedures and to illustrate how they can assist in resolving complex commercial issues and restructuring corporate financial distress.[32] The cases also highlighted that local governments play an important role in the EBL process.

In March 2019, the SPC released the SPC Provisions (III) concerning the Application of the EBL (*Fashi* [2019] No 3), which provided further clarification of the EBL rules about bankruptcy expenses, post-petition lending, debtor's guarantees and creditors' rights and powers.[33] At the press conference where the Provisions were presented,

---

[26] See also ch 13.
[27] Full report at www.gov.cn/xinwen/2017-12/20/content_5248899.htm.
[28] Full report at www.gov.cn/xinwen/2018-12/21/content_5350934.htm.
[29] ibid.
[30] ibid.
[31] ibid.
[32] See Section 4.3.3.
[33] See Section 4.3.1.

Judge Liu Guixiang, a member of the SPC Judicial Committee, said that the guidance aims to ensure a stable, fair, transparent and predictable business environment which would liberate productivity and improve the competitiveness of China and Chinese businesses.[34] It responded to some of the issues that were highlighted at the Shenzhen National Bankruptcy Trial Work Conference in December 2017.[35]

The SPC further discussed the EBL at the SPC Work Conference in July 2019.[36] Judge Liu Guixiang said that courts must do more to enable effective implementation of the EBL. He highlighted, in particular, the need to strengthen the coordination of government and court efforts in cases of corporate bankruptcy. He also acknowledged that the SPC should introduce another judicial interpretation to clarify the law and remove the existing obstacles to insolvent liquidation and reorganisation. Moreover, the SPC and local courts should also issue judicial interpretations and policies concerning issues such as bond defaults, equity pledges of listed companies, and Internet lending practices that directly affect financial security and social stability.

Finally, in March 2020, the SPC released eight more typical EBL cases – this time with a focus on how the courts can help companies deal with the damaging effect of the coronavirus pandemic.[37] The cases were supposed to show that the EBL mechanisms can promote economic recovery after the pandemic, and illustrated what the courts can do to help already struggling companies on practical examples.

As the economy keeps slowing down, the courts' role in improving China's business environment has been repeatedly highlighted. The Central Political and Legal Work Conference in January 2020 concluded that it is necessary to create a better legal environment – one that is stable and predictable, and governed by the rule of law – to support the development of private companies.[38] Importantly, it called for equal protection of private and state companies in court, including when resolving their financial distress and bankruptcy. As was discussed earlier, private companies' EBL petitions are often ignored by courts,[39] a fact that was acknowledged by Professor Li Shuguang and others at the Shenzhen National Bankruptcy Trial Work Conference in December 2017.[40]

Similarly, when the SPC highlighted the significant improvement in China's World Bank ranking for the ease of doing business that was released in early 2020,[41] it drew attention to the fact that the improvement in resolving corporate bankruptcies was one of the reasons for the better overall ranking.[42] The SPC celebrated this success but also warned that more needs to be done.

The remainder of this chapter discusses the main reform initiatives and improvements to the EBL from 2015 to 2020 that have followed from the political and judicial

---

[34] Full text of Judge Liu's speech and the provisions at www.chinatrial.net.cn/news/27254.html.

[35] The SPC Notice concerning the Minutes of the National Work Conference on Bankruptcy Trials (*Fa* [2018] No 53).

[36] G Liu (3.7.2019, Weixin). See also Section 2.4.3.

[37] See Section 4.3.4.

[38] People's Court News (19.1.2020).

[39] See Sections 2.5, 8.1 and 8.3.

[40] Summarised in the SPC Notice concerning the Minutes of the National Work Conference on Bankruptcy Trials (*Fa* [2018] No 53).

[41] The ranking improved from 46th place in 2018 to 31st place in 2019: 'SPC takes up judicial responsibility to improve China's business environment' SPC announcement on 11.6.2020.

[42] China ranked 51st (up from 61st place in 2018): ibid.

statements discussed above. Much has been achieved and the EBL continues to offer essential mechanisms for market exit and corporate restructuring which, together, improve China's business environment.

12.2. Summary of Key Reforms 2015–20

The overview of the political and judicial meetings, statements and decisions concerning the EBL from 2015 to 2020 clearly shows that there has been an increased level of interest in the EBL. Policy-makers, expert observers and judges realised that the EBL has been broken and many proposals and initiatives aimed at fixing the law have been discussed.[43] However, not all issues that were identified in Chapters six to nine have been addressed and even those issues that have been addressed have not yet been fully resolved.

The key reform initiatives that have been tested and implemented between 2015 and 2020 – which are discussed in the remainder of this chapter – originated from three sources: central Party-state, the SPC, and local-level courts and governments. It was the Party-state that authorised the initial commencement of the EBL review process in 2015.[44] However, the detailed rules and improvements have mostly come from the SPC and local-level courts and governments. Some of the reforms were ordered by the SPC – for example, the introduction of specialised bankruptcy courts[45] and the launch of the online EBL platform.[46] The SPC has also set the general approach to the EBL for lower courts and its interpretations and typical cases[47] have provided top-down guidance and preferred solutions to particular problems. However, most of the detailed rules and initiatives that are discussed below were produced and tested locally. Such initiatives usually take a long time to be ready for national implementation. The process off trial-and-error must be concluded at a local level, the issues resolved and the likely obstacles explored and minimised before they can be implemented nationwide. The EBL itself was initially drafted and tested as a local regulation in Shenzhen.[48] Similarly, many of the recent reforms discussed in this chapter were first formulated and are still being tested at local level – for example, the rules governing simplified EBL hearing and personal bankruptcy.[49]

The remainder of this chapter discusses seven major and three smaller, largely underdeveloped reform initiatives. Section 12.3 examines the initiative that set off the reform process in China – the resolution of zombie companies. Section 12.4 discusses the introduction of specialised bankruptcy courts. Section 12.5 looks at the online EBL platform and examines how it reduces information asymmetry and improves transparency and predictability. Section 12.6 considers the judicial and political guidance and its role in improving the functioning of the EBL in practice. Section 12.7 explores local

---

[43] See ch 11.
[44] See Section 12.1.
[45] See Section 12.4.
[46] See Section 12.5.
[47] See Section 4.3.
[48] See Section 4.1.
[49] See Sections 12.8 and 12.9.

initiatives that aim to educate and share local experience in dealing with EBL cases. Section 12.8 examines new rules on simplified EBL hearings, which have been tested at several local courts. Section 12.9 looks at new rules on dealing with personal bankruptcies, a topic that is not expressly covered by the EBL but is nevertheless crucial for effective resolution of financial distress in China. Section 12.10 examines the establishment of bankruptcy assistance funds in several provinces. Section 12.11 focuses on proposals and local rules for evaluating judges' performance in the context of EBL cases. And Section 12.12 looks at some recent developments in defining a proper relationship and the forms of cooperation between the courts and local governments. These initiatives show the determination and creativity of Chinese courts and judges, and the key role that they play in ensuring the proper functioning of the EBL in practice.

12.3. Reform 1: Encourage Greater Use of the EBL – Resolving Zombie Companies

As China's economy started slowing down and the amount of corporate debt kept increasing, the Government realised that it must act in order to stabilise the economy.[50] However, the EBL – which was the most obvious mechanism for restructuring distressed but viable companies and liquidating the rest – was rarely used in practice.[51] This was the case even with regards to zombie companies (*jiangshi qiye* 僵尸企业) – ie heavily indebted companies that rely on continuous financial support to survive[52] – because those in control of the EBL were afraid of liquidating the companies.[53] Local governments were unwilling to let these companies fail due to the fear that the resulting loss of state-owned assets, unemployment and likely social instability would reflect badly on them and so would negatively affect their performance and their career prospects.[54] Banks were afraid of raising the (reported) rate of non-performing assets.[55] And employees – represented by powerful labour unions – were afraid of losing their income which, in the absence of a well-functioning social security system, would be very difficult.[56] Only once the central Party-state ordered that these companies must be resolved – ie liquidated or reorganised under the EBL – did the local governments permit local courts to get to work.[57]

Focusing on zombie companies was an obvious starting point. Given that these companies were already technically insolvent – their debts exceeded their assets – they satisfied the EBL entry requirements.[58] There were many (primarily state-sector) companies that continued to be propped up by a string of (state-directed) bridging loans

---

[50] See Sections 3.1 and 12.1.
[51] See Sections 5.1 and 10.1.
[52] See Sections 9.2.1 and 10.1.2.
[53] Sina (28.3.2016). See also Sections 2.4.2 and 8.3.2.
[54] ibid.
[55] See the commentary on the 2015 Central Economic Work Conference by S Gao, 'Thinking on how to promote the supply-side reform' (10.5.2016).
[56] See Sections 7.2.1 and 11.2.1.
[57] See Section 12.1 and Sina (28.3.2016).
[58] See Section 4.2.2.

and financial injections.[59] There were also 265 listed companies in the A-share market whose earnings per share have been negative for three consecutive years – which were also labelled as zombie companies.[60]

However, resolving zombie companies is complicated as they commonly involve long-term relationships with other companies, a large number of assets (in some cases), many employees, different types of creditors, and political protectionism.[61] In order to detangle the pre-existing legal issues and come up with a fair and effective restructuring or liquidation plan, the hearing court needs a lot of EBL-related experience and expertise.

As a result, in February 2016, the SPC organised a national conference to discuss the disposal of zombie companies. The SPC issued the Memorandum concerning Hearing Bankruptcy Cases in accordance with the Law and Actively and Steadily Promoting Rescue and Liquidation of Bankrupt Companies,[62] which put forward clear and specific requirements and guidance on the disposal of zombie companies. Moreover, at least 10 regional high courts released judicial guidance and actively coordinated and cooperated with local governments in resolving zombie companies.[63] Several local (provincial) courts also issued White Papers on dealing with the disposal of assets.[64] In some cases, local governments also formulated guidance to support court work, to shorten the duration of resolving zombie companies under the EBL, and to ensure timely settlement of EBL matters more generally.[65]

The turning point in the resolution of zombie companies, however, was the creation of specialised bankruptcy courts.[66] In Guangzhou, for example, the creation of a specialised bankruptcy tribunal enabled the Guangzhou Intermediate People's Court to investigate the key issues and deepen the expertise of its judges to deal with zombie companies, which helped them resolve 164 provincial and municipal state-owned zombie enterprises by the end of 2017.[67] In 2018, more than 1,900 SASAC-related zombie companies were resolved in China, which resulted in a drop in SASAC-accounted losses by more than 200 billion RMB.[68] In addition, the Party-state continued to emphasise the need to resolve zombie companies in its annual nationwide strategy announcements.[69] As a result, the number of EBL cases surged, and courts resolved 6,257 EBL cases in 2017 and 11,669 EBL cases in 2018.[70]

However, even with the increase in the number of EBL cases, the cleaning up has not been fast enough – as argued by experts[71] and acknowledged by the Government.

---

[59] See Section 9.2.2.
[60] Gao (n 55).
[61] See Section 8.3.
[62] *Fa* [2016] No 169.
[63] Art 14 of the SPC Notice concerning the Minutes of the National Work Conference on Bankruptcy Trials (*Fa* [2018] No 53).
[64] Liu Guixiang's introduction to the 2018 typical cases, second point: see Section 4.3 and Sohu (8.3.2018).
[65] For example, the Zhejiang Provincial Government's Several Opinions concerning the Acceleration of the Disposal of Zombie Companies (*Zhezheng Banfa* [2017] No 136).
[66] Discussed in detail in Section 12.4.
[67] Liu Guixiang's introduction to the 2018 typical cases, fourth point: see Section 4.3 and Sohu (8.3.2018).
[68] Data quoted in Y Li (17.7.2019, ECNS).
[69] See Section 12.1.
[70] cf average 2,000–3,000 EBL cases per year until 2015: see Section 5.1.
[71] See eg T Huang (23.8.2019, PIIE).

To put more pressure on local governments and so speed up the process, the central Government said in December 2018 that all zombie companies should be resolved using the EBL by the end of 2020.[72] In June 2019, the National Development and Reform Commission (NDRC) – China's top economic planning agency – announced that in 2020 it would focus on researching international experience with clearing zombie companies[73] and called on local governments and courts to put even more effort to closing the remaining zombie companies before the deadline elapses.[74] The NDRC said that local government subsidies and loans would be cut and local governments would have to 'guide or force' zombie companies out of the market in order to improve corporate efficiency in the face of China's economic slowdown.[75]

Although more remains to be done, much has already been achieved. The push to use the EBL to resolve zombie companies has helped break the unhealthy reliance and interconnectedness of some state companies[76] and encouraged the clearing of many heavily indebted companies from the market. Moreover, the increased focus on the EBL that resulted from the removal of zombie companies made courts more willing to explore the use of the EBL in other types of cases as well. While hearing EBL cases, many issues were identified and are being resolved.[77] Many of the remaining reforms discussed below have been made possible, at least indirectly, by the initial push to resolve zombie companies in late 2015.

12.4. Reform 2: Specialised Bankruptcy Courts and Administrator Associations

Initially, EBL cases were heard by generalist civil courts with little or no experience and expertise necessary for resolving complex corporate bankruptcies.[78] Local courts and commentators have long called for an introduction of specialised judges who would be better positioned to deal with EBL-related issues.[79] The importance of establishing specialised bankruptcy courts more widely was reiterated by the SPC's President Zhou Qiang and Professor Li Shuguang at the Shenzhen National Bankruptcy Trial Work Conference in December 2017.[80] It was again repeated by Judge Liu Guixiang at the press conference when releasing the first batch of SPC's typical EBL cases in March 2018.[81]

---

[72] D Jing and L Cheng (5.12.2018, Caixin).
[73] 'Announcement for the collection of research topics of the Finance and Credit Construction Department in 2019' (6.6.2019), available at www.ndrc.gov.cn/fzggw/jgsj/cjd/sjdt/201906/t20190606_1111439.html.
[74] See also Y Li (17.7.2019, ECNS).
[75] ibid.
[76] See Section 7.2.2.
[77] The resolution of zombie companies helped ensure more accurate and objective enforcement of the EBL (Section 11.3.3) and illustrated that corporate bankruptcies could be effectively resolved without excessive reliance on local governments (Sections 8.3 and 11.3.3–11.3.5).
[78] Shenzhen was an exception: a specialised bankruptcy court existed there since 1993: Shenzhen Intermediate Court, Following the Development of the Guangdong-Hong Kong-Macao Greater Bay Area – What Kind of Butterfly Effect Will the Shenzhen Bankruptcy Court Bring? (22.4.2019).
[79] See Section 11.3.2. See also Zhejiang Changxing Court's Corporate Bankruptcy Trial White Paper and Ten Typical Cases (2012–18).
[80] See Section 12.1.
[81] See Sohu (8.3.2018) and Section 4.3.

In response to the prioritisation of resolving zombie companies and reducing overcapacity in China in December 2015,[82] the SPC released a notice calling for establishing specialised divisions in all of China's Intermediate Courts and increasing the number of bankruptcy judges in June 2016.[83] While China had only five (voluntarily created) specialised bankruptcy courts or divisions in 2015, following the SPC Notice, Zhejiang, Shandong and Shenzhen created specialised bankruptcy divisions by the end of July 2016. The rest of the country was supposed to follow by the end of 2016, but the progress has been relatively slow.[84] Nevertheless, by the end of 2018, there were 98 specialised bankruptcy divisions and standalone courts.[85] In 2019, many more specialised bankruptcy divisions were created and three standalone bankruptcy courts were established in Shenzhen, Beijing and Shanghai.[86] More specialised bankruptcy courts opened recently in several other places, including in Jinan, Nanjing and Qingdao in April 2020.[87]

A recent empirical study found that, since the introduction of specialised bankruptcy courts and divisions, corporate bankruptcies in China have benefited from a significant increase in the expertise of judges which has led to a quicker resolution of SOEs' bankruptcies under the EBL.[88] It has also led to an increase in the number of court-based bankruptcies (in particular liquidations) of local SOEs.[89] Interestingly, the study found that following the introduction of specialised bankruptcy courts and divisions, SOEs experience more limited access to bank finance (both in terms of size of loans and probability of getting a loan) while private companies experience better access to bank loans. The introduction of specialised courts, therefore, had a significant impact on the marketisation of China's economy.

To support the work of specialised courts, a number of bankruptcy administrator associations were established as well. In 2018, Chongqing, Jiangxi, and Zhejiang established provincial bankruptcy administrator associations, and more than 20 city-level administrator associations were established nationwide.[90] By September 2019, there were 42 bankruptcy administrator associations across China.[91] Many courts established local guidelines for choosing administrators and created official lists of eligible administrators. For example, Changxing Court in Zhejiang Province created such a list and grouped the administrators according to their qualifications and relevant experience.[92] Guidance notes were also released, stating that administrators for more complex cases should be chosen from the provincial-level court list where there is more expertise and experience.[93]

---

[82] See Section 12.1.
[83] The SPC Memorandum concerning the Establishment of Liquidation and Bankruptcy Trial Divisions in Intermediate People's Courts (*Fa* [2016] No 209).
[84] See SPC Monitor (30.6.2016).
[85] F Wang (29.3.2019, 21st Century Business Herald).
[86] J Sun, 'Current Trends in China's Bankruptcy Filings' (21.8.2019) Perkins Coie report.
[87] People's Court News (15.4.2020); Nanjing Daily (12.6.2020); Sina (23.4.2020).
[88] B Li and J Ponticelli, 'Going Bankrupt in China' (July 2020) NBER Working Paper No 27501.
[89] ibid. Although note that these were most likely zombie companies.
[90] Announced at the press conference when releasing the SPC Interpretation (III): full text available at www.chinatrial.net.cn/news/27254.html.
[91] The Paper (26.10.2019).
[92] Zhejiang Changxing Court's Corporate Bankruptcy Trial White Paper and Ten Typical Cases (2012–18).
[93] ibid.

The introduction of specialised courts and administrator associations addresses some of the issues identified earlier – particularly the lack of expertise, experience and consistency when applying the EBL.[94] Specialised judges quickly gain the necessary experience and tools for resolving complex EBL cases. Similarly, administrators benefit from the training and sharing events organised by the associations. Together, these initiatives have been instrumental in safeguarding more professional and transparent application of the law, more reliable and fairer protection for different groups of stakeholders and, ultimately, more predictable process outcomes which is desirable for an improved business environment. Hopefully, over time, more regions in China will introduce specialised courts and administrators' associations so that they can also benefit from these improvements.

12.5. Reform 3: EBL Platform

Another important initiative which has improved the implementation of the EBL is the introduction of the National Corporate Bankruptcy and Reorganisation Case Information Platform ('EBL platform'), a website about the EBL with information about the law in general and with extensive functions for all EBL participants. It was established by the SPC under the Provisions on Disclosure of Information on Enterprise Bankruptcy Cases (for Trial)[95] in 2016. The EBL platform serves as a centralised information system which provides information about the relevant bankruptcy-related rules and regulations. But, importantly, it is also a working noticeboard which displays notifications of activities relating to individual EBL proceedings such as newly accepted EBL applications, dates of creditors' meetings, auctions, etc.[96] The EBL platform is intended as a comprehensive centralised information system and so, when courts and administrators publish notifications relating to EBL cases in other media, they must also post a copy at the EBL platform.[97] Moreover, it is also a gateway for submitting legal documents, filing creditors' claims and attending and voting at creditors' meetings.[98] All information relating to active EBL cases – except for state secrets and private information – must be disclosed as ordered by the EBL and other relevant laws.[99]

Some local (intermediate) courts also launched their own local EBL platforms with information about bankruptcy case hearings, announcements, case judgments, petition filing, EBL procedures, and, importantly, also specific local rules and guidelines that only affect companies domiciled in that region. Such local EBL platform was launched (for trial operation) in Shenzhen – one of the pilot regions with a specialised bankruptcy court – in January 2016.[100]

The launch of a centralised information system that is free and accessible to all was a significant step towards greater transparency and credibility of China's corporate

---

[94] See Sections 8.1.1 and 11.3.1–11.3.2.
[95] *Fafa* [2016] No 19.
[96] Arts 1, 3–5 of the Notice.
[97] Art 7 of the Notice.
[98] Arts 8–10 of the Notice.
[99] Art 2 of the Notice.
[100] 'The first bankruptcy information disclosure platform in the country was born in Shenzhen, Guangdong' (15.2.2016), available at www.court.gov.cn/zixun-xiangqing-16641.html.

bankruptcy regime. At the same time, it also addresses some of the issues identified earlier – particularly those relating to information asymmetries,[101] discoverability of EBL procedures for the affected stakeholders, and excessive cost and delays that traditionally affected EBL cases.[102] Three additional functions of the EBL platform were highlighted by the SPC.[103] Firstly, the platform allows the SPC to regulate and supervise judicial acceptance and EBL-related activities. By the end of February 2018, the EBL platform was accessed 133 million times; contained 21,745 public documents; and provided 21,762 EBL judgments. The SPC can track overdue cases in real time through the online reservation system for EBL cases in the information network. Secondly, the EBL platform allows for timely and comprehensive notifications in EBL cases. The platform provides valuable public information to the affected parties and the market, and it helps realise the enterprise value faster and more fully. During the reorganisation of Jiamei Tiansheng Wuhan Real Estate Development Ltd, seven prospective investors were recruited through the EBL platform within a week. The company received a deposit of 150 million RMB in advance, which helped get through the reorganisation process. Similarly, the EBL platform was used by the Shenzhen Intermediate People's Court in November 2017 to auction three Boeing 747 aircrafts through an online auction in the EBL Liquidation of the Emerald International Cargo Airlines Ltd with the final sale price exceeding 468 million RMB (the starting price was about 100 million RMB). Finally, the EBL platform encourages proper and efficient disposition of bankrupt companies using the EBL. In May 2017, Dongfeng Electric Group's Dongfeng Motor Ltd started EBL proceedings. Within seven days, 17 social intermediaries[104] in Beijing, Shanghai and other places signed up. By the end of February 2018, the court held 33 online creditor meetings, involving 32,102 creditors and concerning more than 137.4 billion RMB.

The EBL platform, therefore, enables the EBL to be used more effectively and without undue delay caused by late claim filings, late notifications and problems in arranging creditors' meetings and reaching necessary quora. This is a very promising development which has already helped overcome many serious issues that prevented efficient implementation of the EBL in the past – and is likely to continue to overcome information-related problems and help ameliorate delays and excessive cost of EBL procedures which is very desirable.

12.6. Reform 4: Judicial and Political Guidance

The SPC has been releasing interpretative documents – some about the EBL provisions, others focused on other laws but relevant to the EBL in practice – since the EBL was implemented in 2007.[105] However, local courts and local governments – with a

---

[101] See Sections 7.1.1 and 11.2.1.1.
[102] See Section 8.1.2.
[103] Judge Liu Guixiang's speech at the press conference to release the typical cases in 2018: Sohu (8.3.2018).
[104] Art 24 EBL states that 'The liquidating group formed by the members from related sectors or organizations, or the *social intermediary institutions* such as law firms, accounting firms, and bankruptcy liquidating firms may act as the Administrator'. (emphasis added)
[105] See Section 4.3 for details.

few exceptions – only started paying more attention to the EBL and started releasing detailed guidance about its implementation after the EBL was identified as a political priority by the central Party-state in October and December 2015.[106] This Section briefly looks at three types of judicial and political guidance that have influenced how the EBL is implemented in practice. They are judicial interpretations and rules; national and local typical EBL cases; and guidance regarding what tools the courts should use when resolving corporate financial distress.

The SPC has been very active in releasing guidance and explanations of a wide range of issues arising from the EBL. Section 4.3.1 discussed seven such documents, two of which were released in 2015–20. Two interpretative provisions – *Fashi* [2007] No 8 and *Fashi* [2007] No 9 – provided detailed guidance about appointment and remuneration of administrators. Three interpretative provisions – *Fashi* [2011] No 22, *Fashi* [2013] No 22 and *Fashi* [2019] No 3 – provided detailed guidance about a range of EBL-specific issues such as the insolvency test, evidentiary requirements, scope of the debtor's estate, administrators' powers and duties, bankruptcy expenses, post-petition lending, creditors' rights and powers, etc. Finally, the SPC also issued two important regulatory documents – *Fafa* [2009] No 36 and *Fafa* [2020] No 14 – which explained general judicial policy when hearing EBL cases. Together, these documents provide important answers to theoretical and practical issues that arise from the EBL practice. At the same time, the SPC guidance also ensures greater coherence in how the law is applied in different provinces, and it clarifies the underlying principles and policies that should help local courts resolve any further issues that have not been answered by the EBL or the SPC.

Some local courts have also issued guidance on how to hear EBL cases[107] and reports that summarise their experience and tips for effective implementation of the EBL.[108] Although some limited local guidance existed before 2015, the volume and geographical range have increased significantly since the EBL was identified as a political priority in late 2015. Sometimes, local courts go beyond mere guidance and experiment with new initiatives. One example is the Shenzhen regulation that allows natural persons to go bankrupt in China.[109] Another example is the development of simplified EBL procedures which allow for faster and cheaper resolution in smaller, simpler cases.[110] Similarly, local courts have also experimented with the entry requirements. Although Article 2 of the EBL only requires that the company be insolvent or obviously likely to become insolvent to be able to use EBL reorganisation,[111] some courts have issued further rules. For example, courts in Zhejiang and Beijing require a petitioning debtor or creditor to explain whether and how a company can successfully complete the restructuring ('survivability

---

[106] See Section 12.1.

[107] See eg Suzhou Court's guidance on resolving difficult debt enforcement cases: 'Suzhou, Jiangsu: Creating a Wujiang model for bankruptcy cases' (20.5.2018).

[108] See eg Shenzhen White paper in People's Daily (6.11.2017); 'Fujian Court's White Paper on Hearing Bankruptcy Cases' (31.7.2019, Yunqingsuan); 'Guangzhou Intermediate Court Releases White Paper on Hearing Bankruptcy Cases' (30.12.2019, Yunqingsuan).

[109] See Section 12.9.

[110] See Section 12.8.

[111] See Section 4.2.2.

test'), which is often hard to show and prove.[112] Nevertheless, such a test is perceived locally as a key to preventing wasteful delay and abuse of reorganisation where liquidation may be more appropriate. Local guidance tests new ideas and, where successful, they may be adopted by the SPC or incorporated into the EBL once it is reformed.[113]

Another form of guidance are the typical EBL cases. The SPC released two batches – one in 2018 and one in 2020 – with examples of liquidation, reorganisation and composition cases.[114] Many local courts also release their local typical EBL cases; the most active courts do so almost every year while other, less EBL-active ones cover several years in a single batch.[115] There are usually 10 cases in each batch, and each case includes a summary of the facts and of the judgment and – most importantly – a commentary from the releasing court. These cases are not binding, but they illustrate the courts' general approach to corporate bankruptcy and their solutions to the most common and complex problems that arise in EBL practice. Importantly, moreover, they also provide an insight into the political underpinnings of EBL practice and the way how courts cooperate with local governments.[116]

Finally, local governments also release guidance about which tools they prefer the courts to use when resolving EBL cases. Courts generally follow such Party-state's guidance.[117] For example, under the 1986 law, there was a clear policy preference for the use of mergers[118] which impliedly continued under the EBL.[119] The policy was later rejected, but it was reintroduced in 2016 when resolving zombie companies.[120] Although mergers can be an effective (and relatively quick) way of dealing with bankrupt companies – especially when they are a part of a broader group of companies – there are problems associated with this approach.[121]

Another policy that the courts have been told to follow is the preference for settling debts using financial instruments such as debt-for-equity swaps and asset securitisation.[122] The use of such financial instruments was officially supported by the State Council in February 2018,[123] and the use of these tools was highlighted and praised in several important cases.[124] However, note that using debt-for-equity swaps can be unwelcome and problematic.[125]

---

[112] See Section 8.1.1.

[113] This is how the 1993 Shenzhen Corporate Bankruptcy Regulation were used in the context of the EBL.

[114] See Sections 4.3.3–4.3.4.

[115] See typical cases in eg 'Bankruptcy Cases at Jiangsu Court and Ten Typical Bankruptcy Cases in 2018' (6 March 2020); 'Ten Typical Bankruptcy Cases of Wujiang Court (2016–2019)' (17.4.2020); 'Top Ten Typical Bankruptcy Cases of Zhejiang Courts in 2019' (13.4.2020).

[116] For a discussion of how local governments influence Chinese courts, see Sections 2.4.3, 8.3.3 and 11.3.5.

[117] See Sections 2.4.3 and 8.3.3.

[118] See Section 4.1.

[119] See Sections 8.3.5 and 9.2.3.

[120] B Xing (8.4.2016, The Paper). See also the fourth and seventh typical cases in 2018 and the sixth typical case in 2020: Sections 4.3.3–4.3.4. Note that Zhijie Jia has urged that the EBL restructuring should be selective: Several Issues of the Draft of the China Enterprise Bankruptcy Law (2006) *Journal of the China People's Congress* 757.

[121] See Sections 9.2.2–9.2.3 and 12.1.

[122] This was also highlighted by Professor Li Shuguang at the Seminar on the 10th Anniversary of the Implementation of the Corporate Bankruptcy Law in B Lu (12.9.2017, People's Court News).

[123] 'China to further reduce SOE debts' (8.2.2018, China.org).

[124] The fourth typical case (2018) in Section 4.3.3; Bohai Steel Reorganisation in Section 8.3.4.

[125] See Section 10.2.2.

Together, the judicial and political guidance helps address some of the issues identi-fied earlier – most importantly they resolve unclear provisions in the EBL,[126] fix flaws in surrounding rules and practices,[127] and enable a consistent and predictable application of the EBL in practice.[128] They help unify implementation of the EBL nationwide (SPC) and intra-provincially (local courts, local governments) and published local guidance can also serve as an educational and experience-sharing mechanism for lower courts and other provinces.

12.7. Reform 5: Local Conferences and Experience-sharing Events

Conferences, training sessions and inter-provincial help and sharing workshops have also played an important role in educating judges and exchanging experiences and tips on how to deal with various issues that arise in practice. These initiatives have been helping address some of the issues identified earlier, most importantly the lack of judges' expertise and experience[129] and the lack of consistency in the application of EBL provi-sions across provinces.[130]

Conferences have helped bring together experts and stakeholders in order to discuss and agree on a common approach to critical legal issues. As we saw in Section 12.1 above the SPC's 8th National Conference for Civil and Commercial Judges in December 2015 enabled the SPC to transmit central legal policy on dealing with EBL cases. Similarly, the SPC organised a conferences in February 2016 in Zhejiang to discuss and agree on a common approach for dealing with zombie companies. Probably the most important EBL-related SPC conference took place in Shenzhen in December 2017[131] and was used to summarise (and unify) the approach to EBL cases and make a plan for further clari-fication and improvements. Conference summaries,[132] which are released shortly after the conference ends, are considered judicial normative documents which influence how local courts apply the law.[133]

Several successful conferences have also been held by local courts, local law firms and local universities, often jointly or with support of local governments. By way of an example, one of the earlier local conferences was organised by the Wenzhou Intermediate People's Court in November 2013 and discussed the possibility of online auctions to maximise the value of bankruptcy estate.[134] Another local conference was held in Shenzhen in November 2016 and brought together practitioners and judges to

---

[126] See Sections 6.1 and 11.1.
[127] See Sections 7.1-3 and 11.2.1–11.2.3.
[128] See Sections 8.1.1 and 11.3.3.
[129] See Sections 8.1.1 and 11.3.1.
[130] See Section 8.1.
[131] See the SPC Notice concerning the Minutes of the National Work Conference on Bankruptcy Trials (*Fa* [2018] No 53).
[132] *huiyijiyao*会议纪要.
[133] SPC Monitor (17.8.2019).
[134] Sina (7.12.2015); Wenzhou Intermediate Court's Minutes on the Disposal of Corporate Bankruptcy Property through Online Judicial Auction Platform (22.9.2015).

discuss practical challenges of resolving EBL cases.[135] More recently, Zhejiang University and Zhejiang Provincial Higher Court organised an online conference that explored the question of maximising bankruptcy estate and how to effectively dispose of assets using conventional means and modern technology.[136] In addition, many local courts have also held training sessions,[137] interactive workshops[138] and cross-institutional educational events.[139] These local events are very important because they can focus on the particular issues that are most relevant in the given region and so efficiently address and ameliorate local problems that prevent effective implementation of the EBL in practice.

Since some courts – usually those in regions with the more developed market – have more experience and expertise than others, there have been inter-provincial events and assistance visits. They usually involve meetings between judges and Party-state officials from the two regions, a review of their experiences and difficult cases, field trips and an agreement to cooperate in the future.[140] Such inter-provincial help and experience-sharing also help build further expertise and understanding of the EBL across China, which is crucial for ameliorating the implementation of the EBL in practice.

12.8. Reform 6: Simplified EBL Procedure

One of the problems of corporate bankruptcy law in general is that the process tends to be long and costly,[141] which makes it inefficient for smaller, simpler corporate bankruptcies. Some of the other initiatives have already shortened the time it takes to hear an EBL case – for example, creditors can now submit their claims and attend and vote at creditors' meetings online.[142] Nevertheless, more is needed.

The first experimental simplified[143] bankruptcy procedure was tested in Shenzhen in 1993.[144] The Shenzhen Regulation stated that simplified bankruptcy law hearing could take place where three conditions were satisfied: clear facts, clear creditor–debtor relationships, and the bankrupt property or debt amounted to less than 0.5 million RMB.[145] Interestingly, the 2000 draft of the EBL also contained a simplified version of bankruptcy procedure which was inspired by the 1993 Shenzhen Regulation.[146]

---

[135] Y Hu (7.11.2016, Yunqingsuan).

[136] 'Xu Jianxin: Exploring the maximization of bankruptcy assets and corporate reorganization in Zhejiang Province' (23.4.2020, CNR).

[137] eg the Changsha Intermediate People's Court (Hunan Province) held a training session in February 2016 with experts from the SPC and Beijing universities: Weixin (1.3.2016).

[138] eg the Quzhou Intermediate People's Court held a workshop on the EBL's role in economic upgrading in February 2016: ChinaCourt (5.2.2016).

[139] eg the Quanzhou Government (Fujian Province) organised a cross-institutional EBL training in February 2016: DongNanWang (18.2.2016).

[140] See eg Q Zhang (2.4.2020, People's Court News).

[141] See Section 8.1.2.

[142] See Section 12.5.

[143] Also called 'expedited' or 'fast-track'.

[144] Z Song and R Xie, 'A Few Suggestions about the Simplified Bankruptcy Cases' (27.5.2020) Guangdong South-Freedom Law Firm.

[145] The Shenzhen Special Economic Zone Corporate Bankruptcy Regulations (18.12.1993).

[146] Arts 157–163 of the Shenzhen Regulations. See also Y Xu and Y Hua (23.3.2017, Yunqingsuan).

The chapter was, however, deleted from the final version of the EBL due to objections of some commentators.[147]

In recent years, the simplified EBL procedure reappeared. After Wenzhou became China's Comprehensive Financial Reform Pilot Zone in 2012,[148] The Wenzhou Intermediate People's Court released local guidance in March 2013 that permitted simplified EBL hearings.[149] The results were astonishing: the average duration of EBL hearings went from 'two to three years' to 'up to three months' after the regulation was promulgated.[150] In 2015, Wenzhou was chosen to be China's first trial court for simplified EBL hearing.[151] The Wenzhou model was based on the 1993 Shenzhen Regulation but it went further. Besides the original three requirements (clear facts, clear creditor-debtor relationships, but note that '0.5 million RMB' was replaced by 'dispute is not large'), it also stipulated that the bankruptcy must fall into one of five situations:

(i) the volume of debtor's assets and the number of creditors are small;
(ii) the bankruptcy estate does not cover bankruptcy expenses;
(iii) the applicant, the respondent and all major stakeholders agree to use the simplified procedure;
(iv) the debtor and all the creditors reached an agreement about all claims and debts;[152] or
(v) other circumstances which make the case suitable for the simplified procedure.[153]

Some cases – particularly those affecting broader social and economic stability and where the simplified hearing would be unfair – are excluded.[154]

The renewed interest in the use of a simplified EBL procedure was a result of a combination of the slowing economy, the growing corporate debt and the political push to clear out zombie companies from the market.[155] Local governments and courts were told that local zombie companies 'must be removed from the market according to the law'[156] – but the companies had little or no money, and so the procedures had to be as quick as possible in order to minimise the bankruptcy expenses. Moreover, there was pressure from EBL practitioners and some courts to introduce a simplified EBL procedure for smaller, simpler cases which do not need all the safeguards and full mechanisms in the EBL to ensure fair and efficient restructuring or exit from the market.[157]

---

[147] ibid.
[148] J Xu, H Ju and Y Wang, 'Research on simplifying bankruptcy procedures' (2014) *Law Application* 98.
[149] ibid. Wenzhou Intermediate Court's Minutes on the Trial Implementation of Simplified Bankruptcy Case Procedures (27.3.2013).
[150] F Wen (30.12.2019, People's Court News).
[151] X Wen (15.1.2015, JCRB).
[152] This is similar to pre-packs or informal restructuring, which only need the court to confirm the settlement.
[153] Wenzhou Intermediate Court's Minutes (n 149).
[154] ibid.
[155] Zhejiang Changxing Court's Corporate Bankruptcy Trial White Paper and Ten Typical Cases (2012–18).
[156] See Section 12.3.
[157] Y Pang (8.6.2016, Yunqingsuan); Z Song and R Xie (n 144).

Following the successful trial of the simplified EBL procedure in Wenzhou, many other regions released local rules for simplified EBL hearings,[158] and many already report positive results.[159] Several academic studies have also been conducted, proposing the best rules and showing the likely benefits of simplified EBL procedures for China's economy and business environment.[160] It also appears that the Government is actively exploring the option of including a simplified procedure as a part of the EBL itself.[161]

12.9. Reform 7: Personal Bankruptcy

Besides improving existing law, some initiatives have also focused on adding new tools and mechanisms to the courts' arsenal. One such initiative is the introduction of personal bankruptcy rules. Section 11.1.6 explored several economic and personal reasons why it is desirable to introduce personal bankruptcy law in China. The calls to introduce a mechanism for resolving personal bankruptcies in China[162] were eventually heard and the SPC announced in June 2019 that a pilot programme would test and formulate personal bankruptcy rules in select trial regions between 2019 and 2023.[163] In July 2019, the National Development and Reform Commission – China's top economic planner – together with 13 other government departments jointly issued the Notice concerning Reform Plan for Accelerating the Improvement of the Exit Regime for Market Entities[164] which confirmed their intention to formulate personal bankruptcy law.

Several regions – importantly, Wenzhou and Shenzhen, which both have developed private economy and experienced judiciary – were selected to formulate and test rules on centralised personal debt clean-up. The aim was to create efficient rules which would allow fair collective part-repayment of debt to creditors and a fresh start for the debtors while, at the same time preventing abuse of the new regime.

The Wenzhou Intermediate People's Court published trial local personal bankruptcy rules in September 2019.[165] The rules only apply in the Wenzhou area. The rules

---

[158] See eg 'Jiangsu Bankruptcy Trial Work Report in 2019' (3.3.2020); the Shanghai Higher People's Court Guidelines on Simplifying Procedures and Accelerating the Advancement of Bankruptcy Cases 2019 (*Hugaofa* [2018] No 167); the Dalian Municipal Intermediate Court's Guidelines on Simplifying Trial Procedures for Bankruptcy Cases in 2020; the Guangzhou Intermediate Court's Working Guidelines on Promoting Fast-track Bankruptcy Procedure (Trial) (*Suizhongfa* [2020] No 30).

[159] In 2018, the Wujiang Court applied simplified procedures to settle 29 bankruptcy cases throughout the year, with an average time limit of 58.29 days and a minimum time of 39 days: People's Court News (28.2.2019).

[160] See eg J Guo, Theoretical Research of Simplified Bankruptcy Procedure (2017/12), available at www.commerciallaw.com.cn/ueditor/php/upload/file/20180415/1523806445288614.pdf; Xu, Ju and Wang, 'Research' (2014). See also The World Bank, 'Saving Entrepreneurs, Saving Enterprises: Proposals on the Treatment of MSME Insolvency' (World Bank, 2018); The World Bank, 'Report on the Treatment of MSME Insolvency' (World Bank, 2017).

[161] F Wang (29.3.2019, 21st Century Business Herald).

[162] The President of the SPC called for an introduction of personal bankruptcy law in November 2018: 'Zhou Qiang, President of the Supreme People's Court: Promote the Establishment of a Personal Bankruptcy System and Improve the Current Bankruptcy Law' (2.11.2018). NPC deputies and bank governors made a similar call in mid-2019: '"Half Bankruptcy Law" A Dream Journey' (27.8.2019).

[163] The Guidelines for People's Courts on Enforcement Work (2019–2023) (11.6.2019).

[164] (*Fagaicaijin* [2019] No 1104).

[165] Wenzhou Intermediate Court's Implementing Opinions on the Centralised Cleanup of Personal Debt (11.9.2019).

stipulate that the procedure can be initiated by an individual debtor who fails to fulfil a monetary obligation under a pre-existing judgment where they do not have enough assets to repay the debt in full or they clearly lack the ability to repay.[166] They further state that the debtor must also prove the existence of one of the following:

(i) the debtor has a guarantee responsibility with regards to a company that has entered an EBL proceeding or has been declared bankrupt;
(ii) the debtor is responsible for a company's debt because the corporate veil was pierced;
(iii) the debtor is responsible for a debt of an unincorporated organisation;
(iv) the debtor cannot repay a debt because of 'life difficulties'; or
(v) the debtor has proposed a repayment plan which was accepted by all creditors.[167]

Article 7 further states that the debtor must show that:

(i) there are no other cases involving monetary obligation outside Wenzhou (unless the outside creditor agrees to participate in the Wenzhou proceedings);
(ii) the debtor and their spouse made a comprehensive and truthful declaration of their assets;
(iii) the spouse agreed to allow court investigation (including investigation of their bank account) and other family members also agreed to asset investigations, if necessary; and
(iv) the debtor must agree in writing not to engage in 'high consumption activities'[168] or non-essential spending other than for life and work.

Once a petition is accepted, the court appoints an administrator or adds the personal bankruptcy case into a pre-existing EBL case.[169] Alternatively, the debtor and creditors can agree that one of the creditors should act as an administrator. The administrator then informs all creditors in writing within 20 days from the moment when the court accepted the petition to open proceedings.[170] The administrator also makes a public announcement; the announcement period should be within the range of 30 days to three months.[171]

The repayment plan must be voted for by the majority of unsecured creditors.[172] Parties can also agree on different voting rules.[173] Creditors' meeting can vote twice; a failure to approve the repayment plan leads to the termination of the procedure.[174] The court should not approve the repayment plan if:

(i) the plan violates statutory rules or public order and cannot be amended;
(ii) the plan is reached using unfair methods;
(iii) it is impossible to implement the plan;

---

[166] Art 6 of the Wenzhou Opinions.
[167] ibid.
[168] Defined in Art 3 of the SPC Provisions concerning the Restriction on High Consumption and Related Expenses of Persons under Debt Enforcement Order (*Fashi* [2010] No 8).
[169] Art 17 of the Wenzhou Opinions.
[170] Art 19 of the Wenzhou Opinions.
[171] ibid.
[172] Art 24 of the Wenzhou Opinions.
[173] Art 22 of the Wenzhou Opinions.
[174] Art 29 of the Wenzhou Opinions.

(iv) the debtor privately satisfied the interest of one or more creditors, which seriously damages the interests of other creditors;

(v) other circumstances (at court's discretion).[175]

There is no maximum duration of the repayment plan, but there are rules about credit restoration. Article 34 states that:

(i) credit of a debtor with a debt of less than two million RMB and a repayment rate of more than 50 per cent can be restored after one year upon the completion of the repayment plan;

(ii) credit of a debtor with a debt of two to five million RMB and with a repayment rate of more than 30 per cent can be restored after one to three years upon the completion of the repayment plan;

(iii) credit of a debtor with a debt of five to 20 million RMB and with a repayment rate of more than 10 per cent can be restored after two to five years upon the completion of the repayment plan; and

(iv) in all other circumstances, credit can be restored after three to six years upon the completion of the repayment plan.

Finally, Article 35 states that, before credit is restored, the individual debtor cannot:

(i) engage in 'high consumption activities', except for travelling economy class flights or second class high speed train;

(ii) act as a legal representative or being a shareholder in profitable companies;

(iii) act as a legal representative, director or supervisor of an SOE; and

(iv) perform other acts decided by the court.

The rules were first[176] tested in October 2019 where a debtor with over two million RMB of debt reached a settlement with his four creditors. The debtor agreed to pay a one-off sum within the first 18 months and then 50 per cent of his household income over the following six years. The total repayment rate was only 1.5 per cent.[177] In the following months, more personal bankruptcy decisions were handed down by local courts,[178] making a promising start in this very important area.

The introduction of personal bankruptcy rules must deal with Chinese society's suspicion and reluctance to permit personal debt relief. Wenzhou started a quiet revolution and a new trend which is slowly influencing how people perceive personal debt in China. By the end of 2019, the Wenzhou city courts accepted 25 and concluded 11 personal bankruptcy cases.[179] Other courts followed. Taizhou created personal bankruptcy rules around the same time as Wenzhou. By the end of 2019, the two

---

[175] Art 31 of the Wenzhou Opinions.

[176] Note that the first personal bankruptcy rules and case in China – although less famous than the Wenzhou rules and case – were actually in Taizhou (Zhejiang Province): see eg 'Taizhou Court: The year of breaking the ice of personal bankruptcy' (2.1.2020).

[177] Z Xin (10.10.2019, SCMP).

[178] eg in Suzhou (Jiangsu Province): 'Jiangsu's first personal debt liquidation case concluded' (2.6.2020, Yunqingsuan).

[179] 'Top Ten Typical Bankruptcy Cases of Zhejiang Courts in 2019' (13.4.2020, Yunqingsuan).

levels of courts in Taizhou accepted 117 and concluded 23 personal bankruptcy cases.[180]

Shenzhen then released its trial personal bankruptcy rules in June 2020.[181] A couple of weeks earlier, the Central Committee of the Party and the State Council issued the Opinions on Accelerating the Improvement of the Socialist Market Economic System in the New Era[182] which reaffirm the future (nationwide) introduction of personal bankruptcy legislation. Until then, however, the rules need to be tested and perfected at a local level.

12.10. Reform 8: Bankruptcy Assistance Fund

In some cases, the debtor's situation has become so dire that they do not have enough assets to cover the costs of a bankruptcy procedure. In such cases, courts and administrators have been reluctant to accept and carry out EBL liquidation. This issue is particularly pronounced in zombie companies which are deeply indebted. Local courts and governments were ordered in 2015 to resolve zombie companies 'according to the law',[183] but the issue of bankruptcy expenses made this task very difficult. To support the work of courts and administrators, some local governments have established a corporate bankruptcy assistance fund to ensure that bankruptcy expenses are covered even where the debtor's assets are insufficient to cover these costs, which has, in the past, disincentivised courts and administrators from accepting EBL cases.

Such fund was established in Guangzhou in 2017,[184] Shanghai in 2018,[185] and many other locations since then. 76 counties and municipalities in Zhejiang Province established a bankruptcy assistance fund by the end of 2019, each in the amount of 5 to 5.5 million RMB, with a total amount of 128 million RMB.[186] Each court formulated a set of rules to regulate the sources of the aid funds, the scope of use, and the rules about the fund's management, supervision and the approval process.[187]

These bankruptcy assistance funds have proven essential for enabling the removal of the most heavily indebted companies – including zombie companies – from the market. Although their use is not intended for and cannot ensure that the creditors are repaid, they also help the creditors indirectly in that they do not face the uncertainty of not knowing the status of their claim and can make arrangements accordingly. Moreover, the funds help the courts clear out such companies which also helps improve China's business environment and the rule of law.

---

[180] ibid.

[181] K Cai (24.6.2020, Caixin).

[182] Issued on 11.5.2020.

[183] See Section 12.1.

[184] 'Bankruptcy Cases with No Funds Apply for Public Welfare Fund Support' (17.7.2017, Guangzhou Association of Bankruptcy Administrators).

[185] Shanghai Intermediate Court's Administrative Measures for Enterprise Bankruptcy Funds (Trial) (*Hugaofa* [2018] No 300).

[186] 'Xu Jianxin: Exploring the maximization of bankruptcy assets and corporate reorganization in Zhejiang Province' (23.4.2020, CNR).

[187] See eg Zhejiang Changxing Court's Corporate Bankruptcy Trial White Paper and Ten Typical Cases (2012–18).

12.11. Reform 9: Judges' Evaluation System for Resolving EBL Cases

Section 8.1.3 suggested that the courts are often reluctant to accept EBL petitions[188] because of the internal quotas on the number of cases that they have to resolve. EBL cases usually take up a lot of time and resources. As a result, using the EBL is often an unthankful task because it puts courts in conflict with the local government and, more importantly, the delays and complexity of the cases reflect badly on them.[189] It is, therefore, hardly surprising that judges are often reluctant to accept EBL petitions.

To deal with this issue,[190] the SPC released the Notice concerning Compulsory Liquidation and Separate Performance Evaluation of Bankruptcy Cases[191] in 2019 in which it orders the use of a new evaluation regime for judges who hear EBL cases. The Notice acknowledges that EBL cases are often complex and take a long time to resolve, but it also stresses the importance of making sure that corporate bankruptcies are dealt with in practice. The courts can evaluate judges' performance in EBL cases with reference to other types of cases or as a separate category.[192] The SPC also reiterates the importance of establishing specialised courts and providing EBL training to judges in order to empower courts to hear EBL cases more efficiently.[193]

While there is no normative guidance as to the evaluation of EBL cases, courts in Beijing and Wenzhou came up with a formula where they equate one EBL case to 16 second-instance commercial cases.[194] The SPC guidelines were further discussed at a conference organised by the Shenzhen Intermediate People's Court in March 2020.[195]

12.12. Reform 10: Cooperation with Local Party-state

Section 8.3 explained that the Party-state often plays an important role in EBL cases.[196]

The importance of the Party-state support was reiterated by the SPC in its typical EBL cases[197] and other guidance to lower courts.[198] As a result, many courts have been reluctant to accept and hear EBL cases independently.[199] On the one hand, it is understandable why courts welcome the Party-state's support in resolving EBL cases.[200]

---

[188] See also Sections 2.4.3 and 8.3.3.
[189] ibid.
[190] See suggestions in Section 11.3.3.3.
[191] *Faban* [2019] No 49.
[192] ibid, Arts 1–3.
[193] ibid, Art 5.
[194] X Wang, Q Shao, X Liu, 'Analysis of Performance Evaluation Standards of Bankruptcy Cases' (April 2018) *Legal Expo* 20. See also Section 11.3.3.3.
[195] 'Urge enterprises to continue to survive and develop Shenzhen court bankruptcy trial to help resume work and production' (30 March 2020).
[196] The ways how the Party-state interfere in EBL cases were further explored in Section 9.2.
[197] See Sections 4.3.3–4.3.4.
[198] eg the SPC Notice concerning the Correct Hearing of EBL Cases and Judicial Guarantee to Maintain Orderly Market Economy (*Fafa* [2009] No 36). See also Section 8.3.3.
[199] See Sections 2.4.3 and 8.3.3.
[200] See Section 8.3.3.

On the other hand, however, unlimited interference from the Party-state is harmful: it prevents full implementation of the EBL and so realisation of the benefits of bankruptcy law seen elsewhere; such interference is often contrary to the parties' wishes; and it often leads to unfair or inefficient outcomes.[201] In order to keep the benefits of the Party-state support but avoid the undesirable consequences of excessive interference, a framework for court–government cooperation is clearly needed. This was also argued in Section 11.3.5 which suggested that so long as the Party-state only steps in at a court's request and is limited in scope – so as to ensure judicial independence – it is possible and even desirable to allow the cooperation between courts and Party-state in EBL cases.

A mechanism for enabling cooperation between courts, administrators and local governments was proposed at the Shenzhen National Bankruptcy Trial Work Conference in December 2017.[202] Du Wanhua, an SPC judge in charge of EBL reform, called for an establishment of a 'normalised government-courts coordination system', which would help protect the rights of each party on an equal basis.[203] Judge Du argued that this system would help ensure that no EBL cases are ignored (for example, where the hearing court fears their level of complexity). It would also help resolve delays and mismanagement of EBL cases.

Several regions issued formal guidelines and, in some places, set up whole departments for the cooperation of courts and local Party-state. This commonly involves releasing joint guidelines that clarify the powers and responsibilities of the courts and the Party-state.[204] It is often also accompanied by a court's statement of intent to hear all cases according to the law and by a corresponding pledge by the Party-state to unblock market- and law-driven exit for financially distressed companies in the region.[205]

The Zhejiang Provincial High Court discussed its arrangements in a White Paper released in 2019. Xu Jianxin, a member of the Party Leadership Group and Vice-President of Zhejiang Higher People's Court, said that a necessary precondition to successful EBL practice is wide acceptance of the concept of bankruptcy protection among the people in general but, even more importantly, by 'the Party and government departments and all sectors of the society through various forms of media publicity, case hearings, and government coordination meetings'.[206] He said that the key is to pass three important messages to the Party, the government departments and all sectors of society. First, the EBL can not only liquidate distressed companies but also restructure those companies with temporary financial problems but good future prospects (as illustrated by the typical EBL cases that were released on the same day). Moreover, it is also important to highlight that liquidation can sell (and so save) the core business. Second, a high number of EBL cases does not mean that a local economy is struggling. On the contrary,

---

[201] See Section 11.3.5.
[202] See Section 12.1.
[203] SPC Monitor (31.12.2017).
[204] See eg The Paper (17.5.2020).
[205] ibid.
[206] 'Remarks from the press conference of "Zhejiang Court Further Advances the Structural Reform and Economic Transformation and Upgrade of the Bankruptcy Trial Service Supply Side"' (16.4.2018, Zhejiang Court).

the release of economic resources such as land and real estate through the bankruptcy process, and the reallocation of such resources to the most effective user can effectively promote economic transformation and upgrading – especially in provinces with limited resources such as Zhejiang. Third, the EBL provides a centralised settlement procedure that can effectively prevent and resolve the risks of corporate guarantee chains. The EBL helps dispose and resolve corporate risk in a timely manner which prevents the bad debt to add up and become a systemic risk.

12.13. The Future

Much has been achieved since the EBL was implemented in 2007, particularly in the last few years. The increased political focus on the EBL has helped encourage greater use of the law and renewed court and government interest in improving the EBL as written and as implemented. As this chapter has illustrated, the courts are developing guidance and increasing their EBL-specific expertise and experience, supporting infrastructure is being put in place, and local initiatives are testing new approaches and solutions to the most pressing problems.

Nevertheless, more remains to be done. Many of the initiatives discussed in this chapter are in their infancy and most have only been tested in select few locations. Moreover, the provinces and regions which have been proposing and testing the new initiatives – eg Zhejiang, Jiangsu and Shenzhen – are generally already well developed and have active, pro-market courts and governments.[207] Once the reform moves nationwide, however, additional issues are likely to arise.

Moreover, many important issues have not yet been addressed. They include the questions concerning the resolution of the conflict between employees' and creditors' interests;[208] the full implementation of China's social security system and a mechanism to pay out unemployment benefits;[209] the treatment of claims from shadow lenders;[210] the circumstances under which parties can use the EBL before a debtor becomes technically insolvent;[211] further details about the administrators' duties and the practical implications if they fail to carry them out;[212] and clearer willingness of the Party-state to let courts apply the EBL independently and only assist in the precisely defined circumstances that were discussed in Sections 11.3.5 and 12.12.[213]

Given the complexity and the conflicts of interest[214] that are inherent in corporate bankruptcies – and which are particularly pronounced in authoritarian China where the Party-state and the market forces often clash[215] – the reform process is likely to

---

[207] ibid.
[208] See Sections 6.1.1 and 11.1.2.
[209] See Sections 7.2.1 and 11.2.2.1.
[210] See Sections 6.2.2, 7.3 and 11.2.3.
[211] See Sections 6.3 and 11.1.4.1.
[212] See Sections 8.2 and 11.3.3.1.
[213] See also Caixin (10.4.2019).
[214] See Sections 8.3, 10.3.2, 11.1.2 and 11.3.
[215] See Sections 2.2.4 and 2.5.

take many more years before the rules are ready to be implemented nationally.[216] As Section 10.3 highlighted, there are obstacles and challenges ahead. Nevertheless, so long as the reform project has the support of the Government and the SPC – which it does for the time being[217] – it is likely that many of the issues identified in Chapters six to nine will be ameliorated or removed.

The Legislative Affairs Office of the NPC's Financial Economic Committee confirmed in June 2019 that a team was being assembled for drafting amendments to the EBL.[218] The reformers will be able to benefit from the last 13 years of EBL practice, the insights from recent local reform initiatives and international best practice. Given the (acknowledged) pressing need for a more efficient resolution of corporate financial distress in China today, it is likely that further improvements will, in time, be made. However, the success of the changes will largely depend on the scope of the reform and the willingness of the reformers to address all the key issues in the law as written and applied.[219]

---

[216] Note that it took 12 years to draft the EBL: see Section 4.1.

[217] See Section 12.1 and the SPC Memorandum concerning the Minutes of the National Civil and Commercial Trial Work Conference (*Fa* [2019] No 254). See also commentary of some of the SPC proposals in S Xu and S Zhang, 'SPC's Minutes of the National Civil and Commercial Trial Work Conference – Interpretation and recommendations' (23.8.2019, Zhonglun).

[218] See eg Y Shan and J Teng (29.3.2019, Caixin).

[219] See ch 11 for further discussion.

PART IV

Foreign Stakeholders and the EBL

Foreign laws inspired many provisions in the EBL, foreign governments and advisers influenced the wording and implementation of the EBL, foreign stakeholders are affected by courts' handling of EBL cases (both domestic and cross-border), and foreign solutions have been examined and, at times, copied in recent reform initiatives. It is, therefore, desirable to have a brief look at the role and treatment of foreign stakeholders in EBL cases in China. Chapter thirteen, the last substantive chapter of this book, provides an overview of several key issues in this area, including a discussion of the cross-border application of the EBL and several recent cross-border bankruptcy cases.

13

The Role of Foreign Parties in Corporate Bankruptcy Cases in China

China has, over time, become an important player in the global economy. Chinese companies are among the largest and most influential corporate players; Chinese manufacturers are important suppliers to many global companies and governments; foreign investment flows into China, and Chinese Government and companies invest abroad; and since it announced the Belt and Road Initiative in 2013, China has become a global influencer and rulemaker as well. This remarkable transformation of China's economy contributed to China's economic success, but it has also created many challenges that the Chinese Government has to resolve. One such challenge is the need for an effective cross-border dispute settlement – including cross-border bankruptcy rules.[1]

This chapter, therefore, provides an overview of several issues that affect the role of foreign parties – debtors, creditors and other stakeholders – in corporate bankruptcy cases in China. Section 13.1 briefly examines how foreign stakeholders influenced the wording and implementation of the EBL. Section 13.2 then looks at the rules and official guidance that govern cross-border bankruptcies in China. Finally, Section 13.3 concludes with a discussion of several domestic and cross-border EBL cases in which foreign interests were affected.

13.1. Foreign Influence in the Making of the EBL

China has come a long way since Deng Xiaoping's economic reforms in the 1970s and 80s, and arguably one of the most significant changes has been its stepping out of isolation and becoming a member of the international market.[2] For China, it has provided business and investment opportunities, but also pressure to comply with certain international standards and to take steps to protect international interests. The nature of these interests and the way in which foreign stakeholders tried to protect them in China is the focus of this chapter.

Although China's opening up started in the early 1980s and the negotiations to become a member of the World Trade Organization started in 1986, China did not

---

[1] This was acknowledged by the SPC in 2017 in the SPC Opinions concerning Providing Judicial Services and Safeguards to the Construction of the Belt and Road (*Fafa* [2015] No 9).
[2] See Section 2.1 for a detailed discussion about China's economic development.

become a full member of the global market until it acceded to the WTO in 2001. The international community opened up to China, but only subject to certain conditions which aimed to protect key international interests and market rules. China had to promise to reduce tariffs on imports and to remove local protectionism. Importantly, China also had to undertake to gradually open up its domestic market to foreign goods and certain services (especially finance and telecommunications). Foreign companies would gain a large new market, and China's economy would benefit from foreign investment, foreign companies' know-how, new export opportunities, market discipline and greater economic efficiency thanks to foreign competition. It was hoped that, together, the changes would speed up China's economic reform process. It turned out that the hopes were largely fulfilled.[3] China's GDP and the economy grew fast,[4] Chinese businesses and consumers benefited from the new markets and products available to them, and the access to the international capital sped up the spectacular growth and development of China's economy.[5]

Enabling international trade in practice meant providing certain safeguards. China had to introduce market institutions and many laws to protect foreign newcomers against local protectionism and to ensure an equal playing field for all. China started publishing all rules online and in a specialised gazette; it introduced a public hearing system in 2005; and it amended or repealed more than 3,000 laws and regulations[6] – among them the 1986 bankruptcy law which was replaced by the EBL in 2006.

The EBL – like many other laws introduced in the 2000s – was inspired by foreign bankruptcy laws and the law-making process was influenced by foreign stakeholders.[7] Foreign influence was exerted using soft pressure from foreign actors in China (eg investors and entrepreneurs,[8] foreign governments and non-governmental organisations and experts) and through advice and rules arising from China's membership and cooperation with international bodies (eg WTO, IMF, foreign chambers of commerce). During the EBL drafting process, foreign experts, governments, chambers of commerce and international organisations actively lobbied the Chinese Government and took part in the consultation stage of law-making in order to protect their interests, ensure an equal playing field and prevent local protectionism. Foreign academics were also influential in sharing their understanding and experience with bankruptcy laws around the world.[9]

The Chinese Government refused to be bullied into blindly following international trends and standards and instead stressed that the rules that may work elsewhere might

---

[3] See eg L Brandt and TG Rawski, *China's Great Economic Transformation* (Cambridge University Press, 2008) 6 and ch 16.

[4] See Section 2.1.

[5] See eg The Economist (17.6.2014); NR Lardy, 'The Role of Foreign Trade and Investment in China's Economic Transformation' (1995) *The China Quarterly* 1065.

[6] See summary report 'China in the WTO: Past, Present and Future' (WTO, 2011), available at www.wto.org/english/thewto_e/acc_e/s7lu_e.pdf.

[7] See Section 2.4.2.

[8] Large foreign businesses seem to get a similar level of access and influence as large domestic companies – see S Kennedy, *The Business of Lobbying in China* (Harvard University Press, 2005) chs 3–5, and Section 11.2.2.1.

[9] See also Sections 4.1 and 4.2.

not be suitable for the hybrid developing–developed China.[10] Nevertheless, international organisations and governments have had some success in influencing the EBL. This is true especially in the early days after China's accession to the WTO when the later drafts of the EBL were being discussed.[11] It was at that time when additional provisions such as the rules on cross-border bankruptcy were added.[12] The final version of the EBL was a combination of foreign-inspired provisions and Chinese tools and mechanisms. The EBL drafters – many of whom had extensive knowledge and experience of foreign bankruptcy codes, having studied and worked abroad[13] – learned from and copied provisions concerning an insolvency test, employee protection, administrators, avoidable transactions, a moratorium, cramdown powers, a debtor-in-possession mechanism and super-priority financing from bankruptcy laws in Germany, France, the US, the UK and Japan. At the same time, however, the drafters also included several China-specific provisions such as courts' duty to maintain the socialist market economy, prioritisation of employee claims, and the retention of government liquidation committees in some EBL cases.[14] Moreover, some of the provisions that were clearly inspired by or taken from foreign laws were, over time, implemented 'with Chinese characteristics' – that is, to protect politically preferred interests and allow local protectionism rather than being implemented in an objective, independent manner.[15]

One of the areas that were heavily influenced by foreign rules and practices was the cross-border bankruptcy recognition. Its drafting and eventual inclusion in the EBL were influenced by three important international developments. Firstly, the publication of the UNCITRAL Model Law on Cross-Border Insolvency in 1997 shaped drafters' thinking about the desirability and scope of cross-border bankruptcy rules.[16] Secondly, the infamous GITIC case in 1999[17] highlighted the problem of not having cross-border bankruptcy rules. Importantly, one of the hired experts, Professor Wang Weiguo, was also a member of the EBL drafting team; his involvement in the case is likely to have influenced his thinking about cross-border bankruptcy rules in China. And thirdly, as was discussed earlier, China's accession to the WTO in 2001 carried with it obligations to provide access to foreign market participants – in exchange for access to foreign markets for Chinese companies – and provide a level-playing field for all market participants. Cross-border bankruptcy rules are an important tool for this purpose.

---

[10] China preferred to make gradual changes with local adaptations of the rules – also known as *Beijing Consensus* – over shock approach where new rules are introduced everywhere at once, without preparatory stages – known as *Washington Consensus*: M Myant and J Drahokoupil, *Transition Economies: Political Economy in Russia, Eastern Europe, and Central Asia* (Wiley, 2011). Some interpret their reluctance to adopt certain rules as protectionism: eg S Breslin, 'Globalization, International Coalitions, and Domestic Reform' (2004) 36 *Critical Asian Studies* 657.

[11] See Section 4.1.

[12] See J Shi, 'Cross-Border Insolvency' in R Parry (ed), *China's New Enterprise Bankruptcy Law* (Routledge, 2010).

[13] In particular Professor Li Shuguang and Professor Wang Weiguo: Z Zhang, *Corporate Reorganisations in China* (Cambridge University Press, 2018) 226.

[14] For details of the EBL provisions, see Section 4.2.

[15] See Sections 2.4, 8.3, 11.3.3–13.3.4 and 12.12.

[16] See eg J Shi, 'The Chinese Cross-Border Insolvency Law: Reality, Problems and Future' (2002) *Chinese Legal Science* 114.

[17] *CCIC Finance Ltd. v Guangdong International and Investment Corp* [2005] HKEC 1180.

13.2. Rules and Guidance that Govern Cross-border Bankruptcies in China

China had no rules on cross-border bankruptcy until the implementation of the EBL in June 2007. Arguably, China did not need cross-border bankruptcy rules under the 1986 law because it was largely isolated and the bankruptcy law was primarily focusing on disciplining the SOEs.[18] However, as the economy grew and China joined the global economy as a member of the WTO in 2001, it became evident that China needed a mechanism for dealing with the interests of foreign stakeholders in China and Chinese assets located abroad in the context of corporate bankruptcies.[19] There were a handful of pre-2007 cross-border bankruptcy cases which were dealt with by courts, but their approach was inconsistent and mostly unsatisfactory.[20] A new mechanism was, therefore, needed.

China decided not to adopt the UNCITRAL Model Law on Cross-Border Insolvency. Instead, a provision was added into the new EBL to govern cross-border bankruptcies. Article 5 embraces limited universalism.[21] Article 5(1) stipulates that EBL ruling affects all assets (located in China or abroad). However, Article 5(2) only allows foreign bankruptcy ruling to affect assets in China where there is an international or bilateral treaty between China and the relevant foreign jurisdiction, or based on mutual reciprocity so long as the foreign ruling would not violate Chinese laws; state sovereignty, security and social public interests; or harm the legitimate rights and interests of creditors in China.

The last condition in Article 5(2) raises an interesting question of whether the priority of employee claims – which is different from most other countries – would need to be protected under a foreign ruling in order to satisfy this condition. Some guidance was provided by SPC Judge Liu Guixiang at the press conference when releasing the first batch of typical EBL cases in 2018.[22] He said that lower courts must strive to resolve cross-border issues and that equal protection must be offered to domestic and foreign creditors. Nevertheless, he added, employee claims and tax claims must be 'reasonably protected'.[23] Judge Liu further explained that, 'after the satisfaction of domestic secured creditors, employee claims and tax claims', all remaining assets can be distributed in accordance with the provision of the foreign court.[24] This is problematic, however, because in many cases very little or no assets are left at that stage.

There are now several cases where EBL ruling was recognised by a foreign court under Article 5(1) of the EBL, as discussed in Section 3.2 below. This gives EBL administrators

---

[18] See Zhang, *Corporate Reorganisations* (2018) 222–23.

[19] The need became obvious particularly after the liquidation of Guangdong International Trust and Investment Corporate (GITIC), a high-profile failure of a state-owned bank in 1999: see eg J Lam, 'The Bankruptcy of GITIC' (1999) *Journal of International Banking law* 193; Z Xin, 'The Emerging Insolvency Risks of Chinese Financial Institutions' (1999) *Journal of International Banking and Finance Law* 91.

[20] See Shi, 'Cross-Border Insolvency' (2012).

[21] See eg Q Bu, 'China's Enterprise Bankruptcy Law: Cross-Border Perspectives' (2009) *International Insolvency Review* 187.

[22] Sohu (8.3.2018).

[23] ibid, para 49.

[24] ibid, para 50.

a legal basis for recovering debtors' assets that are located abroad. However, it does not give them an explicit power to also take part in bankruptcy proceedings abroad.[25]

On the other hand, recognition of foreign rulings in China under Article 5(2) of the EBL has been more problematic. China has a bilateral treaty on judicial assistance in civil and commercial matters with 39 countries, and 35 of these agreements include agreement on recognition of foreign judgments.[26] The list includes, importantly, Singapore, France, Italy, Poland and Russia. However, China does not have such agreements with some of its major business partners, including the US, Japan, the UK and the EU.[27] Moreover, a treaty does not guarantee automatic recognition because many countries – including China – impose additional conditions.[28]

In the absence of a treaty, the applicant must rely on the principle of reciprocity.[29] Initially, China relied on strict de facto reciprocity, meaning that a precedent had to exist that either country recognised and enforced the other country's judgment in a similar case.[30] The lack of such precedent has empowered many courts in China to refuse to recognise foreign judgments.[31] Based on this approach, Chinese courts are likely to recognise bankruptcy judgments from the US, Hong Kong and the British Virgin Islands, which have recognised EBL rulings in the past.[32]

The strict application of the reciprocity principle has been widely criticised.[33] Some have argued that China should be more proactive in establishing reciprocity with others by being the first to recognise foreign judgments.[34] Such proactivity was endorsed by the SPC's guidance to lower courts in 2015.[35] Pro-cooperation principles among the Belt and Road countries were further developed in the SPC's guidance in 2019,[36] which stressed the importance of equal protection for Chinese and foreign stakeholders, strong international judicial cooperation, recognition of foreign-related civil and commercial judgments. The 2019 document also included a provision which said that courts should 'improve the cross-border bankruptcy coordination mechanism, explore the application of the main bankruptcy procedures and the system of COMI, and

---

[25] cf Art 5 UNCITRAL Model Law on Cross-Border Insolvency.

[26] This is accurate as of 30 June 2020: China's Ministry of Foreign Affairs at www.fmprc.gov.cn/mfa_eng.

[27] Note that China signed the Hague Convention on the Choice of Court Agreements on 12 September 2017. However, it is yet to be ratified (accurate on 30 June 2020).

[28] For an overview of Chinese court decisions involving recognition and enforcement of foreign judgments and foreign court decisions involving Chinese judgments, see G Du and M Yu (16.7.2019).

[29] Note that reciprocity was not included as a prerequisite for recognition in the UNCITRAL Model Law on Cross-Border Insolvency due to the opposition from several countries: LC Ho, *Cross-Border Insolvency: A Commentary on the UNCITRAL Model Law*, 4th edn (Globe Law and Business Publishing, 2017) 7–8.

[30] See eg H Shen, 'Research on Some Difficult Problems in Recognition and Enforcement of Foreign Civil and Commercial Judgments' (2018) *Law Application* 9.

[31] See eg D Hu, 'Cross-border Insolvency Regime in China: Finding the Most Pragmatic Interim Solution for Globalised Companies under Localised Practices' (2018) *American Bankruptcy Law Journal* 523.

[32] See Section 13.3.2.

[33] See eg J Shi and Y Huang, 'Sino-US Milestone of Cross-border Bankruptcy Co-operation – Comment on Topoint Solar Case' (2017) *Journal of Application* 51.

[34] See eg W Zhu, 'Constructing Negative Reciprocity System in the Recognition and Enforcement of Foreign Judgments in China' (2017) *Hebei Law Science* 19.

[35] The SPC Notice concerning Providing Judicial Services and Safeguards to the Construction of the Belt and Road (*Fafa* [2015] No 9).

[36] The SPC Notice concerning the Provision of Judicial Services and Safeguards for the Construction of the 'Belt and Road' by Court (*Fafa* [2019] No 29).

protect the rights of all creditors and investors in accordance with the law'.[37] In addition, the SPC reached an agreement with other ASEAN country courts in Nanning in June 2017 that reciprocity should be presumed vis-à-vis other ASEAN jurisdictions.[38] The Nanning statement is not legally binding, nor is it an international treaty within the meaning of Article 5(1) of the EBL. Nevertheless, when read together with the other SPC documents, it is a clear signal that Chinese courts are moving towards wider recognition of foreign judgments.

The existence of bilateral treaties and the recent broadening of the reciprocity principle makes the recognition of cross-border bankruptcy rulings in China more likely. For the countries without such treaty, prior recognition, or outside of the Belt and Road and ASEAN group of countries, however, it may still be a struggle to get their proceedings recognised in China. These excluded jurisdictions may, nevertheless, benefit from recent changes in the approach of the SPC and may be able to argue that their foreign bankruptcy judgment should be recognised in China because their home jurisdiction 'could theoretically recognise Chinese bankruptcy proceedings were there to be a hypothetical application'.[39] Such extension – although theoretically sound – remains untested and so its validity is unclear.

Although cross-border bankruptcies from some foreign jurisdictions may be recognised in China, the rules are insufficient.[40] Calls for change have been heard from prominent local representatives – for example Yu Jihua, an NPC deputy and vice chairman of the Jiangxi Provincial Overseas Chinese Federation, who proposed that given China's increasingly global role, cross-border bankruptcy rules need to be revised soon.[41]

The need to introduce further rules about cross-border bankruptcy was also acknowledged at a national level by the SPC Judge Liu Guixiang at a press conference in March 2018[42] and again in his keynote speech at the 3rd China–Singapore Law and Judicial Roundtable in August 2019.[43] Judge Liu confirmed that the EBL would be updated 'soon' to provide further rules about cross-border bankruptcies in China.[44]

In the meantime, the recently inaugurated Shenzhen Bankruptcy Court[45] has been tasked with trialling possible cross-border rules and was given jurisdiction over cross-border bankruptcy cases.[46] Several recent studies consider China's options for reform

---

[37] ibid, Art 31.

[38] Nanning Statement of the 2nd China-Association of Southeast Asian Nations (ASEAN) Justice Forum (8.6.2017).

[39] 'China's recognition of foreign insolvency proceedings and VIE structures' (June 2020, Harneys and Fangda) International Insolvency & Restructuring Report 2020/21, available at www.capital-markets-intelligence.com/wp-content/uploads/2020/06/IIRR2020-21_Harneys-Fangda.pdf.

[40] See the Seminar on the 10th Anniversary of the Implementation of the Corporate Bankruptcy Law in B Lu (12.9.2017, People's Court News). See also Shi (n 12); MS Wee, 'The Belt and Road Initiative, China's Cross-Border Insolvency Law, and the UNCITRAL Model Law on Cross-Border Insolvency' (2020) *Chinese Journal of Comparative Law* 116.

[41] Y Li (15.3.2019, People's Court News).

[42] Sohu (8.3.2018).

[43] Full text available at www.court.gov.cn/zixun-xiangqing-179382.html.

[44] ibid.

[45] See Section 12.4.

[46] Y Ping and S Wang (15.1.2019, Yicai).

of its cross-border bankruptcy regime,[47] but it is unclear which of these options will be chosen by the Government in the end.

13.3. Foreign Stakeholders in Corporate Bankruptcy Cases in China

Foreign parties may be affected by a case of corporate bankruptcy in one of three ways. They can be a foreign party affected by an EBL case resolving bankruptcy of a Chinese company – discussed in Section 13.3.1 below. They can be a party based outside of China in a cross-border application of an EBL case – discussed in Section 13.3.2. Or they can be a party affected by corporate bankruptcy that is heard by a foreign court using foreign bankruptcy law – discussed in Section 13.3.3. Each situation gives rise to different rules and challenges.

13.3.1. Foreign Parties in Domestic EBL Cases

Despite the fears of many that foreign creditors would be discriminated against, the EBL, as written, puts foreign and Chinese creditors on the same footing. All my interviewees agreed that, in practice, foreign stakeholders receive the same treatment as domestic ones – that is, their relative power depends on their size and relative economic importance, not their ownership. Those with experience from less developed, more protective regions in central China added that there might be a degree of preferential treatment towards big SOEs.[48] But they all insisted that the clear trend and tendency is to treat foreign and domestic creditors of the same type equally. This was the case even in the much-criticised case of Wuxi Suntech Ltd in 2013.[49] The case concerned EBL reorganisation of Wuxi Suntech, which was incorporated in China and was a subsidiary of Suntech Powers Ltd, a holding company that was incorporated in the Cayman Islands. Most of the foreign creditors that were affected were in fact creditors of the holding company, not the reorganised subsidiary, and so the EBL did not concern their claims at all.

However, it is important to note that equal treatment of foreign and Chinese creditors does not mean that the recovery rates are the same as they may expect in their home jurisdiction or even Hong Kong.[50] What it does mean is that foreign creditors can expect the same treatment as Chinese creditors of similar type (eg large unsecured creditors, secured creditors, trade creditors, etc).[51] This was emphasised by all my

---

[47] See eg R Parry and G Nan, 'The future direction of China's cross-border insolvency laws, related issues and potential problems' (2018) *International Insolvency Review* 5; G Long, F Wang and L Ye, 'China's cross-border bankruptcy development path selection: Singapore's experience and enlightenment' (2020) *People's Justice* 1.

[48] Note that domestic private companies and foreign companies would be treated the same there.

[49] See eg K Bradsher (20.3.2013, New York Times); U Desai and M Price (18.5.2015, Business Insider).

[50] See eg Yiu (11.10.2015, SCMP); Shim (12.4.2013, Business Insider).

[51] See also OHM Yau, H You and HC Steele (eds), *China Business: Challenges in the 21st Century* (The Chinese University Press, 2004) 84.

interviewees – Chinese and foreign – and was also confirmed in an empirical study of Chinese reorganisations in 2007–15, which shows that foreign and Chinese unsecured creditors always received equal treatment.[52]

13.3.2. Cross-border EBL Cases – Article 5(1) EBL

Although slow at first, the recognition and enforcement of Chinese EBL judgments by foreign courts have been increasing. So far, EBL judgments have been recognised by courts in the US, Hong Kong and the British Virgin Islands. Some of these cases are discussed below to illustrate the circumstances in which recognition takes place and to suggest that this trend indicates that it is likely that there will be further recognitions in the future.

The US Bankruptcy Court in New Jersey was the first foreign court to recognise Chinese EBL ruling. The Haining Intermediate People's Court commenced the EBL reorganisation of *Zhejiang Topoint Photoelectric Co Ltd* in 2013. In 2014, the Haining Court applied to the New Jersey Court under Chapter 15 of the US Bankruptcy Code (as a foreign main proceeding) and was granted an interim relief order to prevent creditors in the US from commencing or continuing any action in the US against the debtors' assets.[53] The EBL administrator was allowed to collect the debtor's assets in the US (which he claimed were worth almost USD 12 million) and could sue and be sued in US courts. The US recognition was based on the rules under Chapter 15 of the US Bankruptcy Code rather than Article 5 of the EBL, which is important as there is no treaty nor proven pre-existing reciprocity.[54]

The Hong Kong High Court recognised two Chinese EBL rulings in the first half of 2020. Unlike the position in the US, the recognition by the Hong Kong court was based on reciprocity.[55] The first case – *CEFC Shanghai International Group Limited*[56] – concerned an application from the joint administrators in CEFC's EBL liquidation (with formal support from the Shanghai Intermediate People's Court) to the Hong Kong court. The administrator sought assistance in a claim against CEFC's Hong Kong subsidiary, Shanghai Huaxin Group (Hong Kong) Ltd, which was in liquidation. The recognition order was granted and all proceedings against CEFC's Hong Kong subsidiary were stayed. The main criteria for recognition are that the foreign bankruptcy proceedings must be collective bankruptcy proceedings which are opened in the company's country of incorporation.[57] As a result of this decision, EBL procedures are capable of being recognised in Hong Kong.

---

[52] Zhang (n 13) 231–33.

[53] *In re Zhejiang Topoint Photoelectric Co Ltd* [2015] US Bankruptcy Court for the District of New Jersey 14-24549.

[54] Another prominent Chinese EBL ruling that was recognised in the US was *Reward Science and Technology Industry Group Ltd* in 2019: see eg SL Chenetz and TN Moss (14.1.2020, Perkins Coie).

[55] J Shi, 'Hong Kong Court's Recognition and Assistance of Mainland Bankruptcy Procedures – From the Perspective of Huaxin Bankruptcy' delivered at China Bankruptcy Law Forum, available at qnmlgb.tech/artic les/5ef21bde4e7418bb50ae9dcd.

[56] [2020] HKCFI 167.

[57] ibid.

In the second case – *Shenzhen Everich Supply Chain Ltd.*[58] – the Hong Kong court also recognised an EBL liquidation ruling in China (Shenzhen) and granted assistance to the EBL administrator. This time, the Hong Kong court went further and granted the EBL administrator a right to take control of Shenzhen Nianfu's Hong Kong subsidiaries.[59]

Finally, in the 2018 case of *Industrial Bank Financial Leasing Ltd v Xing Libin*,[60] the British Virgin Islands High Court recognised three EBL judgments. The basis for such recognition was not explained in the case. In order to ensure effective enforcement of the judgment, the court also appointed equitable receivers in the British Virgin Islands to take control of the debtor's assets in the territory (shares in the British Virgin Islands holding company, which owned debtors' assets in Hong Kong).[61]

13.3.3. Cross-border Cases Based on Foreign Bankruptcy Law – Article 5(2) EBL

In principle, Article 5(2) of the EBL permits Chinese courts to recognise bankruptcy rulings from foreign courts so long as there is a treaty or reciprocity, and so long as the additional conditions are satisfied.[62] However, it has been rare for courts to recognise foreign rulings in general[63] – and extremely rare for Chinese courts to recognise foreign bankruptcy rulings in particular.[64]

Nevertheless, judicial recognition of foreign bankruptcy judgments is possible. Under the 1986 law, the Foshan Intermediate People's Court recognised an Italian bankruptcy ruling in the case of *B&T Ceramic Group Srl*.[65] The recognition was based on a bilateral treaty on judicial assistance between Italy and China. Even under the EBL, for the 39 countries that have such bilateral treaties,[66] this is a helpful precedent which suggests that their case may also be recognised on this basis so long as cross-border bankruptcy is within the scope of the treaty and the conditions in Art 5(2) EBL are satisfied.

Under the EBL, judicial recognition of foreign bankruptcy judgments has been very difficult. Some commentators discuss the German case of Zublin International Co. Zublin won an arbitration award against a Chinese company. The award was later set

---

[58] [2020] HKCFI 965.

[59] ibid.

[60] BVIHC (Com) 0032 of 2018.

[61] For a discussion of cross-border insolvency rules in BVI, see eg 'Recognition of foreign insolvency proceedings and foreign insolvency practitioners in the BVI' (April 2017, Mourant Guide) available at www.mourant.com/file-library/media---2017/2017-guides/recognition-of-foreign-insolvency-proceedings-and-foreign-insolvency-practitioners-in-the-bvi-(updated).pdf.

[62] See Section 13.2.

[63] See eg J Huang, *Interregional Recognition and Enforcement of Civil and Commercial Judgments* (Hart Publishing, 2014); W Zhang, 'Sino–Foreign Recognition and Enforcement of Judgments: A Promising "Follow-Suit" Model?' (2017) *Chinese Journal of International Law* 515.

[64] See eg the Shanghai Court's refusal to recognise the English administration order concerning the Lehman Brothers in 2009 on the grounds that China and UK have neither a bilateral treaty nor reciprocity: see Zhang (n 13) 234.

[65] [2000] Foshan Interm Civ No 633.

[66] See Section 13.2.

aside by the Wuxi Court because the arbitration clause was invalid. A German bankruptcy judgment was issued by the Montabaur Regional Court in Germany in 2009. The German administrator applied to the Wuhan Intermediate People's Court, which decided to recognise the German ruling. The recognition was based on established reciprocity between China and Germany.[67] Unfortunately, the case is not publicly available and remains the only case of recognition under Art 5(2) of the EBL.

In practice, Chinese courts have been willing to permit foreign bankruptcy administrators to represent the debtor in local legal proceedings. In the 2014 case of *Sino-Environmental Technology Group v Thumb Environmental Technology Group*,[68] the SPC held that a foreign bankruptcy administrator could act on behalf of the debtor in China in accordance with the law of the place where the debtor is incorporated.[69] Some commentators describe this as a back-door recognition.[70] However, without full recognition of foreign bankruptcy ruling, bankruptcy administrators cannot fully perform functions – in particular their duty to secure the foreign debtor's assets in China for the benefit of all creditors (eg by preventing individual enforcement against debtor's property).

Seeking recognition of a foreign bankruptcy judgment in China is possible in theory, but challenging in practice. If a party cannot show a bilateral agreement between China and its country of domicile or prove reciprocity, Chinese courts are unlikely to recognise the foreign judgment. This is problematic and needs to be addressed in the next round of reform.[71]

---

[67] See J Huang, 'Commercial Issues in Private International Law' in E Douglas, V Bath, M Keyes and A Dickinson (eds), *Commercial Issues in Private International Law* (Hart Publishing, 2019).

[68] (2014) Minsizhongzi No 20 Civil Ruling.

[69] ibid.

[70] A McGinty and S Tait, 'Will the Chinese Courts Grant "Back-Door Recognition" to Overseas Insolvency Practitioners?' (2010) *Corporate Rescue and Insolvency* 195.

[71] China adopt the UNCITRAL Model Law on Cross-Border Insolvency, or do so with modifications: C Jin, 'Recognition of and Assistance in Foreign Insolvency Proceedings in China: Interpretation and Legislation' (2019) *Tribune of Political Science and Law* 143.

Conclusion

This book presented new findings – supported by new qualitative and quantitative data and previously unexplored sources – about how the EBL works, its many limitations, and it proposed improvements that could ensure more efficient implementation of the law in practice. Although the book is in many places critical of the EBL and the environment in which it operates, it is important to note that much has been achieved and much should be celebrated. As Chapter four pointed out, the enactment of the EBL itself was a major legislative success. After years of government- and SOE-centric quasi-resolution of corporate distress, China finally recognised the need to act and provided a modern, market-driven mechanism for resolving corporate financial distress. The law as written had some flaws, but also an enormous potential. Over time, however, it became clear that additional guidance was needed to explain and support the rules in the EBL. This is where the SPC and local government's guidance came into play. In addition, as the level of expertise and experience increased – especially in the most EBL-active regions such as Shenzhen and Wenzhou – the enforcers themselves created further rules and proposals that helped improve the EBL further.

The book started with four questions – their answers are the biggest contribution of this book. The first question focused on how the EBL operates and why it is so rarely used. Chapter four provided a detailed discussion of the EBL rules and supporting guidance. As such, it provides a reference point for those who wish to know more about China's corporate bankruptcy law as written. As the same time, Chapters five and ten also showed that China has a comparatively low number of bankruptcy cases – both in absolute terms and when contextualised. Chapters six to nine then suggested that the limited use of the EBL may be explained by four interlinked groups of constraints that were identified by my interviewees and supported by a variety of primary and secondary sources. The constraints were, firstly, flaws in the EBL; secondly, flaws in the surrounding rules and practices; thirdly, limitations and biases of EBL enforcers; and fourthly, the parties' perception that non-EBL alternatives are better than the EBL. These constraints were repeatedly identified in my interviews as reducing parties' expected payoffs or preventing them from using the law – both of which are likely to disincentivise the parties from using the EBL.

The second question asked whether it matters that the EBL is so rarely used and whether it is desirable to use the EBL more. It was argued in Chapter ten that it does matter, and that there are three reasons why a greater, more efficient use of the EBL may be desirable. Firstly, the Chinese Government recently admitted that bankruptcy law is not used enough to deal with corporate financial distress and that a greater use is needed to deal with companies' under-productivity, over-capacity, inefficiency and bad debt. Secondly, the number of bankruptcy law cases in China is significantly lower than elsewhere – both in terms of absolute numbers and when contextualised as a ratio of bankruptcy cases per total number of companies across several reviewed economies. And thirdly, several economic indicators suggest that China's economy is riddled with (actually or nearly) insolvent companies whose financial distress is either ignored or is dealt with using comparatively less efficient non-EBL alternatives.

It was further argued that greater and more efficient use of the EBL is likely to give rise to several economic benefits. They include comparatively more efficient resolution of financial distress that is currently available under the non-EBL alternatives (particularly for complex cases); fewer cases of debt avoidance; improved control of bad debt; greater amount and lower cost of credit; better allocation of resources; improved business environment, more investment and more entrepreneurship; and a strengthened rule of law in China.

The third question then turned to China's reform options that would ameliorate the identified shortcomings. Chapter eleven put forward three sets of reform proposals that would address the constraints identified in Chapters six to eight, namely changes aimed at the written provisions of the EBL and proposed new provisions to be added to the EBL; changes aimed at improving the surrounding rules and practices; and changes aimed at EBL enforcers. Chapter twelve then provided an overview and a discussion of 10 reform initiatives that have been trialled in several provinces and regions in China between 2015 and 2020.

The fourth, and final, question focused on the role of foreign stakeholders in the making and implementation of the EBL. Chapter thirteen provided an overview of the rules and practices that govern cross-border bankruptcies and domestic EBL cases that affect foreign stakeholders. The discussion also examined several recent cases that shed light on the courts' reasoning. It substantiated the generally perceived fact that enforcing foreign bankruptcy judgments is hard, but it also pointed out the rules that make such recognition possible in the future.

Much has been achieved over the past 13 years – from June 2007 when the EBL was implemented, to June 2020 when this book ends – but, as Chapters ten to twelve suggest, there is still more that needs to be done. China still does not have a national personal bankruptcy law; more specialised bankruptcy courts and professionals are needed; local governments are still heavily involved in many EBL cases; and many questions remain unanswered. Moreover, the scope of the recent reform initiatives has been limited to select regions and their impact on judicial and commercial practice is yet to be seen. Similarly, there is a temptation to only focus on improving the EBL and the surrounding rules and practices.[1] Although important, this book has argued that they are of secondary importance. Instead, the decisive factor for whether the EBL will be used more efficiently in the future is the question of whether the Party-state finally realises that their unlimited and unregulated interference[2] with the EBL process is harmful and undesirable in the long term.[3] China is at a stage where it can no longer afford to

---

[1] See chs 6 and 7 and Sections 11.1–11.2.

[2] Note that there is a difference between the Party-state's 'interference' and 'support'. The latter does not transgress on judicial independence and so can continue. The former, however, cannot. See Section 11.3.5.

[3] See Sections 10.3.2 and 11.3.5. Note also that the EBL was written to be applied independently: Section 4.1.

ignore this argument. With the economy slowing down and the amount of corporate and government debt growing, China needs to allow the EBL – a well-written law with great potential – to impose hard budget constraints and remove all unviable companies from the market without outside interference. This will take time.[4] However, unless and until courts are allowed to hear EBL cases independently, the EBL will not be able to deliver all the predicted benefits that have been observed elsewhere and is unlikely to fully maximise the potential of a well-functioning bankruptcy law.[5]

[4] See Section 10.3.2.
[5] See Sections 1.2 and 10.2.

BIBLIOGRAPHY

Acharya, V and Subramanian, K, 'Bankruptcy Codes and Innovation' (2009) *Review of Financial Studies* 4949.

Ahearne, A and Shinada, N, 'Zombie firms and economic stagnation in Japan' (2005) *International Economics and Economic Policy* 363.

Allen, F, Qian, J and Qian, M, 'Law, finance and economic growth in China' (2005) *Journal of Financial Economics* 57.

Anderlini, J, 'China Orders banks to keep lending to insolvent state projects' (Financial Times, 15.5.2015).

Andreas, J, 'Battling over political and cultural power during the Chinese Cultural Revolution' (2002) *Theory and Society* 463.

Ang, L and Wang, J, 'Judicial Independence in Dominant Party States: Singapore's Possibilities for China' (2019) *Asian Journal of Comparative Law* 337.

Ang, YY and Jia, N, 'Perverse Complementarity: Political Connections and the Use of Courts among Private Firms in China' (2014) 76 *Journal of Politics* 318.

Aoki, M, *Corporations in Evolving Diversity: Cognition, Governance and Institutions* (Oxford, Oxford University Press, 2010).

Araujo, A, Reffeira, R and Funchal, B, 'The Brazilian bankruptcy law experience' (2012) *Journal of Corporate Finance* 994.

Armour, J, 'The Law and Economics of Corporate Insolvency: A Review' (2001) ESRC Centre for Business Research, University of Cambridge Working Paper 197/2001.

—— 'Personal Insolvency and the Demand for Venture Capital' (2004) *European Business Organization Law Review* 87.

—— 'The Rise of the "Pre-Pack": Corporate Restructuring in the UK and Proposals for Reform' in RP Austin and FJG Aoun (eds), *Restructuring Companies in Troubled Times: Director and Creditor Perspectives* (Sydney, Ross Parsons Centre of Commercial, Corporate and Taxation Law, 2012).

—— and Cumming, D, 'Bankruptcy Law and Entrepreneurship' (2008) *American Law and Economics Review* 303.

—— and Deakin, S, 'Norms in Private Insolvency: The 'London Approach' to the Resolution of Financial Distress' (2001) *Journal of Corporate Law Studies* 21.

—— Hansmann, H and Kraakman, R, 'Agency Problems and Legal Strategies' in R Kraakman, J Armour, P Davies, L Enriques, H Hansmann, G Hertig, K Hopt, H Kanda and E Rock, *The Anatomy of Corporate Law: A Comparative and Functional Approach*, 3rd edn (Oxford, Oxford University Press, 2017).

—— Hertig, G and Kanda, H, 'Transactions with Creditors' in R Kraakman, J Armour, P Davies, L Enriques, H Hansmann, G Hertig, K Hopt, H Kanda and E Rock, *The Anatomy of Corporate Law: A Comparative and Functional Approach*, 3rd edn (Oxford, Oxford University Press, 2017).

—— Hsu, A and Walters, A, 'Corporate Insolvency in the United Kingdom: The Impact of the Enterprise Act 2002' (2008) *European Company and Financial Law Review* 1613.

Arner, D, Booth, C, Lejot, P and Hsu, B, 'Property Rights, Collateral, Creditors Rights and Insolvency in East Asia' (2007) *Texas International Law Journal* 515.

Aron, J, 'Growth and institutions: A review of the evidence' (15/2000) *The World Bank Research Observer* 99.

Arsenault, SJ, 'The Westernization of Chinese Bankruptcy: An Examination of China's New Corporate Bankruptcy Law through the Lens of the UNCITRAL Legislative Guide to Insolvency Law' (2008–09) *Penn State International Law Review* 45.

Asia News 'Beijing to maintain restrictions on real estate market' (28.11.2011), available at www.asianews.it/news-en/Beijing-to-maintain-restrictions-on-real-estate-market-23299.html.

Asiaweek, 'The sell-off' (30.11.2001).

Awokuse, TO and Yin, H, 'Intellectual property rights protection and the surge in FDI in China' (2010) *Journal of Comparative Economics* 217.

Aziz, J and Duenwald, C, 'Growth-Financial Intermediation Nexus in China' (2002) IMF Working Paper No 02/194.

Bae, K and Goyal, VK, 'Creditor Rights Enforcement and Bank Loans' (2009) *Journal of Finance* 823.

Bai, C, Lu, J and Tao, Z, 'Property rights protection and access to bank loans' (2006) *Economics of Transition* 611.

Baker, GP, Jensen, MC and Murphy, KJ, 'Compensation and Incentives: Practice vs. Theory' (1988) *Journal of Finance* 593.

Balding, C, 'Sizing up NPL risk in China' (Financial Times, 28.10.2015).

Barbara-Francis, C, 'Quasi-Public, Quasi-Private Trends in Emerging Economies: The Case of China' (2001) *Comparative Politics* 276.

Barboza, D, 'Coin of Realm in China Graft: Phony Receipts' (New York Times, 8.8.2013), available at www.nytimes.com%2F2013%2F08%2F04%2Fbusiness%2Fglobal%2Fcoin-of-realm-in-china-graft-phony-receipts.html.

Baum, R, *Burying Mao: Chinese Politics in the Age of Deng Xiaoping* (Woodstock, Princeton University Press, 1996).

BBVA, 'China's shadow bank lending: a threat to financial stability?' (China Banking Watch, BBVA Research, 23.11.2011), available at www.bbvaresearch.com/KETD/fbin/mult/111123_ChinaBankingWatch_En_tcm348-280630.pdf?ts=2012012.

Bedford, OA and Hwang, K, 'Guilt and Shame in Chinese Culture' (2003) *Journal for the Theory of Social Behaviour* 127.

Berk, JB, Stanton, R and Zechner, J, 'Human Capital, Bankruptcy and Capital Structure' (2010) *Journal of Finance* 891.

Bernstein, L, 'Opting out of the Leal System: Extralegal Contractual Relations in the Diamond Industry' (1992) *Journal of Legal Studies* 115.

Bernstein, T, 'Stalinism, famine and Chinese peasants Grain procurements during the Great Leap Forward' (1984) *Theory and Society* 339.

Bharati, P, Lee, I and Chaudhury, A (eds), *Global Perspectives on Small and Medium Enterprises and Strategic Information Systems: International Approaches* (Hershey, Business Science Reference, 2010).

Bi, H, 'The Role of Court in Corporate Reorganization' (2009) *Shandong Judicial Review* 68.

Blasek, K, *Rule of Law* (Berlin, Springer, 2015).

Bloomberg, 'China has its worst-ever start to a year for defaults' (2.4.2017), available at www.bloomberg.com/news/articles/2017-04-02/china-just-had-its-worst-ever-start-to-a-year-for-bond-defaults.

Booth, C, 'The 2006 PRC Enterprise Bankruptcy Law: the wait is finally over' (2008) *Singapore Academic of Law Journal* 275.

—— and Wang, W, 'Study on Alternative Approaches for Debt Restructuring of Enterprises in China' (World Bank Report for the State Economy and Trade Commission of China, 2002).

—— and Zhang, X, 'Chinese Bankruptcy Law in an Emerging Market Economy: The Shenzhen Experience' (2001) *Columbia Journal of Asian Law* 1.

Borst, N, 'China Shadow Banking Primer' (PIIE, 1.11.2011), available at piie.com/blogs/china-economic-watch/china-shadow-banking-primer.

Bradsher, K, 'Suntech Unit Declares Bankruptcy' (New York Times, 20.3.2013), available at www.nytimes.com/2013/03/21/business/energy-environment/suntech-declares-bankruptcy-china-says.html.

Brandt, L and Rawski, TG, *China's Great Economic Transformation* (Cambridge, Cambridge University Press, 2008).

Branigan, T, 'Chinese figures show fivefold rise in babies sick from contaminated milk' (The Guardian, 2.12.2008), available at www.theguardian.com/world/2008/dec/02/china.

Breslin, S, 'Globalization, International Coalitions and Domestic Reform' (2004) 36 *Critical Asian Studies* 657.

Bris, A, Welch, I and Zhu, N, 'The Costs of Bankruptcy: Chapter 7 Liquidation vs. Chapter 11 Reorganization' (2005) *Journal of Finance* 1298.

Brown, K, *The New Emperors: Power and the Princelings in China* (London, IB Tauris, 2014).

Bu, Q, 'China's Enterprise bankruptcy Law: Cross-Border Perspectives' (2009) *International Insolvency Review* 187.

Buckley, C and Hernandez, J, 'China Seeks to Avoid Mass Layoffs While Cutting Production' (New York Times, 16.3.2016), available at www.nytimes.com/2016/03/17/world/asia/china-premier-li-keqiang-economy.html?src=recg&_r=0.

Bufford, S and Yanagida, K, 'Japan's Revised Laws on Business Reorganization: An Analysis' (2006) *Cornell International Law Journal* 1.

Burns, JP and Zhou, Z, 'Performance management in the Government of the People's Republic of China' (2010) *OECD Journal on Budgeting* 1.

Caballero, R, Hoshi, T and Kashyap, A, 'Zombie Lending and Depressed Restructuring in Japan' (2008) *American Economic Review* 1943.

Cai, H and Treisman, D, 'Did Government Decentralization Cause China's Economic Miracle?' (2006) *World Politics* 505.

Cai, J, 'Private lenders thrive in China as banks neglect small clients' (South China Morning Post, 6.1.2014), available at www.scmp.com/business/banking-finance/article/1398701/private-lenders-thrive-china-banks-neglect-small-clients.

Cai, K, 'Milk scandal firm Sanlu declared bankrupt' (China Daily, 13.2.2009), available at www.chinadaily.com.cn/china/2009-02/13/content_7472161.htm.

—— 'Opinion: Shenzhen Passes Milestone With Personal Bankruptcy Regulation' (Caixin, 24.6.2020), available at www.caixinglobal.com/2020-06-24/opinion-shenzhen-passes-milestone-with-personal-bankruptcy-regulation-101572018.html.

Cai, Y, 'Local Governments and the Suppression of Popular Resistance in China' (2008) *China Quarterly* 24.

Caixin 'CX Daily: A Bankruptcy Law Revamp Must Put Local Governments in Their Place' (10.4.2019), available at www.caixinglobal.com/2019-04-10/cx-daily-a-bankruptcy-law-revamp-must-put-local-governments-in-their-place-101402326.html.

—— 'Chinese Banks Told to Curb Loans to Developers, Homebuyers' (11.9.2019), available at www.caixinglobal.com/2019-09-11/chinese-banks-told-to-curb-loans-to-developers-homebuyers-101461061.html.

Callick, R, *The Party Forever: Inside China's Modern Communist Elite* (New York, Palgrave Macmillan, 2013).

Cao, S, 'Survey Report Concerning the Enterprise Bankruptcy Law' (May 1986).

—— 'The Storm Over Bankruptcy' (1998) 31 *Chinese Law and Government* 12.

Cao, Y, 'NPC mulls end of death penalty for some crimes' (China Daily, 26.11.2014), available at www.chinadaily.com.cn/kindle/2014-11/26/content_18980580.htm.

—— 'Courts told to enforce judgments' (China Daily, 7.1.2016), available at usa.chinadaily.com.cn/epaper/2016-01/07/content_22976702.htm.

—— 'To ease load, more IP courts planned' (China Daily, 30.8.2017), available at www.chinadaily.com.cn/china/2017-08/30/content_31308314.htm.

Carney, RW, *Authoritarian Capitalism* (Cambridge, Cambridge University Press, 2018).

Carruthers, B and Halliday, T, 'Negotiating Globalization: Global Scripts and Intermediation in the Construction of Asian Insolvency Regimes' (2006) *Law & Social Inquiry* 521.

Casey, A, 'Bankruptcy's Endowment Effect' (2016) *Emory Bankruptcy Developments Journal* 141.

Castellucci, I, 'Rule of Law with Chinese Characteristics' (2007) 13 *Annual Survey of International & Comparative Law* 35.

Chan, A, Madsen, R and Unger, J, *Chen Village under Mao and Deng* (Berkeley, University of California Press, 1992).

Chang, T, 'The Making of the Chinese Bankruptcy Law: A Study In the Chinese Legislative Process' (1987) *Harvard International Law Journal* 333.

Chen, D, Deakin, S, Siems, M and Wang, B, 'Law, Trust and Institutional Change in China: Evidence from Qualitative Fieldwork' (2017) *Journal of Corporate Law Studies* 1.

Chen, F, 'Subsistence Crises, Managerial Corruption and Labour Protests in China' (2000) *The China Journal* 41.

Chen, J, 'China: Constitutional Changes and Legal Development' in A Tay and A Leung (eds), *Greater China – Law, Society and Trade* (Sydney, Law Book Company, 1995).

Chen, S, 'Our Legislative Trend in the 1990s' (Guangming Daily, 9.3.1994).

Chenetz, SL and Moss, TN, 'Why Chinese Companies File Chapter 15 Cases in US Bankruptcy Courts' (Perkins Coie, 14.1.2020), available at www.perkinscoie.com/en/news-insights/why-chinese-companies-file-chapter-15-cases-in-us-bankruptcy-courts.html.

Cheung, Y, Jing, L, Lu, T, Rau, PR and Stouraitis, A, 'Tunnelling and propping up' (2009) 17 *Pacific-Basin Finance Journal* 372.

China Bond Rating Co Ltd and Hum, Y, 'A Study on Unsecured Debt Recovery Rates in Corporate Bankruptcies in China' (China Economic Net, 9.4.2014), available at finance.ce.cn/rolling/201404/09/t20140409_2627094.shtml.

China Briefing, 'Obtaining Land-Use Rights for FIEs in China' (19.2.2014), available at www.china-briefing.com/news/2014/02/19/obtaining-land-use-rights-for-fies-in-china.html.

China Labour Bulletin, 'Strikes and protests by China's workers soar to record heights in 2015' (7.1.2016), available at www.clb.org.hk/content/strikes-and-protests-china's-workers-soar-record-heights-2015.

—— 'China starts to shift social insurance burden from employers to workers' (29.6.2016), available at clb.org.hk/content/china-starts-shift-social-insurance-burden-employers-workers.

—— 'Worker protests on the rise as China's car industry shrinks' (30.7.2019), available at www.clb.org.hk/content/worker-protests-rise-china's-car-industry-shrinks.

China Law Translate, 'The Curious Case of China's Guiding Cases System' (21.2.2017), available at www.chinalawtranslate.com/en/the-curious-case-of-chinas-guiding-cases-system.

China's Ministry of Justice, 'New lawyers must make an oath of loyalty' (21.3.2012), available at www.moj.gov.cn/index/content/2012-03/21/content_3445267.htm?node=7318.

Cho, S, 'Continuing Economic Reform in the People's Republic of China: Bankruptcy Legislation Leads the Way' (1996) *Hastings International and Company Law Review* 739.

Chow, G, 'Economic Reform and Growth in China' (2004) *Annals of Economics and Finance* 127.

—— *Interpreting China's Economy* (Singapore, World Scientific Publishing, 2010).

Choyleva, D, 'China has no choice but to walk financial tightrope' (Financial Times, 21.6.2017).

Claessens, S and Klapper, L, 'Bankruptcy Around the World: Explanation of its Relative Use' (World Bank, 2002).

Clarke, D, 'Empirical Research in Chinese Law' in E Jensen and T Heller (eds), *Rule of Law: Legal and Judicial Reform in Developing and Transition Countries* (Stanford, Stanford University Press, 2003).

Collier, A, 'China's shadow finance time-bomb could trigger crisis' (Financial Times, 26.6.2017).

Concise Encyclopaedia of Democracy (London, Routledge, 2013).

Congressional-Executive Commission on China, 'Judicial Independence in the PRC', available at www.cecc.gov/judicial-independence-in-the-prc.

Cook, S, 'After the Iron Rice Bowl: Extending the Safety Net in China' (2000) IDS Discussion Paper 377.

Cooter, R, 'Law from Order' (1997) JMO Working Papers in Law, Economics and Institutions.

—— 'Do Good Laws Make Good Citizens? An Economic Analysis of Internalizing Legal Values' (2000) UC Berkeley Law & Economics Research Paper No 2000-8.

—— and Schäfer, H, *Solomon's Knot* (Princeton, Princeton University Press, 2011).

Coughlin, CC, Chrystal, KA and Wood, GE, 'Protectionist Trade Policies: A Survey of Theory, Evidence and Rationale' (Federal Reserve Bank of St Louis, January/February 1988), available at files.stlouisfed.org/files/htdocs/publications/review/88/01/Protectionist_Jan_Feb1988.pdf.

Credit Suisse, 'Case Studies on the Monitoring of Informal Credit Markets' (Credit Suisse Economics Research, 28.9.2011).

Cull, R and Xu, L, 'Who gets credit? The behaviour of bureaucrats and state banks in allocating credit to Chinese state-owned enterprises' (2003) *Journal of Development Economics* 533.

Dalkir, K, *Knowledge Management in theory and practice* (London, Routledge, 2013).

Dam, K, *Law-Growth Nexus: The Rule of Law and Economic Development* (Washington DC, Brookings Institution Press, 2006).

—— 'The Judiciary and Economic Development' (March 2006) University of Chicago, John M Olin Law & Economics Working Paper No 287.

Danese, P, 'China: Foreign banks fumble over their expansion strategies' (EuroMoney, 29.6.2019), available at www.euromoney.com/article/b18vjw1pb6dykl/china-foreign-banks-fumble-over-their-expansion-strategies.

Davydenko, SA and Franks, JR, 'Do Bankruptcy Codes Matter? A Study of Defaults in France, Germany and the UK' (2008) *Journal of Finance* 565.

Deakin, S, 'Legal Evolution: Integrating Economic and Systemic Approaches' (2011) Centre for Business Research, University of Cambridge Working Paper No 424.

DeLisle, J, 'China's Legal System' in WA Joseph (ed), *Politics in China*, 3rd edn (Oxford, Oxford University Press, 2019).

Desai, U and Price, M, 'China's foreign creditors are running into trouble with the country's court system' (Business Insider, 18.5.2015), available at www.businessinsider.com/r-amid-china-slowdown-foreign-creditors-face-bankruptcy-riddle-2015-5.

Dewaelheyns, N and Van Hulle, C, 'Legal Reform and Aggregate Small and Micro Business Bankruptcy Rates: Evidence from the 1997 Belgian Bankruptcy Code' (May 2006) KU Leuven AFI Working Paper No 0607.

Dey, A, 'Corporate Governance and Agency Conflicts' (2008) *Journal of Accounting Research* 1143.

Ding, X, 'The Socialist Market Economy: China and the World' (2009) 73 *Science & Society* 235.

Djankov, S, McLiesh, C and Schleifer, A, 'Private credit in 129 countries' (2007) *Journal of Financial Economics* 299.

—— Hart, O, McLiesh, C and Shleifer, A, 'Debt Enforcement Around the World' (2008) *Journal of Political Economy* 1105.

Douglas, E, Bath, V, Keyes, M and Dickinson, A (eds), *Commercial Issues in Private International Law* (Oxford, Hart Publishing, 2019).

Drahokoupil, J and Myant M, *Transition Economies: Political Economy in Russia, Eastern Europe and Central Asia* (Hoboken, Wiley & Sons, 2011).

Drehmann, M and Tsatsaronis, K, 'The credit-to-GDP gap and countercyclical capital buffers: questions and answers' (BIS, 9.3.2014), available at www.bis.org/publ/qtrpdf/r_qt1403g.htm.

Dreyer, JT, *China's Political System: Modernization and Tradition* (New York, Longman, 2010).

Du, G and Yu, M, 'List of China's Cases on Recognition of Foreign Judgments' (16.7.2019), available at www.chinajusticeobserver.com/a/list-of-chinas-cases-on-recognition-of-foreign-judgments.

Du, J and Girman, S, 'Red Capitalists: Political Connections and Firm Performance in China' (2010) *Kyklos* 530.

Duan, J, 'Statement on the Rule of Law at the National and International Levels' (2008) *Chinese Journal of International Law* 509.

Durden, T, 'China "Faked, Forged" Documents For Exports And Imports' (ZeroHedge, 25.9.2014), available at www.zerohedge.com/news/2014-09-25/china-faked-forged-documents-exports-and-imports-least-10-billion-fake-trade-exposed.

—— 'Credit Suisse Warns on China' (ZeroHedge, 10.12.2015), available at www.zerohedge.com/news/2015-12-10/credit-suisse-warns-china-some-companies-are-having-borrow-pay-staff-salaries.

—— 'Thousands Of Angry Unpaid Chinese Workers Protest Shocking Bankruptcy Of Major Telecom Supplier' (ZeroHedge, 10.12.2015), available at www.zerohedge.com/news/2015-10-12/thousands-angry-unpaid-chinese-workers-protest-shocking-bankruptcy-major-telecom-sup.

—— 'The Chinese Will Need Another Bailout' (ZeroHedge, 11.7.2016), available at www.zerohedge.com/news/2016-07-11/chinese-will-need-another-bailout.

Eaton, DL, Norley, LE, Huang, H and Asimacopoulos, KM, 'China's New Enterprise Bankruptcy Law' (Kirkland & Ellis LLP, October 2006), available at www.kirkland.com/siteFiles/kirkexp/publications/2272/Document1/Chinas_New_Enterprise_Bankruptcy_Law.pdf.

Edin, M, *Market Forces and Communist Power: Local Political Institutions and Economic Development in China* (Uppsala, Uppsala University Press, 2000).

EEO, 'Runaway bosses are Jiangnan's destiny' (8.10.2011), available at www.eeo.com.cn/2011/1008/213001.shtml.

Eidenmüller, H, 'Comparative Corporate Insolvency Law' (2016) ECGI Law Working Paper 319/2016.

Ellickson, R, *Order Without Law* (Cambridge, Harvard University Press, 1991).

—— Law and Economics Discovers Social Norms (1998) *Journal of Legal Studies* 537.

Elmer, K, 'Chinese debtors shamed with broadcast of names and faces on giant screens on May 1 holiday' (South China Morning Post, 4.5.2018), available at www.scmp.com/news/china/society/article/2144690/chinese-debtors-shamed-broadcast-names-and-faces-giant-screens.

Engdahl, FW, 'The Role of Debt and China's Shadow Banking System: Is Baoshang Bank China's Lehman Brothers?' (Global Research, 8.7.2019), available at www.globalresearch.ca/baoshang-bank-chinas-lehman-brothers/5683006.

Esplugues, C, 'China's Accession to WTO' (2009) *Chinese Business Law* 1.

Euler Hermes, 'Collection Profile: China' (December 2015).

Falke, M, 'China's New Law on Enterprise Bankruptcy: A Story with a Happy End?' (2007) *International Insolvency Review* 63.

Fan, D, 'Wenzhou: the Difficulties of Implementing the Bankruptcy Law' (Nanfang Weekend, 24.1.2014).

Fan, J, Huang, J and Zhu, N, 'Institutions, ownership structures and distress resolution in China' (2013) *Journal of Corporate Finance* 71.

Fan, K and Kaufmann-Kohler, G, 'Integrating Mediation into Arbitration: Why It Works in China' (2008) *Journal of International Arbitration* 479.

Farrell, D, Lund, S, Rosenfeld, J, Morin, F, Gupta, N and Greenberg, E, 'Putting China's Capital to Work: The Value of Financial System Reform' (McKinsey Global Institute, 2006).

Feld LP and Voigt, S, 'Economic growth and judicial independence: cross-country evidence using a new set of indicators' (2003) *European Journal of Political Economy* 497.

Feng, J, 'More than 240,000 Chinese companies declare bankruptcy in the first two months of 2020' (SupChina, 9.4.2020), available at supchina.com/2020/04/09/more-than-240000-chinese-companies-dec lare-bankruptcy-in-the-first-two-months-of-2020.

Fijnaut, C and Paoli, L (eds), *Organised Crime in Europe* (Dordrecht, Springer, 2004).

Finder, S, 'China's Master Plan for Remaking Its Courts' (The Diplomat, 26.3.2015).

—— 'China's Evolving Case Law System In Practice' (2017) *Tsinghua China Law Review* 245.

Forsythe, M, 'China's Chief Justice Rejects an Independent Judiciary and Reformers Wince' New York Times (18.1.2017), available at www.nytimes.com/2017/01/18/world/asia/china-chief-justice-courts-zhou-qiang. html.

Franks, JR and Loranth, G, 'A Study of Inefficient Going Concerns in Bankruptcy' (2004) CEPR Discussion Paper 5035.

—— and Sussman, O, 'Financial Distress and Bank Restructuring of Small to Medium Size UK Companies' (2005) *Review of Finance* 65.

Frisby, S, 'A preliminary analysis of pre-packaged administrations' (Report to The Association of Business Recovery Professionals, August 2007).

Funchal, B, 'The effects of the 2005 Bankruptcy Reform in Brazil' (2008) *Economics Letters* No 101.

Fung, R and Wang, S, *Arbitration in China: A Practical Guide* (Hong Kong, Sweet & Maxwell Asia, 2003).

Gallagher, M, *Authoritarian Legality in China* (Cambridge, Cambridge University Press, 2017).

Gao, S, 'Thinking on how to promote the supply-side reform' (NDRC, 10.5.2016), available at www.ndrc.gov. cn/fggz/fgjh/yxyd/201605/t20160510_1095426.html.

Ge, X, 'Composition' in R Parry, Y Xu and H Zhang (eds), *China's New Enterprise Bankruptcy Law: Context, Interpretation and Application* (Aldershot, Ashgate, 2010).

—— 'Creditors' Meeting and Creditors' Committee' in R Parry, Y Xu and H Zhang (eds), *China's New Enterprise Bankruptcy Law: Context, Interpretation and Application* (Aldershot, Ashgate, 2010).

Gesteland, L, 'China – Jack Rodman thinks bad debt can be golden opportunity' (ChinaOnline, 22.4.2002).

Gilley, B, 'Deng Xiaoping and His Successors' in WA Joseph (ed), *Politics in China*, 3rd edn (Oxford, Oxford University Press, 2019).

Gilson, R and Milhaupt, C, 'Economically Benevolent Dictators: Lessons for Emerging Democracies' (2011) 59 *American Journal of Comparative Law* 227.

Giné, X and Love, I, 'Do Reorganization Costs Matter for Efficiency? Evidence from a Bankruptcy Reform in Colombia' (July 2006) World Bank Policy Research Working Paper No 3970.

Gintis, H, *The Bounds of Reason: Game Theory and the Unification of the Behavioral Sciences* (Princeton, Princeton University Press, 2009).

Glenn, HP (2007) *Legal Traditions of the World*, 3rd edn (Oxford, Oxford University Press).

Global Times, 'How China's debt collectors go to work' (20.6.2016), available at www.globaltimes.cn/ content/989412.shtml.

Goebel, C and Ong, LH, 'Social Unrest in China' (Long Briefing, Europe China Research and Academic Network, 2012).

Goode, R, *Principles of Corporate Insolvency Law*, 4th edn (London, Sweet & Maxwell, 2011).

Gough, N, 'Online lender Ezubao took $7.6 Billion in Ponzi Scheme' (New York Times, 1.2.2016), available at www.nytimes.com%2F2016%2F02%2F02%2Fbusiness%2Fdealbook%2Fezubao-china-fraud.html.

Gregory, N, Tenev, S and Wagle, DM, 'China's Emerging Private Enterprises: Prospects for the New Century' (International Finance Corporation, 2000).

Greif, A, 'Reputation and Coalition in Medieval Trade: Evidence on the Maghribi Traders' (1989) *Journal of Economic History* 857.

Guo, J, 'Theoretical Research of Simplified Bankruptcy Procedure' (2017/12), available at www.commerciallaw. com.cn/ueditor/php/upload/file/20180415/1523806445288614.pdf.

Guo, K and Yao, Y, 'Causes of privatization in China: Testing several hypotheses' (2005) *Economics of Transition* 211.

Guo, S, *Chinese Politics and Government* (London, Routledge, 2013).

Hale, G and Long, C, 'What are the Sources of Financing of the Chinese Firms?' (July 2010) Hong Kong Institute for Monetary Research Working Paper No 19/2010.

Halliday, T, 'The Making of China's Corporate Bankruptcy Law' (2007) The Foundation for Law, Justice and Society, University of Oxford, available at www.fljs.org/sites/www.fljs.org/files/publications/Halliday.pdf.

Han, C, 'A Possible Surge in Bankruptcy Filings after the EBL 2006 Takes Effect' (People's Court News, 31.5.2007).

—— 'The Legislative Evolvement of the Bankruptcy Enterprise Law in China and Its Lessons' (2009) *Citizenship and Law* 2.

Hancock, T, 'China province admits falsifying fiscal data' (Financial Times, 18.1.2017).

Harris, D, 'How to avoid being held hostage in China' (Forbes, 11.1.2016).

—— 'China hostage situations with a new twist' (ChinaLawBlog, 16.5.2016), available at www.chinalawblog. com/2016/05/china-hostage-situations-with-a-new-twist.html.

Hart, O and Moore, J, 'Incomplete Contracts and Renegotiation' (1988) *Econometrica* 755.

He, W, *In the Name of Justice: Striving for the Rule of Law in China* (Washington DC, Brookings Institution Press, 2012).

Heilmann, S (ed), *China's Political System* (Lanham, Rowman & Littlefield, 2017).

Henderson, KE, 'Halfway Home and a Long Way to Go: China's Rule of Law Revolution and the Global Road to Judicial Independence, Judicial Impartiality and Judicial Integrity' in R Peerenboom (ed), *Judicial Independence in China* (Cambridge, Cambridge University Press, 2009).

Hernandez, J, 'Labor Protests Multiply in China as Economy Slows, Worrying Leaders' (New York Times, 14.3.2016), available at www.nytimes.com%2F2016%2F03%2F15%2Fworld%2Fasia%2Fchina-labor-strike-protest.html.

Herrero, AC, Schwartz, S, Xia, L and Xu, G, 'China's shadow bank lending: a threat to financial stability?' (BBVA, 2011), available at www.bbvaresearch.com/KETD/fbin/mult/111123_ChinaBankingWatch_En_tcm348-280630.pdf.

Ho, LC, *Cross-Border Insolvency: A Commentary on the UNCITRAL Model Law*, 4th edn (Woking, Globe Law and Business Publishing, 2017).

Hook, L and Davies, P, 'Suntech a test for China's bankruptcy law' (Financial Times, 21.3.2013).

Hornby, L, 'China rows back on state-sector reforms' (Financial Times, 14.7.2016).

—— and Zhang, A, 'China murder case shines spotlight on loan sharks' (Financial Times, 30.3.2017).

Hsu, S, 'Rumblings in China's Real Estate Market' (The Diplomat, 16.1.2015), available at kuaibao.qq.com/s/20 200403A057HO00?refer=spider.

—— 'China is finally improving property rights protection' (Forbes, 30.11.2016), available at www.forbes. com/sites/sarahsu/2016/11/30/china-improving-property-rights-protections/#752c14386e5c.

Hu, D, 'Cross-border Insolvency Regime in China: Finding the Most Pragmatic Interim Solution for Globalised Companies under Localised Practices' (2018) *American Bankruptcy Law Journal* 523.

Hu, Y, 'Several questions about the case guidance system' (EPaper, 29.1.2014), available at epaper.gmw.cn/ gmrb/html/2014-01/29/nw.D110000gmrb_20140129_2-16.htm.

—— 'Shenzhen's first enterprise bankruptcy law practice forum successfully held' (Yunqingsuan, 7.11.2016), available at www.yunqingsuan.com/news/detail/11822.

Huang, J, *Interregional Recognition and Enforcement of Civil and Commercial Judgments* (Oxford, Hart Publishing, 2014).

—— 'Commercial Issues in Private International Law' in E Douglas, V Bath, M Keyes and A Dickinson (eds) *Commercial Issues in Private International Law* (Oxford, Hart Publishing, 2019).

Huang, P and Wu, H, 'More Order without More Law' (1994) *Journal of Law, Economics and Organization* 390.

Huang, RH, 'Institutional Structure of Financial Regulation in China: Where Is It Now and Where Is It Heading?' in RH Huang and D Schoenmaker (eds), *Institutional Structure of Financial Regulation* (London, Routledge, 2014).

Huang, T, 'China Is Only Nibbling at the Problem of "Zombie" State-Owned Enterprises' (PIIE, 23.8.2019), available at www.piie.com/blogs/china-economic-watch/china-only-nibbling-proble m-zombie-state-owned-enterprises.

Huang, Y, *Capitalism with Chinese characteristics: Entrepreneurship and the State* (Cambridge, Cambridge University Press, 2008).

—— 'Cracking China's debt conundrum' (Financial Times, 6.12.2016).

Hung, J and Chen, Y (eds), *The State of China's State Capitalism* (London, Palgrave Macmillan, 2018).

Islam, R, 'Institutional Reform and the Judiciary: Which Way Forward' (2003) World Bank Policy Research Working Paper 3134.

J Kornai, *Economics of Shortage* (Amsterdam, North-Holland, 1980).

Jackson, T, *The Logic and Limits of Bankruptcy* Law (Washington, Beard Books, 1986).

Jia, Z, 'Explanation on the Draft Law of the People's Republic of China on Enterprise Bankruptcy' (2006) *Journal of the China People's Congress* 575.

Jiang, X, 'The Roles of Insolvency Practitioners in Corporate Reorganisation' (2009) *Journal of Law Application* 77.

Jiang, Y, 'The Curious Case of Inactive Bankruptcy Practice in China: A Comparative Study of US and Chinese Bankruptcy Law' (2014) *Northwestern Journal of International Law & Business* 560.

Jin, C, 'Recognition of and Assistance in Foreign Insolvency Proceedings in China: Interpretation and Legislation' (2019) *Tribune of Political Science and Law* 143.

Jing, D and Cheng, L, 'China Sets Deadline to Deal With 'Zombie' Companies' (Caixin, 5.12.2018), available at www.caixinglobal.com/2018-12-05/china-sets-deadline-to-deal-with-zombie-companies-101355950. html.

Jing, Y, Cui, Y and Li, D, 'The Politics of performance Measurement in China' (2015) *Policy and Society* 49.

Joseph, WA (ed), *Politics in China*, 3rd edn (Oxford, Oxford University Press, 2019).

—— 'Ideology and China's Political Development' in WA Joseph (ed), *Politics in China*, 3rd edn (Oxford, Oxford University Press, 2019).

Kahn, J, 'Dispute leaves US executive in Chinese legal netherworld' (New York Times, 1.11.2005), available at www.nytimes.com%2F2005%2F11%2F01%2Fworld%2Fasia%2Fdispute-leaves-us-executive-in-chinese-legal-netherworld.html.

—— 'When Chinese Sue the State, Cases Are Often Smothered' (New York Times, 28.12.2005), available at www.nytimes.com/2005/12/28/world/asia/when-chinese-sue-the-state-cases-are-often-smothered.html.

Kaiman, J, 'As China's economy slows, workers feel the sting' (Los Angeles Times, 9.1.2016), available at www. latimes.com%2Fworld%2Fasia%2Fla-fg-china-factories-closing-20160108-story.html.

Kaminska, I, 'China treads closer to a day of debt reckoning' (Financial Times, 16.3.2017).

Katz, P, *Divine Justice: Religion and The Development of Chinese Legal Culture* (London, Routledge 2008).

Kaufman Winn, J, 'Creditors' Rights in Taiwan: A Comparison of Corporate Reorganization Law in the United States and the Republic of China' (1998) *North Carolina Journal of International Law and Commercial Regulation* 409.

Ke, Z, 'Commencement of Listed Company Reorganisations in China' (2009) *People's Judicature* 38.

Kennedy, S, *The Business of Lobbying in China* (London, Harvard University Press, 2005).

Kipnis, A, Tomba, L and Unger, J (eds), *Contemporary Chinese Society and Politics* (London, Routledge, 2009).

Klapper L, 'Saving Viable Businesses' (The World Bank, Viewpoint 328, 2011).

Klerman, DM, 'Legal Infrastructure, Judicial Independence and Economic Development' (2007) *Global Business & Development Law Journal* 427.

Kohn, A, 'Why Incentive Plans Cannot Work' (Harvard Business Review, September–October 1993), available at hbr.org/1993/09/why-incentive-plans-cannot-work.

Kornai, J, 'Resource-constrained versus demand-constrained systems' (1979) *Econometrica* 801–19.

Kossov, A and Lovyrev, D, 'Related Party Transactions: International Experience and Russian Challenges' (OECD, 2014), available at www.oecd.org/daf/ca/RPTsInternationalExperienceandRussianChallenges.pdf.

Kraakman, R, Armour, J, Davies, P, Enriques, L, Hansmann, H, Hertig, G, Hopt, K, Kanda, H and Rock, E, *The Anatomy of Corporate Law: A Comparative and Functional Approach*, 3rd edn (Oxford, Oxford University Press, 2017).

Kroeber, AR, *China's Economy* (Oxford, Oxford University Press, 2016).

Kuhn, RL, *How China's Leaders Think* (Singapore, John Wiley & Sons, 2011).

Kynge, J, *China Shakes the World – The Rise of a Hungry Nation* (London, Weidenfeld & Nicolson, 2006).

La Roche, J, 'Kyle Bass: There's a "ticking time bomb" in China' (Business Insider, 10.2.2016), available at www.businessinsider.com/kyle-bass-letter-on-trust-beneficiary-rights-in-china-2016-2.

Ladany, L, *The Communist Party of China and Marxism, 1921–85* (Stanford, Hoover Institution Press, 1988).

—— *Law and Legality in China* (Honolulu, University of Hawaii Press, 1992).

Lam, J, 'The Insolvency of GITIC' (1999) *Journal of International Banking law* 193.

Lampton, D, *Following the Leader* (Berkley, University of California Press, 2014).

Landa, J, 'A theory of the ethnically homogeneous middleman group' (1981) *Journal of Legal Studies* 346.

Landry, PE, *Decentralized Authoritarianism in China: The Communist Party's Control of Local Elites in the Post-Mao Era* (Cambridge, Cambridge University Press, 2008).

Lardy, NR, 'The Role of Foreign Trade and Investment in China's Economic Transformation' (1995) *The China Quarterly* 1065.

Law Time, 'Illegal ghost companies?' (17.2.2016), available at www.lawtime.cn/info/gongsi/gssl/201602173329215.html.

Legal Advice 110, 'How to calculate compensation of insolvent company's executives' (15.11.2012), available at www.110.com/ziliao/article-330177.html.

Legal Daily, 'The Legislative Train is Speeding Up towards market Economy' (2.1.1994).

—— 'Li Shuguang Talking on Bankruptcy Law' (12.2.2007).

—— 'The Status of Listed Company Reorganisation Administrators is Expected to be Clarified' (9.6.2008).

—— 'New lawyers must make an oath of loyalty' (21.3.2012).

—— 'Government intervention in court's work is outdated' (1.3.2016).

Leggett, K, 'Chinese debt collector uses shame as his primary collection weapon' (Wall Street Journal, 21.9.2000), available at www.wsj.com/articles/SB969500305690756665.

Leng, S, 'Coronavirus: nearly half a million Chinese companies close in first quarter as pandemic batters economy' (South China Morning Post, 6.4.2020), available at www.scmp.com/economy/china-economy/article/3078581/coronavirus-nearly-half-million-chinese-companies-close-first.

Leung, JCB, 'Dismantling the "iron rice bowl": welfare reforms in the People's Republic of China' (1994) *Journal of Social Policy* 341.

Li, B and Ponticelli, J, 'Going Bankrupt in China' (July 2020) NBER Working Paper No 27501.

Li, C, 'China's Communist Party-state: The Structure and Dynamics of Power' in WA Joseph (ed), *Politics in China*, 3rd edn (Oxford, Oxford University Press, 2019).

Li, J, 'NPC Weighs Momentous New Bankruptcy Law' (China Daily, 22.6.2004), available at www.chinadaily.com.cn/english/doc/2004-06/22/content_341275.htm.

—— He, N and Xu, J, 'Borrowers face costly payback' (China Daily, 14.2.2014), available at www.chinadaily.com.cn/cndy/2012-02/14/content_14597676.htm.

Li, L, 'Corruption in China's Courts' in R Peerenboom (ed), *Judicial Independence in China* (Cambridge, Cambridge University Press, 2009).

—— The "Production" of Corruption in China's Courts: Judicial Politics and Decision making in a One-Party State' (2012) *Law & Social Inquiry* 848.

Li, S, 'Bankruptcy Law in China: Lessons of the Past Twelve Years' (2001) *Harvard Asia Quarterly* 1.

—— 'Some Problems of Drafting the Chine New Bankruptcy Law' (2002) *China Legal Science* 78.

Li, SA, 'China: Update on Private Lending Rules' (CrowdFundInsider, 3.11.2015), available at www.crowdfundinsider.com/2015/11/76729-china-update-on-private-lending-rules.

Li, Y, 'The bankruptcy process is "difficult to start", the trial mechanism should be improved' (Weixin, 12.6.2017), available at mp.weixin.qq.com/s/JKFMiKVfd9lV32C3EXzInw.

—— 'NPC deputy Yu Jihua: the time is right to establish a personal bankruptcy system' (People's Court News, 15.3.2019), available at www.chinacourt.org/article/detail/2019/03/id/3788906.shtml.

—— 'NDRC measures make bankruptcy easier for failing companies in China' (ECNS, 17.7.2019), available at www.ecns.cn/news/economy/2019-07-17/detail-ifzkzyey4244390.shtml.

Liang, F, Das, V, Kostyuk, N and Hussain, M, 'Constructing a Data-Driven Society: China's Social Credit System as a State Surveillance Infrastructure' (2018) *Policy & Internet* 415.

Liebman, B, 'China's Courts: Restricted Reform' (2008) *Columbia Journal of Asian Law* 1.

Lim, Y and Hahn, C, 'Bankruptcy Policy Reform and Total Factor Productivity Dynamics in Korea: Evidence from Macro Data' (2003) NBER Working Paper 9810.

Lin, C, Lin, P and Song, F, 'Property rights protection and corporate R&D: Evidence from China' (2010) *Journal of Development Economics* 49.

Lin, L and Milhaupt, C, 'We are the (National) Champions: Understanding Mechanisms of State Capitalism in China' (2013) *Stanford Law Review* 697.

Lin, L and Yu, J, 'The Right of Letters and Visits & the System of Letters and Visits' (2008) *Journal of Zhejiang University* (Humanities and Social Sciences) 3.

Lin, W, Wang, J and Guo, Y, '459 Real Estate Bankruptcy Filings Raise Concerns of Homebuyers Losing Out' (Caixin, 19.12.2019), available at www.caixinglobal.com/2019-12-19/459-real-estate-bankruptcy-filings-raise-concerns-of-homebuyers-losing-out-101496055.html.

Little, P and Tomasic, R, *Insolvency Law and Practice in Asia* (Hong Kong, FT Law & Tax Asia Pacific, 1997).

Liu, G, 'Liu Guixing: Speech at the National Civil and Commercial Trial Work Conference' (Weixin, 3.7.2019), available at mp.weixin.qq.com/s/nUE022dqtrx8xLuQ0jDFvw.

Liu, P, 'Bankruptcies among Chinese developers are up by a half amid slowing economy, restrictions on borrowing' (South China Morning Post, 26.7.2019), available at www.scmp.com/business/article/3020099/bankruptcies-among-chinese-developers-are-half-amid-slowing-economy.

Liu, S, 'Beyond Global Convergence: Conflicts of Legitimacy in a Chinese Lower Court' (2006) 31 *Law & Social Inquiry* 75.

Liu, W, 'Base III and Bank Regulation in China' (2014) *Journal of Legal Technology Risk Management* 1.

Livermore, A, 'Mandatory Social Welfare Benefits for Chinese Employees' (China Briefing, 21.2.2012), available at www.china-briefing.com/news/2012/02/21/mandatory-social-welfare-benefits-for-chinese-employees.html.

LLP Gore, *The Chinese Communist Party and China's Capitalist Revolution: The political impact of market* (London, Routledge, 2011).

Long, G, Wang, F and Ye, L, 'China's cross-border bankruptcy development path selection: Singapore's experience and inspiration' (2020) *People's Justice* 1.

Lopez, L, 'Everything just changed for Chinese companies' (Business Insider, 21.12.2015), available at www.businessinsider.com/china-announces-bankruptcy-measures-2015-12.

Lu, B, 'Bankruptcy Law Changes in Ten Years: Proposal to Give Legal Status to Bankruptcy Court' (12.9.2017), People's Court News, available at www.chinacourt.org/article/detail/2017/09/id/2995025.shtml&usg=ALkJrhhx1b0WT9oy2BcyQniaZiWAvK_3CA.

Lu, M and Azar, Z, 'Comparing the Old and New Brazilian Bankruptcy Law' (Inter-American Trade Report in National Law Center for Inter-American Free Trade, Vol 12(3), March 2005).

Lu, X, 'The Balance between Court Control and Autonomy of Affected Parties in Corporate bankruptcy Administrator Appointments' (2015) *People's Judicature* 75.

Lubman, SB, *Bird in a Cage* (Stanford, Stanford University Press, 2002).

Lum, T, 'Social Unrest in China' (Congressional Research Service, 2006), available at digitalcommons.ilr.cornell.edu/crs/19.

Ma, J, 'Analysis of 10 years of People's Courts hearing bankruptcy cases' (China INSOL, 27.6.2014).

MacFarquhar, R, *The Origins of the Cultural Revolution 2: The Great Leap Forward, 1958–1960* (New York, Columbia University Press, 1983).

—— and Schoenhals, M, *Mao's Last Revolution* (London, Harvard University Press, 2006).

Mai, C, 'Court Issues Cramdown and Banks Suffer 23 Billion Yuan Losses' (China Stock Times, 10.10.2016).

Mair, V, 'Rule of Law or Rule by Law? In China, a Preposition Makes All the Difference' (20.10.2014, WSJ), available at blogs.wsj.com/chinarealtime/2014/10/20/rule-of-law-or-rule-by-law-in-china-a-preposition-makes-all-the-difference.

Maliszewski, W, Arslanalp, S, Caparusso, JC, Garrido, J, Guo, S, Kang, JS, Lam, WR, Law, D, Liao, W, Rendak, N, Wingender, P, Yu, J and Zhang, L, 'Resolving China's Corporate Debt Problem' (October 2016) IMF Working Paper 16/203.

Mao, Y, 'Informal Reorganisation of SMEs' (2012) *China Entrepreneur* 112.

—— 'Chongchuan: "Coupling of Houses and Governments" Advances the Trial of Enterprise Bankruptcy Cases' (Yunqingsuan, 18.6.2020), available at www.yunqingsuan.com/news/detail/63643&usg=ALkJrhh5Tqq5Zdly3Ui3nF8RIHlDKEGh_Q.

McGinty, A and Tait, S, 'Will the Chinese Courts Grant "Back-Door Recognition" to Overseas Insolvency Practitioners?' (2010) *Corporate Rescue and Insolvency* 195.

McMahon, D, 'Loan "Guarantee Chains" in China Prove Flimsy' (Wall Street Journal, 23.11.2014), available at www.wsj.com/articles/loan-guarantee-chains-in-china-prove-flimsy-1416775097.

—— 'Cleaning Up Bad banks loans? Do an IPO' (Wall Street Journal, 22.12.2014), available at blogs.wsj.com/chinarealtime/2014/12/22/cleaning-up-bad-bank-loans-do-an-ipo.

—— *China's Great Wall of Debt* (Boston, Little, Brown, 2018).

Megginson, W, Ullah, B and Wei, Z, 'State ownership, soft-budget constraints and cash holdings: Evidence from China's privatized firms' (2014) *Journal of Banking and Finance* 276.

Meisner, M, *The Deng Xiaoping Era: An inquiry into the fate of Chinese socialism* (New York, Hill and Wang, 1996).

—— *Mao's China and After: A History of the People's Republic*, 3rd edn (New York, Free Press, 1999).

Milhaupt, C and Liebman, B (eds), *Regulating the Visible Hand?* (Oxford, Oxford University Press, 2016).

Milhaupt, C and Pistor, K, *Law and Capitalism: What Corporate Crises Reveal about Legal Systems and Economic Development around the World* (Chicago, University of Chicago Press, 2008).

Minzner, CF, 'Xinfang: An Alternative to Formal Chinese Legal Institutions' (2006) *Stanford Journal of International Law* 103.

Mitchell, T, 'Chinese train makers agree $26bn merger' (Financial Times, 31.12.2014).

—— and Wildau, G, 'World Bank warns of China debt risk from backdoor local borrowing' (Financial Times, 6.5.2017).

Montinola, G, Qian, Y and Weingast, B, 'Federalism Chinese Style: The Political Basis for Economic Success in China' (1995) *World Politics* 50.

Morrison, A and Wilhelm Jr, AJ, 'Trust, Reputation and Law: the Evolution of Commitment in Investment Banking' (2015) *Journal of Legal Analysis* 363.

Morrow, R, 'Beijing seeks to prod state banks with private competition' (GlobalCapitalAsia, 6.6.2014).

Moser, M (ed), *Managing Business Disputes in Today's China* (Kluwer Law International, 2007).

Mrockova, N, 'Does Law Matter for Economic Development: the Case of China' in L Scaffardi (ed), *The BRICS Group in the Spotlight: An Interdisciplinary Approach* (Edizioni Schientifiche Italiane, 2015).

Nanjing Daily, 'The province's first bankruptcy court was established in Nanjing and will govern these four types of cases' (12.6.2020), available at www.njdaily.cn/2020/0612/1846679.shtml.

Naughton, B, *Growing out of the plan* (Cambridge, Cambridge University Press, 1996).

—— *The Chinese Economy: Transitions and Growth* (London, MIT Press, 2007).

—— 'Leadership Transition and the "Top Level Design" of Economic Reform' (30.4.2012) *China Leadership Monitor* No 37.

Nee, V and Opper, S, *Capitalism from Below: Markets and Institutional Change in China* (London, Harvard University Press, 2011).

Nevitt, CE, 'Private Business Associations in China: Evidence of Civil Society or Local State Power?' (1996) *The China Journal* 36.

Newsweek, 'Below the radar' (17.11.2007).

Nishihara, M and Shibata, T, 'Dynamic bankruptcy procedure with asymmetric information between insiders and outsiders' (2018) *Journal of Economic Dynamics and Control* 118.

Niu, Z and van Dijck, G, 'The Impact of Culture on Chinese Judges' Decision-Making in Contractual Damages Cases' (2017) *Asian Journal of Law and Society* 1.

North, D, *Structure and Change in Economic History* (London, Norton, 1981).

—— *Institutions, Institutional Change and Economic Performance* (Cambridge, Cambridge University Press, 1990).

—— 'Institutions' (1991) *Journal of Economic Perspectives* 97.

Oesterle, DA, 'Corporate directors' personal liability for "insolvent trading" in Australia, "reckless trading" in New Zealand and "wrongful trading" in England: a recipe for timid directors, hamstrung controlling shareholders and skittish lenders' in IM Ramsay (ed), *Company Directors' Liability for Insolvent Trading* (Melbourne, University of Melbourne, 2000).

Ogus, A, 'The Importance of Legal Infrastructure for Regulation (and Deregulation) in Developing Countries' (2003) CRC Annual Conference ('Innovation and Change in Regulation and Competition'), available at www.competition-regulation.org.uk/publications/working_papers/WP65.pdf.

Oi, JC, 'Fiscal Reform and the Economic Foundations of Local State Corporatism in China' (1992) *World Politics* 99.

Pang, Y, 'Exploring simplified bankruptcy liquidation for "zombie companies"' (Yunqingsuan, 8.6.2016), available at www.yunqingsuan.com/news/detail/10553.

Pargendler, M, 'The Unintended Consequences of State Ownership: The Brazilian Experience' (2012) *Theoretical Inquiries in Law* 503.

Parisi, F (ed), *The Oxford Handbook of Law and Economics* (Oxford, Oxford University Press, 2017).

Parry, R, 'Administrator: Appointment and Remuneration' in R Parry, Y Xu and H Zhang (eds), *China's New Enterprise Bankruptcy Law: Context, Interpretation and Application* (Aldershot, Ashgate, 2010).

—— 'Transaction Avoidance' in R Parry, Y Xu and H Zhang (eds), *China's New Enterprise Bankruptcy Law: Context, Interpretation and Application* (Aldershot, Ashgate, 2010).

—— Xu, Y and Zhang, H (eds), *China's New Enterprise Bankruptcy Law: Context, Interpretation and Application* (Aldershot, Ashgate, 2010).

—— and Nan, G, 'The future direction of China's cross-border insolvency laws, related issues and potential problems' (2018) *International Insolvency Review* 5.

Patel, RI, 'A Practical Evaluation of the PRC's 2007 Enterprise Bankruptcy Law' (2009) *UC Davis Business Law Journal* 109.

Pauly, MV, 'The Economics of Moral Hazard' (1968) *American Economic Review* 531.

Payne, J, *Schemes of Arrangement: Theory, Structure and Operation* (Cambridge, Cambridge University Press, 2014).

Peerenboom, R, *China's Long March Toward Rule of Law* (Cambridge, Cambridge University Press, 2002).

—— (ed), *Judicial Independence in China: Lessons for Global Rule of Law Promotion* (Cambridge, Cambridge University Press, 2009).

—— 'A Tale of Two Judiciaries: Judicial Enforcement of Economic and Social Rights in China and India' (2013), available at ssrn.com/abstract=2211911.

Pei, M, *China's Trapped Transition* (Cambridge, Harvard University Press, 2006).

Pen, G and Zhang, T, 'Entry of Corporate reorganisation Procedures' (2012) *Academic Forum* 72.

Peng, M and Luo, Y, 'Managerial Ties and Firm Performance in a Transition Economy: The Nature of a Micro-Macro Link' (2000) *Academy of Management Journal* 486.

People's Court News, 'Notice of the SPC on Further Promotion of People's Court Work in 2009' (18.2.2009).

—— 'WuJiang Court released its 2018 Work Report and ten typical cases' (28.2.2019), available at wjsfy. chinacourt.gov.cn/article/detail/2019/02/id/3740941.shtml.

—— 'Creating a better legal environment for private enterprises' (19.1.2020), available at www.chinacourt. org/article/detail/2020/01/id/4778739.shtml&usg=ALkJrhijDgJQtH4LOI04EfuDI-NW_t74wQ.

—— 'Jinan Bankruptcy Court was formally established in Jinan, Shandong' (15.4.2020), available at www. chinacourt.org/article/detail/2020/04/id/4965543.shtml&usg=ALkJrhhgU9vKF3sU54cV5415TTHoz48 WHA.

—— 'Clarify creditors' participation in the bankruptcy process' (24.5.2020), available at rmfyb.chinacourt. org/paper/html/2020-05/24/content_168368.htm.

People's Daily, 'The number of cases declining even after implementation of new EBL' (10.10.2015), available at news.cpd.com.cn/n3569/c30632562/content.html.

—— 'Interpretation of the Central Economic Work Conference: Eight Highlights of China's Economy in 2017' (17.12.2016), available at www.gov.cn/zhengce/2016-12/17/content_5149174.htm.

—— 'Shenzhen Intermediate People's Court cleared nearly 100 billion yuan of bankruptcy debt in ten years' (6.11.2017), available at sz.people.com.cn/n2/2017/1106/c202846-30891993.html.

Pieke, F, *The Good Communist* (Cambridge, Cambridge University Press, 2015).

Pierce, D and Yee, L, 'China's Bank Asset Management Companies: Gold in Them Thar Hills?' (Topics in Chinese Law, O'Melveny & Myers LLP, July 2001).

Ping, Y and Wang, S, 'The First Stand-alone Bankruptcy Court in China Opened in Shenzhen' (Yicai, 15.1.2019), available at www.yicai.com/news/100099035.html.

Plazzi, A and Torous, W, 'Does Corporate Governance Matter?' (2016) Swiss Finance Institute Research Paper No 16–54.

Pollard, V, *State Capitalism, Contentious Politics and Large-Scale Social Change* (Koninklijke Brill, 2011).

Posner, R, *Economic Analysis of Law* (Boston, Little, Brown, 1972).

—— 'Social Norms and the Law' (1997) *American Economic Review* 365.

Powell, B, 'China's Property: Bubble, Bubble, Toil and Trouble' (The Times, 22.3.2010).

PR News, 'China City Commercial Bank (CCB) Industry 2011–2020 – Research and Markets' (11.7.2016), available at www.prnewswire.com/news-releases/china-city-commercial-bank-ccb-industry-2011-2020---research-and-markets-300296604.html.

Qi, L, 'The Corporate Reorganization Regime under China's New Enterprise Bankruptcy Law' (2008) *International Insolvency Review* 13.

Qian, J and Strahan, P, 'How law and institutions shape financial contracts: The case of bank loans' (2007) *Journal of Finance* 2803.

Qin, Y, 'The Current Situations of Chinese Judges: Lost in a Cloud of Conflict and Confusion' (2011) *Zeitschrift fur Chinesisches Recht* 241.

Rabinovitch, S, 'Uncertain Foundations' (Financial Times, 2.12.2012).

Ramsay, IM (ed), *Company Directors' Liability for Insolvent Trading* (Melbourne, University of Melbourne, 2000).

Remmert, A, 'Introduction to German Insolvency Law' (Justiz, 2007), available at www.justiz.nrw.de/WebPortal_en/projects/ieei/documents/public_papers/german_insolvency.pdf.

Ren, H, 'My Views about the Flaws and Strengths of China's Bankruptcy Law' (ChinaCourt.org, 21.4.2009), available at www.chinacourt.org/article/detail/2009/04/id/354771.shtml&usg=ALkJrhiMQXNKDVjcdd2lbbsXF8TKrOhqoQ.

Ren, P, 'Duties and functions of a judge in EBL cases' (Weixin, 19.1.2016), available at mp.weixin.qq.com/s?__biz=MzA5MzgwMjU5Ng==&mid=402131983&idx=1&sn=d076aea8c91750c8f32dc7e8b3041d89&scene=5&srcid=0303vS643bv7R4CqDLVfLZQK#rd.

Ren, S, 'China banks: Debt to equity swaps with zombie firms only carry more risk' (Barrons, 10.3.2016), available at www.barrons.com/articles/china-banks-debt-to-equity-swaps-with-zoomie-firms-only-carry-more-risk-1457661271.

Reuters, 'East Star bankrupt, first Chinese airline to fail' (27.8.2009), available at www.reuters.com/article/china-airline-bankrupt/east-star-bankrupt-first-chinese-airline-to-fail-idUSPEK25329120090827.

—— 'China's runaway bosses spotlight underground loan market' (29.9.2011), available at www.reuters.com/article/us-china-economy-runaway-bosses-idUSTRE78S0XJ20110929.

—— 'Insight: China pays high price to spare state firm from bankruptcy' (21.5.2012), available at www.reuters.com/article/us-china-bond-default-idUSBRE84J08320120521.

—— 'China to crack down on fake data "corruption": statistics chief' (12.2.2014), available at www.reuters.com/article/us-china-economy-statistics-idUSBREA1B0H520140212.

—— 'Near-bankrupt Chinese property firm offers lesson in lending risks' (3.4.2014), available at www.reuters.com/article/us-china-realestate/near-bankrupt-chinese-property-firm-offers-lesson-in-lending-risks-idUSBREA320DX20140403.

—— 'China says top judge under investigation for corruption' (12.7.2015), available at www.reuters.com/article/us-china-anticorruption-judge/china-says-top-judge-under-investigation-for-corruption-idUSKCN0PM0K220150712.

—— 'China says pushing for unified property registration by year-end' (10.1.2016), available at www.reuters.com/article/china-property/china-says-pushing-for-unified-property-registration-by-year-end-idUSL3N14U02W20160110.

—— 'Shame on you! China uses public billboards to expose runaway debtors' (19.7.2016), available at www.reuters.com/article/us-china-debt-shaming/shame-on-you-china-uses-public-billboards-to-expose-runaway-debtors-idUSKCN0ZZ0BS.

—— 'China unveils plans to cut corporate debt, to push debt-to-equity swaps' (10.10.2016), available at www.reuters.com/article/us-china-economy-debt-idUSKCN12A0MU.

—— 'Moody's downgrades China, warns of fading financial strength as debt mounts' (23.5.2017), available at www.reuters.com/article/us-china-economy-rating/moodys-downgrades-china-warns-of-fading-financial-strength-as-debt-mounts-idUSKBN18K04Q.

—— 'China cracking down on bank loans redirected to property sector in 32 cities' (9.8.2019), available at www.reuters.com/article/us-china-economy-property-loans/china-cracking-down-on-bank-loans-redirected-to-property-sector-in-32-cities-idUSKCN1UZ0Q1.

—— 'Exclusive: China's Tianjin government orders Bohai Steel restructuring start by September: sources' (21.8.2019), available at www.reuters.com/article/us-china-debt-bohai-steel-exclusive/exclusive-chinas-tianjin-government-orders-bohai-steel-restructuring-start-by-september-sources-idUSKCN1VB0KM.

—— 'China gives P2P lenders two years to exit industry: document' (28.11.2019), available at www.reuters.com/article/us-china-p2p/china-gives-p2p-lenders-two-years-to-exit-industry-document-idUSKBN1Y2039.

Roberts, D, 'China's 85 Million-Strong Communist Party' (Bloomberg, 12.6.2014), available at www.bloomberg.com/news/articles/2014-06-12/chinas-85-million-strong-communist-party-wants-to-slim-down.

Rodano, G, Serrano-Velarde, N and Tarantino, E, 'The Causal Effect of Bankruptcy Law on the Cost of Finance' (2012) Oxford University Centre for Business Taxation Working Paper 12/18.

Saich, T, 'The Blind Man and the Elephant: Analysing the Local State in China' in L Tomba (ed), *East Asian Capitalism: Conflicts and the Roots of Growth and Crisis* (Milano, Annali della Fondazione Giangiacomo Feltrinelly, 2002).

Schipke, A, Rodlauer, M and Zhang, L, 'The Future of China's Bond Market' (IMF, March 2019).

SCMP, 'Debtors held in cages by officials' (South China Morning Post, 4.12.1999), available at www.scmp.com/article/301610/debtors-held-cages-officials.

—— '200 bosses flee their creditors in Zhejiang' (South China Morning Post, 12.10.2011), available at www.scmp.com/article/981606/200-bosses-flee-their-creditors-zhejiang.

Shan, Y and Teng, J, 'China Moves Closer to Overhaul of Bankruptcy Law' (Caixin, 29.3.2019), available at www.caixinglobal.com/2019-03-29/china-moves-closer-to-overhaul-of-bankruptcy-law-101398784.html.

Shandong Provincial People's Court, 'A Study Dealing with Zombie Companies in Shandong' (2016) *People's Judicature* 10.

Shanghai Scrap Blog, 'Scrape trader kidnapped, held for ransom in Ningbo' (25.10.2008), available at shanghaiscrap.com/2008/10/scrap-trader-kidnapped-held-for-ransom-in-ningbo.

Shapiro, D and Tang, Y, 'Business Group Performance in China: Ownership and Temporal Considerations' (2009) *Management and Organization Review* 167.

She, H, 'Discussion on how Chinese courts can participate in the innovation of social management' (17.2.2014), available at court.gmw.cn/html/article/201402/07/150236.shtml.

Sheehy, B, 'Fundamentally Conflicting Views of the Rule of Law in China and the West and Implications for Commercial Disputes' (2005/06) *New Journal of International Law & Business* 225.

Shelling, T, *Micromotives and Macrobehavior* (New York, Norton & Co, 1978).

Shen, H, 'Research on Some Difficult Problems in Recognition and Enforcement of Foreign Civil and Commercial Judgments' (2018) *Law Application* 9.

Shenkar, O and Ronen, S, 'The Cultural Context of Negotiations' (1987) *The Journal of Applied Behavioural Science* 263.

Shenzhen Intermediate Court, 'Following the Development of the Guangdong-Hong Kong-Macao Greater Bay Area – What Kind of Butterfly Effect Will the Shenzhen Bankruptcy Court Bring?' (22.4.2019), available at www.szcourt.gov.cn/article/30049916.

Shi, J, 'The Chinese Cross-Border Insolvency Law: Reality, Problems and Future' (2002) *Chinese Legal Science* 114.

—— 'Bankruptcy Law Reform in China' (The Second Forum for Asian Insolvency Reform, Bangkok, Thailand, 16–17.12.2006).

—— 'Hong Kong Court's Recognition and Assistance of Mainland Bankruptcy Procedures – From the Perspective of Huaxin Bankruptcy' (China Bankruptcy Law Forum: Removal of Zombie Companies, Ruian, Zhejiang, 9.4.2020), available at qnmlgb.tech/articles/5ef21bde4e7418bb50ae9dcd.

—— and Huang, Y, 'Sino-US Milestone of Cross-border Bankruptcy Co-operation – Comment on Topoint Solar Case' (2017) *Journal of Application* 51.

Shim, S, 'Suntech Power: Challenges under PRC Bankruptcy' (Business Insider, 12.4.2013), available at business-finance-restructuring.weil.com/international/suntech-power-challenges-under-prc-bankruptcy.

Sim, KS, *China in Transition*, vol 2 (New York, Nova Science Publishers, 2003).

Simon, H, 'Rational decision-making in business organizations' (1979) *American Economic Review* 493.

Sina, 'Refusal to cooperate leaves EastStar unable to cope with debts and forces it to stop flying' (16.3.2009), available at finance.sina.com.cn/chanjing/b/20090316/06575979066.shtml).

—— 'Seeking employment: company's reputation or company's strength?' (28.9.2015), available at blog.sina.com.cn/s/blog_1543cdb2f0102w01i.html.

—— 'Registered ghost companies avoid 3 million arrests' (1.12.2015), available at news.sina.com.cn/o/2015-12-01/doc-ifxmainy1520040.shtml.

—— 'Wenzhou Intermediate People's Court: Corporate bankruptcy property on the online judicial auction platform' (7.12.2015), available at finance.sina.com.cn/sf/news/2015-12-07/161812451.html.

—— 'Millions of Chinese companies dying every year, calls for a specialised bankruptcy court' (28.1.2016), available at finance.sina.com.cn/sf/news/2016-01-28/103618989.html.

—— 'Bankruptcy difficulties of zombie SOEs: Courts Don't Dare Accept and Governments Don't Allow' (28.3.2016), available at finance.sina.com.cn/sf/news/2016-03-28/101025196.html.

—— 'Qingdao Bankruptcy Court was established' (23.4.2020), available at k.sina.cn/article_6456450127_180d59c4f02000zqre.html.

Smyth, R, Tam, OK, Warner, M and Zhu, CJ (eds), *China's Business Reforms: Institutional Challenges in a Globalised Economy* (London, Routledge, 2015).

Sohu, 'Just released! 50 latest opinions on the trial of bankruptcy and reorganisation cases' (8.3.2018), available at www.sohu.com/a/225145138_481798.

Song, Z and Xie, R, 'A Few Suggestions about the Simplified Bankruptcy Cases' (Guangdong South-Freedom Law Firm, 27.5.2020), available at www.nflawyer.cn/index.php?m=Law&a=content_detail&id=246&class_id=42&type=dynamic&noneed_id=177.

Sorkin, AR, *Too Big to Fail: The Inside Story of How Wall Street and Washington Fought to Save the Financial System – and Themselves* (Penguin Books, 2010).

Soto, H de, *The Mystery of Capital* (New York, Basic Books, 2000).

SPC Monitor, 'The Supreme People's Court and interpreting the law, revisited' (10.7.2015), available at supremepeoplescourtmonitor.com/2015/07/10/the-supreme-peoples-court-and-interpreting-the-law-revisited-part-one.

—— 'Brief report on bankruptcy litigation in the Chinese courts' (14.11.2015), available at supremepeoplescourtmonitor.com/2015/11/14/brief-report-on-bankruptcy-litigation-in-the-chinese-courts.

—— 'Bankruptcy: What to expect in 2016 from the Chinese civil & commercial courts (II)' (16.1.2016), available at supremepeoplescourtmonitor.com/2016/01/16/bankruptcy-what-to-expect-in-2016-from-the-chinese-civil-commercial-courts-ii.

—— 'Chinese bankruptcy courts to become hospitals for sick companies' (3.3.2016), available at supremepeoplescourtmonitor.com/2016/03/03/chinese-bankruptcy-courts-to-become-hospitals-for-sick-companies.

—— 'Chinese courts recruiting more bankruptcy forces' (30.6.2016), available at supremepeoplescourtmonitor.com/2016/06/30/chinese-courts-recruiting-more-bankruptcy-forces.

—— 'What's new in the Supreme People's Court's diversified dispute resolution policy' (5.7.2016), available at supremepeoplescourtmonitor.com/2016/07/05/whats-new-in-the-supreme-peoples-courts-diversified-dispute-resolution-policy.

—— 'Supreme People's Court judge convicted of taking bribes' (10.7.2016), available at supremepeoplescourtmonitor.com/2016/07/10/supreme-peoples-court-judge-convicted-of-taking-bribes.

—— 'Which Chinese cases are most persuasive?' (16.9.2016), available at supremepeoplescourtmonitor.com/2016/09/16/which-chinese-cases-are-most-persuasive.

—— 'Supreme People's Court releases 2016 bankruptcy data' (26.2.2017), available at supremepeoplescourtmonitor.com/2017/02/26/supreme-peoples-court-releases-2016-bankruptcy-data.

—— 'Signals in Zhou Qiang's 2017 Report (Part 2)' (19.3.2017), available at supremepeoplescourtmonitor.com/2017/03/19/signals-in-zhou-qiangs-2017-report-part-2.

—— 'Supreme People's Court reports on its bankruptcy accomplishments' (31.12.2017), available at supremepeoplescourtmonitor.com/2017/12/31/supreme-peoples-court-reports-on-its-bankruptcy-accomplishments.

—— 'How the Supreme People's Court guides the court system through judicial documents (1)' (19.5.2019), available at supremepeoplescourtmonitor.com/2019/05/19/chinese-judicial-documents-1.

—— 'The National Civil Commercial Trial Work Conference Draft Conference Summary or how the SPC guides the lower courts through issuing conference summaries' (17.8.2019), available at supremepeoplescourtmonitor.com/2019/08/17/the-national-civil-commercial-trial-work-conference-draft-conference-summary-or-how-the-spc-guides-the-lower-courts-through-issuing-conference-summaries.

—— 'Supreme People's Court and its normative documents' (28.8.2019), available at supremepeoplescourtmonitor.com/2015/08/28/supreme-peoples-court-and-its-normative-documents.

SputnikNews, 'Why Does China Need to Bankrupt Its Companies?' (20.12.2018), available at sputniknews.com/asia/201812201070828771-china-bankrupt-companies.

Sternberg, J, 'The Bailout that busted China's banks' (28.10.2011, WSJ), available at online.wsj.com/article/SB10001424052970204485304576642542360975276.html.

Sun, J, 'Current Trends in China's Bankruptcy Filings' (Perkins Coie report, 21.8.2019), available at www.jdsupra.com/legalnews/current-trends-in-china-s-bankruptcy-49571.

Szamosszegi, A and Kyle, C, 'An Analysis of State-Owned Enterprises and State Capitalism in China' (US-China Economic and Security Review Commission, 2011).

SZICA, 'Creditors of reputation-debts giving to emotions' (18.2.2013), available at www.szica.com/420.html.

Tamanaha, B, *On the Rule of Law: History, Politics, Theory* (Cambridge, Cambridge University Press, 2004).

Tang, A, *Insolvency in China and Hong Kong: A Practitioner's Perspective* (Hong Kong, Sweet & Maxwell Asia, 2005).

—— and Ward, A, *The Changing Face of Chinese Management* (London, Routledge, 2003).

Tang, F, 'China's spiralling local government debt out of control' (South China Morning Post, 9.3.2017), available at www.scmp.com/news/china/economy/article/2077367/chinas-spiralling-local-govt-debt-still-out-control-says.

Tang, H and Shi, Y, 'Judicial Experiment of Hearing Corporate Reorganisation of Private Companies' (2011) *Legal Research* 102.

Tang, W, 'Several Problems of the Proposed Bill of Enterprise Bankruptcy Law on Reorganisation' (2005) *Jurists* 33.

Tanner, MS, *The Politics of Lawmaking in China: Institutions, Processes and Democratic Prospects* (Oxford, Oxford University Press, 1999).

Teiwes, FC, 'Mao Zedong in Power' in WA Joseph (ed), *Politics in China*, 3rd edn (Oxford, Oxford University Press, 2019).

—— and Sun, W, *The End of the Maoist Era: Chinese Politics During the Twilight of the Cultural Revolution, 1972–1976* (Abingdon, ME Sharpe, 2009).

Tenev, S and Zhang, C, 'Corporate Governance and Enterprise Reform in China: Building the Institutions of Modern Markets' (World Bank & IFC, 2002).

The Economist, 'Bankruptcy in China – Silent Busts' (9.10.2008).

—— 'China's debt-to-GDP level' (17.6.2014).

—— 'China's Crushing of independent lawyers is a blow to rule of law' (15.6.2017).

The Paper, 'Supreme law: World Bank report recognizes bankruptcy system, investor protection increased by 36' (26.10.2019), available at www.thepaper.cn/newsDetail_forward_4785213.

—— 'Langfang Intermediate People's Court released a series of corporate bankruptcy trial documents' (17.5.2020), available at www.thepaper.cn/newsDetail_forward_7430103.

The World Bank, *Bureaucrats in Business* (London, Oxford University Press, 1995).

Thelen, K (2004) *How Institutions Evolve: The Political Economy of Skills in Germany, Britain, the United States and Japan* (Cambridge, Cambridge University Press).

Thireau, I and Hua, L, 'The Moral Universe of Aggrieved Chinese Workers: Workers' Appeals to Arbitration Committees and Letters and Visits Offices' (2003) *The China Journal* 83.

Tirole, J, *The Theory of Corporate Finance* (Woodstock, Princeton University Press, 2006).

Tomasic, R (ed), *Insolvency Law in East Asia* (Aldershot, Ashgate, 2006).

—— The Conceptual Structure of China's New Corporate Bankruptcy Law (2010), available at http://ssrn.com/abstract=1546556.

—— 'The Conceptual Structure of China's New Corporate Bankruptcy Law' in R Parry, Y Xu and H Zhang (eds), *China's New Enterprise Bankruptcy Law: Context, Interpretation and Application* (Aldershot, Ashgate, 2010).

—— Little, P, Francis, A, Kamarul, K and Wang, K, 'Insolvency Law Administration and Culture in Six Asian Legal Systems' (1996) *Australian Journal of Corporate Law* 248.

—— and Wang, M, 'Reforming China's Corporate Bankruptcy Laws' (2005) 18 *Australian Journal of Corporate Law* 220.

—— and Zhang, Z, 'From Global Convergence in China's Enterprises Bankruptcy Law 2006 to Divergent Implementation' (2012) *Journal of Corporate Law Studies* 295.

Trebilcock, LJ and Prado, MM, *What Makes Poor Countries Poor* (Cheltenham, Edward Elgar Publishing, 2011).

Tsai, K, *Back-Alley Banking: Private Entrepreneurs in China,* (Ithaca, Cornell University Press, 2002).

Tushnet, M, 'Preserving Judicial Independence in Dominant Party States' (2015) *New York Law School Law Review* 107.

van der Heijden, J, 'Institutional Layering: A Review of the Use of the Concept' (2011) *Politics* 9.

Visaria, S, 'Legal Reform and Loan Repayment: The Microeconomic Impact of Debt Recovery Tribunals in India' (2009) *American Economic Journal: Applied Economics* 59.

Vogel, E, *Deng Xiaoping and the Transformation of China* (London, Harvard University Press, 2011).

Vollrath, D, *Fully Grown: Why a Stagnant Economy Is a Sign of Success* (Chicago, University of Chicago Press, 2020).

Walter, C and Howie, F, *Red Capitalism* (Singapore, John Wiley & Sons, 2011).

Wang, B, 'Improper Trading in bankruptcy and Director Liabilities' in R Parry, Y Xu and H Zhang (eds), *China's New Enterprise Bankruptcy Law: Context, Interpretation and Application* (Aldershot, Ashgate, 2010).

Wang, F, 'Bankruptcy cases soared by more than 50% for three consecutive years' (21st Century Business Herald, 29.3.2019), available at m.21jingji.com/article/20190329/d04a816437cbdf71fa6f5c6b3d45d629.html.

Wang, L, Several Issues of Amending China's Bankruptcy Law (2002) *Legal Science* 78.

—— Corporate Bankruptcy Legal System (a lecture in the NPC, 6.4.2004), available at www.npc.gov.cn/npc/c541/200404/f5f76c47994746018c0c6944d3823647.shtml.

—— Problems of Amending the Bankruptcy Law (2005) *Legal Science* 3.

Wang, Q, 'China to establish its first personal bankruptcy system' (CGTN, 20.7.2019), available at news.cgtn.com/news/2019-07-20/China-to-establish-its-first-personal-bankruptcy-system-IulITshzeU/index.html.

Wang, S, 'On courts' function in strengthening and innovation of social management' (People's Court News, 3.3.2011).

—— and Chen, W, Empowering Creditors in Filing for Bankruptcy: Lessons from the UK (2014) *Hebei Law Science* 45.

—— and McKee, M, Litigation and arbitration in China: Which is better (Lehman Law briefing paper, 2015), available at www.lehmanlaw.com/fileadmin/lehmanlaw_com/Publications/Briefing_Paper_Series/Litigation_and_arbitration_in_China-Which_is_better.pdf.

Wang, W, 'Adopting Corporate Rescue Regimes in China: A Comparative Survey' (1998) *Australian Journal of Corporate Law* 234.

—— 'Institutional Reasoning in Drafting New Bankruptcy Law of China' (Chinese Insolvency Law Symposium: Developing an Insolvency Infrastructure, Hong Kong, 17-18.11.2000), available at law.hku.hk/aiifl/events/symposium/papers/wang%20weiguo.doc.

—— 'Strengthening Judicial Expertise in Bankruptcy Proceedings in China' (the Forum for Asian Insolvency Reform (FAIR), Bali, 7–8.2.2001).

—— 'Changchun Approach: A New Scheme for Debt Restructuring in China' (the Second Forum for Asian Insolvency Reform, Bangkok, Thailand, 16–17.12.2002).

—— 'The New Enterprise Bankruptcy Law: a Contemporary and Advanced Legislation' (2006) *The People's Congress of China* 17.

—— 'The Order of Payment of Workers' Claims and Securities Interests under China's New Bankruptcy Law' (Fifth Forum for Asian Insolvency Reform (FAIR), Beijing, China, 27-28.4.2006), available at www.oecd.org/dataoecd/41/40/38182499.pdf.

Wang, X, 'Theories and Practice of the Corporate Reorganisation Regime' (2012) *Journal of Law Application* 10.

—— 'Case Registration and Bankruptcy Filings' (2015) *Journal of Law Application* 36.

—— 'On the Marketization Implementation of Bankruptcy Law' (People's Court News, 6.12.2016), available at www.chinacourt.org/article/detail/2017/12/id/3101315.shtml.

—— 'Government-Organized Liquidation Committees in Corporate Bankruptcies' (the China National Bankruptcy Annual Conference, Beijing, China, 2.5.2017).

—— Shao, Q and Liu, X, 'Analysis of Performance Evaluation Standards of Bankruptcy Cases' (April 2018) *Legal Expo* 20.

—— and Xu, Y, 'Several Issues of Making the Enterprise Bankruptcy Law' (2007) *Politics and Law* 89.

Wang, Z, 'Seeking performance or control? Tethered party innovation in China's performance evaluation system' (2020) *Journal of Chinese Governance* 1.

Want China Times, 'Wenzhou fights back against violent debt collection' (29.9.2011), available at www.wantchinatimes.com/news-subclass-cnt.aspx?cid=1103&MainCatID=11&id=20110929000022.

Warren, E and Westbrook, JL, 'The Success of Chapter 11: A Challenge to the Critics' (2009) *Michigan Law Review* 603.

Watson, K, 'Confusion Reigns Over New Legislation' (South China Morning Post, 30.9.2008), available at www.scmp.com/article/654451/confusion-reigns-over-new-legislation.

Wee, MS, 'The Belt and Road Initiative, China's Cross-Border Insolvency Law and the UNCITRAL Model Law on Cross-Border Insolvency' (2020) *Chinese Journal of Comparative Law* 116.

Wei, L, 'China issuing "strict controls" on overseas investment' (Wall Street Journal, 26.11.2016), available at www.wsj.com/articles/china-issuing-strict-controls-on-overseas-investment-1480071529.

Weihai Intermediate People's Court, 'Enhancing the Reorganisation of Limited Liability Companies in China' (2013) *Shandong Justice* 32.

Weinland, D, 'China reopens securitised bad-debt market' (Financial Times, 20.5.2016).

—— 'Corporate defaults in China surge in 2019 to record high $18.6bn' (Financial Times, 26.12.2019).

Wen, F, 'Zhejiang's first bankruptcy court was established in Wenzhou' (People's Court News, 30.12.2019), available at www.chinacourt.org/article/detail/2019/12/id/4749831.shtml.

Wen, X, 'Wenzhou will explore simplified procedures for bankruptcy cases' (JCRB, 15.1.2015), available at news.jcrb.com/jxsw//201501/t20150115_1468553.html.

Whincop, MJ, 'The economic and strategic structure of insolvent trading' in IM Ramsay (ed), *Company Directors' Liability for Insolvent Trading* (Melbourne, University of Melbourne, 2000).

White, LT, *Policies of Chaos: the organizational causes of violence in China's Cultural Revolution* (Princeton, Princeton University Press, 1989).

White, MJ, 'The Cost of Corporate Bankruptcy' in JS Bhandari and LA Weiss (eds), *Corporate Bankruptcy: Economic and Legal Perspectives* (Cambridge, Cambridge University Press, 1996).

—— 'Bankruptcy: Past Puzzles, Recent Reforms and the Mortgage Crisis' (2009) *American Law and Economics Review* 1.

—— 'Economics of Bankruptcy' in F Parisi (ed), *The Oxford Handbook of Law and Economics* (Oxford, Oxford University Press, 2017).

Whiting, SH, *Power and Wealth in Rural China* (Cambridge, Cambridge University Press, 2006).

Wihlborg, C, Gangopadhyay, S and Hussain, Q, 'Infrastructure Requirements in the Area of Bankruptcy Law' (2001) Wharton Financial Institutions Center Working Paper 01-09.

Wildau, G, 'In China, Risking a Chain Reaction of Default' (New York Times, 28.4.2014), available at www.nytimes.com%2F2014%2F04%2F29%2Fbusiness%2Finternational%2Fin-china-risking-a-chain-reaction-of-default.html.

—— 'Bad loans surge at China's biggest banks' (Financial Times, 30.10.2014).

—— 'China Shadow Bank Collapse' (Financial Times, 4.12.2014).

—— 'China's state-owned enterprise reform plans face compromise' (Financial Times, 14.9.2015).

—— 'China state group bailout highlights urgency of reform' (Financial Times, 22.9.2015).

—— 'China's state-owned zombie economy' (Financial Times, 29.2.2016).

—— 'China bankruptcies surge as government targets zombie enterprises' (Financial Times, 23.6.2016).

—— 'Chinese default exposes creditor anger at political interference' (Financial Times, 27.7.2016).

—— 'China regulator launches fresh shadow banking crackdown' (Financial Times, 29.7.2016).

—— 'In search of China's hidden credit' (Financial Times, 12.10.2016).

—— 'China banks risk Lehman moment as wholesale borrowing rises' (Financial Times, 23.11.2016).

—— 'China's Statistics chief admits some economic data are false' (Financial Times, 8.12.2016).

—— 'China's private banks struggle to upend state-owned incumbents' (Financial Times, 12.12.2016).

—— 'Chinese reform plans highlight reluctance to cede control' (Financial Times, 9.1.2017).

Witt, MA and Redding, G (eds), 'China's Authoritarian Capitalism' in MA Witt and G Redding, *Oxford Handbook of Asian Business Systems* (Oxford, Oxford University Press, 2014).

Woodruff, C, 'Review of de Soto's Mystery of Capital' (2001) *Journal of Economic Literature* 1215.

World Bank, Doing *Business in 2004: Understanding Regulation* (World Bank and Oxford University Press, 2004).

Wu, W, 'Commencement of Bankruptcy Proceedings in China: Key Issues in the Proposed New Enterprise Bankruptcy and Reorganization Law' (2004) *Victoria University of Wellington Law Review* 239.

—— 'How the Communist Party controls China's state-owned industrial titans' (South China Morning Post, 17.6.2017), available at www.scmp.com/news/china/economy/article/2098755/how-communist-party-controls-chinas-state-owned-industrial-titans.

Wu, X, *The Decade of Surge with Big Fishes and Flooding Water* (Beijing, CITIC Press Corporation, 2017).

X Wang and Z Yi (eds), *The Chinese Bankruptcy Summit* (Beijing, Law Press, 2010).

Xi, J, 'Secure a Decisive Victory in Building a Moderately Prosperous Society in All Respects and Strive for the Great Success of Socialism with Chinese Characteristics for a New Era' (a report delivered at the NPC, 18.10.2017), available at www.xinhuanet.com/english/download/Xi_Jinping's_report_at_19th_CPC_National_Congress.pdf.

Xia, M, *The People's Congresses and Governance in China* (London, Routledge, 2008).

Xiao, J, 'Bankruptcy Administrator: Status, Powers and Duties' in R Parry, Y Xu and H Zhang (eds), *China's New Enterprise Bankruptcy Law: Context, Interpretation and Application* (Aldershot, Ashgate, 2010).

—— 'Bankruptcy Estate' in R Parry, Y Xu and H Zhang (eds), *China's New Enterprise Bankruptcy Law: Context, Interpretation and Application* (Aldershot, Ashgate, 2010).

Xie, B, *Comparative Insolvency Law: The Pre-pack Approach in Corporate Rescue* (Cheltenham, Elgar Publishing, 2016).

Xin, X, 'Cramdown Approvals in China's Corporate Reorganisation Law' (2011) *Journal of Law Application* 57.

Xin, Z, 'The Emerging Insolvency Risks of Chinese Financial Institutions' (1999) *Journal of International Banking and Finance Law* 91.

—— 'China court approves personal bankruptcy ruling that could pave the way for further debt cases' (South China Morning Post, 10.10.2019), available at www.scmp.com/economy/china-economy/article/3032323/china-court-approves-landmark-bankruptcy-ruling-could-pave.

Xing, B, 'The Supreme Law talks about cleaning up "zombie enterprises": as many mergers and acquisitions as possible, less bankruptcy and liquidation' (The Paper, 8.4.2016), available at www.thepaper.cn/newsDetail_forward_1453939.

Xinhua 'Chinese airline goes bankrupt with huge debts' (27.8.2009), available at news.xinhuanet.com/english/2009-08/27/content_11954674.htm.

—— 'No Deadline for Centrally Managed SOEs' Real Estate Business' (6.12.2010).

—— 'What happens to properties after the expiration of 70 years?' (4.11.2013), available at www.chinasmack.com/chinese-land-use-rights-what-happens-after-70-years.

——'Highlights of China's Central Economic Work Conference' (24.11.2015).

—— 'China to tackle industrial overcapacity' (21.12.2015), available at news.xinhuanet.com/english/2015-12/21/c_134938491.htm.

—— 'China Focus: China releases guideline on protection of property rights' (27.11.2016), available at news.xinhuanet.com/english/2016-11/27/c_135861977.htm.

—— 'China approves launch of five new private banks' (27.12.2016), available at news.xinhuanet.com/english/2016-12/27/c_135936795.htm.

—— 'Central Economic Work Conference held in Beijing. Xi Jinping, Li Keqiang made an important speech' (12.12.2019), available at www.xinhuanet.com/politics/2019-12/12/c_1125340392.htm.

Xu, C, 'The Fundamental Institutions of China's Reforms and Development' (2011) *Journal of Economic Literature* 1076.

Xu, J, Ju, H and Wang, Y, 'Research on simplifying bankruptcy procedures: Taking Wenzhou Court's experience in simplifying bankruptcy trial procedures as a sample' (2014) *Law Application* 98.

Xu, S and Zhang, S, 'SPC's Minutes of the National Civil and Commercial Trial Work Conference – Interpretation and recommendations' (Zhonglun, 23.8.2019), available at www.zhonglun.com/Content/2019/08-23/1455139322.html.

Xu, Y and Hua, Y, 'On Realistic Needs and System Design of Summary Bankruptcy Procedure' (Yunqingsuan, 23.3.2017), available at www.yunqingsuan.com/news/detail/12900.

Xu, Y and Zheng, W, 'Bankruptcies of Financial Institutions' in R Parry, Y Xu and H Zhang (eds), *China's New Enterprise Bankruptcy Law: Context, Interpretation and Application* (Aldershot, Ashgate, 2010).

Yan, D, 'Government Intervention in China's Listed Company Reorganisations' (2016) *Legal Forum* 122.

Yan, S, 'China real estate firm at risk' (CNN, 19.3.2014), available at money.cnn.com/2014/03/19/news/economy/china-property-default/index.html.

Yang, D, *Remaking the Chinese Leviathan: Market Transition and the Politics of Governance in China* (Stanford, Stanford University Press, 2004).

Yang, Y, 'China house price growth slows as lending curbs take hold' (Financial Times, 19.12.2016).

Yang, Z, 'Fragmented Authoritarianism – The Facilitator Behind the Chinese Reform Miracle: A Case Study in Central China' (2013) *China Journal of Social Work* 4.

—— 'Legitimacy Crisis and Legitimation in China' (1996) *Journal of Contemporary Asia* 201.

Yap, C and Orlik, T, 'Life and Death: China's Runaway Bosses' (Wall Street Journal, 15.2.2012), available at blogs.wsj.com/chinarealtime/2012/02/15/life-and-death-chinas-runaway-bosses.

Yau, OHM, You, H and Steele, HC (eds), *China Business: Challenges in the 21st Century* (Beijing, The Chinese University Press, 2004).

Ye, B, 'Filing of Claims' in R Parry, Y Xu and H Zhang (eds), *China's New Enterprise Bankruptcy Law: Context, Interpretation and Application* (Aldershot, Ashgate, 2010).

Yeung, K, 'Coronavirus: China to open US$1.5 trillion distressed debt market as it braces for bad loan blowout' (South China Morning Post, 30.3.2020), available at www.scmp.com/economy/china-economy/article/3077562/coronavirus-china-open-us15-trillion-distressed-debt-market.

Ying, X, 'Risks of New Financing in Listed Company Reorganisations' (2012) *Chinese Lawyer* 46.

Yiu, E, 'Bankruptcies in China pose challenge for foreign creditors' (South China Morning Post, 11.10.2015), available at www.scmp.com/business/china-business/article/1866377/bankruptcies-china-pose-challenge-foreign-creditors.

You, B, 'Risk Management for China's Insolvency Practitioners' (2009) *People's Judicature* 33.

Yu, C, 'Protecting Bank Creditors in Corporate Reorganisation Cramdown Approvals' (2017) *China Urban Finance* 52.

Yu, S, 'China boosts lending to small businesses despite risk' (Financial Times, 30.12.2019).

Yueh, L, *Enterprising China* (Oxford, Oxford University Press, 2009).

Yunqingsuan, 'The Dream journey of half-bankruptcy law' (27.8.2019), available at www.yunqingsuan.com/news/detail/53809.

Zhai, K, 'The Rise and Fall of Bo Xilai' (South China Morning Post, 22.8.2013), available at www.scmp.com/news/china/article/1298386/rise-and-fall-bo-xilai.

Zhang, C, 'Du Wanhua: Legal EBL proceedings appropriate to deal with zombie companies' (Weixin, 3.5.2016), available at mp.weixin.qq.com/s?__biz=MzIwOTA4NzMyOQ==&mid=2651773770&idx=1&sn=67a69dd116111a7fc8c9b137af0c01fb&scene=5&srcid=05034kJNXVWAqYZji26N1Ekx#rd.

Zhang, H, Corporate Rescue in R Parry, Y Xu and H Zhang (eds), *China's New Enterprise Bankruptcy Law: Context, Interpretation and Application* (Aldershot, Ashgate, 2010).

Zhang, Q, 'Mianyang Intermediate People's Court went to Anzhou Court to investigate and guide bankruptcy cases' (People's Court News, 2.4.2020), available at www.chinacourt.org/article/detail/2020/04/id/4879408.shtml.

Zhang, W, 'Sino–Foreign Recognition and Enforcement of Judgments: A Promising "Follow-Suit" Model?' (2017) *Chinese Journal of International Law* 515.

Zhang, X and Liu, M, 'Lending and taking security in China: Overview' (PracticalLaw Guide, 1.7.2019), available at uk.practicallaw.thomsonreuters.com/3-500-9517?transitionType=Default&contextData=(sc.Default)&firstPage=true&bhcp=1.

Zhang, Y, 'On the Strengthening the Socialist Legal System' (1981) *Social Sciences in China* 1.

Zhang, Z, *Corporate Reorganisations in China* (Cambridge, Cambridge University Press, 2018).

Zhang, ZY, 'China's SOE Reforms: What the Latest Round of Reforms Mean for the Market' (China Briefing, 29.5.2019), available at www.china-briefing.com/news/chinas-soe-reform-process.

Zhao, Huimiao, *Government Intervention in the Reorganisation of Listed Companies in China* (Cambridge, Cambridge University Press, 2020).

Zhao, Huanxin, 'China names key industries for absolute state control' (China Daily, 19.12.2006), available at www.chinadaily.com.cn/china/2006-12/19/content_762056.htm.

Zhao, Hongmei and Qing, K, 'China's runaway bosses spotlight underground loan market' (Reuters, 29.9.2011), available at www.reuters.com/article/us-china-economy-runaway-bosses-idUSTRE78S0XJ20110929.

Zheng, H, Bankruptcy Law of the People's Republic of China: Principle, Procedure and Practice (1986) *Vanderbilt Journal of Transnational Law* 683.

Zheng, J, Competition Between Arbitral Institutions in China – Fighting for a Better System? (Kluwer Abitration Blog, 16.10.2015), available at kluwerarbitrationblog.com/2015/10/16/competition-between-arbitral-institutions-in-china-fighting-for-a-better-system.

Zheng, Y and Zhu, Y, 'Bank lending incentives and firm investment decisions in China' (2013) *Journal of Multinational Financial Management* 146.

Zheng, Y, Lu, Y and White, LT (eds), *Politics of Modern China*, vol 2 (London, Routledge, 2010).

Zhou, KX, *How the Farmers Changed China: Power of the people* (Boulder, Westview Press, 1996).

Zhou, L, 'Governing China's Local Officials' (2007) *Economic Research Journal* 36.

Zhou, Z, Chen, J, Zhu, W and Yang, L, 'Firm capability and performance in China: The moderating role of *guanxi* and institutional forces in domestic and foreign contexts' (2014) *Journal of Business Research* 77.

Zhu, W, 'Constructing Negative Reciprocity System in the Recognition and Enforcement of Foreign Judgments in China' (2017) *Hebei Law Science* 19.

Zhu, Z, 'Two get death in tainted milk case' (China Daily, 23.1.2009), available at www.chinadaily.com.cn/china/2009-01/23/content_7422983.htm.

Zou, H, 'An Analysis of China's Corporate Rehabilitation Regimes' (2007) *Journal of China University of Political Science and Law* 48.

—— 'China's Corporate Rehabilitation System – Theories and Practice' (2007) *Journal of China University of Political Science and Law* 48.

Zweig, D, 'China's Political Economy' in WA Joseph (ed), *Politics in China*, 3rd edn (Oxford, Oxford University Press, 2019).

Authorless

'Announcement for the collection of research topics of the Finance and Credit Construction Department in 2019' (NDRC, 6.6.2019), available at www.ndrc.gov.cn/fzggw/jgsj/cjd/sjdt/201906/t20190606_1111439.html.

'Bankruptcy Cases at Jiangsu Court and Ten Typical Bankruptcy Cases in 2018' (Sina, 6.3.2020), available at k.sina.cn/article_2056346650_7a915c1a02000w1xy.html?from=news&subch=onews.

'Bankruptcy Cases with No Funds Apply for Public Welfare Fund Support' (Guangzhou Association of Bankruptcy Administrators, 17.7.2017), available at gzaba.org.cn/faq_view.aspx?TypeId=50005&Id=525&Fid=t8:50005:8.

'BIS Quarterly Review March 2016' (BIS, April 2016), available at www.bis.org/publ/qtrpdf/r_qt1609.pdf.

'Central Economic Work Conference held in Beijing, Xi Jinping Li Keqiang made an important speech' (21.12.2015), available at www.gov.cn/xinwen/2015-12/21/content_5026332.htm.

'China Corporate Bond Market Blue Book' (FitchRatings, 2019), available at your.fitch.group/rs/732-CKH-767/images/china-corporate-bond-market-blue-book_fitch_10083315.pdf.

'China Legal Report: Debt Collection in China' (WenFei Law, April 2014), available at www.wenfei.com/fileadmin/archives/clr/140414_CLR_April_2014.pdf.

'China's recognition of foreign insolvency proceedings and VIE structures' (International Insolvency & Restructuring Report 2020/21 by Harneys and Fangda, June 2020), available at www.capital-markets-intelligence.com/wp-content/uploads/2020/06/IIRR2020-21_Harneys-Fangda.pdf.

'China to further reduce SOE debts' (China.org, 8.2.2018), available at www.china.org.cn/business/2018-02/08/content_50449229.htm.

'East Star Airline goes bankrupt with huge debts' (China.org, 28.8.2009), available at www.china.org.cn/business/2009-08/28/content_18416805.htm.

'Fujian Court's White Paper on Hearing Bankruptcy Cases' (Yunqingsuan, 31.7.2019), available at www.yunqingsuan.com/news/detail/53088.

'Guangzhou Intermediate Court Releases White Paper on Hearing Bankruptcy Cases' (Yunqingsuan, 30.12.2019), available at www.yunqingsuan.com/news/detail/57565?WebShieldDRSessionVerify=IThqAUxyJbcZsQSNAPFz.

'"Half Bankruptcy Law" A Dream Journey' (27.8.2019), available at www.yunqingsuan.com/news/detail/53809

'Jiangsu's first personal debt liquidation case concluded' (Yunqingsuan, 2.6.2020), available at www.yunqingsuan.com/news/detail/62785.

'Jiangsu Higher People's Court's Report on the Commercial Trial Work of Provincial Courts' (28.5.2019), available at www.jsrd.gov.cn/cwhzt/201903/hywj/201905/t20190527_513704.shtml.

'Nanning Statement of the 2nd China-Association of Southeast Asian Nations (ASEAN) Justice Forum' (8.6.2017), available at www.court.gov.cn/zixun-xiangqing-47372.html.

'Recognition of foreign insolvency proceedings and foreign insolvency practitioners in the BVI' (Mourant Guide, April 2017), available at www.mourant.com/file-library/media---2017/2017-guides/recognition-of-foreign-insolvency-proceedings-and-foreign-insolvency-practitioners-in-the-bvi-(updated).pdf.

'Remarks from the press conference of "Zhejiang Court Further Advances the Structural Reform and Economic Transformation and Upgrade of the Bankruptcy Trial Service Supply Side"' (Zhejiang Court, 16.4.2018), available at www.zjcourt.cn/art/2018/4/16/art_105_2318.html.

'Rule of Law Index 2015' (The World Justice Project, 2015).

'SPC takes up judicial responsibility to improve China's business environment' (SPC announcement, 11.6.2020), available at english.court.gov.cn/2020-06/11/content_37536974.htm.

'Statistical Bulletin of Human Resources and Social Security Development in 2015' (Ministry of Human Resources and Social Security, 30.5.2016), available at www.mohrss.gov.cn/SYrlzyhshbzb/dongtaixinwen/buneiyaowen/201605/t20160530_240967.html.

'Suzhou, Jiangsu: Creating a Wujiang model for bankruptcy cases' (20.5.2018), available at jszx.court.gov.cn/1150/ExecuteNewsletter/5695.jhtml.

'Taizhou Court: The year of breaking the ice of personal bankruptcy' (Yunqingsuan, 2.1.2020), available at www.yunqingsuan.com/news/detail/57602.

'Ten Typical Bankruptcy Cases of Wujiang Court (2016-2019)' (Yunqingsuan, 17.4.2020), available at www.yunqingsuan.com/news/detail/60586.

'The first bankruptcy information disclosure platform in the country was born in Shenzhen, Guangdong' (15.2.2016), available at www.court.gov.cn/zixun-xiangqing-16641.html.

'Top Ten Typical Bankruptcy Cases of Zhejiang Courts in 2019' (Yunqingsuan, 13.4.2020), available at www.yunqingsuan.com/news/detail/60428.

'Urge enterprises to continue to survive and develop Shenzhen court bankruptcy trial to help resume work and production' (SPC, 30.3.2020), available at www.court.gov.cn/fabu-xiangqing-224201.html.

'Xu Jianxin: Exploring the maximization of bankruptcy assets and corporate reorganization in Zhejiang Province' (CNR, 23.4.2020), available at finance.cnr.cn/zt/fenghui/kaimushi/20200423/t20200423_525065382.shtml.

'Zaozhuang Xuechen County People's Court, Unsecured Creditor Protection in Corporate Liquidations' (30.11.2016), available at zzxcqfy.sdcourt.gov.cn/zzxcqfy/388369/388372/1455229/index.html.

'Zhejiang Court Advances the Structural Reform of the Bankruptcy Trial Service Supply Side and Economic Transformation and Upgrade' (Zhejiang Higher Court, 16.4.2018), available at www.zjcourt.cn/art/2018/4/16/art_105_2318.html.

'Zhou Qiang, President of the Supreme People's Court: Promote the Establishment of a Personal Bankruptcy System and Improve the Current Bankruptcy Law' (People's Court News, 2.11.2018), available at finance.qq.com/a/20181102/007249.htm

INDEX

Printed in the USA
CPSIA information can be obtained
at www.ICGtesting.com
LVHW021621300324
775854LV00001BA/60